CLASSIC
HOME
COOKING

CLASSIC HOME COOKING

MARY BERRY

AND MARLENA SPIELER

DK Publishing

LONDON, NEW YORK, MELBOURNE,
MUNICH AND DELHI

Editorial consultant JENI WRIGHT
Art editor BILL MASON
Design development GRADE DESIGN CONSULTANTS
Managing editor GILLIAN ROBERTS
Managing art editor KAREN SAWYER
Category publisher MARY-CLARE JERRAM
DTP designer (London) SONIA CHARBONNIER
DTP coordinator (India) PANKAJ SHARMA
Production controller LOUISE DALY

Revised edition
Photographer EDWARD ALLWRIGHT
Food stylist VICKI SMALLWOOD
Stylist ROSIE HOPPER

First American edition, 1995
This revised edition published in the United States in 2003
by DK Publishing, Inc.
375 Hudson Street, New York, New York 10014
Penguin Group (US)

A Cataloging-in-Publication record for this book is available from
the Library of Congress

ISBN 0–7894–9674–7

Color reproduced in Singapore by Colourscan
Printed in China by Toppan Printing Co. (Shenzhen) Ltd.

BEFORE MAKING THE RECIPES IN THIS BOOK, PLEASE REFER
TO COOK'S NOTES ON PAGE 525

SEE OUR COMPLETE PRODUCT LINE AT
www.dk.com

CONTENTS

3

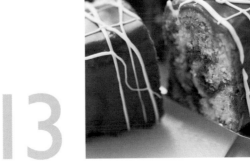

SPECIAL MENU INDEX

The index on pages 8–13 is an easy-to-use reference and visual guide to choosing a special dish, whether you are cooking for a celebration, planning a party, or simply looking to expand your culinary repertoire. Some of the menus, such as Thanksgiving Roast Turkey, present a complete main course. Others – as in Fresh Ways with Salmon Fillets – show how to ring the changes on old favorites. There is inspiration from Italy, India, and Japan as well as indulgent treats to satisfy the sweetest tooth. Whichever dish takes your fancy, we hope you will have as much fun choosing as making and eating it.

FIRST COURSES

TAPAS   68

VEGETABLES WITH GARLIC DIPS Boiled or grilled vegetables with spicy or garlic mayonnaises.
TUNA TOSTADOS Toasted garlic breads topped with tuna, tomato, and melting cheese.
CHICK PEA & RED PEPPER SALAD An earthy salad of contrasting textures.
ANDALUCIAN MUSHROOMS Serrano ham brings the taste of Southern Spain to this dish.

FIRST COURSES

PREPARE-AHEAD FIRST COURSES   78

DOUBLE SALMON TIAN Individual fresh salmon and cream cheese rounds on peppery salad leaves, topped with luxurious smoked salmon.
ASPARAGUS & QUAIL EGG SALAD An extremely simple starter that always impresses.
SMOKED SALMON TERRINE The richness of the salmon is tempered by lowfat cheese and the snap of creamed horseradish.

FISH & SHELLFISH

SIMPLE FISH SUSHI   134

NIGIRI SUSHI Bite-size mouthfuls of shrimp, delicious sticky rice, and fiery wasabi (Japanese horseradish) paste.
HOSO MAKI Rolls of seaweed with vinegared sushi rice, crabmeat, and cucumber.
SUSHI SQUARES WITH SMOKED SALMON A modern interpretation of sushi, topped with palate-cleansing pickled ginger slices.

FISH & SHELLFISH

CLASSIC BUFFET-PARTY SALMON   144

WHOLE POACHED SALMON A perfect centrepiece for a summer celebration. The fish is poached with black peppercorns, bay leaves, and other aromatics for added flavor, then served cold, with jumbo shrimp to garnish, and the traditional accompaniment, fresh dill mayonnaise. Impressive, yet easily made at home.

FRESH WAYS WITH SALMON FILLETS 152

PAN-GRILLED SALMON TRANCHES Served with a sour cream and dill sauce.
THAI CHILI SALMON Spicy salmon fillets with chili, lime, and a coriander garnish.
WARM HONEYED SALMON SALAD Served with a herbed yogurt dressing.
HERB-ROASTED SALMON A bread crumb, parsley, and cheese topping keeps the fish moist.

CHICKEN & TURKEY SALADS 184

TARRAGON CHICKEN WITH AVOCADO A classic combination enlivened with anchovies, and garnished with peppery watercress.
VIETNAMESE TURKEY SALAD With fish sauce, chili, mint, and crunchy white cabbage.
RED BELL PEPPER HERBED CHICKEN SALAD A lowfat and colorful salad with a mouthwatering dressing that includes basil and parsley.

MARINATED BARBECUED CHICKEN 196

ORANGE & ROSEMARY CHICKEN Tangy chicken with a colorful and spicy salsa.
FRUITY CILANTRO CHICKEN Aromatic chicken drumsticks with a fresh mango salsa.
YOGURT & MINT CHICKEN A couscous salad with pine nuts complements the Middle Eastern flavors of this dish.

THANKSGIVING ROAST TURKEY 202

GOLDEN ROAST TURKEY A festive feast with all the traditional trimmings – a chestnut, bacon, and pork sausagemeat stuffing, rich gravy, bread sauce flavored with onion, cloves, bay leaf, and black peppercorns, fruity cranberry sauce, crispy bacon rolls, and mini sausages.

CHICKEN & TURKEY STIR-FRIES 210

LACQUERED DUCK A new take on a classic dish, sticky, sweet, and satisfying.
CHINESE CHICKEN WITH MANGO Marinated chicken stir-fried with cashew nuts, peppers, bok choy, mushrooms, and mango.
TURKEY-TO-GO A serve-yourself combination of spiced turkey and red pepper to wrap in warm, soft tortillas – appetizing, and fun to eat as well.

MEXICAN BUFFET PARTY 250

VEGETARIAN ENCHILADAS Crispy tortillas oozing with cheese, beans, and spicy tomato sauce served with guacamole.
MEXICAN BEAN SALAD Nutritious and tasty, this combination of beans in a herby dressing makes an ideal buffet-party dish.
CHARGRILLED STEAKS WITH RED VEGETABLES Juicy steaks, onions, and peppers served with the Mexican classic, refried beans.

THE BEST BURGERS 260

LAMB BURGERS Served in warm pita bread with a cool cucumber and mint yogurt.
THAI BURGERS Top-quality beef, lightly spiced and formed into burgers, ideal with a crunchy salad or raw vegetable strips alongside.
VEGGIE BURGERS Meatless but protein-packed, made with beans, cheese, carrots, pine nuts, and dried apricots.

KEBABS ON THE BARBECUE 274

BEEF & RED ONION Classic steak and onions with all the flavor of food cooked on the grill.
ORIENTAL PORK Pork, peppers, and pineapple combine to make this a dish with a difference.
SAUSAGE & SESAME Served with their own side-dish of mushrooms, tomatoes, and zucchini.
CURRIED LAMB Chunks of tender lamb in a spicy yogurt marinade with coriander and mint.

VEGETABLE CASSEROLES 306

SPICY PUMPKIN CASSEROLE Sweet-tasting parsnips, pumpkin, potatoes, and onions, lightly curried. Garnished with chopped fresh cilantro.
MUSHROOM STROGANOFF A vegetable twist on the classic (beef) dish – artichoke hearts, bell peppers, and mushrooms in a creamy wine sauce.
ROASTED VEGETABLE MEDLEY Cauliflower, lima beans, carrots, and other tasty vegetables caramelized in a hot oven and dressed with herbs.

VEGETARIAN BAKES 312

TUSCAN CANNELLONI Beans, sun-dried tomatoes, and a creamy blue cheese make up the filling in this Italian pasta dish.
MAJORCAN TUMBET CASSEROLE Layers of vegetables in a tomato sauce flavored with garlic and rosemary.
KILKERRY PIE Potatoes and leeks in a tangy cheese sauce topped with crisp phyllo pastry.

VEGETARIAN CURRIES 318

DHAL A hearty and nutritious lentil dish flavored with cinnamon, coriander seed, and cumin – the perfect accompaniment to any curry.
SAG ALOO Spinach (sag) and potato (aloo) with mustard and cumin seeds, onion, garlic, fresh root ginger, and other spices. Served with a dollop of cooling yogurt.
NIRAMISH Vegetables, including red peppers and green beans, in a rich coconut milk sauce.

ASIAN VEGETARIAN SUPPERS 324

THAI CURRY The heat of the curry is tempered by the coconut milk. Served with jasmine rice.
PEKING TOFU WITH PLUM SAUCE Fried tofu replaces the duck in this classic Chinese dish.
FIRECRACKER STIR-FRY Bok choy, sugarsnap peas, peppers, and mushrooms in a fiery stir-fry.
JAPANESE NOODLE SOUP Delicately spiced, with tofu and green onions – a meal in a bowl.

PASTA & RICE

EASY PASTA SUPPER DISHES   340

RED HOT RAGU A lively pasta dish of pork sausagemeat, chilies, and a spicy tomato sauce.

RIGATONI WITH MUSHROOMS & ARUGULA Wilted arugula leaves add pep to this dish of pasta, mushrooms, and a creamy pesto sauce.

FUSILLI WITH DOUBLE TOMATOES Pasta spirals tossed with asparagus, mushrooms, fresh cherry tomatoes, and sun-dried tomatoes.

PASTA & RICE

RAVIOLI   346

CHICKEN & PROSCIUTTO Parcels of Italian cured ham and chicken in a tomato and basil sauce.

RICOTTA & SPINACH A familiar flavor combination, best simply served with butter, Parmesan, and freshly ground black pepper.

CRAB & SHRIMP Seafood parcels that melt in the mouth, in a fragrant cilantro sauce.

PASTA & RICE

ORIENTAL NOODLE DISHES   352

SINGAPORE NOODLES A simple dish with complex flavors, made with pork and vegetables.

SZECHUAN NOODLES WITH WATER CHESTNUTS Strong contrasts of taste and texture define this favorite Chinese dish.

PAD THAI WITH TIGER SHRIMP Chicken and shrimp transform a traditional Thai side-dish into a hearty yet fragrant main course.

PASTA & RICE

NASI GORENG   358

CHICKEN NASI GORENG A highly-seasoned rice dish with chicken, shrimp, bacon, and the crunch of toasted almonds.

VEGETARIAN NASI GORENG Thinly sliced white cabbage, peppers, and tomatoes in a spicy stir-fry with rice, and a garnish of omelet strips.

QUICK NASI GORENG Fried rice with bean sprouts, mushrooms, and succulent shrimp.

VEGETABLES & SALADS

CHARGRILLED VEGETABLE PLATTER   386

FOR BARBECUE OR GRILL An assortment of fresh vegetables – eggplants, zucchini, red and yellow bell peppers, red onion, asparagus, pattypan squash, and mushrooms – brushed with good olive oil, then grilled until sweet and tender, and lightly charred. Served hot as a side dish with any meat or firm fish, or cold as an unusual salad.

VEGETABLES & SALADS

FRESH & LIGHT SALADS   394

HERB SALAD A tangy orange and mustard dressing is tossed with fine asparagus, sun-dried tomatoes, and leaves including lamb's lettuce.

PUY LENTIL SALAD A simple salad dressed with sharp-sweet balsamic vinegar and olive oil.

TABBOULEH Nutritious, nutty bulgur wheat, lifted by the refreshing taste of mint and lemon.

ITALIAN PESTO SALAD Broccoli, cauliflower, and black olives with the classic Italian basil sauce.

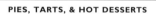

MERINGUES 476

MOCHA MERINGUE MILLE-FEUILLES Thin disks of meringue and almonds layered with sweetened coffee cream.

CHOCOLATE MERINGUE SHELLS Crisp, light meringue shells, drizzled with melted semisweet chocolate, then sandwiched together with a rich chocolate cream.

FRESH FRUIT BASKETS Berries of your choice, cream, and meringue served with raspberry sauce.

FRESH FRUIT SALADS 482

SPICED FRUIT A year-round mix of succulent dried fruits, with vanilla and star anise.

FRUITS OF THE FOREST Balsamic vinegar and green peppercorns add zip to juicy fresh berries.

ORANGE PASSION Just fruit: oranges, papaya, passion fruit, and lime juice, with no added sugar.

TROPICAL ISLAND Physalis (cape gooseberries) and Asian pears (nashi) star in this unusual salad.

SORBETS 490

LIME, APRICOT, RASPBERRY, AND PEAR & GINGER So easy to make, from a basic mixture of sugar, water, and egg white, sorbets capture the vivid colors and pure flavors of your favorite fruits in a light, lowfat, refreshing mouthful. The perfect ending to a rich meal or (for a special occasion) try offering a small serving between courses as a palate cleanser.

SMALL CHOCOLATE CAKES 508

DOUBLE-CHOCOLATE MUFFINS Bitter cocoa powder and best-quality semisweet chocolate chips, enhanced with a little strong coffee, for a deeply chocolatey experience.

BEST-EVER BROWNIES Soft, moist squares of chocolate with the added crunch of walnuts.

CHOCOLATE CUPCAKES Enjoy a whole chocolate cake all to yourself, embellished with smooth chocolate frosting.

FESTIVE FRUITCAKES 514

CANDIED FRUITCAKE A traditional rich fruit cake with a spectacular topping of apricot jam, nuts, and candied fruit and peel. Finished with a colorful ribbon.

SNOW WHITE CAKE Fairytale icing hides a delicious secret – a moist cake packed with dried fruits, nuts, and candied citrus peel, covered with a layer of home-made almond paste. Decorated with fresh cranberries and silver dragees, or as you wish.

CHOUX PASTRIES 522

COFFEE ECLAIRS Oozing with whipped cream and topped with a silky coffee icing.

TOP-HAT CREAM PUFFS Tiny cream-filled choux buns sitting atop larger ones, crowned with a decadent chocolate frosting.

CHOCOLATE CREAM PUFFS Golden choux pastry baked until light as air, then split, filled with whipped cream, and drizzled with a creamy warm chocolate sauce. Who could resist?

FOREWORD

CLASSIC HOME COOKING has been a reliable, trusted kitchen companion for many years. But much has changed since it was first published. We lead busier lives, fulfilling greater dreams. We entertain less formally than in the past, but so much more comfortably, often in the warmth of a cosy kitchen where guests can chat with the cook and enjoy the fun of preparing a meal together. Travel has broadened our horizons, and given us a taste for different foods.

Now, we know what it means to eat well in the modern sense, downplaying butter and sugar and rich sauces, preparing healthier meals using natural ingredients, and letting their flavor and freshness shine through. Fortunately, there's an abundance of good foods available – seasonal fruits and vegetables; fresh fish and lean meat; locally produced cheeses; and interesting breads that are lovingly crafted by hand and baked in the traditional way. Supermarkets as well as small neighborhood stores have responded to our more adventurous tastes – acquired during vactions in exotic destinations – and provide us with all manner of unusual ingredients, including the herbs, spices, and flavorings that enhance the appeal of simple ingredients.

This new edition of the book takes account of all these changes while retaining the features that made the original one so special – the picture for every dish, the visual indexes at the beginning of each chapter, the ease of use, and the knowledge that each one of the tried-and-tested recipes can be made with absolute confidence of a great result. Two people deserve a special mention for their contribution to this edition: Lucy Young, who helped to develop and test the new recipes, and Jeni Wright, who carefully reviewed every recipe and suggested many good changes. Heartfelt thanks to them both.

USEFUL
INFORMATION

EQUIPMENT

GOOD EQUIPMENT MAKES cooking easy. With top-quality knives, pots and pans, and other utensils, you will be able to cook efficiently and with pleasure. If you are equipping your first kitchen, the bare minimum is all that is required – there is no need for fancy utensils to turn out delicious meals. As your experience grows, you can gradually add to your collection, buying more specialist and unusual items as your skills increase.

Always buy the best equipment you can afford – it is false economy to save money, because cheap equipment simply will not last. Using a thin pan in which food always sticks and burns, or trying to chop vegetables with a flimsy knife, will soon turn cooking into a chore.

MEASURING EQUIPMENT

Even experienced cooks need accurate measuring tools to ensure ingredients are in correct proportion to one another – vital when baking – or the right size, or at the optimum temperature.

- KITCHEN SCALES, which all serious bakers will want to have, may be balance, electronic, or spring-operated. Balance scales give the most accurate results, especially for small amounts. Being strong and simple in construction, with no complicated mechanism to wear out, they will last a lifetime. Electronic scales, which run on batteries, are not very accurate with amounts under 1 oz (30 g), but have the advantage that many can be reset to zero when weighing more than one ingredient in the bowl at the same time.
- LIQUID MEASURING CUPS made of toughened glass are very useful – those made from clear plastic or acrylic are usually cheaper but may not withstand the heat of boiling liquid. Buy the biggest measures you can store (they can be used for mixing, too), and marked with standard American (cup and ounce) as well as metric units. New and ingenious is an angled measuring cup that lets you check the accuracy of measurements either from the side or by looking straight down into the cup.
- MEASURING CUPS are normally sold in sets of four, comprising 1 cup, ½ cup, ⅓ cup, and ¼ cup. You can also buy sets of seven cups – the usuals plus ¾ cup, ⅔ cup, and ⅛ cup – as well as additional "odd-size" measures, such as 1½-cup and 2-cup. Measuring cups made of stainless steel will last a lifetime.

- MEASURING SPOONS, for accurate dispensing of small amounts of wet or dry ingredients, usually come in nesting sets of four – 1 tablespoon, 1 teaspoon, ½ teaspoon, and ¼ teaspoon. Some sets also include ⅛ teaspoon. Spoon measures of dry ingredients should always be leveled off with a knife.
- A MEAT THERMOMETER, to measure the internal temperature of meat and poultry during cooking, takes the guesswork out of roasting, and ensures thorough, safe cooking. One type is inserted into the meat or poultry before cooking begins; others, such as instant-read thermometers and thermo forks, are used as a spot check during cooking or at the end of the cooking time (these types are very useful when grilling and broiling).
- A DEEP-FRYING OIL THERMOMETER will check the temperature of the oil to be sure of crisp fried results. To guarantee success, and make frying very easy and safe, use an electric deep-fryer, which has its own built-in thermometer.
- A CANDY THERMOMETER performs the same function as a deep-frying thermometer, but for sugar syrups.
- A TAPE MEASURE and/or a ruler will enable you to roll or cut pastry and pasta to the correct dimensions, and also check that pans are the required size.
- AN AUTOMATIC TIMER helps avoid overcooking disasters when you are busy and forget to watch the clock.

POTS & PANS

On the stovetop, pans need to be heavy enough to sit securely without tipping, yet not so heavy that you have trouble lifting them. A heavy base is important for gentle, even heat distribution. Pots and pans also need to have lids that fit tightly and sturdy handles that stay cool. Heatproof handles make it possible to use pots and pans in the oven too, when necessary.

- A SAUTE PAN is more versatile than a frying pan or skillet because it has deeper sides. Choose from stainless steel or nonstick (the most useful size is 9–11 in/23–28 cm).
- AN OMELET PAN, shallow with curved sides, is often made of cast iron or stainless steel; a nonstick finish is easier to use. A 5½-in (16-cm) pan is the right size for a 2-egg French omelet, a 9-in (23-cm) pan for a thick, flat Spanish or Italian omelet. A shallower crêpe pan is an optional extra.
- A GRILL PAN, traditionally made of heavy cast iron, gives an attractive finish to chops, steaks, and vegetables. Well-defined ridges keep the food out of the fat it renders, and deep sides let you make a sauce in the pan too. Griddles are similar, but have a smooth cooking surface.

MATERIALS FOR COOKWARE

COPPER (an excellent heat conductor) reacts chemically with food, air, and liquid, so copper pans must be lined. Stainless steel has replaced tin and silver as the most common lining. Lined copper pans are truly the best, preferred by many professional chefs, but they are expensive and heavy.

STAINLESS STEEL is lightweight and durable but not a very good heat conductor, so the bases of stainless steel pans for use on the stovetop are usually "sandwiched" with aluminum, copper, or a copper and silver alloy. Pans with such heavy-gauge bases are expensive but should last a lifetime. Ovenware is usually limited to roasting pans.

CAST IRON can be heated to a high temperature, so cast-iron pans are perfect for cooking food quickly and evenly. It also retains and transmits low heat well so is appropriate for long, slow cooking too. Cast-iron pans need to be "seasoned" before use, so food does not stick, and must be thoroughly dried after washing to prevent rusting. Enameled cast iron will not rust, and is good for stovetop casseroles as it makes very strong, sturdy (though heavy) vessels.

ALUMINUM (another efficient heat conductor) scratches easily and can react with acidic foods, giving them a metallic taste. It is usually covered with another material, such as stainless steel, or a nonstick coating.

GLASS is not as good a conductor of heat as metal, so pastry baked in thick, ovenproof glass will never be as crisp as that baked in a metal pan, but it is very useful for baking dishes, and for oven-to-tableware.

PORCELAIN, STONEWARE, AND GLAZED EARTHENWARE are quite tough and sturdy materials for ovenware (take care not to chip or crack them), and most can double as serving dishes.

NONSTICK coatings make pots and pans quick and easy to clean. Some coatings are readily scratched and wear off with time; other, newer versions, such as titanium, are more durable and can be used with metal utensils.

- SAUCEPANS WITH STRAIGHT SIDES have a multitude of uses, from sauces and vegetables to soups and stews. You need a minimum of three in different sizes, starting with one about 1½ quarts (1.5 liters) in capacity. Two handles on larger pans make lifting much easier; if the handles are short and made of metal, the pan can double as a casserole in the oven.
- A SMALL SAUCEPAN, about 1 quart (1 liter) in capacity, with a nonstick coating and pouring spouts on both sides, is invaluable for milk and cream sauces.
- A PASTA COOKER is tall and fairly narrow, with a perforated insert that lifts out for draining. Many stockpots come with the same sort of insert, and so can be used for cooking pasta, plus making stock and large quantities of soup.
- A STEAMER at its simplest is a collapsible basket that fits inside a large saucepan. Special steamer pans have inserts with perforated bases. Chinese stacking bamboo steamers, which fit inside a wok, are a cheaper alternative.
- A WOK with one long handle is easier to use than a wok with two small handles; one with a flat base is most stable on both gas and electric burners. The cheapest Chinese woks are made from unseasoned carbon steel; if pre-seasoned or nonstick, the wok will be easier to clean. A large wok (14 in/35 cm across the top) is the most versatile. Many come complete with lids (very useful) and cooking tools.

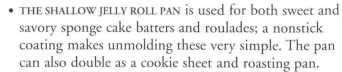

OVENWARE

Cooking in the oven requires sturdy vessels that conduct and retain heat efficiently. For convenience, choose oven-to-table dishes that are attractive enough for serving too. The choice of metal or ceramic, nonstick or uncoated, depends largely on the job you want the pans or dishes to do. Whatever you buy, look after it to avoid rusting and scratching.

- A ROASTING PAN needs to be deep, strong, and rigid. If possible, have two in different sizes, one of them as big as your oven will take. Too small a pan makes it difficult to baste the meat or poultry properly; roasting in a pan that is too large will cause juices to evaporate and burn. With a spout on the edge of the pan you can pour off juices; a rack that fits inside the pan enables meat to be roasted free of its fat. Hinged racks can be folded to cradle a bird.

- BAKING OR COOKIE SHEETS have many uses – to bake cookies, small cakes and pastries, and pizzas – and to provide a heat-conducting base for pastry shells; you will need at least two. Buy the largest that will fit comfortably in your oven, and be sure they are heavy-duty, inflexible, and completely flat. Good-quality nonstick coatings are a boon when it comes to cleaning.

- LOAF PANS with deep sides are used for baking breads and cakes, and for pâtés and meat loaves. Two different sizes are needed: one 1 lb (500 g), or 8½ x 4½ x 2½ in (21 x 11 x 6 cm), and the other 2 lb (1 kg). Some pans have hinged drop-down sides.

- TUBE PANS, deep and round, with a hollow tube in the center, are used for angel food cakes. A bundt pan is similar, but has curved, fluted sides.

- A SPRINGFORM PAN is ideal for delicate cakes and cheesecakes. It has deep, straight sides and a clamp on the side that is opened to release the base. The side can then be lifted off.

- CAKE PANS may be round or square. Layer cake pans are shallow (1½– 2 in/4–5 cm deep) and usually round; you will need at least two. Deeper cake pans (about 3 in/7.5 cm) are used for fruit cakes.

- THE SHALLOW JELLY ROLL PAN is used for both sweet and savory sponge cake batters and roulades; a nonstick coating makes unmolding these very simple. The pan can also double as a cookie sheet and roasting pan.

- A SHEET PAN is similar to a jelly roll pan, but it is deeper. It is used for baking cakes that are cut into squares or rectangles for serving.

- A MUFFIN PAN will bake muffins as well as cup cakes. Pans may have 6, 12, or 24 holes or cups, and the width and depth of the cups varies from mini to giant. Popover pans are similar but slimmer.

- A PIE PAN OR PLATE has plain, sloping sides and a lip for the pie edge. A good all-purpose size is 23 cm (9 in), measured across the top.

- AN OVAL PIE DISH with a wide lip is traditional for deep-dish sweet and savory pies.

- A SHALLOW FLUTED TART PAN, about 9 in (23 cm) in diameter, is best for making quiches and tarts, as the fluted edge helps to strengthen the fragile pastry shell. For easy serving, choose a metal pan with a loose bottom: lift the quiche or tart from the side of the pan and serve it on the pan base. Or, bake in a fluted ceramic dish and serve from it. Individual tartlet pans or molds are available in a wide variety of shapes and sizes.

- A STRAIGHT-SIDED, DEEP SOUFFLE DISH, 6 cups (1.4 liters) in capacity, can double as a baking dish for crisps and other hot desserts. Small soufflé dishes and ramekins are used for individual soufflés, and baked desserts such as crème caramel, baked eggs, and mousses. Average capacity is 5 to 8 oz (150 to 250 ml). Both soufflé dishes and ramekins can be brought straight from the oven to the table.

- GRATIN AND BAKING DISHES come in many different shapes and sizes, and are very versatile. They are used for vegetable and other gratins, baked pasta dishes, shepherd's pie, and moussaka, for baking fish, and for hot puddings. They can be used for roasting, too. Most gratin and baking dishes will resist very high temperatures, which means they can be put under the broiler as well as into a hot oven.

- A RANGE OF CASSEROLES in various sizes, and with tight-fitting lids, is also useful. Choose ones that can be used on the stovetop as well as in the oven.

- A PIZZA STONE reproduces the very hot, dry conditions of a professional pizza oven so you can bake a crisp pizza at home. Some come with a large wooden paddle on which the pizza is shaped for baking.

- RE-USABLE COOKING LINERS, spread out on a baking sheet or in a pan, will prevent food from sticking, and they only need to be wiped clean.

ELECTRICAL EQUIPMENT

There is an almost limitless choice of electrical appliances to help you in the kitchen. Equipping yourself with the full range is costly and wastes storage space, so when buying, think carefully about what you cook and how often you are likely to use the appliance.

- MIXERS work much faster than whisking and mixing by hand. They may be compact and hand-held or large and heavy-duty, standing on the worktop. The hand-held mixer is good for beating egg whites and whipping cream, and can be used in a pan over the heat. Choose a powerful mixer with at least three speeds, and check that the beaters are easy to remove for cleaning. To mix cake batters and bread doughs efficiently, choose a large mixer with a stand and bowl. Most have a dough hook attachment for kneading and some come with a separate blender, grinder, juice extractor, pasta maker, potato peeler, and a shredder and slicer. Of course, mixers like this are expensive and take up space.
- BLENDERS, also called liquidizers, make smooth soups, sauces, vegetable purées, dips, batters, and drinks. Look for a model with a large container, and blades set low to cope with small quantities. A HAND-HELD BLENDER, a less expensive and more portable version, will purée soup directly in a pan or small quantities in a beaker or deep bowl. It is easier to wash than the free-standing blender and takes up less storage space.
- A FOOD PROCESSOR almost eliminates the need for a free-standing blender. Different blades chop, grate, slice, or purée all kinds of ingredients, or mix pastry and bread doughs. The more expensive the processor, the more sophisticated the jobs it will do. Some come with a mini bowl for processing small quantities, which is very useful for herbs, spices, and nuts.
- ELECTRIC GRINDERS will quickly produce freshly ground coffee or spices, and can also be used for grinding nuts and making bread crumbs.
- AN ICE CREAM MACHINE, BREAD MACHINE, PASTA MACHINE, RICE COOKER, SLOW COOKER, CONTACT GRILL, AND THERMOSTATICALLY CONTROLLED DEEP-FRYER are nice items to have if space and budget permit.

CUTTING TOOLS

A set of sturdy, well-made, and sharpened knives is vital for efficient food preparation. Make sure they are comfortable to hold: the best balanced have the metal of the blade running through the handle, which should be securely riveted, or the knife may be made from a whole piece of metal. Keep knives on a wall-mounted magnetic strip, or in a knife block, rather

than in a drawer where they will go blunt quickly and will be a danger to fingers reaching in.

- A PARING KNIFE, with a rigid, pointed 3- or 4-in (7- or 10-cm) blade, makes trimming and peeling (paring) fruit and vegetables easy.
- A UTILITY KNIFE is similar in shape to the paring knife but has a blade 5 or 6 in (12 or 15 cm) long.
- A SMALL SERRATED KNIFE, with a thin, flexible blade, is ideal for slicing lemons, tomatoes, and other fruits and vegetables with tough or slippery skins.
- THE CHEF'S OR COOK'S KNIFE, with a rigid, heavy, wide blade about 8 in (19 or 20 cm) long, tapering to a pointed tip, is the all-purpose cutting tool, unbeatable for slicing and chopping vegetables and fruit into dice, and for chopping herbs.
- A BREAD KNIFE has a long, thin, firm blade with a serrated edge to cut through bread crusts cleanly. Serrated knifes cannot be sharpened.
- A CARVING KNIFE is long, thin, and flexible, with a blade that has a straight, sharp edge curving upward toward the tip. To hold the meat firmly, use with a two-pronged carving fork that has a safety prong to prevent the knife blade from slipping toward you.
- A CLEAVER with a wide, heavy blade is the tool for tough chopping jobs.
- THE MEZZALUNA has a crescent-shaped single or double blade and two handles. It works by being rocked over the food to be chopped, and is especially efficient for large quanities of tender-leaved herbs.
- KNIFE SHARPENERS are available in manual or electric models, or you can have your knives sharpened professionally once or twice a year. It is vital to sharpen knives regularly as blunt knives cause accidents. In between, use a SHARPENING STEEL to "refresh" sharpened knives
- CUTTING BOARDS are indispensable. Have at least two, either wooden or polyethylene/acrylic. One should be kept for raw meat and poultry, to ensure that they do not contaminate cooked food or fruits and vegetables to be eaten raw. Always clean boards thoroughly with hot, soapy water, and dry well.

UTENSILS

Using the right tool for the job may seem like a cliché, but it is a concept that is very important in the kitchen. The wrong tools will only cause frustration and waste valuable time.

- A SET OF MIXING BOWLS in varying sizes is essential. Have at least four, and choose ones that fit inside each other so that they do not take up all your storage space. Toughened glass is heatproof and versatile, and gives you an all-round view of what you are mixing.

- FLEXIBLE RUBBER OR PLASTIC SPATULAS, either flat or spoon-shaped, will scrape bowls clean so nothing is wasted, and they are good for folding mixtures, too. Have at least two, one for savory and the other for sweet mixtures.

- WOODEN SPOONS AND SPATULAS, in varying sizes, are useful for all kinds of tasks, both in preparation and cooking. Wooden spoons will mix and beat; with long handles they are good for stirring mixtures on the stovetop (they won't scratch a pan). A spoon with a corner will reach right to the edges or the bottom corner of the pan. The flat-sided spatula can be used for folding mixtures together. It doubles up as a lifter and turner, too.

- A SLOTTED (OR PERFORATED) SPOON is invaluable when removing food from liquids for serving or testing for doneness, and for skimming fat or scum off the surface of stocks and soups. It is also essential for draining fat or oil from food you have fried, either before further cooking or serving.

- A TURNER OR SPATULA is used for any solid food that needs turning in the pan or lifting carefully from pan to plate. It is especially useful for delicate foods like fish that have a tendency to break up.

- TONGS are also useful for turning and moving pieces of hot food, such as when broiling, and for moving long pasta like spaghetti and tagliatelle from pan to plate. They grasp the food without piercing it, as a fork would do.

- A LONG METAL SPATULA has a flat, thin, flexible blade. It is used for spreading icing and frosting, and for turning and lifting foods such as crêpes. It is useful to have two: one with a blade 9–10 in (23–25 cm) long and the other shorter, about 5 in (13 cm). An angled or offset spatula, which looks like a bent metal spatula, is used to remove slices of tart or pie from rimmed pans.

- A LONG-HANDLED LADLE scoops out hot liquids such as soups, stews, and pasta sauces for serving, so that they don't have to be poured from heavy pans. It can also be used for pouring batter into a crêpe pan.

- WHISKS incorporate air into egg whites to produce a snowy foam and into cream to thicken it. To make light work of these tasks, choose a balloon whisk with a comfortable handle and a large balloon of springy wire. A flat coiled whisk, or whip, is ideal for whisking a sauce over the heat or gravy in a roasting pan to produce smooth, well-blended results.

- GRATERS come in many guises. The most familiar are box or conical graters, which have a different grating surface on each face. Flat graters – like the individual faces on box graters – are less convenient to use as they will not stand up on their own. New-style FLAT GRATERS with handles come in a variety of ultra-sharp surfaces: fine for rapid zesting, grating, or puréeing; coarse for cheese and chocolate; ribbon graters for hard cheeses; and slicers for shavings of chocolate, Parmesan, or fresh ginger. Also useful are a HAND-OPERATED ROTARY GRATER and a NUTMEG GRATER.

- VEGETABLE PEELERS either have a fixed blade, for peeling potatoes and other round fruits and vegetables, or a swivel blade for straight-sided vegetables such as carrots. Some peelers have a pointed end for digging out "eyes" from potatoes.

- A GARLIC PRESS will crush garlic without fuss, although the aroma and taste will be stronger than if the garlic is chopped by hand. Be sure to choose a press with a detachable grille to make cleaning easy.

- A CITRUS ZESTER has a row of small holes in its wide, flat end that remove the zest (the colored, oil-rich part of the peel) from citrus fruits in tiny strips. The zest can then be minced if wanted. To take slightly thicker strips of zest, a canelle knife is used.

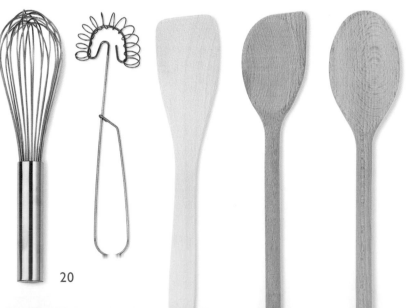

- SCISSORS (kept solely for kitchen use) are perfect for cutting bacon slices into strips, snipping herbs, and a myriad other small tasks. Stainless steel scissors are easy to keep clean.
- STURDY POULTRY SHEARS work like garden secateurs, making light work of cutting up chicken and other birds.
- A LEMON SQUEEZER will juice halved citrus fruits of all kinds very quickly. Choose one with a well-fitting strainer to catch the seeds. The traditional reamer is an attractive alternative, and it extracts a lot of juice, but you will need to strain out the seeds afterward.
- Buy the biggest MORTAR AND PESTLE you can store – apart from grinding herbs, spices, and garlic, it is the traditional vessel for making pounded sauces such as pesto. Porcelain is a good choice as it has the weight of marble without the prohibitive cost.
- SIEVES AND STRAINERS sift dry ingredients and strain wet ones, and can also purée cooked fruit and vegetables. It is handy to have two, large and small. The best material is stainless steel, because it will not rust over time.
- A POTATO MASHER needs to be strong and with a comfortable handle so that it can mash and purée cooked potatoes and other root vegetables efficiently. For the lightest, dry and fluffy results, use a ricer; a dishwasherproof model is easiest to clean.
- A STURDY COLANDER, with legs or a base so it is free-standing, will ensure safe draining of hot cooked vegetables, pasta, and legumes.
- A SALAD SPINNER operated by a handle or pulley uses centrifugal force to remove water from salad leaves without bruising them.
- A GRAVY SEPARATOR enables you to pour fat-free gravies and sauces. The jug either has two spouts, one shallow and one coming up from near the bottom, or just one deep spout. Fat, being lighter, will float to the surface of the gravy and can be poured off through the shallow spout (or the gravy can just be poured from beneath the fat using the deep spout).
- A LONG, HEAVY ROLLING PIN is needed for pastry, hand-rolled pasta, and sweets. One that is 2–3 in (5–7 cm) in diameter is the best choice. Wooden pins are fine, although marble ones stay cooler for rolling pastry and chocolate.

- A PASTRY SCRAPER is a small oblong of flexible plastic that resembles the tool used for smoothing plaster. It is invaluable for scraping up rich doughs that are made directly on the work surface.
- CUTTERS are used for rolled-out cookie doughs, scones, and tartlet cases. They may be plain or fluted, as well as in a wide range of shapes and sizes.
- A PASTRY BRUSH is the best tool for glazing and sealing pastry, greasing cake pans, and basting meat. The flat, paintbrush-type is easier to use than a round brush.
- A WIRE RACK allows air to circulate around cakes, cookies, and breads as they cool.
- A PASTRY BAG WITH A VARIETY OF TUBES is handy for piping cream and icings, and for shaping meringues and choux pastries such as éclairs.
- A CHERRY PITTER, APPLE CORER, AND MEAT POUNDER are inexpensive but useful items that don't take up space.

AND DON'T FORGET…

- paper towels
- foil
- plastic wrap
- wax paper
- parchment paper
- fine white (undyed) string for trussing and tying
- wooden toothpicks
- can opener
- corkscrew and bottle opener (a bottle stopper too, for leftovers)
- salt and pepper mills
- small skewers for testing cakes, meat, and poultry; long metal skewers and bamboo ones for kebabs and satay
- icecube trays

FREEZING

A freezer offers one of the most natural and economical methods of food preservation, and is invaluable in a busy household: most of the fresh food needed for a week, or even a month, can be bought in just one shopping trip and then frozen until it is needed.

Equipment needs to be airtight and moistureproof so the food does not spoil or develop "freezer burn" (dry, gray patches on the surface of the food that are not dangerous but spoil the appearance and texture).

- USE RIGID plastic or foil containers with lids, or freezer bags.
- FREEZER-QUALITY plastic wrap, freezer paper, and foil are convenient for interleaving and wrapping.
- FREEZER TAPE will seal packages securely; ordinary tape peels off.

WAYS TO FREEZE

A few simple techniques will keep frozen items at their freshest and best.

Liquids

Pour liquids into rigid containers, leaving ½-in (1-cm) headroom. Freeze until solid, then remove and rewrap in freezer bags.

Interleaving

Separate individual items like chops and steaks so they do not stick together when frozen, then pack them in a freezer bag.

Tray freezing

Arrange delicate items like berries and meringues on trays so they freeze separately, then pack in freezer bags once solid.

Blanching

Blanch vegetables in boiling water, then plunge into ice water and drain well before freezing. This helps retain color and texture.

WHAT FREEZES WELL?

- FRUIT frozen raw will always be slightly softer after thawing, but is still good. More successful are fruits poached in syrup or juice, puréed, or cut in chunks for pies and puddings. Storage: 12 months
- VEGETABLES usually need to be blanched first (see box, left), or they can be frozen in cooked dishes such as soups and casseroles. Storage: 12 months
- MEAT, POULTRY AND GAME BIRDS, AND FISH must be very fresh; smaller pieces are best. (Shellfish such as crab, lobster, and shrimp are better bought frozen.) Storage: beef 8 months; lamb, veal, and pork 6 months; bacon and sausages 1 month; game birds 12 months; poultry 8 months; white fish 3 months; oily fish and shellfish 2 months
- FRESH PASTA, both filled and unfilled, freezes well. Pasta in sauce tends to be soft when thawed, although made-up pasta dishes work well. Storage: 3 months
- DAIRY PRODUCTS with higher fat contents are best – full-fat hard cheeses are more successful than lower-fat cheeses. Storage: hard cheese 6 months; full-fat cream cheese 6 weeks; butter 3 months; homogenized milk and whole-milk yogurt 1 month
- BREADS, PASTRIES, AND CAKES all freeze well. Pastry can be cooked or uncooked; quiche fillings should be made with cream, not milk. Cakes are best frozen before filling or icing. Storage: most bread 6 months; crusty bread 3 weeks; cakes and pastries 3 months

THAWING & REHEATING

For some foods, thawing before cooking or reheating is not necessary, but others must be thoroughly thawed before cooking. Cook thawed food immediately, to kill any bacteria, and never refreeze foods already thawed unless you cook them first.

- VEGETABLES AND PASTA – add directly to boiling water.
- FISH FILLETS AND SHELLFISH – cook from frozen.
- SAUCES AND SOUPS – heat gently until thawed.
- THICKER PIECES OF MEAT – thaw before cooking.
- POULTRY – unwrap, cover loosely, and thaw completely on a lipped plate in the refrigerator (bacteria multiply at room temperature).

MICROWAVING

The microwave has revolutionized cooking for people with busy lifestyles. It can cook fish and many vegetables and fruit to perfection, retaining vitamins, color, and texture, and it thaws frozen food quickly and successfully. It also performs myriad other tasks that speed preparation in the kitchen.

Special equipment is not essential for cooking in a microwave, as many containers and implements used for conventional cooking are suitable. For convenience, use the dish you want to eat from.

- ROUND OR OVAL DISHES with straight sides are the most efficient for even heat distribution.
- OVENPROOF GLASS and ceramic dishes are excellent, as are plastics specially made for the microwave (other plastic containers may soften and distort, or even melt and collapse). Metal pans should not be used.
- USE LARGE CONTAINERS for liquids, and keep stirring to avoid a buildup of hot spots and to prevent liquids from boiling over.

TIPS FOR SUCCESS

Arranging food properly (see box, below) will ensure even cooking. Just remember that microwaves penetrate food from the outside toward the middle. Covering food with a lid or plastic wrap (not foil) prevents it from drying out during cooking and traps steam, which helps to heat the food.

- MOST MICROWAVES contain a turntable, which rotates the food and exposes it evenly to the microwaves.
- IF COOKING in a dish that does not have a lid, cover it securely with plastic wrap, or put the food in a roasting bag and fasten with a plastic (not metal) tie.
- PAPER TOWELS are useful for soaking up moisture and covering foods loosely to prevent spattering (do not use recycled paper, which may contain tiny fragments of metal). You can also use wax paper.
- FOR THOROUGH, EVEN COOKING, stir foods halfway, or regularly, during microwaving. The microwaves will continue to produce heat inside the food after it has come out of the oven, so always let food stand for a few minutes to finish cooking before serving.

THAWING KNOW-HOW

Thawing must be done slowly and gently, so that the outside does not begin to cook before the inside is thawed. For this reason always use the Defrost setting.

- BREAK UP and stir stews, soups, and sauces as they thaw.
- SET FROZEN BREAD, pastry, and cakes on paper towels so that moisture will be absorbed as they thaw.
- BE SURE meat and poultry are completely thawed before cooking.
- COOK FOOD as soon as possible once it is thawed.

ARRANGING FOODS

Simple, but clever, techniques will help you microwave food as quickly and efficiently as possible.

Arrange unevenly shaped food in a circle with the densest parts – for example, the thick stems of broccoli or the meaty parts of chicken drumsticks – facing outward in the dish.

Position foods of the same size and shape, or small individual dishes, in a circle, with space between them, so that the microwaves can penetrate and reach the food from all sides.

USE A MICROWAVE TO …

- Soften or melt cold butter
- Toast nuts
- Warm bread, rolls, croissants, bagels, and the like
- Cook bacon perfectly crisp
- Soften a wedge of Brie or Camembert
- Make deliciously creamy scrambled eggs
- Soften chopped onions
- Cook rice to perfection
- Make breakfast oatmeal or bedtime cocoa
- Cook corn on the cob (set it on paper towels)
- Melt chocolate (stir halfway)
- Soften crystallized honey (take lid off jar) and ice cream
- Warm citrus fruit so it yields more juice

THE WELL-PROVISIONED KITCHEN

With a supply of useful ingredients always on hand, you should never be short of ideas for an impromptu meal or interesting flavorings to add zest to your cooking, or the basics for a cake, a loaf of bread, or a favorite dessert. Everyone will have a different list of essential staples, according to what they prefer to cook and eat, but most of our pantries, refrigerators, and freezers will contain many of the same basic elements.

THE PANTRY

Gone are the days when every home had a pantry, a dry, often dark, cold room in which to keep foodstuffs like vegetables and fruit that would otherwise quickly deteriorate in the warmth of the kitchen.

Nowadays most of us have to manage with a cupboard in the kitchen, using the refrigerator for storage more than we used to, if only because it is the only cold place we have. You will find advice on storing different foods in the Know-How pages of individual chapters, but here are some general tips:

- CHOOSE A CUPBOARD in the coolest part of your kitchen – not next to a radiator, boiler, or oven – and make sure it is dry.
- PACK THE SHELVES logically – bags of flour together, alongside packages of sugar or of rice and pasta, for example – with the things that you use most often arranged at the front.
- MARK PURCHASE DATES on cans, packages, and jars, and regularly check them. Note pull dates or date codes on bought chilled and frozen food. Also check if foods need to be refrigerated once opened.

DRY GOODS

Grains, pasta, and dried beans and peas form the backbone of the pantry – combined with fresh foods they will provide an infinite variety of nutritious meals. Other dry staples to keep on hand are sugars and flours, as well as nuts and seeds, dried fruits, spices and dried herbs, a selection of crackers, and breakfast cereals. If you like to bake cakes and cookies or breads, baking powder, baking soda, and active dry yeast are a must. You might also want to stock cream of tartar, gelatin (leaves and/or granules), unsweetened cocoa powder, and bouillon cubes or powder, plus, of course, salt and pepper, coffee, and tea.

- RICE is so versatile – it can be served as an accompaniment or used as an ingredient in both savory and sweet dishes. Many types are available, varying in size and shape of grain, color, and texture, whether wholegrain or polished (white). Wholegrain rice has had only the outer, inedible husk removed, which makes it more nutritious than white rice. It is worth keeping a selection of different rices in your pantry.

  Long-grain rices, which stay in separate grains once cooked, include flavorful and aromatic basmati, Texmati (a cross between basmati and American long-grain), red rice (which is a wholegrain rice), Thai fragrant rice, also called jasmine rice, and long-grain (patna or Carolina) rice. Parboiled or converted rice is a very nutritious white long-grain rice; instant or quick white rice is fully or partially cooked and its grains never stick together.

  Medium- and short-grain rices have starchy grains that tend to cling together after cooking. Types include risotto rice (sometimes labeled as arborio or carnaroli rice), which has plump, oval grains, and a similar paella rice, the best of which is said to come from Valencia, Spain; sticky rice (also called glutinous rice – a misnomer because it contains no gluten); sweet mochi rice, very glutinous and with a high starch content; and sushi rice.

- **OTHER-GRAINS** offer interesting and tasty alternatives to rice, as well as meals or flours, and flakes for granola and hot cereals. They include:

  Bulgur, which is part-cooked, cracked, and crushed wheat grains. It is very easy to prepare – it needs only soaking or a few minutes cooking – and is popular in the Mediterranean and Middle East. Cracked wheat is similar but takes longer to cook.

  Cornmeal, a yellow, white, or blue granular meal ground from dried corn kernels. Cooked with water or stock until it thickens, it makes the northern Italian dish called polenta. It is also used to make quick breads, hot cereal, and cakes.

  Couscous, not a true grain but a type of pasta made from semolina flour. It is used much like rice as an accompaniment or as part of a salad or other dish.

  Oat groats and rolled oats, which are cooked and eaten as cereal. Groats can also be prepared like rice.

  Pearl barley, and its wholegrain form hulled barley, most often used in soups and casseroles. They can also be cooked like rice for side dishes and pilafs.

- **DRIED PASTA** is available in myriad shapes and sizes, the majority of which are interchangeable in recipes. Italian pasta is made from wheat flour, sometimes enriched with egg, whereas Asian and non-wheat pastas can be made from mung-bean starch (cellophane or bean thread noodles), rice flour (rice sticks), buckwheat flour (Japanese soba), cornstarch, potato flour, and soybean or yam starch. Spaghetti, tagliatelle or fettuccine, penne, and fusilli are basic Italian pasta shapes to keep in your pantry, plus some Asian noodles to partner quick stir-fries.

- **DRIED BEANS, PEAS, AND LENTILS** are easy to prepare, although (with the exception of lentils and split peas) they take time to cook. For speed, use canned beans, which are just as nutritious as dried.

UNUSUAL GRAINS TO TRY

- **KASHA**, which is roasted whole or cracked buckwheat groats, tends to break down when cooked, so it is good used in risotto-type dishes.
- **QUINOA** (pronounced "keen-wa") is a very nutritious and ancient grain from South America. It contains more protein than any other grain, and is also higher in unsaturated fats and lower in carbohydrates than most – all of which make it a useful addition to a healthy diet. Quinoa is quite bland, with a flavor similar to that of couscous. It can be cooked in the same ways as rice.
- **WHOLE GRAINS** of oat, rye, and wheat, also known as kernels, groats, and berries, make an unusual substitute for brown rice.

LEGUMES

Dried beans, peas, and lentils make up the family of legumes. All but lentils and split peas are usually presoaked, and need 10 minutes' hard boiling at the beginning of cooking.

Red Kidney Beans
Popular in Mexican cooking, especially in chile con carne, their deep red skins add color to many salads and stews.

Cannellini Beans
These Italian white kidney beans are good in soups and salads. Other white beans are the larger great Northern and smaller navy.

Black Beans
Traditional in Caribbean, Mexican, Chinese, and Brazilian dishes, these slightly sweet beans go well with rice and spicy sauces.

Cranberry Beans
Creamy in consistency, these are large beans with a delicious flavor. They are also known as shell beans and, in Italy, borlotti beans.

Azuki Beans
Tender-textured beans with a strong flavor, azuki are used in Chinese and Japanese rice dishes and soups, and in red bean paste.

Chickpeas
Famous in hummus and other Middle Eastern dishes, chickpeas (or garbanzos) are also used in Indian and Spanish cooking.

Split Peas
These are field peas that are dried and split. Yellow and green are available, and are interchangeable in soups, purées, and bakes.

Lentils
Reddish-orange and yellow lentils cook quickly and become mushy, while greenish-brown lentils and lentilles de Puy retain their shape.

TOMATOES

These three tomato-based products are useful to keep in the pantry for boosting the flavor of fresh tomatoes or adding a rich tomato taste on their own.

Sun-Dried Tomatoes

If sold packed in oil, sun-dried tomatoes can be used as they are; those tomatoes dry-packed in cellophane usually need to be soaked in oil or another liquid first

Tomato Paste

Available in cans and tubes, this is a richly flavored concentrate, useful for adding depth of color and flavor to cooked dishes. Sun-dried tomato versions are milder and sweeter.

Tomato Purée

Tomatoes are crushed or cooked briefly and then strained to make this smooth, thick liquid, sold in cans or jars. Purée is useful in sauces, soups, and stews.

SAUCES, PRESERVES, SYRUPS, OILS & VINEGARS

For use at the table and as quick-and-easy instant flavorings, here are some pantry possibilities.

- HOT PEPPER SAUCES, such as Tabasco, Asian chili, and Moroccan harissa, are fiery condiments that will give a kick to any bland food. Hot HORSERADISH SAUCE is another way to add zest.
- WORCESTERSHIRE SAUCE has a piquant salty flavor, good in sauces and marinades.
- PESTO SAUCE (made from basil, Parmesan, and pine nuts) and TAPENADE (black olive paste) can be stirred into hot pasta and rice, and used in dips.
- MAYONNAISE is a favorite in sandwiches and salad dressings, such as the classic Thousand Island, as well as making a base for dips. Reduced-fat, fat-free, and flavored versions are available.
- TOMATO KETCHUP is good for mixing into sauces and dressings, as well as topping burgers. A spoonful or two of TOMATO PASTE will add flavor and color to sauces, soups, and stews, while TOMATO PUREE can form the basis of a pasta sauce or soup.
- ASIAN SAUCES – soy and tamari, oyster, chili, hoisin, teriyaki, and bean, plus miso, sesame, and wasabi pastes – are traditional in Chinese and Japanese dishes and can also add exciting flavors to Western ones. For Southeast-Asian cooking, you might want to keep fish sauce (also called nam pla), tamarind paste, and coconut milk and cream.

- CURRY PASTES come in varying strengths, and are ideal for quickly spicing curries as well as soups and creamy dressings for poultry salads.
- PRESERVES, such as mango chutney, red-currant jelly, and marmalade, add fruity sweetness to a dish; other chutneys offer hot and spicy flavors. Pickles and relishes may be sweet or tangy.
- MUSTARD appears in many different flavors, colors, and textures, and all types can be used in cooking or as a condiment. It is useful to stock the three basics: strong Dijon mustard, coarse-grain mustard, and very hot and pungent English mustard.
- OILS are used for frying, brushing, and basting, as well as in marinades and dressings. Two types – a neutral-flavored general-purpose oil such as sunflower and a more flavorful olive oil – are the basics to keep in stock. In addition, you might want to add walnut, hazelnut, or toasted sesame oils, plus an oil or two flavored with your favorite herbs or spices.
- VINEGARS add pep to dressings and sauces as well as being essential in pickles and relishes. Red or white wine vinegar is a must, with cider, sherry, and balsamic vinegars being optional choices. The cheaper balsamics are satisfactory for cooking, while the more expensive varieties are best kept for drizzling on food before serving or at the table.
- SYRUPS – honey and maple – make instant sweet sauces for ice cream and hot puddings.

CANNED GOODS

Pantry shelves laden with a variety of canned foods are a boon for a busy cook. If you keep a basic stock of canned fish, vegetables, and fruits, you will be able to rustle up a meal at a moment's notice.

- FISH, such as salmon, tuna, sardines, anchovies, crab, and clams, are available in many different forms – packed in various oils or in water or brine, or in flavorful sauces. Use your favorites in dips and sandwich fillings, on pizzas, in salads, and in pasta sauces and fish casseroles.

- TOMATOES come whole or crushed, in natural juice or purée, plain or flavored with herbs and garlic. Fresh tomatoes are always available, but can lack flavor when out of season; canned tomatoes taste good year round. They are also wonderfully convenient, needing no peeling or seeding before using in soups, sauces, and stews.

- LEGUMES, such as chickpeas and red kidney and cannellini beans, are a quick alternative to their dried form, as they only have to be drained and rinsed well, and they are just as nutritious. They are excellent in salads and to make dips such as hummus as well as in all kinds of hot dishes, from chile con carne to pasta e fagioli (pasta and bean soup).

- ASIAN VEGETABLES, such as bamboo shoots and water chestnuts, will add crunch to stir-fries and other Chinese or Japanese dishes.

- FRUITS – canned in natural juice for the best and truest flavor – are great standbys for quick desserts. You can also use them to bulk up a fresh winter fruit salad, and for fruit smoothies.

THE COLD STORE

The refrigerator and freezer are natural extensions of the pantry, the places where more perishable standbys can be kept safely on hand. Stocking a good selection of chilled and frozen foods means you can have the makings of all kinds of quickly prepared meals.

- DAIRY PRODUCTS – milk and the foods based on it such as butter, cheese, cream, and yogurt – are found in most people's refrigerator. There is such an amazing choice of types of milk and cream, varieties of cheese, and flavors of yogurt, and what you stock is up to you, but two very useful staples are: a piece of Parmesan cheese to grate as needed, and some thick plain yogurt to serve with and/or in sweet and savory dishes, or to blend with fruit to make delicious smoothies. In the freezer, you can keep milk, butter, cream, and whole-milk yogurt for emergencies, and grated cheese to add frozen to sauces or to use as a topping for gratins and other baked dishes. For instant desserts, ice cream and frozen yogurt are a must in the freezer.

- EGGS are another essential standby. They can be the basis of simple, nutritious meals by themselves, or be added to countless other dishes, both sweet and savory.

- VEGETABLES, bought ready-prepared in bags for refrigerator storage or frozen, are a real time-saver. Chilled prepared vegetables range from trimmed carrots, green beans, and broccoli, to shelled fresh peas, cut-up root vegetables for soups and stews, and ready-washed spinach and salad leaves. Frozen vegetables, which can be more nutritious than fresh, are usually best cooked from frozen, which makes them the ultimate convenience food.

- FRUITS such as apples stay deliciously crisp in the refrigerator, ideal for snacks or adding to fruit salads; citrus fruits also store well in the refrigerator. Soft fruits – raspberries, strawberries, boysenberries, loganberries, cranberries, and so on – are very useful to have in the freezer for quick desserts and cereal toppings, as are grated citrus zest, apple or other fruit purée or chunks (for pie fillings), and fruit juice concentrates.

- BREAD is a top freezer standby. With a sliced loaf, you can take out slices as you need them – they can be toasted from frozen, as can pita bread. If you prefer unsliced bread, cut loaves into halves or quarters and freeze in separate bags so you can take out what you need – that way you will always have fresh bread. Also handy are croûtons and bread crumbs, good ways to use up the last of a staling loaf.

- SEAFOOD such as fish fillets, raw and cooked shrimp, crab, and other shellfish bought ready-frozen does not need to be thawed before cooking.

- OTHER FOODS useful in the freezer are chicken fillets – skinless, boneless breast halves – and sausages (both must be thoroughly thawed before cooking), fresh pasta (drop it frozen into a big pot of boiling salted water), herbs, unsalted nuts (they stay fresher in the freezer than in the cupboard), and coffee.

FLAVORING FOOD

Herbs, spices, and the essential seasonings, salt and pepper, enhance the flavors of the food we eat, and also often add enticing aromas and vibrant colors. It is hard to imagine cooking without them.

HERBS

With their wonderful flavors, scents, and colors, herbs can transform even the simplest dish into something very special. Most savory dishes benefit from the inclusion of one or more herbs to add flavor during cooking, or as a garnish to be sprinkled over the top of a dish just before serving. Sweet dishes, too, can be perfumed with herbs such as mint and lemon balm, and decorated with delicate herb flowers such as borage. Herbs are also used to make drinks known as infusions or tisanes.

PRESERVING HERBS
Preserve fresh herbs by freezing them. This is a better method for most herbs than drying because a fresher flavor is retained. Herbs that freeze well include parsley, tarragon, chives, dill weed, and fennel. Chop or pull off leaves or small sprigs, then mix with water in icecube trays or freeze in small plastic bags.

Herbs that can be dried successfully at home include bay leaves, sage, and rosemary. Hang them in a warm place, such as above the boiler, until dry, then pull or rub off the leaves from the stems. Pack whole bay leaves into jars; chop or crumble sage and rosemary first.

STORING HERBS
Buy or gather fresh herbs only when they are needed. If you have to store them for a day or so, keep them in a cool place or in the refrigerator. If they have stems, stand them in water, like cut flowers, and cover with a plastic bag. Dried herbs must be stored correctly or they will quickly lose their flavor. Dark glass jars or earthenware pots with airtight lids are the best for wall-mounted storage, but if you only have clear glass jars, keep them in a dark cupboard or drawer, because light causes dried herbs to deteriorate. Make sure they are kept in a cool, dry place, away from kitchen heat and steam.

Dried herbs will not keep forever, even if they are stored correctly. Herbs you have dried yourself will keep for 1 year, but purchased herbs much less, so it is best to buy in small quantities. Mark the purchase date on the bottom of the jar so you will know when to replenish your supplies.

USING HERBS
Always try to use fresh herbs, particularly in salads and sauces, as they always taste better than dried or frozen. Bunches of a wide variety of fresh herbs are available now, so there is usually no need to use dried.

Fresh herbs are often chopped or shredded before being added to a dish, and this is best done at the last possible moment. The volatile oils in herbs are released by heat or oxidation, so unless the herbs are used as soon as they are prepared, they will quickly lose their flavor and they may start to discolor (this is especially true of basil). If whole herb sprigs or leaves are used to flavor a dish, lift them out before serving. For easy removal, tie with string or wrap in cheesecloth, as in a bouquet garni (see box, page 29).

Herbs that dry well include sage, oregano and marjoram, bay, and dill weed, and these are good used in dishes that require long cooking. When buying dried herbs, look for those that are freeze-dried, because they have the best flavor, color, and aroma.

Another option you might want to try are the preserved herbs in oil packed in tubes or bottles – they are very convenient, and useful to keep in the refrigerator for those times when you run out of fresh herbs at the last moment.

Dried herbs are more pungent than fresh, so a smaller quantity is required. Use ½ teaspoon finely powdered dried herb or 1 teaspoon crumbled dried herb in place of 1 tablespoon chopped fresh herb.

HERB FLAVORS

The range of herbs in the shops is exciting for adventurous cooks, and even more varieties can be grown at home. These are the most commonly used.

- FRESH-TASTING HERBS: parsley (used both as a flavoring and garnish; flat-leaf has a more pronounced, spicier flavor than curly) and chives (a delicate taste of onion with a crunchy texture).
- SWEET HERBS: basil (spicy and aromatic; many varieties in addition to sweet basil, such as opal or purple basil and anise-flavored Thai basil), bay leaves (with a pungent, resinous aroma), mint (including cool and mellow spearmint or garden mint, pungent peppermint, spicy Moroccan mint, and fruity apple mint), and oregano and marjoram (marjoram is subtly spicy while oregano has a more peppery or lemony bite; they can be used interchangeably).
- ANISE-FLAVORED HERBS: chervil (delicate taste and pretty leaves), tarragon (pungent), dill weed (fragrant and tangy; seeds are used as a spice), and fennel (mild and slightly sweet; seeds are used as a spice).
- PUNGENT HERBS: rosemary (aroma and flavor are not reduced by long cooking), sage (spicy, often slightly musky), thyme (pleasantly strong and slightly peppery), cilantro (spicy citrus aroma and taste), and garlic (whole cloves roasted or simmered are mellow, crushed and sautéed much stronger; new garlic is milder in flavor than dried garlic).

PREPARING HERBS

Rinse the herbs well under cold running water and dry with paper towels. Then remove leaves or sprigs from the stems.

Chopping
Gather the leaves or sprigs into a compact pile on a chopping board. Chop the leaves with a sharp knife, rocking the blade back and forth, until the herbs are as fine as you want them. A mezzaluna (see page 19) is useful for chopping a large quantity.

Snipping
A pair of sharp scissors is best for snipping chives. Hold the stalks in one hand and snip into short lengths, either into a bowl or directly into the dish you are flavoring. This technique is also good for finely shredding large-leaved herbs such as sage.

Making a Bouquet Garni

Hold 2–3 sprigs each of thyme and parsley with 1–2 bay leaves. If you like, wrap in two pieces of pared orange zest, or two pieces of celery, then tie into a bouquet with kitchen string. Orange and celery work well in beef and pork casseroles.

HERB MIXTURES

There are classic combinations of herbs, most of them from France, that are often used in cooking, especially in dishes like stews and casseroles that need long, slow simmering or cooking in the oven.

- A BOUQUET GARNI is used in many long-cooked dishes. The traditional combination for a fresh bouquet garni is parsley, thyme, and bay, but this may be varied according to the dish being flavored (see box, above). If using dried herbs, or adding other flavorings such as peppercorns or spice berries, wrap them all in a cheesecloth bag. Remember to remove the bouquet garni before serving (if you use a long piece of string, this can be tied to the pan handle for easy removal after cooking).
- HERBES DE PROVENCE, an aromatic mixture of sage, basil, summer savory, thyme, rosemary, fennel seed, lavender, and marjoram, is a classic French mixture. Good in poultry, meat, and vegetable dishes, it should be used sparingly.
- FINES HERBES combines equal quantities of tarragon, chervil, parsley, and chives. It works well in omelets and with fish and poultry.
- DRIED HERB MIXTURES, such as Italian seasoning (basil, oregano, and rosemary) and poultry seasoning (sage plus thyme, marjoram, savory, or rosemary), are also widely available.

GROWING YOUR OWN HERBS

The range of fresh herbs available in wholefood markets and supermarkets is extensive, but buying them is much more expensive than using those you grow yourself, especially if you use large amounts. Also, growing your own gives you the chance to try more unusual varieties of herbs. Cultivation, indoors or out, is simple and satisfying. Herbs can be grown in the garden, in pots on a paved terrace or patio, in a hanging basket, or in a window box. Indoors, they will flourish in a box or in pots on a sunny windowsill.

SPICES

In the past, spices were often used to mask the taste of less-than-perfect food, and at one time were so precious and expensive that they would be locked away in special spice boxes or cupboards. Today, spices are no longer a luxury seasoning, and modern cooks use them to enhance flavors rather than to disguise them.

BUYING AND STORING SPICES

If they are whole, spices do not deteriorate as quickly as herbs (which is why it is best to buy whole spices and grind them as you need them). Store in tightly sealed containers in a cool, dark, dry place. Whole spices will keep for 1 year, ground spices for about 6 months.

USING SPICES

Because spices need time to release their aromas and flavors, they are usually added near the start of cooking. If the cooking process is prolonged, whole, cracked, or bruised spices are normally used rather than ground spices, which may become bitter.

Toasting or warming whole or ground spices before use brings out their flavors, and is a good thing to do if the spices are to be added to a dish that is cooked for only a short time. When toasting, use a heavy frying pan over a low heat because the spices can scorch easily; if toasting ground spices add a little oil to the pan. Warm the spices just until they smell aromatic.

SALT

Salt is the essential seasoning, both for cooking and as a table condiment. It enhances the natural flavors of all savory foods and some sweet ones, and is important in baking and in the preservation of food. Most salt is mined from deposits of dried salt lakes underground; the rest (sea salt) is evaporated from sea water. Salt may be coarse-grained (kosher salt is one example) or fine-grained (examples are table salt, which has additives to keep it free-flowing, and iodized salt, which is table salt with added iodine).

Monosodium glutamate (MSG) is used in a similar way to salt, to accentuate flavors.

SPICE FLAVORS

Spices come in many shapes and sizes, with subtly differing flavors and fragrances. They can be as exotic as rosebuds and licorice root or as familiar as cinnamon and cloves. Here are some of the most commonly used.

- HOT SPICES stimulate the palate and sharpen the appetite as well as encouraging the body to produce perspiration – an excellent means of cooling down in a hot climate. The best known hot spice is chili, which is available as whole chili peppers (fresh or dried), dried chili flakes (also called dried red pepper flakes), and ground into chili powder (usually a blend of ground chilies and other spices), very hot cayenne pepper, and paprika (may be mild or hot). In addition there are chili sauces and pastes, oils, and

PREPARING SPICES

The way in which spices are prepared depends on the recipe in which they are used and the depth of flavor required.

Whole spices
Whole spices (and herbs) that are to be removed before a dish is served are best tied in a piece of cheesecloth, so they can be lifted out all at once.

Toasting spices
Heat a heavy frying pan until hot. Add the spices and cook over a low heat for 1–2 minutes, stirring occasionally, until the aromas are released. Let cool, then grind.

Grinding spices
Put the whole spices into a mortar; crush them with a pestle to the required consistency. Or, grind in a small electric mill kept specially for grinding spices.

Soaking saffron
Put saffron threads into a small bowl and add hot water (usually an amount is specified in the recipe). Let soak for 10 minutes. Use the threads and liquid.

jam. Just as the hundreds of different varieties of chili pepper vary from pleasantly warm through to burning hot, so do the spices and mixtures derived from them.

- PEPPER is an aromatic hot spice. Black, white, green, and red or pink peppercorns are available, each different in taste and fragrance. Freshly ground black pepper is used in almost every savory dish plus a few sweet ones and is an essential table condiment. There are also two Asian peppers: fragrant Sichuan pepper and Japanese sansho.
- OTHER HOT SPICES are the familiar mustard, plus ginger and galangal. Mustard is available as whole seeds, powder, or readymade paste, and in blended mixtures that include herbs, other spices, or even fruit flavors – the French *moutarde au cassis*, for example, contains crème de cassis (black-currant liqueur) for a rich taste and vibrant red color. Ginger and the less familiar galangal are similar in appearance and in taste; they are actually knobby rhizomes, not roots. Both are available fresh (try Asian markets or a large supermarket), as powder, and in dried slices that need to be soaked in water before using (they are good to flavor soups and stews, but take care to remove the slices before serving).
- WARM, FRAGRANT SPICES provide a sweet note. They are usually added at the beginning of cooking so that their flavor and aroma can permeate the dish, be it sweet or savory. Warm spices include allspice (a single spice that is like a peppery mixture of cloves and cinnamon), green cardamom (pods contain tiny, sticky black seeds), cinnamon, cloves, coriander seed, pretty star anise and anise seed (both licorice-like), nutmeg and mace (nutmeg is the seed and mace its wrapping), and vanilla (use beans or pure extract).
- NUTTY SPICES include poppy seeds and sesame seeds.
- PUNGENT SPICES are assertive in taste so should be used judiciously. They include juniper berries (slightly sweet and resinous), cumin (warm and a bit sharp), and caraway.
- FRUITY SPICES may be sweet or refreshingly tart. They range from sourish tamarind (available as dried pulp in a block, paste, or concentrate) to lemon grass stalks and kaffir lime leaves.
- COLORING SPICES will tint as well as flavor a dish. Saffron is expensive but only a pinch is needed to color a dish yellow (and add a warm, musky taste). Turmeric gives a richer, yellow-ocher hue, and is slightly more bitter. The dark red color of goulash and chorizo sausages comes from paprika (ground chili peppers).

THE CHILI SPICE FAMILY

The different powders derived from dried chili peppers can be confusing. Some are much hotter than others, so it is wise to know which is which.

Paprika
The mildest of the chili family, paprika is available in three forms – sweet (mild), sharp (hot), and smoked (musky).

Cayenne or Red Pepper
A pungent, hot powder made from one of the hottest varieties of chili pepper with nothing added. Use with caution.

Chili Powder
A blend of ground chili pepper with herbs and other spices, usually oregano and cumin, plus garlic. Strength varies.

SPICE MIXTURES

Although there is nothing like the thrill of inventing and grinding your own mixtures from whole spices, readymade blends of ground spices do save time for the busy cook. Mixtures vary according to individual manufacturers and brands; try different brands to find which you prefer. These are the most common.

- CURRY POWDER may be hot or perfumed and mild, according to the blend of spices (usually turmeric, fenugreek, coriander, cumin, cardamom, chili, cinnamon, and paprika). It gives curries an authentic flavor, which is often difficult to achieve yourself.
- GARAM MASALA, an aromatic curry spice, is usually a mixture of cumin, coriander, cardamom, cinnamon, pepper, cloves, turmeric, and ginger, sometimes with mace and bay. It is best added to a dish toward the end of the cooking time to preserve its fine aroma.
- APPLE PIE SPICE is a mixture of allspice, cinnamon, cloves, mace, and nutmeg. PUMPKIN PIE SPICE combines cinnamon, nutmeg, ginger, and cloves.
- FIVE-SPICE POWDER is a Chinese blend of five flavors (salty, sour, bitter, pungent, and sweet) – hence its name. It is a mixture of ground star anise, fennel, cloves, cinnamon, and Sichuan pepper. Dried ginger, cardamom, or licorice can be added to the mixture, although commercial powders rarely include these.

SAFE & HEALTHY COOKING

It is important to handle and store perishable foods with care, so they remain at their best, and to help prevent food poisoning. The common-sense food safety guidelines are easy to follow and will ensure that you can enjoy what you eat without worries.

DAIRY PRODUCTS

Eggs should be stored in the refrigerator. It is best to leave them in their carton so you can keep an eye on the date stamp. Some have a Julian date (1–365), which indicates the day of the year the eggs were packed; others show a date 30 days after the packing date. Keeping eggs in their carton will also prevent them from absorbing the odors of other foods in the refrigerator.

Eggs can harbor the salmonella bacterium, which can cause severe food poisoning. While the risk of salmonella infection is low, it is wise to handle and cook eggs with care. Thorough cooking (firm whites and thickened yolks, and to a temperature of 145°F/63°C) will destroy any bacteria that may be present. People in vulnerable groups (pregnant women, babies and young children, the elderly, the sick, and people with compromised immune systems) should avoid eating raw eggs (such as in homemade mayonnaise) and lightly cooked eggs (e.g. runny scrambled eggs), unless the eggs have been pasteurized.

Soft cheeses ripened using molds (such as Brie and Camembert) and soft blue cheeses (whether made from pasteurized or unpasteurized milk) may harbor the listeria bacterium, which can cause an illness similar to flu. Listeria is of no concern to adults in normal health, but those people in vulnerable groups (as listed above) may want to avoid these sorts of soft cheeses.

MEAT & POULTRY

Raw meat can contain bacteria that cause food poisoning, so it must be handled safely. Keep it in the refrigerator, in its original wrapping or transferred to fresh wrapping or a covered dish, and away from any food that will not be cooked before eating, such as salad ingredients. Normal cooking – even if just to rare – will destroy any surface bacteria that may be present, but ground meat should be cooked thoroughly – to 155°F (68°C).

Poultry such as chicken and turkey can be infected with food-poisoning bacteria, commonly salmonella and campylobacter. So, as with meat, keep poultry in the refrigerator and cook it thoroughly. To ensure this, it is recommended that the body cavity not be stuffed (this could prevent heat from penetrating to the center of the bird). If you do want to stuff the body cavity, fill it loosely and only two-thirds full, and stuff no more than 3 hours before cooking. Then at the end of the cooking time test the internal temperature of the bird and of the stuffing using an instant-read thermometer: the thigh meat and the stuffing should be at least 170°F (75°C) and the breast meat 160°F (71°C). Cool any leftovers as quickly as possible (no more than 2 hours at room temperature), then wrap them and store in the refrigerator or freezer.

SEAFOOD

Mussels, clams, and oysters bought alive are very perishable. Store, covered with a damp cloth, in the coldest part of the refrigerator, and use the same day. When preparing mussels and clams for cooking, discard any that have broken shells or with gaping shells that do not close when sharply tapped (these are not safe to eat). After cooking, discard any that have not opened.

Crab, shrimp, and lobster must also be very fresh; they become poisonous when stale. If they smell of ammonia or at all unpleasant, do not buy them.

Fish bought as fresh may previously have been frozen, so be sure to check. If it was previously frozen it must not be frozen again (unless it is used in a cooked dish such as a casserole).

GRAINS & LEGUMES

Leftover cooked rice should always be cooled quickly and stored in a covered container in the refrigerator (for no longer than a day or so) or in the freezer – if not kept cool it could develop food-poisoning toxins. Be sure to reheat cooked rice until it is very hot.

Most legumes contain toxic proteins that can cause severe food-poisoning symptoms. To destroy the toxins, give all dried beans and peas (with the exception of chickpeas, split peas, and lentils) a fast boil for 10–15 minutes at the start of cooking, then reduce the heat and continue to simmer until tender.

HOT & CHILLED SOUPS

UNDER 30 MINUTES

30–60 MINUTES

ASIAN CLASSIC

THAI SPICED SOUP

Fresh and chunky: shredded chicken, bean sprouts, and leafy vegetables simmered in coconut milk and stock. Served over noodles.

SERVES 4 238 calories per serving

Takes 25 minutes   Page 55

DINNER PARTY

ASPARAGUS SOUP

Fresh asparagus blended with stock and potatoes, and richly flavored with garlic. Garnished here with nuggets of butter.

SERVES 6 96 calories per serving

Takes 25 minutes   Page 42

LOW FAT

FRENCH PEA SOUP

Smooth and summery: onion blended with frozen or fresh peas (in season) and stock, and flavored with mint sprigs.

SERVES 4–6 179–119 calories per serving

Takes 35 minutes   Page 40

ECONOMICAL

WATERCRESS SOUP

Smooth and creamy: blended onion, potatoes, watercress, stock, and milk, lightly flavored with a bay leaf. Can be served hot or cold.

SERVES 6 140 calories per serving

Takes 25 minutes   Page 43

FAMILY CHOICE

TOMATO SOUP

Tomatoes, onions, and garlic blended with stock. Enriched with readymade pesto sauce and flavored with a bay leaf.

SERVES 6–8 134–101 calories per serving

Takes 25 minutes   Page 45

CUBAN CORN &

CUBAN CORN & SEAFOOD SOUP

Firm white fish with corn, pumpkin, potato, stock, and tomato purée, simmered with chili and garlic.

SERVES 4 379 calories per serving

Takes 40 minutes   Page 50

TASTY MUSHROOM SOUP

Mushrooms, garlic, and onion cooked with stock and white wine, and generously flavored with thyme and marjoram.

SERVES 4–6 109–73 calories per serving

Takes 25 minutes   Page 41

ASIAN CLASSIC

CHINESE CRAB & CORN SOUP

Blended corn kernels cooked with crabmeat and stock, and flavored with soy sauce, green onions, garlic, and ginger.

SERVES 4 216 calories per serving

Takes 20 minutes   Page 55

HIGH PROTEIN

LENTIL & BACON SOUP

Nourishing and hearty: diced vegetables, bacon, and lentils simmered in stock, and richly flavored with garlic and herbs.

SERVES 4–6 301–201 calories per serving

Takes 50 minutes   Page 53

30–60 MINUTES

AMERICAN CLASSIC

CLAM CHOWDER

Fresh clams cooked in fish stock, then simmered with milk, onion, and potatoes, and flavored with bacon and bay leaf.

SERVES 4 497 calories per serving

Takes 50 minutes Page 48

ANGLO-INDIAN FAVORITE

INDIAN-SPICED SMOKED HADDOCK CHOWDER

Vegetables and spices, simmered with smoked haddock and stock, make a rich and piquant soup.

SERVES 4 500 calories per serving

Takes 50 minutes Page 46

PUMPKIN SOUP

Nourishing and smooth: blended pumpkin, leeks, and stock, enriched with cream, and combined with peas and spinach.

SERVES 6 329 calories per serving

Takes 50 minutes Page 52

GAME SOUP

Rich and aromatic: bacon and mushrooms simmered in game stock, flavored with a citrus and herb bouquet and red-currant jelly.

SERVES 4 223 calories per serving

Takes 50 minutes Page 53

DINNER PARTY

CURRIED PARSNIP SOUP

Smooth and spicy: parsnips blended with mild curry powder, onion, garlic, and stock, and enriched with cream.

SERVES 6–8 197–147 calories per serving

Takes 35 minutes Page 44

VEGETARIAN

SPICED AUTUMN SOUP

Potatoes, carrots, apples, orange zest and juice, tomatoes, and stock blended with onion, garlic, curry powder, and dried basil.

SERVES 8 171 calories per serving

Takes 50 minutes Page 47

HIGH PROTEIN

BLUE CHEESE & ONION SOUP

Creamy and rich: finely sliced onions combined with stock, blue Stilton cheese, bay leaves, and nutmeg make a tasty soup.

SERVES 8 255 calories per serving

Takes 50 minutes Page 47

FAMILY CHOICE

WINTER VEGETABLE SOUP

Assortment of seasonal vegetables simmered with stock, seasoned with dill and turmeric, and colored with spinach.

SERVES 6 153 calories per serving

Takes 55 minutes Page 44

HOT & SOUR SOUP

Rich and tangy: dried mushrooms, sliced cabbage, tofu, bamboo shoots, and chicken simmered with stock, and enriched with eggs.

SERVES 4–6 249–166 calories per serving

Takes 50 minutes Page 54

OVER 60 MINUTES

TZATZIKI SOUP

Cool and refreshing: yogurt, cucumber, and garlic blended with olive oil, white wine vinegar, and mint, and served chilled.

SERVES 4–6 138–92 calories per serving
Takes 15 minutes, plus chilling   Page 56

TRADITIONAL RUSSIAN

BORSCHT

Beets, cabbage, potatoes, and tomatoes simmered with stock, vinegar, sugar, and dill for a rich sweet-sour flavor.

SERVES 4 244 calories per serving
Takes 1¼ hours   Page 45

BOUILLABAISSE

Mediterranean favorite: assorted white fish and shellfish simmered in stock with vegetables, orange zest, and Provençal herbs.

SERVES 8 337 calories per serving
Takes 1¼ hours   Page 51

GAZPACHO

Tomatoes, pimientoes, and garlic blended with stock, olive oil, and red wine vinegar make a rich iced soup. Served with garlic croûtons.

SERVES 4–6 249–166 calories per serving
Takes 15 minutes, plus chilling   Page 57

LOW FAT

RICH FISH SOUP

White fish fillets blended with stock, dry white wine, and mixed vegetables, and richly flavored with garlic and herbs.

SERVES 4 419 calories per serving
Takes 1¼ hours   Page 48

SHRIMP GUMBO

Red bell pepper and tomatoes cooked with chorizo, stock, and okra make a piquant base for shrimp. Served with a rice timbale.

SERVES 4 512 calories per serving
Takes 1¼ hours   Page 50

FRENCH CLASSIC

FRENCH ONION SOUP

Thinly sliced caramelized onions simmered in beef stock and topped with a traditional Gruyère croûte.

SERVES 8 353 calories per serving
Takes 1¼ hours   Page 42

VEGETARIAN

CREAMY CARROT & ORANGE SOUP

Smooth and tangy: carrots and stock mixed with crème fraîche or sour cream, orange zest and juice, and fresh chives.

SERVES 6–8 300–201 calories per serving
Takes 1¼ hours   Page 40

DINNER PARTY

LOBSTER BISQUE

Rich-tasting and luxurious: lobster, shallots, brandy, wine, stock, and spices combined with cream (optional) and lemon juice.

SERVES 6 192 calories per serving
Takes 1½ hours   Page 49

OVER 60 MINUTES

CHILLED STRAWBERRY SOUP

White wine sweetened with sugar and blended with strawberries and orange juice, then chilled for a refreshing fruit soup.

SERVES 4 169 calories per serving

Takes 15 minutes, plus chilling   Page 58

GOULASH SOUP

Rich and wholesome: beef, roasted red bell peppers, onions, potatoes, and tomatoes cooked in stock, and flavored with paprika.

SERVES 4–6 544–363 calories per serving

Takes 2¹/4 hours   Page 52

ROASTED TOMATO & GARLIC SOUP

Light and well flavored: roasted ripe tomatoes cooked with onion and stock, and richly flavored with garlic.

SERVES 4 127 calories per serving

Takes 40 minutes, plus standing   Page 41

BLUEBERRY & RED WINE SOUP

Chilled and fruity: cranberry juice, red wine, cinnamon, and sugar simmered with blueberries, and enriched with cream.

SERVES 4 364 calories per serving

Takes 30 minutes, plus chilling   Page 57

VICHYSSOISE

Leeks, onion, and potatoes blended with chicken stock, chilled, then combined with cream, result in this renowned velvety soup.

SERVES 4–6 251–167 calories per serving

Takes 45 minutes, plus chilling   Page 56

VEGETABLE MINESTRONE

Hearty soup: dried beans cooked and added to a tomato sauce with stock, leeks, cabbage, and arborio rice.

SERVES 4–6 250–167 calories per serving

Takes 1³/4 hours, plus soaking   Page 43

CHILLED CURRIED APPLE & MINT SOUP

Apples blended with onion, curry powder, stock, mango chutney, lemon juice, yogurt, and mint.

SERVES 6 110 calories per serving

Takes 40 minutes, plus chilling   Page 58

CHICKEN NOODLE SOUP

Rich and warming: simmered chicken, carrots, and stock, flavored with garlic, parsley, and dill, and served over noodles.

SERVES 6 261 calories per serving

Takes 2¹/2 hours   Page 54

SPLIT PEA & HAM SOUP

Green split peas and flavorsome ham hock, simmered with onion, celery, potatoes, and leeks, make a substantial meal.

SERVES 6–8 451–338 calories per serving

Takes 3³/4 hours, plus soaking   Page 46

SOUPS KNOW-HOW

A BATCH OF SOUP in the refrigerator is one of the best convenience foods ever, highly nutritious and wonderfully versatile. On a cold day, a bowl of soup is warming and sustaining, and with a sandwich or some good bread it can make a well-balanced lunch or supper. Soup is great for entertaining too, the ideal prepare-ahead first course. And soup is comforting at bedtime or, indeed, at any time of day.

There are all kinds of soups: light and delicate or rich and hearty; simple and quick to prepare or cooked long and slow to extract maximum flavor from the ingredients; velvety smooth in texture or full of delicious pieces of meat, vegetables, beans, or pasta. Soups may be served hot or chilled, in a mug, a bowl, or a soup plate, plain or attractively garnished. There are even sweet and fruity soups that can double up as desserts.

Clarifying stock

Skimming will make a stock quite clear, but for crystal-clear results it needs to be clarified. When cold pour into a large pan. For every 2 cups (500 ml) add an egg white and crushed egg shell. Heat slowly, whisking. When frothy and starting to rise up, stop whisking and remove from the heat to subside. The crust that forms will act as a filter, collecting all the impurities. Repeat the rising up and subsiding 2 or 3 times, then simmer for 45 minutes. Strain through a cheesecloth-lined sieve, holding back the crust.

STOCKS

A well-flavored stock forms the base of many soups, and nothing tastes as good as homemade. Stock is economical to make because it is based on meat, poultry, or fish bones and trimmings, and vegetables. Although it usually takes time to make stock – several hours of gentle simmering for meat and poultry stocks – it is easy to prepare, and can be made well in advance and in large quantities. It can then be frozen until needed. Recipes for stocks can be found on pages 122, 170, 235, and 276. If you don't have any homemade stock, you can use stock made from bouillon powder or a cube, or canned broth (either ready to serve – already diluted – or condensed). Remember, though, that these stocks and broths may be salty. If you use low-sodium canned broth you can adjust the seasoning to your taste.

SKIMMING SOUPS

As a soup is brought to a boil, foam or scum may form on the surface. This is most likely with soups that contain meat or poultry, particularly on the bone, or root vegetables, and dried beans and lentils. This foam, which contains impurities, should be removed as it forms.

Use a large metal spoon or skimmer (slotted if there are herbs and whole spices in the soup) to skim off the foam.

If there is a lot of fat on the surface of a soup, skim it off with a large metal spoon, or blot it with paper towels, before serving.

MICROWAVING

For many soups, a microwave cannot give the same results as conventional long, slow cooking, but it can produce light vegetable soups in minutes. And it is useful for thawing frozen stocks and soups, and for reheating soups. The most efficient way of heating soup in the microwave is to transfer the soup to individual bowls or mugs, because soup in larger containers will take longer to heat up than it would in a pan on the stovetop. For cooking soup in the microwave, use a container that is large enough to allow the soup to rise up slightly. Stir once or twice during cooking or heating, and just before serving, because the soup at the edge will be hot and bubbling long before that in the center. Add cream, sour cream, or plain yogurt and any garnish just before serving.

FREEZING

Soups taste best if freshly made, but most can be frozen without major impairment of flavor and texture. Avoid freezing soups containing ingredients such as pasta, potatoes, and rice, as they become mushy. It is always best to underseason, because further seasoning can be added when reheating. Add any cream, eggs, and milk at the reheating stage, because freezing could cause separation or curdling.

To thaw a soup to be served hot, heat from frozen in a heavy saucepan over a low heat, stirring occasionally. If the soup appears to be separating, whisk briskly until smooth, or work in a blender or food processor, or directly in the pan with a hand-held blender, for a few seconds. Thaw soup to be served cold in its freezer container, in the refrigerator.

THICKENING SOUPS

Many soups can be slightly thickened simply by being puréed to a smooth consistency. Puréed soups that contain starchy ingredients such as rice, pasta, and potatoes will be even thicker.

In some soup recipes, flour is used as a thickener. Normally it is added to the softened vegetables, to bind the fat and juices together. The mixture is then cooked to remove the raw flour taste before the stock is stirred in. Flour can also be added to puréed soups at the end of cooking if they are not thick enough: blend the flour with cold stock, whisk in, and simmer until thickened.

GARNISHES

An attractive garnish can lift a soup, adding a contrast in color, texture, and flavor. Here are some ideas.
• Fresh herbs, either chopped or as whole leaves – mint, chives, thyme, parsley, basil, tarragon, and cilantro are all popular. Choose an herb that complements or mirrors any herbs in the soup, and add at the last minute so that it retains its freshness.
• Shredded or crumbled cheese
• Chopped hard-boiled egg
• Fine shreds of citrus zest or whole berries

• Crisp pieces of bacon; diced meat or poultry
• Toasted nuts; sunflower seeds
• Croûtons
• Chopped, diced, sliced, or grated vegetables such as green onions, cucumber, carrots, bell peppers, and fennel
• A spoonful of a sauce such as pesto
• A blob or decorative swirl of cream or plain yogurt (see box, below)

Adding cream & yogurt

Heavy or whipping cream and crème fraîche can be added to a hot soup and heated further, with no danger of curdling.

Light cream, sour cream, and yogurt will curdle if overheated, so add them just before serving and warm through over a low heat. For chilled soups, add cream or yogurt once the soup has been chilled, before serving.

Garnishing with cream

With a teaspoon, quickly swirl light or whipping cream in a spiral on each serving.

PUREEING SOUPS

Soups are often puréed to give them a velvety smooth texture. This also gives them a thicker texture. Starchy vegetables and a little flour will help to thicken them even more.

Blender or food processor
Either of these can be used to process the cooked ingredients in batches. Scrape the sides of the container once or twice to ensure there are no solid pieces left unprocessed.

Hand-held blender
Use this to purée directly in the saucepan (which should be deep to prevent splashes). It's not useful for large quantities, but is ideal for blending in a final addition of cream or yogurt.

Sieve or strainer
To make a puréed soup ultra smooth, and remove any fibers, seeds, or skins, work it through a fine sieve with a wooden spoon. This is much easier to do if the soup is first puréed in a blender or food processor.

FRENCH PEA SOUP

SERVES 4–6

2 tbsp (30 g) butter

1 large onion, coarsely chopped

1 tbsp all-purpose flour

3½ cups (500 g) frozen peas

5 cups (1.25 liters) vegetable chicken or stock

½ tsp sugar

2 large mint sprigs

salt and black pepper

shredded fresh mint for garnish

1 Melt the butter in a large saucepan, add the chopped onion, and cook very gently, stirring occasionally, for about 10 minutes until soft but not colored.

2 Sprinkle in the flour and stir for a further 1–2 minutes, then add the frozen peas, stock, sugar, and sprigs of mint.

3 Bring to a boil, cover, and simmer gently, stirring occasionally, for 5 minutes or until the peas are soft. Do not simmer any longer than this or the peas will lose their fresh green color.

4 Remove the mint sprigs and discard. Purée the soup in a food processor or blender until smooth.

5 Return the soup to the rinsed-out pan, reheat, and add salt and pepper to taste. Serve hot, garnished with shredded fresh mint.

Cook's know-how

Use fresh peas when in season. You will need about 2 lb (1 kg) peas in their pods to give you 1 lb (500 g) after shelling, and they will take 20 minutes to cook in step 3.

CREAMY CARROT & ORANGE SOUP

SERVES 6–8

2 tbsp (30 g) butter

1 onion, coarsely chopped

2 lb (1 kg) carrots, thickly sliced

6 cups (1.5 liters) vegetable stock

grated zest of ½ orange

1¼ cups (300 ml) orange juice

salt and black pepper

1¼ cups (300 ml) crème fraîche or sour cream

3 tbsp snipped fresh chives

1 Melt the butter in a large saucepan, add the onion, and cook gently, stirring occasionally, for a few minutes until soft but not colored. Add the carrots, cover, and cook gently, stirring from time to time, for 10 minutes.

2 Add the stock and bring to a boil. Cover and simmer, stirring from time to time, for 30–40 minutes until the carrots are soft.

3 Purée the soup in a food processor or blender until smooth. Return the soup to the rinsed-out pan, and add the orange zest and juice, and salt and pepper to taste. Stir in the crème fraîche or sour cream, then gently reheat the soup.

4 Stir in half of the snipped chives, and garnish individual servings with the remaining chives.

Healthy option

Crème fraîche or sour cream make this soup rich and creamy for a dinner party first course, but for an everyday soup that is full of zest and vitality, you can easily omit it and increase the stock by 1¼ cups (300 ml) in step 2. Another healthy option is to cook the onion in step 1 in 1 tbsp each olive oil and water rather than using butter.

ROASTED TOMATO & GARLIC SOUP

This soup is light in consistency but full of flavor, making it perfect for late summer when tomatoes are at their ripest and best. Charring the tomatoes in the oven gives the soup a wonderful smoky flavor.

SERVES 4

2 lb (1 kg) ripe tomatoes

2 tbsp olive oil

1 onion, chopped

3 garlic cloves, coarsely chopped

6 cups (1.5 liters) chicken or vegetable stock

salt and black pepper

pesto sauce for serving

1 Cut the tomatoes in half and arrange them, cut-side down, in a large roasting pan. Roast in a preheated oven at 425°F (220°C) for 15 minutes or until the skins are charred.

2 Remove the pan of tomatoes from the oven and leave until they are cool enough to handle, then peel off the skins and discard them. Chop the tomato flesh coarsely, retaining the juice.

3 Heat the oil in a large saucepan, add the onion and garlic, and cook gently, stirring occasionally, for a few minutes until soft but not colored.

4 Add the stock and the tomato flesh and juices, and bring to a boil. Lower the heat and simmer for 5 minutes, then add salt and pepper to taste.

5 Serve the soup hot, with a bowl of pesto sauce so everyone can stir in a spoonful to taste before they eat.

MEXICAN ROASTED TOMATO SOUP

Add 1/4 tsp each ground cumin and dried chili flakes to the onion and garlic in step 3. Instead of pesto, serve with a relish made with 3–4 tbsp chopped fresh cilantro leaves, 1 tbsp chopped red or sweet onion, and 1–2 tbsp lime or lemon juice.

SUN-DRIED TOMATO SOUP

Cook 2–3 chopped sun-dried tomatoes and add them to the saucepan with the onion and garlic in step 3. Serve garnished with finely shredded fresh basil.

TASTY MUSHROOM SOUP

SERVES 4–6

2 tbsp (30 g) butter

1 small onion, minced

1 garlic clove, minced

1 lb (500 g) mushrooms, sliced

5 cups (1.25 liters) vegetable or chicken stock

2/3 cup (150 ml) dry white wine

2 tsp chopped fresh oregano

2 tbsp chopped fresh thyme

salt and black pepper

1 Melt the butter in a large saucepan, add the onion and garlic, and cook gently, stirring occasionally, for a few minutes until soft but not colored. Add the mushrooms and cook, stirring from time to time, for 10 minutes.

2 Pour in the stock and wine, then add the oregano and half of the thyme. Season with salt and pepper. Bring to a boil, cover, and simmer gently for 10 minutes or until the mushrooms are tender.

3 Taste for seasoning and serve hot, sprinkled with the remaining fresh thyme.

ASPARAGUS SOUP

SERVES 6

2 cups (250 g) chopped potatoes

6 cups (1.5 liters) vegetable or chicken stock

1 lb (500 g) asparagus

2 garlic cloves, minced

2 tbsp chopped fresh basil (optional)

salt and black pepper

2 tbsp (30 g) butter (optional)

1 Put the potatoes into a large saucepan, add the stock, and bring to a boil. Cover and simmer for 15 minutes or until the potatoes are tender.

2 Meanwhile, cut any woody ends off the asparagus and discard. Cut off the tips and chop the stalks into chunks.

3 Add the asparagus and garlic to the pan and cook for 5 minutes, stirring from time to time, until the asparagus is tender. Remove 9 tips; reserve for the garnish.

4 Purée the soup in a food processor or blender until smooth. Return the soup to the rinsed-out pan and reheat.

5 Add the basil, if using, and salt and pepper to taste. Slice the reserved asparagus tips lengthwise in half. Serve the soup hot, garnished with the asparagus tips and small nuggets of butter, if wished.

ARTICHOKE SOUP

Use 14 oz (400 g) canned artichoke hearts or bottoms, drained and diced, instead of the asparagus, and garnish with basil.

Healthy option

This is a soup for a special occasion, and the butter garnish makes it an absolute classic — melted butter is traditional with asparagus. If you are concerned about the fat content, you can garnish with torn basil instead.

FRENCH ONION SOUP

SERVES 8

3 tbsp (45 g) butter

1 tbsp sunflower oil

2 lb (1 kg) large onions, thinly sliced

2 tsp sugar

2 tbsp all-purpose flour

7 cups (1.8 liters) vegetable, chicken, or beef stock

salt and black pepper

8 Gruyère croûtes (page 49)

1 Melt the butter with the oil in a large saucepan, and caramelize the onions with the sugar (see box, right). Sprinkle the flour into the pan and cook, stirring constantly, for 1–2 minutes.

2 Gradually stir in the stock and bring to a boil. Season with salt and pepper, then cover and simmer, stirring from time to time, for 35 minutes.

3 Taste the soup for seasoning, then ladle into warmed bowls. Float a Gruyère croûte in each bowl and serve immediately.

Cook's know-how

Cooking with sugar is the key to developing a rich, golden brown color and sweet caramel flavor in onions. It is this that produces the characteristic appearance and taste of this classic soup.

Caramelizing onions

Cook the onions in the butter and oil for a few minutes until soft. Add the sugar and continue cooking over a low heat, stirring occasionally, for 20 minutes or until the onions are golden brown.

VEGETABLE MINESTRONE

SERVES 4–6

2 tbsp olive oil

1 onion, chopped

2 celery stalks, chopped

2 carrots, diced

14 oz (400 g) canned crushed plum tomatoes

1 tbsp tomato paste

1 garlic clove, minced

salt and black pepper

6 cups (1.5 liters) chicken or vegetable stock

14 oz (400 g) canned cannellini or red kidney beans, drained

8 oz (250 g) leeks, trimmed and finely sliced (about 2 1/2 cups)

1 1/2 cups (125 g) finely shredded Savoy cabbage

2 tbsp arborio (risotto) rice

grated Parmesan cheese for serving

1 Heat the oil in a large saucepan, add the onion, celery, and carrots, and cook gently, stirring, for 5 minutes.

2 Add the tomatoes, tomato paste, and garlic, and season with salt and pepper. Stir, then pour in the stock and bring to a boil over a high heat.

3 Cover the pan and lower the heat so the soup is gently simmering. Cook for 15 minutes, stirring from time to time.

4 Add the beans, leeks, cabbage, and rice, and simmer for 20 minutes longer. Taste for seasoning.

5 Serve hot, with a bowl of grated Parmesan cheese for everyone to help themselves.

Cook's know-how

If you don't have arborio or any other type of risotto rice, use broken spaghetti instead. You will need 1/4 cup (30 g).

WATERCRESS SOUP

SERVES 6

2 tbsp (30 g) butter

1 onion, minced

2 potatoes, coarsely chopped

1 bunch (125 g) watercress, tough stems removed

4 cups (1 liter) vegetable or chicken stock

1 1/4 cups (300 ml) milk

1 bay leaf

salt and black pepper

light cream for garnish (optional)

1 Melt the butter in a large saucepan, add the onion, and cook gently, stirring from time to time, for a few minutes until soft but not colored.

2 Add the potatoes and the watercress to the saucepan and cook for about 5 minutes until the watercress is wilted.

3 Pour in the chicken or vegetable stock and milk, add the bay leaf, and season with salt and pepper.

4 Bring the mixture to a boil, cover, and simmer very gently for 15 minutes or until the potatoes are tender.

5 Remove the bay leaf and discard. Purée the soup in a food processor or blender until smooth. Return the soup to the rinsed-out pan and reheat, then taste for seasoning.

6 Serve hot, garnishing each bowl with a little cream, if desired.

Cook's know-how

Watercress soup is delicious served chilled in summer. After puréeing, pour the soup into a large bowl, then cover, cool, and chill for at least 3 hours. Taste for seasoning before serving because chilling dulls the flavor slightly. You can also freeze this soup for up to 3 months.

CURRIED PARSNIP SOUP

SERVES 6–8

2 tbsp (30 g) butter

1 1/2 lb (750 g) parsnips, coarsely chopped

1 large onion, chopped

1 large garlic clove, minced

2 tsp mild curry powder

7 cups (1.8 liters) vegetable or chicken stock

salt and black pepper

1 cup (250 ml) light cream

fresh chives for garnish

1 Melt the butter in a large saucepan, add the chopped parsnips, onion, and garlic, and cook gently, stirring from time to time, for 5 minutes or until the onion is softened but not colored.

2 Stir in the curry powder and cook for 1 minute, then blend in the stock, and season with salt and pepper. Bring to a boil, stirring, then cover and simmer gently for 20 minutes or until the parsnips are tender.

3 Purée the soup in a food processor or blender until smooth. Return the soup to the rinsed-out pan and heat through, stirring constantly, then taste for seasoning.

4 Stir in the cream and reheat gently. Serve at once, garnished with fresh chives.

Healthy option

If you are concerned about the fat content, omit the cream and use stock or water instead.

WINTER VEGETABLE SOUP

SERVES 6

3 tbsp (45 g) butter

1 leek, trimmed and diced

1 onion, chopped

1 celery stalk, diced

1 small potato, diced

1 turnip, diced

1 small carrot, diced

3 garlic cloves, minced

6 cups (1.5 liters) vegetable or chicken stock

4 cups (250 g) coarsely shredded spinach (see box, right)

3 green onions, thinly sliced

salt and black pepper

1 Melt the butter in a large saucepan, add the leek, and cook gently, stirring occasionally, for 5 minutes or until softened. Add the onion, celery, potato, turnip, carrot, and garlic, and cook for 8 minutes.

2 Pour in the stock and bring to a boil. Cover and simmer, stirring occasionally, for 25 minutes or until the vegetables are tender.

3 Add the spinach and green onions, and cook for just 3 minutes until the spinach is wilted but still bright green. Season well, and serve hot.

Shredding spinach

Remove the stems. Stack up several spinach leaves and roll up tightly, then cut crosswise into shreds.

BORSCHT

SERVES 4

1 heaped cup (175 g) coarsely shredded white cabbage

1½ cups (200 g) diced waxy potatoes

1 cup (225 g) canned crushed tomatoes

1 small carrot, chopped

1 small onion, chopped

6 cups (1.5 liters) vegetable or chicken stock, more if needed

1 lb (500 g) cooked beets, peeled and diced (about 3 cups)

3–4 dill weed sprigs, chopped

2½ tbsp (30 g) sugar

2 tbsp wine vinegar

salt and black pepper

sour cream and dill weed sprigs for garnish

1 Put the cabbage, potatoes, tomatoes, carrot, and onion into a large pan with the stock.

2 Bring to a boil, then simmer for 30–40 minutes until the vegetables are very tender. Add extra stock if necessary.

3 Add the diced beets, dill, sugar, and vinegar, and simmer for 10 minutes to let the sweet-sour flavors develop. Add salt and pepper to taste, and more sugar and vinegar if necessary.

4 Serve at once, garnished with spoonfuls of sour cream and sprigs of dill.

TOMATO SOUP

SERVES 6–8

2 tbsp (30 g) butter

2 onions, coarsely chopped

1 garlic clove, minced

1 tbsp all-purpose flour

5 cups (1.25 liters) vegetable or chicken stock

28 oz (800 g) canned tomatoes

1 bay leaf

salt and black pepper

4 tbsp pesto sauce

light cream (optional) and fresh basil leaves for garnish

Healthy option

For a really healthy version of this soup, omit the butter, flour, and pesto, and simply simmer the onions and garlic with the stock, tomatoes, and bay leaf. Cook for 30–40 minutes to develop the flavors before puréeing, then serve topped with torn basil.

1 Melt the butter in a large saucepan, add the onions and garlic, and cook gently, stirring from time to time, for a few minutes until soft but not colored.

2 Add the flour to the pan and cook, stirring constantly, for 1 minute.

3 Pour in the stock, then add the tomatoes and their juice and the bay leaf. Season with salt and pepper. Bring to a boil, then cover the pan and simmer gently for 20 minutes.

4 Remove the bay leaf and discard. Purée the soup in a food processor or blender until smooth.

5 Return the soup to the rinsed-out pan, add the pesto sauce, and heat through. Taste for seasoning.

6 Serve at once, garnished with cream (if desired) and fresh basil leaves.

QUICK TOMATO SOUP

Tomato purée (sieved tomatoes) makes a beautiful deep red soup. Substitute 3 cups (750 ml) of bottled or canned tomato purée for the canned tomatoes and then cook as directed.

SPLIT PEA & HAM SOUP

SERVES 6–8

2½ cups (500 g) green split peas

1-lb (500-g) meaty ham hock

10 cups (2.5 liters) water

1 large onion, minced

4 celery stalks, minced

3 potatoes, diced

3 leeks, trimmed and sliced

3 tbsp chopped parsley (optional)

salt and black pepper

1 Put the split peas and the ham hock into separate large bowls and cover each generously with cold water. Let soak overnight.

2 Drain the split peas and ham hock, then put them both into a large saucepan with the measured water. Bring to a boil, then simmer, uncovered, for about 1 hour.

3 Add the onion, celery, potatoes, and leeks to the pan, cover, and simmer gently for 2½ hours until the ham is tender and the peas are cooked. Add more water, if needed, during cooking.

4 Skim the surface if necessary. Remove the ham hock from the saucepan and let it cool slightly. Pull the meat off the bone, discarding any skin and fat.

5 Coarsely chop the meat and return it to the saucepan. Add the parsley, if using, and salt and pepper to taste, then heat gently to warm through. Serve hot.

Cook's know-how

Ham hocks, the lower portion of the hog's hind leg, are inexpensive and give wonderful flavor to soups.

INDIAN-SPICED SMOKED HADDOCK CHOWDER

SERVES 4

4 tbsp (60 g) butter

1 small onion, thinly sliced

6 celery stalks, sliced

2 carrots, chopped into ½ in (1 cm) dice

1 lb (500 g) potatoes, cut into ¾ in (2 cm) chunks (about 3 cups)

3 tbsp all-purpose flour

2 tsp curry powder

½ tsp turmeric

½ tsp ground ginger

2½ cups (600 ml) fish or vegetable stock

freshly ground black pepper

14 oz (400 g) canned crushed tomatoes

1½ lb (750 g) smoked haddock (finnan haddie), skinned and chopped into bite-sized pieces

2½ cups (600 ml) whole milk

salt (optional)

chopped fresh dill weed for garnish

1 Melt the butter in a large saucepan, and add the onion, celery, and carrots. Stir to coat the vegetables in the butter, cover, and cook gently until they begin to soften. Add the potatoes and cook for a further 1–2 minutes.

2 Add the flour and spices to the vegetables and stir to mix together, then add the stock and season with pepper (do not add salt at this stage, as smoked fish is salty). Bring to a boil, and simmer until the vegetables are tender, about 10–15 minutes.

3 Add the tomatoes, smoked haddock, and milk to the vegetable mixture in the pan, and simmer gently for 10–15 minutes until the fish is cooked.

4 Taste the soup for seasoning. Serve hot in warmed bowls, garnished with chopped fresh dill weed.

SPICED AUTUMN SOUP

SERVES 8

4 tbsp (60 g) butter

2 large onions, coarsely chopped

2 potatoes, coarsely chopped

2 carrots, coarsely chopped

3 garlic cloves, minced

pared zest and juice of 1 orange

2 tsp mild curry powder

7 cups (1.8 liters) vegetable or chicken stock

28 oz (800 g) canned crushed tomatoes

2 apples, peeled and chopped

salt and black pepper

herb croûtes (page 49) for serving

1 Melt the butter in a large saucepan, add the onions, potatoes, carrots, garlic, and orange zest, and cook gently, stirring from time to time, for about 5 minutes.

2 Add the curry powder, and cook, stirring constantly, for 1–2 minutes.

3 Add the stock, orange juice, tomatoes, and apples, and season with salt and pepper. Bring to a boil, then cover and simmer gently for 30 minutes until the vegetables are tender. Discard the orange zest.

4 Purée the soup in a food processor or blender until smooth. Return to the rinsed-out pan, reheat, and taste for seasoning. Serve hot, with herb croûtes.

Paring orange zest

With a vegetable peeler, remove strips of zest, excluding the bitter white pith.

BLUE CHEESE & ONION SOUP

SERVES 8

2 1/2 cups (600 ml) milk

2 bay leaves

1/4 tsp grated nutmeg

6 tbsp (90 g) butter

2 large onions, finely sliced

7 tbsp all-purpose flour

6 cups (1.5 liters) vegetable or chicken stock

salt and black pepper

5 oz (150 g) blue Stilton cheese, crumbled (about 1 heaped cup)

light cream for serving (optional)

1 Pour the milk into a saucepan, add the bay leaves and nutmeg, and bring almost to a boil. Remove from the heat, cover, and let infuse for 20 minutes.

2 Meanwhile, melt the butter in a large pan, add the onions, and cook very gently, stirring occasionally, for about 10 minutes or until they are soft but not colored.

3 Add the flour, and cook, stirring, for 2 minutes. Strain the milk and gradually blend it into the onion and flour. Add the stock, and season with salt and pepper. Bring to a boil and simmer, half covered, for 10 minutes.

4 Add the cheese and stir over a very low heat until it melts (do not boil or the cheese will be stringy). Taste for seasoning, and stir in a little cream if desired. Serve hot.

Healthy option

There are ways of making this soup lighter if you are concerned about the fat content. Use 2 percent milk in step 1 and only 2 tbsp (30 g) butter in step 2, and omit the flour in step 3. At the end, whisk the flour to a paste with a little cold stock or water, then whisk into the soup and boil, whisking, until thickened. Add only 2–3 oz (60–90 g) cheese in step 4.

CLAM CHOWDER

SERVES 4

1 lb (500 g) hard-shell clams, cleaned (page 124)

1 cup (250 ml) fish stock

3 tbsp (45 g) butter

1 onion, chopped

3 thick bacon slices, diced

2 tbsp all-purpose flour

2 potatoes, diced

3 cups (750 ml) milk

1 bay leaf

salt and black pepper

1 Put the clams into a large saucepan, add the fish stock, and bring to a boil. Lower the heat, cover, and cook over a medium heat for 5–8 minutes until the clam shells open.

2 Discard any clams that have not opened. Set aside 12 clams in their shells for garnish and keep warm. Remove the remaining clams from their shells and chop them if large. Discard the shells and strain the cooking juices.

3 Melt the butter in a large pan, add the onion, and cook gently for a few minutes until soft but not colored. Add the bacon and flour, and cook, stirring, for 1–2 minutes.

4 Add the potatoes, milk, strained clam juices, and bay leaf to the pan. Bring to a boil, then lower the heat and simmer for 15 minutes. Add the chopped clams, and heat gently for about 5 minutes. Remove the bay leaf and discard.

5 Add salt and pepper to taste. Serve hot, garnished with the reserved clams in their shells.

Cook's know-how

If fresh clams are not available or you want to save time, use 7 oz (200 g) canned chopped clams. Omit steps 1 and 2 and increase the fish stock to 1 1/4 cups (300 ml), then just heat the clams through in step 4.

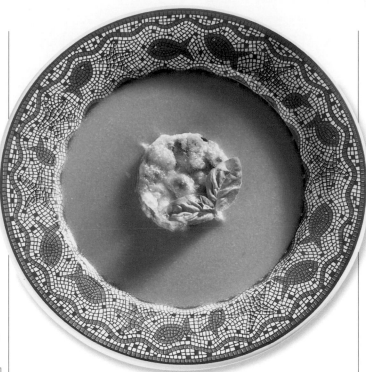

RICH FISH SOUP

SERVES 4

4 tbsp olive oil

2 leeks, trimmed and chopped

1 celery stalk, chopped

1 potato, chopped

1 carrot, chopped

1 small red bell pepper, halved, seeded, and chopped

3 garlic cloves, roughly chopped

2 cups (375 g) seeded and chopped ripe tomatoes, or 14 oz (400 g) canned crushed tomatoes

1 lb (500 g) mixed white fish fillets, chopped (see box, right)

4 cups (1 liter) fish stock

2 cups (500 ml) dry white wine

1/4 tsp cayenne pepper

salt and black pepper

Gruyère croûtes (page 49) and basil sprigs for garnish

Cook's know-how

This fine puréed soup is based on the French "soupe de poisson." For an interesting flavor, ask your fishmonger for a mixture of different fish – whatever is cheapest and best on the day. Bony fish, small pieces, and scraps will all do very well, because the fish is puréed and then sieved.

1 Heat the oil in a large saucepan, add the leeks, celery, potato, carrot, red bell pepper, and garlic, and cook gently, stirring occasionally, for 5 minutes or until the vegetables are just soft.

2 Add the tomatoes and fish. Cook for 3 minutes, then add the stock, wine, and cayenne pepper, and bring to a boil. Simmer for 35 minutes.

3 Purée the soup in a food processor or blender, then work it through a sieve or fine strainer to make it velvety smooth.

4 Return the soup to the rinsed-out pan and reheat gently, stirring occasionally. Add salt and pepper to taste.

5 Serve hot, each bowl garnished with a Gruyère croûte and a sprig of basil.

LOBSTER BISQUE

A bisque is a purée flavored with brandy, white wine, and cream, prepared by a complex process that brings out the maximum flavor. When made with lobster, it is perfect for a special occasion. This lighter and healthier version of the traditional recipe is just as delicious.

SERVES 6

2 tbsp (30 g) butter
6 shallots, coarsely chopped
1/2 carrot, minced
1 cooked large lobster
pinch of cayenne pepper
1/2 tsp paprika
juice of 1 small lemon
4 tbsp brandy
1 1/4 cups (300 ml) dry white wine
6 cups (1.5 liters) fish stock
1/3 cup (60 g) long-grain rice
about 3 tbsp light cream (optional)

1 Melt the butter in a large saucepan, add the shallots and carrot, and cook gently for about 5 minutes until softened.

2 Using a mallet or wooden rolling pin, crack the lobster shell, remove the cooked meat (page 125), and set aside. Reserve a single large piece of the shell to add to the bisque, and discard the rest.

3 Slice the meat from the large claws and the tail of the lobster; reserve a few pieces for garnish.

4 Add the cayenne, paprika, lemon juice, and brandy to the shallots and carrot in the pan, and reduce over a high heat to about 2 tablespoons.

5 Add the wine, fish stock, rice, and reserved lobster shell to the pan and cook for about 15 minutes until the rice is tender. Remove the lobster shell and discard.

6 Add the lobster meat (except the garnish) to the pan, and season lightly with salt and pepper. Cook the soup over a low heat just until the lobster is heated through, about 5 minutes.

7 Purée the soup in a food processor or blender until smooth. Press the purée through a sieve to remove any tiny pieces of lobster shell.

8 Return the purée to the pan and add the cream if using. Taste for seasoning and adjust if necessary.

9 Serve the soup at once, garnished with the reserved pieces of lobster meat.

Cook's know-how

Most fishmongers and supermarkets sell cooked lobsters, although you might have to pre-order it. Buy only from a reputable fish market or supermarket with a quick turnover. The lobster should feel heavy for its size, and smell fresh. Keep it as cool as possible until you get home, then unwrap it, cover with a clean cloth or paper towels, and store in the coldest part of the refrigerator. Use the lobster the same day, or within 24 hours.

CROUTES & CROUTONS

These need not be reserved for special occasions. They can turn the most basic of everyday soups into a special dish.

HERB CROUTES

Trim the crusts from slices of bread. Cut each slice into a square or decorative shape. Heat a very thin film of oil in a nonstick frying pan, add the bread, and brown on both sides. Mince some parsley or separate into small sprigs. Drain the croûtes on paper towels. Roll the edges of the croûtes in the parsley or put a leaf on top of each one.

GARLIC CROUTONS

Trim the crusts from slices of bread and cut into 1/2-in (1-cm) cubes. Heat a very thin film of oil in a nonstick frying pan. Peel and mince 1 garlic clove, and cook for 1 minute. Add the bread cubes and cook, stirring occasionally, until brown all over. Remove and drain on paper towels.

GRUYERE CROUTES

Cut slices from a baguette and toast on one side under the broiler. Remove from the heat and turn the slices over. Grate Gruyère cheese evenly over the untoasted sides of the slices. Return to the broiler and cook until the cheese has melted and is gently bubbling.

CUBAN CORN & SEAFOOD SOUP

SERVES 4

2 tbsp (30 g) butter

I small onion, chopped

2 garlic cloves, minced

3 cups (500 g) frozen corn kernels

2 cups (200 g) pumpkin or sweet potato (yam), peeled and cut into chunks

I fresh, mild red chili pepper, halved, seeded, and chopped, or 1/4 tsp dried chili flakes

5 cups (1.25 liters) fish, chicken, or vegetable stock

I cup (250 ml) tomato purée

I bay leaf

1/2 tsp dried thyme

salt and black pepper

8 oz (250 g) any firm white fish fillets, cut into large chunks

lime wedges for serving

1 Melt the butter in a large pan, add the onion and garlic, and cook gently for a few minutes until soft but not colored. Add the pumpkin or sweet potato and the chili pepper, and cook, stirring occasionally, for about 5 minutes.

2 Add the stock, purée, bay leaf, and thyme, and season with salt and pepper. Bring to a boil, cover, and simmer, stirring occasionally, for 15 minutes or until the pumpkin or sweet potato pieces are just tender.

3 Add the fish to the soup and cook very gently for 3–5 minutes, just until the chunks become opaque.

4 Discard the bay leaf and taste for seasoning. Serve hot, with lime wedges.

Cook's know-how

Monkfish is the firmest white fish, but it is expensive. You could use cod, haddock, or pollack, but take care not to let the fish break up — they are not as firm as monkfish.

SHRIMP GUMBO

SERVES 4

3 tbsp sunflower oil

I small onion, diced

I red bell pepper, halved, seeded, and diced

I celery stalk, diced

3 garlic cloves, minced

2 tbsp chopped parsley

3 tbsp all-purpose flour

I tsp each ground cumin and dried oregano

1 1/2 lb (750 g) ripe tomatoes, chopped, or 28 oz (800 g) canned crushed tomatoes

6 oz (175 g) smoked chorizo or other spicy sausage, sliced

5 cups (1.25 liters) fish stock

8 oz (250 g) okra, sliced

8–12 oz (250–375 g) cooked peeled shrimp

pinch of cayenne pepper

salt and black pepper

rice timbales (see box, right) for serving

4 large cooked shrimp and 4 green onions for garnish

1 Heat the oil, add the onion, red bell pepper, celery, garlic, and parsley, and cook for 8 minutes or until softened. Add the flour, and cook, stirring, for 1 minute.

2 Sprinkle in the cumin and oregano, and cook, stirring, for 1 minute, then add the tomatoes, chorizo, and stock. Bring to a boil, then simmer, stirring occasionally, for about 30 minutes or until the soup has thickened slightly.

3 Add the okra and cook for 5–7 minutes until tender, then add the shrimp and heat through. Add the cayenne, and season with salt and pepper.

4 Serve the gumbo hot, with rice timbales. Garnish each serving with a large cooked shrimp and a green onion.

Making a rice timbale

Oil a small mold or ramekin, fill with cooked rice, and press down lightly. Turn upside-down onto a warmed soup plate or wide bowl and lift off the mold.

BOUILLABAISSE

Bouillabaisse, the classic fish soup-stew with the authentic flavors of Provence, is one of the most satisfying and delectable dishes you can bring to your table. In France, it is traditionally served with thick slices of toasted bread spread with "rouille," a chili-flavored mayonnaise.

SERVES 8

2 tbsp olive oil

1 large onion, chopped

1 small fennel bulb, sliced

4 garlic cloves, minced

1 tbsp chopped parsley

1 bay leaf

4 cups (1 liter) water

2¹/₂ cups (600 ml) fish stock

3 cups (500 g) finely chopped ripe tomatoes

¹/₂ tsp dried herbes de Provence or Italian seasoning

a strip of orange zest

¹/₄ tsp fennel seeds (optional)

2–3 potatoes, cut into chunks

1 lb (500 g) assorted fish, cut into bite-sized pieces

1 lb (500 g) assorted shellfish, shucked or peeled

pinch of saffron threads

salt and black pepper

8 toasted baguette slices for serving

ROUILLE

3 garlic cloves

¹/₂ cup (125 ml) mayonnaise

2 tsp paprika

1 tsp chili powder

3 tbsp olive oil

1 fresh, hot red chili pepper, halved, seeded, and minced

1 tbsp lemon juice

salt

1 Heat the olive oil in a large, heavy saucepan. Add the onion, fennel, garlic, parsley, and bay leaf, and cook, stirring occasionally, for 5 minutes.

2 Add the water, stock, tomatoes, herbs, orange zest, and fennel seeds (if using). Bring to a boil, then cover, and simmer for 30 minutes.

3 Meanwhile, make the rouille (see box, right). Keep chilled until needed.

4 Add the potatoes to the soup, cover, and simmer for 10 minutes. Do not stir or the potatoes will break up.

5 Add the fish, shellfish, and saffron, and season with salt and pepper. Cover and cook for a few minutes, just until the fish turns opaque.

6 Remove the bay leaf and orange zest, and discard. Serve the bouillabaisse with slices of toasted baguette spread with the rouille.

Cook's know-how

Ask your fishmonger to recommend a variety of white fish and shellfish. Ideally, you should have a combination of pieces of chunky white fish with small whole fish, plus two or three different shellfish such as clams, mussels, and shrimp.

Making rouille

Use a knife blade to crush the garlic to a paste. Mix in a bowl with the mayonnaise, paprika, and chili powder.

Pour in the olive oil, drop by drop, whisking constantly as the oil is absorbed into the spicy mayonnaise.

Add the chili pepper and lemon juice to the sauce; add salt to taste and stir well to combine.

Cook's know-how

Controversy surrounds the ingredients that should be included in bouillabaisse, with some cooks insisting that saffron, orange zest, and fennel seeds are essential.

PUMPKIN SOUP

SERVES 6

3 lb (1.5 kg) pumpkin or butternut squash

2/3 cup (150 g) butter

2 leeks, trimmed and sliced

4 cups (1 liter) chicken or vegetable stock

1/4 tsp grated nutmeg

salt and black pepper

1/4 cup (30 g) frozen peas

4 cups (250 g) chopped spinach leaves

1 1/4 cups (300 ml) light cream

1 Peel the pumpkin and discard the seeds and fibers. Cut the flesh into 3/4-in (2-cm) chunks.

2 Melt two-thirds of the butter in a large saucepan. Add the leeks and cook very gently, covered, for 10 minutes or until soft.

3 Add the stock, pumpkin chunks, and nutmeg, and season with salt and pepper. Bring to a boil, then cover, and simmer for 30 minutes or until the vegetables are very soft.

4 Meanwhile, cook the peas in boiling salted water for 5 minutes. Drain thoroughly.

5 Melt the remaining butter in a saucepan. Add the spinach, cover, and cook gently for 3 minutes until wilted.

6 Purée the soup in a food processor or blender until smooth, in batches if necessary. Return to the pan and stir in the cream. Stir the peas and spinach into the soup, heat through, and serve hot.

Cook's know-how

You can serve the soup in hollowed-out small pumpkins, scalloping the edges as illustrated above. Other possibilities include leaving the soup chunky rather than puréeing it, using double the amount of spinach and omitting the peas, and halving the butter and cream to reduce the fat content.

GOULASH SOUP

SERVES 4–6

2 red bell peppers

2 tbsp sunflower oil

1 lb (500 g) beef chuck, trimmed and cut into 1 1/2-in (3.5-cm) pieces

2 large onions, thickly sliced

1 tbsp all-purpose flour

2 tsp paprika

6 cups (1.5 liters) beef stock

14 oz (400 g) canned crushed tomatoes

2 tbsp tomato paste

1 tbsp red wine vinegar

1 garlic clove, minced

1 bay leaf

salt and black pepper

3 cups (750 g) coarsely chopped potatoes

dash of hot pepper sauce

sour cream and snipped fresh chives for garnish (optional)

1 Roast and peel the red bell peppers (page 388). Cut the flesh into chunks.

2 Heat the oil in a large pan. Add the beef and brown all over. Add the onions, peppers, flour, and paprika, and stir over a high heat for 1–2 minutes.

3 Add the stock, tomatoes, tomato paste, vinegar, garlic, and bay leaf, and season with salt and pepper. Bring to a boil, cover tightly, and simmer for 1 1/2 hours.

4 Add the potatoes and cook for 30 minutes or until the beef and potatoes are tender. Remove the bay leaf and discard.

5 Add a little hot pepper sauce, and taste for seasoning. Serve hot, garnished with sour cream and snipped chives, if desired.

Cook's know-how

To save time, you can use canned or bottled pimientoes, preserved in oil or brine, instead of roasting bell peppers yourself.

GAME SOUP

SERVES 4

2 tbsp (30 g) butter

4 oz (125 g) thick bacon slices, diced

1 onion, sliced

1³/4 cups (125 g) sliced crimini mushrooms

1 tbsp all-purpose flour

5 cups (1.25 liters) game stock (page 170)

salt and black pepper

1 tbsp red-currant jelly

ORANGE-HERB BOUQUET

6 parsley stems

pared zest of 1 orange

1 bay leaf

1 large thyme or marjoram sprig

Orange-herb bouquet

Tie the parsley, orange zest, bay leaf, and thyme or marjoram with a piece of kitchen string. Leave a length of string to tie to the saucepan handle, so that the orange and herb bouquet can be easily lifted from the pan at the end of cooking.

1 Make the orange-herb bouquet (see box, above right) and set aside.

2 Melt the butter in a large saucepan, add the bacon, and cook over a high heat, stirring occasionally, for 5–7 minutes until crisp.

3 Lower the heat, add the onion to the pan, and cook gently, stirring from time to time, for a few minutes until softened but not colored.

4 Add the mushrooms to the pan, and cook for about 5 minutes, then add the flour and cook, stirring constantly, for 1 minute. Add the stock and the orange-herb bouquet, season with salt and pepper, and bring to a boil. Cover and simmer for 30 minutes.

5 Discard the bouquet, then stir in the red-currant jelly. Taste for seasoning before serving.

LENTIL & BACON SOUP

SERVES 4–6

2 tbsp (30 g) butter

1 onion, chopped

1 carrot, diced

1 celery stalk, diced

3 garlic cloves, minced

2–3 lean, thick bacon slices, diced

1 cup (175 g) red lentils

1 cup (125 g) peeled and diced potato, rutabaga, or turnip

2 bay leaves

1/2 tsp dried sage (optional)

8 cups (2 liters) vegetable or chicken stock

salt and black pepper

chopped parsley for garnish

1 Melt the butter in a large saucepan, add the onion, carrot, celery, and garlic, and cook, stirring, for 5–6 minutes until soft and lightly colored.

2 Add the bacon, lentils, potato, rutabaga, or turnip, bay leaves, and sage (if using). Cook for 15 minutes.

3 Pour in the stock and bring to a boil, then simmer gently, uncovered, for about 20 minutes or until the lentils and vegetables are tender. Add salt and pepper to taste.

4 Remove the bay leaves and discard. Serve hot, sprinkled with chopped parsley.

LENTIL & FRANKFURTER SOUP

For a hearty main-dish soup, add 8 oz (250 g) frankfurters. Chop them into 1/2-in (1-cm) pieces and add to the soup about 5 minutes before the end of the cooking time, so that they warm through but do not overcook. Other smoked sausages can also be used.

CHICKEN NOODLE SOUP

SERVES 6

2 lb (1 kg) chicken thighs

1 lb (500 g) carrots, sliced

1/2 bunch celery, chopped

1 small onion, peeled but left whole

2–3 garlic cloves, coarsely chopped

a few parsley sprigs

12 cups (3 liters) water

2–3 chicken bouillon cubes

salt and black pepper

4 oz (125 g) thin noodles

chopped fresh dill weed for garnish

1 Put the chicken pieces into a large saucepan with the carrots, celery, onion, garlic, and parsley. Pour in the measured water and bring to a boil. Using a slotted spoon, skim off the foam that rises to the surface.

2 Lower the heat, crumble in the bouillon cubes, and season with salt and pepper. Cover and simmer gently for 1 hour.

3 Skim any fat from the surface of the soup. With a slotted spoon, lift out the parsley, onion, and chicken. Discard the parsley. Chop the onion, and shred the chicken meat, discarding the skin and bones. Set aside.

4 Break the noodles into 5-cm (2-in) pieces and drop them into the soup. Bring to a boil, then cover, and simmer for about 10 minutes or until tender.

5 Return the onion and chicken to the soup, heat through, and taste for seasoning. Serve hot, garnished with dill weed.

Healthy option

To reduce the fat content of the soup, strip the skin off the chicken thighs before cooking. Chicken meat is low in fat and calories; the majority of the fat is in the skin.

HOT & SOUR SOUP

SERVES 4–6

2 dried Chinese mushrooms

1/4 head Napa cabbage, sliced

6 cups (1.5 liters) chicken or vegetable stock

2 oz (60 g) Chinese noodles, such as rice sticks

salt

4 oz (125 g) firm tofu, diced

1/3 cup (90 g) drained canned, sliced bamboo shoots

3/4 cup (90 g) diced cooked, lean chicken meat

1/3 cup (30 g) bean sprouts

3 tbsp cornstarch mixed with 3 tbsp cold water

2 eggs, lightly beaten

2 tbsp white wine vinegar

1 tbsp dark soy sauce

1/4 tsp cayenne pepper

FOR SERVING

2 tsp toasted sesame oil

2 green onions, thinly sliced

cilantro sprigs

1 Put the dried mushrooms into a bowl, cover with hot water, and let soak for about 30 minutes.

2 Meanwhile, put the sliced Napa cabbage into a large saucepan, add the stock, and bring to a boil. Simmer for 15 minutes. Set aside.

3 Break the noodles into pieces. Simmer in boiling salted water for 3–4 minutes until just tender. Drain.

4 Drain the mushrooms, reserving the soaking liquid. Squeeze the mushrooms dry, then cut them into thin strips.

5 Add the tofu, bamboo shoots, chicken, bean sprouts, noodles, and the mushrooms and their liquid to the Napa cabbage and stock. Heat until almost boiling, then stir in the cornstarch mixture. Simmer until the soup thickens slightly, then drizzle in the beaten eggs to form strands.

6 Combine the vinegar, soy sauce, and cayenne pepper, and pour into the soup. Taste for seasoning. Drizzle a little sesame oil over each serving, and garnish with green onion slices and cilantro sprigs.

CHINESE CRAB & CORN SOUP

SERVES 4

2 1/3 cups (375 g) frozen corn kernels

4 cups (1 liter) hot chicken stock

3 green onions, thinly sliced

1/2-in (1-cm) piece of fresh ginger, peeled and grated

1 garlic clove, minced

1 tbsp light soy sauce

8 oz (250 g) cooked crabmeat

1 tbsp cornstarch mixed with 2 tbsp cold water

salt and black pepper

toasted sesame oil and cilantro sprigs for serving

1 Purée the corn with one-fourth of the hot stock in a food processor or blender until smooth.

2 Pour the remaining stock into a pan, and add the green onions, ginger, garlic, and soy sauce. Heat until bubbles form at the edge.

3 Add the crabmeat and the corn purée, and continue to heat until bubbles form again. Blend the cornstarch mixture into the soup and cook, stirring occasionally, for 10 minutes or until it thickens slightly. Season to taste with salt and pepper.

4 Pour the soup into bowls, drizzle a little sesame oil over each serving, and garnish with cilantro. Serve hot.

THAI SPICED SOUP

SERVES 4

3 oz (90 g) thin egg noodles

salt and black pepper

2 cups (500 ml) chicken stock

14 oz (400 g) canned coconut milk

1 small carrot, coarsely chopped

1/4 cup (30 g) fine green beans, cut into 1/2-in (1-cm) pieces

3 green onions, thinly sliced

2 cups (250 g) shredded cooked, lean chicken meat

2 cups (125 g) shredded mixed green leaves, such as spinach and bok choy

1/3 cup (30 g) bean sprouts

2 tbsp fish sauce

2 tsp Thai curry paste (green or red)

1/4 hothouse cucumber, cut into matchstick-thin strips, and cilantro sprigs for garnish

1 Cook the noodles in boiling salted water for 2–3 minutes, or according to package directions, until just tender. Drain and rinse in cold water. Set aside while preparing the soup.

2 Put the stock, coconut milk, carrot, green beans, and green onions into a large saucepan, and bring to a boil.

3 Lower the heat, add the chicken, green leaves, bean sprouts, fish sauce, and curry paste, and cook for 2 minutes or until the green leaves are just wilted. Season to taste with salt and pepper.

4 To serve, divide the cooked noodles among warmed bowls. Ladle the hot soup over the noodles, and garnish with cucumber strips and cilantro sprigs.

Cook's know-how

For a vegetarian version, omit the cooked chicken and use vegetable stock instead of the chicken stock. You can also vary the vegetables, but note that their cooking times may be different. Try shredded white cabbage instead of the green leaves, and snow peas instead of green beans. Shredded Swiss chard would also be good in this soup, as would a small quantity of corn kernels or peas, and even a little diced eggplant.

VICHYSSOISE

SERVES 4–6

4 tbsp (60 g) butter

3 large leeks, trimmed and sliced

1 small onion, chopped

2 potatoes, coarsely chopped

5 cups (1.25 liters) chicken stock

salt and black pepper

FOR SERVING

2/3 cup (150 ml) light cream

milk (optional)

2 tbsp fresh snipped chives

1 Melt the butter in a large saucepan, add the leeks and onion, and cook very gently, stirring occasionally, for 10–15 minutes until soft but not colored.

2 Add the potatoes, stock, and salt and pepper to taste. Bring to a boil, then cover and simmer gently for 15–20 minutes until the potatoes are tender.

3 Purée the soup in a food processor or blender until smooth. Pour into a large bowl or pass through a sieve for a smoother finish. Cover and chill for at least 3 hours.

4 To serve, stir in the cream. If the soup is too thick, add a little milk. Taste for seasoning, and garnish with snipped chives before serving.

Cook's know-how

For an elegant, pale-colored soup, trim off the dark green parts of the leeks (both the ends and the outside leaves) and only use the white and pale green parts. After you have sliced them, swish them in lots of cold water in the sink and change the water several times to get rid of all traces of grit. Finally, rinse the leeks thoroughly in a colander.

TZATZIKI SOUP

SERVES 4–6

2 1/2 cups (600 g) plain yogurt

1 cup (250 ml) water

1 hothouse cucumber, seeded (see box, right) and diced

4 garlic cloves, coarsely chopped

1 tbsp olive oil

1 tsp white wine vinegar

1 tsp dried mint

salt and black pepper

2–3 tbsp chopped fresh mint and 3 green onions, thinly sliced, for garnish

1 Purée the yogurt, measured water, one-quarter of the diced cucumber, the garlic, oil, vinegar, and dried mint in a food processor or blender until smooth. Season well with salt and add pepper to taste.

2 Transfer the soup to a large bowl and stir in the remaining cucumber. Cover and chill for at least 1 hour.

3 Taste for seasoning. Sprinkle the soup with chopped fresh mint and green onions before serving.

Seeding a cucumber

Trim the cucumber with a small knife, then cut it in half lengthwise. With a teaspoon, scoop out and discard the seeds from each cucumber half.

Cook's know-how

You may be surprised to find dried mint in this recipe. Although fresh mint is generally far superior to dried, here the mint is left to steep in the yogurt for a minimum of an hour, and this brings the dried mint to life, giving it a more intense flavor than fresh, which would discolor in this time: Once chopped, fresh mint is best used as soon as possible.

BLUEBERRY & RED WINE SOUP

SERVES 4

1 1/2 cups (350 ml) cranberry juice

1 cup (250 ml) red wine

1 cinnamon stick

about 2/3 cup (125 g) sugar

2 cups (250 g) blueberries

1 tbsp cornstarch mixed with
  2 tbsp cold water

1/2 cup (125 ml) sour cream

1/2 cup (125 ml) light cream

1 Put the cranberry juice, wine, and cinnamon stick into a large saucepan and add the sugar (the amount depends on the sweetness of the fruit). Bring to a boil and simmer for 15 minutes.

2 Stir most of the blueberries into the pan, reserving a few for garnish, and cook for 5 minutes. Taste and add more sugar, if you think it needs it.

3 Gradually blend the cornstarch mixture into the soup, and return to a boil. Cook for 3 minutes or until the soup thickens slightly. Remove the pan from the heat and discard the cinnamon stick, then pour the soup into a bowl. Let cool for about 30 minutes.

4 Stir the sour cream and the light cream into the soup until evenly blended. Cover and chill for at least 3 hours. Serve well chilled, garnished with the reserved blueberries.

Cook's know-how

Served chilled, this fruit soup makes a cooling and refreshing summer first course. To prevent it from tasting too sweet, use a robust red wine, such as a Zinfandel or Cabernet Sauvignon. When in season, dark sweet cherries can be used instead of blueberries.

GAZPACHO

SERVES 4–6

2 lb (1 kg) tomatoes, peeled (see box, right), quartered, and seeded

1 large, mild onion

7 oz (200 g) canned or bottled pimientoes, drained

2 large garlic cloves

2 1/2 cups (600 ml) cold vegetable or chicken stock

1/3 cup (75 ml) olive oil

4 tbsp red wine vinegar

juice of 1/2 lemon

salt and black pepper

FOR GARNISH

1/2 hothouse cucumber, diced

1 small green bell pepper, halved, seeded, and diced

garlic croûtons (page 49)

1 Coarsely chop the tomatoes, onion, bell peppers, and garlic. Purée in a food processor or blender with the stock, oil, and vinegar until smooth.

2 Turn the mixture into a bowl and add the lemon juice, and salt and pepper to taste. Cover and chill for at least 1 hour.

Peeling tomatoes

Cut the cores from the tomatoes and score an "x" on the base. Immerse the tomatoes in boiling water for 8–15 seconds until their skins start to split. Transfer at once to cold water. When the tomatoes are cool enough to handle, peel off the skin with a small knife.

3 Serve the soup well chilled in bowls, each one garnished with spoonfuls of diced cucumber, green bell pepper, and garlic croûtons.

CHILLED CURRIED APPLE & MINT SOUP

SERVES 6

2 tbsp (30 g) butter

1 onion, coarsely chopped

1 tbsp mild curry powder

3³/4 cups (900 ml) vegetable stock

1¹/2 lb (750 g) apples, peeled, cored, and coarsely chopped (about 6 cups)

2 tbsp mango chutney

juice of ¹/2 lemon

7–8 sprigs of fresh mint

salt and black pepper

¹/2 cup (100 g) plain yogurt

a little milk, if needed

1 Melt the butter in a large saucepan, add the onion, and cook gently, stirring occasionally, for a few minutes until soft but not colored. Add the curry powder and cook, stirring constantly, for 1–2 minutes.

2 Add the stock and chopped apples, and bring to a boil, stirring. Cover and simmer for 15 minutes or until the apples are tender.

3 Purée the apple mixture, mango chutney, and lemon juice in a food processor or blender until very smooth.

4 Strip the mint leaves from the stems, reserving 6 small sprigs for garnish. Mince the mint leaves.

5 Pour the soup into a large bowl, stir in the minced mint, and add salt and pepper to taste. Cover and chill in the refrigerator for at least 3 hours.

6 Whisk in the yogurt, then taste for seasoning. If the soup is too thick, add a little milk. Garnish with the reserved mint before serving.

Cook's know-how

This soup is equally delicious served hot. After puréeing, return the soup to the rinsed-out pan and reheat it gently, stirring occasionally. Stir in the minced mint, then remove from the heat and swirl in the yogurt. Serve at once.

CHILLED STRAWBERRY SOUP

SERVES 4

1 cup (250 ml) dry white wine

7 tbsp (90 g) sugar

1 very small piece of pared lime zest (optional)

2 cups (250 g) strawberries

1 cup (250 ml) orange juice

4 mint sprigs for garnish

1 Put the wine and sugar into a saucepan and bring to a boil. Continue boiling for 5 minutes, then remove the pan from the heat and add the lime zest, if using. Let cool.

2 Remove and discard the lime zest, if used. Hull and chop the strawberries, reserving 4 whole for garnish.

3 Purée the wine syrup and chopped strawberries in a food processor or blender until very smooth.

4 Pour the purée into a large bowl and stir in the orange juice. Cover and chill for at least 3 hours.

5 Serve well chilled, garnished with the reserved whole strawberries and mint sprigs.

STRAWBERRY & CHAMPAGNE SOUP

Omit the white wine and lime zest. Purée the strawberries, reserving a few for garnish, with the sugar and orange juice. Divide the mixture among chilled glass serving bowls and top with chilled Champagne or dry sparkling wine. Garnish and serve.

STRAWBERRY & WATERMELON SOUP

Remove the seeds from a 2-lb (1-kg) piece of watermelon. Chop the flesh and purée until smooth, then combine with the wine syrup, strawberries, and a little lime juice. Omit the orange juice.

2

FIRST COURSES

UNDER 30 MINUTES

QUICK & EASY

MIMOSA FISH SALAD

Rich, creamy salad of white fish fillets, sour cream, hard-boiled egg, mayonnaise, and parsley. Served on tomatoes.

SERVES 4 213 calories per serving
Takes 10 minutes   Page 84

AVOCADO WITH TOMATOES & MINT

Light and refreshing: chopped tomatoes combined with mint and vinaigrette dressing, and piled into avocado halves.

SERVES 4 232 calories per serving
Takes 15 minutes   Page 88

FRENCH CLASSIC

COQUILLES ST. JACQUES

Rich and luxurious: scallops poached with white wine and bay leaf, then stirred into a Mornay sauce flavored with Gruyère cheese.

SERVES 4 297 calories per serving
Takes 25 minutes   Page 80

QUICK & EASY

HUMMUS

Smooth and summery: chick peas blended with rosemary, olive oil, and lemon juice, and richly flavored with garlic.

SERVES 6 150 calories per serving
Takes 10 minutes   Page 75

CHEVRE CROUTES

Goat cheese and pesto, on toasted baguette slices and sprinkled with olive oil, give a tangy flavor to this inviting appetizer.

SERVES 4 450 calories per serving
Takes 20 minutes   Page 66

SARDINES WITH CORIANDER

Broiled sardines, flavored with a butter that combines coriander and shallot with lime juice, make a refreshing first course.

SERVES 4 511 calories per serving
Takes 25 minutes   Page 82

SPICY SHRIMP

Shrimp in a dressing of mayonnaise, creamed horseradish, and tomato paste, spiked with lemon juice and hot pepper sauce.

SERVES 4 338 calories per serving
Takes 10 minutes   Page 83

JUMBO SHRIMP WITH AIOLI

Stir-fried jumbo shrimp served with a Provençal mayonnaise made with garlic, egg yolks, mustard, olive oil, and lemon juice.

SERVES 4 482 calories per serving
Takes 20 minutes   Page 82

DINNER PARTY

ASPARAGUS WITH QUICK HOLLANDAISE

Tender fresh asparagus served with an easy version of hollandaise sauce, garnished with lemon twists.

SERVES 4 384 calories per serving
Takes 20 minutes   Page 86

UNDER 30 MINUTES

30–60 MINUTES

VEGETARIAN

BRIOCHES WITH WILD MUSHROOMS & WATERCRESS
Light-textured, rich bread filled with a mixture of mushrooms, watercress, and cream.

SERVES 6 295 calories per serving
Takes 20 minutes   Page 86

SMOKED CHICKEN SALAD WITH WALNUTS
Sliced smoked chicken in an orange dressing, on a bed of salad leaves, orange segments, and walnuts.

SERVES 6 472 calories per serving
Takes 15 minutes   Page 85

PREPARE AHEAD

SALMON & SHRIMP PHYLLO PURSES
Salmon and shrimp in light phyllo pastry purses. Served with a wine, cream, and dill sauce.

SERVES 8 448 calories per serving
Takes 55 minutes   Page 71

WARM SALAD WITH BACON & SCALLOPS
Crisp bacon, scallops, salad leaves tossed in walnut oil, and a hot wine vinegar and shallot dressing.

SERVES 4 276 calories per serving
Takes 20 minutes   Page 85

MOULES MARINIERE
Traditional French dish: mussels cooked with dry white wine, onion, garlic, parsley, thyme, and a bay leaf. Served in a light sauce.

SERVES 6 302 calories per serving
Takes 25 minutes   Page 80

CANAPES
Lightly toasted bread served with a selection of toppings: anchovy and shrimp, cheese and green onion, salami, and asparagus.

SERVES 4 251 calories per serving
Takes 40 minutes   Page 65

SPICY MEATBALLS
Tiny warm meatballs seasoned with garlic, onion, paprika, fresh cilantro, and tomato paste. Served with a sesame dip.

SERVES 6 481 calories per serving
Takes 25 minutes   Page 65

DINNER PARTY

CHEESE AIGRETTES
Warm nuggets of choux pastry, flavored with sharp Cheddar cheese, then deep-fried and served warm.

SERVES 10–12 238–198 calories per serving
Takes 25 minutes   Page 67

CHEESE & OLIVE BITES
Pimiento-stuffed olives wrapped in cheese pastry flavored with paprika and mustard. Baked, then served warm or cold.

SERVES 4 317 calories per serving
Takes 40 minutes   Page 66

30–60 MINUTES

WARM SALAD WITH PEARS & STILTON

Toast topped with Stilton cheese on a bed of watercress and pears. Served with a warm red onion and balsamic vinegar dressing.

SERVES 4 563 calories per serving
Takes 35 minutes   Page 90

TEX-MEX CLASSIC

NACHOS GRANDE

Spicy and nourishing: refried beans, tomatoes, chili, onion, garlic, and green bell pepper, surrounded by tortilla chips. Topped with cheese.

SERVES 4–6 594–396 calories per serving
Takes 45 minutes   Page 70

OVER 60 MINUTES

PAN-FRIED PATES

Blended chicken livers with bacon, spinach, shallots, parsley, garlic, and sage. Molded into ovals and wrapped in bacon.

SERVES 4 392 calories per serving
Takes 60 minutes   Page 75

SARDINE PATE

Individual pâtés of sardines blended with butter, cream cheese, and lemon juice, seasoned with black pepper, then chilled.

SERVES 8 197 calories per serving
Takes 10 minutes, plus chilling   Page 72

LEEK PARCELS WITH PROVENÇAL VEGETABLES

Layers of eggplant, pesto, red bell pepper, zucchini, and tomato, wrapped in leek strips.

SERVES 4 283 calories per serving
Takes 40 minutes   Page 77

LOW CALORIE

SUMMER MELONS

Contrastingly colored melon balls, mixed with tomato strips, and dressed in vinaigrette. Chilled and served with mint.

SERVES 4 282 calories per serving
Takes 15 minutes, plus chilling   Page 88

ITALIAN CLASSIC

ANTIPASTI

Two popular Italian appetizers: crostini, made from thin slices of baguette brushed with garlic and olive oil and baked until crisp, which are topped with sun-dried tomato butter; and mozzarella, tomato, and basil salad, dressed with olive oil and balsamic vinegar.

SERVES 8 311 calories per crostini serving 180 calories per salad serving

Takes 45 minutes   Page 89

EGG PATE

Hard-boiled eggs mixed with crème fraîche, consommé, and whipped cream, and garnished with large shrimp.

SERVES 8 243 calories per serving
Takes 45 minutes, plus chilling   Page 77

OVER 60 MINUTES

PREPARE AHEAD

GRAVADLAX

Scandinavian specialty: fresh salmon fillets pickled in sugar, sea salt, dill weed, and black pepper, sandwiched together, and chilled. Served in slices, with a rich sauce combining mustard, sugar, white wine vinegar, egg yolk, sunflower oil, and dill weed.

SERVES 16 395 calories per serving
Takes 30 minutes, plus chilling   Page 83

CAPONATA

Eggplant cooked with celery, onions, tomato paste, sugar, and vinegar, then mixed with olives, garlic, and parsley.

SERVES 4–6 297–198 calories per serving
Takes 35 minutes, plus standing   Page 90

SALMON QUENELLES

Little dumplings of salmon, egg whites, and cream, shaped and poached, and served with a luxurious asparagus sauce.

SERVES 4–6 766–511 calories per serving
Takes 30 minutes, plus chilling   Page 81

PICNIC FARE

SMOKED CHICKEN TART

Strips of smoked chicken mixed with onion, mushrooms, and spinach in a light pastry shell, baked with an egg and crème fraîche topping.

SERVES 6 290 calories per serving
Takes 1¼ hours, plus chilling   Page 74

SMOKED HADDOCK MOUSSE

Tender smoked fish blended with cream cheese and mayonnaise, with turmeric added for a rich color and flavor.

SERVES 6 217 calories per serving
Takes 45 minutes, plus chilling   Page 76

RUSSIAN-STYLE

SHRIMP BLINI

Russian blini (puffy yeast pancakes) made with buckwheat flour. Served with red and black caviar, shrimp, and crème fraîche.

SERVES 6–8 369–277 calories per serving
Takes 35 minutes, plus standing   Page 84

PREPARE AHEAD

THREE-FISH TERRINE

Layers of smoked fish pâtés – trout with cream cheese and lemon juice; salmon with lemon juice, tomato paste, cream cheese, and dill weed; mackerel with cream cheese and lemon juice – wrapped in smoked salmon slices. Served here on a bed of watercress.

SERVES 10 424 calories per serving
Takes 40 minutes, plus chilling   Page 73

OVER 60 MINUTES

SMOKED SALMON ROULADE

Spinach roulade rolled around layers of smoked salmon, a mixture of cream cheese, yogurt, and green onions, and tomato slices.

SERVES 4–6   407–271 calories per serving
Takes 45 minutes, plus chilling   Page 87

INDIVIDUAL FISH PATES

Rich and delicate: haddock blended with smoked salmon, white sauce, mayonnaise, and cream, and flavored with white wine.

SERVES 8   217 calories per serving
Takes 50 minutes, plus chilling   Page 72

DINNER PARTY

DIPS WITH CRUDITES

Three unusual dips: bagna cauda, a warm anchovy and garlic dip; taramasalata, a chilled mixture of smoked cod roe, lemon juice, garlic, and oil; and "poor man's caviar," in which eggplant, shallots, and garlic are blended with parsley and tahini paste.

SERVES 12   120 calories per serving
Takes 1½ hours, plus chilling `   Page 67

AMERICAN FAVORITE

SPICY CHICKEN WINGS

Chicken wings marinated in oil, lemon juice, and spices, then baked. Served with blue cheese dressing for dipping into.

SERVES 4–6   206–137 calories per serving
Takes 60 minutes, plus marinating   Page 70

BROCCOLI TERRINE

Broccoli florets blended with milk and egg yolk, flavored with grated nutmeg, and thickened with gelatin and whipped cream.

SERVES 4–6   236–157 calories per serving
Takes 50 minutes, plus chilling   Page 76

PREPARE AHEAD

BRANDIED CHICKEN LIVER PATE

Chicken livers blended with bread, bacon, thyme, egg, and nutmeg, and flavored with brandy. Baked, then chilled.

SERVES 8   268 calories per serving
Takes 1¼ hours, plus chilling   Page 74

CANAPES

Homemade canapés are an excellent accompaniment for drinks, served as an appetizer before dinner. These use toasted bread as a base, but if you prefer you can fry the bread in a mixture of oil and butter instead.

SERVES 4

4 slices of white bread, crusts removed

ANCHOVY TOPPING

| 1 tbsp mayonnaise |
| 1 or 2 green onion tops |
| 8 anchovy fillets, drained |
| 4 cooked peeled shrimp |

CHEESE TOPPING

| 2 tbsp (30 g) cream cheese |
| 2 green onion tops, very finely sliced |
| 4 capers |

SALAMI TOPPING

| 1 tbsp (15 g) butter |
| 2 slices of salami |
| 4 slices of gherkin |

ASPARAGUS TOPPING

| 1 tbsp mayonnaise |
| 6 asparagus tips, cooked and drained |
| 2 slices of radish |
| a few parsley leaves for garnish |

1 Make the canapé bases: Toast the white bread lightly on both sides. Let cool.

2 Make the anchovy topping: Spread 1 piece of toast with mayonnaise and cut into 4 squares. Cut the green onion tops into 4 pieces, then make vertical cuts to separate each piece into strands. Cut the anchovies in half and arrange in a lattice pattern on each square. Place a shrimp on top, and garnish with the green onions.

3 Make the cheese topping: Spread 1 piece of toast with cream cheese and cut into 4 squares. Arrange the green onion slices diagonally across the cream cheese. Place a caper on each square.

4 Make the salami topping: Butter 1 piece of toast and cut into 4 rounds with a pastry cutter.

5 Cut each slice of salami in half to make 2 half-moon-shaped pieces. Roll each piece to form a point at the straight end so that a cornet shape is made. Put 1 cornet and 1 piece of gherkin on each canapé.

6 Make the asparagus topping: Spread 1 piece of toast with mayonnaise and cut into 4 squares. Halve the asparagus tips lengthwise. Halve the radish slices and cut away the centers to form 4 crescents. Put 3 halved asparagus tips on each square, arrange the radish on top, and garnish.

Cook's know-how

Try using different types of salami. Some, such as Danish salami, are mild in flavor, but you may prefer spicier Italian salami, such as salame di Milano or salame di Napoli.

SPICY MEATBALLS

SERVES 8

| 2 lb (1 kg) lean ground beef |
| 1 small onion, grated |
| 2 garlic cloves, minced |
| 1 egg, beaten |
| 2 cups (90 g) fresh bread crumbs |
| 2 tbsp tomato paste |
| 2 tbsp paprika |
| 2 tbsp chopped fresh cilantro |
| salt and black pepper |
| 3 tbsp olive oil for frying |
| chopped parsley for garnish |
| crudités for serving |

SESAME DIP

| 2 tbsp soy sauce |
| 2 tbsp toasted sesame oil |
| 1 tbsp rice wine or dry sherry |
| 1 green onion, thinly sliced |
| 1 tbsp sesame seeds, toasted |

1 Make the sesame dip: Whisk all the ingredients together and set aside.

2 Combine the meatball ingredients in a bowl. Using your hands, roll the mixture into little balls.

3 Heat the oil in a frying pan, and cook the meatballs, in batches, over a medium heat for 5 minutes or until browned, firm, and cooked through. Garnish, and serve warm with the sesame dip and crudités.

CHEVRE CROUTES

SERVES 4

½ baguette

about 2 tbsp pesto sauce

1 log-shaped goat cheese

olive oil for sprinkling

black pepper

radicchio and curly endive leaves
  for serving

chervil sprigs for garnish

1 Cut the baguette into 8 slices, each ½ in (1 cm) thick, and toast under the broiler on one side only. Lightly spread the untoasted sides with the pesto sauce.

2 Cut the goat cheese into 8 slices, each ½ in (1 cm) thick, and place on the pesto. Toast the croûtes under the broiler, 3 in (7 cm) from the heat, for 3 minutes or until the cheese just begins to soften. Remove the broiler pan from the heat.

3 Lightly sprinkle a little olive oil and grind a little pepper over each cheese croûte. Return the croûtes to the broiler, close to the heat, for 3 minutes or until the cheese begins to bubble and is just tinged golden brown.

4 Line a serving platter with radicchio and endive leaves, arrange the croûtes on top, and garnish with chervil sprigs. Serve at once.

ITALIAN BRUSCHETTA WITH GOAT CHEESE

Substitute 8 slices of Italian ciabatta (slipper bread), or other rustic bread, for the baguette. After toasting the topped croûtes in step 3, sprinkle chopped black olives over them and drizzle with extra virgin olive oil. Serve sprinkled with fresh basil leaves.

CHEESE & OLIVE BITES

SERVES 4

1½ cups (175 g) grated sharp
  Cheddar cheese

⅔ cup (90 g) all-purpose flour

1 tbsp (15 g) butter, plus extra for
  greasing

1 tsp paprika

½ tsp mustard powder

20 pimiento-stuffed green olives

cayenne pepper and parsley sprigs
  for garnish

1 Work the cheese, flour, butter, paprika, and mustard powder in a food processor until the mixture resembles fine bread crumbs.

2 Tip the dough mixture into a bowl and use to wrap the olives (see box, right).

3 Butter a baking sheet. Put the wrapped olives on it and bake in a preheated oven at 400°F (200°C) for 15 minutes or until the pastry is golden.

4 Remove the cheese and olive bites from the baking sheet and let cool slightly.

5 Serve warm or cold, sprinkled with cayenne pepper and garnished with parsley sprigs.

Wrapping the olives in the dough

Take a thumb-sized piece of the dough mixture and flatten it on the work surface.

Place an olive in the middle of the piece of dough. Wrap the dough around the olive, pressing to make it stick. If the dough mixture is too crumbly and will not stick, add a little water to help bind it.

DIPS WITH CRUDITES

For an informal start to a meal, a selection of dips served with fresh, crisp vegetables and some good bread is hard to beat. Bagna cauda, meaning "hot bath," is a rustic Italian dip that should be put over a gentle heat to keep it warm.

POOR MAN'S CAVIAR

SERVES 4

1 1/2 lb (750 g) eggplants

salt and black pepper

2 shallots, halved

1–2 garlic cloves

4 tbsp lemon juice

4 tbsp olive oil

4 tbsp chopped parsley

2 tbsp tahini paste

1 Cut the eggplants in half lengthwise. Score the flesh in a lattice pattern, sprinkle with salt, and let stand for 30 minutes.

2 Rinse the eggplant halves with cold water, and pat dry with paper towels. Place on a baking sheet and bake in a preheated oven at 400°F (200°C) for 20 minutes.

3 Add the shallots and garlic to the baking sheet, and bake for 15 more minutes.

4 Purée the eggplants, shallots, and garlic with the lemon juice, oil, parsley, tahini paste, and salt and pepper to taste in a food processor until smooth.

5 Turn the dip into a bowl. Cover and chill for at least 1 hour before serving.

TARAMASALATA

SERVES 4

1 lb (500 g) smoked cod or other fish roe, skinned and coarsely chopped

4 small slices of white bread, crusts removed

4 tbsp lemon juice

1 large garlic clove, chopped

1 cup (250 ml) olive oil

salt and black pepper

1 Work the cod roe in a food processor or blender until smooth. Break the bread into a bowl, add the lemon juice, and let the bread soak for 1 minute. Add to the cod roe with the garlic, and work until smooth.

2 Pour the oil into the mixture, a little at a time, processing until all the oil has been absorbed. Add salt and pepper to taste. Turn the taramasalata into a bowl. Cover and chill for at least 1 hour before serving.

BAGNA CAUDA

SERVES 4

2/3 cup (150 ml) good-quality olive oil

2 garlic cloves, minced

2 oz (60 g) canned anchovy fillets, drained and chopped

black pepper

1 Heat the oil in a frying pan, add the garlic, and cook gently, stirring occasionally, for a few minutes until soft but not colored. Add the anchovies and cook over a very low heat until they dissolve in the oil. Season with black pepper.

2 To serve, carefully pour the bagna cauda into an earthenware pot (or a cheese fondue pot) and place over a flame to keep warm while it is being served.

CHEESE AIGRETTES

SERVES 10–12

1 1/4 cups (300 ml) water

4 tbsp (60 g) butter

3/4 cup + 2 tbsp (125 g) self-rising flour

2 egg yolks

2 eggs

1 cup (125 g) grated sharp Cheddar cheese

salt and black pepper

vegetable oil for deep-frying

1 Put the water and butter into a saucepan and bring to a boil. Remove from the heat, and add the flour. Beat well until the mixture is smooth and glossy and leaves the side of the pan clean. Let cool slightly.

2 In a bowl, lightly mix the yolks and eggs, then beat into the flour mixture a little at a time. Stir in the cheese. Add salt and pepper to taste.

3 Heat the oil to 375°F (190°C). Lower the mixture a teaspoonful at a time into the oil, and cook until golden brown. Lift out and drain on paper towels. Serve warm.

Cook's know-how

These little deep-fried puffs made from choux pastry are traditionally flavored with cheese, but chopped anchovies are sometimes added for extra piquancy.

TAPAS

Tapas are Spanish appetizers: little plates of savory foods traditionally served in bars, and accompanied
by drinks (often chilled dry sherry) and good conversation. All sorts of hot and cold dishes make
excellent tapas: just make sure they can easily be eaten with the fingers or a fork.

VEGETABLES WITH GARLIC DIPS

SERVES 4

1½ lb (750 g) small new potatoes

2 eggplants, cut into chunky wedges

olive oil for brushing

2 red bell peppers, roasted and peeled (page 388)

small bunch of watercress for serving

rouille and aïoli (pages 51 and 82) for serving

1 Boil the potatoes for 10–15 minutes until just tender. Drain and let cool, or keep warm, as desired.

2 Arrange the eggplant wedges in the broiler pan and brush with olive oil. Cook under the broiler, 4 in (10 cm) from the heat, for 10 minutes or until tender and lightly browned, turning occasionally. Cut the roasted peppers into chunks.

3 Arrange the vegetables on a serving plate, garnish with the watercress, and serve with rouille and aïoli.

CHICK PEA & RED PEPPER SALAD

SERVES 4

14 oz (400 g) canned chick peas (garbanzo beans), drained

½ red onion or 3 green onions, chopped

3 garlic cloves, minced

3 tbsp olive oil

2 tbsp white wine vinegar

salt and black pepper

a bunch of flat-leaf parsley

1 red bell pepper, roasted and peeled (page 388)

about 12 pimiento-stuffed olives

1 Combine the chick peas with the onion, garlic, oil, vinegar, and salt and pepper to taste. Remove the parsley leaves from the stems, chop them roughly and stir in.

2 Cut the red pepper into small chunks; chop the olives if you like. Stir into the chick pea mixture until evenly mixed.

TUNA TOSTADOS

SERVES 4

½ baguette, sliced on the diagonal

1 garlic clove, minced

3 tbsp olive oil

2 ripe tomatoes, thinly sliced

½ 7-oz (200-g) can tuna, drained

1 cup (125 g) grated manchego or Cheddar cheese

1 Lightly toast the bread on both sides under the broiler. Meanwhile, combine the garlic with the olive oil.

2 Brush each slice of toasted bread with a little of the garlic oil, then top with a thin slice of tomato. Place a little tuna on each, then top with cheese.

3 Return to the broiler and cook, about 4 in (10 cm) from the heat, for 2–3 minutes, until the cheese has melted. Serve piping hot.

TRADITIONAL TAPAS

An appetizing selection of tapas does not have to involve a lot of work. In addition to the dishes on this page, serve some of the following – they require little or no preparation.

- pan-fried and salted almonds
- black or green olives
- slices or chunks of manchego cheese
- squares of Spanish omelet (page 101)
- slices of smoked chorizo (spicy sausage)
- chunks of crusty bread
- jumbo shrimp (good with aïoli)

ANDALUCIAN MUSHROOMS

SERVES 4

8 oz (250 g) button mushrooms

2 tbsp olive oil

6 shallots, chopped

3 garlic cloves, minced

1 oz (30 g) Serrano ham, cut into strips

¼ tsp chili powder

¼ tsp paprika (preferably sweet smoked)

1 tsp lemon juice

6 tbsp dry red wine

chopped flat-leaf parsley for garnish

1 Pull the mushroom stems from the caps. Heat the olive oil in a frying pan until hot, add the shallots and half of the garlic, and cook, stirring, for 5 minutes or until soft but not colored. Add the mushroom caps and stems, and cook, stirring, for 3 minutes or until lightly browned.

2 Add the Serrano ham, chili powder, and paprika, and cook, stirring constantly, for 1 minute.

3 Add the lemon juice, and cook over a high heat for a few minutes until the liquid has almost evaporated and the mushrooms are just tender.

4 Add the red wine and continue to cook over a high heat until the liquid is reduced and flavorful. Stir in the remaining garlic, sprinkle with the chopped parsley, and serve at once.

CLOCKWISE FROM TOP: Vegetables with Garlic Dips (Rouille and Aïoli), Chick Pea & Red Pepper Salad, Andalucian Mushrooms, Tuna Tostados.

SPICY CHICKEN WINGS

SERVES 4–6

1 lb (500 g) chicken wings

2 tbsp sunflower oil

1 tsp lemon juice

1 tbsp paprika

1 tsp ground cumin

1/2 tsp dried oregano

1/2 tsp chili powder

black pepper

parsley sprigs for garnish

FOR SERVING

1/2 red bell pepper, cut into strips

1/2 bunch celery, cut into sticks, plus leaves

blue cheese dressing (page 372)

1 Cut the chicken wings in half and put the pieces in a shallow dish.

2 In a large bowl, combine the oil, lemon juice, paprika, cumin, oregano, chili powder, and black pepper. Brush the mixture over the chicken, cover, and let marinate at room temperature for at least 1 hour.

3 Line a large roasting pan with foil and place a rack on top. Lay the chicken wings in a single layer on the rack, and cook in a preheated oven at 400°F (200°C) for 40 minutes or until the wings are browned, sizzling, and crisp.

4 Remove the chicken from the rack and drain on paper towels. Serve with red pepper strips, celery sticks, and blue cheese dressing, and garnished with parsley sprigs.

Healthy option

The skin is the crispest part of these chicken wings, but it is also the fattiest. If you strip off the skin before marinating, the chicken will still taste good but it will not have a crisp baked coating.

NACHOS GRANDE

SERVES 4–6

2 tbsp sunflower oil

1 onion, minced

1/2 green bell pepper, chopped

3 garlic cloves, minced

1 cup (225 g) canned crushed tomatoes

1/2–1 fresh, hot green chili pepper, halved, seeded, and minced

1/2 tsp chili powder

1/2 tsp paprika

14 oz (400 g) canned refried beans

1/3 cup (75 ml) water

2–3 handfuls tortilla chips

1/4 tsp ground cumin

1 1/2 cups (175 g) grated Cheddar cheese

paprika for garnish

1 Heat the oil in a frying pan, add the onion, green bell pepper, and garlic, and cook gently, stirring occasionally, for 5 minutes or until softened.

2 Add the tomatoes and chili pepper, and cook over a medium heat for 5 minutes or until most of the liquid has evaporated.

3 Stir in the chili powder and paprika. Cook for 3 more minutes, then add the refried beans, breaking them up with a fork. Add the measured water and cook, stirring from time to time, for 8–10 minutes or until the mixture thickens.

4 Spoon the beans into a baking dish, arrange the tortilla chips around the edge, and sprinkle with the cumin. Sprinkle the cheese over the beans and tortilla chips.

5 Bake in a preheated oven at 400°F (200°C) for 15–20 minutes until the cheese has melted. Sprinkle paprika in a lattice pattern on top.

Cook's know-how

The spicy bean mixture makes a tasty filling for soft flour tortillas. Make it up to the end of step 3 and serve it in a bowl for everyone to help themselves, with a bowl of sour cream or plain yogurt to spoon on top. There is enough to fill 8 tortillas.

SALMON & SHRIMP PHYLLO PURSES

These crisp, golden purses and their creamy sauce are ideal for a party as they can be prepared up to
24 hours ahead, kept covered with a damp dish towel in the refrigerator, and cooked at the last minute.
For a really special occasion, use scallops instead of shrimp.

MAKES 8 PURSES

1-lb (500-g) tail end piece of
salmon, boned, skinned, and cut
into bite-sized pieces

8 oz (250 g) cooked peeled shrimp

lemon juice for sprinkling

8 oz (250 g) phyllo pastry

4 tbsp (60 g) butter, melted

butter for greasing

salt and black pepper

lemon slices and dill weed sprigs for
garnish

WHITE WINE SAUCE

1/2 cup (125 ml) dry white wine

1 1/4 cups (300 ml) heavy cream

1 tsp chopped fresh dill weed

Healthy option

You can use about 2 tbsp
olive oil to brush the phyllo
rather than melted butter, and
serve the purses with lemon
halves for squeezing rather
than the creamy sauce.

1 Combine the salmon pieces
and shrimp. Sprinkle with
lemon juice, and add salt and
pepper to taste. Set aside.

2 Cut the phyllo into sixteen
7-in (18-cm) squares. Brush
2 squares with the melted
butter, covering the remaining
squares with a damp dish towel.
Make a phyllo purse (see box,
right). Repeat to make 8 purses.

3 Butter a baking sheet. Add
the phyllo purses, lightly
brush with the remaining
melted butter, and bake in a
preheated oven at 375°F
(190°C) for 15–20 minutes or
until crisp and golden.

4 Meanwhile, make the sauce:
Pour the wine into a
saucepan and boil rapidly until
it has reduced to about 3 tbsp.
Add the cream and simmer
until it reaches a light coating
consistency. Remove from the
heat, and add the dill and salt
and pepper to taste.

5 Pour the sauce into a bowl
and garnish with a dill
sprig. Garnish the purses with
the lemon slices and dill sprigs,
and serve with the warm sauce.

Making a phyllo purse

Place one-eighth of the salmon
and shrimp mixture in the
middle of one buttered phyllo
pastry square.

Fold 2 opposite sides of pastry
over the mixture to form a
rectangle. Take the 2 open ends
and fold one over the filling and
the other underneath.

Place this parcel on the second
buttered pastry square and
draw up the edges. Squeeze the
pastry together at the neck to
seal the purse.

INDIVIDUAL FISH PATES

Rich in flavor, these little pâté parcels make an ideal appetizer for a special occasion. With the gelatin, they are firm enough to be sliced. For softer pâtés, omit the gelatin and wine, and serve in ramekin dishes.

SERVES 8

8 oz (250 g) haddock fillet

2/3 cup (150 ml) milk

1 1/2 tbsp (20 g) butter

2 tbsp all-purpose flour

1 tsp powdered gelatin

4 tbsp dry white wine

8 oz (250 g) smoked salmon pieces

2 tbsp mayonnaise

4 tbsp heavy cream

dash of lemon juice

black pepper

oil for greasing

smoked salmon and lemon slices, and dill weed sprigs for garnish

1 Put the haddock into a saucepan and add the milk. Bring almost to a boil, then simmer gently for 10 minutes or until the fish is opaque and flakes easily.

2 Lift the haddock out of the pan, remove the skin and bones, and discard. Flake the fish and let cool. Reserve the cooking liquid.

3 Melt the butter in a small pan, add the flour, and cook, stirring, for 1 minute. Gradually blend in the reserved cooking liquid, and bring to a boil, stirring constantly, until the mixture thickens. Place a piece of damp parchment paper over the surface of the sauce to prevent a skin from forming, and leave until cold.

4 Sprinkle the gelatin evenly over the wine in a small bowl. Let stand for about 3 minutes or until the gelatin becomes spongy.

5 Put the bowl into a saucepan of gently simmering water and heat for about 3 minutes or until the gelatin has dissolved. Let cool slightly.

6 Purée the haddock, cold white sauce, smoked salmon, and mayonnaise in a food processor or blender until almost smooth. Gradually add the gelatin mixture, pulsing between each addition. Add the cream and lemon juice, season with pepper, and pulse again.

7 Grease 8 small molds. Spoon the pâté into the molds, cover, and chill for at least 2 hours.

8 To serve, unmold each pâté and garnish with smoked salmon and lemon slices, and dill sprigs.

SARDINE PATE

SERVES 8

8 oz (250 g) canned sardines in oil, drained and bones removed

1/2 cup (125 g) butter, softened

1/2 cup (125 g) lowfat cream cheese

3 tbsp lemon juice

black pepper

lemon twists and parsley sprigs for garnish

1 Purée the sardines, butter, cheese, and lemon juice in a food processor until almost smooth. Add pepper and more lemon juice to taste.

2 Divide the sardine mixture among 8 small ramekins (or put into a large bowl) and smooth the surface. Cover and chill for at least 30 minutes.

3 Serve chilled, garnished with lemon twists and parsley sprigs.

SHRIMP PATE

Substitute 8 oz (250 g) cooked peeled shrimp for the sardines.

Healthy note

Sardines are an oily fish, rich in omega-3 fatty acids, which can help to prevent heart disease and blood clots. They also provide vitamin D. If you eat the bones, which are removed for this pâté, they are a source of calcium.

THREE-FISH TERRINE

Three kinds of smoked fish – trout, salmon, and mackerel – are blended with cream cheese, arranged in layers, and wrapped in smoked salmon, for a subtle variety of flavors. The finished terrine can be frozen for up to 1 month.

SERVES 10

sunflower oil for greasing

6–8 oz (175–250 g) smoked salmon slices

salt and black pepper

watercress for serving

TROUT PATE

6 oz (175 g) smoked trout

6 tbsp (90 g) butter

6 tbsp (90 g) cream cheese

1 1/2 tbsp lemon juice

SALMON PATE

4 oz (125 g) smoked salmon pieces

4 tbsp (60 g) butter

1/4 cup (60 g) cream cheese

1 1/2 tbsp lemon juice

1 tbsp tomato paste

1 tbsp chopped fresh dill weed

MACKEREL PATE

6 oz (175 g) smoked mackerel

6 tbsp (90 g) butter

6 tbsp (90 g) cream cheese

1 1/2 tbsp lemon juice

5-CUP (1.25-LITER) LOAF PAN OR TERRINE MOLD

1 Make the trout pâté: Remove the skin and bones from the trout and purée with the butter, cheese, lemon juice, and salt and pepper to taste in a food processor until smooth and well blended. Turn into a bowl, cover, and chill.

2 Make the salmon pâté: Purée the smoked salmon pieces, butter, cheese, lemon juice, tomato paste, dill, and salt and pepper to taste in a food processor until smooth and well blended. Turn into a bowl, cover, and chill.

3 Make the mackerel pâté: Remove the skin and bones from the mackerel and purée with the butter, cheese, lemon juice, and salt and pepper to taste in a food processor until smooth and well blended. Turn into a bowl, cover, and chill.

4 Assemble the terrine (see box, right). Cover and chill overnight.

5 To serve, carefully unmold the terrine, cut into thick slices, and arrange on beds of watercress on individual serving plates.

Assembling the terrine

Oil the loaf pan and line with overlapping slices of smoked salmon. Arrange them crosswise and allow 1 1/2–2 in (3.5–5 cm) to overhang the sides.

Turn the trout pâté into the loaf pan and spread it evenly with a metal spatula, leveling the surface. If necessary, wet the spatula to prevent sticking. Add the salmon pâté in the same way, and then top with the mackerel pâté.

Fold the smoked salmon over the mackerel pâté, tucking in the ends.

SMOKED CHICKEN TART

SERVES 6

8 oz (250 g) piecrust dough

1 tbsp (15 g) butter

1/2 small onion, minced

1 cup (60 g) thinly sliced mushrooms

1 cup (60 g) baby spinach leaves, washed

salt and black pepper

scant 1 cup (200 ml) crème fraîche or sour cream

2 extra large eggs

2 tbsp chopped parsley

1 cup (90 g) cooked smoked chicken, sliced into thin strips

1/4 cup (30 g) grated Cheddar cheese

7-IN (18-CM) TART DISH OR PAN

1 Roll out the dough and use to line the tart dish or pan. Prick the bottom of the pastry shell with a fork. Line the shell with foil or wax paper, and fill with ceramic baking beans or raw rice or pasta.

2 Place the dish or pan on a heated baking sheet, and bake in a preheated oven at 425°F (220°C) for 15 minutes, removing the foil and beans for the final 5 minutes. Remove from the oven and turn the temperature down to 350°F (180°C).

3 Melt the butter in a frying pan, add the onion, cover, and cook gently for 10–15 minutes until soft. Remove the lid, increase the heat, add the mushrooms, and cook for 1–2 minutes. Add the spinach and cook until just wilted, then season and let cool.

4 Mix the crème fraîche, eggs, and parsley in a bowl, and season with salt and pepper. Mix the chicken with the cold spinach, spread in the pastry shell, and top with the grated cheese. Pour the egg mixture over the top and bake for 25–30 minutes until golden brown and set. Serve warm.

BRANDIED CHICKEN LIVER PATE

SERVES 8

4 slices (125 g) bread, crusts removed

1 garlic clove, coarsely chopped

4 oz (125 g) thick bacon slices, coarsely chopped

2 tsp chopped fresh thyme

1 lb (500 g) chicken livers, trimmed

1 egg

4 tbsp brandy

1/2 tsp grated nutmeg

salt and black pepper

4 tbsp (60 g) butter, melted

2-LB (1-KG) LOAF PAN

1 Line the loaf pan with foil, leaving 2 in (5 cm) foil overhanging on each side.

2 Cut the bread into thick chunks, and work with the garlic in a food processor to form fine crumbs. Add the bacon and thyme, and work until finely chopped.

3 Add the chicken livers, egg, brandy, and nutmeg, season with salt and pepper, and purée until smooth. Add the butter and purée again.

4 Put the pâté mixture into the prepared loaf pan, level the surface, and fold the foil over the top. Set in a roasting pan. Pour boiling water into the roasting pan to come about halfway up the side of the loaf pan. Bake in a preheated oven at 325°F (170°C) for 1 hour.

5 Test the pâté for doneness (see box, below). Let the pâté cool completely, then cover and chill overnight.

6 To serve, cut the pâté into slices.

Is it cooked?

Insert a skewer into the middle of the pâté. If it comes out hot and clean, the pâté is cooked.

PAN-FRIED PATES

These little bacon-wrapped chicken liver and spinach pâtés are easy to make, and they are at their most delicious when served with a tangy salad of sliced tomatoes and chopped onions in an herb vinaigrette dressing.

SERVES 4

2 tbsp (30 g) butter

4 oz (125 g) chicken livers, trimmed

5 shallots, coarsely chopped

4 oz (125 g) lean, thick bacon slices or Canadian bacon, coarsely chopped

1 cup (60 g) shredded spinach leaves

2 tbsp chopped parsley

1 tsp chopped fresh thyme leaves

1 garlic clove, minced

salt and black pepper

8 bacon slices

1 Melt half of the butter in a frying pan, add the chicken livers, and cook gently, stirring occasionally, for 3 minutes or until they are browned on the outside but still pink inside.

2 Purée the chicken livers in a food processor until smooth. Turn into a large bowl and set aside.

3 Melt the remaining butter in the frying pan, add the shallots, and cook gently, stirring occasionally, for a few minutes until soft but not colored.

4 Add the shallots to the chicken livers along with the chopped bacon, spinach, parsley, garlic, and thyme. Season with salt and pepper. Purée half of this mixture until smooth, then stir it into the remaining mixture in the bowl.

5 Shape and wrap the chicken liver pâtés (see box, right).

6 Heat a frying pan, add the pâtés, and cook them gently until browned all over. Lower the heat, cover, and cook over a very gentle heat for 35–40 minutes.

7 Serve the pan-fried pâtés either warm or at room temperature.

Cook's know-how

To trim the chicken livers, use kitchen scissors to cut away any membranes.

Shaping and wrapping the pâtés

Mold the pâté mixture into 8 equal-sized oval shapes, using your hands.

Lay a bacon slice flat, put a pâté oval at one end, and roll the bacon around it.

Twist the slice around the ends to enclose the pâté, then tuck it in underneath to secure. Repeat with the remaining bacon slices and pâté.

HUMMUS

SERVES 6

28 oz (800 g) canned chick peas (garbanzo beans), drained

2–3 garlic cloves, coarsely chopped

1 tbsp tahini paste, or to taste

3 tbsp olive oil, or to taste

juice of 1 lemon, or to taste

salt and black pepper

FOR GARNISH (OPTIONAL)

6 rosemary sprigs

1 red bell pepper, halved, seeded, and cut into strips

12 small black olives

1 Purée the chick peas, garlic, tahini paste, oil, and lemon juice in a food processor or blender until smooth.

2 Add salt and pepper to taste, and more oil, tahini, and lemon juice if you think it needs it, then purée again.

3 Spoon into dishes and level the surface. If you like, garnish with rosemary, red pepper, and olives.

Cook's know-how

There are no hard-and-fast rules about the amounts of oil, tahini paste, and lemon juice when making hummus. The best method is to purée the amount suggested,, then taste it and see before adding more. Serve chilled, if you like.

SMOKED HADDOCK MOUSSE

SERVES 6

8 oz (250 g) smoked haddock (finnan haddie) fillet, skinned

juice of 1/2 lemon

salt and black pepper

1 cup (250 g) cream cheese

2 tbsp mayonnaise

1 tbsp turmeric

6 SMALL RAMEKINS

1 Line a baking sheet with a long, wide piece of foil and place the haddock on it. Sprinkle the fish with the lemon juice, and season with pepper. Bring the long edges of the foil together and fold to seal. Bring each of the short edges together and fold to seal, forming a parcel.

2 Bake the fish in a preheated oven at 350°F (180°C) for 7–10 minutes or until the fish is just cooked and flakes easily with a fork. Set aside in the foil parcel until cold.

3 Flake the fish, removing any bones. Place in a food processor or blender, adding any juices that are left on the foil. Add the cream cheese, mayonnaise, and turmeric. Season lightly with salt.

4 Process or blend the mixture until smooth, then check and adjust the seasoning if necessary.

5 Lightly oil the ramekins and spoon in the fish mixture. Cover and chill for at least 3 hours, when the mixture will be set to a soft mousse.

6 Serve with thin slices of whole-wheat toast (the cheese adds richness to the mousse, so you don't really need any butter).

Cook's know-how

Turmeric comes from the same family as ginger, but the root is rarely used in cooking and it is only seen in its powdered form in recipes. It is often used to add warm color and flavor to Indian dishes, especially curries (it is the spice that makes curry powder the color it is), and is known to be an important source of curcumin, a phytochemical with anti-cancer and anti-inflammatory effects.

BROCCOLI TERRINE

SERVES 4–6

1 lb (500 g) broccoli florets

salt and black pepper

2 envelopes (15 g) powdered gelatin

1/2 cup (125 ml) milk

1 egg yolk

pinch of grated nutmeg

1/2 cup (125 ml) heavy cream

oil for greasing

carrot julienne salad (page 391) for serving

2-LB (1-KG) LOAF PAN

1 Cook the broccoli in boiling salted water for 3–4 minutes or until just tender. Drain well, pouring 1/3 cup (75 ml) of the cooking liquid into a small bowl.

2 Let the reserved cooking liquid cool slightly, then sprinkle the gelatin evenly over the top. Let stand for 3 minutes or until the gelatin becomes spongy. Set the bowl in a pan of gently simmering water for 3 minutes or until the gelatin has dissolved.

3 Put the milk and egg yolk into a small saucepan and beat together. Heat gently, stirring, until the mixture thickens enough to coat the back of the spoon. Let cool slightly.

4 Reserve a few broccoli florets for garnish. Roughly chop half of the remaining broccoli, and purée the rest with the milk and egg mixture in a food processor until smooth. Pour the puréed broccoli mixture into a large bowl and add the chopped broccoli, gelatin mixture, and nutmeg. Season with salt and pepper, and mix together.

5 Whip the cream until it forms firm peaks, then fold into the broccoli mixture. Oil the loaf pan and pour in the broccoli mixture. Cover and chill for at least 3 hours.

6 Unmold the terrine and cut into slices. Garnish with the reserved broccoli florets, and serve with the carrot julienne salad.

LEEK PARCELS WITH PROVENÇAL VEGETABLES

Punchy pesto features twice in this stunning first course – inside the parcels and in the dressing. The flavors of basil, pine nuts, garlic, and Parmesan complement the leeks, zucchini, and eggplant, three vegetables that go together surprisingly well.

SERVES 4

| I large leek, green part only, trimmed and cut in half lengthwise |
| I eggplant, cut into 8 slices |
| I zucchini, sliced |
| olive oil for brushing |
| 1/2 tsp herbes de Provence or Italian seasoning herbs |
| salt and black pepper |
| 3 tbsp pesto sauce |
| I red bell pepper, halved, seeded, roasted, and peeled (page 388), or I bottled pimiento, drained and chopped |
| I cup (225 g) canned tomatoes, drained and chopped |
| carrot julienne for garnish |

PESTO DRESSING

| 3 tbsp olive oil |
| 3 tbsp white wine vinegar |
| I tsp pesto sauce |

1 Blanch the leek in boiling water for 1 minute. Drain and rinse. Separate the green layers to give 13 strips.

2 Brush the eggplant and zucchini with the oil, and sprinkle with the herbs, salt, and pepper. Cook under a hot broiler about 4 in (10 cm) from the heat, for 5 minutes. Brush the eggplant with pesto.

3 Cut one of the strips of leek into 4 long strands and set aside. Take 3 strips of leek and lay on top of one another in a star formation. Assemble the leek parcels (see box, right).

4 Put the leek parcels on a baking sheet and bake in a preheated oven at 350°F (180°C) for 10 minutes.

5 Whisk the dressing ingredients together, and spoon onto 4 serving plates. Place the leek parcels on top, garnish, and serve.

Assembling the leek parcels

Place a slice of eggplant where the strips of leek cross. Place a piece of red pepper on top, then 1–2 slices of zucchini, a piece of tomato, and, finally, another slice of eggplant.

Fold the leek strips over the filling so they meet on top in the middle and enclose the filling completely.

Tie the parcel with one of the long strands of leek, or with a length of string. Repeat with the remaining leek strips, vegetables, and leek strands.

EGG PATE

SERVES 8

| 2 envelopes (15 g) powdered gelatin |
| 2 tbsp water |
| 14 oz (400 g) canned consommé or beef broth |
| 2/3 cup (150 ml) heavy cream |
| 6 hard-boiled eggs, peeled and chopped |
| 2/3 cup (150 ml) crème fraîche |
| salt and black pepper |
| 8 large cooked shrimp in shell, lemon slices, and dill weed sprigs for garnish |

1 Sprinkle the gelatin over the water in a bowl. Let stand for 3 minutes or until the gelatin is spongy. Set the bowl in a saucepan of simmering water for 3 minutes or until the gelatin has dissolved.

2 Pour the consommé or broth into a bowl and stir in the gelatin liquid.

3 Whip the cream in a large bowl until it forms soft peaks. Fold in the eggs, crème fraîche, and three-fourths of the consommé. Season with salt and pepper.

4 Divide the mixture among 8 ramekins and level the surface. Let stand for about 30 minutes until set. If it has already set, reheat the remaining consommé gently, then spoon it over the pâté. Chill for at least 3 hours.

5 To serve, unmold the pâté and garnish with the shrimp, lemon slices, and dill.

PREPARE-AHEAD FIRST COURSES

If you are having friends over for a party, it is always best to try to get the first course made ahead of time. Then, before you sit down to eat, you can concentrate on the main course and vegetables, which almost always need last-minute attention. These three dishes can all be made several hours ahead of serving.

ASPARAGUS & QUAIL EGG SALAD

SERVES 6

12 quail eggs

18 asparagus spears

12 oz (340 g) bottled roasted artichokes hearts in oil

FOR SERVING

1 tbsp balsamic vinegar

salt and black pepper

about 1/4 cup (30 g) Parmesan shavings

1 Put the eggs in a pan of cold water, bring to a boil, and boil for 3 minutes (start timing as soon as the water comes to a boil). Drain and rinse under cold running water, then peel immediately. The shells come off very easily when the eggs are just cooked.

2 Peel the asparagus stems with a potato or vegetable peeler if they are woody, then cut the asparagus into 2-in (5-cm) lengths. Cook in boiling salted water for about 2 minutes until only just tender. Drain and rinse thoroughly under cold running water, then pat dry with paper towels.

3 Drain the artichoke hearts, reserving the oil. Cut the artichokes and eggs lengthwise in half. Divide the artichokes and asparagus among 6 plates, and top each serving with 4 egg halves.

4 Make a dressing by mixing 3 tbsp of the reserved oil from the artichoke jar with the balsamic vinegar, and season with salt and pepper.

5 Drizzle the dressing over the salad and top with the Parmesan shavings. Serve with crusty rolls.

DOUBLE SALMON TIAN

SERVES 6

1 lb 5 oz (650 g) fresh salmon fillet, skinned

scant 1 cup (200 g) lowfat cream cheese

4 tbsp chopped fresh dill weed

salt and black pepper

FOR SERVING

few handfuls mizuna leaves, or any other peppery leaves such as arugula

6 small slices of smoked salmon, total weight about 7 oz (200 g)

6 lemon wedges

6 3-IN (7.5-CM) METAL RINGS OR 5-OZ (150-ML) RAMEKIN DISHES

1 Wrap the fresh salmon tightly in foil and bake in a preheated oven at 375°F (190°C) for 15–20 minutes or until just cooked. Let cool in the foil.

2 Mix the cream cheese and dill weed in a large bowl until smooth. Flake the cooled salmon into the bowl, including any fish juices and jelly, but discarding any bones. Season well with salt and pepper, and fold gently together.

3 Put the metal rings on a flat tray or baking sheet (if using ramekins, line them with plastic wrap). Divide the salmon and cheese mixture among the rings, smoothing the surface with the back of a metal spoon. Cover and refrigerate for at least 2 hours, up to 8 hours if possible.

4 To serve, divide the salad leaves among 6 plates. Lift a ring filled with salmon onto the leaves, using a slotted spatula, then carefully ease off the ring. (If using ramekins, invert the salmon tian onto the leaves, then gently remove the plastic wrap.) Top each tian with a loosely curled piece of smoked salmon and serve with wedges of lemon for squeezing.

SMOKED SALMON TERRINE

SERVES 8

9 oz (275 g) thinly sliced smoked salmon

black pepper

1 cup (250 g) lowfat cream cheese

1/2 cup (125 g) unsalted butter, softened

4 canned anchovy fillets (more if you wish)

2 tbsp creamed horseradish

1–2 tbsp chopped fresh parsley or dill weed, or a mixture of the two

FOR SERVING

salad leaves, tossed in your favorite dressing

lime or lemon wedges

1-LB (500-G) LOAF PAN

1 Dampen the loaf pan and line with plastic wrap, letting it hang over the sides. Divide the smoked salmon into four equal piles. Cover the bottom of the pan with one-fourth of the salmon and sprinkle with black pepper.

2 Put the cream cheese, butter, anchovies, horseradish, and parsley or dill into a blender or food processor, season with black pepper, and work to a very smooth paste. Do not add salt. (If you don't have a blender or food processor, beat the mixture vigorously with a wooden spoon.)

3 Spread one-third of the paste over the salmon in the pan, then cover with a second layer of salmon. Continue the layering, finishing with salmon. Tightly pull the plastic wrap over the top and press down firmly. Refrigerate for at least 6 hours, preferably overnight.

4 To serve, put the terrine in the freezer for 30 minutes (this will make it easy to slice). Unmold it from the pan and discard the plastic wrap, then cut into 16 thin slices. Serve 2 slices on each plate, on a bed of dressed salad leaves, with lime or lemon wedges for squeezing.

CLOCKWISE FROM TOP: Smoked Salmon Terrine, Asparagus & Quail Egg Salad, Double Salmon Tian.

COQUILLES ST. JACQUES

SERVES 4

8 sea scallops, with 4 shells if possible

2/3 cup (150 ml) water

4 tbsp medium dry white wine

1 bay leaf

salt and black pepper

lemon wedges and bay leaves for garnish

MORNAY SAUCE

3 tbsp (45 g) butter

3 tbsp all-purpose flour

4 tbsp light cream

1/2 cup (60 g) grated Gruyère cheese

1 Cut each scallop into 2–3 pieces. Put the measured water, wine, and bay leaf into a small pan, and season with salt and pepper. Bring to a boil, then lower the heat and add the scallops.

2 Poach for 1 minute or until the scallops are just tender when tested with the tip of a knife. Lift out the scallops with a slotted spoon. Strain the cooking liquid and reserve.

3 Make the Mornay sauce: Melt the butter in a saucepan, add the flour, and cook, stirring, for 1 minute. Gradually stir in the reserved cooking liquid and bring to a boil, stirring constantly, until the mixture thickens. Simmer gently for about 5 minutes. Lower the heat and stir in the cream and half of the grated cheese. Taste for seasoning.

4 Stir the scallops into the sauce, then divide among the shells. Sprinkle with the remaining cheese.

5 Place the filled shells under the broiler, 3 in (7 cm) from the heat, and cook for 5 minutes or until the cheese has melted and the sauce is bubbling. Garnish with lemon wedges and bay leaves.

Cook's know-how

If you can't get scallop shells for serving, use individual baking dishes or gratin dishes. The French type with two small handles, or "ears," are traditional for this dish.

MOULES MARINIERE

SERVES 6

6 tbsp (90 g) butter

1 small onion, minced

1 garlic clove, minced

6 lb (3 kg) mussels, cleaned (page 124)

2 cups (500 ml) dry white wine

6 parsley sprigs

3 thyme sprigs

1 bay leaf

salt and black pepper

1 tbsp all-purpose flour

3 tbsp chopped parsley for garnish

1 Melt two-thirds of the butter in a large saucepan, add the onion and garlic, and cook gently, stirring from time to time, for a few minutes until soft but not colored.

2 Add the mussels, wine, parsley, thyme, and bay leaf, and season with salt and pepper. Cover the saucepan tightly and bring to a boil.

3 Cook, shaking the saucepan frequently, for 5–6 minutes or until the mussels open.

4 Throw away any mussels that are not open. Transfer the open mussels to a warmed large serving bowl.

5 Strain the cooking juices into a small pan and boil until reduced by one-third.

6 Mix the remaining butter and the flour on a plate to make a paste (beurre manié).

7 Whisk the beurre manié into the cooking liquid and bring to a boil, stirring constantly. Taste for seasoning, then pour over the mussels. Garnish and serve at once.

Healthy option

This classic recipe is made with a butter-and-flour beurre manié, which thickens the sauce. For a healthier option, cook the onion and garlic in 2 tbsp olive oil and omit the flour. To compensate for the lack of thickening, boil the cooking liquid in step 5 until reduced by about half.

SALMON QUENELLES

Quenelles are delicate little dumplings, traditionally oval but sometimes round, which can be made with fish, meat, or chicken. The name comes from "Knödel," the German word for dumpling. They are simple to make, yet they look elegant and impressive, as if they require professional skills.

SERVES 4–6

1 lb (500 g) salmon fillet, skinned and cut into chunks

2 egg whites

salt and white pepper

2/3 cup (150 ml) heavy cream

lemon slices and flat-leaf parsley sprigs for garnish

ASPARAGUS SAUCE

6 tbsp dry white wine

8 oz (250 g) young asparagus, trimmed

1 1/4 cups (300 ml) heavy cream

1 Make the quenelles: Purée the salmon, egg whites, and salt and pepper to taste in a food processor until completely smooth.

2 With the machine still running, pour in the cream in a steady stream until it is thoroughly blended. Turn the mixture into a large bowl, cover, and chill for 2 hours.

3 Bring a saucepan of salted water to a simmer. Shape and cook the quenelles (see box, right). Keep the quenelles warm while you make the sauce.

4 Make the asparagus sauce: Pour the wine into a saucepan and boil rapidly for about 2 minutes until it is reduced to a thin syrup.

5 Cook the asparagus in a pan of boiling salted water for 3–5 minutes until tender. Drain, then cut off the asparagus tips and reserve them for garnish.

6 Purée the reduced wine with the asparagus stalks until very smooth.

7 Boil the cream in a saucepan for 4 minutes or until it is thick enough to coat the back of a metal spoon. Stir in the asparagus purée, and taste for seasoning.

8 Pour the sauce onto warmed plates, arrange the quenelles on top, and garnish with the reserved asparagus tips, lemon slices, and parsley sprigs.

Cook's know-how

Take care not to overprocess the purée when blending the quenelle mixture. If you work it too hard, it could cause the cream to curdle.

Shaping and cooking the quenelles

Dip a table spoon into the simmering water, then take a spoonful of the chilled quenelle mixture. Using a second warm, wet spoon, or your fingers, mold into an oval. Repeat with the remaining mixture.

Lower some quenelles into the simmering water and cook for 6–10 minutes until they are firm when pressed with a finger. Do not put too many into the pan at one time.

Remove the quenelles with a slotted spoon, drain well, and keep them warm while you cook the remainder.

SARDINES WITH CORIANDER

SERVES 4

12–16 large sardines or small herring

olive oil for brushing

salt and black pepper

lime wedges and flat-leaf parsley sprigs for garnish

CORIANDER-LIME BUTTER

1 tsp ground coriander

4 tbsp (60 g) unsalted butter, at room temperature

1 1/2 tsp lime juice

1 shallot, minced

1/4 tsp finely grated lime zest

1 Scale the sardines with the back of a kitchen knife. With a sharp knife, cut the stomachs open and scrape out the contents.

2 Rinse the sardines inside and out, and pat dry. Brush all over with oil, and sprinkle with salt and pepper.

3 Prepare the coriander-lime butter: Heat a heavy pan, add the coriander, and toast lightly. Transfer the coriander to a bowl and let cool slightly.

4 Add the butter and lime juice to the coriander and whisk until thick. Stir in the shallot and lime zest, and salt and pepper to taste.

5 Place the sardines under a hot broiler, 4 in (10 cm) from the heat, and cook for 1 1/2–2 minutes on each side until they begin to feel firm.

6 Transfer the sardines to a platter, and spread a little coriander-lime butter on each one. Garnish with lime wedges and flat-leaf parsley sprigs, and serve at once.

JUMBO SHRIMP WITH AÏOLI

SERVES 4

2 tbsp olive oil

12 raw jumbo shrimp in shell

1 tbsp chopped parsley

lemon wedges and flat-leaf parsley sprigs for garnish

AÏOLI

2 garlic cloves, coarsely chopped

salt and black pepper

1 egg yolk

1 tsp mustard powder

2/3 cup (150 ml) olive oil

1 tbsp lemon juice

1 Make the aïoli: In a small bowl, crush the garlic with a pinch of salt until it forms a smooth paste. Add the egg yolk and mustard powder, and beat well. Beat in the oil, drop by drop, as if making mayonnaise, whisking constantly until the mixture is thick and smooth, and all the oil has been absorbed. Beat in the lemon juice, and add pepper to taste.

2 Heat the oil in a large frying pan, add the shrimp, and toss over a high heat for 3–4 minutes, just until the shells turn bright pink. Remove the shrimp from the frying pan and drain on paper towels.

3 To serve, arrange the shrimp on warmed plates, sprinkle with chopped parsley, and garnish with lemon wedges and parsley sprigs. Serve with individual bowls of aïoli.

Cook's know-how

Uncooked, or raw, shrimp are usually gray in color – it is only when they are cooked that they turn into the pink shrimp we are familiar with. The golden rule when cooking shrimp is never to overcook them, so be sure to remove them from the heat as soon as they turn pink. Overcooked shrimp are rubbery, chewy, and tasteless.

GRAVADLAX

You can buy this Scandinavian "pickled" salmon, but it is easy (and less expensive) to make it yourself – and your guests will be very impressed. Serve it with thin slices of dark rye bread. You will find the gravadlax easier to slice if it has been frozen for about 4 hours beforehand.

SERVES 16

4¹/₂-lb (2.25-kg) whole fresh salmon, boned and cut lengthwise in half into 2 fillets (ask your fishmonger to do this)

dill weed sprigs and lemon segments for garnish

PICKLING MIXTURE

¹/₃ cup (75 g) sugar

4 tbsp coarse sea salt

4 tbsp chopped fresh dill weed

MUSTARD-DILL SAUCE

3 tbsp Dijon mustard

2 tbsp sugar

1 tbsp white wine vinegar

1 egg yolk

²/₃ cup (150 ml) sunflower oil

salt and black pepper

2 tbsp chopped fresh dill weed

1 Make the pickling mixture: Put the sugar, sea salt, and chopped dill weed into a small bowl, season generously with black pepper, and stir well to mix.

2 Sandwich the salmon fillets together (see box, right).

3 Wrap the fillets in a double thickness of foil and place in a large dish. Weigh down with heavy cans of food, and keep in the refrigerator for 24 hours. Halfway through this time, turn the salmon over.

4 Make the mustard-dill sauce: In a medium bowl, whisk together the mustard, sugar, vinegar, and egg yolk, then add the oil a little at a time, whisking constantly. The sauce should have the consistency of mayonnaise. Add salt and pepper to taste, then stir in the chopped dill weed.

5 Unwrap the salmon. A lot of sticky, salty liquid will have drained from the fish during the pickling: this is quite normal. Remove the fish from the pickling liquid, and dry well. Separate the 2 salmon fillets and lay them skin-side down.

6 To serve, slice each fillet on a slant, cutting the flesh away from the skin. The slices should be a little thicker than for smoked salmon and each one should have a fringe of dill. Garnish with dill sprigs and lemon segments, and serve with the mustard-dill sauce.

Sandwiching the salmon

Put 1 salmon fillet skin-side down on a board, cover the surface with the pickling mixture, and place the second fillet on top, skin-side up.

SPICY SHRIMP

SERVES 4

²/₃ cup (150 ml) mayonnaise

2 tbsp creamed horseradish

1 tbsp lemon juice

1 tsp Worcestershire sauce

1 tsp tomato paste

¹/₄ tsp sugar

few drops of hot pepper sauce

black pepper

8 oz (250 g) cooked peeled shrimp

salad leaves for serving

thin lemon wedges, parsley sprigs, and 4 large cooked shrimp in shell for garnish

1 Make the dressing: In a medium bowl, combine the mayonnaise, creamed horseradish, lemon juice, Worcestershire sauce, tomato paste, sugar, and hot pepper sauce, and season well with a little black pepper.

2 Add the peeled cooked shrimp and stir to coat with the dressing.

3 Line 4 individual glass serving bowls with the salad leaves and top with the shrimp mixture. Garnish each serving with a thin lemon wedge, a parsley sprig, and a large shrimp in shell.

SHRIMP BLINI

Blini are small Russian crêpes made with yeast and buckwheat flour. Buckwheat flour is available from healthfood stores, but if you cannot find any, use whole-wheat flour instead. This mixture makes about 24 blini.

SERVES 6–8

BLINI

3/4 cup (125 g) all-purpose flour

1 1/4 cups (125 g) buckwheat flour

1/2 tsp salt

1/2 tsp rapid-rise dry yeast

scant 2 cups (450 ml) milk, warmed

1 egg, separated

sunflower oil for frying

FOR SERVING

2 1/2 oz (75 g) black lumpfish caviar

2 1/2 oz (75 g) red salmon caviar

4 oz (125 g) cooked peeled shrimp

1/2 cup (125 ml) crème fraîche or light sour cream

lemon segments and fresh chives for garnish

1 Put both types of flour into a large bowl. Add the salt and yeast, and stir together.

2 Gradually beat in the warm milk to make a smooth batter. Cover the bowl and leave in a warm place for about 40 minutes until the batter is frothy and has doubled in volume.

3 Beat the egg yolk into the batter. Put the egg white into a clean bowl and whisk until stiff but not dry, then fold into the batter.

4 Heat a large non-stick frying pan or griddle, brush with oil, and heat until the oil is hot. Spoon about 2 tbsp batter into the pan for each blini (you should be able to cook 3 or 4 at a time), and cook over a moderate heat for 2–3 minutes or until bubbles rise to the surface and burst.

5 Turn the blini over with a metal spatula and cook for a further 2–3 minutes until golden on the other side. Wrap the cooked blini in a dish towel and keep them warm.

6 Cook the remaining blini in batches until all the batter is used up, lightly oiling the pan between each batch.

7 To serve, arrange the blini on warmed plates, with spoonfuls of red and black caviar, shrimp, and crème fraîche or sour cream. Garnish with lemon and chives.

Cook's know-how

You can buy blini, rather than making your own. They will need to be gently heated.

MIMOSA FISH SALAD

SERVES 4

2 hard-boiled eggs

10 oz (300 g) firm white fish fillets, cooked, skinned, and flaked

3 tbsp sour cream

3 tbsp mayonnaise

1 tbsp chopped parsley

1 tsp chopped fresh dill weed

a few drops of hot pepper sauce

salt and black pepper

4 large tomatoes, halved

lemon twists, flat-leaf parsley sprigs, and celery leaves for garnish

1 Remove the yolk from one egg and reserve. Chop the white and the remaining egg.

2 Mix the fish with the chopped egg, sour cream, mayonnaise, parsley, dill, and hot pepper sauce. Add salt and pepper to taste.

3 Top the tomatoes with the fish mixture. Press the egg yolk through a sieve, sprinkle it over the mixture, and garnish with lemon, parsley, and celery.

SMOKED CHICKEN SALAD WITH WALNUTS

SERVES 6

1 smoked chicken, weighing about 2¹/₂ lb (1.25 kg)
7 tbsp sunflower oil
2 tbsp walnut oil
5 tbsp orange juice
¹/₄ tsp ground coriander
¹/₄ tsp sugar
salt and black pepper
12 oz (375 g) mixed salad leaves
4 oranges, peeled and segmented
¹/₂ cup (60 g) walnut pieces

1 Remove the meat from the chicken carcass, and discard all of the skin and any gristle. Cut the meat into thin, neat slices. Put the chicken into a shallow, non-metallic dish.

2 In a small bowl, combine the sunflower and walnut oils, orange juice, ground coriander, and sugar. Season with salt and pepper. Pour the dressing over the chicken slices and toss them gently until evenly coated.

3 Arrange the salad leaves, orange segments, and chicken slices on individual serving plates, scatter the walnut pieces over the top, and serve immediately.

WARM DUCK SALAD

Substitute 12 oz (375 gz) smoked duck or turkey breast meat for the chicken. Gently heat the poultry slices in the dressing, and add warm garlic croûtons (page 49) to the salad.

WARM SALAD WITH BACON & SCALLOPS

SERVES 4

12 oz (375 g) mixed salad leaves, such as radicchio, corn salad, curly endive, and arugula
8 shallots, minced
1 tbsp sunflower oil
8 oz (250 g) lean, thick bacon slices, diced
12 sea scallops, halved
3 tbsp white wine vinegar
2 tbsp walnut oil
salt and black pepper

1 Put the salad leaves into a large bowl and sprinkle with half of the shallots.

2 Heat the oil in a frying pan, add the bacon, and cook quickly, stirring occasionally, for 5 minutes or until crisp. Add the scallops and cook quickly for 1–2 minutes until just opaque. Remove from the pan and keep warm.

3 Add the remaining shallots and cook for 1 minute. Add the vinegar and boil rapidly, stirring to incorporate all the pan juices.

4 Sprinkle the walnut oil over the salad leaves and toss together until the leaves are evenly coated and shiny. Add the bacon and scallops, hot vinegar and shallots, and seasoning to taste.

Cook's know-how

Stirring vinegar into the frying pan loosens and dissolves the flavorsome juices from the bacon and scallops that are on the bottom of the pan, so they are not wasted. This is called deglazing.

ASPARAGUS WITH QUICK HOLLANDAISE

SERVES 4

1 1/4 lb (625 g) asparagus

salt and black pepper

lemon twists for garnish

QUICK HOLLANDAISE

1 tbsp lemon juice

1 tbsp white wine vinegar

4 egg yolks, at room temperature

2/3 cup (150 g) unsalted butter, melted

1 Cut any woody ends off the asparagus and discard. Lay the spears flat in salted boiling water in a shallow pan (a sauté pan or frying pan is ideal), and simmer gently for 3–4 minutes until the asparagus is tender but still firm.

2 Meanwhile, make the quick hollandaise: Three-fourths fill a food processor or blender with hot water and pulse or process briefly, to warm the bowl. Pour the water away and dry the bowl.

3 Put the lemon juice and vinegar into the warm processor bowl, add the egg yolks, and pulse briefly.

4 With the machine running, gradually pour in the melted butter, and work until thick and creamy. Season to taste.

5 To serve, drain the asparagus. Ladle the hollandaise sauce onto warmed plates, arrange the asparagus on top, and garnish with lemon twists.

Healthy option

An alternative way to cook asparagus, and one that gives it lots of flavor, is to pan-grill it. Heat a ridged nonstick or castiron grill pan until very hot. While it is heating up, roll the asparagus spears in a little olive oil, seasoned with sea salt and freshly ground black pepper. As soon as the pan is hot but not smoking, lay the spears across the ridges and cook for 3–4 minutes, turning them with tongs so they become evenly charred on all sides. Instead of serving with a buttery Hollandaise, sprinkle with a little extra-virgin olive oil and freshly grated Parmesan cheese.

BRIOCHES WITH WILD MUSHROOMS & WATERCRESS

SERVES 6

2 tbsp (30 g) butter

8 oz (250 g) wild mushrooms, such as porcini and shiitake, trimmed and sliced

1 cup (60 g) chopped watercress

4 tbsp heavy cream

squeeze of lemon juice

salt and black pepper

6 brioches (page 416)

watercress sprigs for garnish

1 Melt the butter in a large frying pan, add the mushrooms, and cook over a high heat, stirring from time to time, for 3 minutes or until all the liquid has evaporated. Add the watercress, cream, lemon juice, and salt and pepper to taste, and cook until the watercress is just wilted.

2 Hollow out the brioches (see box, right). Spoon in some of the mixture.

Preparing brioches

Remove the brioche top and set aside. Using your fingers, pull out the soft inside, leaving a 1/4-in (5-mm) crust. Repeat with the remaining brioches.

3 To serve, transfer the brioches to warmed serving plates and replace the brioche tops. Spoon the remaining mushroom and watercress mixture onto the plates beside the brioches, and garnish with watercress sprigs.

SMOKED SALMON ROULADE

The richness of the cheese and smoked salmon layers is offset by a thin layer of tomatoes to provide a fresh and tangy contrast. Here the roulade is served in slices, but you could serve it whole, with just a few slices cut at one end.

SERVES 4–6

1 tbsp (15 g) butter

1 garlic clove, minced

1 cup (150 g) cooked, squeezed dry, and chopped spinach

4 eggs, separated

1 tsp chopped fresh rosemary

pinch of grated nutmeg

salt and black pepper

salad leaves and lemon slices for garnish

FILLING

1 cup (250 g) cream cheese

3 tbsp plain yogurt or 2 tbsp milk

4 green onions, thinly sliced

4 oz (125 g) smoked salmon

2 ripe tomatoes, thinly sliced

13- × 9-IN (33- × 23-CM) JELLY ROLL PAN

1 Make the roulade: Line the jelly roll pan with a sheet of parchment paper, cutting the corners of the paper so that it fits snugly into the pan.

2 Put the butter into a saucepan, add the garlic, and cook gently until the butter melts. Remove from the heat. Stir in the spinach.

3 Add the egg yolks, rosemary, and nutmeg, season to taste, and beat into the spinach mixture.

4 In another bowl, whisk the egg whites until firm but not dry. Fold 2–3 spoonfuls into the spinach mixture, then fold in the remainder.

5 Spread the batter in the jelly roll pan, and bake in a preheated oven at 375°F (190°C) for 10–12 minutes until the roulade feels firm. Remove from the oven, cover with a damp dish towel, and let cool.

6 Meanwhile, make the filling: Beat the cream cheese and yogurt or milk together until smooth, then stir in the green onions.

7 Unmold the cooled roulade and peel off the paper. Fill and roll the roulade (see box, right).

8 Wrap the roulade in foil, then overwrap with a damp dish towel, and chill overnight.

9 To serve, trim off the hard edges of the roulade, cut into thick slices, and arrange on a serving platter. Garnish with salad leaves and lemon slices.

PROSCIUTTO ROULADE

Substitute 4 oz (125 g) thinly sliced prosciutto for the smoked salmon.

Cook's know-how

This roulade can be prepared up to the end of step 8 up to 2 days ahead, making it ideal for a dinner party or other special occasion.

Filling and rolling the roulade

Arrange the slices of smoked salmon on top of the roulade, leaving a 1-in (2.5-cm) border on each side.

Spread the cheese filling over the salmon, using a metal spatula. Arrange the tomato slices over half of the cheese filling, looking at it widthwise.

Roll up the roulade, starting from the end where the tomato slices have been placed.

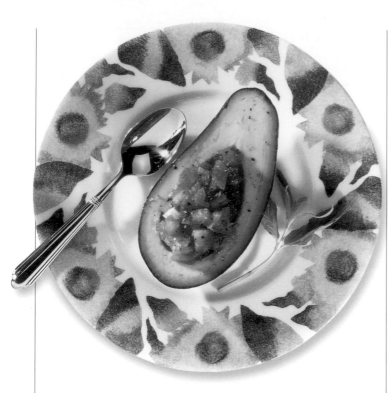

AVOCADO WITH TOMATOES & MINT

SERVES 4

| 4 small, firm tomatoes |
| 2 ripe avocados |
| 1 tbsp chopped fresh mint |
| mint sprigs for garnish |

DRESSING

| 2 tsp white wine vinegar |
| 1 tsp Dijon mustard |
| 2 tbsp olive oil |
| 1/4 tsp sugar |
| salt and black pepper |

1 Peel the tomatoes: Cut out the cores and score an "x" on the base of each one, then immerse in a bowl of boiling water until the skins start to split. Transfer at once to a bowl of cold water. Peel and seed the tomatoes, then coarsely chop the flesh.

2 Make the dressing: In a small bowl, whisk together the vinegar and mustard. Gradually whisk in the oil, then add the sugar, and salt and pepper to taste.

3 Halve and pit the avocados. Brush the flesh with a little dressing to prevent any discoloration.

4 Combine the tomatoes, chopped mint, and dressing. Pile the tomato mixture into the avocado halves, garnish with mint sprigs, and serve at once.

Healthy note

Avocados are full of heart-healthy nutrients, such as vitamin E, folate, and potassium. They are also high in fat (and calories) but the fat is the "healthy" monounsaturated kind.

SUMMER MELONS

SERVES 4

| 2 ripe melons with different colored flesh (see box, right), about 1 1/2 lb (750 g) each |
| 1 lb (500 g) tomatoes |
| 1 tbsp chopped fresh mint |
| mint sprigs for garnish |

DRESSING

| 6 tbsp sunflower oil |
| 2 tbsp white wine vinegar |
| 1/4 tsp sugar |
| salt and black pepper |

1 Cut the melons in half, and remove and discard the seeds. Using a melon baller or a knife, cut balls or neat cubes of flesh and put into a bowl.

2 Peel the tomatoes: Cut out the cores and score an "x" on the base of each one, then immerse in a bowl of boiling water until the skins start to split. Transfer at once to a bowl of cold water. Peel and seed the tomatoes, then cut the flesh into long strips. Add the strips to the melon.

3 Make the dressing: In a small bowl, whisk together the sunflower oil and vinegar, then add the sugar, and salt and pepper to taste. Pour the dressing over the melon and tomato mixture. Cover and chill for at least 1 hour.

4 To serve, stir the chopped mint into the melon and tomato mixture, spoon the salad into chilled bowls, and garnish each serving with a mint sprig.

Cook's know-how

Choose two different varieties of melon to make an attractive color combination. Honeydew has pale greenish-yellow or creamy flesh, as does casaba melon, while cantaloupe and crenshaw have deep orange flesh. You can also use watermelon for even more contrast.

ANTIPASTI

This is the Italian version of the French hors d'oeuvre or Spanish tapas – a selection
of appetizers offered to guests with drinks before a meal, or just for snacking
on informally at any time of day.

MOZZARELLA, TOMATO, & BASIL SALAD

SERVES 8

4 beefsteak tomatoes

8 oz (250 g) mozzarella cheese

4 tbsp shredded fresh basil

4 tbsp olive oil

1 tbsp balsamic vinegar or wine vinegar

salt and black pepper

basil sprig for garnish

1 Peel the tomatoes: Cut out the cores and score an "x" on the base of each one, then immerse in boiling water until the skins start to split. Transfer at once to cold water; when cool, peel off the skin. Thinly slice the tomatoes.

2 Slice the mozzarella and arrange with the tomato slices alternately on a plate, slightly overlapping them.

3 Just before serving, sprinkle with the basil, olive oil, vinegar, and salt and pepper to taste. Garnish with a basil sprig.

Cook's know-how

As well as the salad and crostini, make up a platter of sliced prosciutto, mortadella, bresaola, and salami. Another good choice for antipasti is a seafood salad of shrimp, mussels, and squid, which you can sometimes buy at delicatessens.

SUN-DRIED TOMATO CROSTINI

SERVES 8

1 baguette

2 garlic cloves, minced

about 3 tbsp olive oil

4 sun-dried tomatoes in oil

2 tbsp (30 g) butter

salt and black pepper

12 pitted black olives, chopped

1/4 tsp dried rosemary

1 Cut the baguette into 24 thin slices and arrange them on 2 baking sheets. Add the garlic to the olive oil, then brush about half of the oil onto the slices of bread. Bake in a preheated oven at 350°F (180°C) for 10 minutes.

2 Remove the baking sheets from the oven, turn the slices of bread over, brush with a little more garlic oil, and bake for a further 10 minutes or until crisp and golden. Let cool.

3 Dry the sun-dried tomatoes with a paper towel and cut them into pieces. Put the tomato and butter in the small bowl of a food processor and work until finely chopped (or pound them with a mortar and pestle). Season with salt and pepper to taste.

4 Spread the sun-dried tomato butter over the crostini, arrange the chopped olives on top, and sprinkle with rosemary.

CAPONATA

SERVES 4–6

about 4 tbsp olive oil

1 large eggplant cut into ¹/2-in (1-cm) chunks

¹/2 bunch celery, diced

2 onions, thinly sliced

¹/2 cup (125 g) tomato paste

5 tbsp sugar

¹/2–³/4 cup (125–175 ml) red wine vinegar

1 cup (125 g) pitted green olives

3 tbsp capers (optional)

1–2 garlic cloves, minced

¹/2 cup (30 g) chopped parsley

salt and black pepper

1 Heat 3 tbsp of the oil in a large saucepan, add the eggplant, and cook gently, stirring, for 8 minutes or until tender. Remove the eggplant from the pan with a slotted spoon.

2 Heat the remaining oil in the pan, add the celery, and cook gently, stirring occasionally, for 7 minutes or until browned.

3 Return the eggplant to the pan, along with the onions, tomato paste, sugar, and vinegar. Cook over a medium heat for 10 minutes to reduce the harshness of the vinegar. Add a little water if the mixture becomes too thick and starts sticking to the pan.

4 Remove from the heat, and add the green olives, capers, if using, garlic, and half of the parsley. Add salt and pepper to taste. Cover and let cool. To serve, transfer to serving plates and sprinkle with the remaining parsley.

WARM SALAD WITH PEARS & STILTON

SERVES 4

8 thin slices of white bread (crusts removed), cut into small rounds

2 garlic cloves, halved

8 oz (250 g) blue Stilton cheese, sliced

2 bunches of watercress, trimmed and chopped

2 pears, peeled and cut into thin wedges

4 tbsp sunflower oil

1 small red onion, minced

2 tbsp balsamic vinegar

1 Toast the bread shapes on both sides under the broiler. Rub both sides of the bread with the garlic cloves and arrange the slices of Stilton cheese on top of each piece.

2 Arrange the chopped watercress and pear wedges on 4 individual serving plates, then set aside.

3 Heat the sunflower oil in a frying pan, add the onion, and cook gently for 5 minutes or until soft but not colored.

4 Meanwhile, put the Stilton-topped toasts under the broiler, close to the heat, for 1–2 minutes until the cheese has melted. Cut the toasts in half.

5 Add the vinegar to the onion in the frying pan, and let it heat through, stirring occasionally. Pour the onion mixture over the watercress and pears. Arrange the toasts on the plates and serve at once.

WARM SALAD WITH PEARS & BRIE

For a milder flavor, substitute 8 oz (250 g) French Brie or Italian Dolcelatte for the Stilton. As they are softer in texture, slice them thickly.

EGGS & CHEESE

3

SPINACH & MUSHROOM FRITTATA

Flat Italian omelet chunky with bacon, mushrooms, and spinach, sprinkled with Parmesan, and browned under the broiler.

SERVES 2–3 673–449 calories per serving
Takes 25 minutes   Page 100

ECONOMICAL

SPANISH OMELET

Traditional Spanish dish: diced potatoes, onions, and eggs cooked slowly until set, to make a nourishing and simple meal.

SERVES 4 389 calories per serving
Takes 25 minutes   Page 101

RACLETTE

Boiled new potatoes topped with Swiss raclette cheese and heated in the oven until sizzling. Served with gherkins and onions.

SERVES 4 446 calories per serving
Takes 25 minutes   Page 111

OEUFS EN COCOTTE

Warm creamy snack: whole eggs in ramekins, topped with cream and parsley, and steamed or baked.

SERVES 4 176 calories per serving
Takes 25 minutes   Page 114

PICNIC FARE

PROSCIUTTO & ZUCCHINI FRITTATA

Light and easy to make: thinly sliced zucchini and diced prosciutto cooked with beaten eggs make a colorful Italian omelet. Browned under the broiler, cut into wedges, and garnished with shredded fresh basil. Served hot or cold.

SERVES 4 270 calories per serving
Takes 25 minutes   Page 101

TEX-MEX CLASSIC

HUEVOS RANCHEROS

Spicy dish of tomatoes simmered with onion, garlic, green bell pepper, chili pepper, and cumin. Topped with a poached egg.

SERVES 4 196 calories per serving
Takes 25 minutes   Page 114

MUSHROOM OMELET WITH CIABATTA

Italian slipper bread filled with an omelet brimming with sliced shiitake mushrooms.

SERVES 2 673 calories per serving
Takes 25 minutes   Page 100

BRUNCH FAVORITE

EGGS BENEDICT

A classic: poached eggs and bacon slices on toasted English muffins, topped with lemony hollandaise sauce.

SERVES 4 602 calories per serving
Takes 25 minutes   Page 113

30–60 MINUTES

SWISS CLASSIC

HIGH PROTEIN

CHEESE FONDUE
Gruyère and Emmental cheeses melted in a fondue pot with wine, garlic, and kirsch. Served with bread and apple for dipping.

SERVES 6 813 calories per serving
Takes 30 minutes   Page 111

SAVORY SOUFFLE OMELET
Light and summery: zucchini, red bell pepper, and tomatoes combined with soufflé mixture. Flavored with garlic, onion, and thyme.

MAKES 2 479 calories per serving
Takes 35 minutes   Page 99

MEDITERRANEAN ZUCCHINI PIE
Wholesome and rich: zucchini mixed with Parmesan and mozzarella cheeses, eggs, pesto, garlic, and mint. Topped with puff pastry.

SERVES 4 545 calories per serving
Takes 50 minutes   Page 104

VEGETARIAN

CROQUE SENOR
Sandwich of Cheddar cheese and ham given a Mexican flavor with salsa of tomatoes, chili pepper, and red bell pepper. Cooked until golden.

SERVES 4 413 calories per serving
Takes 30 minutes   Page 112

MEXICAN OMELET
Folded omelet with a substantial filling of onion and garlic cooked with green bell pepper, tomatoes, mushrooms, and hot pepper sauce.

MAKES 2 547 calories per serving
Takes 50 minutes   Page 99

BROCCOLI SOUFFLES
Broccoli, shallots, and blue cheese combined with soufflé mixture and flavored with nutmeg and cayenne pepper.

SERVES 4 499 calories per serving
Takes 45 minutes   Page 110

PREPARE AHEAD

EGGS FLORENTINE
Nutritious and creamy: spinach mixed with green onions and cream, topped with a poached egg and Parmesan cheese sauce.

SERVES 4 475 calories per serving
Takes 30 minutes   Page 113

PIZZA TARTLETS
Rich and tangy: tomatoes, black olives, and fontina or mozzarella cheese, complemented by the robust Mediterranean flavors of garlic and oregano, set in

MAKES 12 198 calories each
Takes 55 minutes   Page 105

short-pastry tartlet shells spread with pesto. Sprinkled with Parmesan cheese to give a tasty, crisp finish.

30–60 MINUTES

VEGETARIAN

SWISS CHEESE & TOMATO RAREBIT

Variation of Welsh rarebit: tomatoes, Swiss cheese, wine, and mushrooms. Served on buttered toast.

SERVES 4 640 calories per serving
Takes 30 minutes   Page 112

FAMILY CHOICE

STRATA WITH CHEESE & PESTO

Savory custard of eggs, crème fraîche, and milk, poured over slices of bread and pesto. Sprinkled with Italian cheeses.

SERVES 4 600 calories per serving
Takes 50 minutes   Page 106

DINNER PARTY

GARLIC & GOAT CHEESE SOUFFLES

Tangy soufflés combining garlic-flavored sauce base with goat cheese, egg yolks, and whisked egg whites.

SERVES 6 267 calories per serving
Takes 55 minutes   Page 110

OVER 60 MINUTES

SOUFFLE CREPES WITH BROCCOLI & CHEESE

Crêpes with a soufflé filling combining tiny broccoli florets, Cheddar cheese, and mustard.

MAKES 8 300 calories per serving
Takes 45 minutes, plus standing   Page 108

BROCCOLI & RICOTTA GRATIN

Ricotta, Cheddar, and Parmesan cheeses mixed with broccoli, eggs, garlic, and thyme, baked in a buttered bread-crumb crust.

SERVES 4–6 689–460 calories per serving
Takes 1 hour 5 minutes   Page 106

FRENCH CLASSIC

QUICHE LORRAINE

Classic savory tart: short-pastry shell spread with lightly cooked onion and crisp pieces of bacon. Sprinkled with grated Gruyère cheese, then filled with an egg and cream mixture, and baked until golden brown. Served warm or cold.

SERVES 4–6 756–504 calories per serving.
Takes 60 minutes, plus chilling   Page 102

OVER 60 MINUTES

DINNER PARTY

CREAMY SEAFOOD CREPES

Pieces of cod fillet cooked with onion, garlic, tomatoes, fresh dill, cream, and shrimp, and flavored with fresh basil. The creamy filling is spread over crêpes, which are then folded into triangles, and garnished with shrimp, sprigs of basil, and lemon twists.

SERVES 6 308 calories per serving
Takes 50 minutes, plus standing   Page 107

FAMILY CHOICE

CHICKEN CREPES FLORENTINE

Crêpes filled with chicken, mushrooms, and thyme, served on a bed of spinach. Sprinkled with Gruyère cheese and baked.

SERVES 4 721 calories per serving
Takes 50 minutes, plus standing   Page 108

SPINACH, LEEK, & GRUYERE TART

Nourishing and creamy: leeks and spinach in a short-pastry shell with a mixture of eggs, milk, cream, and Gruyère cheese.

SERVES 4–6 721–480 calories per serving
Takes 60 minutes, plus chilling   Page 104

SMOKED SALMON & ASPARAGUS QUICHE

Salmon and asparagus set in a short-pastry shell with a savory custard of yogurt, eggs, and dill.

SERVES 6–8 321–241 calories per serving
Takes 1¼ hours, plus chilling   Page 103

TRADITIONAL

CLASSIC CHEESE SOUFFLE

Delicate and light: milk flavored with bay leaf, parsley, and onion, combined with butter, flour, eggs, and Cheddar cheese.

SERVES 4 363 calories per serving
Takes 1¼ hours   Page 109

VEGETARIAN

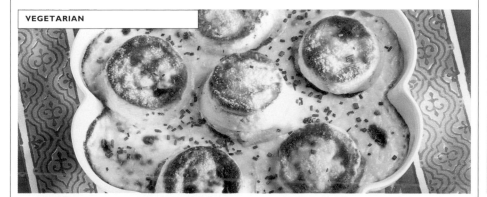

SWISS DOUBLE CHEESE SOUFFLES

Rich and very creamy: individual soufflés flavored with Gruyère cheese and chives. Baked until golden and firm, then unmolded and topped with cream and Parmesan cheese. Baked again until golden, and garnished with snipped fresh chives.

SERVES 6 465 calories per serving
Takes 1 hour 5 minutes   Page 110

ROQUEFORT QUICHE

Roquefort and cream cheese combined with eggs, crème fraîche, and chives, poured into a short-pastry shell, and baked.

SERVES 4–6 504–336 calories per serving
Takes 1 hour 5 minutes   Page 103

EGGS & CHEESE KNOW-HOW

EGGS ARE ONE of the most useful foods in a cook's repertoire. They can be cooked in many delicious ways, from simple boiling, poaching, and scrambling to omelets and soufflés that require a little more skill. Eggs are also used to enrich pastries and doughs, give volume and moistness to cakes and many puddings, thicken sauces and custards, bind mixtures ranging from burgers to pâtés, and provide a coating for foods to be fried.

Cheese has countless culinary uses. Apart from its everyday use as a sandwich filling, it is found in sauces, fondues, and pizza toppings; it flavors savory pastries, doughs, and quiche fillings; it is essential in many pasta dishes; and it is popular in desserts such as cheesecake and tiramisu.

BUYING & STORING

Most of the eggs we eat are hens' eggs, although there are also tiny quail eggs, large duck eggs, and even larger goose eggs. Hens' eggs are usually classified according to quality and size under USDA standards, the highest grade being AA, and they may also be described according to the farming method used – for example, "cage-free" – or the diet of the hen ("vegetarian-fed"). In-shell pasteurized eggs, which will be free of any possibility of salmonella infection, are also becoming available. Whichever eggs you buy, check the date stamp, and check that none is damaged or cracked. Store eggs in their carton in the refrigerator (away from strong foods so that they do not absorb flavors and odors through their shells). If you place them pointed end down, the yolk will remain centered in the white.

Cheese deteriorates once cut, so do not buy it in a large piece unless you know it will be used up quickly. Keep all cheeses well wrapped in the refrigerator or in a cool place (soft cheeses must be stored in the refrigerator and used within a few days).

SEPARATING EGGS

For best results, take eggs straight from the fridge so they are well chilled.

1 Holding an egg over a bowl, break open the shell. Carefully transfer the yolk from one half shell to the other, letting the egg white run into the bowl. Repeat several times.

2 Put the yolk in another bowl. Remove any yolk from the white with the tip of a spoon (the white will not whisk stiff if there is any trace of yolk).

COOKING WITH CHEESE

Cheese needs to be cooked with care as heat can spoil its texture, making it rubbery or stringy. Hard and firm cheeses can withstand heat best, melting and blending smoothly. When adding cheese to a sauce, do this at the end of cooking and melt gently; do not boil. If broiling a cheese topping, cook as briefly as possible.

MICROWAVING

Never microwave an egg that is still in its shell, because it will burst. Even out of its shell, a whole egg may burst, so always pierce the membrane on the yolk with a toothpick before cooking. The yolk cooks more quickly than the white, so standing time should be allowed to let the white continue cooking. Where yolks and whites are combined, as for scrambled eggs, the mixture will appear undercooked but will firm up during the standing time.

Cheeses melt quickly in the microwave, so take care not to overcook or burn them. Hard or firm, sharp cheeses and processed cheeses are the best. Frozen soft, ripened cheeses can be softened and brought to room temperature in the microwave before serving.

FREEZING

Shelled raw eggs freeze very successfully, and can be stored for up to 6 months. If whole, whisk gently to mix the yolk and white; add a little salt to whole eggs and egg yolks for use in savory foods or sugar for use in sweet dishes (nothing needs to be added to whites). Thaw at room temperature. Egg-based dishes such as quiches, custards, and mousses can also be frozen.

Hard and firm cheeses freeze well, as do soft, ripened cheeses such as Brie. Store them for up to 1 month. Thaw in the refrigerator before use. Note that the texture of hard cheeses may change after freezing, becoming more crumbly, making the cheeses suitable only for cooking. Soft, fresh cheeses and soft, blue-veined cheeses do not freeze well.

COOKING EGGS

Eggs are one of the cheapest sources of protein and could not be easier to cook. Once you have mastered the basic techniques you will be able to produce a wide range of nutritious meals in minutes.

BOILING

Use eggs at room temperature (the shells are less likely to crack). Put the eggs into a pan of simmering water. Bring back to a boil, then simmer gently. Cooking times are calculated from the time the water comes back to a boil, and can vary according to individual taste and on the size and freshness of the eggs. For soft-boiled eggs, simmer gently for 4–5 minutes; for hard-boiled eggs, allow 8–10 minutes. After cooking hard-boiled eggs, lift them out of the water and crack the shell to allow steam to escape, then plunge the eggs into ice water. Peel when cool enough to handle. (An unsightly black line may form around the yolk if you cook them too long, or keep them in the shell.) Use right away or keep in a bowl of cold water in the refrigerator for up to 24 hours.

ALL ABOUT EGGS

Hens' eggs are graded by their minimum weight per dozen. The sizes are: jumbo, extra large, large, medium, small, and peewee. The shell – usually white and sometimes brown, now also occasionally blue, green, pink, or speckled – is a result of the breed of hen. The color of the yolk depends on the hen's diet. Blood spots on the yolk do not indicate that the egg is fertile.

SCRAMBLING

Scrambled eggs can be served plain, or flavored with herbs, cheese, ham, or smoked salmon. Allow 2 eggs per person.

1 Lightly beat the eggs with salt and pepper to taste and a little milk, if you like. Melt a nugget of butter in a pan. Add the eggs.

2 Cook over a medium heat, stirring constantly with a wooden spatula or spoon, until almost set – they will continue to cook after they have been removed from the heat. Serve at once.

FRYING

Fresh eggs are essential for successful frying because they keep their shape during cooking. Fry the eggs in your favorite oil, adding a nugget of butter for extra flavor, if you like.

1 Heat a thin layer of oil in a nonstick frying pan. When the oil is very hot and starting to sizzle, slip in an egg and cook over a medium heat.

2 Spoon the oil over once or twice to give a white top. Remove and serve, or turn over and cook for a few seconds, to set the yolk a little more.

POACHING

The classic method for poaching eggs is in a pan of simmering water. Use the freshest eggs possible, because they will keep a neat shape.

1 Bring a wide pan of water to a boil. Lower the heat so that the water is simmering, and slide in an egg. Swirl the water around the egg to give it a neat shape. Simmer for 3–4 minutes until the egg is cooked to your taste.

2 Lift out the egg with a slotted spoon and drain briefly on paper towels. To keep them warm, or to reheat them if they have been prepared ahead, immerse them in a bowl of hot water (they will take 1 minute to reheat).

MAKING AN OMELET

Omelets are best made in a special pan kept solely for the purpose: then they are less likely to stick. If you do not have one, use a small frying pan, no more than 8 in (20 cm) in diameter.

1 Beat 2–3 eggs with salt and pepper, plus chopped fresh herbs if you like. Heat the pan, then add a nugget of butter. When the butter is foaming, tilt the pan to coat the bottom. Pour in the eggs.

2 Cook over a medium heat. As the eggs begin to set, lift and pull back the edge of the omelet toward the middle, and tilt the pan so the liquid egg runs underneath.

3 Continue cooking until the omelet is just set and the underside is golden. Tilt the pan, loosen the edge of the omelet, and flip over in half, to fold it. Slide onto a plate to serve.

Omelet know-how

Gently stir to combine the yolks with the whites: vigorous beating will make the omelet rubbery.

Make sure the pan is hot and the butter foaming when you add the eggs.

The omelet will continue to cook after you remove it from the heat, so the middle should still be a little moist.

MAKING CREPES

The quantities given here will make enough batter for about 12 thin crêpes, using a 7- to 8-in (18- to 20-cm) pan. Do not worry if the first crêpe or two is a failure: it acts as a test for the consistency of the batter and the heat of the pan. If you are new to crêpe-making you may prefer to make them slightly thicker, to be on the safe side, in which case you may only make 8 crêpes. Any uneaten crêpes will keep for 24 hours, or they can be frozen.

1 Sift 3/4 cup (125 g) all-purpose flour into a bowl and make a well in the middle. Whisk together 1 egg, 1 egg yolk, and a little milk taken from 1 1/4 cups (300 ml), then pour into the well. Whisk with a little of the flour.

2 Gradually whisk in half of the remaining milk, drawing in the rest of the flour a little at a time, to make a smooth batter. Stir in the remaining milk. Cover and let stand for about 30 minutes.

3 Heat the frying pan and brush with a little oil. Ladle 2–3 tbsp batter into the pan and tilt the pan so that the batter spreads out evenly over the bottom.

4 Cook the crêpe over a medium-high heat for 45–60 seconds until small holes appear on the surface, the underside is lightly browned, and the edge has started to curl. Loosen the crêpe and turn it over by tossing or flipping it with a metal spatula. Cook the other side for about 30 seconds until golden.

5 Slide the crêpe out of the pan. Heat and lightly grease the pan again before making the next crêpe. Serve the crêpes as they are made, or stack them on a plate and reheat before serving. (If the crêpes are hot when you stack them they will not stick together; there is no need to interleave them with wax paper.)

MEXICAN OMELET

An omelet is one of the most useful of all egg dishes, quick and easy to make, and nutritious either plain or with a filling. This recipe combines a classic French omelet with a piquant filling, but you can add whatever filling you like.

MAKES 2

6 eggs

2 tbsp (30 g) butter

chopped parsley for garnish

FILLING

2 tbsp olive oil

I onion, minced

I garlic clove, minced

I green bell pepper, halved, seeded, and minced

2 ripe tomatoes, minced

1 3/4 cups (125 g) thinly sliced button mushrooms

1/4 tsp Worcestershire sauce

a few drops of hot pepper sauce

salt and black pepper

1 Make the filling: Heat the oil in a frying pan, add the onion and garlic, and cook for 5 minutes or until softened. Add the bell pepper and cook, stirring, for 5 minutes.

2 Add the tomatoes and mushrooms, and cook, stirring, for 10 minutes. Add the Worcestershire and pepper sauces, season with salt and pepper, and simmer for about 5 minutes. Keep warm.

3 Beat 3 of the eggs in a bowl with salt and pepper. Heat an omelet pan or small frying pan and add half of the butter.

4 When the butter is foaming, add the eggs. Cook over a medium heat, pulling back the edge as the eggs set, and tilting the pan so the liquid egg runs underneath. Continue until lightly set and golden.

5 Spoon half of the filling onto the half of the omelet farthest from the pan handle. With a metal spatula, lift the uncovered half of the omelet and flip it over the filling.

6 Slide the omelet onto a warmed plate and garnish with chopped parsley. Make the second omelet in the same way, reheating the pan before adding the butter.

MUSHROOM OMELET

Substitute 2 1/2 cups (175 g) sliced button mushrooms for the filling. Cook in a little melted butter, and season with salt and pepper.

SMOKED CHICKEN OMELET

Substitute I cup (125 g) diced smoked chicken and I tbsp snipped fresh chives for the filling.

TOMATO OMELET

Substitute 5 minced ripe tomatoes for the filling. Cook the tomatoes in a little butter for 2–3 minutes. Season well, and stir in a few snipped fresh chives.

SAVORY SOUFFLE OMELET

MAKES 2

4 eggs, separated

2 tbsp (30 g) butter

FILLING

2 tbsp olive oil

1/2 onion, thinly sliced

I garlic clove, minced

I zucchini, sliced

I red bell pepper, halved, seeded, and sliced

I cup (200 g) canned crushed tomatoes

I tbsp chopped fresh thyme leaves

salt and black pepper

1 Make the filling: Heat the oil in a frying pan, add the onion and garlic, and cook gently for 5 minutes or until softened. Add the zucchini and red pepper, and cook for about 2 minutes. Add the tomatoes and thyme, season with salt and pepper, and simmer for about 20 minutes.

2 Whisk together the egg yolks, salt, and pepper. Whisk the egg whites until stiff, then fold into the yolks.

3 Melt half of the butter in an omelet pan. When it foams, add half of the egg mixture, and cook over a gentle heat for 3 minutes. Add half of the filling, fold the omelet in half, and serve. Repeat with the remaining eggs and filling.

MUSHROOM OMELET WITH CIABATTA

SERVES 2

4 eggs

salt and black pepper

2 tbsp (30 g) butter

1 cup (60 g) sliced shiitake mushrooms

1 tbsp snipped fresh chives

1 loaf of ciabatta (Italian slipper bread), warmed and split open lengthwise

1 Break the eggs into a small bowl, season with salt and pepper, and beat with a fork.

2 Melt half of the butter in a small frying pan, add the mushrooms, and cook over a high heat for 3–5 minutes until all the liquid has evaporated. Remove from the heat, stir in the chives, season with salt and pepper, and keep hot.

3 Heat an omelet pan or small frying pan until very hot. Add the remaining butter and swirl the pan to coat the bottom and sides. When the butter is foaming, pour in the seasoned egg mixture.

4 Cook the omelet over a medium heat, pulling back the edge as the eggs set, and tilting the pan so the uncooked egg can run to the side of the pan. Continue until the omelet is lightly set and the underside is golden brown. Remove from the heat.

5 Scatter the mushrooms over half of the omelet, then flip the uncovered half over them. Fill the warmed split ciabatta with the omelet, cut the ciabatta in half crosswise, and serve at once.

SPINACH & MUSHROOM FRITTATA

SERVES 2–3

1 tbsp olive oil

2 thick slices (60 g) bacon, diced

8 oz (250 g) crimini mushrooms, quartered

2 cups (125 g) coarsely chopped spinach leaves

6 eggs

salt and black pepper

2 tbsp grated Parmesan cheese

1 Heat the oil in a large frying pan. Add the bacon and mushrooms, and cook over a high heat, stirring, for about 7 minutes or until the bacon is crisp. Add the spinach and turn it in the oil for 1–2 minutes. Do not let the spinach wilt. Lower the heat.

2 Break the eggs into a bowl, season with salt and pepper, and beat with a fork.

3 Pour the eggs over the mushrooms and spinach, and cook over a medium heat for 10 minutes. As the eggs set, lift the frittata with a metal spatula and tilt the pan so the uncooked egg runs underneath.

4 When the eggs are set, sprinkle with grated Parmesan and place the pan under the broiler, 4 in (10 cm) from the heat. Cook for 1–2 minutes or until the top is golden brown and firm when pressed. Cut in half and serve.

Healthy option

You can omit the bacon to lower the saturated fat content of this frittata (and make it vegetarian too), but increase the oil to 3 tbsp. To compensate for the lack of bacon flavor, add a splash of soy sauce in step 2.

SPANISH OMELET

SERVES 4

3 tbsp olive oil
2 large potatoes, diced
2 large onions, chopped
6 eggs
salt and black pepper
1 tbsp chopped parsley

1 Heat the oil in a frying pan, add the potatoes and onions, and stir until coated with the oil. Cook gently for about 10 minutes until golden brown. Pour the excess oil from the pan.

2 Break the eggs into a bowl, season with salt and pepper, and beat with a fork.

3 Pour the eggs into the pan, and mix gently with the vegetables. Cook for about 10 minutes until the eggs are almost set, then brown the top of the omelet under the broiler for 1–2 minutes.

4 Slide the omelet onto a warmed plate and cut into quarters. Sprinkle with chopped parsley and serve warm or cold.

MIXED BEAN OMELET

Lightly cook 1/2 cup (60 g) cut fine green beans and 3/4 cup (125 g) shelled fresh or frozen lima beans. Add to the pan in step 3, when mixing the potatoes and onions with the eggs.

PROSCIUTTO & ZUCCHINI FRITTATA

SERVES 4

2 tbsp olive oil
1 1/4 lb (625 g) small zucchini, thinly sliced on the diagonal
6 eggs
salt and black pepper
2/3 cup (60 g) diced prosciutto
shredded fresh basil or chopped flat-leaf parsley for garnish

1 Heat the oil in a large frying pan. Add the zucchini and cook gently for 5 minutes or until just tender.

2 Break the eggs into a bowl, season with salt and pepper, and beat with a fork.

3 Add the prosciutto to the zucchini in the frying pan, then pour in the eggs.

4 Cook over a medium heat for about 10 minutes. As the eggs set, lift the frittata with a metal spatula and tilt the pan so the uncooked egg can run underneath. Continue until almost set and the underside is golden brown.

5 Place the frying pan under the broiler, 4 in (10 cm) from the heat. Cook for 1–2 minutes until the top is a light golden brown and the frittata is cooked through and quite firm when pressed.

6 Cut the frittata into wedges, and lightly garnish with shredded fresh basil or parsley. Serve hot or cold.

Cook's know-how

The true prosciutto is Parma ham (prosciutto di Parma), which comes from a very small area in and around the town of Parma in northern Italy. Another fine Italian prosciutto comes from San Daniele.

QUICHE LORRAINE

This most famous of all quiches is named after the area it comes from – Alsace Lorraine in north-eastern France – where it was traditionally served on May Day, following a dish of roast sucking pig.

SERVES 4–6

2 tbsp (30 g) butter

1 onion, chopped

6 oz (175 g) thick bacon slices, diced

1 cup (125 g) grated Gruyère cheese

1 cup (250 ml) light cream or milk

2 eggs, beaten

salt and black pepper

SHORT PASTRY

3/4 cup (125 g) all-purpose flour

4 tbsp (60 g) butter

about 1 tbsp cold water

8-IN (20-CM) QUICHE DISH OR PAN

CERAMIC BAKING BEANS

1 Make the pastry with the flour, butter, and water (see box, right). Wrap in plastic wrap and chill for 30 minutes.

2 Roll out the pastry on a lightly floured work surface, and use to line the quiche dish or pan. Prick the bottom of the pastry shell with a fork.

3 Line the pastry shell with a sheet of foil or wax paper, and fill with ceramic baking beans (or raw rice or pasta if you have no beans). Place the dish or pan on a heated baking sheet and bake in a preheated oven at 425°F (220°C) for 15–20 minutes, removing the foil and beans for the final 10 minutes.

4 Meanwhile, make the filling: Melt the butter in a frying pan, add the onion and bacon, and cook gently, stirring occasionally, for 10 minutes or until the onion is golden brown and the bacon is crisp.

5 Spoon the onion and bacon into the pastry shell and sprinkle the cheese on top. Mix the cream and eggs together, season with salt and pepper, and pour into the pastry shell.

6 Reduce the oven setting to 350°F (180°C) and bake the quiche for 25–30 minutes until the filling is golden and set. Serve warm or cold.

Making short pastry

Tip the flour into a bowl and rub in the butter lightly with your fingertips until the mixture looks like fine crumbs.

Add the water and mix with a round-bladed knife to form a soft but not sticky dough.

SMOKED SALMON & ASPARAGUS QUICHE

SERVES 6–8

4 oz (125 g) fine asparagus, cooked, drained, and cut into 1 1/2-in (3.5-cm) lengths (about 1 cup)

3 oz (90 g) smoked salmon, cut into strips

1 1/4 cups (300 ml) thick plain yogurt or crème fraîche

2 eggs

1 tbsp chopped fresh dill weed

black pepper

SHORT PASTRY

1 1/4 cups (175 g) all-purpose flour

6 tbsp (90 g) butter

about 2 tbsp cold water

9-IN (23-CM) QUICHE DISH OR PAN

CERAMIC BAKING BEANS

1 Make the pastry: Tip the flour into a bowl and rub in the butter with your fingertips, then add enough water to bind to a soft dough. Wrap in plastic wrap and chill for 30 minutes.

2 Roll out the pastry, and use to line the quiche dish or pan. Prick the pastry shell with a fork.

3 Line the pastry shell with foil or wax paper and fill with baking beans (or raw rice or pasta if you have no beans). Place the dish or pan on a heated baking sheet and bake in a preheated oven at 425°F (220°C) for 15–20 minutes, removing the foil and beans for the final 10 minutes.

4 Arrange the asparagus and half of the salmon in the pastry shell. Mix the yogurt or crème fraîche, eggs, dill weed, and plenty of pepper, and pour into the shell. Arrange the remaining salmon on top.

5 Reduce the oven setting to 350°F (180°C) and bake for 35 minutes or until the filling is golden and set. Serve warm or cold.

ROQUEFORT QUICHE

SERVES 4–6

2/3 cup (90 g) crumbled Roquefort or other blue cheese

3/4 cup (175 g) cream cheese

2 eggs, beaten

2/3 cup (150 ml) crème fraîche or sour cream

1 tbsp snipped fresh chives

salt and black pepper

SHORT PASTRY

3/4 cup (125 g) all-purpose flour

4 tbsp (60 g) butter

about 1 tbsp cold water

8-IN (20-CM) QUICHE DISH OR PAN

CERAMIC BAKING BEANS

1 Make the pastry: Tip the flour into a bowl and rub in the butter with your fingertips. Add enough water to bind to a soft dough. Wrap in plastic wrap and chill for 30 minutes.

2 Roll out the pastry, and use to line the quiche dish or pan. Prick the bottom of the pastry shell with a fork.

3 Line the pastry shell with foil or wax paper and fill with baking beans (or raw rice or pasta if you have no beans). Place the dish or pan on a heated baking sheet and bake in a preheated oven at 425°F (220°C) for 15–20 minutes, removing the foil and beans for the final 10 minutes.

4 Meanwhile, make the filling: Mix the Roquefort and cream cheese in a bowl, then beat in the eggs, crème fraîche or sour cream, and chives, and season with salt and pepper. Take care when adding salt as blue cheese is quite salty.

5 Pour the mixture into the pastry shell, reduce the oven setting to 350°F (180°C), and bake the quiche for 30 minutes until golden and set. Serve warm or cold.

SPINACH, LEEK, & GRUYERE TART

SERVES 4–6

2 tbsp (30 g) butter

2 cups (175 g) trimmed and finely sliced leeks

3 1/2 cups (250 g) coarsely chopped young spinach leaves

2 eggs, beaten

2/3 cup (150 ml) each heavy cream and milk, or 1 1/4 cups (300 ml) milk

3/4 cup (90 g) grated Gruyère cheese

salt and black pepper

SHORT PASTRY

1 1/4 cups (175 g) all-purpose flour

6 tbsp (90 g) butter

about 2 tbsp cold water

9-IN (23-CM) QUICHE DISH OR PAN

CERAMIC BAKING BEANS

1 Make the pastry: Tip the flour into a bowl and rub in the butter with your fingertips. Add enough water to bind to a soft dough. Wrap in plastic wrap and chill for 30 minutes.

2 Roll out the pastry and use to line the quiche dish or pan. Prick the bottom of the pastry shell with a fork.

3 Line the pastry shell with foil or wax paper and fill with baking beans (or raw rice or pasta if you have no beans). Put the dish or pan on a heated baking sheet and bake in a preheated oven at 425°F (220°C) for 15–20 minutes, removing the foil and beans for the final 10 minutes.

4 Make the filling: Melt the butter in a frying pan, add the leeks, and cook over a high heat for 5 minutes or until just beginning to turn golden brown. Add the spinach and cook for about 2 minutes until it just begins to wilt. Spoon the filling into the pastry shell.

5 Mix together the eggs, milk, cream, and Gruyère cheese, season with salt and pepper, and pour into the pastry shell.

6 Reduce the oven setting to 350°F (180°C) and bake for 25 minutes or until the filling is golden and set. Serve warm or cold.

MEDITERRANEAN ZUCCHINI PIE

SERVES 4

1 lb (500 g) zucchini

3/4 cup (90 g) grated Parmesan cheese

3/4 cup (90 g) shredded mozzarella or fontina cheese

2 eggs, lightly beaten

2–3 tbsp pesto sauce

2–3 garlic cloves, minced

1 tsp dried mint

salt and black pepper

8 oz (250 g) puff pastry

beaten egg for glazing

9-IN (23-CM) SQUARE BAKING DISH OR PAN

1 Grate the zucchini into a large bowl, then blot off any excess moisture with paper towels. Add the Parmesan, mozzarella, eggs, pesto, garlic, and mint, and season with salt and pepper. Stir well to mix, then spoon into the dish or pan.

2 Roll out the pastry into a rough square, about 1 in (2.5 cm) larger than the dish or pan and 1/8–1/4 in (3–5 mm) thick. Cover the dish or pan with the pastry, trimming the edges. Cut slits in the top with a knife.

3 Cut out shapes from the pastry trimmings, using a shaped pastry cutter if you like. Brush the top of the pie with beaten egg, arrange the pastry shapes on top, and glaze them with the beaten egg.

4 Bake the pie in a preheated oven at 400°F (200°C) for 15–20 minutes until lightly browned on top and puffy. Serve hot.

PIZZA TARTLETS

These tartlets, with their traditional pizza flavors, will serve 4 people as a light lunch or supper dish, accompanied by a crisp, green salad. They also make a tasty appetizer to serve with pre-dinner drinks. They taste just as good cold as hot, so they can be prepared well in advance.

MAKES 12

1/3 cup (90 g) red or green pesto sauce
1 1/2 cups (250 g) minced ripe tomatoes
9 black olives, pitted and quartered
1 cup (125 g) shredded fontina or mozzarella cheese
2–3 garlic cloves, minced
2–3 tbsp grated Parmesan cheese
1 tsp dried oregano

SHORT PASTRY

1 1/4 cups (175 g) all-purpose flour
6 tbsp (90 g) butter
about 2 tbsp cold water

1 Make the pastry: Tip the flour into a bowl and rub in the butter with your fingertips. Add enough water to bind to a soft dough. Wrap in plastic wrap and chill for 30 minutes.

2 Make the tartlet shells (see box, right).

3 Spread the pesto in the tartlet shells, then fill the shells with the tomatoes, garlic, black olives, and fontina cheese.

4 Sprinkle the grated Parmesan cheese over the tartlets, covering the pastry edges as well as the filling. Sprinkle the dried oregano on top.

5 Bake the tartlets in a preheated oven at 400°F (200°C) for 20–30 minutes until the edges are golden brown and the cheese topping has melted and become crisp.

6 Serve the tartlets warm or cold.

GOAT CHEESE TARTLETS

Cut a log of goat cheese into 12 slices and use instead of the shredded fontina or mozzarella.

Making tartlet shells

Sprinkle the work surface lightly with flour, then roll out the short pastry until 1/8–1/4 in (3–5 mm) thick

Cut out 12 rounds from the pastry, using a 4-in (10-cm) pastry cutter or the rim of a glass or small saucer.

Fold up the edges of the rounds to form rims; put the rounds on a baking sheet.

STRATA WITH CHEESE & PESTO

SERVES 4

4–6 thick slices of stale bread, crusts removed

1/3 cup (90 g) pesto sauce

4 eggs, lightly beaten

1/2 cup (125 ml) crème fraîche

1/2 cup (125 ml) milk

1 1/2 cups (175 g) grated fontina or sharp Cheddar cheese

1/2 cup (60 g) shredded mozzarella cheese

1/4 cup (30 g) grated Parmesan cheese

1 Spread the bread slices with pesto, then arrange them in a single layer in a baking dish.

2 In a bowl, combine the eggs with the crème fraîche and milk, then pour this over the bread. Sprinkle with all of the cheeses.

3 Bake the strata in a preheated oven at 400°F (200°C) for 35–40 minutes until golden brown. It will puff up slightly as it bakes, but, unlike a soufflé, it can be safely left to stand for about 5 minutes before serving.

Cook's know-how

You need stale bread to make a good, moist strata, which makes it great for using up leftover bread. If the bread is fresh, the strata will be soggy.

BROCCOLI & RICOTTA GRATIN

SERVES 4–6

8 oz (250 g) broccoli

salt and black pepper

1 1/2 cups (375 g) ricotta or cottage cheese, lightly mashed

1 cup (125 g) grated sharp Cheddar cheese

1/2 cup (60 g) grated Parmesan cheese

2 eggs, lightly beaten

2–3 garlic cloves, minced

1 tsp chopped fresh thyme

5 tbsp (75 g) butter

4 cups (175 g) fresh bread crumbs

9-IN (23-CM) QUICHE DISH

1 Trim the broccoli and cut the stems from the heads. Peel and dice the stems; break the heads into small florets. Plunge the florets and stems into a pan of boiling salted water for 1 minute. Drain, rinse under cold running water, and drain again.

2 Put the ricotta into a large bowl with the Cheddar, Parmesan, eggs, garlic, and thyme. Season with salt and pepper, and mix until smooth, then add the broccoli stems.

3 Melt the butter in a saucepan, remove it from the heat, and stir in the bread crumbs.

4 Line the quiche dish with about three-fourths of the buttered bread crumbs, pushing them up the side of the dish to form a loose crust. Spoon in the cheese mixture, then sprinkle with the remaining buttered crumbs. Arrange the broccoli florets on top.

5 Bake in a preheated oven at 350°F (180°C) for about 40 minutes or until quite firm. Serve warm or cold.

CREAMY SEAFOOD CREPES

The succulent filling of shrimp and white fish in an herby cream sauce makes these crêpes really rich and special – ideal for a weekend lunch served with a crisp green salad. You could also serve them as a dinner-party first course, allowing one per person. The unfilled crêpes can be made in advance and stored in the freezer for up to 1 month.

SERVES 6

FILLING

8 oz (250 g) cod fillet, skinned
12 oz (375 g) cooked shrimp in shell
2 tbsp olive oil
1 small onion, minced
1 garlic clove, minced
4 tomatoes, minced
1 tbsp chopped fresh dill weed
salt and black pepper
3 tbsp light cream
2 tbsp chopped fresh basil
basil and lemon for garnish

CREPES

3/4 cup (125 g) all-purpose flour
1 egg, plus 1 egg yolk
1 1/4 cups (300 ml) milk
sunflower oil for frying

1 Make the crêpe batter: Sift the flour into a large bowl and make a well in the middle. Add the whole egg, egg yolk, and a little of the milk.

2 Gradually blend in the flour, beating until smooth. Add the remaining milk to make a thin, creamy batter. Let stand while you make the filling.

3 Cut the cod fillet into 1/2-in (1-cm) pieces. Reserve 12 shrimp for the garnish, and peel the remainder.

4 Heat the oil in a medium saucepan, add the onion and garlic, and cook very gently, stirring occasionally, for about 10 minutes until soft but not colored.

5 Add the cod, tomatoes, and dill, and season with salt and pepper. Cook over a medium heat, stirring, for 10 minutes or until thick.

6 Stir in the cream and peeled shrimp, and heat gently. Remove from the heat and stir in the basil. Keep warm.

7 Make the crêpes: Heat a small frying pan and brush with a little oil. Stir the batter, then ladle about 3 tbsp into the pan. Cook for 1 minute until the underside is golden. Turn and cook the second side, then slide out of the pan and keep hot. Repeat to make 12 crêpes.

8 Fill the crêpes with the seafood mixture and fold (see box, right). Garnish with basil and lemon, and the reserved shrimp in shell.

Filling and folding the crêpes

Put a crêpe on a serving plate. Put 2–3 spoonfuls of the seafood filling on one half and spread it to within 1/4 in (5 mm) of the edge.

Fold the unfilled half of the crêpe over the seafood filling to enclose it.

Fold the crêpe in half again, to form a triangle. Transfer to a serving plate and keep warm. Repeat with the remaining crêpes and filling.

SOUFFLE CREPES WITH BROCCOLI & CHEESE

MAKES 8

8 crêpes (page 107)

butter for greasing

2 tbsp grated Parmesan cheese

FILLING

1 cup (125 g) tiny broccoli florets

salt and black pepper

3 tbsp (45 g) butter

3 tbsp all-purpose flour

1¼ cups (300 ml) milk

½ tsp Dijon mustard

1 cup (125 g) grated sharp Cheddar cheese

4 eggs, separated

1 Make the filling: Blanch the broccoli florets in boiling salted water for 1 minute. Drain, rinse under cold running water, and drain again.

2 Melt the butter in a small saucepan, add the flour, and cook, stirring occasionally, for about 1 minute.

3 Remove the pan from the heat and gradually blend in the milk. Bring to a boil, stirring until thickened. Remove from the heat, add the mustard and cheese, and season with salt and pepper. Stir, then let cool slightly.

4 Beat the egg yolks into the sauce. In a large bowl, whisk the egg whites until soft peaks form, then fold into the cheese sauce, along with the broccoli.

5 Lay the crêpes on two lightly buttered baking sheets. Divide the soufflé mixture among the crêpes, arranging it down the middle of each one. Fold the sides of each crêpe loosely over the top of the filling, then sprinkle with grated Parmesan cheese.

6 Bake in a preheated oven at 400°F (200°C) for 15–20 minutes until the soufflé filling has risen and the crêpes are crisp. Serve immediately.

CHICKEN CREPES FLORENTINE

SERVES 4

1 lb (500 g) spinach leaves, coarsely chopped

2 tbsp (30 g) butter

pinch of grated nutmeg

8 crêpes (page 107)

1 cup (125 g) grated Gruyère cheese

FILLING

4 tbsp (60 g) butter

12 oz (375 g) crimini mushrooms, quartered

3 tbsp all-purpose flour

1¼ cups (300 ml) chicken stock

12 oz (375 g) cooked chicken meat, cut into bite-sized pieces (about 2½ cups)

1 tbsp chopped fresh tarragon

salt and black pepper

1 Make the filling: Melt the butter in a heavy pan, add the mushrooms, and cook, stirring often, for 2–3 minutes.

2 Add the flour and cook, stirring, for 1 minute. Remove the pan from the heat and gradually blend in the stock. Bring to a boil, stirring, then simmer for 2–3 minutes. Add the chicken and tarragon, and season with salt and pepper.

3 Rinse the spinach and put into a saucepan with only the water that clings to the leaves. Cook for 2 minutes or until tender. Drain well, squeezing to extract any excess water, then stir in the butter and nutmeg. Spoon into a shallow baking dish.

4 Divide the chicken and mushroom mixture among the 8 crêpes. Roll up the crêpes and arrange them, in a single layer, on top of the spinach.

5 Sprinkle with the cheese, then bake in a preheated oven at 375°F (190°C) for about 25 minutes until golden. Serve hot.

Healthy option

There are several ways in which you can cut the amount of fat and calories in this dish. For the filling, halve the butter and cook the mushrooms in a nonstick pan; also halve the amount of chicken and shred it finely. The Gruyère cheese can also be halved, or you could use a reduced-fat cheese instead.

CLASSIC CHEESE SOUFFLE

SERVES 4

1 1/4 cups (300 ml) milk

1 bay leaf

a few parsley stems

1/2 onion, peeled

pinch of cayenne pepper

salt and black pepper

3 tbsp (45 g) butter, plus extra for greasing

3 tbsp all-purpose flour

3 eggs, separated

1 tbsp Dijon mustard

1 cup (125 g) grated sharp Cheddar cheese

5-CUP (1.25-LITER) SOUFFLE DISH

1 Bring the milk to a boil in a saucepan with the bay leaf, parsley stems, and onion half. Remove from the heat, cover, and let infuse for about 20 minutes. Strain, then add the cayenne and season with salt and pepper.

2 Melt the butter in a large pan, add the flour, and cook, stirring, for 1 minute. Remove from the heat and slowly blend in the milk, then bring to a boil. Simmer for 2–3 minutes, stirring, until thickened. Remove from the heat and let cool for about 10 minutes.

3 Beat the egg yolks in a bowl. Stir them into the cooled white sauce, then stir in the mustard and all but 2 tbsp of the Cheddar.

4 Whisk the egg whites until they will hold firm but not dry peaks. Fold 1–2 tbsp egg whites into the cheese mixture until evenly combined, then fold in the remaining whites.

5 Lightly butter the soufflé dish. Pour in the soufflé mixture and sprinkle with the reserved cheese.

6 Set on a preheated baking sheet and bake near the top of a preheated oven at 350°F (180°C) for about 25 minutes or until risen and just set in the middle. Serve at once.

BROCCOLI SOUFFLES

SERVES 4

3 tbsp (45 g) butter, plus extra for greasing

3 tbsp all-purpose flour

1 cup (250 ml) milk

pinch of grated nutmeg

salt and cayenne pepper

12 oz (375 g) broccoli florets

3–4 shallots, minced

2 tbsp grated Parmesan cheese

4 egg yolks

1 1/3 cups (175 g) crumbled blue cheese

6 egg whites

4 8-OZ (250-ML) SOUFFLE DISHES

1 Melt 2 tbsp (30 g) butter in a large pan, add the flour, and stir for 1 minute. Remove from the heat and gradually blend in the milk, then bring to a boil, stirring until thickened. Add the nutmeg, season with salt, and stir in a pinch of cayenne pepper. Let cool.

2 Steam the broccoli for 2–3 minutes until just tender. Rinse under cold running water, then chop coarsely.

3 Heat the remaining butter in a pan, add the shallots, and cook gently for 3 minutes or until soft.

4 Prepare the soufflé dishes (see box, below).

5 Beat the egg yolks and add to the cooled sauce, along with the broccoli, shallots, and blue cheese.

6 Whisk the egg whites until they form firm but not dry peaks. Fold 1–2 tbsp of the egg whites into the broccoli mixture, then fold in the remaining egg whites.

7 Pour the mixture into the soufflé dishes. Bake the soufflés near the top of a preheated oven at 350°F (180°C) for 30 minutes. Serve at once.

Preparing the soufflé dishes

Butter the bottoms and sides of the soufflé dishes. Sprinkle with a thin layer of grated Parmesan cheese.

SWISS DOUBLE-CHEESE SOUFFLES

SERVES 6

3 tbsp (45 g) butter, plus extra for greasing

3 tbsp all-purpose flour

1 1/4 cups (300 ml) milk

1/2 cup (60 g) grated Gruyère cheese

2 tbsp snipped fresh chives

salt and black pepper

3 eggs, separated

1/2 cup (60 g) grated Parmesan cheese

1 1/4 cups (300 ml) heavy cream

snipped fresh chives for garnish

1 Melt the butter in a large saucepan, add the flour, and cook, stirring, for 1 minute. Remove from the heat and gradually blend in the milk. Return to the heat and bring to a boil, stirring until thickened.

2 Remove the pan from the heat and beat in the Gruyère cheese and chives. Season with salt and pepper, then stir in the egg yolks.

3 Whisk the egg whites until stiff but not dry. Stir 1 tbsp into the mixture, then fold in the rest.

4 Generously butter 6 small ramekins, and divide the mixture equally among them. Place the ramekins in a small roasting pan and pour boiling water into the pan to come halfway up the sides of the ramekins.

5 Bake the soufflés in a preheated oven at 425°F (220°C) for 15–20 minutes until golden and springy to the touch. Let the soufflés stand for 5–10 minutes; they will shrink by about one-third.

6 Butter a large, shallow gratin dish. Sprinkle half of the Parmesan cheese over the bottom. Run a metal spatula around the edge of each soufflé, unmold carefully, and arrange on top of the Parmesan in the gratin dish.

7 Season the cream with salt and pepper, then pour this over the soufflés. Sprinkle the remaining Parmesan over the top. Return to the oven and bake for 15–20 minutes until golden. Garnish with snipped chives.

GARLIC & GOAT CHEESE SOUFFLES

SERVES 6

1 head of garlic

1 cup (250 ml) milk

1/2 cup (125 ml) water

3 tbsp (45 g) butter, plus extra for greasing

3 tbsp all-purpose flour

5 oz (150 g) goat cheese, diced

6 eggs, separated

salt and black pepper

fresh chives for garnish

6 5-OZ (150-ML) SOUFFLE DISHES

1 Separate and peel the garlic cloves. Put the milk, measured water, and all but one of the garlic cloves into a saucepan. Bring to a boil, then simmer for 15–20 minutes until the garlic is tender and the liquid has reduced to 1 cup (250 ml). Let cool, then lightly mash the garlic in the milk.

2 Melt the butter in a saucepan, add the flour, and stir for 1 minute. Remove from the heat and gradually blend in the garlic-flavored milk.

3 Return to the heat and bring to a boil, stirring constantly until the mixture thickens. Simmer for 2–3 minutes. Transfer to a large bowl and let cool for about 10 minutes. Chop the remaining garlic clove.

4 Add the chopped garlic, diced goat cheese, and egg yolks to the cooled sauce. Season with salt and pepper.

5 In a large bowl, whisk the egg whites until stiff but not dry. Stir 1 tbsp of the egg whites into the garlic and cheese mixture, then fold in the remaining egg whites.

6 Lightly butter the soufflé dishes. Pour in the soufflé mixture and bake in a preheated oven at 350°F (180°C) for 15–20 minutes. Serve at once, garnished with chives.

CHEESE FONDUE

SERVES 6

1 large loaf of crusty bread, crusts left on, cut into 1-in (2.5-cm) triangles

2 cups (250 g) shredded Gruyère cheese

2 cups (250 g) shredded Emmental cheese

¼ cup (30 g) cornstarch

2 cups (500 ml) dry white wine

1 garlic clove, lightly crushed

2 tbsp kirsch

pinch of grated nutmeg

salt and black pepper

FOR SERVING (OPTIONAL)

2 apples, quartered and sliced

6 tbsp sesame seeds, toasted

3 tbsp cumin seeds, toasted

1 FONDUE SET

1 Place the pieces of bread on a large baking sheet and put into a preheated oven at 325°F (170°C). Warm them for 3–5 minutes until dried out slightly.

2 Put the Gruyère and Emmental cheeses into a medium bowl and toss with the flour.

3 Put the wine and garlic into a fondue pot and boil for 2 minutes, then lower the heat so that the mixture is barely simmering. Add the cheese mixture, a spoonful at a time, stirring constantly with a fork and letting each spoonful melt before adding the next.

4 When the fondue is creamy and smooth, stir in the kirsch, nutmeg, and salt and pepper to taste.

5 Set the fondue pot over the burner; the mixture should barely simmer. Serve with the baked bread for dipping into the fondue, as well as the optional apple slices and sesame seeds and cumin seeds.

RACLETTE

SERVES 4

2 lb (1 kg) new potatoes, halved

salt

8 oz (250 g) Swiss raclette cheese, cut into 16 thin slices

1 red onion, thinly sliced

12 small gherkins

12 cocktail pickled onions

1 Cook the potatoes in boiling salted water for 12–15 minutes until just tender. Drain and keep the potatoes warm.

2 Put 4 heavy, oven-to table serving plates into a preheated oven at 475°F (240°C) to warm for 3–5 minutes.

3 Divide the potatoes among the plates, then arrange 4 slices of raclette cheese on top of each serving. Return the plates to the oven and heat for 1–2 minutes until the cheese is melted and sizzling.

4 Divide the red onion slices, gherkins, and pickled onions among the plates, and serve at once.

Cook's know-how

Gruyère or Emmental cheese can be used instead of raclette.

CROQUE SENOR

SERVES 4

8 slices of white bread

4 slices of sharp Cheddar cheese

4 slices of cooked ham

2 tbsp (30 g) butter, softened

lemon wedges and cilantro sprigs for serving

SPICY TOMATO SALSA

3 ripe but firm tomatoes, minced

1 red bell pepper, halved, seeded, roasted, and peeled (page 388), then minced

1 garlic clove, minced

2 green onions, thinly sliced

1 fresh, hot, green chili pepper, halved, seeded, and minced

1 tbsp red wine vinegar

salt

1 Make the salsa: Combine the tomatoes, red bell pepper, garlic, green onions, chili pepper, and vinegar in a bowl. Season with salt, then set aside.

2 Put 4 slices of bread on a board. Arrange the cheese slices and then the ham slices on top. Spoon the salsa over the ham.

3 Lightly spread the butter over one side of the remaining slices of bread and put them, butter-side up, on top of the salsa.

4 Heat a heavy frying pan. Toast each sandwich in the pan, butter-side down, over a medium-high heat until the cheese begins to melt and the bread turns golden. Lightly spread the second side of each sandwich with butter. Turn over and cook the other side until golden.

5 Garnish with lemon wedges, cilantro sprigs, and any remaining spicy tomato salsa. Serve hot.

SWISS CHEESE & TOMATO RAREBIT

SERVES 4

3 garlic cloves

2 tbsp (30 g) butter, plus extra for spreading

3 tbsp all-purpose flour

1 1/3 cups (250 g) minced ripe tomatoes

1/2 cup (125 ml) dry white wine

3 cups (375 g) grated Swiss or Gruyère cheese

2 cups (125 g) chopped mushrooms

1 tbsp chopped fresh tarragon

salt and black pepper

4 slices of bread, crusts removed

chopped parsley for garnish

1 Mince 2 of the garlic cloves. Melt the butter in a saucepan, add the minced garlic, and cook gently, stirring, for 1–2 minutes. Add the flour and stir for 1 minute. Add the minced tomatoes and cook for 2 more minutes.

2 Pour in the wine and cook, stirring, for 5 minutes or until the mixture thickens. Add the Swiss cheese, a little at a time, and stir until it has melted. Add the chopped mushrooms and tarragon, season with salt and pepper, and cook for 3 minutes or until the mushrooms are tender.

3 Cut the remaining garlic clove in half. Toast the bread on both sides under the broiler. Rub one side of the toast with the cut sides of the garlic, then discard it.

4 Spread the garlic side of the toast with butter, place on warmed plates, and top with the cheese mixture. Serve at once, sprinkled with chopped parsley.

EGGS BENEDICT

SERVES 4

8 lean bacon slices or slices of Canadian bacon

2 English muffins, split in half

4 eggs

butter for spreading

fresh flat-leaf parsley for garnish

HOLLANDAISE SAUCE

2 tsp lemon juice

2 tsp white wine vinegar

3 egg yolks, at room temperature

1/2 cup (125 g) unsalted butter, melted

salt and black pepper

1 Cook the bacon under the broiler, 3 in (7 cm) from the heat, for 5–7 minutes until crisp. Keep the bacon warm.

2 Toast the cut sides of the muffin halves under the broiler. Keep warm.

3 Make the hollandaise sauce: Put the lemon juice and wine vinegar into a small bowl, add the egg yolks, and whisk with a balloon whisk until light and frothy.

4 Place the bowl over a pan of simmering water and whisk until the mixture thickens. Gradually add the melted butter, whisking constantly until thick. Season with salt and pepper. Keep warm.

5 Poach the eggs: Bring a large, wide pan of water to a boil. Lower the heat so that the water is simmering, then slide in the eggs. Swirl the water around the eggs to make neat shapes. Simmer for about 4 minutes. Lift out with a slotted spoon.

6 Butter the muffin halves and put onto warmed plates. Put 2 bacon slices and an egg on each one, and top with the sauce. Serve at once, garnished with parsley.

SPICY LIME HOLLANDAISE

Substitute 2 tsp lime juice for the lemon juice in the hollandaise sauce, and add 1/2 tsp each of paprika and chili powder.

EGGS FLORENTINE

SERVES 4

8 oz (250 g) spinach leaves

3 green onions, thinly sliced

2 tbsp heavy cream

4 eggs

3 tbsp grated Parmesan cheese

CHEESE SAUCE

2 tbsp (30 g) butter

2 tbsp all-purpose flour

1 cup (250 ml) milk

1 1/2 cups (175 g) grated sharp Cheddar cheese

pinch each of cayenne pepper and grated nutmeg

salt and black pepper

1 Rinse the spinach and put into a saucepan with only the water that clings to the leaves. Cook for 2 minutes or until wilted and tender. Drain and set aside.

2 Make the cheese sauce: Melt the butter in a saucepan, add the flour, and stir for 1 minute. Remove from the heat and gradually blend in the milk. Bring to a boil, stirring constantly until the mixture thickens. Simmer for 2–3 minutes.

3 Stir in the Cheddar cheese, add the cayenne pepper and nutmeg, and season with salt and pepper. Keep warm.

4 Combine the spinach in a bowl with the green onions and cream, and season with salt and pepper. Set aside.

5 Poach the eggs: Bring a large, wide pan of water to a boil. Lower the heat so that the water is simmering, then slide in the eggs, one at a time. Swirl the water around the eggs to make neat shapes. Simmer for about 4 minutes. Lift out with a slotted spoon.

6 Divide the spinach and green onion mixture among 4 warmed oven-to-table dishes. Arrange the poached eggs on the spinach, and spoon the cheese sauce over the eggs.

7 Sprinkle the grated Parmesan cheese over the sauce, then place the dishes under the broiler, 3 in (7 cm) from the heat. Cook until the cheese has melted and is lightly browned, and the whole dish is heated through. Serve hot.

OEUFS EN COCOTTE

SERVES 4

1 tbsp (15 g) butter

4 eggs

salt and black pepper

4 tbsp heavy cream

1 tbsp chopped parsley

4 SMALL RAMEKINS

1 Melt the butter, and pour a little into each ramekin.

2 Break each egg into a saucer, then slide into a prepared ramekin. Sprinkle with salt and pepper, and top each egg with 1 tbsp cream.

3 Place the ramekins in a roasting pan and pour boiling water into the pan to come halfway up the sides of the ramekins. Cover with foil.

4 Bake in a preheated oven at 400°F (200°C) for about 10 minutes or until the whites are opaque and firm but the yolks still soft. Or, put the ramekins into a large frying pan, add boiling water to the pan to come halfway up the sides, cover, and cook over a medium heat for 10 minutes.

5 Sprinkle a little parsley over each baked egg 1–2 minutes before the end of cooking time.

FETA CHEESE COCOTTES

After pouring the butter into the ramekins, divide ½ cup (125 g) diced feta cheese, tossed with minced fresh herbs and hot red chili pepper, among the ramekins. Also, substitute 2–3 thinly sliced green onions for the parsley.

HUEVOS RANCHEROS

SERVES 4

2 tbsp sunflower oil

1 onion, minced

3 garlic cloves, minced

1 green bell pepper, halved, seeded, and chopped

1–2 fresh, hot green chili peppers, halved, seeded, and chopped

2¾ cups (500 g) minced ripe tomatoes, or 14 oz (400 g) canned crushed tomatoes

1 tsp ground cumin

¼ tsp sugar

salt

4 eggs

cilantro sprigs for garnish

1 Heat the oil in a frying pan, add the onion, garlic, green bell pepper, and chili pepper, and cook gently, stirring occasionally, for 5 minutes or until the onion is soft.

2 Add the tomatoes, cumin, and sugar, season with salt, and simmer, stirring from time to time, for 10 minutes or until the mixture is thick.

3 Meanwhile, poach the eggs: Bring a large, wide pan of water to a boil. Lower the heat so that the water is simmering, then slide in the eggs, one at a time. Swirl the water around the eggs to make neat shapes. Simmer for 4 minutes. Lift out with a slotted spoon.

4 Taste the tomato sauce for seasoning, and ladle onto serving plates. Top each of the servings with a poached egg and garnish with a cilantro sprig.

HUEVOS RANCHEROS WITH CHEESE

Fry the eggs instead of poaching them. Transfer the eggs to serving plates, top with the sauce, and sprinkle with ½ cup (60 g) grated sharp Cheddar cheese.

4

FISH & SHELLFISH

UNDER 30 MINUTES

DINNER PARTY

THAI SHRIMP STIR-FRY

Spicy Asian dish: shrimp, red bell pepper, ginger, chili pepper, and lemon grass, stir-fried with rice noodles, soy sauce, and lime juice.

SERVES 4 522 calories per serving

Takes 15 minutes   Page 127

SCALLOPS WITH ASPARAGUS & LEMON

Fresh and aromatic: scallops cooked with asparagus and garlic, with a parsley, lemon, and tarragon sauce.

SERVES 6 159 calories per serving

Takes 20 minutes   Page 130

DEVILED CRAB

Crabmeat in a sauce flavored with nutmeg, sherry, green onion, and hot pepper sauce. Topped with bread crumbs and baked.

SERVES 4 502 calories per serving

Takes 25 minutes   Page 128

TIGER SHRIMP WITH TARRAGON SAUCE

Shrimp simmered with wine, garlic, and parsley. Served with a tarragon sauce.

SERVES 4 252 calories per serving

Takes 20 minutes   Page 126

HERRING WITH AN OAT CRUST

Crisp and heart-healthy: butterflied fresh herring coated in finely ground oats and mustard, then broiled. Garnished with parsley and lemon.

SERVES 4 461 calories per serving

Takes 15 minutes   Page 137

OYSTER STEW WITH PERNOD & SAFFRON

An unusual Mediterranean-style dish: fresh oysters simmered with Pernod, cream, white wine, fish stock, leek, carrot, watercress, saffron, and lemon juice. Lightly seasoned with cayenne pepper, and garnished with fresh chervil.

SERVES 4 251 calories per serving

Takes 25 minutes   Page 133

UNDER 30 MINUTES

SEVERN SALMON

Baked salmon flavored with pepper, in a pool of sauce made from cream, watercress, lemon juice, butter, and egg yolk.

SERVES 6 414 calories per serving

Takes 25 minutes   Page 142

LOW FAT

BROILED TROUT WITH CUCUMBER & DILL

Trout with a stuffing of lightly cooked cucumber, dill weed, and lemon juice.

SERVES 4 435 calories per serving

Takes 25 minutes   Page 138

HIGH PROTEIN

SCALLOPS WITH SPICY CASHEW SAUCE

Scallops stir-fried with mustard seeds and garlic, served in a cashew and chili sauce.

SERVES 6 276 calories per serving

Takes 25 minutes   Page 130

DINNER PARTY

CHINESE-STYLE OYSTERS

Oysters wrapped in bacon and stir-fried with green bell pepper, garlic, and water chestnuts, then sprinkled with green onion slices.

SERVES 4 248 calories per serving

Takes 25 minutes   page 133

LOW CALORIE

SALMON WITH SPINACH

Broiled salmon served with a salsa of lightly cooked green onions mixed with spinach, lemon juice, and mustard.

SERVES 4 454 calories per serving

Takes 25 minutes   Page 142

FAMILY FARE

BEST-EVER FRIED FISH

Temptingly crisp: sole fillets coated in flour, beaten egg, and fresh bread crumbs. Cooked until golden and served with lemon.

SERVES 4 298 calories per serving

Takes 25 minutes   Page 148

HERRING WITH MUSTARD SAUCE

Baked herring served with a classic sauce made from mustard powder, sugar, and white wine vinegar.

SERVES 4 479 calories per serving

Takes 25 minutes   Page 137

FILLETS OF SOLE MEUNIERE

Fresh and summery: slim sole fillets lightly floured and cooked in butter, then served with parsley and lemon-flavored butter.

SERVES 4 274 calories per serving

Takes 20 minutes   Page 146

SHRIMP TACOS

Hot and crunchy: taco shells with a spicy filling of shrimp, cilantro, tomatoes, onion, garlic, green bell pepper, and paprika.

SERVES 4 414 calories per serving

Takes 25 minutes   Page 126

30–60 MINUTES

CAJUN-SPICED RED SNAPPER

Red snapper fillets marinated in a piquant mixture of garlic, paprika, cumin, and chili powder. Topped with cilantro butter.

SERVES 4 258 calories per serving

Takes 15 minutes, plus marinating   Page 154

HOT & SOUR MACKEREL

Red bell pepper, fresh chili pepper, carrots, and green onions stir-fried, then broiled with mackerel fillets. Served with a hot and sour sauce.

SERVES 4 539 calories per serving

Takes 35 minutes   Page 136

MUSSEL GRATIN

Mussels simmered with wine, shallot, and garlic, topped with cream and parsley sauce and bread crumbs, then broiled.

SERVES 4 448 calories per serving

Takes 35 minutes   Page 131

FAMILY CHOICE

GOLDEN FISH CAKES

Cod or haddock simmered in milk flavored with bay leaf and peppercorns. Mixed with potato, shaped, and coated in crumbs.

SERVES 4 613 calories per serving

Takes 50 minutes   Page 158

LOBSTER WITH BLACK BEAN SALSA

Lobster tails spread with garlic and oregano-flavored butter, and broiled. Served with black bean salsa.

SERVES 4 531 calories per serving

Takes 35 minutes   Page 129

CHEESE-TOPPED BAKED RED PORGY

Porgy fillets baked with lemon, then covered in a white sauce, sprinkled with cheese, and broiled.

SERVES 4 401 calories per serving

Takes 40 minutes   Page 155

MACKEREL WITH GREEN GRAPE SAUCE

Broiled mackerel served with a tangy grape sauce enriched with butter, sugar, and ginger.

SERVES 4 489 calories per serving

Takes 35 minutes   Page 136

SALMON WITH AVOCADO

Succulent salmon steaks baked with tarragon, and served with a rich sauce of avocado, yogurt, and lime zest and juice.

SERVES 4 543 calories per serving

Takes 35 minutes   Page 143

MUSHROOM-STUFFED SOLE FILLETS

Sole fillets rolled and stuffed with onion and mushrooms. Baked with tarragon and wine, which form the base for a cream sauce.

SERVES 4 568 calories per serving

Takes 35 minutes   Page 146

30–60 MINUTES

STEAMED CLAMS WITH PARSLEY

Clams cooked in a delicious sauce made from white wine, onion, garlic, and lots of parsley, enriched with butter.

SERVES 4 207 calories per serving

Takes 40 minutes   Page 132

SPICED FISH WITH COCONUT

Sweet and spicy: monkfish pieces lightly coated in flour, then cooked with coconut milk, onion, coriander, cumin, and turmeric.

SERVES 4 389 calories per serving

Takes 45 minutes   Page 151

SPICY CLAMS WITH CILANTRO PESTO

Clams richly flavored with tomatoes, stock, garlic, and chili. Served with cilantro pesto.

SERVES 4–6 349–233 calories per serving

Takes 45 minutes   Page 132

MONKFISH WITH GINGER-ORANGE SAUCE

Monkfish fillets cooked with orange, ginger, onion, and stock; served with a sauce spiked with lime.

SERVES 4 221 calories per serving

Takes 40 minutes   Page 150

DINNER PARTY

COD STEAKS WITH ANCHOVY & FENNEL

Cod steaks baked with a topping of anchovies, fennel, parsley, and bread crumbs.

SERVES 4 429 calories per serving

Takes 40 minutes   Page 154

SEA BASS WITH LEMON BUTTER SAUCE

Whole sea bass baked in foil with tarragon, lemon, and wine. Served with a creamy sauce.

SERVES 4 363 calories per serving

Takes 40 minutes   Page 157

LOW FAT

ASIAN FISH PARCELS

An aromatic Asian dish: sole fillets sprinkled with ginger, green onion, soy sauce, and rice wine, baked in parchment paper.

SERVES 4 312 calories per serving

Takes 35 minutes   Page 157

RED PORGY NIÇOISE

Baked red porgy on a bed of fennel, onion, and garlic, sprinkled with lemon juice, olives, and chopped parsley.

SERVES 4 356 calories per serving

Takes 50 minutes   Page 155

CRISP-TOPPED SEAFOOD PIE

Cod poached in milk, then baked with shrimp, leeks, and broccoli. Topped with white sauce, Gruyère, and grated piecrust dough.

SERVES 4 575 calories per serving

Takes 55 minutes   Page 158

30–60 MINUTES

OVER 60 MINUTES

GINGERED SOLE

Light and tangy: sole fillets marinated in sunflower and sesame oils, fresh ginger, garlic, sherry, and vinegar, then broiled.

SERVES 4 247 calories per serving

Takes 15 minutes, plus marinating   Page 147

DINNER PARTY

LOBSTER TAILS WITH MANGO & LIME

Lobster tail meat coated in a sauce of wine, cream, mango, and grated lime zest and juice. Sprinkled with Parmesan cheese and baked.

SERVES 4 442 calories per serving

Takes 40 minutes   Page 128

SEAFOOD & AVOCADO SALAD

Poached monkfish with crabmeat and shrimp on a bed of salad leaves, avocado, and tomatoes, dressed with crème fraîche.

SERVES 4 396 calories per serving

Takes 35 minutes, plus cooling   Page 129

MEDITERRANEAN STUFFED SQUID

Tender squid pouches filled with bread crumbs, onion, garlic, chopped squid, parsley, and dill weed, and pan-fried in butter.

SERVES 4 224 calories per serving

Takes 40 minutes   Page 127

ROAST MONKFISH NIÇOISE

Succulent monkfish cooked with roasted garlic, lemon, wine, artichoke hearts, herbs, olives, and sun-dried tomatoes.

SERVES 4 448 calories per serving

Takes 50 minutes   Page 150

SOLE FLORENTINE

Sole fillets baked on a bed of white sauce and spinach and topped with Parmesan. Served with hot lemon bread.

SERVES 4 422 calories per serving

Takes 1 hour 5 minutes   Page 147

MUSSELS WITH POTATOES & CHORIZO

Mussels cooked with potatoes, spicy chorizo sausage, garlic, stock, sherry, and cumin seeds.

SERVES 6 523 calories per serving

Takes 40 minutes   Page 131

HADDOCK WITH MUSHROOMS & CREAM

Baked haddock topped with mushrooms, a creamy sauce, bread crumbs, and Parmesan.

SERVES 4–6 429–286 calories per serving

Takes 55 minutes   Page 149

HALIBUT IN PHYLLO PASTRY

Delicate and moist: leek and carrot strips, cooked with wine, stock, and saffron, form a bed for halibut in phyllo pastry packages.

SERVES 4 564 calories per serving

Takes 1 hour 5 minutes   Page 156

OVER 60 MINUTES

LOW FAT

TUNA TERIYAKI

Light and simple: tuna steaks marinated in garlic, ginger, soy sauce, and sesame oil. Broiled, then sprinkled with green onion.

SERVES 4 339 calories per serving

Takes 15 minutes, plus marinating   Page 139

TUNA WITH FENNEL & TOMATO RELISH

Tuna marinated in oil, lemon juice, garlic, and herbs, broiled, and topped with relish.

SERVES 4 467 calories per serving

Takes 25 minutes, plus marinating   Page 139

MONKFISH KEBABS

Pieces of monkfish marinated in oil, lemon zest and juice, and dill weed, threaded with lightly cooked cucumber, lemon, and bay leaves.

SERVES 4 286 calories per serving

Takes 30 minutes, plus marinating   Page 151

KOULIBIAC

Flaked salmon mixed with rice, onion, tomatoes, parsley, and lemon. Wrapped in puff pastry and decorated with a pastry braid.

SERVES 8–10 518–414 calories per serving

Takes 1 1/4 hours   Page 141

INDIAN-SPICED HADDOCK

Pieces of haddock marinated in a mixture of coriander, cayenne, and turmeric. Simmered with ginger, chili pepper, and potato.

SERVES 4 365 calories per serving

Takes 40 minutes, plus marinating   Page 149

DINNER PARTY

SALMON EN CROUTE

Salmon fillets marinated in dill weed and lemon zest and juice, baked in puff pastry with spinach, green onions, and cream cheese.

SERVES 8 745 calories per serving

Takes 1 1/2 hours, plus marinating   Page 143

SWORDFISH WITH ORANGE RELISH

Swordfish steaks marinated in orange and lemon juices, olive oil, and garlic. Broiled, then served with an orange relish.

SERVES 4 429 calories per serving

Takes 20 minutes, plus marinating   Page 140

OUTDOOR COOKING

SHARK WITH TROPICAL SALSA

Shark steaks marinated in cumin, garlic, lemon juice, and cilantro. Served with a salsa of pineapple, papaya, and chili pepper.

SERVES 4 534 calories per serving

Takes 25 minutes, plus marinating   Page 140

BAKED TROUT WITH ORANGE

Fresh and hearty: whole trout stuffed with mushrooms, shallots, orange zest and juice, white wine vinegar, thyme, and parsley.

SERVES 4 378 calories per serving

Takes 45 minutes, plus chilling   Page 138

FISH & SHELLFISH KNOW-HOW

SEAFOOD IS DELICIOUS, versatile, and quick to cook. Compared with other protein foods, it is excellent value for money as there is usually little wastage. In addition, it is very nutritious: all fish and shellfish are good sources of essential vitamins and minerals, but oily fish are particularly rich in vitamins A and D and also provide beneficial omega-3 fatty acids.

Seafood is divided into two broad categories: fish and shellfish. Fish may be white (its oil is found mainly in the liver) or oily (the oil is distributed in the flesh); white fish are further sub-divided according to body shape (round or flat). Of the shellfish, crustaceans (crab, shrimp) have shells and legs; mollusks (clams, scallops) just have shells. Squid is a mollusk with an internal "shell."

FISH STOCK

Ask your fishmonger for heads, bones, and trimmings from lean white fish (not oily fish, which make a bitter-tasting stock).

1 Rinse 1 1/2 lb (750 g) bones and trimmings and put them into a large pan. Add 4 cups (1 liter) water and 1 cup (250 ml) dry white wine. Bring to a boil, skimming the surface.

2 Add 1 sliced onion, 1 sliced carrot, 1 chopped celery stalk, 1 bay leaf, a few parsley sprigs, and a few black peppercorns. Simmer for 20–25 minutes. Strain. Use immediately, or cool, cover, and refrigerate to use within 2 days. It can also be frozen for up to 3 months.

CLEANING & BONING ROUND FISH

Round fish such as trout, mackerel, herring, and salmon are often cooked whole, and boning makes them easier to serve and eat. When boned they can also be stuffed. Fishmongers will prepare the fish for you, but if you want to do it yourself, here's how.

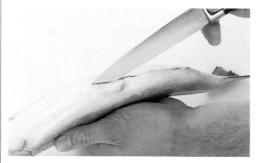

1 To clean the fish, first snip off the fins. Cut along the belly, from the vent end to just below the head. Remove the innards, scraping away any dark blood. Lift the gill covering and remove the concertina-shaped gills. Rinse well.

2 To bone, extend the belly opening so that it goes all the way to the tail. Hold the belly open and carefully run the knife between the flesh and the bones along one side, from tail to head, to cut the flesh from the ribcage.

3 Turn the fish around and cut the flesh from the ribcage on the other side. Snip through the backbone at each end and gently pull it away from the flesh, removing it with the ribcage in one piece.

4 If the head and tail have been cut off, open out the fish and lay it skin-side up. Press along the backbone to loosen the bones. Turn over and lift or cut out the ribcage and backbone. The fish is now "butterflied."

SCALING

Unless skinning a fish before cooking, the scales should be removed. Dip your fingers in salt to ensure a firm grip and grasp the fish tail. Using the blunt side of a knife, with firm strokes scrape off the scales, from tail to head. Rinse well. Or, ask your fishmonger to do this.

MICROWAVING

One of the best uses for a microwave is for cooking fish and shellfish: they retain their texture and all of their flavorful juices. However, care must be taken not to overcook the delicate flesh. Whether cooking or thawing, arrange pieces of fish so that the thicker areas are at the outside of the dish; overlap thin areas or fold them under. With whole fish, shield delicate areas, such as the tail and head, with smooth strips of foil. If thawing seafood, again protect thin, delicate areas by shielding them with smooth strips of foil. Except when doing this, never put metal or metal containers in microwave ovens (see also page 23.)

FREEZING

It's best to buy fish already frozen, as it will have been processed and frozen at very low temperatures immediately after being caught – while still at sea – to prevent there being any deterioration.

If you have fish to freeze yourself, clean it and wrap tightly. For the best flavor, store white fish for no longer than 3 months, oily fish and shellfish for 2 months. (When buying, be aware that some seafood sold as "fresh" may have been frozen and then thawed, so it should not be frozen again at home.)

Fish fillets and some shellfish can be cooked very successfully from frozen, but if you need to thaw seafood before cooking, do so slowly in the refrigerator or quickly in the microwave.

BUYING & STORING

When buying fish and shellfish, aroma and appearance are your guides. Seafood should have the clean smell of the sea. If it has an unpleasantly "fishy" or ammonia-like odor, it is not fresh.

Whole fresh fish should have clean, red gills, the scales should be firmly attached, and it should be covered in a clear slime; the flesh should feel firm and springy. The flesh of fillets and steaks should be firm, moist, and lustrous. If at all possible ask for steaks to be cut while you wait. If buying pre-packaged fish, check the color of any liquid that has accumulated in the pack: it should not be cloudy or off-white.

Shellfish is sold both in the shell and shucked, raw and cooked. The shells of crabs, lobsters, and shrimp become pink or red when cooked. Live shellfish, such as mussels, clams, and oysters, should have tightly closed shells. If any shells are open they should close if lightly tapped; if they do not, the shellfish is dead and should be discarded. Shucked oysters, scallops, and clams should be plump; scallops should smell slightly sweet. Shrimp should also smell faintly sweet, and feel firm.

Keep the fish or shellfish cool until you get home, then unwrap it, cover with a wet cloth or wet paper towels, and store in the coldest part of the refrigerator. Use oily fish and shellfish the same day; keep white fish no more than 24 hours.

FILLETING FLATFISH
Either 2 wide or 4 narrow fillets can be cut from a small flatfish. Larger flatfish will yield 4 good-sized fillets. Keep the bones for making stock.

1 Make a shallow cut through the skin around the edge of the fish, where the fin bones meet the body. Cut across the tail and make a curved cut around the head. Then cut down the center of the fish, cutting through the flesh to the bone.

2 Insert the knife between the flesh and the bones on one side at the head end. Keeping the knife almost parallel to the fish, cut close to the bones, loosening the flesh to detach the fillet in one piece.

3 Repeat to remove the second fillet on the same side. Then turn the fish over and remove both of the fillets from the other side. Check the fillets for any stray bones, pulling them out with tweezers.

4 To skin, lay each fillet skin-side down and hold the tail with salted fingers to ensure a firm grip. Cut through the flesh at the tail end, then, holding the knife at an angle, cut the flesh from the skin.

PREPARING SHRIMP

Both raw and cooked shrimp can be used successfully in a variety of tasty dishes. When buying, take into account that shrimp lose at least half of their weight when the heads and shells are removed.

1 Gently pull off the head and then the legs. Peel the shell from the body, leaving on the last tail section of shell if you like.

2 Make a shallow cut along the center of the back of the shrimp. Lift out the black intestinal vein, then rinse the shrimp under cold running water.

PREPARING MUSSELS & CLAMS

Most mussels and clams are sold alive, in shell, and are cooked by steaming. If clams are very sandy, soak them overnight in very salty water; otherwise, just rinse them to remove sand. Both mussels and clams need to be scrubbed.

1 To clean the shells of mussels and clams, hold under cold running water and scrub with a small stiff brush. Use a small knife to scrape off any barnacles.

2 To remove a mussel's "beard" (anchoring thread), hold it firmly between your thumb and the blade of a small knife and pull it away from the shell.

PREPARING A COOKED CRAB

The sweet, succulent meat inside a crab is of two types – lump (pieces of the white body meat) and flaked (small bits of light and dark meat from the body and claws).

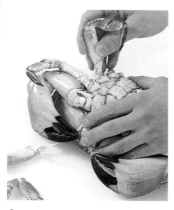

1 Put the crab on its back and twist off the legs and claws, close to the body.

2 Using nutcrackers, a small hammer, or a rolling pin, crack the shells of the claws without crushing them. Break open the shells and carefully remove the meat, using a small fork or skewer.

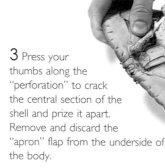

3 Press your thumbs along the "perforation" to crack the central section of the shell and prize it apart. Remove and discard the "apron" flap from the underside of the body.

4 Pull the central body section up and away from the shell. Scoop out any brown meat and put it into the bowl (or keep it separate if you prefer). Scoop out any roe. Discard the stomach sac, which is located between the eyes.

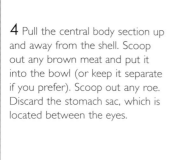

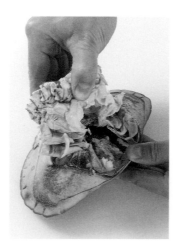

5 Pull the spongy gills (known as "dead man's fingers") from the body and discard them.

6 Cut the body in half with a large knife and pick out all the white meat from the crevices. Add to the other meat in the bowl.

PREPARING A COOKED LOBSTER

Cooked lobster meat can be added to cooked dishes for a brief heating, or it can be served cold with mayonnaise (most attractively in the shell) or in a salad.

To remove the meat

1 Twist off the large claws. Using a sturdy nutcracker, small hammer, or rolling pin, crack the shells of the claws without crushing them. Pick out the meat, in 1 or 2 large pieces. If the shell is not to be used for serving, pull apart the body and tail. Twist off the small legs, crack them, and remove the meat with a skewer or lobster pick.

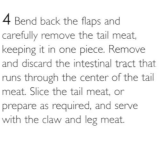

2 Lift off the top of the body shell. Scoop out the gray-green liver (tomalley) and any coral-colored roe, both of which are edible, and reserve. Discard the stomach and spongy gills ("dead man's fingers").

To serve in the shell

1 Use a sharp, heavy knife to split the lobster in half lengthwise, cutting from the head to the tail. Pull the halves apart.

4 Bend back the flaps and carefully remove the tail meat, keeping it in one piece. Remove and discard the intestinal tract that runs through the center of the tail meat. Slice the tail meat, or prepare as required, and serve with the claw and leg meat.

3 With scissors or a sharp knife, cut along the soft underside of the tail.

2 Scoop out the liver and roe, and discard the intestine. Twist off the legs and claws (remove the meat). Loosen the meat in the shell.

PREPARING OYSTERS

To shuck oysters, use an oyster knife or other small, sturdy knife.

Hold oyster round-side down and insert the knife near the hinge. Lever the shells apart. Slide in the knife to sever the top muscle. Lift off the shell. Run the knife under the oyster to loosen it.

PREPARING A SQUID

Once cleaned, fresh squid yields a tube-like body, which can be stuffed or sliced, and separate tentacles. You can buy it already cleaned or do this yourself as shown here.

1 Pull the head and tentacles away from the body (the innards will come away with the head as will the long, narrow ink sac if it is present). Cut off the tentacles, just in front of the eyes.

2 Squeeze the tentacles near the cut end so that the hard beak can be removed. Discard it. Rinse the tentacles well and set aside. Discard the head and innards (and the ink sac unless using it in a sauce).

3 Peel the skin from the body. Pull the long piece of cartilage (quill) out of the body and discard. Rinse the body thoroughly, inside and out, and pull off the two flaps (slice these for cooking).

SHRIMP TACOS

SERVES 4

2 tbsp sunflower oil

2 onions, chopped

3 garlic cloves, minced

1 green bell pepper, halved, seeded, and diced

1 tbsp paprika

2 tsp chili powder

1/2 tsp ground cumin

4 ripe, firm tomatoes, chopped

1 lb (500 g) cooked peeled shrimp

2 tbsp chopped fresh cilantro

salt and black pepper

12 taco shells

1 head butter lettuce, shredded

sliced pickled jalapeños, large cooked peeled shrimp, and cilantro leaves for garnish

1 Heat the oil in a large frying pan, add the onions, and cook gently, stirring from time to time, for 3–5 minutes until softened but not colored. Add the garlic and diced green bell pepper, and cook, stirring occasionally, for 3 minutes or until the pepper is soft.

2 Stir in the paprika, chili powder, and cumin, and cook, stirring, for 1 minute. Add the tomatoes and cook for 3–5 minutes until soft.

3 Lower the heat and stir in the shrimp and chopped cilantro. Season with salt and pepper.

4 Meanwhile, heat the taco shells in a preheated oven at 350°F (180°C) according to package directions.

5 Spoon the shrimp mixture into the taco shells, top with the shredded lettuce, and garnish with jalapeños, large shrimp, and cilantro leaves. Serve at once.

Healthy note

Shrimp, like most shellfish, are a healthy food low in calories and fat. They are rich in the antioxidant selenium, which is linked to a healthy heart and circulation, and they are also a good source of iodine, zinc, and calcium.

TIGER SHRIMP WITH TARRAGON SAUCE

SERVES 4

12 raw tiger shrimp in shell

olive oil for brushing

1 1/4 cups (300 ml) dry white wine

1 garlic clove, minced

4 tbsp chopped parsley

lemon and tarragon for garnish

TARRAGON SAUCE

2/3 cup (150 ml) sour cream

4 tbsp chopped fresh tarragon

1 tsp Dijon mustard

squeeze of lemon juice

salt and black pepper

1 Make the tarragon sauce: Combine the sour cream, tarragon, mustard, and lemon juice, and season with salt and pepper.

2 Heat a heavy frying pan. Brush the shrimp with oil, add to the pan, and cook over a high heat for 2 minutes or until the shrimp turn pink.

3 Keeping the heat high, add half of the wine and the garlic. Boil rapidly for 2–3 minutes, then stir in 2 tbsp of the parsley.

4 When the wine has reduced slightly, lower the heat and add the remaining wine. Season with salt and pepper. Simmer for 5 minutes or until the shrimp have released their juices into the wine.

5 To serve, spoon the cooking juices over the shrimp, sprinkle with the remaining parsley, and garnish with lemon and sprigs of fresh tarragon. Accompany with the tarragon sauce.

MEDITERRANEAN STUFFED SQUID

SERVES 4

8 small, whole squid, cleaned (page 125)

2 tbsp (30 g) butter, plus a little extra for frying

1 large onion, minced

2 garlic cloves, minced

1 1/3 cups (60 g) fine fresh bread crumbs

1 tbsp chopped fresh dill weed

1 tbsp chopped parsley

salt and black pepper

lemon slices and chopped parsley for serving

1 Chop the squid tentacles roughly and set aside.

2 Make the stuffing: Melt the butter in a frying pan, add the onion and garlic, cover, and cook over a low heat for about 15–20 minutes until very soft.

3 Add the chopped squid tentacles, bread crumbs, dill, and parsley to the onion and garlic, and fry over a high heat for 2–3 minutes. Season with salt and pepper. Let cool.

4 Fill the squid bodies with the cold stuffing, and secure the tops (see box, below).

5 Heat a little butter in a clean frying pan and fry the stuffed squid for 4–5 minutes until golden brown all over and firm to the touch, and the filling is heated through.

6 Garnish the squid with lemon slices and parsley, and serve at once.

Securing the squid

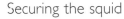

Thread a wooden toothpick through the top of each stuffed squid to secure the opening.

THAI SHRIMP STIR-FRY

SERVES 4

8 oz (250 g) rice noodles

salt

3 tbsp sunflower oil

1 red bell pepper, halved, seeded, and cut into thin strips

1 carrot, cut into thin strips

1 fresh, hot green chili pepper, halved, seeded, and cut into thin strips

1-in (2.5-cm) piece of fresh ginger, peeled and cut into thin strips

1 garlic clove, minced

8 green onions, sliced

2 lemon grass stalks, trimmed and sliced

1 lb (500 g) cooked peeled tiger or jumbo shrimp

2 tbsp white wine vinegar

2 tbsp soy sauce

juice of 1/2 lime

1 tbsp toasted sesame oil

3 tbsp chopped fresh cilantro for garnish

1 Put the rice noodles into a large saucepan of boiling salted water and stir to separate the noodles. Remove from the heat, cover, and let stand for 4 minutes. Drain well and set aside.

2 Heat 1 tbsp of the sunflower oil in a wok or large frying pan. Add the red pepper, carrot, chili pepper, ginger, garlic, green onions, and lemon grass, and stir-fry over a high heat for 2 minutes.

3 Add the shrimp and stir-fry for 1 minute, then stir in the noodles.

4 Add the remaining sunflower oil, the vinegar, soy sauce, lime juice, and sesame oil, and stir-fry for 1 minute.

5 Sprinkle with the chopped fresh cilantro, and serve at once.

SCALLOP STIR-FRY

Substitute 1 lb (500 g) sea scallops for the tiger shrimp, cutting each scallop into two or three pieces if they are very large. Stir-fry for about 2 minutes, then add the red bell pepper, carrot, chili pepper, fresh ginger, garlic, green onions, and lemon grass, and stir-fry for a further 2 minutes. Add the soaked and drained noodles, then continue with the recipe from the beginning of step 4.

DEVILED CRAB

SERVES 4

5 tbsp (75 g) butter

1 1/2 tbsp all-purpose flour

3/4 cup (175 ml) milk

1/4 tsp mustard powder

1/4 tsp grated nutmeg

1 egg yolk

1 1/2 tbsp dry sherry

1 tsp Worcestershire sauce

2–3 dashes of hot pepper sauce

1 lb (500 g) cooked crabmeat

1 green onion, thinly sliced

salt and black pepper

2 3/4 cups (125 g) fresh bread crumbs

paprika and minced green onions for garnish

1 Melt 3 tbsp (45 g) of the butter in a saucepan, add the flour, and cook, stirring, for 1 minute. Remove from the heat, and gradually blend in the milk. Bring to a boil, stirring constantly until the mixture thickens. Simmer for 2–3 minutes. Remove from the heat and stir in the mustard and nutmeg.

2 Put the egg yolk into a small bowl and whisk in a little of the sauce. Stir this mixture back into the sauce in the pan.

3 Add the dry sherry, Worcestershire sauce, hot pepper sauce, crabmeat, green onion, and salt and pepper to taste, and stir to mix. Spoon the mixture into 4 cleaned crab shells, or into ramekins, and set them on a baking sheet.

4 Melt the remaining butter in a saucepan, add the bread crumbs, and cook, stirring, for 5 minutes or until golden brown.

5 Spoon the buttered crumbs over the crabmeat mixture. Bake in a preheated oven at 400°F (200°C) for 10 minutes or until the tops are browned and bubbling. Sprinkle with paprika and minced green onions before serving.

LOBSTER TAILS WITH MANGO & LIME

SERVES 4

4 cooked rock lobster tails

6 tbsp dry white wine

1 cup (250 ml) heavy cream

1 small mango, peeled, pitted, and cut into cubes (page 430)

grated zest and juice of 1 lime

1/4 cup (30 g) grated Parmesan cheese

1 Remove the meat from the lobster tails (see box, below), then cut each piece of lobster meat in half lengthwise. Arrange the pieces of lobster meat, cut-side up, in a large, shallow baking dish.

2 Pour the white wine into a small saucepan and boil rapidly until it has reduced to about 2 tbsp.

3 Add the cream to the saucepan and boil until the mixture has reduced to a coating consistency. Stir in the mango cubes and grated lime zest and juice.

4 Spoon the mixture over the lobster in the dish. Sprinkle with the Parmesan cheese and bake in a preheated oven at 425°F (220°C) for about 20 minutes or until hot and bubbling. Serve hot.

Removing the meat from a lobster tail

Hold the tail in one hand. With a pair of scissors, cut along both sides of the underside of the shell, toward the end, without damaging the meat.

Pull back the underside of the shell, and lift out the lobster meat, making sure it is all in one piece.

LOBSTER TAILS WITH BLACK BEAN SALSA

SERVES 4

4 cooked rock lobster tails

lime twists and cilantro sprigs for garnish

BLACK BEAN SALSA

4 ripe but firm tomatoes, minced

1 small onion, chopped

1 garlic clove, minced

1 fresh, mild green chili pepper, halved, seeded, and chopped

2 tbsp chopped fresh cilantro

14 oz (400 g) canned black beans, drained

salt and black pepper

GARLIC BUTTER

2/3 cup (150 g) butter

5 garlic cloves, minced

2 tsp minced fresh oregano

1 Make the black bean salsa: In a bowl, combine the tomatoes, onion, garlic, chili pepper, and cilantro. Add the beans, and season with salt and pepper to taste.

2 With a sharp knife, cut each lobster tail in half lengthwise and loosen the meat, keeping it in the shell.

3 Make the garlic butter: Cream the butter in a bowl, add the garlic, oregano, and salt and pepper to taste, and mix well. Spread half of the butter mixture over the lobster meat.

4 Place the lobster under the broiler, 4 in (10 cm) from the heat. Broil for 5 minutes or until slightly browned in patches and heated through.

5 Spread the lobster with the remaining garlic butter, then garnish with lime twists and cilantro sprigs. Serve hot, with the black bean salsa.

Healthy option

Instead of garlic butter, drizzle the lobster with a little olive oil, either plain or flavored with garlic and herbs. Or, use a chili-flavored oil, which would also work well.

SEAFOOD & AVOCADO SALAD

SERVES 4

1 lb (500 g) monkfish fillets, trimmed and skinned

2/3 cup (150 ml) fish stock

1 slice of onion

6 black peppercorns

squeeze of lemon juice

1 bay leaf

mixed salad leaves, such as curly endive, radicchio, and arugula

2 avocados

lemon juice for brushing

2 large tomatoes, peeled (page 57), seeded, and cut into strips

4 oz (125 g) cooked peeled shrimp

3/4 cup (90 g) cooked crabmeat

flat-leaf parsley for garnish

CREME FRAICHE DRESSING

1/2 cup (125 ml) crème fraîche

3 tbsp lemon juice

salt and black pepper

1 Put the monkfish into a saucepan with the stock, onion, peppercorns, lemon juice, and bay leaf. Bring to a gentle simmer, cover, and poach very gently, turning once, for 10 minutes until opaque throughout and firm.

2 Remove the pan from the heat and let the fish cool in the liquid, then lift it out and cut into bite-sized pieces.

3 Make the crème fraîche dressing: Put the crème fraîche and lemon juice into a bowl, add salt and pepper to taste, and stir to mix.

4 To serve, arrange the salad leaves on individual plates. Halve, pit (page 88), and peel the avocados, and brush with lemon juice. Slice lengthwise and arrange in a fan shape on the leaves. Add the strips of tomato, the monkfish, shrimp, and crabmeat. Spoon the crème fraîche dressing over the salad, garnish with parsley, and serve at once.

Healthy option

You can use reduced-fat sour cream (light sour cream or nonfat sour cream) for the dressing, because it is cold — lower fat sour creams have a tendency to separate if they are heated.

SCALLOPS WITH ASPARAGUS & LEMON

SERVES 6

1 lb (500 g) fresh asparagus tips, cut into 1-in (2.5-cm) lengths

4 tbsp (60 g) butter

1 lb (500 g) bay scallops

3 garlic cloves, minced

juice of 1 lemon

2 tbsp minced parsley

1 tbsp chopped fresh tarragon

salt and black pepper

1 Blanch the asparagus in boiling salted water for about 2 minutes, then drain and refresh in cold water to stop the cooking and set the bright green color.

2 Melt half the butter in a frying pan and fry the scallops for about 30 seconds on each side until just opaque and firm to the touch (you may need to do this in batches). Remove the scallops with a slotted spoon and keep warm.

3 Heat the remaining butter in the frying pan. Add the garlic, lemon juice, parsley, and tarragon, and season with salt and pepper.

4 Return the scallops and asparagus to the pan, and heat them through very gently, shaking the pan to coat them in the sauce. Serve hot.

Cook's know-how

If bay scallops are not available, use the larger sea scallops instead. Slice each one in half horizontally, and they will then cook in the same amount of time. If scallops are not available at all, or if you prefer, you can substitute an equal quantity of raw tiger shrimp. Peel them, but leave the tails on for a decorative touch.

SCALLOPS WITH SPICY CASHEW SAUCE

SERVES 6

2/3 cup (100 g) toasted, salted cashew nuts

3 tbsp sunflower oil

3 garlic cloves, minced

1 lb (500 g) sea scallops

1 onion, chopped

1 green bell pepper, halved, seeded, and cut into thin strips

1 fresh, hot red chili pepper, halved, seeded, and minced

1/2 tsp turmeric

1 cup (250 ml) fish stock

1 tsp grain mustard

salt and black pepper

1 Grind the cashew nuts in a food processor or nut grinder until smooth.

2 Heat the oil in a large frying pan, add the garlic and scallops, and stir-fry for 2 minutes or just until the scallops turn opaque. Remove with a slotted spoon.

3 Add the onion, green bell pepper, and chili pepper to the frying pan, and cook gently, stirring occasionally, for 3–5 minutes until the onion is soft but not colored. Add the turmeric and cook, stirring, for 1 minute.

4 Add the ground cashew nuts and stock to the mixture in the frying pan. Bring to a boil and simmer for 5–10 minutes until the sauce thickens.

5 Stir the scallops into the sauce, add the mustard, and season with salt and pepper. Gently warm through. Serve hot.

Cook's know-how

If you are short of time, instead of grinding the cashews in step 1, use 2 heaped tablespoons of cashew nut butter or peanut butter (smooth or crunchy).

MUSSEL GRATIN

SERVES 4

2/3 cup (150 ml) dry white wine

1 shallot, minced

1 garlic clove, minced

6 lb (3 kg) large mussels, cleaned (page 124)

1 1/4 cups (300 ml) light cream

3 tbsp chopped parsley

salt and black pepper

2/3 cup (30 g) fresh white bread crumbs

2 tbsp (30 g) butter, melted

1 Pour the wine into a large saucepan, add the minced shallot and garlic, and bring to a boil. Simmer for 2 minutes.

2 Add the mussels, cover tightly, and return to a boil. Cook, shaking the pan frequently, for 5–6 minutes until the mussels open.

3 Using a slotted spoon, transfer the mussels to a large bowl. Discard any that have not opened; do not try to force them open.

4 Strain the cooking liquid into another saucepan, bring to a boil, and simmer until reduced to about 3 tbsp. Add the cream and heat through. Stir in half of the parsley, and season with salt and pepper.

5 Remove the top shell of each mussel and discard. Arrange the mussels, in their bottom shells, on a large, oven-to-table serving dish.

6 Spoon the sauce over the mussels and sprinkle with the bread crumbs and melted butter. Cook under the broiler, 4 in (10 cm) from the heat, for 3–5 minutes until golden. Garnish with the remaining parsley and serve at once.

Cook's know-how

The common or blue (actually black) mussel is found along both the Atlantic and Pacific coasts of the North America.

MUSSELS WITH POTATOES & CHORIZO

SERVES 6

2 tbsp olive oil

2 large potatoes, diced

12 oz (375 g) smoked chorizo sausage, diced

3 garlic cloves, minced

1/2 cup (125 ml) fish stock

4 tbsp dry sherry or white wine

about 2 dozen large mussels, cleaned (page 124)

salt and black pepper

chopped flat-leaf parsley for garnish

1 Heat the olive oil in a large saucepan, add the potatoes, and cook gently, stirring from time to time, for 12–15 minutes until golden and softened. Add the chorizo sausage and garlic, and cook, stirring constantly, for about 2 minutes.

2 Add the fish stock, sherry or wine, and mussels, and season with salt and pepper. Cover the pan tightly and bring to a boil. Cook, shaking the pan frequently, for 5–8 minutes or until the mussels have opened.

3 Discard any mussels that have not opened; do not try to force them open.

4 Transfer the mussel, potato, and chorizo mixture to a large serving dish, and pour the cooking juices over. Serve hot, garnished with parsley.

Healthy option

Mussels, potatoes, and chorizo make a delicious combination, popular in traditional Spanish cooking. Chorizo gives this dish its characteristic russet color, but it is a fatty sausage so you may prefer to use less – just 4 oz (125 g) will give some color and flavor, and you could make up the remaining weight by adding frozen lima beans in step 2.

SPICY CLAMS WITH CILANTRO PESTO

SERVES 4–6

4 tbsp olive oil

6 ripe, firm tomatoes, diced

4 garlic cloves, minced

1 tbsp chili powder

about 4 dozen littleneck clams, cleaned (page 106)

2 1/2 cups (600 ml) fish stock, or 1 1/4 cups (300 ml) each dry white wine and fish stock

juice of 1/2 lime

CILANTRO PESTO

12 cilantro sprigs

2 tbsp olive oil

1 large garlic clove, roughly chopped

1 fresh, mild green chili pepper, halved, seeded, and chopped

salt and black pepper

1 Make the cilantro pesto: Strip the cilantro leaves from the stems. Purée the cilantro leaves, olive oil, garlic, and chili pepper in a food processor or blender until smooth. Season with salt and pepper, and set aside.

2 Heat the oil in a large saucepan, add the tomatoes, garlic, and chili powder, and cook gently, stirring from time to time, for 8 minutes or until slightly thickened.

3 Add the clams and stir for about 1 minute, then pour in the stock. Cover the pan tightly and cook over a medium heat, shaking the pan frequently, for 5–8 minutes until the clams open. Discard any that have not opened; do not try to force them open.

4 Using a slotted spoon, transfer the clams to a warmed bowl.

5 Pour the cooking juices into a small pan and boil until reduced by about half. Add the lime juice and season to taste, then pour the sauce over the clams.

6 Serve the clams hot, topped with the cilantro pesto.

STEAMED CLAMS WITH PARSLEY

SERVES 4

about 3 dozen littleneck clams, cleaned (page 124)

1 tbsp (15 g) butter

2 onions, coarsely chopped

2 garlic cloves, minced

1 1/4 cups (300 ml) dry white wine

2/3 cup (150 ml) water

2 tbsp (30 g) butter

about 6 tbsp chopped parsley

1 Melt the butter in a large, deep saucepan. Add the onions and garlic, and fry for 2–3 minutes.

2 Pour in the wine and water, and add 2 tbsp of the parsley. Add the clams, cover the pan, and bring to a boil. Cook, shaking the pan, for about 12 minutes until the clams open. Discard any that have not opened; do not try to force them open.

3 Using a slotted spoon, transfer the clams to a warmed bowl or serving dish.

4 Bring the sauce to a boil, then whisk in the remaining butter and parsley.

5 Pour the sauce over the clams, and serve them immediately.

Cook's know-how

Hardshell clams come in different sizes. On the East Coast, the smallest are littlenecks (with a shell diameter less than 2 in/5 cm); the next are medium-sized cherrystones, and the largest are chowder clams (at least 3 in/7 cm shell diameter). On the West Coast. there are also littlenecks, as well as small butter clams and big Pismos (5 in/12 cm shells). This recipe is also suitable for cherrystones and for mussels.

OYSTER STEW WITH PERNOD & SAFFRON

SERVES 4

12 oysters in their shells

1 1/2 cups (375 ml) light cream

1 cup (250 ml) dry white wine

1 cup (250 ml) fish stock

1 small bulb of fennel, trimmed and minced

1 small carrot, diced

1/4 cup (30 g) chopped watercress leaves

2 tbsp Pernod or vermouth

1 tbsp lemon juice

pinch of saffron threads (optional)

pinch of cayenne pepper (optional)

salt

chervil sprigs for garnish

1 Shuck the oysters (page 125). Strain the liquid from the shells into a measuring cup. Set aside.

2 Put the cream, wine, stock, leek, and carrot into a saucepan and bring to a boil. Simmer for 7–10 minutes until the vegetables are just tender.

3 Add the oyster liquid to the pan with the watercress, Pernod or vermouth, lemon juice, saffron, and cayenne pepper (if using). Season with salt. Bring to a boil, then add the oysters and simmer until the oysters are just heated through and curling slightly at the edges. Serve at once, garnished with chervil sprigs.

CHINESE-STYLE OYSTERS

SERVES 4

8 bacon slices, cut crosswise in half

3 1/2 oz (100 g) canned smoked oysters, drained

1 small green bell pepper, halved, seeded, and cut into bite-sized pieces

1 garlic clove, minced

1 1/3 cups (250 g) canned water chestnuts, drained

1 green onion, thinly sliced

lemon wedges and hot pepper sauce for serving

Healthy note

Oysters are rich in zinc and iron, two minerals that are essential in a healthy diet.

1 Wrap half a bacon slice around each oyster and fasten securely with a wooden toothpick.

2 Heat a frying pan, add the bacon-wrapped oysters, and cook gently for 6–8 minutes until browned and crisp. Add the green pepper, garlic, and water chestnuts, and stir-fry over a high heat for 2 minutes.

3 Sprinkle with the green onion slices, and serve with lemon wedges and hot pepper sauce.

SIMPLE FISH SUSHI

Making your own sushi is easy as long as you keep it simple, as here. The three different
types of sushi shown are made from one batch of rice and just a few ingredients in addition to the fish.
Presented in a stylish way, the finished result is stunning.

HOSO MAKI

MAKES 20

2 sheets of nori (dried Japanese seaweed)

a bowl of vinegar water (see box, in third
column)

prepared Simple Sushi Rice (see recipe, bottom
of next column)

a little wasabi (Japanese horseradish paste)

1½ cups (175 g) cooked or drained, canned
crabmeat, flaked

½ hothouse cucumber, halved lengthwise,
seeded, and cut into long, thin strips

BAMBOO ROLLING MAT

1 Lay the rolling mat on a flat surface
with one of the longest sides nearest to
you. Lay one sheet of nori shiny side down
on the mat.

2 Dip your hand in vinegar water, take a
handful of the sushi rice, and spread it
over the nori, leaving a 1-in (2.5-cm) gap
along the edge farthest away from you.

3 Spread a thin layer of wasabi – about
½ in (1 cm) wide – lengthwise along
the middle of the rice (from left to right).
Cover the wasabi with half the crab, then
put a strip of cucumber on either side of
the crab.

4 Moisten the uncovered edge of the nori
with a little cold water. Using the mat
and starting from the side nearest to you,
roll the rice in the nori, squeezing it to
make a tight roll. Seal the moistened edge
around the roll, then wrap in plastic wrap.
Make a second roll in the same way.

5 To serve, unwrap the rolls and cut each
one into 10 pieces using a very sharp
knife that has been dipped in cold water
(trim off the ends first so you get neat
slices).

SUSHI SQUARES WITH SMOKED SALMON

MAKES 40

a bowl of vinegar water (see box, next column)

prepared Simple Sushi Rice (see recipe, below)

4 thin slices of smoked salmon

a few strips of sushi pickled ginger (gari), from a
jar

13- x 9-IN (32.5- x 23-CM) JELLY ROLL PAN

1 Line the jelly roll pan with plastic wrap
(if you don't have a pan of about this
size, cover a chopping board with plastic
wrap). Dip your hand in vinegar water,
take a handful of the sushi rice, and press it
into the pan, patting it level with your
hand. Repeat with more handfuls of rice
until the pan is full. Refrigerate for about
15 minutes until firm.

2 Turn the pan upside-down onto a
board and remove the plastic wrap. Cut
into about 40 small squares with a very
sharp, wet knife. Cut the smoked salmon
into little strips to fit on each square and
top with a little pickled ginger.

SIMPLE SUSHI RICE

1 lb (500 g) sushi rice (2½ cups)

4 tbsp rice wine vinegar

4 tbsp Japanese rice wine (mirin or sake)

¼ tsp salt

1 Put the rice in a strainer and rinse
under cold running water. Tip it into a
saucepan and pour in 3 cups (750 ml) cold
water. Bring to a boil, then lower the heat
and simmer, covered, for 15 minutes or
until all the water has been absorbed.

2 Remove the pan from the heat and
cover it immediately with a dish towel
and lid (this is to make sure no steam can
escape). Leave for about 10 minutes.

3 Mix together the vinegar, rice wine, and
salt in a small bowl, then fold gently
into the rice. Continue to cut and fold
through the rice while cooling with a fan or
a piece of cardboard (it is important to cool
the rice quickly so that it remains sticky).

NIGIRI SUSHI

MAKES 10

10 raw tiger shrimp in shell

salt

a little wasabi

a bowl of vinegar water (see box, below)

prepared Simple Sushi Rice (see recipe, previous
column)

10 SMALL METAL SKEWERS

1 Push a skewer lengthwise through each
shrimp so the shrimp becomes straight.
Boil for 1–2 minutes in salted water until
pink, then drain and let cool. Remove the
skewers and gently peel the shrimp, leaving
the tails intact.

2 Make a slit down the length of the belly
of each shrimp (without cutting right
through) and gently open out the shrimp.
Remove the black vein from the back.

3 Using your finger, spread a little wasabi
along the middle of the slit in the belly.
Dip your hand in vinegar water and take a
small amount of rice, about the size of a
small walnut. Shape the rice with your
hand (it will be very sticky) so that it fills
the slit on top of the wasabi, then reshape
the shrimp around the rice by squeezing.
Turn the right way up to serve.

Cook's know-how

The secret of good sushi is to make a
good sticky rice, which is very simple.
Directions are usually on the package;
the recipe here includes a little rice wine
for sweetness, plus a little salt.

To stop the rice sticking to your hand
you will need a bowl of vinegar water
(water with a little vinegar added).

Always use sushi rice on the day it is
made. After you have made all the
sushi, you can refrigerate them for up
to 24 hours until ready to serve.

CLOCKWISE FROM TOP: Nigiri Sushi, Hoso Maki,
Sushi Squares with Smoked Salmon.

134

HOT & SOUR MACKEREL

SERVES 4

2 carrots

1 red bell pepper, seeded

1 fresh, hot green chili pepper, halved and seeded

6 garlic cloves

8 green onions

1 lemon grass stalk, slit lengthwise and bruised

2 tbsp sunflower oil

4 mackerel fillets, 6 oz (175 g) each

cilantro sprigs for garnish

HOT AND SOUR SAUCE

4 tbsp Thai fish sauce or light soy sauce

4 tbsp cider vinegar, white wine vinegar, or rice vinegar

2 tbsp lime juice

2 tbsp sugar

1 Make the hot and sour sauce: In a small bowl, combine the fish sauce, vinegar, lime juice, and sugar.

2 Cut the carrots, bell pepper, chili pepper, and garlic into matchstick-thin strips. Slice the green onions.

3 Line the broiler pan with foil. Arrange the mackerel on the foil and cook under the broiler, 4 in (10 cm) from the heat, for 3 minutes on each side. Continue to broil until the fish is opaque and will flake easily.

4 Meanwhile, stir-fry the vegetables: Heat the sunflower oil in a wok or large frying pan. Add the carrots, bell and chili peppers, garlic, green onions, and lemon grass, and stir-fry over a high heat for 3 minutes or until the vegetables are just tender.

5 Remove and discard the lemon grass. Arrange the vegetable mixture on top of the fish, pour the sauce over, and garnish with cilantro sprigs.

MACKEREL WITH GREEN GRAPE SAUCE

SERVES 4

4 whole mackerel, 8 oz (250 g) each, cleaned and heads removed (page 122)

salt and black pepper

GREEN GRAPE SAUCE

2 cups (375 g) tart green grapes

2 tbsp water

2 tbsp sugar

2 tbsp (30 g) butter

1/2 tsp ground ginger

1 Cut the fins off the mackerel and make 3–4 diagonal cuts on both sides of each fish. Season the mackerel inside and out with salt and pepper.

2 Make the green grape sauce: Put the grapes into a saucepan with the water and sugar. Cover tightly and simmer very gently, shaking the pan occasionally, for 5 minutes or until tender.

3 Reserve 12 of the cooked grapes for garnish, then press the remainder through a nylon strainer. Beat in the butter and ginger. Return the sauce to the pan and keep warm.

4 Cook the mackerel under the broiler, 4 in (10 cm) from the heat, for 7–8 minutes on each side until the fish is opaque and will flake easily.

5 Serve the mackerel hot, garnished with the reserved whole grapes. Pass the sauce separately.

MACKEREL WITH CRANBERRY SAUCE

Substitute 2 cups (375 g) fresh cranberries for the grapes. You can use frozen cranberries too, but they will take slightly longer to cook – simmer them until they pop open.

HERRING WITH AN OAT CRUST

SERVES 4

1¹/₃ cups (125 g) rolled oats

2 tsp mustard powder

salt and black pepper

4 fresh whole herring, 6–8 oz (175–250 g) each, cleaned and "butterflied" (page 122)

8 parsley sprigs

parsley and lemon wedges for garnish

1 Work the rolled oats in a food processor until reduced to a fine meal. In a shallow dish, combine the oat meal, mustard powder, and salt and pepper to taste.

2 Open out the herring and press them into the oat-meal mixture to coat well on both sides.

3 Cook the herring under the broiler, 4 in (10 cm) from the heat, for 4 minutes on each side or until the fish is opaque and will flake easily.

4 Arrange the herring on a warmed serving platter and garnish with parsley and lemon wedges.

Healthy note

Herring are an inexpensive oily fish, and enjoying oily fish regularly (once a week) is one of the best ways to eat for good health. This is because they contain omega-3 fatty acids, which help discourage heart disease and blood clots. Herring also provide vitamin D, which is good for healthy bones, teeth, nerves, and muscles.

HERRING WITH MUSTARD SAUCE

SERVES 4

4 fresh whole herring, 6–8 oz (175–250 g) each, cleaned and boned (page 122)

salt and black pepper

butter for greasing

lemon wedges and parsley sprigs for garnish

MUSTARD SAUCE

2 tbsp (30 g) butter

2 tbsp all-purpose flour

1¹/₄ cups (300 ml) milk

2 tsp mustard powder

1 tsp sugar

2 tsp white wine vinegar

1 Season the herring inside and out with salt and black pepper. Reshape the fish and place side by side in a buttered baking dish.

2 Cover and bake in a preheated oven at 400°F (200°C) for 12 minutes or until the fish is opaque and will flake easily.

3 Meanwhile, make the mustard sauce: Melt the butter in a saucepan, add the flour, and cook, stirring, for 1 minute. Remove from the heat and gradually blend in the milk. Bring to a boil, stirring constantly until the mixture thickens. Simmer for 2–3 minutes. Add the mustard powder, sugar, and vinegar, and season with salt and pepper. Cook for a further minute.

4 To serve, garnish the herring with lemon wedges and parsley sprigs. Pass the mustard sauce separately.

Healthy option

Instead of the mustard sauce, make a quick, cold sauce by mixing a teaspoonful or two of Dijon mustard and a squeeze of lemon juice into your favorite reduced-fat mayonnaise or into light or nonfat sour cream.

BROILED TROUT WITH CUCUMBER & DILL

SERVES 4

1 hothouse cucumber, peeled

2 tbsp (30 g) butter

small bunch of dill weed, chopped

salt and black pepper

juice of 1 lemon

4 whole trout, 12–14 oz (375–400 g) each, cleaned (page 122)

dill weed and chives for garnish

dill-cream sauce (page 148) for serving

1 Cut the cucumber in half lengthwise and scoop out the seeds, then cut the flesh across into 1/4-in (5-mm) slices. Melt the butter in a saucepan, add the cucumber, and cook gently for 2 minutes.

2 In a bowl, combine two-thirds of the cooked cucumber with the chopped dill, season with salt and pepper, and sprinkle with the lemon juice. Stuff the trout with the mixture.

3 Line the broiler pan with foil. Arrange the trout on the foil and put the remaining cucumber around them.

4 Cook the trout under the broiler, 4 in (10 cm) from the heat, for 4–7 minutes on each side until the flesh will flake easily.

5 Garnish the trout with dill sprigs and chives, and serve with the extra cucumber and the dill-cream sauce.

TROUT WITH ALMONDS

Dip the trout in seasoned flour. Melt 4 tbsp (60 g) butter in a large frying pan and cook the trout, in batches if necessary, for 6–8 minutes on each side until the fish is opaque and will flake easily. Drain on paper towels and keep warm. Wipe out the pan, then melt 1 tbsp (15 g) butter in it and fry 2/3 cup (60 g) sliced almonds until lightly browned. Add a squeeze of lemon juice, then pour the lemon and almond mixture over the trout. Serve at once.

BAKED TROUT WITH ORANGE

SERVES 4

4 whole trout, 12–14 oz (375–400 g) each, cleaned (page 122)

4 large thyme sprigs

4 large parsley sprigs

2 cups (125 g) sliced button mushrooms

2 shallots, chopped

4 tbsp white wine vinegar

grated zest and juice of 1 orange

salt and black pepper

orange and thyme for garnish

1 With a sharp knife, make 2 diagonal cuts through the skin and into the flesh on both sides of each trout.

2 Strip the thyme and parsley leaves from their stems. In a bowl, combine the mushrooms, shallots, vinegar, orange zest and juice, thyme, parsley, and salt and pepper to taste.

3 Reserve one-fourth of the mushroom and herb mixture to spoon over the stuffed trout.

4 Stuff the trout with the remaining mushroom and herb mixture (see box, below).

5 Arrange the trout in a non-metallic baking dish and spoon the reserved mushroom mixture over them. Cover and marinate in the refrigerator for up to 4 hours.

6 Bake in a preheated oven at 350°F (180°C) for 20–25 minutes until the fish is opaque and will flake easily. Garnish with orange and thyme before serving.

Stuffing the trout

Hold each fish open and spoon in an equal portion of the mushroom and herb mixture, then press firmly closed.

TUNA WITH FENNEL & TOMATO RELISH

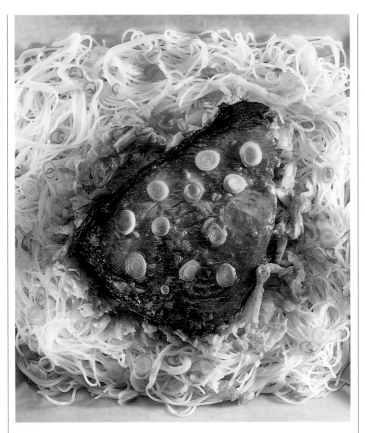

TUNA TERIYAKI

SERVES 4

4 tuna steaks, about 1 in (2.5 cm) thick, 6 oz (175 g) each

2 green onions, thinly sliced, for garnish

MARINADE

3 tbsp dark soy sauce

2 tbsp toasted sesame oil

1 tbsp Japanese rice wine or sweet sherry

3 garlic cloves, chopped

1 tbsp sugar

1/2-in (1-cm) piece of fresh ginger, peeled and grated

1 Make the marinade: Put the soy sauce, sesame oil, rice wine, garlic, sugar, and ginger into a non-metallic dish. Add the tuna steaks to the marinade and turn to coat. Cover the dish and let marinate in the refrigerator for up to 4 hours.

2 Reserve the marinade. Cook the steaks under the broiler, 3 in (7 cm) from the heat, for 3–4 minutes on each side; brush regularly with the marinade. Serve at once, garnished with green onions.

GRILLED SALMON TERIYAKI

Cut 4 salmon fillets into 1-in (2.5-cm) cubes and marinate in the refrigerator for up to 4 hours, as in step 1, then thread onto metal skewers. Grill over hot coals, turning and brushing frequently with the marinade, for 6–8 minutes.

Healthy note

Fresh ginger, a key ingredient in Asian cooking, is known to have healing properties. It helps stimulate the circulation, fights coughs and colds, and soothes indigestion. It may also relieve rheumatism.

SERVES 4

4 tbsp olive oil

juice of 1/2 lemon

3 garlic cloves, minced

4 tuna steaks, about 1 in (2.5 cm) thick, 6 oz (175 g) each

salt and black pepper

lime wedges and fennel tops for garnish

FENNEL AND TOMATO RELISH

1 small fennel bulb, chopped

2 ripe but firm tomatoes, minced

2 tbsp olive oil

1 tbsp lemon juice

1 tbsp tapenade (see box, right)

1 garlic clove, chopped

1 Combine the olive oil, lemon juice, and garlic in a large, non-metallic dish. Add the tuna steaks and turn to coat. Cover the dish and let marinate in the refrigerator, turning occasionally, for about 1 hour.

2 Meanwhile, make the relish: Put the fennel, tomatoes, olive oil, lemon juice, tapenade, and garlic into a bowl and stir well to combine.

3 Remove the tuna from the marinade, reserving the marinade. Cook the tuna under the broiler, 3 in (7 cm) from the heat, for 3–4 minutes on each side, basting once or twice with the reserved marinade.

4 Season the tuna with salt and pepper, and top with the fennel and tomato relish. Garnish with lime wedges and fennel tops before serving.

Cook's know-how

Tapenade comes from Provence in the south of France. It is a tangy paste made of typical Provençal ingredients: black olives, anchovies, capers, and fruity olive oil. It is sold in tubes, jars, and tubs in supermarkets.

SWORDFISH WITH ORANGE RELISH

SERVES 4

4 swordfish steaks, 6 oz (175 g) each

MARINADE

3 tbsp olive oil

juice of 1 orange

juice of 1 lemon

3 garlic cloves, minced

salt and black pepper

ORANGE RELISH

2 oranges, peeled and diced

3 tbsp olive oil

2 tbsp chopped fresh basil

1 Make the marinade: In a shallow, non-metallic dish, combine the olive oil, orange and lemon juices, and garlic, and season with salt and pepper. Turn the swordfish steaks in the marinade, cover, and let marinate in the refrigerator for about 1 hour.

2 Make the orange relish: In a bowl, combine the oranges, olive oil, and basil, and season with salt and pepper to taste.

3 Remove the swordfish from the marinade, reserving the marinade. Place the steaks under the broiler, 3 in (7 cm) from the heat, and cook, basting once or twice with the marinade, for 5 minutes on each side or until the flesh is opaque and will flake easily. Serve hot, with the relish.

TUNA WITH ORANGE RELISH

Substitute tuna steaks for the swordfish steaks, and fresh cilantro for the basil.

Cook's know-how

When marinating fish, leave it for no more than 4 hours: after this time the acid in the marinade will start to seep deep into the fish, which will make it dry when it is cooked.

SHARK WITH TROPICAL SALSA

SERVES 4

4 shark steaks, 6 oz (175 g) each

MARINADE

1/2 cup (125 ml) olive oil

juice of 1/2 lemon

3 garlic cloves, minced

1 tbsp chopped fresh cilantro

1 tsp ground cumin

pinch of cayenne pepper

salt and black pepper

TROPICAL SALSA

2 cups (275 g) canned pineapple pieces in natural juice, drained

1 small, ripe papaya or mango, peeled, seeded, and diced

1 small red bell pepper, halved, seeded, and diced

1 fresh, mild red or green chili pepper, halved, seeded, and diced

2 tbsp chopped fresh cilantro

1 tbsp white wine vinegar

sugar (optional)

1 Make the marinade: In a non-metallic dish, combine the oil, lemon juice, garlic, cilantro, cumin, and cayenne. Season with salt and pepper.

2 Turn the shark steaks in the marinade, then cover and let marinate in the refrigerator for about 1 hour.

3 Make the tropical salsa: In a large bowl, combine the pineapple, papaya or mango, red bell pepper, chili pepper, cilantro, and vinegar. Season with salt and pepper. If the fruit is sour, add a little sugar.

4 Remove the steaks from the marinade, reserving the marinade. Cook the steaks under the broiler, 3 in (7 cm) from the heat, basting once or twice with the marinade, for 3–4 minutes on each side until the flesh is opaque and will flake easily. Serve with the salsa.

Cook's know-how

Try this cranberry and orange salsa instead of the tropical salsa: Peel and dice 1 orange. Mix with 2 cups (250 g) chopped cranberries and 2/3 cup (125 g) sugar. Serve chilled, with the hot fish.

KOULIBIAC

This pie – a salmon and rice mixture enclosed in crisp puff pastry – makes an impressive dish for a dinner party or other special occasion. In Russia, its country of origin, there is an appropriate saying: "Houses make a fine street, pies make a fine table."

SERVES 8–10

1/2 cup (75 g) long grain rice
salt and black pepper
4 tbsp (60 g) butter, plus extra for greasing
1 large onion, chopped
14 oz (400 g) canned crushed tomatoes, drained
1 lb (500 g) fresh salmon fillet, cooked, skinned, and flaked
2 tbsp chopped parsley
grated zest and juice of 1 lemon
1 lb (500 g) puff pastry
1 egg, beaten
4 tbsp (60 g) butter, melted, and juice of 1/2 lemon for serving
lemon twists and watercress sprigs for garnish

1 Cook the rice in boiling salted water for 12 minutes or until just tender.

2 Meanwhile, melt the butter in a saucepan, add the onion, and cook very gently for about 10 minutes until soft but not colored. Add the tomatoes, stir, and cook for 15 minutes. Let cool.

3 Drain the rice thoroughly, then combine with the onion and tomato mixture, the flaked salmon, parsley, and lemon zest and juice. Season with salt and pepper.

4 Roll out the puff pastry and cut out an 11- x 16-in (28- x 40-cm) rectangle. Reserve the pastry trimmings.

5 Arrange the salmon mixture down the middle of the rectangle, leaving a 3 in (7 cm) border on each side. Brush the border with a little of the beaten egg. Wrap and decorate the koulibiac (see box, right).

6 Bake the koulibiac in a preheated oven at 425°F (220°C) for 30–45 minutes until golden.

7 Transfer to a warmed serving dish, and pour the melted butter and lemon juice into the cuts. Serve in thick slices, garnished with lemon twists and watercress.

Wrapping and decorating the koulibiac

Fold the shortest pastry ends over the salmon filling and brush the top of the folded pastry with beaten egg.

Fold the longest sides over the filling to make a long parcel. Turn the parcel over and place on a buttered baking sheet. Brush all over with beaten egg.

Make 2 decorative cuts in the top of the pastry. Cut a 2- x 12-in (5- x 30-cm) strip from the rolled-out pastry trimmings, then cut into 3 equal strips. Press the ends together and braid the strips. Lay the braid down the middle of the parcel and glaze with beaten egg.

SEVERN SALMON

SERVES 6

6 salmon steaks, 6 oz (175 g) each

butter for greasing

salt and black pepper

watercress sprigs for garnish

WATERCRESS SAUCE

1 1/4 cups (300 ml) light cream

1 cup (60 g) watercress leaves

6 tbsp (90 g) butter, melted

1 tsp all-purpose flour

juice of 1 lemon

1 egg yolk

Cook's know-how

You can vary this recipe by using pieces of salmon fillet, about 5 oz (150 g) each, instead of salmon steaks. They will take 10 minutes at the most to cook in the oven. Instead of watercress, you can use a small bunch of fresh dill weed or tarragon for the sauce.

---

1 Arrange the salmon steaks in a single layer in a buttered roasting pan and sprinkle with black pepper.

2 Cover tightly with foil and bake in a preheated oven at 350°F (180°C) for 15 minutes or until the fish is opaque and will flake easily.

3 Meanwhile, make the watercress sauce: Put the cream, watercress, butter, flour, lemon juice, and egg yolk into a food processor, season with salt and pepper, and purée until smooth.

4 Transfer the cream and watercress mixture to a small saucepan and cook over a gentle heat, stirring, until the sauce thickens. Taste for seasoning.

5 Serve the salmon hot on a pool of watercress sauce, garnished with fresh sprigs of watercress.

SALMON WITH SPINACH

SERVES 4

4 salmon steaks, 6 oz (175 g) each

salt and black pepper

1 tbsp (15 g) butter

lemon twists for garnish

SPINACH SALSA

2 tbsp olive oil

8 green onions, finely sliced

1 garlic clove, minced

4 tbsp lemon juice

1 tsp grain mustard

1 lb (500 g) spinach, finely chopped

Healthy note

Although spinach is rich in iron, the iron is not well absorbed by the body due to the oxalic acid in the vegetable. However, spinach has other things to offer, including an antioxidant called lutein, which can help protect against age-related degeneration of eyesight.

---

1 Season the salmon steaks with black pepper and dot with the butter.

2 Cook the salmon steaks under the broiler, 3 in (7 cm) from the heat, for 2–3 minutes on each side until the fish is opaque and will flake easily. Let rest.

3 Make the spinach salsa: Heat the oil in a frying pan, add the green onions and garlic, and cook, stirring, for about 1 minute. Stir in the lemon juice, mustard, and spinach, and cook, stirring, for about 2 minutes. Transfer to a bowl, and season with salt and pepper.

4 Garnish the salmon with lemon twists and serve at once, with the salsa.

SALMON EN CROUTE

SERVES 8

I whole salmon, 3¹/2–4 lb (1.7–2 kg), cleaned and boned (page 122), then cut lengthwise in half and skinned
I tbsp chopped fresh dill weed
grated zest and juice of I lemon
salt and black pepper
2 tbsp (30 g) butter
8 green onions, sliced
4 cups (250 g) coarsely shredded spinach
I cup (250 g) lowfat cream cheese
all-purpose flour for dusting
1¹/2 lb (750 g) puff pastry
I egg, beaten
lemon slices, cherry tomatoes, and parsley sprigs for garnish

1 Put the 2 pieces of salmon into a shallow non-metallic dish and sprinkle with the dill, lemon zest and juice, salt, and pepper. Cover and let marinate in the refrigerator for about 1 hour.

2 Melt the butter in a small pan, add the onions, and cook gently for 2–3 minutes until soft but not colored.

3 Remove from the heat. Add the spinach and toss in the butter, then let cool. Stir in the cheese and season.

4 Roll out half of the pastry on a lightly floured surface to an 8- x 15-in (20- x 38-cm) rectangle. Lay the pastry on a baking sheet and place a piece of salmon, skinned side down, on top. Spread with the spinach mixture, then put the second piece of salmon on top, skinned side up. Brush the pastry border with a little beaten egg.

5 Roll out the remaining pastry to a slightly larger rectangle, cover the salmon completely, and trim and seal the edges. Make "scales" on the top with the edge of a spoon, then make 2 small holes to let steam escape during baking.

6 Brush with beaten egg and bake in a preheated oven at 400°F (200°C) for 40–45 minutes until the pastry is risen and browned. Serve hot, garnished with lemon, tomatoes, and parsley.

SALMON WITH AVOCADO

SERVES 4

2 tbsp (30 g) butter, melted
4 salmon steaks, 6 oz (175 g) each
salt and black pepper
4 tarragon sprigs
4 slices of lime

AVOCADO SAUCE

2 avocados, halved, pitted (page 88), and peeled
2/3 cup (150 ml) plain yogurt
grated zest and juice of I lime

1 Brush 4 large squares of foil with melted butter. Put a salmon steak on each square, season, and top with a tarragon sprig and a slice of lime. Wrap the foil around the salmon. Put on a baking sheet and bake in a preheated oven at 300°F (150°C) for 25 minutes or until the fish is opaque and will flake easily.

2 Meanwhile, make the avocado sauce: Put the flesh of 1 avocado into a food processor with the yogurt and lime zest and juice. Season with salt and pepper, and purée until smooth. Transfer to a serving bowl. Dice the remaining avocado and stir into the sauce.

3 Unwrap the salmon, transfer to warmed serving plates, and serve with the avocado sauce.

CLASSIC BUFFET-PARTY SALMON

This is the perfect dish for a buffet party. The salmon is gently poached, with the skin and head for added flavor, then cooled in the cooking liquid to keep it moist. A fish poacher is useful, but you can improvise with a large, wide pot and a wire rack that fits inside.

SERVES 10

1 whole salmon, 5½ lb (2.75 kg), cleaned (page 122)
salt and black peppercorns
4 bay leaves
1 onion, sliced
4 tbsp white wine vinegar
3 tbsp chopped fresh dill weed
about 1 cup (250 ml) mayonnaise (page 372)

FOR GARNISH

about 14 cooked jumbo shrimp, peeled but with heads on (if available)
1–2 bunches of fresh dill weed
lemon wedges or slices

1 Lift out the rack from the fish poacher and set aside. Half fill the pan with cold water and add 2 tbsp salt, 12 black peppercorns, the bay leaves, onion, and vinegar.

2 Set the salmon on the rack and lower into the pan. Bring to a boil, then simmer for 1 minute only. Remove from the heat, cover, and let stand for about 2 hours, until the fish is just warm.

3 Lift the rack and salmon out of the fish poacher. Strain the cooking liquid and reserve. Cover the salmon with a large piece of plastic wrap and flip the fish over onto the wrap. Bone and skin the salmon (see box, below). Cover and chill in the refrigerator for at least 1 hour.

4 Mix the dill into the mayonnaise, then taste for seasoning. Spoon into a serving bowl and chill until ready to serve.

5 Arrange the shrimp in a line along the middle of the salmon so that the heads are facing in opposite directions (this will hide the line where the backbone was). The number of shrimp will depend on the length of your salmon, so buy extra just in case – you can always use any leftover shrimp around the edge of the plate as an extra garnish.

6 Arrange dill sprigs around the edge of the salmon and on the plate, along with lemon slices or wedges. Serve with the dill mayonnaise.

Boning and skinning a cooked salmon

1 Using a chef's knife, neatly remove the head from the salmon.

2 Run the knife along the backbone of the fish to loosen the top fillet.

3 Flip the top fillet over and remove the bones from the fish.

4 Use the plastic wrap to help flip the bottom fillet back onto the top, and remove the skin and any dark flesh.

5 Use the plastic wrap to help flip the fish over onto a large serving plate, then remove the skin from the other side.

6 With a small knife, gently scrape away the brownish flesh from the top, leaving behind only the pink flesh.

FILLETS OF SOLE MENIERE

SERVES 4

all-purpose flour for coating

salt and black pepper

4 small, whole sole or flounder,
  each cut into 4 fillets and skinned
  (see box, right)

4 tbsp (60 g) butter

1 tbsp chopped parsley

juice of 1/2 lemon

lemon slices and parsley sprigs for
  garnish

1 Sprinkle flour onto a plate
  and season with salt and
pepper. Dip the 16 fillets into
the flour and shake off excess.

2 Melt half of the butter in a
  large frying pan. When it is
foaming, add the fillets and
cook for 2 minutes on each side
or until the flesh is opaque and
flakes easily. Transfer to warmed
serving plates and keep warm.

3 Wipe the pan with paper
  towels. Melt the remaining
butter and heat quickly until
golden. Stir in the parsley and
lemon juice, then pour over the
fillets. Serve hot, garnished with
lemon and parsley.

Cook's know-how

You can fillet and skin the sole
yourself (page 123), but a
fishmonger will do it for you,
and this will save a lot of time.
Explain that you need
"quarter" fillets from each
sole, that is two slim fillets
from each side of the fish. For
a special occasion you can use
Dover sole, which is imported
from Europe. It is less widely
available than other sole
(which are really founders),
and more expensive, but the
flavor and texture are superb.

MUSHROOM-STUFFED SOLE FILLETS

SERVES 4

4 tbsp (60 g) butter

1 onion, minced

5 cups (375 g) minced mushrooms

2 large, whole sole or flounder,
  each cut into 4 fillets and skinned
  (see box, below left)

1 cup (250 ml) dry white wine

2 tsp chopped fresh tarragon

salt and black pepper

1 cup (250 ml) heavy cream

squeeze of lemon juice

1 Melt half of the butter in a
  saucepan, add the onion
and mushrooms, and cook
gently for 5 minutes.

2 Roll the fillets (see box,
  right), with the skinned
sides in. Arrange them in a
shallow baking dish and fill
with the mushrooms.

3 Add the wine, tarragon, and
  salt and pepper to taste.
Cover and bake in a preheated
oven at 350°F (180°C) for
15 minutes or until the fish is
opaque and flakes easily.

4 Remove the fish from the
  dish and keep warm. Pour
the juices into a saucepan and
boil for 3 minutes or until
reduced by half. Stir in the
cream and lemon juice, heat
through gently, and taste for
seasoning before serving.

Rolling the fillets

Bring around the 2 ends of
each fillet to form a circle, with
the smaller tail end outside.

Thread a wooden toothpick
through both ends of each fillet,
to secure.

GINGERED SOLE

SERVES 4

4 large sole or flounder fillets

green onions for garnish (optional)

GINGER MARINADE

1-in (2.5-cm) piece of fresh ginger, peeled and finely sliced

1 large garlic clove, sliced

2 tbsp sunflower oil

1 tbsp toasted sesame oil

1 tbsp dry sherry

1 tbsp sherry vinegar

2 tsp light soy sauce

1 Put the sole fillets into a shallow, non-metallic dish.

2 Make the marinade: Combine the ginger, garlic, sunflower and sesame oils, sherry, sherry vinegar, and soy sauce. Pour this over the fish.

3 Cover the fish and let marinate in the refrigerator, turning once, for 30 minutes.

4 Cook the fillets, skin-side down, under the broiler, 3 in (7 cm) from the heat, for 4–5 minutes until the fish is opaque and flakes easily. Serve hot, garnished with green onions, if you like.

SOLE FLORENTINE

Here, fillets of sole are topped with a cheese sauce and baked on a bed of spinach, so they stay moist while cooking. Slices of hot lemon bread – an interesting variation of garlic bread – make an unusual accompaniment.

SERVES 4

4 large, whole sole or flounder, each cut into 4 fillets and skinned (see box, opposite page)

juice of 1/2 lemon

salt and black pepper

3 tbsp (45 g) butter

3 tbsp all-purpose flour

scant 2 cups (450 ml) milk

1 1/2 lb (750 g) spinach

1/4 cup (30 g) grated Parmesan cheese

hot lemon bread (see box, below)

1 Sprinkle the sole fillets with the lemon juice and some salt and pepper. Fold the fillets in half widthways and set aside.

2 Melt the butter in a saucepan, add the flour, and cook gently, stirring, for 1 minute. Remove from the heat and gradually blend in the milk. Bring to a boil, stirring constantly until the sauce thickens. Simmer for 2–3 minutes, stirring frequently, then season with salt and pepper to taste.

3 Wash the spinach and put into a pan with only the water remaining on the leaves. Cook for 2 minutes or until wilted. Drain well.

4 Stir half of the sauce into the cooked spinach and spoon into a shallow baking dish. Arrange the sole on top. Pour the remaining sauce over the top and sprinkle with the cheese. Bake in a preheated oven at 400°F (200°C) for 30 minutes. Serve hot, with hot lemon bread.

Hot lemon bread

Beat the grated zest of 1/2 lemon into 1/2 cup (125 g) softened butter, using a fork. Work in the juice of 1/2 lemon, and salt and pepper to taste.

Cut a baguette into 1/2-in (1-cm) slices, leaving the slices attached underneath.

Spread the butter in between the slices, and a little on top. Wrap in foil and bake in a preheated oven at 400°F (200°C) for 20 minutes, opening the foil for the last 5 minutes to crisp the top.

BEST-EVER FRIED FISH

These sole fillets are shallow-fried in a crisp coating of fresh bread crumbs. This is far superior to a batter coating in both flavor and texture, and it protects the fish from the heat of the oil and keeps it moist, in the same way as batter.

SERVES 4

3 tbsp all-purpose flour

salt and black pepper

1 extra large egg, beaten

2/3 cup (30 g) fresh white bread crumbs

4 large sole or flounder fillets, skinned

2 tbsp sunflower oil

lemon wedges for garnish

1 Sprinkle the flour into a shallow dish and season with salt and pepper. Pour the beaten egg into another dish, and sprinkle the bread crumbs into a third.

2 Bread all the fish fillets (see box, below).

3 Heat the oil in a large frying pan, add the breaded fillets, and fry over a high heat for 2–3 minutes on each side until they are crisp and golden. (You may have to fry the fish in 2 batches, depending on the size of your pan.)

4 Lift the fillets out of the frying pan with a slotted spatula and let drain briefly on paper towels. Serve the fish hot, garnished with lemon wedges.

Breading a fish fillet

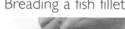

Dip the fillet into the seasoned flour, to coat. Shake off any excess.

Dip the floured fillet into the beaten egg, letting any excess drain off.

Dip the fillet into the bread crumbs, making sure it is lightly and evenly coated.

SAUCES FOR FISH

DILL-CREAM SAUCE

Work 1 1/4 cups (300 ml) light cream, 6 tbsp (90 g) butter, 1 egg yolk, the juice of 1 lemon, and 1 tsp all-purpose flour in a food processor until smooth. Transfer the mixture to a small saucepan and heat gently, stirring constantly, until the sauce has thickened and will coat the back of the spoon. Season with salt and pepper, then stir in 2 tbsp chopped dill weed and 1 tbsp snipped chives.

TARTAR SAUCE

Work 1 egg, 1 1/2 tsp sugar, 1/2 tsp mustard powder, and salt and pepper to taste in a food processor or blender until smooth. Add 1 1/4 cups (300 ml) sunflower oil, pouring it in in a steady stream, and work until the mixture is very thick and all of the oil has been incorporated. Add the juice of 1 lemon and mix. Transfer to a bowl and stir in 1 tbsp each chopped gherkins, capers, and parsley, and 2 tbsp chopped fresh tarragon. Cover and let stand for at least 1 hour so the flavors can blend.

INDIAN-SPICED HADDOCK

SERVES 4

1 1/2-lb (750-g) thick piece of haddock fillet, skinned

1 tsp ground cumin

1 tsp ground coriander

pinch of cayenne pepper

1/4 tsp turmeric

1 tsp salt

2 tbsp sunflower oil

1 small onion, sliced

1-in (2.5-cm) piece of fresh ginger, peeled and grated

1 fresh, hot green chili pepper, halved, seeded, and minced

1 small head cauliflower, cut into small florets

2 potatoes, diced

1 large green bell pepper, halved, seeded, and cut into strips

2/3 cup (150 ml) water

black pepper

plain yogurt for serving

1 Cut the haddock into 2-in (5-cm) cubes and put them into a bowl.

2 Mix the spices and salt together, sprinkle over the haddock, and stir to coat evenly. Cover and chill for about 1 hour.

3 Heat half of the oil in a frying pan, add the onion, and cook over a high heat for 5 minutes. Stir in the ginger and chili pepper, and cook for 2 minutes. Add the cauliflower, potatoes, and green bell pepper, and cook for 5–7 minutes. Remove the vegetables with a slotted spoon and set aside.

4 Heat the remaining oil, add the haddock, and brown lightly all over. Add the cooked vegetables and measured water, and simmer for about 10 minutes or until the fish is cooked and the vegetables are tender. Taste for seasoning, then serve hot, with plain yogurt.

HADDOCK WITH MUSHROOMS & CREAM

SERVES 4–6

1 1/4 cups (300 ml) milk

1 slice of onion

6 black peppercorns

1 bay leaf

4 tbsp (60 g) butter, plus extra for greasing

1 1/2-lb (750-g) thick piece of haddock fillet, skinned

salt and black pepper

squeeze of lemon juice

3 1/2 cups (250 g) sliced button mushrooms

3 tbsp all-purpose flour

3 tbsp light cream (optional)

2/3 cup (30 g) fresh white bread crumbs

1/4 cup (30 g) grated Parmesan cheese

chopped parsley for garnish

1 Put the milk into a small saucepan with the onion, peppercorns, and bay leaf, and bring just to a boil. Remove from the heat, cover, and let infuse for 10 minutes. Lightly butter a shallow baking dish.

2 Cut the haddock into 3-in (7-cm) pieces and place in a single layer in the dish. Sprinkle with salt and pepper.

3 Melt half of the butter in a saucepan, add the lemon juice and mushrooms, and season with salt and pepper. Cook gently, stirring from time to time, for 3 minutes or until just tender. Remove the mushrooms with a slotted spoon and put them on top of the fish.

4 Strain the infused milk and set aside. Melt the remaining butter in the saucepan, add the flour, and cook, stirring, for 1 minute. Remove from the heat and gradually blend in the infused milk. Bring to a boil, stirring until the mixture thickens. Simmer for 2–3 minutes. Stir in the cream, if using, and season with salt and pepper.

5 Pour the sauce over the fish and mushrooms, then sprinkle with the bread crumbs and Parmesan. Bake in a preheated oven at 375°F (190°C) for 25–30 minutes until the fish is cooked and the top is golden and bubbling. Garnish with parsley and serve at once.

149

ROAST MONKFISH NIÇOISE

SERVES 4

3 tbsp olive oil

1 head of garlic, separated into cloves

1 lemon, thickly sliced

1 lb (500 g) monkfish fillets, skinned and cut into chunky pieces

1 tsp dried herbes de Provence

1 cup (250 ml) dry white wine

1/2 cup (125 ml) fish stock

14 oz (400 g) canned artichoke hearts, drained and rinsed

15 pitted black olives

10 sun-dried tomatoes in oil, drained

squeeze of lemon juice

salt and black pepper

lemon wedges and thyme sprigs for garnish

1 Put 1 tbsp of the oil into a baking dish, add the garlic cloves, and roast in a preheated oven at 375°F (190°C) for 10 minutes or until softened.

2 Arrange the lemon slices in the dish, and put the garlic and monkfish on top.

3 Sprinkle with the remaining oil and the herbs, and pour in the wine and stock. Return to the oven for 10 minutes.

4 Add the artichoke hearts, olives, and sun-dried tomatoes, and bake for about 5 minutes to heat through.

5 Transfer the fish and vegetables to a serving dish, discarding the lemon slices. Keep warm.

6 Pour the cooking juices into a small saucepan and boil for about 8 minutes until reduced to about 1/2 cup (125 ml). Add the lemon juice, season with salt and pepper, and pour this over the fish. Garnish with lemon and thyme, and serve at once.

ROAST MONKFISH BASQUAISE

Instead of the artichokes, use 2 bell peppers (1 yellow and 1 red), halved, seeded, and cut into strips, and roast with the garlic cloves.

MONKFISH WITH GINGER-ORANGE SAUCE

SERVES 4

1 orange, washed and thinly sliced

1 onion, chopped

1/2-in (1-cm) piece of fresh ginger, peeled and grated

1 lb (500 g) monkfish fillets, skinned

1 cup (250 ml) fish stock

grated zest of 1/2 lime

5 tbsp lime juice

salt and cayenne pepper

4 tbsp (60 g) unsalted butter, chilled and cubed

sugar or honey to taste (optional)

orange and chives for garnish

1 Put the orange slices, onion, and ginger into a pan. Add the monkfish, green onions, and stock. Bring to a boil, and simmer for 10 minutes or until the fish is firm. With a slotted spoon, transfer the fish to a serving dish. Keep hot.

2 Put a strainer over a bowl, tip in the contents of the pan, and press hard with the back of a spoon to extract all the juices.

3 Pour the juices into a small saucepan and boil rapidly for about 12 minutes until the liquid has reduced to about 2 tbsp.

4 Add the lime zest and juice, and season with salt and cayenne. Heat gently, stirring, until warm. Remove from the heat and finish the sauce (see box, below).

5 Pour the sauce over the fish, garnish, and serve at once.

Finishing the sauce

Add the cubes of butter one at a time, whisking between each addition until the butter melts. The sauce will become glossy at the end. Taste and add a little sugar or honey, if you like.

SPICED FISH WITH COCONUT

SERVES 4

1 1/2 lb (750 g) monkfish fillets, skinned
all-purpose flour for coating
salt and black pepper
2 tbsp sunflower oil
1 onion, finely sliced
1 garlic clove, minced
1 tsp ground coriander
1 tsp ground cumin
1/2 tsp turmeric
2/3 cup (150 ml) canned coconut milk
14 oz (400 g) canned crushed tomatoes
3 tbsp chopped fresh cilantro
cilantro sprigs for garnish

2 Heat the oil in a large frying pan, add the onion, garlic, coriander, cumin, and turmeric, and cook gently, stirring from time to time, for 3 minutes or until the onion begins to soften.

3 Pour in the coconut milk and tomatoes, stir well, and bring to a boil. Simmer for about 5 minutes.

4 Add the monkfish, cover, and cook gently, stirring occasionally, for 10 minutes or until the fish is opaque and the flesh flakes easily. Add the chopped cilantro and taste for seasoning. Serve hot, garnished with cilantro sprigs.

1 Cut the monkfish into 2-in (5-cm) pieces. Season flour with salt and pepper. Lightly coat the monkfish pieces with the flour.

MONKFISH KEBABS

SERVES 4

1 lb (500 g) monkfish fillets, skinned
4 tbsp olive oil
grated zest and juice of 1 large lemon
1 tbsp chopped fresh dill
salt and black pepper
1/2 hothouse cucumber
2 tbsp (30 g) butter
12 fresh bay leaves
2 lemons, sliced
dill weed sprigs for garnish

1 Cut the monkfish fillets into 1-in (2.5-cm) pieces and put them into a bowl. Whisk together the olive oil, lemon zest and juice, dill, and salt and pepper to taste. Pour this over the fish. Cover and let marinate in the refrigerator for up to 4 hours.

2 Peel the cucumber and cut it in half lengthwise. Scoop out the seeds from each half, then cut the flesh across into 3/4-in (2-cm) slices. Melt the butter in a small saucepan, add the cucumber slices, and cook gently for 1 minute or until they begin to soften.

3 Lift the monkfish out of the marinade with a slotted spoon, reserving the marinade. Thread the kebabs (see box, below).

4 Brush the kebabs with marinade, then put under the broiler, 3 in (7 cm) from the heat. Cook the kebabs, brushing them occasionally with the marinade, for 5–6 minutes on each side until the fish is cooked through. Serve at once, garnished with dill sprigs.

Threading the kebabs

Push a piece of fish and a fresh bay leaf onto a metal skewer. Fold a lemon slice around a cucumber slice and push onto the skewer. Keep threading the fish, bay leaves, and lemon and cucumber in turn until you have filled 4 skewers.

FRESH WAYS WITH SALMON FILLETS

Fresh salmon is inexpensive and available all year round, either wild or farmed. Quick, easy, and light, these four recipes using salmon fillets can all be prepared in advance, making them perfect stress-free main dishes for dinner parties.

HERB-ROASTED SALMON

SERVES 4

4 salmon tail fillets, 5 oz (150 g) each, skinned

salt and black pepper

a little vegetable oil

1/2 cup (125 g) garlic and herb soft cheese

TOPPING

2/3 cup (30 g) fresh white bread crumbs

1/4 cup (30 g) grated sharp Cheddar cheese

2 tbsp chopped fresh flat-leaf parsley

finely grated zest of 1 lime

FOR SERVING

lemon wedges

flat-leaf parsley sprigs

1 Season the salmon on both sides with salt and pepper. Place on lightly oiled foil on a baking sheet and spread with the soft cheese, not going quite to the edges.

2 Mix the topping ingredients together, adding seasoning to taste, then sprinkle over the salmon. (You can prepare ahead to this stage, cover the salmon, and keep it in the refrigerator for up to 12 hours.)

3 Cook in a preheated oven at 425°F (220°C) for 15 minutes or until the salmon is opaque and the flesh flakes easily. Garnish with lemon and parsley.

THAI CHILI SALMON

SERVES 4

4 middle-cut salmon fillets, 5–6 oz (150–175 g) each, skinned

MARINADE

2 tbsp Thai fish sauce (nam pla)

finely grated zest and juice of 1 lime

1 large, fresh, hot red chili pepper, halved, seeded, and minced

1-in (2.5-cm) piece of fresh ginger, peeled and finely grated

a few fresh cilantro stems, minced

FOR SERVING

fresh cilantro leaves

1 lime, cut into wedges

1 Put the salmon fillets in a single layer in a shallow, non-metallic dish. Add the marinade ingredients and turn to coat. Cover and marinate in the refrigerator for 2–3 hours, turning the salmon once.

2 Lift the salmon from the marinade and cook under the broiler, 3 in (7 cm) away from the heat, for 5–6 minutes on each side until the salmon is opaque and the flesh flakes easily. Serve hot, with cilantro and lime.

PAN-GRILLED SALMON TRANCHES

SERVES 4

a little olive oil

4 middle-cut salmon fillets, 5–6 oz (150–175 g) each, skinned

salt and black pepper

SAUCE

1 cup (250 ml) crème fraîche or light sour cream

2-in (5-cm) piece of hothouse cucumber, peeled, seeded, and minced

4 tbsp chopped fresh dill weed

pinch of sugar

1 tbsp capers

large squeeze of lemon juice

1 Heat a grill pan until hot, and lightly oil a sheet of foil on a baking sheet. Lightly oil and season the salmon.

2 Cook the salmon in the hot pan on one side only for 1½ minutes until golden underneath. Transfer, cooked-side up, to the foil and finish cooking in a preheated oven at 375°F (190°C) for 10 minutes or until the salmon is opaque and the flesh flakes easily. Let cool.

3 Mix the sauce ingredients in a bowl with salt and pepper to taste. Cover and refrigerate. When the salmon is cold, cover and refrigerate too – for up to 12 hours.

4 To serve, let the salmon come to room temperature and serve with the chilled sauce spooned alongside.

WARM HONEYED SALMON SALAD

SERVES 4

4 middle-cut salmon fillets, 5–6 oz (150–175 g) each, skinned

3 tbsp honey

1 tbsp olive oil

juice of 1 lemon

about 2 tbsp chopped fresh thyme

new potatoes for serving

SALAD

1 fennel bulb, thinly sliced

6 green onions, thinly sliced

3 tbsp extra virgin olive oil

1 tbsp lemon juice

1 tbsp honey

4 tbsp thick plain yogurt

salt and black pepper

1 head romaine lettuce, shredded

2 tbsp chopped parsley

2 tbsp snipped fresh chives

1 Make the salad: Mix the fennel and green onions in a bowl with the olive oil, lemon juice, honey, yogurt, and seasoning. Toss the lettuce in a large salad bowl with the chopped fresh herbs and seasoning. Cover both bowls and refrigerate for about 1 hour.

2 Cut each salmon fillet lengthwise into 4 pieces – they will look like flat sausages. Toss in the honey and season well. Heat the oil in a large nonstick frying pan and fry the salmon over a high heat for 2–3 minutes on each side or until just opaque. Take care when turning the salmon as it breaks up quite easily. Add the lemon juice and thyme to the pan and heat until bubbling.

3 Toss the fennel salad with the lettuce and herbs, then spoon the honeyed salmon on top. Serve warm.

CLOCKWISE FROM TOP: Pan-Grilled Salmon Tranches, Warm Honeyed Salmon Salad, Herb-Roasted Salmon, Thai Chili Salmon.

HALIBUT IN PHYLLO PASTRY

Halibut is a very fine fish with a delicate flavor and firm texture. Enclosing the halibut steaks in phyllo pastry with matchstick-thin vegetables keeps the fish moist and seals in all the flavors, while the pastry trimmings on top provide an attractive, crunchy finish.

SERVES 4

2 halibut steaks, 12 oz (375 g) each, skinned and boned

1 carrot

1 leek, trimmed

2/3 cup (150 ml) fish stock

2 tbsp dry white wine

2 tsp lemon juice

3 strands of saffron or 1/4 tsp turmeric

salt and black pepper

8 large sheets of phyllo pastry

4 tbsp (60 g) butter, melted

lemon slices and dill weed sprigs for garnish

1 Cut the halibut steaks crosswise to make 4 equal pieces. Cut the carrot and leek into matchstick-thin strips.

2 Put the vegetables into a pan with the stock, wine, lemon juice, and saffron.

3 Bring to a boil, then cook for 5 minutes or until the vegetables are just tender. Drain, then season with salt and pepper.

4 Cut the phyllo pastry into eight 10-in (25-cm) squares; reserve the pastry trimmings. Brush 1 square with a little melted butter, put a second square on top, and brush with more melted butter. Make a phyllo parcel (see box, far right). Repeat to make 4 phyllo parcels.

5 Place the phyllo parcels on a baking sheet and bake in a preheated oven at 400°F (200°C) for 20 minutes or until golden and crisp. Garnish with lemon and dill, and serve.

Cook's know-how

Sheets of phyllo pastry are usually sold in a roll, fresh or frozen. The size of the sheets may vary with different brands, so don't worry if they are slightly smaller than 10 in (25 cm) wide – just be sure there is sufficient pastry to cover the filling.

SALMON IN PHYLLO PASTRY

Substitute skinned salmon fillets for the halibut, and 1 zucchini and 4 green onions, both cut into matchstick-thin strips, for the carrot and leek.

Making a phyllo parcel

Spoon one-fourth of the vegetable mixture into the middle of the pastry square. Put 1 piece of halibut on top of the vegetable mixture.

Fold 2 opposite sides of the pastry over the halibut and vegetables, and tuck the remaining 2 ends underneath to form a neat parcel. Brush the top of the parcel with a little melted butter.

Crumple some of the reserved pastry trimmings, and arrange them on top of the parcel. Brush with melted butter.

SEA BASS WITH LEMON BUTTER SAUCE

SERVES 4

sunflower oil for greasing
2 1/4-lb (1.1-kg) whole sea bass, cleaned and boned (page 122)
4 tarragon sprigs
1 lemon, sliced
salt and black pepper
2 tbsp dry white wine

LEMON BUTTER SAUCE

2/3 cup (150 ml) light cream
juice of 1/2 lemon
3 tbsp (45 g) butter, melted
1 egg yolk
1 tsp all-purpose flour
white pepper
1 tsp chopped fresh tarragon

1 Put a large piece of foil on a baking sheet and brush lightly with oil. Put the sea bass on the foil. Tuck 3 of the tarragon sprigs and all but 1–2 of the lemon slices inside the cavity, and sprinkle with salt and black pepper.

2 Season the outside of the fish. Lift up the sides of the foil, pour the wine over the fish, and seal the foil into a loose package. Bake in a preheated oven at 400°F (200°C) for 30 minutes or until the flesh is opaque and flakes easily.

3 Meanwhile, make the sauce: Whisk the cream in a pan with the lemon juice, butter, egg yolk, and flour until mixed. Heat very gently, stirring constantly, until the mixture is thick enough to coat the back of a spoon. Season with salt and white pepper, and stir in the tarragon. Keep warm.

4 Remove the sea bass from the foil and arrange on a warmed serving dish. Pour the cooking juices over. Garnish with the remaining lemon slices and tarragon sprig, and serve at once. Pass the warm lemon butter sauce separately.

ASIAN FISH PARCELS

SERVES 4

3 tbsp (45 g) butter
4 sole or flounder fillets, 8 oz (250 g) each, skinned
3/4-in (2-cm) piece of fresh ginger, peeled and thinly sliced
3 green onions, thinly sliced
2–3 garlic cloves, minced
2 tbsp light soy sauce
1 tbsp rice wine or dry sherry
1/2 tsp sugar

1 Cut 8 sheets of parchment paper into oval shapes, each one measuring about 12 x 5 in (30 x 37 cm). Put the ovals together in pairs to make a double thickness.

2 Melt 2 tbsp (30 g) of the butter. Brush the butter over the top of each pair of parchment ovals, and over 2 large baking sheets.

3 Place a fish fillet on the buttered side of one of the paired paper ovals, positioning it on one side. Top with ginger, green onions, and garlic, and dot with one-fourth of the remaining butter.

4 Whisk together the soy sauce, rice wine, and sugar, and drizzle one-fourth of this mixture over the fish. Fold the paper over the fish, and fold and pleat the edges together like a turnover to seal in the fish and juices. Repeat to make 4 parcels altogether.

5 Put the paper cases on the prepared baking sheets and bake in a preheated oven at 450°F (230°C) for 8–10 minutes until the paper has turned brown and the cases have puffed up. Serve at once, on individual plates.

GOLDEN FISH CAKES

SERVES 4

1 lb (500 g) potatoes, cut into chunks

salt and black pepper

1 lb (500 g) cod, haddock or salmon fillet (or a mixture of white fish and salmon)

1¼ cups (300 ml) milk

1 bay leaf

9 black peppercorns

4 tbsp (60 g) butter

4 tbsp chopped parsley

finely grated zest of 1 lemon

dash of hot pepper sauce (optional)

1 egg, beaten

4 cups (175 g) fresh bread crumbs

sunflower oil for frying

tartar sauce (page 148) for serving

1 Cook the potatoes in boiling salted water for 15–20 minutes until tender.

2 Meanwhile, put the fish into a pan with the milk, bay leaf, and peppercorns. Bring slowly to a boil, then simmer for 10 minutes or until the fish is just opaque.

3 Drain the fish, reserving the liquid. Cool the fish, then flake the flesh, discarding the skin and bones.

4 Drain the potatoes, put them in a bowl, and mash with the butter and 3 tbsp of the fish cooking liquid. Add the fish, parsley, lemon zest, hot pepper sauce, if using, and salt and pepper to taste. Mix well.

5 Shape the mixture into 8 flat cakes, 3 in (7 cm) in diameter. Coat with beaten egg, then with bread crumbs.

6 Heat a little oil in a frying pan and fry the fish cakes, a few at a time, for 5 minutes on each side or until golden. Serve hot, with the tartar sauce.

CRISP-TOPPED SEAFOOD PIE

SERVES 4

1 lb (500 g) cod fillet

1¼ cups (300 ml) milk

1 bay leaf

2 leeks, trimmed and sliced

2 cups (175 g) broccoli florets

6 oz (175 g) cooked peeled shrimp

1 tbsp (15 g) butter

1 tbsp all-purpose flour

salt and black pepper

8 oz (250 g) piecrust dough, well chilled

¼ cup (30 g) grated Gruyère cheese

1 Put the cod into a saucepan with the milk and bay leaf, bring slowly to a boil, and poach gently for 10 minutes or until the fish flakes easily.

2 Meanwhile, blanch the leeks and broccoli in a saucepan of boiling salted water for 3 minutes. Drain.

3 Lift out the fish, remove and discard the skin and bones, and flake the fish. Strain and reserve the milk.

4 Put the leeks and broccoli into a baking dish and add the cod and shrimp.

5 Melt the butter in a small saucepan, add the flour, and cook, stirring, for about 1 minute. Remove from the heat and gradually blend in the reserved milk. Bring to a boil, stirring constantly until thickened. Simmer for 2–3 minutes. Season to taste, then pour into the baking dish.

6 Grate the piecrust dough, using the coarse holes of a grater, then scatter evenly over the sauce. Sprinkle with the grated cheese. Bake in a preheated oven at 400°F (200°C) for 25–30 minutes. Serve at once.

5

POULTRY
& GAME

UNDER 30 MINUTES

BARBECUE

HERB GRILLED CHICKEN

Fresh and summery: chicken quarters brushed with parsley, chives, and garlic in melted butter, then grilled or broiled.

SERVES 8 297 calories per serving

Takes 25 minutes   Page 182

CHICKEN KEBABS

Pieces of chicken marinated in soy sauce, vinegar, oil, and thyme. Broiled with green bell pepper, mushrooms, and cherry tomatoes.

SERVES 6 441 calories per serving

Takes 25 minutes   Page 190

DINNER PARTY

WARM CHICKEN SALAD WITH MANGO & AVOCADO

Marinated chicken with mango and avocado, and rum-flavored cooking juices.

SERVES 4 411 calories per serving

Takes 25 minutes   Page 200

MUSTARD CHICKEN

Hot and creamy: strips of chicken coated with garlic, in a cream sauce piquantly flavored with mustard.

SERVES 4 380 calories per serving

Takes 25 minutes   Page 189

DINNER PARTY

TURKEY WITH SOUR CREAM & CHIVES

Strips of turkey breast in a bacon, mushroom, and sour cream sauce.

SERVES 4 542 calories per serving

Takes 25 minutes   Page 204

LOW FAT

STIR-FRIED CHICKEN WITH CRISP VEGETABLES

Strips of chicken dry marinated in spices including ginger and turmeric. Stir-fried with vegetables.

SERVES 4 405 calories per serving

Takes 25 minutes   Page 188

GREEK CHICKEN SALAD

Creamy and intensely flavored with herbs: pieces of cooked chicken coated in yogurt, sour cream, green onions, and herbs.

SERVES 6 264 calories per serving

Takes 15 minutes   Page 200

QUICK & EASY

CHICKEN STIR-FRY

Light oriental dish: strips of chicken stir-fried with green onions, ginger, carrots, and peppers. Flavored with soy sauce and sherry.

SERVES 4 381 calories per serving

Takes 15 minutes   Page 191

HOT & SPICY STIR-FRIED DUCK

Strips of duck marinated in soy sauce, vinegar, ginger, chili, and orange. Stir-fried with vegetables and water chestnuts.

SERVES 4 453 calories per serving

Takes 25 minutes   Page 215

30–60 MINUTES

CORONATION CHICKEN

Bite-size pieces of chicken in a sauce made from green onions, curry paste, wine, lemon, apricot jam, mayonnaise, and yogurt.

SERVES 6 580 calories per serving

Takes 15 minutes, plus cooling   Page 199

HERB-MARINATED CHICKEN BREASTS

Chicken pieces marinated in lemon juice, herbs, and garlic. Cooked until crispy, and served with a hot stock sauce.

SERVES 4 641 calories per serving

Takes 30 minutes, plus marinating   Page 194

ORIENTAL CLASSIC

THAI CHICKEN WITH WATER CHESTNUTS

Aromatic stir-fry: chicken with water chestnuts, lemongrass, garlic, ginger, cilantro, chili, and tofu.

SERVES 4 272 calories per serving

Takes 30 minutes   Page 188

DINNER PARTY

DUCK BREASTS WITH RASPBERRY SAUCE

Rich and fruity: slices of broiled duck breast served with a sauce of raspberries, port, and orange juice.

SERVES 4 975 calories per serving

Takes 45 minutes   Page 214

STIR-FRIED TURKEY MEATBALLS

Mixture of ground turkey, garlic, soy sauce, and ginger, stir-fried with onion, pepper, zucchini, mushrooms, and bean sprouts.

SERVES 4 232 calories per serving

Takes 30 minutes   Page 207

TARRAGON CHICKEN WITH LIME

Chicken breasts coated with lime butter and sprinkled with lime juice and tarragon. Baked, and served with a sour cream sauce.

SERVES 4 428 calories per serving

Takes 45 minutes   Page 192

TURKEY SCHNITZEL

Golden and tender: turkey breast scalopes coated in seasoned flour, beaten egg, and fresh bread crumbs, and decorated with a crisscross pattern. Chilled in the refrigerator, then cooked until golden. Garnished with lemon slices and chopped parsley.

SERVES 4 394 calories per serving

Takes 25 minutes, plus chilling   Page 205

CHEESE & GARLIC STUFFED CHICKEN

Chicken breasts stuffed with cream cheese, onion, garlic, fresh tarragon, egg yolk, and nutmeg, then baked. Served cut into slices.

SERVES 6 628 calories per serving

Takes 45 minutes   Page 192

30–60 MINUTES

DEVILED CHICKEN DRUMSTICKS

Crispy and piquant: chicken drumsticks covered with a mixture of wine vinegar, ketchup, mustard, and sugar, then baked.

MAKES 12 138 calories each

Takes 45 minutes   Page 198

TURKEY WITH CHEESE & PINEAPPLE

Bite-size pieces of turkey with a cheese and pineapple sauce, sprinkled with fresh brown bread crumbs, then baked.

SERVES 6 450 calories per serving

Takes 40 minutes   Page 208

CHICKEN SATAY

Pieces of chicken marinated in soy sauce, lemon juice, garlic, and spring onions. Served with a peanut and coconut sauce.

SERVES 4 815 calories per serving

Takes 25 minutes, plus marinating   Page 190

HIGH PROTEIN

CHICKEN THIGHS NORMANDE

Chicken thighs baked with leeks, bacon, cider, and thyme, richly flavored with garlic. Served with a creamy sauce.

SERVES 4 599 calories per serving

Takes 55 minutes   Page 195

BACON-WRAPPED CHICKEN BREASTS

Tender and tangy: boneless chicken breasts spread with coarse-grain mustard, and wrapped in bacon slices.

SERVES 6 528 calories per serving

Takes 50 minutes   Page 193

LOW FAT

TURKEY & LEMON STIR-FRY

Turkey breast strips marinated in white wine and lemon zest and juice, stir-fried with courgettes, green pepper, and baby corn cobs.

SERVES 4 342 calories per serving

Takes 20 minutes, plus marinating   Page 205

CHICKEN PINWHEELS

Pounded chicken breast halves spread with a cheese and basil mixture, rolled up, simmered, then sliced. Served with a tomato and herb sauce.

SERVES 4 423 calories per serving

Takes 50 minutes   Page 191

FRAGRANT CHICKEN CURRY WITH ALMONDS

Chicken breasts cooked in an authentic blend of Indian spices, including cinnamon, cardamom seeds, cloves, cumin seeds, ginger, and garam masala, with a creamy yogurt sauce. Served with golden raisins and toasted almonds.

SERVES 4 527 calories per serving

Takes 45 minutes   Page 186

30–60 MINUTES

ORIENTAL POUSSINS

Tangy and succulent: poussins brushed with soy and hoisin sauces, sherry, garlic, and ginger, and baked.

SERVES 4 395 calories per serving
Takes 50 minutes   Page 179

CHICKEN THIGHS WITH CHESTNUT STUFFING

Delicious and filling: boneless chicken thighs stuffed with diced bacon, chestnuts, onion, fresh wholemeal

SERVES 4 598 calories per serving
Takes 55 minutes   Page 195

bread crumbs, chopped parsley, and egg yolk, and then roasted until golden brown. Served with a fruity cranberry-jelly sauce.

FAMILY CHOICE

BARBEQUE

PICNIC FARE

TURKEY BURGERS HOLSTEIN

Golden and tasty: ground turkey combined with chopped ham, parsley, and onion, then shaped into burgers. Served with a fried egg.

SERVES 4 429 calories per serving
Takes 30 minutes, plus chilling   Page 207

JERK CHICKEN

Crispy and spicy: chicken pieces spread with blended lime juice, rum, green onions, chili, garlic, and spices, then barbecued.

SERVES 4 304 calories per serving
Takes 30 minutes, plus marinating   Page 183

LEMON & HERB DRUMSTICKS

Fresh and easy to make: chicken drumsticks marinated in olive oil, lemon juice and zest, onion, garlic, and parsley, then broiled.

MAKES 12 200 calories each
Takes 25 minutes, plus marinating   Page 198

ORIENTAL CLASSIC

TEX-MEX CHICKEN

Chicken breasts marinated in oil, orange juice, and cumin, then broiled. Served with sliced avocado, and a tomato and lime salsa.

SERVES 4 659 calories per serving
Takes 30 minutes, plus marinating   Page 183

ORIENTAL DUCK WITH GINGER

Duck marinated in orange, soy sauce, sesame oil, rice wine, honey, and ginger. Served with baby corn cobs and toasted sesame seeds.

SERVES 4 445 calories per serving
Takes 30 minutes, plus marinating   Page 215

TURKEY MOLE

Hot and spicy: turkey pieces cooked with a blended sauce of tomatoes, almonds, chocolate, chili, cinnamon, and cloves.

SERVES 6 334 calories per serving
Takes 55 minutes   Page 206

30–60 MINUTES

OVER 60 MINUTES

SWEET & SOUR CHINESE CHICKEN
Pieces of chicken marinated in soy sauce and rice wine. Stir-fried with bell peppers, celery, onion, ketchup, pineapple, and lychees.

SERVES 4–6 458–305 calories per serving

Takes 30 minutes, plus marinating Page 189

DUCK BREASTS WITH RED WINE SAUCE
Duck marinated in garlic, balsamic, and rosemary, then cooked, sliced, and served with a wine sauce.

SERVES 4 906 calories per serving

Takes 40 minutes, plus chilling Page 214

FAMILY CHOICE

AMERICAN FRIED CHICKEN
Pieces of buttermilk-soaked chicken coated in flour seasoned with paprika. Cooked until golden, and served with bacon.

SERVES 4 683 calories per serving

Takes 40 minutes, plus standing Page 182

SAFFRON CHICKEN
Chicken breasts marinated in saffron, ginger, lemon, cardamom, cilantro, and cinnamon, then roasted. Served with a sour cream sauce.

SERVES 6 527 calories per serving

Takes 40 minutes, plus marinating Page 187

POUSSINS WITH ROMESCO SAUCE
Spatchcocked poussins and green onions marinated in oil, vinegar, and cinnamon. Served with sauce of tomatoes and almonds.

SERVES 2 845 calories per serving

Takes 60 minutes, plus marinating Page 179

CHICKEN TIKKA
Chicken marinated in yogurt, tomato paste, garlic, tamarind paste, paprika, and ginger. Served with cucumber raita.

SERVES 4–6 266–177 calories per serving

Takes 20 minutes, plus marinating Page 187

CHICKEN WITH SAGE & ORANGE
Fresh and tangy: chicken breasts marinated in orange juice, soy sauce, sage, and ginger. Served with a sage and orange sauce.

SERVES 6 435 calories per serving

Takes 40 minutes, plus marinating Page 193

MOROCCAN POUSSINS
Spatchcocked poussins marinated in lime, garlic, cilantro, paprika, curry powder, cumin, and saffron, then broiled.

SERVES 2 467 calories per serving

Takes 45 minutes, plus marinating Page 178

DINNER PARTY

CHICKEN CORDON BLEU
Golden and tender: pounded chicken breast halves filled with ham and Gruyère cheese, and folded. Coated with egg and bread crumbs.

SERVES 4 602 calories per serving

Takes 45 minutes, plus chilling Page 194

OVER 60 MINUTES

LEMON POUSSINS WITH ARTICHOKE HEARTS

Roasted poussins served with artichokes marinated in lemon, garlic, and parsley.

SERVES 4 555 calories per serving

Takes 1¹/4 hours   Page 178

FAMILY CHOICE

TURKEY CASSEROLE WITH PEPPERS & CIDER

Turkey pieces cooked with cider, red and yellow peppers, onion, and garlic.

SERVES 6 234 calories per serving

Takes 1¹/2 hours   Page 206

PROVENÇAL-STYLE ROAST CHICKEN

Chicken cooked on a bed of vegetables that forms the basis of a delicious sauce.

SERVES 6 547 calories per serving

Takes 1¹/2 hours   Page 176

FRENCH CLASSIC

COQ AU VIN

Rich and nourishing: chicken pieces cooked with bacon, shallots, mushrooms, red wine, stock, and a medley of fresh herbs.

SERVES 4 531 calories per serving

Takes 1¹/2 hours   Page 181

TRADITIONAL ROAST PHEASANT

Two pheasants, buttered and covered with bacon slices, then roasted and served with red currant-flavored gravy, and the traditional accompaniments of game chips, fried bread crumbs, and bread sauce. Garnished with watercress sprigs.

SERVES 4 660 calories per serving

Takes 1¹/2 hours   Page 217

MUSHROOM-STUFFED QUAIL

Whole boned quail stuffed with shallots, mushrooms, and bread crumbs, and served with a lime and sour cream sauce.

SERVES 6 651 calories per serving

Takes 1¹/4 hours   Page 216

TURKEY SALAD WITH MANGO & GRAPES

Turkey breast poached with peppercorns, coated in lemon mayonnaise. Served with walnuts and fruit.

SERVES 4 734 calories per serving

Takes 1¹/2 hours, plus cooling   Page 208

CHICKEN MARENGO

Chicken pieces cooked with shallots, wine, stock, tomatoes, mushrooms, garlic, parsley, thyme, bay leaf, and shrimp.

SERVES 4 479 calories per serving

Takes 1³/4 hours   Page 181

OVER 60 MINUTES

NORMANDY PHEASANT

Rich and tangy: pheasant cooked with apples, celery, onion, stock, and wine. Served with a creamy sauce and apple rings.

SERVES 6–8 751–563 calories per serving
Takes 1³/4 hours   Page 218

TRADITIONAL

BRAISED RABBIT WITH MUSHROOMS & CIDER

Rabbit cooked with shallots, mushrooms, cider, herbs, and enriched with cream.

SERVES 4 506 calories per serving
Takes 2 hours   Page 220

FRENCH ROAST CHICKEN

Tender and succulent: a whole chicken spread with softened butter, seasoned with black pepper, and roasted with chicken stock and a sprig of tarragon. Served with gravy made from the cooking juices, and garlic flowers that are drizzled with olive oil, then roasted.

SERVES 4 433 calories per serving
Takes 2 hours   Page 175

FAMILY CHICKEN CASSEROLE

Popular wholesome meal: chicken quarters cooked with bacon, carrots, celery, onion, stock, bay leaf, thyme, and parsley.

SERVES 4 659 calories per serving
Takes 1³/4 hours   Page 180

ROAST CHICKEN WITH ORANGE & PEPPERS

Chicken with red bell pepper and garlic, flambéed with brandy, and served with orange sauce.

SERVES 4 411 calories per serving
Takes 1³/4 hours   Page 176

SUNDAY ROAST CHICKEN

Traditional English Sunday lunch: chicken flavored with parsley and thyme, and cooked with an apple, lemon, and herb stuffing.

SERVES 4 534 calories per serving
Takes 2 hours, plus cooling   Page 174

OVER 60 MINUTES

ROAST TURKEY WITH GARLIC & TARRAGON

Turkey joint marinated in lemon, tarragon, thyme, and garlic, roasted with the marinade.

SERVES 4 296 calories per serving
Takes 1³/4 hours, plus marinating   Page 204

PHEASANT STEW

Pieces of pheasant simmered with red wine, game stock, bacon, celery, mushrooms, shallots, and garlic.

SERVES 6–8 633–475 calories per serving
Takes 2 hours   Page 218

CHICKEN POT PIE

Hearty meal: chicken simmered with stock, garlic, carrots, and potatoes. Flavoured with nutmeg and parsley, and baked with a pastry topping.

SERVES 6 508 calories per serving
Takes 2 hours, plus cooling   Page 177

MARINATED CHICKEN WITH PEPPERS

Chicken roasted with strips of red and yellow bell peppers, cooled, then tossed with a honey and herb marinade. Served with black olives.

SERVES 6 376 calories per serving
Takes 1³/4 hours, plus cooling   Page 199

GAME PIE WITH FENNEL & CARROTS

Richly flavored with fennel, carrots, onion, stock, and wine, and baked with a puff pastry lid.

SERVES 6 672 calories per serving
Takes 2 hours   Page 219

GUINEA FOWL MADEIRA

Pieces of guinea fowl cooked with shallots, stock, wine, and Madeira, enriched with heavy cream and green grapes.

SERVES 6 613 calories per serving
Takes 1³/4 hours   Page 216

RABBIT WITH MUSTARD & MARJORAM

Pieces of rabbit marinated in mustard and marjoram, and cooked with garlic, bacon, and stock. Served with a mustard sauce.

SERVES 4 548 calories per serving
Takes 2 hours, plus marinating   Page 220

CHICKEN CACCIATORE

Pieces of chicken sprinkled with thyme, and cooked with bacon, onion, green bell pepper, garlic, mushrooms, wine, tomatoes, and sage.

SERVES 4 540 calories per serving
Takes 1³/4 hours   Page 180

RUBY HARE CASSEROLE

Rich and full of flavor: hare marinated in port wine, and cooked with shallots, bacon, crimini mushrooms, and herbs.

SERVES 4 1068 calories per serving
Takes 2¹/2 hours, plus marinating   Page 219

OVER 60 MINUTES

ORIENTAL CLASSIC

PEKING DUCK
Oriental specialty: whole duck brushed before cooking with sherry, honey, and soy sauce. Served with Chinese-style pancakes.

SERVES 6 848 calories per serving

Takes 2¹/2 hours, plus drying   Page 212

POT ROAST VENISON
Rolled shoulder of venison marinated in red wine, orange and lemon zests, and juniper berries, and slowly braised in the marinade with chopped carrots, celery, and onions. Red-currant jelly is added to the sauce just before serving.

SERVES 6 454 calories per serving

Takes 3¹/2 hours, plus marinating   Page 221

ROAST DUCK WITH CRANBERRIES
Duck with a stuffing of onion, fresh wholemeal bread crumbs, and cranberries, roasted until crisp. Served with cranberry sauce.

SERVES 4 580 calories per serving

Takes 2¹/2 hours, plus cooling   Page 213

VENISON CASSEROLE
Rich stew: cubes of venison marinated in wine, parsley, and allspice, and cooked with celery, mushrooms, and carrots.

SERVES 6 466 calories per serving

Takes 2¹/4 hours, plus marinating   Page 221

PREPARE AHEAD

RATHER SPECIAL GAME PIE
A selection of meats marinated in port. Baked in a pastry case filled with jellied stock, then chilled.

SERVES 20 507 calories per serving

Takes 6 hours, plus marinating   Page 222

BALLOTINE OF CHICKEN
Boned chicken pounded and stuffed with pork, liver, bacon, brandy, ham, and pistachio nuts. Rolled, cooked, chilled, and sliced.

SERVES 8–10 617–494 calories per serving

Takes 2³/4 hours, plus chilling   Page 201

TRADITIONAL

CHRISTMAS ROAST GOOSE
Succulent and fruity: goose stuffed with pork sausagemeat, sage, and apple, and roasted. Served with wine-flavored gravy, enriched with goose stock, and baked apples with a stuffing of Calvados, ground cinnamon, ground allspice, and prunes.

SERVES 6–8 1228–921 calories per serving

Takes 5¹/4 hours, plus cooling   Page 209

POULTRY & GAME KNOW-HOW

POULTRY IS THE TERM FOR all domesticated and farmyard birds, including chickens, turkeys, geese, ducks, and rock Cornish hens. The classification "poultry" can also be applied to game birds that once lived in the wild, but are now farmed. These include doves, guinea fowl, pheasants, partridges, quail, squabs, and wild ducks and turkeys. The cooking method you use for most birds will determine their tenderness and often the flavor. Many small game birds lack natural fat, so moist methods, such as braising and stewing, often produce the best results. Marinades are also commonly used to boost flavor and tenderness in poultry and game birds.

BUYING & STORING

Poultry and game birds should have a plump breast and moist skin. Poultry should smell fresh and not "off." Game birds, which are often aged to tenderize their flesh and enhance a "gamy" flavour, should nevertheless have an appealing odor.

Poultry is one of the most popular family mealtime ingredients, and it is sold in a variety of market forms. Fresh poultry is cleaned and ready for cooking. You can buy it plain and natural tasting, or rubbed with flavorings. Most game birds, available from specialty food stores, mail-order suppliers and some supermarkets, are sold frozen.

Frozen birds will have been frozen before they reach the store, and must be completely thawed before they are cooked. Transport frozen poultry as quickly as possible in an insulated bag, and if it has started to thaw before you get home, do not put in the freezer. It will have to be thawed completely and cooked. Thaw whole birds and pieces on a plate with a lip on the bottom shelf of the refrigerator and allow 5 hours for each 1 lb (500 g). Or, put the bird, still in its wrappings, in a sink of cold water and allow 30 minutes for each 1 lb (500 g). It is not recommended to thaw frozen poultry at room temperature.

MICROWAVING

Casseroles and stews made with poultry and game can be cooked very easily in the microwave oven. They are quick to prepare and the meat stays tender and juicy. You can choose to brown the poultry or game and any vegetables on the stovetop first, then transfer to a microwave-safe dish to finish cooking in the microwave. Be sure to transfer the flavorsome pan drippings to the microwave-safe dish as well.

The microwave is also really good for reheating cooked poultry and game dishes, particularly when the meat is off the bone.

For roasting poultry and game, a conventional oven gives better results than the microwave.

FREEZING

Frozen poultry and game is very good and a useful standby. When buying frozen poultry, check it is completely frozen and get it home as quickly as possible. Chicken, turkey, and wild game birds can be stored for up to 6 months; duck, goose, and guinea fowl for 4 months.

Poultry and game must be thoroughly thawed before cooking. This can take time – a 10 lb (4.5 kg) turkey needs 22–24 hours. Unwrap the bird, cover loosely with fresh wrapping, and set on a plate to thaw in the refrigerator. Remove any giblets as soon as possible. Keep in mind that raw poultry or game should never be re-frozen once it has been thawed.

TYPES OF BIRDS

Broilers-fryers, weighing from 2½–5 lb (1.1–2.5 kg), are chickens that can be broiled, baked, fried, roasted and simmered. Roasting chickens are a little larger and suitable for roasting and broiling. Stewing chickens, or boiling fowl, are old laying hens. Poussins are small single-serving birds that are slaughtered at 3 or 4 weeks. Turkey is sold whole, and in numerous pieces, boned or on the bone. Duck is sold whole and in legs or boneless breasts. Other birds, such as geese, guinea fowl, squabs, quail, wild ducks, partridges, and pheasants are sold whole or boned.

THOROUGH COOKING

Cook poultry thoroughly to kill any bacteria.

To test a whole roasted bird, lift it on a long fork – the juices that run out should be clear. For joints, insert a skewer into the thickest part of the meat and check the color of the juices. Alternatively, use an instant-read thermometer: the thigh meat should register 170°F (75°C), breast 160°F (70°C).

POULTRY OR GAME STOCK

To make 2 1/2 quarts (2.5 liters) stock, use 3 lb (1.5 kg) raw poultry or game pieces or bones, or the carcass and trimmings from a roast bird. Don't mix raw and cooked bones.

1 Crush or break up bones and carcasses. Put the bones (or pieces) into a stockpot or large pan. Add 2 or 3 halved, unpeeled onions and cook until browned.

2 Add 4 quarts (4 liters) water. Bring to a boil, skimming any foam from the surface. Add 3 chopped carrots, 3 chopped celery stalks, 1 large bouquet garni, and a few black peppercorns.

3 Half cover the pan and simmer for 2 1/2–3 hours. Strain the stock into a bowl. Leave to cool, then remove the solidified fat from the surface and discard. Cover and keep in the refrigerator for up to 3 days, or freeze for 3 months. (You can keep raw or cooked bones in the freezer too, for making stock at a later date.)

GIBLET STOCK

Giblets are packaged inside birds, and they make a really good stock.

1 Put the giblets (the heart, kidneys, and gizzard but not the liver) in a stockpot or large saucepan and cook until lightly browned. Stir in 1 quart (1 liter) water (or previously made stock). Bring to a boil, skimming any foam that forms on the surface.

2 Add 1 or 2 quartered, unpeeled onions, 1 chopped celery stalk, 1 chopped carrot, 1 bouquet garni, and a few black peppercorns. Simmer for about 1 hour. Strain, then cool, cover, and keep in the refrigerator for up to 3 days, or freeze for 3 months.

JELLIED STOCK

This stock is used in cold dishes such as Rather Special Game Pie (page 222), where it forms a jelly around the meat. Make it in the same way as other stocks, but use bones only, because they contain a high level of gelatin. Crack the bones before adding them to the pot. The stock will set when cool.

Stock know-how

If you do not have a carcass from a whole bird, chicken wings make a good base for a stock.

•

Peppercorns, instead of ground black pepper, are used in stock: prolonged cooking can turn ground black pepper bitter.

•

Skim off fat with a large spoon, soak it up with paper towel, or cool and lift it off.

JOINTING A BIRD

Chicken portions are widely available, but cutting a bird into 4 or 8 serving pieces is not at all difficult to do yourself, and it can be done before or after cooking. A pair of special poultry shears makes the job particularly easy, otherwise use good, strong scissors or a sharp chef's knife.

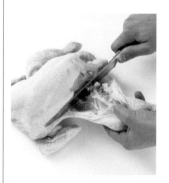

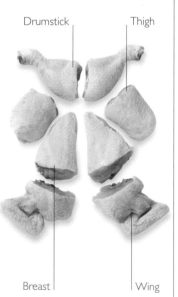

Drumstick   Thigh

Breast   Wing

1 Cut through to the joint between one of the legs and the body. Twist the leg out and away from the body to pop the ball-and-socket joint, then cut through the joint to remove the leg. Remove the other leg.

2 To remove the breast halves, cut through the skin and flesh along both sides of the breastbone. Cut through the bones of the ribcage where it joins the sides of the breastbone, then remove the breastbone.

3 Turn over and cut along the backbone, to give 2 breasts with wings attached. For 8 pieces, cut each breast half diagonally in two: the wing half should be slightly smaller. Cut each leg through the joint into thigh and drumstick.

BONING A WHOLE CHICKEN

Although boning a chicken requires a little time and effort, the result is impressive. Stuffed and rolled into a ballotine, it is ideal for entertaining because it is so easy to carve. Other birds can be boned in the same way.

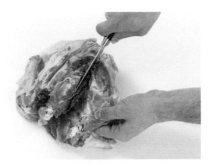  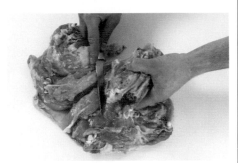

1 Set the bird breast-side down and slit the skin along the backbone. Remove the wishbone (page 172). Slide the knife into the cut and gently pull and scrape the flesh away from the ribcage. Continue cutting away the flesh until you reach the leg and wing joints. Repeat on the other side.

2 Scrape away the flesh from the ribcage, working on one side at a time. Take care not to make any holes in the skin as you are doing this. Cut through the ball-and-socket joints connecting the legs to the carcass (they will still be attached to the skin).

3 Keep cutting the flesh from the bone on both sides until you reach the ridge of the breastbone in the middle. Cut the breastbone free, without cutting through the skin, and lift it away with the carcass.

4 Cut through the tendons in the legs that join the flesh to the bone. Scrape back the flesh until the bones of each leg have been exposed, then pull out the bones, cutting them free of the skin.

5 Bone the wings in the same way as the legs. Push the legs and wings skin-side out. The chicken is now ready for stuffing and rolling. Keep the carcass and bones for making chicken stock.

BONING A QUAIL

For a special occasion, tiny quail can be boned but left whole. It is then quite simple to fill them with a savory stuffing and secure with a toothpick ready for roasting. Make sure you use a very small knife and be careful not to pierce the skin.

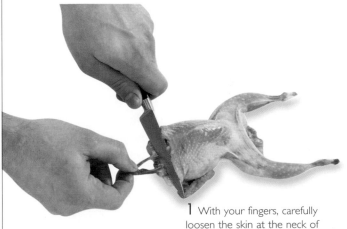  

1 With your fingers, carefully loosen the skin at the neck of the quail, and push it back to reveal the wishbone. With a small, sharp knife, cut the flesh from around the wishbone and remove it.

2 Loosen 1 wing by carefully cutting through the tendon at the base. Repeat with the other wing.

3 Insert the knife between the ribcage and the flesh and, working all around the bird, scrape the flesh from the bones, pushing it back as you go. Remove the ribcage. The bird is now ready to stuff.

SPATCHCOCKING

This method of splitting and flattening a bird makes it quicker to cook and suitable for broiling or grilling over a barbecue. Poussins, chickens, guinea fowl, and most game birds can all be spatchcocked.

1 With poultry shears or a knife, cut along both sides of the backbone and discard. Cut off the wing tips and the ends of the legs. Remove the wishbone.

2 Turn the bird over. Put your hands on top of the breast and press down firmly with the heels of your hands to break the breastbone and flatten the bird.

3 Thread a long metal skewer through the bird at the neck end, passing through the wings. Thread another skewer below the breast, passing through the legs. If small birds are spatchcocked, 2 or 3 can be threaded on the same skewers.

PREPARING POULTRY FOR ROASTING

Tying or skewering a bird before roasting holds it together so it keeps a neat shape during cooking. It will also prevent any stuffing from falling out. To be sure that heat can penetrate into the middle of the bird and cook it thoroughly, it is best to put stuffing into the neck end and not into the large body cavity.

Trussing with string
1 Thread a trussing needle with string. Put the bird breast-side up. Push the legs back and down. Insert the needle into a knee joint. Pass it through the bird and then out through the other knee.

2 Pull the neck skin over the end of the bird and tuck the wing tips over it. Push the needle through both sections of one wing, through the neck skin and beneath the backbone, and out the other wing.

3 With the bird on its side, pull the string tightly, tie the ends together, and trim. Tuck the tail into the cavity and fold the top skin over it.

4 Push the needle through the top skin. Loop the string around one of the drumsticks, under the breastbone, and then around the other drumstick. Pull the string tight and tie the ends.

Simple trussing
1 Put the bird breast-side up and push the legs back and down. Holding the legs with one hand, insert a skewer below the knee joint and push it through the bird.

2 Turn the bird over. Pull the neck skin over the end and tuck the wing tips over it. Push a skewer through 1 wing, the neck skin, and out through the other wing.

REMOVING THE WISHBONE

A bird is easier to carve if the wishbone is removed before cooking.

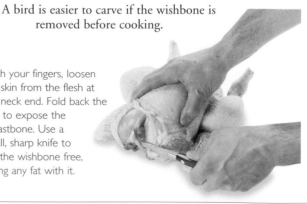

With your fingers, loosen the skin from the flesh at the neck end. Fold back the skin to expose the breastbone. Use a small, sharp knife to cut the wishbone free, taking any fat with it.

CARVING DUCKS & GEESE

Once cooked, small ducks need simply to be cut into quarters or even halves for serving.
Larger ducks and geese can be carved as for other poultry (below).

3 Carve the breast meat in diagonal slices. For a larger bird, carve the breast meat without removing it first, as for a chicken (below).

1 Remove trussing. Cut through the joints between legs and body to remove the legs. (Cook them longer if necessary.) Cut off the wings in the same way.

2 Slit the skin along both sides of the breastbone. Slide the knife blade into the cut on one side to free the breast meat in a single piece. Repeat on the other side.

CARVING POULTRY

After roasting, wrap bird in foil and leave to rest before carving – at least 15 minutes and up to 45 minutes for a large bird – to allow the juices to settle. Remove any trussing first.

1 Put the bird breast-side up on a carving board (ideally one with a well to catch all the juices). Insert a carving fork into one breast to keep the bird steady, then cut into the joint between the far leg and body.

2 Turn the bird on its side and cut away the meat close to the backbone, cutting around the "oyster" meat on the back so that it remains attached to the thigh. Turn the bird over.

3 Twist the leg outward to break the joint, then cut it to remove the leg. If preferred, divide into thigh and drumstick, cutting through the ball-and-socket joint. Remove the other leg.

4 Make a horizontal cut into the breast above the wing joint on one side, cutting all the way to the bone. Carve neat slices from the breast, holding the knife blade parallel to the ribcage. Repeat on the other side.

ROASTING TIMES

These times are a guide only; always test a bird to make sure it is thoroughly cooked (page 169).

Bird	Oven temperature	Time
Poussin	375°F (190°C)	40–45 minutes total cooking, depending on size
Chicken	375°F (190°C)	20 minutes per pound (500 g) plus 20 minutes
Duck	400°F (200°C)	25 minutes per per pound (500 g) for "just cooked"
Goose	350°F (180°C)	20 minutes per pound (500 g) plus 20 minutes
Pheasant	400°F (200°C)	50 minutes total cooking
Turkey 7–9 lb (3.5–4.5 kg)	375°F (190°C)	2½–3 hours total cooking
10–12 lb (5–6 kg)	375°F (190°C)	3½–4 hours total cooking
13–17 lb (6.5–8.5 kg)	375°F (190°C)	4½–5 hours total cooking

Roasting know-how

To calculate roasting time, weigh the bird after you have added any stuffing.

•

Cover large birds loosely with foil if the skin is becoming too browned.

•

Place fatty birds, such as duck and goose, on a rack, to allow the fat to drain away and keep the skin crisp.

SUNDAY ROAST CHICKEN

Traditional roast chicken is very much a family favorite on weekends. With its crisp skin, light, juicy stuffing of onion, apple, herbs, and lemon zest, and accompaniment of rich gravy, it is hard to beat.

SERVES 4

a few parsley and thyme sprigs

chicken, 3 1/2–4 lb (1.7–2 kg)

1/2 lemon, sliced

1/2 onion, sliced

4 tbls (60 g) butter, softened

APPLE & HERB STUFFING

2 tbls (30 g) butter

1 small onion, finely chopped

1 cooking apple, peeled, cored, and grated

1 1/2 cups (60 g) fresh white breadcrumbs

1 small egg, beaten

1 tbsp chopped parsley

1 tbsp chopped fresh thyme

grated zest of 1 lemon

salt and black pepper

GRAVY

2 tsp all-purpose flour

1 1/4 cups (300 ml) chicken stock or giblet stock (page 170)

splash of red wine or sherry and a spoonful of red-currant jelly or cranberry sauce (optional)

1 Make the apple and herb stuffing: melt the butter in a saucepan, add the onion, and cook gently for a few minutes until softened. Remove from the heat, cool slightly, then stir in the apple, breadcrumbs, egg, parsley, thyme, and lemon zest. Season with salt and pepper, then leave until cold.

2 Put the parsley and thyme sprigs into the cavity of the chicken, add the lemon and onion, and season well with black pepper. Tie the legs together with string.

3 Spoon the stuffing into the neck end of the chicken, secure the skin flap over the stuffing with a small skewer, and pat into a rounded shape. Put any remaining stuffing into a baking dish.

4 Weigh the stuffed chicken, and calculate the roasting time at 20 minutes per pound (500 g), plus an extra 20 minutes. Rub the butter over the breast, and season with salt and pepper.

5 Place the chicken, breast-side down, in a roasting pan. Roast in a heated oven at 375°F (190°C) for the calculated time, turning the bird over when lightly browned and basting it every 20 minutes. Put any stuffing in the oven for the last 40 minutes.

6 Check that the chicken is done (page 170), then transfer to a warmed serving platter, and cover with foil. Make the gravy (see box, right).

7 Carve the chicken (page 173). Remove the stuffing from the neck cavity and transfer to a serving dish with any other stuffing. Serve hot, with the gravy.

Making gravy

Tilt the roasting pan, and spoon off all but 1 tbsp of the fat that is on the surface, leaving behind the cooking juices and sediment. Put the roasting pan on the stovetop.

Add the flour, and cook over medium heat for 1–2 minutes, stirring constantly with a whisk or metal spoon to dissolve any sediment from the bottom of the pan.

Pour in the stock, and bring to a boil, stirring. Simmer for 2 minutes, then add wine or sherry, red-currant jelly or cranberry sauce, and salt and pepper to taste. Strain.

FRENCH ROAST CHICKEN

Chicken roasted in the traditional French style is particularly moist and succulent because of the stock added to the roasting pan. In France, the chicken liver is often cooked in a little butter, then sliced and added to the gravy, but this is optional.

SERVES 4

a small bunch of tarragon or rosemary

6 tbls (90 g) butter, softened, plus extra for greasing

chicken, 3 1/2–4 lb (1.7–2 kg)

salt and black pepper

1 1/4 cups (300 ml) 1 chicken stock or giblet stock (page 170)

4 heads of roast garlic (see box, right) to serve

a good splash of red or white wine

1 Put the bunch of herbs and 2 tbls (30 g) of the butter into the cavity of the chicken. Tie the legs together with string. Weigh the chicken and calculate the roasting time at 20 minutes per pound (500 g), plus an extra 20 minutes.

2 Rub the remaining butter all over the chicken and sprinkle with salt and pepper.

3 Put the chicken, breast-side down, into a small roasting pan. Pour the stock into the bottom of the pan, and cover the chicken with buttered waxed paper or foil. Roast in a heated oven at 375°F (190°C) for the calculated time. At regular intervals, baste the chicken and turn it first onto one side, then onto the other, and finally onto its back.

4 Check that the chicken is done (page 169), then transfer to a warmed serving platter, and cover with foil.

5 Leave the chicken to rest for about 15 minutes, then carve and serve with the cooking juices, boiled in the roasting pan with some red or white wine.

ITALIAN ROAST CHICKEN

Roast the chicken in a large roasting pan. Forty minutes before the end of the roasting time, add 1 trimmed and thinly sliced fennel bulb and 2 red onions, peeled and quartered lengthwise, to the pan.

Roast garlic

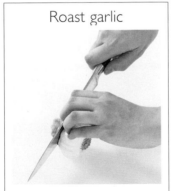

Cut the stem ends off 4 heads of garlic, arrange in an oiled baking dish, and drizzle a little olive oil over the tops. Roast in a heated oven at 375°F (190°C) for 45–60 minutes. To eat, squeeze the soft cloves of garlic from the papery skins.

ROAST CHICKEN WITH ORANGE & PEPPERS

SERVES 4

3 oranges

a few parsley sprigs

1 head of garlic, separated into cloves

3 1/2–4 lb (1.7–2 kg) chicken

salt and black pepper

1 tsp paprika

pinch of cayenne pepper

1 tbls (15 g) butter, softened

1 red pepper, halved, seeded, and diced

6 tbls (90 ml) orange juice

5 tbls (75 ml) brandy

chopped fresh basil to garnish

1 Cut 2 of the oranges lengthwise into quarters, leaving them unpeeled. Peel the remaining orange, and separate into segments, without the tough membranes.

2 Put the parsley, orange quarters, and half of the garlic cloves into the cavity of the chicken.

3 Weigh the chicken, and calculate the roasting time at 20 minutes per pound (500 g), plus an extra 20 minutes.

4 Rub the chicken with salt and pepper, and the paprika, cayenne, and butter. Place the chicken, breast-side down, in a roasting pan. Add the red pepper and the remaining garlic cloves.

5 Roast in a preheated oven at 375°F (190°C) for the calculated time, turning the chicken breast-side up halfway through cooking.

6 Check that the chicken is done (page 169), then remove it from the tin with the red pepper and garlic. Carve the chicken, and arrange on a warmed serving platter with the red pepper and garlic. Keep hot.

7 Spoon off all but 1 tbsp fat from the pan, leaving behind the cooking juices. Add the orange juice and brandy and boil on the stovetop until reduced. Add the orange segments and heat through.

8 Spoon the orange segments and sauce over the chicken, sprinkle with the basil, and serve at once.

PROVENÇAL-STYLE ROAST CHICKEN

SERVES 6

1 large onion, cut into wedges

2 large carrots, peeled and sliced

4 oz (125 g) whole button mushrooms

3 garlic cloves, peeled

1 cup (250 m) dry white wine

1 1/2 cups (375 ml) chicken stock

3 1/2 lb (1.7 kg) chicken, with any giblets removed

14 oz (400 g) canned crushed tomatoes

1 tbsp tomato paste

salt and black pepper

chopped parsley to garnish

1 Arrange the onion wedges, carrot slices, whole mushrooms and garlic cloves in a single layer in a roasting pan, and pour over the wine and stock.

2 Place the chicken breast-side up on a small roasting rack, and place in the middle of the roasting pan on top of the vegetables. Roast in a preheated oven at 400°F (200°C) for 1 1/2 hours or until the chicken is tender and done (page 169).

3 Remove the chicken from the pan, transfer to a large warmed serving dish, and keep warm.

4 Make the sauce: add the chopped tomatoes and tomato paste to the vegetables in the pan, stir well, and return to the oven for 5 minutes or until hot.

5 Carefully pour the contents of the pan into a food processor or blender, and puree until smooth. Season with salt and pepper.

6 Pour the sauce over the roast chicken, garnish with chopped parsley, and serve at once.

CHICKEN POT PIE

This recipe makes a great family dish, packed with tender chicken and colorful vegetables.
You can vary the vegetables according to season and availability.
The pie will be a great success any time of the year.

SERVES 6

2 lb (1 kg) chicken

2 pints (1.25 liters) chicken stock

1 onion, quartered

1 celery stalk, thickly sliced

pared zest and juice of 1 lemon

2 carrots

2 waxy potatoes

3 tbls (45 g) butter

1/3 cup (45 g) all-purpose flour, plus extra for dusting

salt and black pepper

4 oz (125 g) frozen peas

6 oz (175 g) shortcrust pastry

beaten egg yolk for glazing

3 1/2 PINT (2 LITER) PIE DISH

1 Put the chicken, stock, onion, celery, and lemon zest into a large saucepan. Bring to a boil, cover, and simmer for 30 minutes.

2 Add the carrots and potatoes, cover, and simmer for about 20 minutes or until the vegetables are cooked and the chicken is just tender. Remove the vegetables from the liquid and set aside. Leave the chicken to cool in the liquid.

3 Remove the meat from the chicken, and cut into bite-sized pieces, discarding the skin and bones. Dice the vegetables.

4 Skim the fat from the cooking liquid, then bring 1 pint (600 ml) to a boil. Melt the butter in another pan, add the flour, and cook, stirring occasionally, for 1 minute. Stir in the hot stock, whisking until it comes to a boil and thickens. Add the lemon juice and season with salt and pepper.

5 Stir the chicken, diced vegetables, and peas into the sauce, then leave to cool.

6 On a lightly floured work surface, roll out the pastry, then cut out the lid, and fill, cover, and decorate the pie (see box, right).

7 Bake in a preheated oven at 375°F (190°C) for 30 minutes or until the top is crisp and golden brown. Serve hot.

Cook's know-how

The chicken, vegetables, and sauce need to be cold before covering with pastry or the pastry will become soggy. This is a good dish to make ahead up to the end of step 5, then all you have to do is assemble the pie and bake it for half an hour. You can make the filling up to 24 hours ahead and keep it covered in the refrigerator.

Filling, covering, and decorating the pie

Invert the pie dish on to the pastry, and use a small knife to cut around the edge, keeping the blade close to the dish. Reserve all trimmings. Transfer the cold filling to the pie dish, and top with the pastry.

Press the pastry with your fingertips on to the rim of the pie dish. Crimp the edge of the pastry with a fork. Brush the pastry with the beaten egg yolk, making a lattice pattern.

Cut decorative shapes from the reserved pastry trimmings with a pastry cutter. Arrange on top of the pie, and glaze the shapes with the beaten egg yolk.

MOROCCAN POUSSINS

SERVES 2

2 x 12 oz (375 g) poussins,
   spatchcocked (page 172)

MARINADE

3 tbsp olive oil

grated zest of 1 lime and juice
   of 2 limes

1 small onion, finely chopped

2–3 garlic cloves, crushed

2 tbsp chopped fresh cilantro

1 tbsp paprika

2 tsp curry powder

pinch of cayenne pepper

salt

1 Mix all the marinade
  ingredients, except salt, in a
nonmetallic dish. Turn the
poussins in the marinade,
cover, and marinate in the
refrigerator for at least 3 hours
(or overnight), turning
occasionally.

2 When ready to cook,
  preheat the broiler to hot,
and sprinkle the poussins with
a little salt.

3 Put the poussins, skin-side
  down, on a rack under the
broiler, 6 in (15 cm) from the
heat, and grill for 15–20
minutes on each side, turning
once and brushing with the
marinade. Check the poussins
are done by pricking with a
fork – the juices should run
clear, not pink or red. Serve hot
or cold.

Cook's know-how

It is quick and easy to
spatchcock poussins, but you
can buy them already
spatchcocked at most
gourmet food stores,
especially during the barbecue
season.

LEMON POUSSINS WITH ARTICHOKE HEARTS

SERVES 4

4 x 12 oz (375 g) poussins

salt and black pepper

4 garlic cloves

1 lemon, cut into quarters
   lengthwise

4 rosemary sprigs

4 tbls (60 g) butter, softened

1 x 10 oz (300 g) jar antipasta
   artichoke hearts in oil

3/4 cup (175 ml) dry white wine

fresh rosemary and lemon wedges
to garnish

1 Season the poussins inside
  and out, and put a garlic
clove, lemon quarter, and
rosemary sprig into each one.
Tie the legs together with
string, then rub the birds with
the softened butter.

2 Put the poussins upside
  down on a rack in a
roasting pan. Roast in a
preheated oven at 375°F
(190°C) for 40–45 minutes,
turning them the right way up
halfway through.

3 While the poussins are
  roasting, drain the artichoke
hearts, reserving 2–3 tbsp of the
oil, and cut each artichoke
heart in half.

4 Check the poussins are
  done by pricking with a
fork – the juices should run
clear, not pink or red. Remove
them from the pan, and keep
warm. Spoon off all but 1 tbsp
fat from the pan, leaving
behind the cooking juices.

5 Add the wine to the pan,
  mix with the juices, then
boil on the stovetop until
reduced to about 6 tbls (90 ml).

6 Stir in the artichokes and
  the reserved oil, and heat
through gently. Serve the
poussins with the artichokes
and sauce, garnished with
rosemary and lemon wedges.

POUSSINS WITH ROMESCO SAUCE

SERVES 2

2 x 12 oz (375 g) poussins, spatchcocked (page 172)

8 green onions, trimmed (optional)

cilantro sprigs to garnish

MARINADE

2 tbsp olive oil

1 tbsp balsamic vinegar

4 garlic cloves, crushed

1/2 tsp ground cinnamon

salt and black pepper

ROMESCO SAUCE

1 x 8 oz (250 g) canned crushed tomatoes

3/4 cup (90 g) blanched almonds

1 slice of stale bread, broken into pieces

2 tbsp olive oil

1 tbsp balsamic vinegar

1 garlic clove

1 small dried red chili, crumbled

a few sprigs of parsley

1/2 tsp ground cinnamon

1 Make the marinade: combine the oil, vinegar, garlic, and cinnamon, and season with salt and pepper. Brush over the poussins and green onions (if using), cover, and marinate in the refrigerator for 1 hour, or overnight.

2 Place the poussins skin-side down under a hot broiler, 6 in (15 cm) from the heat, and broil for 15–20 minutes on each side. Broil the green onions close to the heat for 5–8 minutes on each side until the onions are slightly charred.

3 Meanwhile, make the romesco sauce: put all the ingredients in a food processor with a pinch of salt and purée until smooth.

4 Check the poussins are done by pricking with a fork – the juices should run clear, not pink or red. Serve hot, with the romesco sauce and the green onions (if used). Garnish each serving with a cilantro sprig.

ORIENTAL POUSSINS

SERVES 4

2 x 1 1/4 lb (625 g) poussins

4 tbsp dark soy sauce

3 tbsp dry sherry

3 tbsp hoisin sauce

3 tbsp sunflower oil

3 garlic cloves, crushed

2 tbsp brown sugar

1 tsp five-spice powder

1 in (2.5 cm) piece of fresh ginger, peeled and grated

green onions to garnish

1 Halve the poussins, and remove the backbones (see box, right).

2 Combine the soy sauce, sherry, hoisin sauce, oil, garlic, sugar, five-spice powder, and ginger. Brush this mixture on both sides of the poussins.

3 Put the poussins, skin-side up, into a roasting tin, and roast in a preheated oven at 375°F (190°C) for 30 minutes. Check the poussins are done by pricking with a fork – the juices should run clear, not pink or red.

4 With a sharp knife, finely shred the green tops of the green onions, working on the diagonal. Serve the poussins hot, garnished with the green onion slices.

Halving a poussin

Cut along the middle of the breast with poultry shears or sturdy kitchen scissors. Take the 2 sides and open out slightly.

Turn the poussin over and cut in half, along one side of the backbone. Remove and discard the backbone.

CHICKEN CACCIATORE

SERVES 4

8 small chicken portions (4 legs and 4 breasts or 8 thighs)

all-purpose flour for dusting

salt and black pepper

3–4 tbsp olive oil

3 oz (90 g) streaky slab bacon or pancetta, cut into strips

1 large onion, chopped

1 small green bell pepper, halved, seeded, and diced

2 garlic cloves, crushed

8 oz (250 g) mushrooms, quartered

1/2 cup (125 ml) red or white wine

14 oz (400 g) canned crushed tomatoes

5 tbls (75 ml) tomato paste

2 tsp chopped fresh sage

4 tbsp chopped parsley

grated zest of 1 lemon

2 tbsp capers, chopped

fresh sage sprigs to garnish

1 Lightly dust the chicken pieces with flour seasoned with salt and pepper, and shake off any excess.

2 Heat half of the oil in a large skillet, add the bacon and chicken, and cook for 10–12 minutes until browned all over. Transfer to a flameproof casserole or a Dutch oven with a slotted spoon, then pour off the fat from the frying pan.

3 Heat the remaining oil in the skillet, add the onion, green bell pepper, and half of the garlic, and cook gently, stirring, for 5 minutes until soft but not colored. Transfer to the casserole with a slotted spoon. Add the mushrooms, and cook for 2 minutes. Add to the casserole.

4 Pour the wine into the skillet, and boil until reduced to about 4 tbsp. Add to the casserole with the tomatoes, tomato paste, and the sage. Cover and cook in a preheated oven at 350°F (180°C) for 45 minutes or until the chicken is tender.

5 Combine the remaining garlic with the chopped parsley, lemon zest, and capers. Stir into the casserole, and taste for seasoning. Serve hot, garnished with sage sprigs.

FAMILY CHICKEN CASSEROLE

SERVES 4

2 tbsp sunflower oil

4 chicken portions (legs or thighs)

4 oz (125 g) bacon slices, cut into strips

1 1/2 cups (250 g) carrots, thickly sliced

2 celery stalks, thickly sliced

1 large onion, sliced

2 tbls (30 g) all-purpose flour

2 1/2 cups (600 ml) chicken stock

1 bouquet garni

salt and black pepper

4 potatoes, cut into large chunks

chopped parsley to garnish

1 Heat the oil in a large flameproof casserole. Add the chicken, skin-side down, and cook for 10–12 minutes until browned all over. Lift out and drain on paper towels. Add the bacon, carrots, celery, and onion, and cook over a high heat, stirring, until golden. Lift out with a slotted spoon, and drain on paper towels.

2 Spoon off all but 1 tbsp fat from the casserole. Add the flour, and cook, stirring constantly, for 3–5 minutes until lightly browned. Gradually pour in the chicken stock, stirring until smooth. Add the bouquet garni, and season with salt and pepper.

3 Return the chicken, bacon, carrots, celery, and onion to the casserole, add the potatoes, and bring to a boil. Cover and cook in a preheated oven at 325°F (160°C) for 1–1 1/4 hours or until the chicken is tender when pierced with a fork. Serve hot, garnished with parsley.

ITALIAN CHICKEN CASSEROLE

Substitute 1 1/2 cups (250 g) sliced zucchini for the carrots, and 14 oz (400 g) canned crushed tomatoes and 1 tbsp tomato paste for the chicken stock. If the mixture is too thick, add a splash of water, chicken stock, or wine.

CHICKEN MARENGO

SERVES 4

2 tbls (30 g) butter

I tbsp sunflower oil

I chicken, 3 lb (1.5 kg), cut into 8 serving pieces (page 170)

8 small shallots or pickling onions

2 tbls (30 g) all-purpose flour

1 1/4 pint (300 ml) dry white wine

2/3 cup (150 ml) chicken stock

14 oz (400 g) canned crushed tomatoes

8 oz (250 g) button mushrooms

I tbsp tomato paste

2 garlic cloves, crushed

I bouquet garni

salt and black pepper

250 g (8 oz) cooked peeled shrimp

chopped parsley to garnish

1 Melt the butter with the oil in a large flameproof casserole or Dutch oven. Add the chicken pieces, and cook for 10–12 minutes until browned all over. Lift out and leave to drain on paper towels.

2 Add the shallots or onions, and cook over a high heat for about 8 minutes or until golden brown.

3 Lift out the shallots or onions and leave to drain on paper towels. Spoon off all but 1 tbsp of the fat from the casserole, add the flour, and cook, stirring, for 3–5 minutes until lightly browned.

4 Lower the heat, and stir in the wine and stock until combined. Add the tomatoes, mushrooms, tomato paste, garlic, and bouquet garni. Season with salt and pepper.

5 Return the shallots or onions and the chicken to the casserole, and bring to a boil. Cover and cook in a preheated oven at 350°F (180°C) for 35 minutes or until the chicken is almost tender. Stir in the shrimp, and return to the oven for another 10 minutes or until the chicken is tender when pierced with a fork. Garnish each serving with chopped parsley before serving.

COQ AU VIN

SERVES 4

2 tbls (30 g) butter

I tbsp sunflower oil

I chicken, 3 lb (1.5 kg), cut into 8 serving pieces (page 170)

4 oz (125 g) bacon slices, cut into strips

8 small shallots or pickling onions

8 oz (250 g) button mushrooms

2 tbls (30 g) all-purpose flour

1 1/4 cups (300 ml) chicken stock

1 1/4 cups (300 ml) red wine

I bouquet garni

I large garlic clove, crushed

salt and black pepper

2 tbsp chopped parsley to garnish

croûtes (page 49) to serve

1 Melt the butter with the oil in a large flameproof casserole. Add the chicken, and cook for 10–12 minutes until browned all over. Lift out and leave to drain on paper towels.

2 Spoon off any excess fat, then add the bacon, shallots or onions, and mushrooms, and cook over a high heat, stirring, until golden brown.

3 Lift the mixture out of the pan with a slotted spoon and leave to drain thoroughly on paper towels.

4 Add the flour to the pan, and cook for 3–5 minutes, stirring constantly until lightly browned. Gradually pour in the stock, then the wine, stirring until smooth.

5 Return the chicken, bacon, shallots, and mushrooms to the casserole, and add the bouquet garni, and garlic. Season with salt and pepper. Bring to a boil, cover, and cook in a preheated oven at 350°F (180°C) for 45 minutes or until the chicken is tender when pierced with a fork.

6 Sprinkle the chicken with the chopped parsley, and serve hot, with croûtes.

Healthy option

To reduce the saturated fat content of this classic dish, skin the chicken before cooking, use 2 tbsp oil and no butter, and half the amount of bacon (or omit it altogether).

AMERICAN FRIED CHICKEN

SERVES 4

3/4 cup (350 ml) buttermilk

8 chicken thighs

3/4 cup (125 g) all-purpose flour

1 1/2 tsp salt

1 tsp paprika

1/2 tsp black pepper

1/2 tsp garlic granules (optional)

large pinch of grated nutmeg

sunflower oil for deep-frying

TO SERVE (OPTIONAL)

4 bacon slices, broiled

parsley sprigs

1 Pour the buttermilk into a large nonmetallic bowl. Add the chicken, and turn to coat. Cover and chill, turning occasionally, for 2–3 hours.

2 In a large bowl, combine the flour with the salt, paprika, pepper, garlic granules (if using), and nutmeg.

3 Lift the chicken pieces out of the buttermilk and shake off any excess liquid. Coat with the seasoned flour.

4 Pour 3/4 in (2 cm) oil into a deep skillet, and heat to 350°F (180°C), or until a cube of bread browns in 1 minute.

5 Fry the chicken in the oil, in 2–3 batches if necessary. Cook each batch for 10–15 minutes or until the pieces are tender when pierced with a fork, turning them several times so they cook evenly.

6 Remove the chicken from the oil with a slotted spoon, and drain on paper towels. Serve hot, with broiled bacon rashers and parsley if you like.

HERB GRILLED CHICKEN

SERVES 8

8 chicken portions (legs or breasts)

HERB BUTTER

6 tbls (90 g) butter, softened

3 tbsp chopped parsley

3 tbsp snipped fresh chives

2 garlic cloves, crushed (optional)

salt and black pepper

1 Mix the butter with the parsley, chives, and garlic, if using, and a good pinch each of salt and pepper.

2 Spread the chicken with the butter, and put, skin-side down over a hot barbecue, or skin-side up under a hot broiler, 4 in (10 cm) from the heat. Cook for 10 minutes on each side or until the juices run clear when the chicken is pierced.

JAMAICAN CHICKEN

Substitute 1/2 tsp crushed peppercorns (red, green, and black), 1 tsp chopped fresh thyme, and 3 chopped green onions for the parsley and chives.

HOT PAPRIKA CHICKEN

Substitute 2 tsp paprika and 2 tsp mustard powder for the parsley and chives.

THAI CILANTRO CHICKEN

Substitute 1–2 tbsp chopped fresh cilantro and 2 tbsp Thai green curry paste for the parsley and chives.

Healthy option

Butter makes the chicken luscious and golden brown, but it is high in saturated fat and calories. You can reduce this by using half the amount of butter or 2 tbsp olive oil. Skinning the chicken before cooking is another option.

JERK CHICKEN

SERVES 4

4 chicken legs or drumsticks

JERK PASTE

3 tbsp lime juice

2 tbsp dark rum

2 tbsp sunflower oil

4 green onions, roughly chopped

1–2 fresh green chilies, halved, seeded, and roughly chopped

2 garlic cloves, roughly chopped

1 tbsp ground allspice

2 tsp fresh thyme leaves

salt and black pepper

TO SERVE

chopped fresh thyme

broiled pineapple rings (optional)

1 Make the jerk paste: purée the ingredients in a food processor with a pinch each of salt and pepper.

2 Put the chicken pieces in a nonmetallic dish and brush them all over with the jerk paste. Cover and marinate in the refrigerator for at least 30 minutes, or overnight.

3 Put the chicken over a hot barbecue, or under a hot broiler, 4 in (10 cm) from the heat. Cook for 10 minutes on each side or until the juices run clear when the chicken is pierced.

4 Serve the chicken hot or cold, sprinkled with thyme and accompanied by broiled pineapple rings, if you like.

TEX-MEX CHICKEN

SERVES 4

4 skinless, boneless chicken breast halves

2 avocados

2 tbsp lime juice

1 red onion, finely chopped

MARINADE

4 tbsp olive oil

4 tbsp orange juice

1 tsp ground cumin

SALSA

(1 lb (500 g) tomatoes, chopped

1 small red onion, finely chopped

3 tbsp olive oil

2 tbsp lime juice

3 tbsp chopped fresh cilantro

2 garlic cloves, crushed

1 fresh green chili, halved, seeded, and chopped

salt

1 Make several diagonal slashes in each chicken breast half, then put the chicken in a nonmetallic dish. Mix the marinade ingredients together, and pour over the chicken. Cover and marinate in the refrigerator for at least 30 minutes, or overnight.

2 Make the salsa: combine the tomatoes, onion, oil, lime juice, coriander, garlic, chilli, and salt to taste. Cover and chill until ready to serve.

3 Remove the chicken from the marinade, and put under a hot broiler, 4 in (10 cm) from the heat. Broil for 3–5 minutes on each side, depending on the size of the chicken, until the juices run clear when the chicken is pierced.

4 Meanwhile, halve, pit (page 88), and peel the avocados. Slice lengthwise, and brush with lime juice.

5 Thinly slice the chicken breasts, following the slashes made before marinating. Arrange the avocado and chicken slices on plates, and sprinkle the chopped red onion around the edges. Spoon a little of the salsa into the middle of each serving, and hand the remainder separately.

CHICKEN AND TURKEY SALADS

Lean, low-fat chicken and turkey teamed with fresh seasonal salad ingredients and vegetables make healthy meals for every day and special occasions, and if you buy cooked meat they are very quick to put together. These salads are good for buffets, too, as most of the preparation can be done well in advance.

TARRAGON CHICKEN WITH AVOCADO

SERVES 6

1 lb (500 g) skinless, boneless cooked chicken

3 green onions, finely sliced

SAUCE

5 tbsp sunflower oil

3 tbsp white wine vinegar

2 tsp Dijon mustard

2–3 tsp sugar, to taste

2 canned anchovy fillets, finely chopped

scant 1 cup (200 ml) lowfat sour cream

1 tbsp chopped fresh tarragon

1 tbsp chopped parsley

salt and black pepper

TO SERVE

2 perfectly ripe avocados

juice of ½ lemon

1 bunch of watercress

2 green onions, trimmed and cut lengthwise into fine slices

1 Cut the chicken into bite-sized pieces and mix with the green onions in a bowl. Whisk all the sauce ingredients together in another bowl, adding salt and pepper to taste. Mix the sauce with the chicken, cover, and marinate in the refrigerator for at least 2 hours, overnight if possible.

2 Just before serving, halve, pit, and peel the avocados, slice the flesh into ½ in (1 cm) strips, and toss in the lemon juice. Gently mix the avocado into the salad, and spoon into a serving dish. Garnish with watercress and green onions, and serve.

VIETNAMESE TURKEY SALAD

SERVES 4

4 tbsp fish sauce (nam pla)

1 lb (500 g) turkey breast steaks

4 tbsp lime juice

1 tbsp sugar, or more to taste

¼ tsp ground black pepper

1 small fresh red chili, halved, seeded, and finely chopped

1½ cups (250 g) hard white cabbage, finely shredded

2 medium carrots, finely shredded

1 small onion, finely sliced

1 large bunch of fresh mint

1 Half fill a medium wok or deep skillet with water, sprinkle in half the fish sauce and bring to a boil. Turn the heat down to a simmer, lower in the turkey breast steaks, and cover the pan with a lid. Simmer for 10 minutes or until the turkey is cooked through. Lift the turkey out of the water, and leave until cool enough to handle.

2 Meanwhile, mix the remaining fish sauce in a large bowl with the lime juice, 1 tbsp sugar, the black pepper and chili. Add the cabbage, carrots, and onion, and mix well.

3 Cut the turkey into bite-sized strips and roughly chop 2 tbsp mint. Toss the turkey and chopped mint into the salad, and mix again. Cover and marinate in the refrigerator for 2–4 hours.

4 To serve, toss the salad again, then taste for seasoning and add more sugar if you like. Serve on a bed of the remaining mint leaves.

RED BELL PEPPER HERBED CHICKEN SALAD

SERVES 6

1 lb (500 g) skinless, boneless cooked chicken

SAUCE

1 bunch of fresh parsley

1 bunch of fresh basil

2 oz (60 g) red bell pepper in oil or brine (from a jar), drained

juice of 1 small lemon

2 tsp sugar

6 tbls (90 g) lowfat thick plain yogurt

4 tbsp lowfat mayonnaise

6 tbls (90 g) reduced-fat cream cheese

salt and black pepper

TO SERVE

fresh basil

strips of red bell pepper

tossed salad leaves

1 Make the sauce. Put the parsley, basil, red bell pepper, lemon juice, and 2 tsp sugar in a food processor and pulse for about 30 seconds until coarsely chopped. Add the yogurt, mayonnaise, cream cheese, and seasonings and pulse again for about 30 seconds. The sauce should be mixed but not finely chopped – it should have texture and flecks of herbs. Taste and add more sugar and seasoning if you like. (If you haven't got a food processor, coarsely chop the parsley, basil, and red bell pepper. Mix the other ingredients together, then mix in the chopped herbs and red bell pepper.)

2 Cut the chicken into strips, mix into the sauce, and turn into a shallow serving dish. Cover and leave in the refrigerator for at least 4 hours, or overnight, for the flavors to infuse.

3 Before serving, check the seasoning, and garnish with basil and strips of red bell pepper. Serve on a bed of tossed salad.

CLOCKWISE FROM TOP: Tarragon Chicken with Avocado, Red Bell Pepper Herbed Chicken Salad, Vietnamese Turkey Salad.

Almonds

FRAGRANT CHICKEN CURRY WITH ALMONDS

The spices in this recipe are among those used in store-bought curry powders, but using your own individual blend of spices gives a truly authentic flavor to a curry. This is a creamy, mild dish – not too hot or spicy.

SERVES 4

2 cloves

2 tsp cumin seeds

seeds of 4 cardamom pods

1 tsp garam masala

pinch of cayenne pepper

2 tbsp sunflower oil

4 skinless, boneless chicken breast halves

1 large onion, finely chopped

2 garlic cloves, crushed

1 in (2.5 cm) piece of fresh ginger, peeled and grated

salt and black pepper

1 1/4 cups (300 ml) chicken stock

2/3 cup (150) light cream

2/3 cup (150) plain yogurt

golden raisins and whole almonds, blanched, shredded, and toasted

1 Crush the cloves in a mortar and pestle with the cumin and cardamom seeds. Mix in the garam masala and cayenne.

2 Heat the oil in a flameproof casserole. Add the chicken, and cook for 2–3 minutes on each side until golden. Remove with a slotted spoon and leave to drain on paper towels.

3 Add the onion, garlic, and ginger to the pan, and cook gently, stirring occasionally, for a few minutes until just beginning to soften. Add the spice mixture and season with salt and pepper, then stir over a high heat for 1 minute.

4 Return the chicken to the casserole. Pour in the stock, and bring to a boil. Cover and simmer gently for 15 minutes or until the chicken is tender.

5 Stir in the cream and yogurt, heat through very gently, then taste for seasoning.

6 Spoon the curry into a serving dish, and sprinkle with the raisins and toasted shredded almonds. Serve hot.

Cook's know-how

Cardamom comes in 3 forms: as pods, whole seeds, and ground seeds. As the seeds lose their flavor quickly, it is best to buy whole cardamom pods and remove the seeds when you need them.

If you like, use 1 3/4 cups (400 ml) coconut milk instead of the stock in step 4, and omit the light cream in step 5. You can then finish the curry with just a swirl of yogurt and a scattering of chopped fresh cilantro.

Blanch the almonds and loosen the skins: immerse in a bowl of boiling water. When cool enough to handle, squeeze the almonds between your fingers to slide and pull off the skins.

Slice the almonds in half lengthwise. Cut the halves into shreds.

Place the shredded almonds on a baking tray, and toast in a preheated oven at 350°F (180°C), stirring the almonds occasionally to make sure they color evenly, for 8–10 minutes until lightly browned.

SAFFRON CHICKEN

SERVES 6

6 boneless chicken breast halves, with the skin left on

1 tbsp vegetable oil

scant 1 cup (200 ml) sour cream

salt and black pepper

chopped cilantro to garnish

MARINADE

2 pinches of saffron threads

1 in (2.5 cm) piece of fresh ginger, peeled and grated

juice of 1 lemon

1 tsp ground cardamom

1 tsp ground cilantro

1 tsp ground cinnamon

1 Make the marinade: put the saffron and the ginger into a mortar and grind with a pestle. Add the lemon juice, cardamom, coriander, and cinnamon, and mix well.

2 Put the chicken into a non-metallic dish, and brush the marinade over it. Cover and marinate in the refrigerator for at least 20 minutes.

3 Pour the oil into a small roasting tin. Turn the chicken breasts in the oil, and put them, skin-side up, in the roasting tin. Cook in a preheated oven at 375°F (190°C) for 15–20 minutes or until the juices run clear when the chicken is pierced with a fork. Remove from the tin and keep warm.

4 Put the pan on the stovetop, pour in the sour cream, and stir to combine with the juices. Do not boil. Season with salt and pepper, and heat through.

5 Divide the sauce among 6 warmed plates. Place the chicken breasts on top, and sprinkle with chopped cilantro before serving.

CHICKEN TIKKA

SERVES 4–6

1 1/2 lb (750 g) skinless, boneless chicken breasts, cut into 1 in (2.5 cm) cubes

cucumber raita (see box, right) to serve

MARINADE

2 tbsp plain yogurt

2 tbsp tomato paste

1 small onion, finely chopped

1 in (2.5 cm) piece of fresh ginger, peeled and grated

3 garlic cloves, crushed

1 tbsp tamarind paste (optional)

1 tbsp paprika

1 tsp ground cumin

large pinch of cayenne pepper

4–6 METAL SKEWERS

1 Make the marinade: in a large bowl, combine the yogurt, tomato paste, onion, ginger, garlic, tamarind paste (if using), paprika, cumin, and cayenne pepper.

2 Toss the chicken in the marinade. Cover and marinate in the refrigerator for at least 2 hours (or overnight), stirring occasionally.

3 Thread the chicken on to skewers, put under a hot broiler, 4 in (10 cm) from the heat, and broil for 3–5 minutes on each side or until cooked through. Serve hot, with raita.

Cucumber raita

Cut half a cucumber in half lengthwise. Scoop out the seeds, then coarsely grate the flesh into a strainer set over a bowl. Sprinkle with salt, and leave to drain for 10 minutes. Press hard to extract the juices.

Tip the cucumber into a bowl and add ⅔ cup (150 g) carton plain yogurt, 3 thinly sliced green onions, 3 heaped tbsp chopped fresh mint, and pepper to taste. Stir well to combine. Serve chilled.

STIR-FRIED CHICKEN WITH CRISP VEGETABLES

SERVES 4

4 skinless, boneless chicken breast halves, cut diagonally into 1/4 in (5 mm) strips

2 tbsp mild curry powder

black pepper

8 green onions

8 oz (250 g) carrots

3 tbsp sunflower oil

6 oz (175 g) baby corn cobs

6 oz (175 g) sugar snap peas

2–3 tbsp lemon juice

2 tbsp honey

1 in (2.5 cm) piece of fresh gingerroot, peeled and grated

salt

4 oz (125 g) bean sprouts

noodles to serve

1 Put the chicken strips in a bowl with the curry powder and season with black pepper. Toss until the chicken is coated, then set aside while you prepare the vegetables.

2 Finely slice the white parts of the green onions, reserving the green tops to garnish the finished dish.

3 Peel the carrots and cut them into matchstick-thin strips.

4 Heat 2 tbsp of the oil in a wok or large skillet. Add the chicken strips and stir-fry over a high heat for 3–4 minutes until golden brown.

5 Add the sliced green onions, the carrot matchsticks, the whole baby corn cobs, and the sugar snap peas, then add the lemon juice, honey, ginger, and a pinch of salt. Stir-fry over a high heat for 4 minutes or until the vegetables are tender-crisp and the chicken is cooked through.

6 Toss in the bean sprouts, and stir-fry over a high heat for 1–2 minutes until heated through. Taste for seasoning. Serve on a bed of noodles, and garnish with the reserved green onions.

THAI CHICKEN WITH WATER CHESTNUTS

SERVES 4

4 skinless, boneless chicken breasts, cut into 2.5 cm (1 in) pieces

3 tbsp sunflower oil

2 garlic cloves, crushed

1 in (2.5 cm) piece of fresh gingerroot, peeled and grated

1/2 –1 fresh green chili, halved, seeded, and chopped

1 tsp light soy sauce, or more to taste

1/2 tsp sugar

salt and black pepper

2 1/2 cups (600 ml) chicken stock

1 stem of lemongrass, bruised

grated zest of 1 lime

7 oz (200 g) canned water chestnuts, drained, rinsed, and sliced

1 small bunch of fresh cilantro, coarsely chopped

lime wedges, sliced green onions, and peanuts to garnish

1 Put the chicken into a dish, and add the oil, garlic, ginger, chili, soy sauce, and sugar. Season with black pepper, stir well, then leave to stand for a few minutes.

2 Heat a nonstick wok or skillet, add the chicken mixture, in batches if necessary, and stir-fry for 2–3 minutes or until lightly browned.

3 Pour in the stock, add any marinade left in the dish, then add the lemongrass, lime zest, water chestnuts, and cilantro. Continue stir-frying for a few minutes more until the chicken is tender.

4 Taste the stir-fry and add more soy sauce, if you like. Serve at once, garnished with lime wedges, green onion slices, and peanuts.

SWEET & SOUR CHINESE CHICKEN

SERVES 4–6

1 lb (500 g) skinless, boneless chicken breast halves, cut into 1 in (2.5 cm) pieces

2 tbsp dark soy sauce

1 tbsp Chinese rice wine or dry sherry

8 oz (250 g) canned pineapple chunks in natural juice, drained and juice reserved

2 tbsp cornstarch

3 tbsp sunflower oil

1 green bell pepper, halved, seeded, and cut into bite-sized pieces

1 red pepper, halved, seeded, and cut into bite-sized pieces

1 celery stalk, thickly sliced

1 onion, cut into bite-sized chunks

4 tbsp tomato ketchup

8 oz (250 g) canned lychees, drained and juice reserved

salt and black pepper

chopped fresh cilantro to garnish

1 Toss the chicken pieces in a large bowl with the soy sauce and rice wine. Cover, and marinate in the refrigerator for at least 30 minutes.

2 Meanwhile, make the reserved pineapple juice up to 1 cup (250 ml) with water and blend with the cornstarch. Set aside.

3 Heat the oil in a wok or large skillet, add the chicken, in batches if necessary, and stir-fry for 3–4 minutes until golden all over. Lift out with a slotted spoon.

4 Add the green and red bell peppers, celery, and onion to the wok, and stir-fry for about 5 minutes.

5 Add the cornstarch and pineapple juice mixture, ketchup, and reserved lychee juice to the wok, and cook for 3–5 minutes until thickened.

6 Return the chicken to the wok with the lychees and pineapple chunks, and heat through. Season with salt and pepper, and serve at once, garnished with chopped fresh cilantro.

MUSTARD CHICKEN

SERVES 4

1 tbsp olive oil

4 skinless, boneless chicken breast halves, cut diagonally into 1 in (2.5 cm) strips

1 garlic clove, crushed

1 cup (250 ml) light cream

1 tbsp all-purpose flour

1 tbsp coarse-grain mustard

salt and black pepper

flat-leaf parsley sprigs to garnish

1 Heat the oil in a skillet until hot. Add the chicken strips and garlic, in batches if necessary, and cook over a medium heat, stirring frequently, for 3–4 minutes.

2 With a slotted spoon, lift the chicken and garlic out of the skillet, and keep them warm.

3 In a small bowl, mix a little of the cream with the flour to make a smooth paste, then mix in the remaining cream.

4 Lower the heat and pour the cream into the pan. Cook gently for 2 minutes, stirring constantly until the sauce has thickened. Stir in the mustard and heat through gently, then season with salt and pepper.

5 Return the chicken to the pan, coat with the sauce, and cook gently for a few minutes more until the chicken is tender when pierced with a fork. Serve hot, garnished with parsley sprigs.

Cook's know-how

Do not let the sauce boil once you have added the mustard or it may taste bitter. Coarse-grain mustard gives an interesting texture to this dish, but if you prefer a smooth sauce, use Dijon mustard.

MARINATED BARBECUED CHICKEN

Smoke-scented, crisp-skinned, and with tender flesh, marinated chicken is full of delicious flavor when cooked on the barbecue. These three recipes use different parts of the bird, all cooked with the skin on for the juiciest results.

ORANGE & ROSEMARY

SERVES 4

4 chicken breasts halves, with the skin left on

a few rosemary sprigs

MARINADE

5 tbls (75 ml) olive oil

5 tbls (75 ml) white wine vinegar

juice of 1 orange

2 tbsp honey

4 garlic cloves, crushed

salt and black pepper

ORANGE SALSA

2 oranges, peeled, segmented, and diced

1 red bell pepper, halved, seeded, and diced

1/4 tsp crushed dried red chilies (chili flakes)

1 tbsp honey

1 Combine the marinade ingredients in a shallow nonmetallic dish. Add the chicken and turn to coat, then cover and leave to marinate in the refrigerator for up to 24 hours.

2 Lay the rosemary sprigs on the barbecue rack, put the chicken on top, and barbecue for 15–20 minutes until the juices run clear. Turn the chicken over several times during cooking, and baste or brush with the marinade.

3 Mix together the ingredients for the salsa. Serve the chicken breasts sliced diagonally, with the salsa alongside.

FRUITY CILANTRO

SERVES 4

8 chicken drumsticks, with the skin left on

MARINADE

5 tbls (75 ml) olive oil

juice of 1 lime

2 tbsp mango chutney

1 in (2.5 cm) piece of fresh gingerroot , peeled and grated

1/2 cup (30 g) fresh cilantro, chopped

salt and black pepper

MANGO SALSA

1 ripe large mango, diced (page 466)

1/2 in (1 cm) piece of fresh gingerroot, peeled and grated

3 green onions, finely chopped

1 tbsp mango chutney

1 tbsp lime juice

1 Combine the marinade ingredients in a shallow nonmetallic dish. Slash the drumsticks, add to the marinade, and turn to coat. Cover and leave to marinate in the refrigerator for up to 24 hours.

2 Barbecue the drumsticks, turning and basting or brushing with the marinade, for 15–20 minutes or until the juices run clear.

3 Mix together the ingredients for the salsa. Serve the drumsticks hot, with the mango salsa alongside.

YOGURT & MINT

SERVES 4

8 chicken thighs on the bone, with the skin left on

couscous salad (made with chopped fresh mint, green onions, red bell pepper, cherry tomatoes, and pine nuts tossed in vinaigrette dressing) to serve

MARINADE

4 tbsp olive oil

juice of 1/2 lemon

3 garlic cloves, crushed

1/2 cup (30 g) fresh mint, chopped

2/3 cup (150 g) plain yogurt

1/4 tsp each ground cumin and turmeric

salt and black pepper

1 Combine the marinade ingredients in a shallow nonmetallic dish. Add the chicken and turn to coat, then cover and leave to marinate in the refrigerator for up to 24 hours.

2 Barbecue the chicken, turning and basting or brushing with the marinade, for 15–20 minutes or until the juices run clear.

3 Serve the chicken thighs hot or cold, on a bed of couscous salad, or with couscous salad served separately in a bowl.

SUCCESSFUL MARINATING

A marinade will give poultry or meat extra flavor before it is cooked over a barbecue, and it may help tenderize it at the same time.

A marinade is a mixture of liquids and seasonings. There is always an acid such as lemon juice, wine, or vinegar, which helps make poultry or meat more tender.
An oil, such as olive, sesame, or sunflower, keeps the meat or poultry moist and carries the flavors of the seasonings into the food. Seasonings usually include salt and pepper, but all kinds of spices and herbs can be used as well. Marinades often include garlic, onions, and fresh gingerroot, which also add flavor.
Allow enough time for large pieces of poultry or meat to pick up the flavor of the marinade. Smaller pieces will pick up the flavor more quickly.
Turn the food in the marinade occasionally for an even coating, and baste or brush with the marinade when barbecuing.

CLOCKWISE FROM TOP: Orange & Rosemary, Fruity Cilantro, Yogurt & Mint.

LEMON & HERB DRUMSTICKS

MAKES 12

12 chicken drumsticks

MARINADE

2/3 cup (150 ml) olive oil

grated zest and juice of 1 lemon

6 large parsley sprigs, chopped

1 onion, thinly sliced

2 large garlic cloves, crushed

salt and black pepper

1 Make the marinade: in a bowl, combine the olive oil, lemon zest and juice, parsley sprigs, onion, and garlic. Season with salt and pepper.

2 Turn the drumsticks in the marinade. Cover and leave to marinate in the refrigerator for at least 30 minutes.

3 Place the drumsticks under a hot broiler, (4 in)10 cm from the heat, and broil, turning frequently and basting with the marinade, for 20 minutes until crisp, brown, and cooked through. Serve the drumsticks hot or cold.

STICKY HONEYED DRUMSTICKS

Use a different marinade: combine 1 cup (250 g) plain yogurt, 2 tbsp honey, and 1 tsp ground cilantro, and season with salt and black pepper.

DEVILED CHICKEN DRUMSTICKS

MAKES 12

12 chicken drumsticks

2 tbsp sesame seeds

SPICY COATING

2 tbsp olive oil

2 tbsp white wine vinegar

2 tbsp tomato ketchup

1 tbsp Dijon mustard

1 small onion, quartered

2 tbsp dark brown sugar

1 large garlic clove, coarsely crushed

1/4 tsp cayenne pepper

salt and black pepper

tortilla chips to serve

1 Make the spicy coating: put the oil, vinegar, ketchup, mustard, onion, sugar, garlic, and cayenne in a food processor. Season with salt and pepper, and purée until fairly smooth.

2 Make 3 deep cuts in each chicken drumstick, arrange in a single layer in a shallow baking dish, and spoon the coating over them. Sprinkle with half of the sesame seeds.

3 Roast in a preheated oven at 375°F (190°C) for 30 minutes or until the drumsticks are cooked through. Turn and baste halfway through cooking, and sprinkle with the remaining sesame seeds. Serve hot or cold, with tortilla chips.

CHILI-ROASTED DRUMSTICKS WITH BACON

Use a different spicy coating: combine 3 tbsp lemon juice, 4 crushed garlic cloves, 1 1/2 tbsp paprika, 1 tbsp mild chili powder, 1 tsp ground cumin, and 1/4 tsp oregano. Coat the drumsticks with the mixture, then wrap each one in a bacon slice.

Healthy note

Chicken is a very lean meat, but the skin is high in fat. If you want to reduce the fat content of these drumsticks, strip the skin off before marinating. The marinade will compensate for the lack of skin, and will keep the chicken moist during cooking.

CORONATION CHICKEN

SERVES 6

1 tbsp sunflower oil

1 cup (125 g) green onions, chopped

4 tsp mild curry paste

2/3 cup (150 ml) red wine

pared zest and juice of 1 lemon

1 tbsp tomato paste

2 tbsp apricot jam

1 1/4 cups (300 ml) mayonnaise

2/3 cup (150 g) plain yogurt

salt and pepper

1 lb (500 g) cooked chicken, cut into bite-sized pieces

watercress sprigs to garnish

1 Heat the oil in a small saucepan, add the green onions, and cook for about 2 minutes until beginning to soften but not color. Stir in the curry paste, and cook, stirring, for 1 minute.

2 Add the red wine, lemon zest and juice, and tomato paste. Simmer, uncovered, stirring, for 5 minutes or until reduced to 4 tbsp. Strain into a bowl, cover, and leave to cool.

3 Work the apricot jam through the strainer, then stir it into the curry paste and wine mixture. Add the mayonnaise and yogurt, season with salt and pepper, then stir well to blend evenly. The mixture should have a coating consistency, and be the color of pale straw.

4 Add the chicken pieces to the mayonnaise mixture, and stir to coat evenly. Garnish with watercress sprigs before serving.

MARINATED CHICKEN WITH PEPPERS

SERVES 6

3 1/2 lb (1.7 kg) chicken

2 tbsp olive oil

1 large red pepper, halved, seeded, and cut into thin strips

1 large yellow bell pepper, halved, seeded, and cut into thin strips

3/4 cup (125 g) pitted black olives

MARINADE

4 tbsp olive oil

2 tbsp honey

juice of 1/2 lemon

1 tbsp chopped mixed fresh herbs, such as parsley, thyme, and basil

salt and black pepper

1 Put the chicken into a roasting pan, rub the breast with oil, and roast in a preheated oven at 375°F (190°C) for 20 minutes per pound (500 g). Twenty minutes before the end of the roasting time, remove from the oven, and spoon off the fat. Add the peppers and return to the oven for 20 minutes.

2 Remove the chicken and peppers from the pan, and leave to stand until cool.

3 Meanwhile, make the marinade: in a large bowl, combine the olive oil, honey, lemon juice, and herbs, and season with salt and pepper.

4 Strip the chicken flesh from the carcass, and cut it into small bite-sized strips. Toss the strips in the marinade, cover, and leave to cool completely.

5 Spoon the chicken onto a platter, arrange the peppers and olives around the edge, and serve at room temperature.

Cook's know-how

If time is short, use a pre-cooked chicken and toss with roasted bell peppers from a jar. If the peppers are packed in oil they will be very moist, so you will only need half the amount of marinade.

GREEK CHICKEN SALAD

SERVES 6

1 lb (500 g) cooked chicken, cut into bite-sized pieces

pita bread to serve

1 green onion, cut into strips, to garnish

SAUCE

²/3 cup (150 g) thick plain yogurt

150 ml (¼ pint) sour cream

8 green onions, thinly sliced

2 tbsp chopped fresh mint

1 tbsp chopped flat-leaf parsley

2 tbsp lemon juice

a pinch of sugar

salt and black pepper

1 Make the sauce: in a large bowl, combine the yogurt, sour cream, green onions, mint, parsley, lemon juice, and sugar, and season with salt and pepper.

2 Toss the chicken pieces in the sauce.

3 Sprinkle the bread with a little water and cook under a hot grill for 1 minute on each side. Garnish the chicken with the green onion strips, and serve with the pita bread.

WARM CHICKEN SALAD WITH MANGO & AVOCADO

This unusual salad combines refreshing slices of mango and avocado with spicy chicken breast and a warm, rum-flavored dressing. The combination of flavors makes a truly tropical dish.

SERVES 4

3 skinless, boneless chicken breasts, cut into 1 in (2.5 cm) strips

1 round lettuce, leaves separated

1 bunch of watercress, trimmed

1 avocado, peeled, pitted (page 88), and sliced lengthwise

1 mango, peeled, pitted (page 430), and sliced lengthwise

4 tbsp dark rum

paprika to garnish

MARINADE

2 tbsp olive oil

2 tbsp lemon juice

2 tsp balsamic vinegar

2 garlic cloves, crushed

1 tbsp paprika

1 mild fresh red chili, halved, seeded, and finely chopped

¹/2 tsp ground cumin

salt

1 Make the marinade: combine the oil, lemon juice, vinegar, garlic, paprika, chili, and cumin, and season with salt. Toss in the chicken strips, cover, and leave to marinate for a few minutes.

2 Arrange beds of lettuce and watercress on 4 serving plates. Arrange the avocado and mango slices on top.

3 Heat a large skillet, and add the chicken strips with the marinade. Cook over a high heat, stirring, for 5–6 minutes until golden on all sides and cooked through.

4 Using a slotted spoon, remove the chicken strips from the pan, and arrange on top of the avocado and mango.

5 Return the skillet to the heat, and pour in the rum. Let it bubble, stirring constantly to dissolve any sediment in the skillet and incorporate the cooking juices, for about 1 minute. Pour the hot rum mixture over the salads, sprinkle with a little paprika, and serve at once.

BALLOTINE OF CHICKEN

A ballotine is a bird or cut of meat that has been boned, stuffed, and rolled. It is slowly cooked in the oven,
left to cool, and then chilled for several hours or overnight until firm. With its colorful, pistachio-studded filling,
this ballotine makes an excellent centerpiece for a buffet party, and is easy to slice and serve.

SERVES 8–10

4 lb (2 kg) chicken, boned (page 171)

4 thin slices of cooked ham

1 cup (125 g) pistachio nuts, shelled

4 tbls (60 g) butter, softened

2½ cups (600 ml) chicken stock

STUFFING

1 lb (500 g) fresh pork side

12 oz (375 g) chicken livers, trimmed

8 oz (250 g) bacon slices, coarsely chopped

2 shallots, quartered

2 garlic cloves

4 tbsp brandy

2 tsp chopped fresh thyme

1 tsp chopped fresh sage

½ tsp ground ginger

½ tsp ground cinnamon

salt and black pepper

1 Make the stuffing: chop the pork into 1/4 in (5 mm) pieces, and place in a bowl.

2 Puree the chicken livers, bacon, shallots, garlic, and brandy in a food processor until smooth. Add to the pork in the bowl with the thyme, sage, ginger, and cinnamon, and season generously with salt and pepper. Stir well to combine.

3 Place the boned chicken, skin-side down, between 2 pieces of plastic wrap and pound to an even thickness with a rolling pin.

4 Remove the plastic wrap from the chicken, and assemble the ballotine (see box, right). Tie several pieces of string around the chicken to keep it in shape.

5 Spread the softened butter over the chicken skin, and season generously with salt and pepper. Place the chicken roll on a wire rack in a roasting pan.

6 Bring the stock to a boil, and pour over the chicken in the roasting pan. Cook in a preheated oven at 325°F (160°C), basting occasionally and adding more stock if necessary, for 2 hours or until the juices run clear when the chicken is pierced.

7 Transfer the ballotine to a plate, and leave to cool. Cover and chill overnight. Cut into thin slices to serve.

Assembling the ballotine

Spread half of the stuffing over the chicken, to within 1 in (2.5 cm) of the edges. Arrange the ham slices on top. Scatter the pistachio nuts on top of the ham.

Spoon on and spread the remaining stuffing over the pistachio nuts.

Fold the chicken over the stuffing to form a sausage shape, and sew the edges together with thin string or fasten them with small metal skewers.

Cook's know-how

Classic French ballotine recipes wrap the chicken roll in cheesecloth before cooking, but this is not necessary.

THANKSGIVING ROAST TURKEY

If you have a large number to cater for on Thanksgiving, be sure to order a fresh turkey well in advance from your butcher or supermarket. You can collect it on the day before or store it for up to 2 days in the refrigerator. If you buy a frozen turkey, make sure that it is thoroughly thawed before cooking – see page 169 for thawing times.

SERVES 12

pared zest of 1 lemon

a few parsley sprigs

a few thyme sprigs

2 celery stalks, roughly sliced

10 lb (5 kg) oven-ready turkey, with giblets

5 tbls (75 g) butter, softened

salt and black pepper

8 oz (250 g) bacon slices (optional)

CHESTNUT STUFFING

2 tbls (30 g) butter

1 onion, finely chopped

3 oz (90 g) slab bacon, finely chopped

12 oz (375 g) frozen chestnuts, thawed, or 6 oz (175 g) dried chestnuts, soaked, finely chopped

6 oz (175 g) pork sausagemeat

3 tbsp chopped parsley

1 tbsp chopped fresh thyme

salt and black pepper

1 medium egg, beaten

GRAVY

2 tbls (30 g) all-purpose flour

2½ cups (600 ml) giblet stock (page 170) or chicken stock

about 2 tbsp port wine, Madeira or sherry

red-currant jelly to taste (optional)

TO SERVE

bread sauce

cranberry sauce

bacon rolls

mini sausages

1 Prepare the stuffing: melt the butter in a skillet, add the onion and bacon, and cook until the onion is soft and both the onion and bacon are golden. Transfer to a large bowl, mix in the remaining stuffing ingredients, and leave until cold.

2 Place the lemon zest, parsley sprigs, thyme, and celery into the cavity of the turkey. Fill the neck end with stuffing. Put the leftover stuffing into a baking dish and set aside.

3 Shape the stuffed end of the turkey into a neat round and secure the loose skin with fine skewers. Tie the legs with string to give a neat shape.

4 Weigh the turkey and calculate the cooking time, allowing 20 minutes per pound (500 g). Arrange 2 large sheets of foil across a large roasting pan. Place the turkey on top and spread the butter over the bird, concentrating on the breast in particular.

5 Season with a little salt and plenty of pepper. If you are using the bacon rashers, overlap them across the turkey, again concentrating on the breast.

6 Fold the sheets of foil loosely over the turkey, leaving a large air gap between the turkey and the foil. Cook the turkey in a preheated oven at 425°F (220°C) for 30 minutes.

7 Reduce the oven temperature to 325°F (160°C) and cook for the remainder of the calculated cooking time.

8 Thirty minutes before the end of the cooking time, fold back the foil and remove the bacon (if used), to allow the breast to brown, then baste with the cooking juices. To check if the turkey is thoroughly cooked, pierce the thickest part of the thigh with a fine skewer: the juices should run clear, not pink or red.

9 Lift the turkey on to a warmed serving platter, cover with fresh foil, and leave to stand in a warm place for 30 minutes before carving.

10 Meanwhile, put the dish of stuffing in the oven and cook for 25–30 minutes. Now make the gravy: spoon all but 2 tbsp of fat from the roasting pan, leaving behind the cooking juices. Place the pan over a low heat on the stovetop, add the flour, and cook, stirring, for 1 minute. Add the stock and port wine, Madeira, or sherry to taste, then cook, stirring, until thickened. Season to taste, and add some red-currant jelly if you think the gravy is too sharp.

11 Carve the turkey and serve with the extra stuffing, gravy, bread sauce, cranberry sauce, bacon rolls, and mini sausages.

BREAD SAUCE

Insert 8 whole cloves into 1 onion. Put it into a pan with 3¾ cups (900 ml) milk, 1 bay leaf, and 6 whole black peppercorns. Bring to a boil, remove from the heat, cover, and leave to infuse for 1 hour. Strain the milk and return to the pan. Gradually add about 3¾ cups (175 g) fresh white bread crumbs, then bring to a boil, stirring. Simmer for 2–3 minutes. Season with salt and black pepper, and stir in 4 tbls (60 g) butter. If liked, stir in 4 tbsp heavy cream before serving. Serve hot.

CRANBERRY SAUCE

Put 1 lb (500 g) fresh cranberries into a saucepan with ½ cup (125 ml) water. Bring to a boil and simmer for about 5 minutes, until the cranberries have begun to break down. Stir in ½ cup (125 g) caster sugar and simmer until the sugar has dissolved. Stir in 2 tbsp port wine before serving. Serve hot or cold.

BACON ROLLS

With the back of a knife, stretch 6 streaky bacon rashers until twice their original size. Cut in half and roll up loosely. Thread on to skewers and cook under a hot grill, turning, for 6 minutes or until browned.

MINI SAUSAGES

Twist 6 thin link pork in the middle and cut in half, to make 12 small sausages. Cook under a hot broiler for 10–15 minutes until cooked through and browned all over.

ROAST TURKEY WITH GARLIC & TARRAGON

SERVES 4

2 1/2 lb (1.25 kg) turkey breast joint

1 tsp all-purpose flour

1 1/4 cups (300 ml) chicken stock

salt and black pepper

watercress sprigs to garnish

MARINADE

3 tbsp sunflower oil

grated zest and juice of 1 lemon

1 small onion, sliced

1 garlic clove, crushed

1 large tarragon sprig

1 large lemon thyme sprig

1 Make the marinade: combine the oil, lemon zest and juice, onion, garlic, tarragon, and thyme. Spoon the marinade over the turkey, cover, and leave to marinate in the refrigerator, turning occasionally, for 8 hours.

2 Put the turkey into a roasting pan. Strain the marinade, and pour around the turkey. Cover with foil, and cook in a preheated oven at 375°F (190°C) for 20 minutes per pound (500 g). Remove the foil after 20 minutes of cooking to brown the turkey.

3 Test whether the turkey is done by inserting a fine skewer into the thickest part: the juices will run clear when it is cooked. Remove the turkey from the roasting pan, and keep warm while you make the gravy.

4 Put the pan on the stovetop, add the flour to the juices in the pan, and cook, stirring, for 1 minute until lightly browned. Add the stock, and bring to a boil, stirring constantly until thickened slightly. Simmer for 2–3 minutes, season with salt and pepper, and strain into a warmed gravy boat.

5 Garnish the turkey with watercress, and serve the gravy separately.

Cook's know-how

Turkey breast joints are widely available from supermarkets. They are excellent if you like roast turkey but don't want to buy a whole bird, or if you find carving a whole turkey difficult. They either come with the breastbone (and sometimes the wings) attached, or as a boned and rolled joint.

TURKEY WITH SOUR CREAM & CHIVES

P SERVES 4

2 tbls (30 g) butter

2 tbsp sunflower oil

1 1/4 lb (600 g) boneless turkey breast tenderloin, cut diagonally into 1/2 in (1 cm) strips

4 bacon slices, diced

1 large onion, sliced

8 oz (250 g) button mushrooms, halved (about 3 1/4 cups)

2 tbls (30 g) all-purpose flour

2/3 cup (150 ml) turkey or chicken stock

salt and black pepper

2/3 cup (150 g) sour cream

2 tbsp snipped fresh chives

1 Melt the butter with the oil in a large skillet until foaming. Add the turkey, and cook over a high heat, stirring, for 8 minutes. Remove the turkey from the pan with a slotted spoon, and keep warm.

2 Lower the heat and add the bacon, onion, and mushrooms. Cook gently, stirring occasionally, for 3–5 minutes until the onion is soft but not colored. Sprinkle in the flour and cook, stirring, for about 1 minute.

3 Pour in the stock, and bring to a boil, stirring until thickened. Add the turkey, and season with salt and pepper. Cover and simmer for about 5 minutes or until the turkey is tender.

4 Stir in the sour cream, and heat gently without boiling. Serve at once, sprinkled with the chives.

Healthy option

To lower the fat content of this dish, omit the butter and bacon and use just 4 tbsp lowfat plain yogurt instead of the sour cream.

TURKEY & LEMON STIR-FRY

SERVES 4

600 g (1 1/4 lb) turkey breast tenderloin, cut diagonally into 1 in (2.5 cm) strips

375 g (12 oz) courgettes

1 large green bell pepper

1 tbsp olive oil

250 g (8 oz) baby corn cobs

salt

chopped parsley and lemon twists to garnish

MARINADE

1/2 cup (125 ml) dry white wine

grated zest and juice of 1 large lemon

2 tbsp olive oil

black pepper

1 Make the marinade: combine the wine, lemon zest and juice, oil, and season with pepper. Toss the turkey strips in the marinade, cover, and marinate in the refrigerator for at least 30 minutes.

2 Slice the zucchini thickly on the diagonal. Halve the green bell pepper and remove the seeds, then cut the bell pepper halves into long thin strips.

3 Heat the oil in a wok, add the zucchini, corn cobs, and green bell pepper, and stir-fry over a high heat for 2 minutes. Remove with a slotted spoon, and keep warm.

4 Remove the turkey strips from the marinade, reserving the marinade. Add the turkey to the wok, and stir-fry over a high heat for 5 minutes or until golden.

5 Pour the reserved marinade over the turkey and cook for 3 minutes or until tender. Return the vegetables to the wok, and heat through. Taste for seasoning. Serve at once, garnished with parsley and lemon twists.

TURKEY SCHNITZEL

SERVES 4

3 tbsp all-purpose flour

salt and black pepper

1 large egg, beaten

1 1/2 cups (60 g) fresh bread crumbs

4 x 6 oz (175 g) turkey breast scallops

2 tbsp sunflower oil

1 tbls (15 g) butter

lemon slices and chopped parsley to garnish

1 Sprinkle the flour onto a plate, and season generously with salt and pepper. Pour the beaten egg onto another plate, and sprinkle the bread crumbs onto a third plate.

2 Coat each scallop with the seasoned flour, shaking off any excess. Dip each floured scallop into the beaten egg, then dip into the bread crumbs.

3 With a sharp knife, score the scallops in a crisscross pattern. Cover and chill in the refrigerator for 30 minutes.

4 Heat the oil with the butter in a large skillet. When the butter is foaming, add the scallops, and cook over a high heat until golden on both sides.

5 Lower the heat and cook for 10 minutes or until the scallops are tender. Test the scallops by piercing with a fine skewer: the juices should run clear.

6 Lift the scallops out of the pan, and drain on paper towels. Garnish with lemon slices and chopped parsley, and serve at once.

Cook's know-how

If you can't find turkey breast scallops, buy breast cutlets. Put them between 2 sheets of plastic wrap, and pound with the bottom of a saucepan until they are about 1/4 in (5 mm) thick.

TURKEY MOLE

SERVES 6

2 tbsp sunflower oil

1 1/2 lb (750 g) turkey pieces

1 1/4 cups (300 ml) turkey or chicken stock

salt and black pepper

MOLE SAUCE

14 oz (400 g) canned crushed tomatoes

1 small onion, coarsely chopped

3/4 cup (90 g) blanched almonds

2 tbls (30 g) raisins (optional)

3/4 square (20 g) semisweet chocolate, coarsely chopped

1 garlic clove

1 tbsp sesame seeds

1 tbsp hot chili powder

1 tsp ground cinnamon

1/2 tsp ground cloves

1/2 tsp ground coriander

1/2 tsp ground cumin

1/4 tsp ground aniseed (optional)

1 Make the mole sauce: put the tomatoes, onion, almonds, raisins (if using), chocolate, garlic, sesame seeds, chili powder, cinnamon, cloves, coriander, cumin, aniseed (if using), and 4 tbsp water into a food processor and process briefly.

2 Heat the sunflower oil in a large saucepan, add the turkey pieces, and cook over a high heat for about 5 minutes until golden on all sides.

3 Add the mole sauce mixture, and cook, stirring, for 2 minutes. Pour in the stock, and bring to a boil. Cover and simmer very gently for 40 minutes or until the turkey is tender. Season with salt and pepper before serving.

Cook's know-how

If you would rather not use the almonds, you can use 2 heaping tbls all-purpose flour to thicken the sauce instead.

TURKEY CASSEROLE WITH PEPPERS & CIDER

SERVES 6

2 tbls (30 g) butter

1 tbsp sunflower oil

1 1/2 lb (750 g) turkey pieces

1 onion, sliced

1 garlic clove, crushed

1 red bell pepper, halved, seeded, and thinly sliced

1 yellow bell pepper, halved, seeded, and thinly sliced

1 1/4 cups (300 ml) dry cider

salt and black pepper

chopped parsley to garnish

1 Melt the butter with the oil in a flameproof casserole. When the butter is foaming, add the turkey pieces, and cook over a high heat for 5 minutes or until golden on all sides. Use a slotted spoon, and drain on paper towels.

2 Lower the heat, add the onion, garlic, and red and yellow bell pepper slices to the casserole, and cook for 5 minutes or until the vegetables are just beginning to soften.

3 Return the turkey to the casserole, pour in the cider, and bring to a boil. Season with salt and pepper, cover, and cook in a preheated oven at 325°F (160°C) for 1 hour or until the turkey is tender.

4 Using a slotted spoon, transfer the turkey and vegetables to a warmed platter. Put the casserole on the stovetop and boil, stirring, until the cooking juices are thickened slightly. Taste for seasoning.

5 Spoon the sauce over the turkey and vegetables, garnish with chopped parsley, and serve at once.

TURKEY & APPLE CASSEROLE

Substitute 2 cored, halved, and sliced eating apples for the red and yellow bell peppers, and add them 20 minutes before the end of the cooking time.

STIR-FRIED TURKEY MEATBALLS

SERVES 4

3 tsp sunflower oil

1 onion, thinly sliced

1 green bell pepper, halved, seeded, and cut into bite-sized pieces

1 zucchini, sliced

4–6 mushrooms, thinly sliced

1 1/3 cup (125 g) bean sprouts

MEATBALLS

12 oz (375 g) ground turkey

3 tbls (45 g) parsley stuffing mix, or bread crumbs

1 onion, finely chopped

4 garlic cloves, crushed

3 tbsp soy sauce

1/2 in (1 cm) piece of fresh gingerroot, peeled and grated

salt and black pepper

1 Make the meatballs: in a bowl, combine the turkey, stuffing or bread crumbs, onion, garlic, 1 tbsp of the soy sauce, and the ginger. Season with salt and pepper, then shape into meatballs (see box, right).

2 Heat 1 tsp of the oil in a wok, add the onion, green bell pepper, and zucchini, and stir-fry for 2–3 minutes.

3 Remove the vegetables with a slotted spoon. Heat another 1 tsp of the oil, add the mushrooms, and stir-fry for 2–3 minutes. Remove with a slotted spoon.

4 Heat the remaining oil in the wok, add the meatballs, and cook gently, turning, for 6–7 minutes or until cooked through. Return the vegetables to the wok, add the bean sprouts and the remaining soy sauce, and heat for 1 minute.

Shaping meatballs

Break off pieces of the turkey mixture and, with wet hands to prevent the mixture sticking, roll into 2 in (5 cm) meatballs.

TURKEY BURGERS HOLSTEIN

SERVES 4

4 tbls (60 g) butter

1 small onion, very finely chopped

1 lb (500 g) ground turkey

3/4 cup (90 g) sliced cooked ham, finely chopped

1 tbsp chopped parsley

salt and black pepper

2 tbsp sunflower oil

4 eggs to serve

1 Melt half of the butter in a small saucepan, add the onion, and cook gently, stirring occasionally, for 3–5 minutes until soft but not colored. Leave to cool.

2 Put the onion into a large bowl, add the turkey, ham, and parsley, and season with salt and pepper. Mix well, then shape into 4 burgers. Cover and chill for 30 minutes.

3 Melt the remaining butter with the oil in a skillet. When the butter is foaming, add the burgers, and cook over a high heat for 2–3 minutes on each side until golden.

4 Lower the heat, and cook, turning once, for about 10 minutes until the burgers are cooked through.

5 Lift the burgers out of the skillet with a slotted spoon and drain on paper towels.

6 Break the eggs into the skillet, and fry over a medium heat until the whites are firm and the yolks are still soft. Divide the turkey burgers among serving plates, top each burger with an egg, and serve at once.

BLUE CHEESE TURKEY BURGERS

Make the burgers as directed. Omit the eggs. Crumble 4 oz (125 g) blue cheese, such as Roquefort, Stilton, or Danish blue, over the burgers 5 minutes before the end of the cooking time.

TURKEY WITH CHEESE & PINEAPPLE

SERVES 6

4 tbsp (60 g) butter

1 onion, sliced

1/2 cup (60 g) all-purpose flour

2 cups (500 ml) turkey or chicken stock

8 oz (250 g) can pineapple pieces in natural juice, drained and juice reserved

8 oz (250 g) mature Cheddar cheese, grated

salt and black pepper

1 lb (500 g) cooked turkey, cut into bite-sized pieces

3 tbsp fresh wholemeal bread crumbs

chopped parsley to garnish

1 Melt the butter in a saucepan, add the onion, and cook gently, stirring occasionally, for 3–5 minutes until soft but not colored. Add the flour, and cook, stirring, for 1 minute.

2 Gradually blend in the stock and the pineapple juice, and bring to a boil, stirring until thickened.

3 Add the pineapple pieces, reserving 6 for garnish. Stir in three-quarters of the cheese, and season with salt and pepper.

4 Divide the turkey pieces among 6 individual gratin dishes, or put into 1 large baking dish. Pour the sauce over the turkey, and sprinkle with the remaining cheese and then the bread crumbs.

5 Bake in a preheated oven at 400°F (200°C) for 15–20 minutes until the turkey has heated through and the topping is golden. Garnish with chopped parsley and the reserved pineapple pieces, and serve at once.

TURKEY SALAD WITH MANGO & GRAPES

SERVES 4

2 1/2 lb (1.25 kg) turkey breast joint

1 onion, quartered

1 carrot, sliced

a few parsley sprigs

pared zest of 1 lemon

6 black peppercorns

1 bay leaf

1 scant cup (200 ml) lemon mayonnaise

1 bunch of watercress, tough stems removed

1 ripe mango, peeled and cut into cubes (page 466)

4 oz (125 g) seedless green grapes

1/2 cup (90 g) walnut pieces

1 Put the turkey into a large saucepan, and cover with cold water. Add the onion, carrot, parsley, lemon zest, peppercorns, and bay leaf, and bring to a boil. Cover and simmer very gently for 1 hour or until the turkey is tender. Remove from the heat, and leave the turkey to poach in the cooling liquid.

2 Lift the turkey out of the poaching liquid, and remove the flesh from the carcass. Discard the skin and bones, then cut the meat into bite-sized pieces.

3 Put the turkey pieces into a large bowl, and add the lemon mayonnaise. Stir well to coat the turkey pieces thoroughly and evenly.

4 Arrange the watercress on individual serving plates, and pile the turkey mixture on top. Arrange the mango cubes and grapes around the edge, sprinkle with the walnut pieces, and serve at room temperature.

Healthy option

To reduce the fat content of this salad, use equal quantities of lowfat plain yogurt and reduced-calorie mayonnaise instead of the lemon mayonnaise, and omit the walnuts.

WALDORF TURKEY SALAD

Substitute 2 cored and cubed red apples, and 2 sliced celery stalks for the mango and grapes, and then add to the turkey and lemon mayonnaise mixture.

CHRISTMAS ROAST GOOSE

Goose is a traditional Christmas bird in Britain and northern Europe, and it is a favorite festive alternative to turkey when a small group of people is to be served. It is simple to cook and tastes delicious with a fruit stuffing and spicy accompaniments.

SERVES 6–8

10–12 lb (5–6 kg) goose, with giblets reserved for stock

1 onion, quartered

1 cooking apple, quartered

a few sage sprigs

salt and black pepper

1/4 cup (30 g) all-purpose flour

2 cups (500 ml) goose giblet stock (page 170)

2/3 cup (150 ml) dry white wine

spiced stuffed apples (see box, right) to serve

watercress sprigs to garnish

PORK & APPLE STUFFING

10 oz (300 g) pork sausagemeat

1/4 cup (60 g) fresh bread crumbs

2 tsp dried sage

2 tbsp (30 g) butter

1 onion, finely chopped

1 large cooking apple, peeled, cored, and finely chopped

1 Make the pork and apple stuffing: in a bowl, combine the sausagemeat, bread crumbs, and sage.

2 Melt the butter in a pan, add the onion, and cook gently, stirring occasionally, for 3–5 minutes until soft but not colored.

3 Add the cooking apple, and cook for 5 minutes. Stir the onion and apple into the sausagemeat mixture, season with salt and pepper, and leave to cool.

4 Remove any fat from the cavity of the goose. Put the onion and apple quarters into the cavity together with the sage. Spoon the stuffing into the neck end of the goose, pat it into a rounded shape, and secure the skin flap with a small skewer. Weigh the goose.

5 Prick the skin of the goose all over with a fork, and rub with salt and pepper. Place the goose, breast-side down, on a wire rack in a large roasting pan, and cook in a preheated oven at 425°F (220°C) for 30 minutes.

6 Turn the goose breast-side up, and cook for 20 minutes. Reduce the oven temperature to 350°F (180°C) and cook for 20 minutes per 1 lb (500 g).

7 Test the goose by inserting a fine skewer into the thickest part of a thigh: the juices should run clear when the meat is thoroughly cooked.

8 Lift the goose on to a warmed serving platter, and then leave to rest, covered with foil, for about 20 minutes.

9 Make the gravy while the goose is resting: pour off all but 2 tbsp of the fat from the roasting pan. Put the pan on the stovetop, add the flour, and cook, stirring, for 1 minute. Add the stock and wine, and bring to a boil, stirring constantly. Simmer for 2–3 minutes, then taste for seasoning. Strain into a warmed gravy boat.

10 To serve, arrange the spiced stuffed apples around the goose, and garnish with watercress. Hand the gravy separately.

Spiced stuffed apples

Core 8 apples, keeping them whole. For the stuffing, combine 2 tbsp Calvados in a small bowl with 1 tsp ground cinnamon, 1/2 tsp ground allspice, and 8 finely chopped prunes.

Place the apples in a buttered baking dish, and spoon the stuffing into the centers. Melt 60 g (2 oz) butter, pour over the apples, and cover with foil. Bake in a preheated oven at 350°F (180°C) for 1 hour or until tender.

Cook's know-how

Goose is even richer and fattier than duck. Putting it on a wire rack in the roasting pan ensures it does not sit in the fat during cooking and this gives it a good, crisp skin.

CHICKEN AND TURKEY STIR-FRIES

Fresh and colorful, these light, healthy stir-fries cook in minutes. If time is short, just marinate the meat while you prepare the other ingredients. Another alternative, for a more intense flavor, is to prepare ahead and marinate overnight.

CHINESE CHICKEN WITH MANGO

SERVES 6

3 skinless, boneless chicken breast halves (about 4 oz/125 g each), cut into thin strips

about 2 tbsp sunflower oil

1 large red bell pepper, cored, seeded, and cut into strips

8 oz (250 g) button chestnut mushrooms, halved

2 tsp cornstarch blended with 5 tbsp cold chicken stock or water

salt and black pepper

250 g (8 oz) bean sprouts

about 3 cups (200 g) bok choy, coarsely sliced

½ cup (60 g) roasted cashew nuts, salted or unsalted

1 large ripe mango, peeled and sliced lengthwise (see page 466)

chopped fresh cilantro to serve (optional)

MARINADE

1 tbsp soy sauce

3 tbsp rice wine vinegar or white wine vinegar

3 tbsp honey

1 Put the chicken in a bowl with the marinade ingredients and mix well. Cover and marinate in the refrigerator for about 2 hours, longer if time allows.

2 Heat 1 tbsp oil over a high heat in a wok or large skillet. Lift half the chicken from the marinade (reserving it), and stir-fry for 1–2 minutes until golden all over and nearly cooked. Remove the chicken and set aside, then repeat with the remainder.

3 Heat the remaining oil in the pan, add the red bell pepper and mushrooms, and stir-fry for 1–2 minutes.

4 Return the chicken to the wok. Stir the cornstarch mixture and pour it into the wok, then add the reserved marinade. Season with salt and pepper and bring to a boil. Add the bean sprouts and bok choy, and stir-fry until the bok choy has just wilted, about 2 minutes. Stir in the cashew nuts and mango slices, and serve at once, sprinkled with chopped cilantro if you like.

TURKEY-TO-GO

SERVES 6

about 1½ lb (750 g) turkey breast tenderloin, cut into thin strips

1 tsp ground cilantro

1 tsp ground cumin

salt and black pepper

12 soft tortilla wraps

about 2 tbsp sunflower oil

1 large red bell pepper, cored, seeded and thinly sliced

TO SERVE

sour cream

tomato salsa or mango chutney

shredded Romaine lettuce

1 Put the turkey strips in a bowl with the cilantro and cumin. Season with salt and pepper, then mix well to coat the turkey in the spices. Cover and marinate in the refrigerator for about 30 minutes, longer if time allows.

2 When you are ready to cook the turkey, warm the tortillas (see page 226). Heat the oil in a wok or large skillet and fry the turkey in batches with the red bell pepper strips until golden brown and cooked through, about 4 minutes. You may need to add more oil with each batch.

3 Transfer the warm tortillas to a basket and spoon the turkey and peppers into a serving dish. Let each person spread their tortillas with sour cream and salsa or chutney, top this with some shredded lettuce and turkey, then roll into a fat cigar shape. The filled tortillas are easy to eat with your hands if they are sliced in half on the diagonal.

Cook's know-how

Soft tortillas are flat Mexican breads that can be made from wheat or corn. (Both are suitable for this recipe). They are sold at supermarkets, and some are flavored with tomato, garlic, or herbs.

LACQUERED DUCK

SERVES 4

4 skinless duck breast halves, 5–6 oz (150–175 g) each, cut diagonally into ½ in (1 cm) strips

2 tbsp sunflower oil

8 green onions, trimmed and cut into 1 in (2.5 cm) lengths

salt and black pepper

1 tbsp sesame seeds, toasted

MARINADE

2 large garlic cloves, crushed

1 tbsp soy sauce

1 tbsp olive oil

2 tbsp honey

1 Put the duck in a bowl with the marinade ingredients and mix well. Cover and marinate in the refrigerator for about 2 hours, or overnight if time allows.

2 Heat the sunflower oil in a wok or large skillet. Lift the duck from the marinade (reserving it), and stir-fry over a high heat for 3–4 minutes or until browned all over. Add the green onions, and stir-fry for a further 2–3 minutes or until the duck is cooked.

3 Pour the marinade and 5 tbsp water into the pan, bring quickly to a boil, then simmer for a few moments until the sauce has a syrupy consistency – take care not to overcook or the marinade might burn. Season with salt and pepper, scatter over the sesame seeds, and serve immediately.

CLOCKWISE FROM TOP: Lacquered Duck, Chinese Chicken with Mango, Turkey-to-Go.

PEKING DUCK

This Chinese dish is great fun to make, but you can buy the pancakes if you are short of time – they are sold at most large supermarkets. Let everyone help themselves to some crisp-skinned duck, green onions, cucumber, and hoisin sauce, so they can assemble their own pancakes.

SERVES 6

5 lb (2.5 kg) duck, with any giblets removed

3 tbsp dry sherry

3 tbsp honey

3 tbsp soy sauce

CHINESE PANCAKES

2 cups (275 g) all-purpose flour

1 scant cup (200 ml) boiling water

2 tbsp sesame oil

TO SERVE

6 green onions, cut into matchstick-thin strips

1/2 cucumber, peeled and cut into matchstick-thin strips

6 tbls (90 ml) hoisin sauce, sprinkled with sesame seeds

green onions to garnish

1 Remove any fat from the cavity of the duck. Put the duck into a bowl, pour boiling water over it, then remove and dry inside and out.

2 Mix together the sherry, honey, and soy sauce, and brush over the duck. Leave to stand, uncovered and at room temperature, for 4 hours or until the skin is dry.

3 Put the duck, breast-side down, on a wire rack in a roasting pan, and roast in a preheated oven at 400°F (200°C) for 25 minutes or until browned. Turn over and roast for a further 1–1¼ hours or until tender.

4 Meanwhile, make the pancake dough: sift the flour into a large bowl, add the boiling water, and mix to form a soft dough. Knead until smooth. Cover and leave to stand for about 30 minutes.

5 Knead the dough for 5 minutes. Shape into a roll about 1 in (2.5 cm) in diameter. Cut into 18 pieces, then roll into balls. Shape and cook the pancakes (see box, right).

6 When the duck is cooked, leave it to stand for about 15 minutes. Meanwhile, stack the pancakes on a plate in a steamer, cover, and steam for 10 minutes. Cut the duck into small pieces. Serve with the pancakes, green onions, cucumber, and hoisin sauce, and garnish with green onions.

Shaping and cooking Chinese pancakes

Pour the sesame oil into a bowl. Take 2 balls of dough, dip half of 1 ball into the oil, then press the oiled half onto the second ball.

Flatten the dough balls with the palms of your hands and roll out to a pancake about 6 in (15 cm) in diameter. Heat a skillet. Put the double pancake into the pan and cook for 1 minute. Flip over and cook the other side for 1 minute.

Remove from the pan, and peel the 2 pancakes apart. Repeat with the remaining dough, to make 18 pancakes in all. Cover the pancakes with a damp dish towel to stop them drying out.

ROAST DUCK WITH CRANBERRIES

Many people like the flesh of roast duck breast a little pink, but the legs need to be well cooked, or they can be tough. To accommodate the difference, serve the breast meat first, and return the duck to the oven for 15 minutes to finish cooking the legs.

SERVES 4

5 lb (2.5 kg) duck, with any giblets reserved for stock

cranberry sauce to serve (page 202)

watercress sprigs to garnish

CRANBERRY STUFFING

2 tbls (30 g) butter

I small onion, finely chopped

3³/4 cups (175 g) fresh whole-wheat bread crumbs

125 g (4 oz) cranberries

I tbsp chopped parsley

¹/4 tsp spice

salt and black pepper

I egg, beaten

GRAVY

I tsp all-purpose flour

1¹/4 cups (300 ml) duck giblet stock (page 170)

1 Make the cranberry stuffing: melt the butter in a pan, add the onion, and cook gently for 3–5 minutes until softened.

2 Stir in the bread crumbs, cranberries, parsley, and spice mixture, and season with salt and pepper. Bind with the egg, and leave to cool.

3 Remove any fat from the cavity of the duck. Spoon the stuffing into the neck end of the duck, secure the skin flap over the stuffing with a small skewer, and pat into a rounded shape. Put any leftover stuffing into an baking dish and set aside.

4 Prick the skin of the duck all over with a fork, and rub salt and pepper into the skin. Place the duck, breast-side down, on a wire rack in a deep roasting pan, and roast in a preheated oven at 400°F (200°C) for 25 minutes or until golden brown.

5 Pour off some of the fat from the pan to reduce splashing. Turn the duck breast-side up, and roast for another 20 minutes or until brown.

6 Reduce the oven temperature to 350°F (180°C), and roast the duck, without basting, for 1–1¹/4 hours. Cook any leftover stuffing with the duck for the last 40 minutes.

7 Test the duck by inserting a fine skewer into the thickest part of a thigh: the juices will run clear when it is cooked. Keep warm, uncovered, while you make the gravy.

8 Pour off all but 1 tbsp of the fat from the roasting pan. Put the pan on the stovetop, add the flour, and cook, stirring, for 2 minutes. Pour in the stock, and bring to a boil, stirring until thickened. Taste for seasoning, and strain into a warmed gravy boat.

9 Put the stuffing into a serving dish, carve the duck (page 173), and garnish with watercress. Serve with the gravy and cranberry sauce.

Cook's know-how

If there are no giblets in the duck, use chicken stock and add a splash of port wine or sherry and some grated orange zest to the gravy.

SAUCES FOR DUCK

ORANGE SAUCE

Put 2 finely chopped shallots, 1¹/4 cups (300 ml) chicken stock, and the juice of 2 oranges into a pan, and bring to a boil. Simmer until reduced by half, then season with salt and pepper. Push through a strainer, add the pared zest of I large orange, cut into fine strips, and reheat gently. Serve hot.

HONEY SAUCE

Cook 2 finely chopped shallots in 2 tbls (30 g) butter until soft. Add I tbsp all-purpose flour, and cook, stirring, for I minute. Blend in 1¹/4 cups (300 ml) chicken stock and 5 tbls (75 ml) dry white wine. Boil, stirring, until thick. Add 3 tbsp honey, I tbsp white wine vinegar, and a pinch each of salt and pepper, and cook for I minute. Push through a strainer, and add 3 tbsp finely chopped parsley. Serve hot.

BLACK-CURRANT SAUCE

Put 1¹/3 cups (250 g) black-currants and 1¹/4 cups (300 ml) water into a saucepan, and bring slowly to a boil. Simmer for 10 minutes until tender. Add 1¹/4 cups (250 g) caster sugar and I tbsp port wine, and cook gently until the sugar has dissolved. Serve hot or cold.

DUCK BREASTS WITH RASPBERRY SAUCE

SERVES 4

4 duck breast halves, 8–10 oz (250–300 g) each, with the skins left on

salt and black pepper

RASPBERRY SAUCE

2/3 cup (150 ml) port wine

5 tbls (75 ml) water

1/4 cup (45 g) caster sugar

8 oz (250 g) raspberries

1 tsp cornstarch

juice of 2 oranges

salt and black pepper

1 Make the raspberry sauce: pour the port and measured water into a small saucepan. Add the sugar, and boil, stirring until the sugar has dissolved. Add the raspberries, bring back to a boil, then cover and simmer very gently for 5 minutes.

2 With a wooden spoon, push the raspberry mixture through a strainer to extract the seeds. Return the raspberry puree to the saucepan, and bring back to a boil.

3 Mix the cornstarch with the orange juice. Add a little of the raspberry puree to the cornstarch mixture, and blend together. Return to the saucepan, and bring back to a boil, stirring constantly until thickened. Season with salt and pepper, and set aside.

4 Score and season each duck breast (see box, below right).

5 Place the duck breasts under a hot broiler, 4 in (10 cm) from the heat, and cook for 8 minutes on each side or until the skin is crisp and the duck is tender but still slightly pink inside.

6 Slice the duck breasts, skin-side up, and arrange in a fan shape on warmed plates. Spoon raspberry sauce around each of the servings, and serve at once.

DUCK BREASTS WITH RED WINE SAUCE

SERVES 4

4 duck breasts halves, 250–300 g (8–10 oz) each, with the skins left on

1/2 cup (125 ml) beef stock

1/2 cup (125 ml) red wine

1 tsp tomato paste

1 tsp lemon juice

1 tbls (15 g) butter

salt and black pepper

1 tbsp chopped fresh rosemary to garnish

MARINADE

5 garlic cloves, sliced

2 tbsp balsamic vinegar

1 tbsp chopped fresh rosemary

1 Make the marinade: in a bowl, combine the garlic, vinegar, and rosemary. Score the duck breasts (see box, right), and put them, skin-side down, in a shallow dish. Spoon the marinade over the top. Chill for 30 minutes.

2 Put the meat, skin-side down, with the marinade, in a skillet and cook for 5–7 minutes. Turn, and cook for 5 more minutes. Remove from the pan, and keep warm.

3 Spoon any excess fat from the skillet. Add the stock and wine, and boil over a high heat until reduced to a dark glaze, then add the tomato paste and lemon juice.

4 Remove from heat, and whisk in the butter, letting it thicken the sauce as it melts. Taste for seasoning.

5 Slice the duck, and arrange on warmed plates. Spoon the sauce around the duck, sprinkle with the chopped rosemary, and serve hot.

Scoring and seasoning the duck

With a sharp knife, score the skin of each duck breast with crisscross lines. Season both sides with salt and pepper.

HOT & SPICY STIR-FRIED DUCK

SERVES 4

4 skinless duck breast halves, 250–300 g (8–10 oz) each, cut diagonally into 1/2 in (1 cm) strips

2 tbsp sunflower oil

8 green onions, cut into 1 in (2.5 cm) lengths

125 g (4 oz) carrots, cut into matchstick-thin strips

8 oz (250 g) snow peas

7 oz (200 g) canned water chestnuts, drained, rinsed, and sliced

MARINADE

2 tsp dark soy sauce

2 tsp red wine vinegar

1 in (2.5 cm) piece of fresh gingerroot, peeled and grated

2 fresh red chilies, cored, seeded, and coarsely chopped

grated zest and juice of 1 orange

1 tsp sesame oil

1 tsp cornstarch

1 tsp sugar

salt and black pepper

1 Make the marinade: in a large bowl, combine the soy sauce, vinegar, ginger, chilies, orange zest and juice, sesame oil, cornstarch, and sugar, then season with salt and pepper.

2 Toss the duck strips in the marinade, cover, and leave to stand for 10 minutes.

3 Lift the duck strips out of the marinade, reserve the marinade, and drain the duck on paper towels.

4 Heat the oil in a wok or large skillet, add the duck, and stir-fry over a high heat for 5 minutes or until browned all over. Add the green onions and carrots, and stir-fry for 2–3 minutes. Add the snow peas, and stir-fry for 1 minute.

5 Pour the marinade into the wok, and stir-fry for about 2 minutes or until the duck is just tender. Stir in the water chestnuts, heat through, and taste for seasoning. Serve hot.

ORIENTAL DUCK WITH GINGER

SERVES 4

4 skinless duck breast halves, 8–10 oz (250–300 g) each

1 tbsp sunflower oil

8 baby corn cobs

bean sprouts and 1 tbsp toasted sesame seeds to garnish

MARINADE

1 scant cup (200 ml) orange juice

3 tbsp dark soy sauce

1 tbsp sesame oil

1 tbsp Chinese rice wine or dry sherry

1 tbsp honey

2 in (5 cm) piece of fresh gingerroot, peeled and grated

1 garlic clove, crushed

salt and black pepper

1 Make the marinade: in a large bowl, combine the orange juice, soy sauce, sesame oil, rice wine, honey, fresh ginger, and garlic, then season with salt and pepper.

2 With a sharp knife, make several diagonal slashes in each duck breast. Pour the marinade over the duck breasts, turn them over, then cover and marinate in the refrigerator for about 30 minutes.

3 Lift the duck breasts out of the marinade, reserving the marinade. Heat the oil in a large skillet, add the duck breasts, and cook over a high heat, turning frequently, for 10–12 minutes until tender. Add the marinade and simmer for 2–3 minutes until slightly reduced.

4 Meanwhile, blanch the baby corn cobs in boiling salted water for 1 minute. Drain, then make lengthwise cuts in each one, leaving them attached at the stem.

5 To serve, slice each duck breast, and arrange on 4 individual plates. Spoon the hot sauce over the duck, add the corn cobs, then garnish with bean sprouts and the toasted sesame seeds. Serve hot.

GUINEA FOWL MADEIRA

SERVES 6

2 tbsp sunflower oil

2 guinea fowl, 2¹/₂ lb (1.25 kg) each, cut into serving pieces (page 170)

4 shallots, halved

1 tbsp all-purpose flour

2¹/₂ cups (600 ml) chicken stock

²/₃ cup (150 ml) dry white wine

4 tbsp Madeira

salt and black pepper

12 oz (375 g) seedless green grapes

²/₃ cup (150 ml) heavy cream

chopped parsley to garnish

1 Heat the oil in a flameproof casserole, and cook the guinea fowl in batches for a few minutes until browned all over. Lift out and drain. Lower the heat, add the shallots, and cook, stirring, for 5 minutes or until softened. Lift out and drain.

2 Add the flour, and cook, stirring, for 1 minute. Pour in the stock, and bring to a boil, stirring. Add the wine and Madeira, and season with salt and pepper. Add the guinea fowl and shallots, and bring to a boil. Cook in a preheated oven at 325°F (160°C) for 1 hour or until tender.

3 Transfer the casserole to the stovetop, add the grapes, and cook for 15 minutes. Add the cream, and heat gently. Garnish with parsley and serve hot.

MUSHROOM-STUFFED QUAIL

Whole quail make an impressive dinner party-dish. They can be fiddly to eat, so boning and stuffing them makes it much easier for your guests. If you are short of time to bone the birds yourself, you can buy them already boned at supermarkets, or ask a butcher to do it.

SERVES 6

12 quail, boned (page 171)

30 g (1 oz) butter, plus extra for greasing

1 tbsp lime marmalade

MUSHROOM STUFFING

4 tbls (60 g) butter

3 shallots, finely chopped

5 cups (375 g) button mushrooms, coarsely chopped

1¹/₃ cups (60 g) fresh white bread crumbs

salt and black pepper

1 egg, beaten

LIME SAUCE

²/₃ cup (150 ml) chicken stock

juice of 1 lime

1 scant cup (200 ml) sour cream

4 tbsp chopped parsley

1 Make the mushroom stuffing: melt the butter in a saucepan, add the shallots, and cook gently, stirring occasionally, for 3–5 minutes until soft but not colored.

2 Add the mushrooms and cook for 2 minutes, then remove from the heat. Stir in the bread crumbs, season with salt and pepper, then stir in the egg and leave to cool. Stuff the quail (see box, right).

3 Put the quail into a buttered roasting pan. Melt the butter gently in a saucepan, add the lime marmalade, and heat gently, stirring, until combined. Brush over the quail, and cook in a preheated oven at 400°F (200°C) for 15–20 minutes until golden brown and tender. Remove from the pan and keep warm.

4 Make the lime sauce: put the roasting pan on the stovetop. Add the stock and boil, stirring for 5 minutes or until reduced a little.

5 Stir in the lime juice and sour cream, and heat gently, stirring constantly, until the sauce has a smooth, creamy consistency.

6 Add half of the parsley and season with salt and pepper. Serve the quail with the lime sauce, and garnish with the remaining parsley.

Stuffing the quail

Spoon some of the stuffing into the cavity of each quail; secure the skin with a wooden toothpick.

STUFFED PHEASANT BREASTS

Use 6 pheasant breasts, with their skin on, and put the stuffing between the skin and the meat. Roast in the oven for 35 minutes.

TRADITIONAL ROAST PHEASANT

Pheasants are often sold in pairs (called a brace) – a cock and a hen. Make sure you get young pheasants for this recipe; old ones are not suitable for roasting and can be very tough unless they are cooked slowly in a casserole.

SERVES 4

2 pheasants, any giblets reserved

6 tbls (90 g) butter, softened

salt and black pepper

4 bacon slices

1 tsp all-purpose flour

1 1/4 cups (300 ml) pheasant giblet stock or chicken stock (page 170)

1 tsp red-currant jelly

watercress sprigs to garnish

TO SERVE

fried bread crumbs (far right)

game fries (far right)

bread sauce (page 202)

1 Spread the pheasants with the butter, and season. Lay 2 bacon slices crosswise over each breast.

2 Put the pheasants into a roasting pan, and cook in a preheated oven at 400°F (200°C), basting once, for 1 hour or until tender.

3 Test the pheasants by inserting a fine skewer in the thickest part of a thigh: the juices should run clear when they are cooked.

4 Lift the pheasants on to a warmed serving platter, cover with foil, and keep warm. Pour off all but 1 tbsp of the fat from the roasting pan, reserving any juices. Put the pan on the stovetop, add the flour, and cook, stirring, for 1 minute.

5 Add the stock and red-currant jelly, and bring to a boil, stirring until lightly thickened. Simmer for 2–3 minutes, then taste for seasoning. Strain into a warmed gravy boat.

6 To serve, garnish the pheasants with the watercress sprigs, and serve with fried bread crumbs, game fries, bread sauce, and the gravy.

Healthy option

The breast meat of pheasant is lean, which means it dries out easily. Covering it liberally with butter is the traditional way to help keep the meat moist, but you can use a drizzle of olive oil instead.

EXTRAS FOR GAME

These traditional accompaniments can be served with roast pheasant and many other game dishes, including quail and partridge.

FRIED BREAD CRUMBS

Melt 2 tbls (30 g) butter with 1 tbsp sunflower oil. When the butter is foaming, add 2 cups (90 g) fresh white bread crumbs and cook, stirring, for 3–5 minutes until golden.

GAME FRIES

Using a mandoline or the finest blade on a food processor, slice 1 lb (500 g) old potatoes finely, then dry them. Heat some sunflower oil in a deep-fryer, add the potato slices, and deep-fry for 3 minutes or until crisp and golden. Drain, then sprinkle with salt.

STUFFING BALLS

Combine 2¾ cup (125 g) fresh white bread crumbs, 4 tbls (60 g) grated cold butter, 1 beaten egg, 2 tbsp chopped parsley, and the finely grated zest of 1 lemon. Season with salt and pepper, stir to mix well, then roll into 12 small balls. Melt 2 tbls (30 g) butter with 1 tbsp olive oil in a skillet. When the butter is foaming, add the stuffing balls, and cook for 5 minutes or until golden all over. Drain thoroughly.

PHEASANT STEW

SERVES 6–8

2 tbsp sunflower oil

2 pheasants, cut into serving pieces (page 170)

2 cups (375 g) shallots, chopped

4 oz (125 g) piece of smoked bacon, cut into strips

3 garlic cloves, crushed

1 tbsp all-purpose flour

2 1/2 cups (600 ml) game stock or chicken stock (page 170)

1 1/4 cups (300 ml) red wine

1 head of celery, separated into stalks, sliced

8 oz (250 g) button mushrooms

1 tbsp tomato paste

salt and black pepper

chopped parsley to garnish

1 Heat the oil in a large flameproof casserole. Add the pheasant pieces and cook over a high heat until browned. Lift out and drain.

2 Add the shallots and bacon and cook for 5 minutes. Add the garlic and flour and cook, stirring, for 1 minute. Add the stock and wine and bring to a boil. Add the celery, mushrooms, tomato paste, and season. Simmer for 5 minutes.

3 Add the pheasant, bring back to a boil, cover, and cook in a preheated oven at 325°F (160°C) for 2 hours. Garnish with parsley.

NORMANDY PHEASANT

Apples and cream are traditional ingredients in the cuisine of Normandy. Here, apples and a rich sauce perfectly complement the pheasant, which is cooked slowly and gently in wine and stock to keep it moist and tender.

SERVES 6–8

2 tbls (30 g) butter

1 tbsp sunflower oil

2 pheasants, cut into serving pieces (page 170)

2 cooking apples, quartered, cored, and sliced

4 celery stalks, sliced

1 onion, sliced

1 tbsp all-purpose flour

1 1/4 cups (300 ml) chicken or game stock (page 170)

2/3 cup (150 ml) dry white wine

salt and black pepper

2/3 cup (150 ml) heavy cream

apple rings to serve (see box, right)

chopped parsley to garnish

1 Melt the butter with the oil in a flameproof casserole. When the butter is foaming, add the pheasant pieces, and cook for about 5 minutes until browned. Lift out and drain.

2 Lower the heat, add the apples, celery, and onion, and cook for 5–6 minutes until soft.

3 Add the flour and cook, stirring, for 1 minute. Pour in the stock and wine, season with salt and pepper, and bring to a boil, stirring until lightly thickened.

4 Return the pheasant to the casserole and spoon the sauce over the top. Bring back to a boil, cover with parchment paper and the casserole lid, and cook in a preheated oven at 350°F (180°C) for 1–1 1/2 hours until tender. Remove the pheasant from the casserole with a slotted spoon and keep warm.

5 Strain the sauce into a saucepan. Whisk in the cream, taste for seasoning, then reheat gently. Arrange the pheasant on serving plates with the apple rings. Spoon the sauce over the pheasant and serve at once, garnished with parsley.

Apple rings

Core 2 cooking apples, leaving them whole, and slice crosswise into 1/4 in (5 mm) rings. Melt 2 tbls (30 g) butter in a frying pan, add the apple rings, and sprinkle with a little sugar. Cook over a high heat for 3 minutes, turning once, until caramelized and golden.

Healthy option

Instead of cream, use lowfat sour cream and only 2/3 cup (150 ml) stock.

RUBY HARE CASSEROLE

SERVES 4

1 hare, cut into serving pieces

2 tbls (30 g) butter

2 tbsp olive oil

4 oz (125 g) piece of slab bacon, cut into strips

16 small shallots

8 oz (250 g) crimini mushrooms, halved (about 4 cups)

2 tbls (30 g) all-purpose flour

3 3/4 cups (900 ml) game stock or chicken stock (page 170)

2 large thyme sprigs

2 large parsley sprigs

salt and black pepper

stuffing balls (page 217)

fresh thyme to garnish

MARINADE

1 1/4 cups (300 ml) ruby port wine

4 tbsp olive oil

1 large onion, sliced

2 bay leaves

1 Make the marinade: in a large bowl, combine the port wine, oil, onion, and bay leaves. Add the hare pieces, turn in the marinade, cover, and leave to marinate in the refrigerator for 8 hours.

2 Remove the hare from the marinade, reserving the marinade. Melt the butter with the oil in a large flameproof casserole. When the butter is foaming, add the hare pieces and cook over a high heat until browned all over. Lift out and drain on paper towels.

3 Lower the heat, add the bacon and shallots, and cook for 5 minutes or until lightly browned. Add the mushrooms and cook for 2–3 minutes. Remove and drain on paper towels. Add the flour and cook, stirring, for 1 minute. Gradually add the stock and bring to a boil, stirring until thickened.

4 Return the hare, bacon, shallots, and mushrooms to the casserole with the strained marinade. Add the thyme and parsley, season with salt and pepper, and bring to a boil. Cover and cook in a preheated oven at 325°F (160°C) for 2 hours.

5 Taste for seasoning. Place the stuffing balls on top, garnish with fresh thyme, and serve hot.

GAME PIE WITH FENNEL & CARROTS

SERVES 6

2 tbsp sunflower oil

1 1/2 lb (750 g) boneless game meat, cut into strips or dice

2 large carrots, sliced

1 fennel bulb, sliced

1 large onion, chopped

2 tsp all-purpose flour

1 1/4 cup (300 ml) game stock or chicken stock (page 170)

2/3 cup (150 ml) red wine

1 tbsp red-currant jelly

salt and black pepper

all-purpose flour for dusting

8 oz (250 g) store-bought puff pastry dough

beaten egg for glazing

chopped parsley to garnish

2-QUART (2-LITER) PIE DISH

1 Heat the oil in a large flameproof casserole. Add the game in batches and cook over a high heat until browned all over. Lift out and drain on paper towels.

2 Lower the heat, add the carrots, fennel, and onion, and cook, stirring occasionally, for 5 minutes or until softened. Add the flour and cook, stirring, for about 1 minute.

3 Gradually pour in the stock and bring to a boil, stirring until thickened. Add the game, wine, and red-currant jelly, and season with salt and pepper. Cover tightly and simmer very gently for 1 hour. Leave to cool.

4 Lightly flour a counter top. Roll out the puff pastry dough until 1 in (2.5 cm) larger than the pie dish. Invert the dish on to the dough and cut around the edge. Cut a long strip of pastry from the trimmings and press onto the rim of the pie dish. Reserve the remaining trimmings. Spoon in the game and vegetable mixture. Brush the dough strip with water, top with the dough lid, and crimp the edge with a fork.

5 Make a hole in the top of the pie to let the steam escape. Roll out the reserved dough and cut decorative shapes with a cookie cutter. Brush the bottoms of the shapes with beaten egg, and arrange on the pie. Glaze with beaten egg.

6 Bake the pie in a preheated oven at 400°F (200°C) for 25–30 minutes until the pastry is well risen and golden. Garnish with parsley.

RABBIT WITH MUSTARD & MARJORAM

SERVES 4

4 tbsp Dijon mustard

1 tsp chopped fresh marjoram

4 rabbit portions

2 tbls (30 g) butter

2 tbsp olive oil

1 large onion, chopped

2 garlic cloves, crushed

3 oz (90 g) piece of smoked slab bacon, cut into pieces

1 tsp all-purpose flour

2 cups (500 ml) chicken stock

salt and black pepper

2/3 cup (150 ml) light cream

2 tbsp chopped parsley to garnish

1 Mix the mustard and marjoram and spread over the rabbit pieces. Place in a shallow dish, cover, and leave to marinate in the refrigerator for 8 hours.

2 Melt the butter with the oil in a large flameproof casserole. When the butter is foaming, add the rabbit, and cook for about 5 minutes until browned all over. Lift out and drain on paper towels.

3 Add the onion, garlic, and bacon to the casserole and cook for 3–5 minutes. Add the flour and cook, stirring, for 1 minute. Gradually blend in the stock and bring to a boil, stirring until thickened.

4 Return the rabbit to the casserole, season with salt and pepper, and bring back to a boil. Cover and cook in a preheated oven at 325°F (160°C) for 1 1/2 hours or until the rabbit is tender.

5 Transfer the rabbit to a warmed platter and keep hot. Boil the sauce for 2 minutes until reduced. Stir in the cream, taste for seasoning, and spoon over the rabbit. Garnish with parsley.

Healthy option

To decrease the amount of saturated fat, omit the bacon and use lowfat sour cream instead of cream.

BRAISED RABBIT WITH MUSHROOMS & CIDER

SERVES 4

2 tbls (30 g) butter

1 tbsp sunflower oil

4 rabbit portions

8 small shallots

12 oz (375 g) mushrooms, quartered (about 6 1/4 cups)

1 1/4 cups (300 ml) hard cider

a few parsley sprigs

3–4 tarragon sprigs

salt and black pepper

1 1/4 cups (300 ml) light cream

2 tbsp chopped parsley to garnish

1 Melt the butter with the oil in a flameproof casserole. When the butter is foaming, add the rabbit, and cook for about 5 minutes until browned all over. Lift out the rabbit with a slotted spoon and drain on paper towels.

2 Add the shallots to the casserole and cook over a high heat, stirring, for about 3 minutes until golden. Add the mushrooms, and cook, stirring occasionally, for 3–4 minutes until softened.

3 Return the rabbit to the casserole, and add the cider, parsley sprigs, and tarragon. Season with salt and pepper, and bring to a boil. Cover and cook in a preheated oven at 325°F (160°C) for 1 1/2 hours or until the rabbit is tender.

4 Transfer the rabbit to a warmed platter and keep warm. Remove and discard the parsley and tarragon. Bring the sauce in the casserole to a boil on the stovetop, then boil until slightly reduced. Stir in the cream, taste for seasoning, and reheat gently.

5 Pour the sauce over the rabbit, and serve at once, garnished with parsley.

BRAISED RABBIT WITH PRUNES

Substitute 1 heaping cup (125 g) pitted prunes for the mushrooms. Add to the casserole 30 minutes before the end of the cooking time.

POT ROAST VENISON

SERVES 6

2½–3 lb (1.25–1.5 kg) venison shoulder, boned, rolled and tied

2 tbls (30 g) butter

2 tbsp sunflower oil

1 large onion, chopped

2 large carrots, sliced

2 celery stalks, sliced

1¼ cups (300 ml) beef stock

salt and black pepper

1 tbsp red-currant jelly

MARINADE

1¼ cups (300 ml) red wine

2 tbsp olive oil

pared zest of 1 orange

pared zest of 1 lemon

2 tsp crushed juniper berries

6 black peppercorns

1 garlic clove, crushed

1 large thyme sprig

1 large parsley sprig

1 Make the marinade: in a large bowl, combine the wine, oil, orange and lemon zests, juniper berries, black peppercorns, garlic, thyme, and parsley. Turn the venison in the marinade, cover, and marinate in the refrigerator, turning occasionally, for 2–3 days.

2 Lift the venison out of the marinade, straining and reserving the marinade, and pat dry. Melt the butter with the oil in a large flameproof casserole. When the butter is foaming, add the venison and cook over a high heat for 5 minutes or until well browned all over. Remove the venison from the casserole.

3 Lower the heat and add the onion, carrots, and celery to the casserole. Cover and cook very gently for 10 minutes. Place the venison on top of the vegetables, add the stock and the strained marinade, then season with salt and pepper and bring to a boil. Cover with a piece of waxed paper and the casserole lid, and cook in a preheated oven at 325°F (160°C) for 2½–3 hours until tender.

4 Lift out the venison and keep warm. Strain the liquid in the casserole, spoon off the fat, then return the liquid to the casserole. Add the red-currant jelly, and boil for a few minutes until syrupy. Slice the venison, and arrange on a warmed platter. Pour the sauce over, and serve hot.

VENISON CASSEROLE

SERVES 6

2 lb (1 kg) stewing venison, cut into 1 in (2.5 cm) cubes

2 tbsp olive oil

6 celery stalks, thickly sliced on the diagonal

5 oz (150 g) crimini mushrooms, quartered (about 2 cups)

2 tbls (30 g) all-purpose flour

salt and black pepper

4 oz (125 g) small carrots

chopped parsley to garnish

MARINADE

2 cups (500 ml) dry red wine

3 tbsp sunflower oil

1 onion, sliced

1 tsp ground allspice

a few parsley sprigs

1 bay leaf

1 Make the marinade: in a large bowl, combine the red wine, oil, onion, allspice, parsley sprigs, and bay leaf. Toss the venison cubes in the marinade to coat them thoroughly, cover, and leave to marinate in the refrigerator, turning occasionally, for 2 days.

2 Lift the venison and onion out of the marinade and pat dry. Strain and reserve the marinade.

3 Heat the oil in a large flameproof casserole, add the venison and onion, and cook for 3–5 minutes until well browned. Lift out and drain on paper towels.

4 Lower the heat, add the celery and mushrooms, and cook for 2–3 minutes until softened. Remove with a slotted spoon. Add the flour and cook, stirring, for 1 minute. Gradually blend in the marinade and bring to a boil, stirring until thickened.

5 Return the venison, onion, celery, and mushrooms to the casserole, and season with salt and pepper. Bring to a boil, cover, and cook in a preheated oven at 325°F (160°C) for 1½ hours.

6 Add the carrots, and return to the oven for 30 minutes or until the venison is tender. Serve hot, garnished with parsley.

RATHER SPECIAL GAME PIE

This raised game pie follows a classic British recipe that takes about 6 hours to make, over 3 days, but it is worth the effort. Boned mixed game meats – usually pheasant, rabbit or hare, and venison – are available from some specialist mail-order game dealers. There is chicken in the pie too, which goes very well with game, but you can use turkey.

SERVES 20

4 lb (2 kg) chicken, boned and skinned (page 171)

2 lb (1 kg) boneless mixed game meats, cut into 1/2 in (1 cm) pieces

375 g (12 oz) belly pork, coarsely chopped

1 lb (500 g) piece of slab bacon, cut into small pieces

butter for greasing

hot-water crust pastry dough (see box, right)

about 2 tsp salt

black pepper

1 egg, beaten

2 cups (500 ml) jellied stock (page 170)

MARINADE

2/3 cup (150 ml) port wine

1 small onion, finely chopped

3 garlic cloves, crushed

leaves of 4 thyme sprigs, chopped

1 tsp grated nutmeg

11 1/2 IN (29 CM) SPRINGFORM OR LOOSE-BOTTOMED CAKE PAN

1 Make the marinade: in a bowl, combine the port wine, onion, garlic, thyme, and grated nutmeg.

2 Cut the chicken into long strips, about 1/2 in (1 cm) wide, and set aside. Cut the rest of the chicken into 1/2 in (1 cm) chunks. Add the chunks to the marinade with the game meats, belly pork, and bacon. Cover and leave to marinate in the refrigerator for 8 hours.

3 Lightly butter the tin. Take two-thirds of the hot-water crust pastry, pat it out over the bottom of the tin, and push it up the side, until it stands 1 cm (1/2 in) above the rim.

4 Season the meat mixture with plenty of salt and pepper and spoon half into the dough. Smooth the surface evenly.

5 Arrange the reserved chicken breast strips on top of the meat, radiating from the middle. Season with salt and pepper.

6 Top with the remaining meat mixture. Brush the top edge of the dough with beaten egg. Roll out the remaining dough, and cover the pie, reserving the trimmings. Pinch around the edge to seal, then crimp.

7 Decorate the pie with the dough trimmings, attaching them with beaten egg. Make 3 steam holes in the dough lid, and glaze the pie with beaten egg.

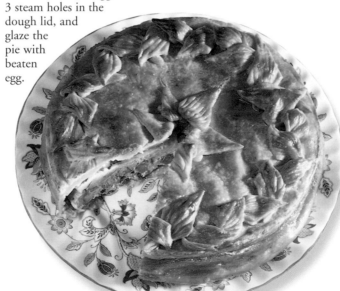

8 Bake in a preheated oven at 425°F (220°C) for 1 hour. If the pastry browns too quickly, cover with foil. Reduce the heat to 325°F (160°C) and cook for 2–2 1/4 hours.

9 Test the pie by piercing the centre with a skewer: the juices will run clear and the meat will feel tender when it is done. Leave the pie to cool in the pan for 8 hours.

10 Put the jellied stock into a saucepan and heat until melted. Using a funnel, slowly pour the stock through the holes in the pie. Cover and chill for 6 hours or until the stock has set. Unmold the pie and cut into wedges to serve.

Hot-water crust

Sift 5 1/3 cups (750 g) all-purpose flour and 1 tsp salt into a large bowl. Put 1 1/3 cups (400 ml) water and 1 1/4 cups (300 g) white vegetable shortening into a pan and heat until the water is boiling and the fat has melted.

Pour onto the flour and mix quickly with a wooden spoon until the mixture holds together.

Turn the dough out onto a floured surface, invert the bowl over the top to keep the dough moist, and leave to cool until lukewarm.

6

MEAT DISHES

UNDER 30 MINUTES

BEEF STROGANOFF

Classic Russian dish: strips of lean beef cooked with shallots and button mushrooms, and mixed with sour cream.

SERVES 6 329 calories per serving

Takes 20 minutes   Page 249

HIGH PROTEIN

LAMB CHOPS WITH MINTED HOLLANDAISE SAUCE

Broiled chops served with hollandaise sauce, flavored with lemon juice and fresh mint.

SERVES 4 611 calories per serving

Takes 20 minutes   Page 278

STEAK DIANE

Flambéed steaks served with a light sauce that combines onion, beef stock, lemon juice, Worcestershire sauce, and parsley.

SERVES 4 373 calories per serving

Takes 25 minutes   Page 248

BARBECUE

STEAKS WITH SMOKED OYSTER RELISH

Steaks rubbed with garlic, and sprinkled with smoked oyster relish flavored with parsley.

SERVES 4 278 calories per serving

Takes 15–20 minutes   Page 247

HERBED CHOPS

Lamb chops brushed with olive oil, sprinkled with pepper, and flavored with rosemary, mint, and thyme sprigs, then broiled.

SERVES 4 320 calories per serving

Takes 15 minutes   Page 278

FAMILY CHOICE

LIVER & BACON WITH ONION SAUCE

Strips of liver simmered with onion, bacon, beef stock, ketchup, and Worcestershire sauce.

SERVES 4 441 calories per serving

Takes 15 minutes   Page 269

FRENCH CLASSIC

TOURNEDOS ROQUEFORT

Crunchy and nutritious: broiled tournedos steaks topped with a mixture of melted Roquefort cheese, butter, and chopped walnuts.

SERVES 4 430 calories per serving

Takes 20 minutes   Page 248

PEPPER STEAKS

Piquant and creamy: fillet mignon encrusted with black peppercorns. Served in a flavorsome pool of cream and brandy sauce.

SERVES 4 489 calories per serving

Takes 25 minutes   Page 246

CALF'S LIVER WITH SAGE

Slices of calf's liver, coated with seasoned flour, and cooked quickly. Served with pan juices flavored with sage and lemon juice.

SERVES 4 364 calories per serving

Takes 10 minutes   Page 270

UNDER 30 MINUTES

SALTIMBOCCA
Veal scallops topped with sage leaves and proscuitto, and then cooked with garlic. Served with a wine and cream sauce.

SERVES 4 342 calories per serving

Takes 25 minutes   Page 267

MEXICAN CLASSIC

BEEF TACOS
Ground beef and tomatoes richly seasoned with garlic, chili, and cilantro. Served in taco shells with lettuce and sour cream.

SERVES 4 407 calories per serving

Takes 25 minutes   Page 263

DINNER PARTY

CHATEAUBRIAND WITH BEARNAISE SAUCE
Broiled steak basted with butter, served with a béarnaise sauce flavored with tarragon.

SERVES 2 761 calories per serving

Takes 25 minutes   Page 246

30–60 MINUTES

VEAL MARSALA
Veal scallops lightly coated in seasoned flour and cooked until golden. Served in a Marsala sauce, and garnished with parsley.

SERVES 4 239 calories per serving

Takes 30 minutes   Page 268

ECONOMICAL

CORNED BEEF HASH
Quick and nourishing: chunks of corned beef cooked with onion, pieces of potato, and stock, and broiled until crispy and brown.

SERVES 4 444 calories per serving

Takes 30 minutes   Page 258

BEEF & BEAN BURRITOS
Popular and piquant: strips of steak cooked with garlic, chili, tomatoes, and pinto beans. Wrapped in soft flour tortillas.

SERVES 4 471 calories per serving

Takes 35 minutes   Page 249

HIGH PROTEIN

BROILED PORK CHOPS WITH MANGO SAUCE
Sweet and tender: chops served with a sauce combining fresh mango and mango chutney.

SERVES 4 347 calories per serving

Takes 35 minutes   Page 288

PORK CHOPS WITH ORANGES
Fresh and tangy: pork chops spread with course mustard, topped with orange slices and sugar, and baked.

SERVES 6 361 calories per serving

Takes 55 minutes   Page 289

HIGH PROTEIN

PORK CHOPS WITH MIXED PEPPERCORNS
Lean loin chops encrusted with peppercorns, served with a white wine, beef stock, and cream sauce.

SERVES 4 567 calories per serving

Takes 30 minutes, plus standing   Page 290

30–60 MINUTES

BARBECUE

LAMB WITH MINT GLAZE

Lamb chops glazed with white wine, vinegar, mint sprigs, honey, and Dijon mustard, then barbecued or broiled.

SERVES 4 304 calories per serving

Takes 15 minutes, plus marinating   Page 277

MADEIRA PORK WITH PAPRIKA

Rich and creamy: pork tenderloin simmered with Madeira, stock, onion, mushrooms, red bell pepper, and paprika, then mixed with cream.

SERVES 4 560 calories per serving

Takes 50 minutes   Page 287

HIGH PROTEIN

VEAL CHOPS WITH MUSHROOMS & CREAM

A classic. Veal chops cooked with mushrooms, cream, shallots, garlic, wine, and tarragon.

SERVES 4 604 calories per serving

Takes 30 minutes, plus soaking   Page 266

BRAISED MEATBALLS

Balls of ground beef and pork in a sauce of hard cider and tomato paste, with onion, garlic, celery, red bell pepper, and mushrooms.

SERVES 4 416 calories per serving

Takes 40 minutes   Page 259

FRENCH CLASSIC

KIDNEYS TURBIGO

Lamb kidneys cooked with thin pork sausages, then simmered with stock, sherry, onions, mushrooms, and bay leaf.

SERVES 4 455 calories per serving

Takes 50 minutes   Page 284

WEINER SCHNITZELS

A classic Viennese dish: veal scallops coated in beaten egg and fresh white bread crumbs, chilled, then cooked until light golden brown.

SERVES 4 373 calories per serving

Takes 20 minutes, plus chilling   Page 267

Traditionally served with piquant anchovy fillets, chopped capers, lemon wedges, and a few parsley sprigs.

OVER 60 MINUTES

JAPANESE CLASSIC

TERIYAKI BEEF

Strips of tender steak marinated in soy sauce, Japanese rice wine, and sugar for an authentic Japanese taste. Stir-fried with onion and red bell pepper.

SERVES 4 329 calories per serving

Takes 15 minutes, plus marinating   Page 252

LAMB NOISETTES WITH ORANGE & HONEY

Broiled noisettes served with a sauce made from the marinade of orange, honey, olive oil, and herbs.

SERVES 4 457 calories per serving

Takes 20 minutes, plus marinating   Page 279

HIGH PROTEIN

LEMON-BROILED LAMB

Butterflied leg of lamb marinated in a tangy mixture of lemon juice, honey, garlic, and mustard, and broiled.

SERVES 6–8 425–318 calories per serving

Takes 45 minutes, plus marinating   Page 273

DINNER PARTY

BACON-WRAPPED PORK IN VERMOUTH SAUCE

Pork tenderloin wrapped in bacon and served with a vermouth and mushroom sauce.

SERVES 6 547 calories per serving

Takes 1¼ hours   Page 287

FAJITAS

Beef steak marinated in orange and lime juices, tequila, garlic, cilantro, and chili, and then broiled. Served with relish and tortillas.

SERVES 4 543 calories per serving

Takes 40 minutes, plus marinating   Page 252

MEAT LOAF

Ground beef mixed with tomatoes, stuffing, onion, carrot, parsley, and garlic, wrapped in bacon and baked.

SERVES 6 478 calories per serving

Takes 1½ hours   Page 262

ORIENTAL CLASSIC

PORK WITH CHILI & COCONUT

Strips of tender pork in a dry marinade of ginger, chili, and curry powder. Cooked with coconut, green onions, and red bell pepper.

SERVES 6 332 calories per serving

Takes 40 minutes, plus marinating   Page 288

CREAMED SWEETBREADS

Veal sweetbreads simmered with onion, parsley, and bay leaf. Served with a lemon-flavored sauce.

SERVES 6 230 calories per serving

Takes 40 minutes, plus soaking   Page 270

HIGH PROTEIN

PORK CHOPS WITH SPINACH & MUSHROOM STUFFING

Loin chops with a savory mixture of spinach and mushrooms, and topped with Gruyère cheese.

SERVES 6 345 calories per serving

Takes 40 minutes   Page 289

OVER 60 MINUTES

AFRICAN CLASSIC

EXOTIC BEEF
Ground beef mixed with garlic, apricots, almonds, chutney, lemon, and milk-soaked bread. Topped with eggs and almonds and baked.

SERVES 6–8 656–492 calories per serving
Takes 1 hour 5 minutes   Page 263

DANISH MEATBALLS
Ground pork seasoned with onion, thyme, and paprika and shaped into ovals. Cooked in a tomato sauce, and topped with plain yogurt.

SERVES 4–6 586–391 calories per serving
Takes 1¹⁄₂ hours   Page 292

TRADITIONAL

SHEPHERD'S PIE
Ground lamb flavored with mushrooms, carrot, onion, garlic, stock, and mushroom ketchup. Topped with mashed potatoes and baked.

SERVES 6 383 calories per serving
Takes 1¹⁄₂ hours   Page 283

ORIENTAL CLASSIC

SPICED LAMB WITH COCONUT
Cubes of lamb, dry marinated in ginger and spices, are cooked with tomato, lime, mango chutney, and coconut, then mixed with yogurt.

SERVES 6 496 calories per serving
Takes 1¹⁄₄ hours   Page 282

FAMILY CHOICE

PASTICCIO
Ground pork simmered with red wine, tomatoes, garlic, herbs, and cinnamon. Baked with macaroni and a cheese-flavored custard.

SERVES 6 679 calories per serving
Takes 1¹⁄₄ hours   Page 292

BEEF WITH ROAST VEGETABLE SALAD
Roast beef served with a salad of roasted eggplant, zucchini, fennel, and bell peppers.

SERVES 4–6 522–348 calories per serving
Takes 1³⁄₄ hours, plus cooling   Page 244

SPANISH CLASSIC

SAUSAGES WITH POTATOES & PEPPERS
Bite-sized pieces of spicy sausage in a casserole with potatoes, red and green bell peppers, and garlic.

SERVES 4 381 calories per serving
Takes 1¹⁄₄ hours, plus cooling   Page 284

MARINATED LOIN OF PORK WITH PINEAPPLE
Pork marinated in pineapple juice, maple syrup, soy sauce, and herbs, and then roasted.

SERVES 8 320 calories per serving
Takes 2¹⁄₂ hours, plus marinating   Page 286

BEEF FLORENTINE
A filling mixture of ground beef, tomato, and garlic, topped with spinach and three types of cheese. Covered with crisp phyllo pastry.

SERVES 8 576 calories per serving
Takes 1¹⁄₂ hours   Page 259

OVER 60 MINUTES

HIGH FIBRE

SAUSAGE & LENTIL CASSEROLE

Herby pork sausages baked with lentils, stock, and vegetables. Flavored with bay leaves, parsley, and sage.

SERVES 6   522 calories per serving

Takes 1¾ hours   Page 296

RACK OF LAMB WITH A WALNUT & HERB CRUST

A dinner party special. Rack of lamb coated with a walnut and parsley crust and roasted.

SERVES 4–6   626–417 calories per serving

Takes 1¾ hours, plus chilling   Page 277

FRENCH CLASSIC

BLANQUETTE OF LAMB

Chunks of boneless lamb shoulder simmered with onion, carrot, bay leaves, lemon juice, and mushrooms. Served with a cream and egg sauce.

SERVES 6   439 calories per serving

Takes 2 hours   Page 281

GREEK CLASSIC

LIGHT MOUSSAKA WITH FRESH MINT

Ground lamb in a tomato-mint sauce, layered with eggplant, and topped with yogurt, egg, and cheese.

SERVES 8   351 calories per serving

Takes 1¾ hours   Page 283

ECONOMICAL

TOAD-IN-THE-HOLE WITH ONION SAUCE

Pork sausage combined with leek, sage, and parsley, and baked in a batter.

SERVES 4   802 calories per serving

Takes 45 minutes, plus standing   Page 296

FAMILY CHOICE

MEAT PIES WITH CHEESY POTATO TOPPING

Ground beef cooked with vegetables and stock. Topped with mashed potatoes and cheese.

SERVES 6   567 calories per serving

Takes 1½ hours   Page 262

LEMON ROAST VEAL WITH SPINACH STUFFING

Boneless veal roast marinated in lemon and thyme, with spinach, shallot, and bacon stuffing.

SERVES 6–8   444–333 calories per serving

Takes 1¾ hours, plus marinating   Page 265

TRADITIONAL

ROAST LEG OF LAMB WITH RED WINE GRAVY

A British classic: lamb flavored with herbs, roasted and served with red wine gravy and mint sauce.

SERVES 4–6   517–344 calories per serving

Takes 2 hours   Page 271

LAMB TAGINE

Cubes of lamb cooked with apricots, fennel, green bell peppers, and stock. Flavored with saffron, ginger, and orange.

SERVES 8   412 calories per serving

Takes 1¾ hours   Page 282

OVER 60 MINUTES

HIGH PROTEIN

CHILI CON CARNE

Tex-Mex speciality: cubes of chuck steak cooked with red kidney beans, chili, onion, garlic, stock, tomato paste, and red pepper.

SERVES 6 362 calories per serving

Takes 3¼ hours, plus soaking   Page 257

SPINACH-STUFFED LAMB

Succulent and nutritious: boned leg of lamb stuffed with spinach and garlic, and roasted with wine and anchovies.

SERVES 6–8 459–344 calories per serving

Takes 2½ hours, plus cooling   Page 272

FRENCH CLASSIC

SHOULDER OF LAMB WITH GARLIC & HERBS

Rich lamb flavored with garlic, rosemary, mint, and thyme. Served with great northern beans.

SERVES 6 464 calories per serving

Takes 1¾ hours   Page 276

FAMILY CHOICE

FARMER'S BACON BAKE

Cut-up lean slab bacon simmered with vegetables, parsley, and peppercorns, and baked with a cheese sauce.

SERVES 6–8 510–383 calories per serving

Takes 2¼ hours   Page 294

PORK IN RED WINE

Cubes of pork marinated in red wine, cilantro seeds, and cinnamon, cooked with wine, and sprinkled with cumin seeds.

SERVES 4 582 calories per serving

Takes 2 hours, plus marinating   Page 291

TRADITIONAL

WINTER BEEF CASSEROLE

Cubes of beef chuck and strips of bacon cooked with stock, celery, and carrots, and flavored with wine and passata.

SERVES 4–6 680–454 calories per serving

Takes 2¾ hours   Page 253

SWEET & SOUR CHINESE SPARERIBS

Spareribs baked until tender, and coated in a sauce combining ginger, garlic, soy and hoisin sauces, tomato paste, and sherry.

SERVES 4 491 calories per serving

Takes 2 hours   Page 290

INDIAN CLASSIC

CURRIED LAMB WITH ALMONDS

Rich and creamy: chunks of lamb cooked with an aromatic blend of ginger, chilies, cardamom, and other spices, in a creamy yogurt sauce.

SERVES 6 508 calories per serving

Takes 2½ hours   Page 280

BEEF ROLLS WITH VEGETABLE JULIENNE

This slices of beef wrapped around stir-fried vegetables, and cooked with beef stock.

SERVES 6 257 calories per serving

Takes 2¼ hours   Page 257

OVER 60 MINUTES

BONED LOIN OF PORK WITH APRICOT STUFFING

A boneless piece of pork filled with an apricot and herb stuffing, then rolled and roasted.

SERVES 8 428 calories per serving
Takes 2¼ hours, plus cooling   Page 285

BEEF WITH HORSERADISH

Tender beef chuck slowly cooked with stock, shallots, curry powder, sugar, ginger, and horseradish cream. Garnished with parsley.

SERVES 6 298 calories per serving
Takes 3 hours   Page 255

AROMATIC LAMB WITH LENTILS

Boneless shoulder of lamb marinated in orange juice, garlic, ginger, and cilantro. Cooked with apricots, stock, onion, and lentils.

SERVES 8 475 calories per serving
Takes 2½ hours, plus marinating   Page 281

CORNED BEEF WITH MUSTARD SAUCE

A hearty meal of meat and fresh vegetables served with a wine-vinegar flavored mustard sauce.

SERVES 6-8 575–431 calories per serving
Takes 2¼ hours, plus soaking   Page 243

HUNGARIAN GOULASH

Beef chuck cooked with stock, onion, tomatoes, red bell pepper, potatoes, paprika, and sour cream.

SERVES 6 474 calories per serving
Takes 2½ hours   Page 254

CHIANTI BEEF CASSEROLE

Taste of Italy: cubes of steak cooked until meltingly tender with Chianti, garlic, thyme, artichoke hearts, sun-dried tomatoes, and olives.

SERVES 4-6 512–342 calories per serving
Takes 2½ hours   Page 255

THAI RED BEEF CURRY

Cubes of beef chuck cooked with cardamom, cinnamon, bay leaves, cloves, ginger, garlic, paprika, tomatoes, yogurt, and red bell pepper.

SERVES 6 327 calories per serving
Takes 2½ hours   Page 256

BEEF WELLINGTON

Roasted beef tenderloin coated with mushrooms, onion, and liver pâté, and encased in puff pastry. Served with a mushroom gravy.

SERVES 8 580 calories per serving
Takes 2¼ hours, plus cooling   Page 245

FRENCH-STYLE BRAISED BEEF

Beef marinated in wine, vinegar, garlic, orange, and herbs, and cooked with bacon, carrots, mushrooms, tomatoes, and olives.

SERVES 4-6 604–402 calories per serving
Takes 2½ hours, plus marinating   Page 243

OVER 60 MINUTES

FRENCH CLASSIC

BOEUF BOURGUIGNON

Rich classic French casserole: cubes of beef chuck cooked with shallots, bacon, red Burgundy, beef stock, mushrooms, and herbs.

SERVES 6 490 calories per serving

Takes 2³/4 hours   Page 253

OSSO BUCO

Slices of veal shin cooked with onion, tomato, carrots, celery, garlic, white wine, and stock. Sprinkled with gremolata just before serving.

SERVES 6 354 calories per serving

Takes 2³/4 hours   Page 268

FAMILY CHOICE

COUNTRY BEEF CASSEROLE

Chunky and nourishing: cubes of beef chuck slowly cooked in a casserole with stock and vegetables. Served with herb dumplings.

SERVES 8 405 calories per serving

Takes 3 hours   Page 256

DINNER PARTY

VEAL STEW WITH OLIVES & PEPPERS

Cubes of stewing veal cooked in a casserole of bell peppers, wine, tomatoes, and olives, flavored with garlic and rosemary.

SERVES 8 355 calories per serving

Takes 2 hours   Page 269

TRADITIONAL

SHOULDER OF LAMB WITH LEMON & OLIVES

Boneless lamb rolled with an olive, lemon, and herb stuffing, and roasted in wine and stock.

SERVES 6–8 460–345 calories per serving

Takes 2³/4 hours   Page 273

TRADITIONAL ROAST BEEF

A traditional succulent family roast: rolled beef rib roast basted and cooked until deliciously tender. Served with a variety of vegetables, traditional British Yorkshire puddings, a rich red wine gravy, and creamy horseradish sauce.

SERVES 8 394 calories per serving

Takes 3¹/4 hours   Page 241

OVER 60 MINUTES

ROAST FRESH HAM
Tender and nourishing: fresh ham roasted with carrot and onion until crisp. Served with a rich gravy and apple sauce.

SERVES 6–8 338–254 calories per serving
Takes 2¼ hours   Page 286

IRISH STEW
Traditional Irish family meal: lamb chops cooked in layers of potato and onion, and flavored with bay leaf, thyme, and parsley.

SERVES 4 539 calories per serving
Takes 3¼ hours   Page 280

HEARTY PORK CASSEROLE
Shoulder of pork cut into cubes, cooked in a casserole with stock, white wine vinegar, honey, soy sauce, mushrooms, and prunes.

SERVES 8 402 calories per serving
Takes 3¼ hours   Page 291

MEAT HOT POT
Lamb chops and kidneys cooked with potatoes, carrots, and onions, and flavored with thyme, parsley, and bay leaf.

SERVES 4 689 calories per serving
Takes 3 hours   Page 279

TEXAS BARBECUE BEEF BRISKET
Spicy and rich: beef baked in a marinade of barbecue sauce, beer, lemon juice, onions, garlic, and Worcestershire sauce.

SERVES 6 693 calories per serving
Takes 3½ hours, plus marinating   Page 242

SAUSAGE BAKE
Slices of pork sausage with layers of vegetables, lentils, and potatoes, slowly cooked in a casserole or Dutch oven with stock, bay leaves, and cloves.

SERVES 6 712 calories per serving
Takes 3¼ hours   Page 295

TRADITIONAL STEAK & KIDNEY PIE
Rich and satisfying: cubes of beef and kidney cooked with stock, Worcestershire sauce, and mushrooms. Topped with a pastry crust.

SERVES 6 577 calories per serving
Takes 3¼ hours, plus cooling   Page 258

SAUSAGE CASSOULET
Garlic flavored sausage, pork sausages, and bacon baked with beans, tomatoes, wine, onion, and herbs. Topped with bread crumbs.

SERVES 8 619 calories per serving
Takes 3 hours, plus soaking   Page 295

TRINIDAD PEPPERPOT BEEF
Boneless beef simmered with stock, vinegar, Worcestershire sauce, chilies, sugar, parsley, peppercorns, cinnamon, and thyme.

SERVES 4–6 697–465 calories per serving
Takes 3¾ hours   Page 244

OVER 60 MINUTES

TRADITIONAL

BEEF POT ROAST WITH WINTER VEGETABLES

Round of beef in a casserole with onions, rutabaga, celery, carrot, wine, and herbs.

SERVES 6 360 calories per serving

Takes 3¹/2 hours   Page 242

FAMILY CHOICE

GREEK ROAST LAMB

Traditional Greek dish: leg of lamb richly flavored with garlic, rosemary, and lemon juice, and cooked until tender.

SERVES 6 328 calories per serving

Takes 4¹/4 hours   Page 272

OXTAIL STEW

Tender thick stew: slices of oxtail slowly simmered with beef stock, onions, tomato paste, celery, and herbs. Served with chunky potatoes.

SERVES 6 337 calories per serving

Takes 4¹/2 hours   Page 264

CARBONNADE OF BEEF

Cubes of beef chuck slowly cooked with onion, garlic, fresh herbs, brown ale, and stock, and topped with mustard croutes.

SERVES 6 465 calories per serving

Takes 3¹/2 hours   Page 254

DINNER PARTY

INDIAN SPICED LAMB

Lamb coated in a mixture of spices, honey, yogurt, and saffron that is roasted, and garnished with cashew nuts and chopped cilantro.

SERVES 6 379 calories per serving

Takes 4¹/4 hours, plus marinating   Page 276

AMERICAN CLASSIC

BOSTON BAKED BEANS

Great northern beans, bacon, and onions cooked with dark brown sugar, tomato paste, molassas, syrup, and dry mustard.

SERVES 6–8 433–325 calories per serving

Takes 5³/4 hours, plus soaking   Page 294

VEAL WITH TUNA MAYONNAISE

Veal flavored with garlic and rosemary, and roasted in white wine. Served chilled with a tuna-flavored mayonnaise.

SERVES 8 636 calories per serving

Takes 3¹/2 hours, plus cooling   Page 266

DINNER PARTY

MUSTARD-GLAZED HAM

Smoked ham roasted with hard cider, glazed with sugar and mustard, and served with a lemon mustard sauce.

SERVES 16–20 477–382 calories per serving

Takes 4 hours, plus soaking   Page 293

PRESSED TONGUE

Salted ox tongue simmered with bay leaf and onion, then covered with gelatin, pressed, and chilled until set.

SERVES 10 392 calories per serving

Takes 4¹/4 hours, plus chilling   Page 264

MEAT KNOW-HOW

FOR CENTURIES, MEAT HAS BEEN the protein food around which the majority of meals have been planned. Today, however, that tradition has been turned on its head, with healthy eating advice to make meat and other protein foods just one part of a healthy diet, not the major part. Nevertheless, meat is enjoyed by most families several times a week, and it still forms the traditional centerpiece for many celebration meals. By making sure the cooking method suits the cut of meat you are preparing – quick cooking for lean meats and long, slow cooking for tougher cuts – you will always have perfectly moist and tender results.

BUYING & STORING

If possible, buy your meat from a good local butcher, or the butcher in a supermarket, because he or she's most likely to have just the cut you want (or will be prepared to cut it for you), and will also advise you how to cook it. Wherever you shop, choose meat that looks fresh and moist (not wet), with a good color and no grayish tinge. Check that pieces are neatly trimmed, without excess fat and splinters of bone. If the meat is packaged, check the use-by date. Appetites vary, but as a general guide, allow 4–6 oz (125–175 g) of lean boneless meat per person, and about 8 oz (250 g) each if the meat has a reasonable amount of bone.

Store all meat in the refrigerator, with raw kept separate from cooked and on a lower shelf (also below any food that will not be cooked before eating). Ground meat and variety meats are more perishable than other kinds of meat, so cook them within 1 or 2 days of purchase. Chops, steaks, and joints can be kept for 3–5 days: remove the wrapping and replace with fresh. Eat cooked meat within 3–4 days.

PREPARING MEAT FOR COOKING

Trim off excess fat before cooking and remove any visible gristle, sinew, and tough connective tissue. If broiling or panfrying steaks or chops, slash or snip any fat at intervals to prevent the meat from curling up during cooking.

Marinate very lean joints to be roasted or lean cuts to be broiled or barbecued to keep them moist during cooking.

MICROWAVING

Because microwave cooking is so fast, meat does not have time to brown and become crisp. This can be overcome by using a special browning dish, which sears meat in the way a skillet does.

The microwave is very useful for defrosting frozen meat. This must be done evenly at the manufacturer's recommended setting to prevent some parts of the meat beginning to cook before others are totally defrosted. All wrapping should be removed from the meat before defrosting to make sure that the meat does not start to cook.

FREEZING

Meat to be frozen must be very fresh. Wrap it tightly and thoroughly so that all the air is excluded. Pad any sharp bones so that they don't pierce the wrapping. If packing chops, cutlets, steaks, or hamburgers, separate them with plastic wrap or freezer wrap. The larger the piece of meat the longer it will keep. Ground meat can be stored in a freezer for 3 months; variety meats, chops, and cutlets for 4 months; roasts and steaks for 6 months. Defrost frozen meat, in its wrapping and on a plate to catch any juices, at the bottom of the refrigerator.

MEAT STOCK

Ask your butcher to saw 2 kg (4 lb) bones into 6 cm (2½ in) pieces. Beef and veal bones are best.

1 Roast the bones in a preheated oven at 450°F (230°C) for 30 minutes. If you have time. Add 2–3 roughly chopped onions, carrots, and celery stalks and roast for another 30 minutes.

2 Transfer the bones and vegetables to a large stockpot. Add 4 quarts (4 liters) water, a bouquet garni made of 1–2 bay leaves, a few parsley sprigs, and 1–2 sprigs of thyme, and a few black peppercorns.

3 Bring to a boil. Skim off scum, then cover and simmer for 4–6 hours. Use a ladle to strain. Skim off fat, or let cool and lift off solidified fat.

BASIC COOKING TECHNIQUES

Tougher pieces of meat should be cooked slowly by stewing or braising to make them meltingly tender.
Those cuts that are naturally tender can be cooked quickly by frying, broiling, or roasting.

Frying and sautéing

1 Dry the meat with paper towels (if too moist it will not brown quickly and evenly). Heat oil or a mixture of oil and butter in a heavy skillet until it is very hot, then add the meat, taking care not to crowd the pan.

2 Cook until well browned on both sides. Reduce the heat and continue cooking until the meat is done to your taste. When turning meat, use tongs rather than a fork, as a fork pierces the meat and allows the juices to run out.

Roasting

1 Take the meat from the refrigerator and allow it to reach room temperature.

2 Preheat the oven. Rub the meat with fat or oil and seasonings, or make incisions all over and insert herbs or slivers of garlic. Insert a meat thermometer, if using.

3 Put the meat and vegetables in a roasting pan. Roast, basting with the fat and juices in the pan, until

cooked to your taste (page 240). If not using a meat thermometer (or an instant-read thermometer), test whether the meat is cooked by inserting a skewer into the middle. If the juices that run out are bloody, the meat is rare; if pink, medium; if clear, well-done.

4 Transfer the roast to a carving board and leave to rest for 10–15 minutes while making gravy. Carve the roast (page 213) and serve.

Broiling and barbecuing

1 Preheat the broiler to hot, or light the barbecue (it will take 20–30 minutes to reach cooking temperature unless it is gas, which will heat up immediately.)

2 Put the meat on the broiler pan and put under the hot broiler, or arrange on the grid over charcoal. Brush with oil or a marinade, and cook the meat until it is browned on both sides, turning and rebrushing as necessary.

3 For sausages or thicker pieces of meat that need to be well cooked, reduce the heat or move the meat farther away from the heat, and complete cooking.

Stir-frying

1 Cut the meat into uniform pieces for even cooking. Heat a wok or heavy skillet, then add a little oil.

2 When the oil is hot, start adding the meat, a little at a time – adding too much at once will lower the temperature of the oil. Using a slotted spoon or a spatula, stir and toss the meat constantly until it is evenly browned.

3 If some of the pieces of meat are cooked before others, they can be pushed up the side of the wok or to the side of the pan where they will keep warm but not overcook.

Stewing

Cut the meat into cubes. Put into a flameproof casserole with any vegetables and liquid to cover plus any flavorings. Bring to a boil, then cover and simmer on the stovetop, or cook in the oven. Alternatively, heat some oil in the casserole and brown the cubes of meat, then brown the vegetables. Add the liquid and any flavorings. Bring to a boil, cover, and simmer as above.

Braising

1 Brown the meat on all sides in a flameproof casserole, to add flavor and a rich color. Remove the meat from the casserole.

2 Add chopped vegetables and cook until they are beginning to brown. Return the meat and add liquid and any flavorings. Bring to a boil, then cover and simmer on the stovetop or in the oven, as instructed in the recipe.

BONING & BUTTERFLYING A LEG OF LAMB

A boned leg of lamb is much easier to carve than meat still on the bone. Tunnel boning leaves a pocket that can be filled with a savory stuffing. If the leg is cut open to lie flat, this is known as "butterflying."

1 To tunnel bone, trim the skin and most or all of the fat from the lamb. Cut around the pelvic bone, at the wide end of the leg, to separate it from the meat. Sever the tendons that connect it to the leg bone. Remove the pelvic bone.

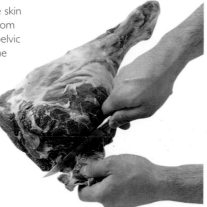

2 At the narrow end of the leg, cut around the shank bone and then scrape the meat away from the whole length of the bone using short strokes.

3 Cut away the meat to expose the joint that joins the shank bone to the leg bone. Sever the tendons and then remove the shank bone.

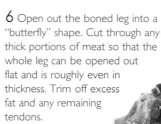

6 Open out the boned leg into a "butterfly" shape. Cut through any thick portions of meat so that the whole leg can be opened out flat and is roughly even in thickness. Trim off excess fat and any remaining tendons.

4 Cut around each end of the leg bone. Ease the leg bone out, cutting and scraping away the meat as you twist and pull the bone out. Trim off the tendons.

5 If you want to butterfly the boned leg, carefully insert a large chef's knife into the cavity left by the leg bone and cut to one side to slit open the meat.

BONING A SHOULDER OF LAMB

A special boning knife, with a narrow, pointed blade, is useful for preparing shoulders of lamb, pork, and veal. If you don't have such a knife, a small, sharp chef's knife can be used instead.

1 Remove the skin and fat. Set the shoulder meat-side up. Cut through the meat to the blade bone, and then cut away the meat on either side, keeping the knife as close to the bone as possible, until the bone is revealed.

2 Cut through the ball-and-socket joint that lies between the blade bone and the central shoulder bone. This will separate the 2 bones.

3 Cut beneath the ball-and-socket joint to free the end. Hold it firmly in one hand and pull the blade bone away from the meat

4 Cut around the central shoulder bone, severing the tendons, and cutting and scraping away the meat. Pull out the bone. If necessary, enlarge the pocket left by the bone so that it will accommodate a stuffing.

PREPARING A RACK OF LAMB

Rack of lamb is a tender joint for roasting or broiling. A single rack, which is one side of the upper ribcage, comprises 6–9 cutlets and serves 2–3 people. Two racks can be used to make impressive cuts such as a guard of honor or crown roast.

Rack of lamb

1 If the butcher hasn't done so, remove the backbone from the meaty end. Pull off the skin. Score through the fat and meat 2 in (5 cm) from the ends of the rib bones.

2 Turn the rack over and set it at the edge of the cutting board, so the ends of the rib bones are suspended. Score the meat along the rack, about 2 in (5 cm) from the ends of the rib bones, cutting through the meat to the bones.

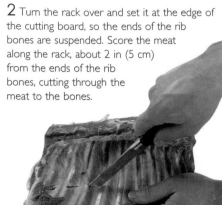

3 Cut out the meat from between the bones, cutting from the crosswise cuts to the ends. Turn the rack over and scrape the ends of the bones clean.

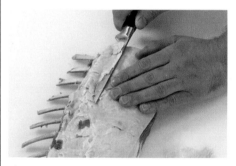

4 Trim away most of the fat from the meat. Repeat the procedure with the second rack, if using.

GUARD OF HONOUR

Hold 1 rack in each hand, fat-side out, and push them together, interlocking the rib bones. Cover the exposed bones with foil, if desired, to prevent them from charring during cooking, then cook as directed in the recipe.

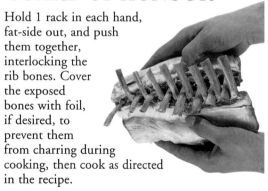

CROWN ROAST

Two racks of lamb are tied together in the shape of a crown

1 Prepare 2 racks as above. Slit the membrane between the rib bones at the meaty end so the racks can be bent.

2 Stand the racks, meat-side innermost, on a work surface and curve to form a crown shape. Bend the bones so the crown will stand upright.

3 Tie string around the middle of the 2 racks, to hold them in place.

4 Fill the center of the roast with a stuffing, then roast (or add a filling just before serving). Carve the roast by cutting down between the rib bones.

STUFFING, ROLLING, & TYING A JOINT

Joints that have been boned and opened out can be rolled around a savory stuffing, which adds moisture and flavor to the meat during cooking.

1 Open out the meat and spread with an even layer of stuffing, leaving a small border clear around the edge.

2 Roll up or fold the meat around the stuffing, to make a compact bolster shape. Turn it so the seam is underneath.

3 Tie string around the meat at regular intervals, to hold it in shape during cooking. Remove the string before carving.

CARVING A JOINT ON THE BONE

Once a roast has finished cooking, transfer it to a carving board, cover with foil, and let it "rest" in a warm place for 10–15 minutes. During this time, the temperature of the meat will even out, and the flesh will reabsorb most of the juices. To carve, use a very sharp, long carving knife and a 2-pronged carving fork.

Shoulder of lamb

1 Insert the fork into the shank end. Cut a narrow, wedge-shaped piece from the middle, in the meatiest part between the angle formed by the blade bone and the shoulder bone.

2 Carve neat slices from either side of this wedge-shaped cut until the blade and central shoulder bones are reached. Turn the shoulder over and cut horizontal slices lengthwise.

Beef rib roast

1 Set the roast upright on a carving board, insert the carving fork into the meaty side, to steady the roast, and cut close to the large rib bones at the base of the meat, to remove them.

2 Hold the now boneless roast upright on the board. With the knife at a slight angle, carve the meat into slices that are about 3/4 in (2 cm) thick.

Leg of lamb

1 Set the roast with the meaty side upward, and insert the carving fork firmly into the meat at the knuckle end. Cut a narrow, wedge-shaped piece from the middle of the meaty portion, cutting all the way to the bone.

2 Carve neat slices from either side of this wedge-shaped cut, gradually changing the angle of the knife to make the slices larger. Turn the leg over. Trim off the fat, then carve off horizontal slices.

Whole ham

1 Cut a few horizontal slices from one side of the ham, to make a flat surface. Turn the ham over onto this surface. Insert the carving fork into the meat at the shank end. Make 3 or 4 cuts through to the bone at the shank end.

2 Insert the knife into the last cut and slide it along the bone, to detach the slices. Make a few more cuts in the ham and continue to remove the slices in the same way. Turn over and carve off horizontal slices.

MAKING GRAVY

A delicious gravy can be made from the richly flavored sediment and juices from roasting meat. Boost flavor with a splash of red or fortified wine, red-currant jelly, Worcestershire sauce, or lemon juice, to taste.

 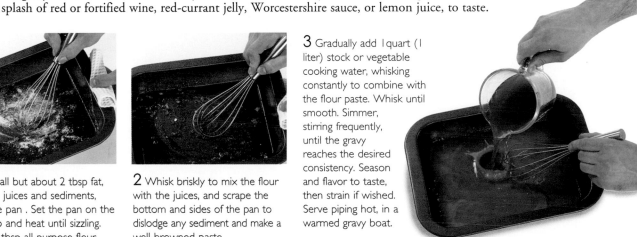

3 Gradually add 1 quart (1 liter) stock or vegetable cooking water, whisking constantly to combine with the flour paste. Whisk until smooth. Simmer, stirring frequently, until the gravy reaches the desired consistency. Season and flavor to taste, then strain if wished. Serve piping hot, in a warmed gravy boat.

1 Pour all but about 2 tbsp fat, with the juices and sediments, from the pan . Set the pan on the stovetop and heat until sizzling. Stir in 2 tbsp all-purpose flour.

2 Whisk briskly to mix the flour with the juices, and scrape the bottom and sides of the pan to dislodge any sediment and make a well-browned paste.

ROASTING MEAT

As all ovens are different, these times are intended as a general guide only. When calculating timings, add an extra pound (500 g) on the weight of your roast if it weighs less than 3 lb (1.5 kg). Be sure to preheat the oven before putting the meat in to cook.

Meat		Oven temperature	Time	Internal temperature
Beef	Rare	350°F (180°C)	15 mins per pound (500 g)	140°F (60°C)
	Medium	350°F (180°C)	20 mins per pound (500 g)	160°F (70°C)
	Well-done	350°F (180°C)	25 mins per pound (500 g)	175°F (80°C)
Veal	Well-done	350°F (180°C)	25 mins per pound (500 g)	175°F (80°C)
Lamb	Medium rare	350°F (180°C)	20 mins per pound (500 g)	170°F (75°C)
	Well-done	350°F (180°C)	25 mins per pound (500 g)	175°F (80°C)
Pork	Medium	350°F (180°C)	25 mins per pound (500 g)	175°F (80°C)
	Well-done	350°F (180°C)	30 mins per pound (500 g)	180°F (85°C)

USING A MEAT THERMOMETER

The most accurate way to test if a large piece of meat is cooked is to use a meat thermometer, which registers the internal temperature. Before cooking, insert the spike of the thermometer into the middle or thickest part of the meat. Make sure the thermometer does not touch a bone because bones become hotter than meat and will, therefore, give a false reading. Start checking the temperature reading toward the end of the suggested cooking time. Alternatively, use an instant-read thermometer, which is inserted near the end of the calculated cooking time. A roast will continue to cook by retained heat for 5–10 minutes after it is removed from the oven.

PREPARING VARIETY MEATS

Although not as popular as they used to be, variety meats, which include liver, kidneys, sweetbreads, and tongue, are both nutritious and delicious. Flavor and texture vary according to the animal from which the meat comes – variety meat from veal has the most delicate flavor and texture; variety meat from pork has the strongest and toughest.

Sweetbreads

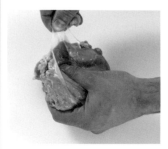 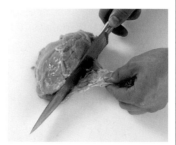

1 Soak the sweetbreads in cold water with 1 tbsp lemon juice for 2–3 hours to clean them. Drain and rinse well. Cut away any discolored parts. Use your fingers to carefully peel off the thin membrane surrounding the sweetbreads.

2 Cut away the ducts and any fat and discard. Don't remove too much or the sweetbreads will break up. Put into a saucepan of cold water and bring to a boil. Blanch calf's sweetbreads for 5 minutes, and lamb's sweetbreads for 3 minutes.

Lamb's kidneys

1 (If using beef or veal kidneys, first separate them.) Carefully cut through any fine membrane around each kidney and use your fingers to peel it off.

2 Set each kidney rounded-side up and slice lengthwise in half (or leave attached at the base, according to recipe directions). With a sharp pair of scissors, snip out the small fatty, white core and the tubes.

Yorkshire puddings

Sift 1 cup (125 g) all-purpose flour and a pinch of salt into a bowl. Make a well, and add 3 beaten eggs and a little milk taken from 1 scant cup (200 ml).

Whisk the milk and egg together in the well with a little of the flour from the side, then whisk in the remaining milk, gradually drawing in all of the flour to make a smooth batter.

TRADITIONAL ROAST BEEF

SERVES 8

6¹/₂ lb (3.25 kg) rolled beef rib roast

vegetable oil for brushing

salt and black pepper

1 onion, quartered

TO SERVE

Yorkshire puddings (see box, right)

gravy of your choice (page 265)

horseradish sauce (see box, below)

1 Insert a meat thermometer, if using, into the middle of the meat. Put the beef into a roasting pan, brush all over the meat with oil, and season with salt and pepper. Add the onion quarters to the pan and roast with the beef in a preheated oven at 400°F (200°C) for 20 minutes.

2 Meanwhile, make the Yorkshire pudding batter (see box right) and set aside.

3 After the beef has been roasting for 20 minutes, baste it with the juices from the pan, and lower the oven temperature to 350°F (180°C).

4 Roast, basting frequently, for 1¹/₂ hours longer for rare beef, 1³/₄ hours for medium, and 2 hours for well-done, or until the meat thermometer registers 140°F (60°C), 160°F (70°C), or 175°F (80°C).

5 Transfer the beef to a carving board, cover with foil, and leave to stand in a warm place. Increase the oven temperature to 425°F (220°C) and bake the Yorkshire puddings.

6 While the puddings are in the oven and the meat is resting, make the gravy in the roasting pan according to the instructions on page 265.

7 Serve the beef with the Yorkshire puddings, gravy, and horseradish sauce.

Put some white vegetable shortening into each cup of a 12-hole muffin pan and heat in a preheated oven at 425°F (220°C) until very hot. Remove the pan from the oven. Whisk the batter and pour into the cups in the pan. Bake the Yorkshire puddings in the oven for 15 minutes or until well risen, golden, and crisp. Serve immediately.

Horseradish sauce

Mix 2–3 tbsp grated fresh horseradish with 1 tbsp white wine vinegar in a bowl. In another bowl, whisk ²/₃ cup (150 ml) whipping cream until thick.

Fold the cream into the horseradish mixture, and add salt, black pepper, and sugar to taste. Cover and leave to chill until ready to serve.

BEEF POT ROAST WITH WINTER VEGETABLES

SERVES 6

2 tbsp sunflower oil

2¹/₂ lb (1.15 kg) beef bottom round or rump

4 onions, quartered

1 large rutabaga, cut into thick chunks

2 celery stalks, thickly sliced

2 large carrots, thickly sliced

²/₃ cup (150 ml) dry white wine

²/₃ cup (150 ml) hot water

1 bouquet garni

salt and black pepper

chopped parsley to garnish

1 Heat the sunflower oil in a large flameproof casserole or Dutch oven. Add the beef and cook over a high heat, turning occasionally, for about 10 minutes until browned all over.

2 Lift the beef out of the casserole and put in the onions, rutabaga, celery, and carrots. Stir well to coat the vegetables in the oil, then cook, stirring occasionally, for about 5 minutes.

3 Push the vegetables to the side of the casserole, and place the meat in the middle, with the vegetables around it.

4 Add the wine, measured water, and bouquet garni, and season with salt and pepper. Bring to a boil, then cover tightly, and cook in a preheated oven at 300°F (150°C) for 2¹/₂–3 hours until the meat is tender.

5 Transfer the meat and vegetables to a warmed platter, cover, and keep warm.

6 Spoon the fat from the surface of the cooking liquid, then boil over a high heat until the liquid is reduced by half. Taste for seasoning, and strain into a warmed gravy boat. Carve the meat into thin slices, garnish with parsley, and serve with the gravy.

TEXAS BARBECUE BEEF BRISKET

SERVES 6

2¹/₂–3 lb (1.15–1.5 kg) beef brisket

2 tbsp sunflower oil

cayenne pepper

MARINADE

3 cups (750 ml) ready made spicy barbecue sauce

1 cup (250 ml) beer

juice of 1 lemon

2 tbsp Worcestershire sauce

3 onions, chopped

5 garlic cloves, crushed

3 tbsp brown sugar

2 tsp ground cumin

¹/₂ tsp ground ginger

1 Make the marinade: in a large bowl, combine the barbecue sauce, beer, lemon juice, Worcestershire sauce, onions, garlic, brown sugar, cumin, and ginger. Turn the brisket in the marinade, cover, and leave to marinate in the refrigerator, turning occasionally, for 1–2 days.

2 Remove the beef from the marinade, reserving the marinade, and pat dry with paper towels.

3 Heat the vegetable oil in a flameproof casserole, add the brisket, and brown.

4 Pour the marinade over, cover, and cook in a preheated oven at 325°F (160°C) for 2¹/₂–3 hours until tender, adding a little water if the sauce becomes too thick.

5 Remove the casserole from the oven and leave to stand for 15–20 minutes. Remove the meat and slice. Season the sauce with cayenne pepper to taste, then heat through. Arrange the meat on a serving platter, and pour over the sauce.

Healthy note

If you cook this dish a day ahead of serving, the fat will rise to the surface as it cools. When it is completely cold, put it in the refrigerator overnight. The next day, spoon off the solidified fat from the surface before reheating – this will make the dish less fatty.

FRENCH-STYLE BRAISED BEEF

SERVES 4–6

2 lb (1 kg) boneless beef chuck or other braising meat

2 tbsp olive oil

4 oz (125 g) piece of lean slab bacon, cut into strips

1 onion, sliced

8 oz (250 g) carrots, thickly sliced

8 oz (250 g) mushrooms, quartered

2 tomatoes, seeded and chopped

1 cup (125 g) pitted black olives

2 1/2 cups (600 ml) beef stock

salt and black pepper

chopped parsley to garnish

MARINADE

2 cups (500 ml) red wine

3 tbsp red wine vinegar

2 large garlic cloves

1 strip of orange zest

1 bouquet garni

1 Make the marinade: combine the wine, vinegar, garlic, orange zest, and bouquet garni in a large nonmetallic bowl. Add the beef, cover, and leave to marinate in the refrigerator overnight.

2 Remove the beef from the marinade and pat dry with paper towels. Strain the marinade and reserve. Heat the oil in a large flameproof casserole, add the beef and bacon, and brown all over. Lift out and drain on paper towels.

3 Add the onion, carrots, and mushrooms and cook, stirring, for 5 minutes or until lightly browned.

4 Add the beef, bacon, tomatoes, olives, and reserved marinade. Pour in sufficient stock to cover the meat and season with salt and pepper.

5 Bring to a boil, cover tightly, and cook in a preheated oven at 350°F (180°C) for 1 1/2–2 hours or until the meat is very tender.

6 Slice the meat and arrange on a warmed platter with the vegetables. Skim the sauce and pour over the meat. Garnish with parsley before serving.

CORNED BEEF WITH MUSTARD SAUCE

SERVES 6–8

2 lb (1 kg) boned and rolled corned beef

1 lb (500 g) baby carrots

8 potatoes, halved

8 celery stalks, cut into chunks

1 1/3 cups (250 g) turnips, cut into chunks

chopped parsley to garnish

MUSTARD SAUCE

2 tbls (30 g) butter

1/4 cup (30 g) all-purpose flour

2/3 cup (150 ml) milk

4 tsp white wine vinegar

2 tsp dry mustard

2 tsp sugar

salt and black pepper

1 Put the corned beef into a large bowl. Cover with cold water and leave to soak overnight to remove any excess salt.

2 Rinse the beef under cold running water, place in a large saucepan, and cover with cold water. Cover the pan with its lid, bring to a boil, and simmer very gently, topping up the water in the pan when necessary, for about 1 hour.

3 Add the carrots, potatoes, celery, and turnips and cook for 40 minutes or until the beef and vegetables are tender.

4 Transfer the meat to a warmed platter. Lift out the vegetables with a slotted spoon, reserving the liquid, and arrange around the meat. Cover and keep warm.

5 Make the sauce: melt the butter in a saucepan, add the flour, and cook, stirring, for 1 minute. Remove from the heat and gradually blend in the milk and 2/3 cup (150 ml) of the cooking liquid from the beef. Bring to a boil, stirring constantly, until the sauce thickens. Simmer for 2 minutes.

6 In a bowl, combine the vinegar, mustard powder, and sugar, and stir into the sauce. Cook for 1 minute, then season with salt and pepper. (Be careful not to add too much salt because the liquid from the beef is salty.)

7 Slice the beef and arrange on warmed serving plates with the vegetables. Pour the mustard sauce over the beef, and sprinkle with parsley.

TRINIDAD PEPPERPOT BEEF

SERVES 4–6

2 lb (1 kg) boneless beef, such as brisket, trimmed

2–3 quarts (2–3 liters) beef stock

2 large onions, coarsely chopped

2–4 fresh red chilies, cored, seeded, and chopped

2 tbsp chopped parsley

4 tbsp vinegar, plus extra if necessary

2 tbsp dark brown sugar

1 tbsp Worcestershire sauce

1 tbsp mixed peppercorns (see box, right), coarsely crushed, plus extra if necessary

1 tsp ground cinnamon

1 tsp dried thyme

large pinch of ground allspice

salt

1 Put the beef into a large pan, add enough stock to cover, and bring to a boil, skimming off any scum that rises to the surface. Lower the heat, cover, and simmer for 1 1/2 hours or until the meat feels just tender when pierced with a skewer.

2 Add the onions, chilies, and half of the parsley, then add the vinegar, sugar, Worcestershire sauce, peppercorns, cinnamon, thyme, allspice, and salt to taste. Cover and simmer for 2 hours or until the beef is very tender.

3 Transfer the beef to a carving board, cover, and keep warm.

4 Skim any fat from the cooking liquid, and boil for about 10 minutes until reduced to1 1/4 cups (300 ml). Season, adding more vinegar and peppercorns if needed. Slice the beef thickly, discarding the fat. Pour the sauce over the beef, and sprinkle with the parsley.

Cook's know-how

Mixed peppercorns come as a combination of black, green, pink, and white peppercorns. They look pretty, and have an intense, complex taste. If you cannot get them, use as many colors as you have.

BEEF WITH ROAST VEGETABLE SALAD

SERVES 4–6

2 lb (1 kg) beef tenderloin cut from the center, trimmed

2 tbsp tapenade (black olive paste)

1 tbsp black peppercorns, coarsely crushed

2 tbsp olive oil

chopped parsley to garnish

ROAST VEGETABLE SALAD

1 tbsp olive oil

1 eggplant, cut into 1/4 in (5 mm) slices

3 zucchini, cut into 1/4 in (5 mm) slices

1 fennel bulb, cut lengthwise into 1/4 in (5 mm) pieces

1 red bell pepper, cored, seeded, and cut into 1/4 in (5 mm) strips

1 yellow bell pepper, cored, seeded, and cut into 1/4 in (5 mm) strips

salt and black pepper

2 tsp balsamic vinegar

1 Tie the beef to retain its shape, if necessary. Spread the black olive paste all over the beef, then press on the peppercorns.

2 Pour the oil into a roasting pan and heat in a preheated oven at 425°F (220°C).

3 Insert a meat thermometer, if using, into the middle of the beef.

4 Put the beef into the hot oil, and roast for 25 minutes for rare beef, 35 minutes for medium, or 40 minutes for well-done, or until the meat thermometer registers 60°C (140°F), 70°C (160°F), or 75°C (170°F).

5 Meanwhile, put the olive oil for the roast vegetable salad into a large bowl. Add the eggplant, zucchini, fennel, and red and yellow bell peppers, and toss in the oil.

6 When the beef is cooked to your liking, remove it from the roasting pan and leave until cold. Meanwhile, put the vegetables into the hot pan and sprinkle with salt and pepper. Cook in the oven, turning the vegetables once, for 30 minutes or until tender. Leave to cool, then sprinkle with the balsamic vinegar and toss to coat.

7 When the beef is cold, slice very thinly and serve with the roast vegetable salad. Garnish with parsley.

BEEF WELLINGTON

Inside a puff pastry case is a succulent piece of prime beef and a rich stuffing of liver pâté and mushrooms. The pastry locks in all the juices and ensures none of the wonderful flavors are lost. Serve with a mushroom and red wine gravy.

SERVES 8

3 lb (1.5 kg) beef tenderloin, trimmed and tied

salt and black pepper

2 tbsp sunflower oil

3 tbls (45 g) butter

1 small onion, finely chopped

8 oz (250 g) flat mushrooms, finely chopped

6 oz (175 g) smooth liver pâté

14 oz (400 g) store-bought puff pastry dough

1 egg, beaten

thin mushroom gravy to serve (page 265)

1 Season the beef with black pepper. Heat the oil in a large skillet, add the beef, and cook over a high heat until browned all over.

2 Put the beef tenderloin in a roasting pan and cook in a preheated oven at 425°F (220°C) for 25 minutes for rare beef, 35 minutes for medium, or 40 minutes for well-done. Leave to cool completely.

3 Meanwhile, melt the butter in the skillet, add the onion and mushrooms, and cook, stirring, for 3 minutes or until softened. Increase the heat to high, and cook until the excess moisture has evaporated. Turn into a bowl and leave to cool completely.

4 Add the liver pâté to the mushroom and onion mixture, season with salt and pepper, and stir well to combine.

5 Wrap the beef in the pastry dough (see box, right).

6 Bake at 425°F (220°C) for 45 minutes or until the pastry is crisp and golden. Cover with foil after 30 minutes to prevent the pastry becoming too brown. Leave to stand for about 10 minutes, then slice and serve with the gravy.

INDIVIDUAL BEEF WELLINGTONS

Cut the raw beef into 8 slices. Brown the slices in a skillet, cool, then wrap each one in dough with a little of the pâté mixture. Bake for 25–30 minutes.

Wrapping the beef in pastry

Roll out 3/4 of the pastry to a 12 x 16 in (30 x 40 cm) rectangle. Spread half of the pâté mixture down the middle, leaving a 4 in (10 cm) border on each side.

Remove the string from the beef and place on the pâté mixture. Cover with remaining pâté mixture.

Brush the dough border with beaten egg. Fold the short sides of the dough over the beef.

Fold the long ends over and turn the parcel over. Brush with beaten egg. Roll out the remaining dough, and cut into strips, 1/4 in (5 mm) wide. Arrange in a lattice pattern on top of the dough, then glaze the strips with beaten egg.

PEPPER STEAKS

SERVES 4

4 fillet mignons, 5–6 oz (150–175 g) each, about 1 in (2.5 cm) thick, trimmed

salt and black pepper

2 tbsp black peppercorns

2 tbls (30 g) butter

1 tbsp sunflower oil

2 tbsp brandy

2/3 cup (150 ml) heavy cream

chopped parsley to garnish

1 Season the steaks on both sides with salt. Crush the peppercorns and spread them on a plate. Coat the steaks with the peppercorns (see box, right).

2 Melt the butter with the oil in a skillet. When the butter is foaming, add the steaks, and cook over a high heat for 2 minutes on each side.

3 Lower the heat and continue cooking until the steaks are to your liking: rare steaks need 1–2 minutes on each side, medium steaks 3 minutes on each side, and well-done steaks 4–5 minutes on each side. Lift out of the pan and keep warm.

4 Pour the brandy into the skillet, and boil rapidly to drive off the alcohol. When the brandy has almost disappeared, stir in the cream, and add salt and pepper to taste. Gently reheat the sauce, pour it over the steaks, and garnish with parsley. Serve hot.

Coating steaks

Press each steak firmly on to the peppercorns, until both sides are well coated.

Healthy option

Instead of the classic brandy-creamy sauce, deglaze the pan with 2 tbsp Madeira, port wine, or sherry, and make a gravy with 5 tbls (75 ml) each red wine and stock. Season well.

CHATEAUBRIAND WITH BEARNAISE SAUCE

SERVES 2

14 oz (400 g) Chateaubriand steak (a thick piece of tenderloin cut from the middle)

2 tbls (30 g) butter, melted

black pepper

béarnaise sauce (see box, right)

1 Cut the steak crosswise in half. Brush one side of each half with melted butter and season with pepper.

2 Put the steaks, buttered-side up, under a hot broiler, 3 in (7 cm) from the heat, and cook for 2 minutes or until browned. Turn the steaks over, brush with melted butter, and season with pepper. Broil for about 2 minutes until browned.

3 Lower the heat and cook, turning once and brushing with the butter, for 4–5 minutes. Cover and leave to stand for 5 minutes. Slice the steaks, and serve with the béarnaise sauce.

Béarnaise sauce

Put 4 tbsp tarragon vinegar, 1 finely chopped shallot, and 1 tbsp chopped tarragon into a pan and boil for a few minutes until reduced by one-third. Leave to cool. Pour 2 egg yolks into a bowl over a saucepan of simmering water, add the vinegar mixture, and whisk over a gentle heat until thick and fluffy.

Melt 6 tbls (90 g) butter and gradually add to the sauce, whisking constantly until thick. Season with salt and white pepper.

STEAKS WITH SMOKED OYSTER RELISH

SERVES 4

4 x 6 oz (175 g) sirloin steaks

salt and black pepper

2 garlic cloves, crushed

1 tbsp olive oil

smoked oyster relish (see box, below) and lemon wedges to serve

1 Season the steaks with salt and pepper, rub with the garlic, and brush with the oil.

2 Heat a skillet over a high heat, add the steaks, and cook for 3–4 minutes on each side for rare steaks, 4–5 minutes for medium steaks, or 7–8 minutes for well-done steaks. Transfer the steaks to warmed serving plates.

3 Generously spoon the smoked oyster relish over the steaks, and serve at once, accompanied by lemon wedges.

CLASSIC CARPETBAG STEAKS

Melt 1 tbls (15 g) butter and cook 2 chopped shallots until softened. Remove from the heat and add 6 chopped fresh oysters, 2 cups (125 g) fresh bread crumbs, 1 tbsp chopped parsley, and salt and pepper. Cut a pocket in each steak and fill with the stuffing.

Smoked oyster relish

Drain 3 1/2 oz (100 g) canned smoked oysters. Finely chop 1 small onion and 1 handful of parsley sprigs.

Chop the drained smoked oysters with a large, sharp chef's knife.

Put the oysters, onion, and parsley into a small bowl and mix well. Chill until needed.

SAVORY BUTTERS

These simple butters are quickly made, and ideal for adding an elegant touch to plain broiled meats such as steaks, chops, and noisettes.

CILANTRO BUTTER

Soften 1/2 cup (125 g) butter and blend in 2 tbsp chopped fresh cilantro, 1 tbsp lemon juice, 1 tsp ground cilantro, and season with salt and black pepper. Chill. Garnish with a coriander sprig and a sprinkling of ground cilantro.

ANCHOVY BUTTER

Soften 1/2 cup (125 g) butter and blend in 2 tbsp finely chopped anchovies, 1 tbsp lemon juice, 1 tsp ground cilantro, and season with black pepper. Chill. Garnish with anchovy fillets.

PARSLEY BUTTER

Soften 1/2 cup (125 g) butter and blend in 2 tbsp chopped parsley, 1 tbsp lemon juice, and seson with salt and black pepper. Chill. Garnish with a lemon twist and a parsley sprig.

MUSTARD BUTTER

Soften 1/2 cup (125 g) butter and blend in 2 tbsp Dijon mustard, 2 tbsp chopped fresh tarragon, and season with salt and black pepper. Chill. Garnish with a tarragon sprig.

STEAK DIANE

SERVES 4

4 x boneless steaks. 4–6 oz (125–175 g) each, trimmed

2 tbls (30 g) butter

2 tbsp sunflower oil

3 tbsp brandy

1 small onion, finely chopped

1 1/4 cups (300 ml) beef stock

2 tbsp Worcestershire sauce

1 tbsp lemon juice

1 tbsp chopped parsley

salt and black pepper

1 Place the steaks between 2 sheets of waxed paper and pound with a rolling pin until 1/4 in (5 mm) thick.

2 Melt the butter with the sunflower oil in a large skillet. When the butter is foaming, add the pounded steaks and cook over a high heat for about 3 minutes on each side until browned. Lift the steaks out of the skillet and cover with foil to keep warm.

3 Pour the brandy into the pan, and add the onion. Cook over a high heat, stirring occasionally, for a few minutes until the onion has softened and absorbed most of the brandy. Stir in the stock, Worcestershire sauce, lemon juice, and parsley, season with salt and pepper, and cook for about 2 minutes.

4 Return the steaks to the pan and spoon over the sauce. Reheat quickly and briefly, and serve hot.

Cook's know-how

In the classic Steak Diane the brandy is flambéed at the table and poured over the steaks at the last minute. This version is more practical.

TOURNEDOS ROQUEFORT

SERVES 4

1 cup (125 g) Roquefort cheese, crumbled

1/2 cup (60 g) walnut pieces, roughly chopped

2 tbls (30 g) butter, softened

salt and black pepper

4 x 4 oz (125 g) tournedo steaks, 1 in (2.5 cm) thick

chopped parsley to garnish

1 In a small bowl, combine the Roquefort, walnuts, butter, and pepper to taste.

2 Season the tournedos steaks on both sides with salt and pepper, and place them under a hot broiler, 3–4 in (7–10 cm) from the heat. Broil for 3–4 minutes on each side for rare steaks, 4–5 minutes for medium steaks, or 7–8 minutes for well-done steaks.

3 Two minutes before the steaks are ready, sprinkle with the Roquefort mixture, and return to the hot broiler until the cheese has melted. Serve hot, garnished with chopped parsley.

Healthy option

Roquefort cheese and walnuts are a classic French topping for steak, but they are both high in fat and calories. If you prefer to keep these down, try this tasty mushroom topping instead. Finely chop 8 oz (250 g) crimini mushrooms in a food processor, then finely chop 1 shallot with a sharp knife, and crush 1 garlic clove. Cook the shallot and garlic with a few tablespoons of water, stock, or wine in a nonstick skillet for 2–3 minutes until softened. Add the mushrooms, stir well, and cook for 15 minutes until softened and dry. Stir in 2 tbsp chopped parsley and 1 tsp finely grated lemon zest, and season with salt and pepper. Spoon the mixture on top of the steaks, and serve at once.

Cook's know-how

Roquefort is a superb blue-veined cheese that melts beautifully under the broiler. A blue cheese will melt well too – and taste just as good.

BEEF & BEAN BURRITOS

SERVES 4

12 oz (375 g) boneless round or sirloin steak, trimmed of fat and cut into thin strips

salt and black pepper

2 tbsp olive oil

1 garlic clove, crushed

1/2–1 fresh red chili, cored, seeded, and chopped

1/2 tsp cumin seeds

14 oz (400 g) canned tomatoes, drained, juice reserved

14 oz (400 g) canned pinto or black beans, drained

8 soft flour tortillas

4 tbsp sour cream

chopped fresh cilantro to garnish

1 Season the steak strips with salt and pepper. Heat the olive oil in a large skillet, add the steak, crushed garlic, chopped chili, and cumin seeds, and cook, stirring, for 5 minutes or until lightly browned.

2 Add the tomatoes to the pan and cook for about 3 minutes. Pour in the reserved tomato juice and boil for 8–10 minutes until the liquid is reduced.

3 Add the beans and cook until heated through. Taste for seasoning, cover, and keep hot. Warm the tortillas (page 252).

4 Divide the steak and tomato mixture among the tortillas and roll them up. Serve topped with sour cream and garnished with cilantro.

BEEF STROGANOFF

SERVES 6

2 tbls (30 g) butter

1 tbsp sunflower oil

1 1/2 lb (750 g) rump steak, trimmed and cut into strips (see box, right)

8 shallots, quartered

10 oz (300 g) button mushrooms, halved

salt and black pepper

1 1/4 cups (300 ml) sour cream

chopped parsley to garnish

1 Melt the butter with the oil in a large skillet. When the butter is foaming, add the steak strips, in batches if necessary, and cook over a high heat for 5 minutes or until browned all over. Remove from the pan with a slotted spoon.

2 Add the shallots and mushrooms and cook for about 5 minutes until soft and browned.

3 Return the steak strips to the pan, and season with salt and pepper. Stir in the sour cream and heat gently. Garnish with parsley, and serve at once.

Cutting the beef

Slice the beef at an angle into thin strips, 1/4 in (5 mm) wide and 2 in (5 cm) long, using a sharp chef's knife.

Healthy option

Stroganoff is a classic dish of steak panfried in butter and oil with mushrooms and sour cream, but there are ways of cutting down on the fat without compromising the flavors in the dish. Use a nonstick pan and omit the butter, then use just 2/3 cup (150 ml) lowfat sour cream.

MEXICAN BUFFET PARTY

Mexican food is ideal for an informal party where everyone helps themselves because it is the tradition in Mexico to put lots of different dishes on the table together rather than serving separate courses. In this hearty menu for 6 people there is something for everyone – meat eaters and vegetarians alike.

CHARGRILLED STEAKS WITH RED VEGETABLES

SERVES 6

6 x 5 oz (150 g) boneless sirloin steaks

2 roasted red bell peppers in olive oil (from a jar), cut into strips, with oil reserved

salt and black pepper

2 red onions, cut into chunky wedges

2 garlic cloves, coarsely chopped

2 tbsp lime juice

fresh cilantro to garnish

1 Heat a ridged cast-iron chargrill pan over a medium heat until very hot. Brush the steaks with a little of the reserved oil from the peppers, and season with salt and pepper. When the pan is hot, chargrill the steaks for about 3–4 minutes on each side for rare meat, 4–5 minutes on each side for medium, and 7–8 minutes on each side for well-done. Remove the steaks from the pan and leave to rest.

2 Turn down the heat under the pan to low, add the red onion wedges, and cook for 5–8 minutes, turning them occasionally, until they are charred and softened. Add the red pepper strips, the garlic and lime juice, and stir-fry for 1–2 minutes until hot and sizzling. Season with salt and pepper.

3 Serve the steaks whole or sliced thickly on the diagonal, with a garnish of fresh cilantro and the red peppers and onions spooned alongside.

GUACAMOLE

Roughly mash the flesh of 1 large ripe avocado in a bowl with a fork. Add 1/2 finely chopped onion, 1 tbsp chopped fresh cilantro, and the juice of 1 lime, Mix well, and season to taste. Chill for no more than 30 minutes before serving, or the avocado will discolor.

VEGETARIAN ENCHILADAS

SERVES 6

4 large soft flour tortilla wraps, about 9 in (23 cm) in diameter

6 oz (175 g) canned red kidney beans, drained

1/2 cup (60 g) feta cheese, grated

1/2 cup (60 g) Cheddar cheese, grated

1 tbsp olive oil

MEXICAN TOMATO SAUCE

1 tbsp olive oil

1/2 small onion, finely chopped

1 green chili, cored, seeded, and finely chopped

1 garlic clove, crushed

14 oz (400 g) canned chopped tomatoes

grated zest of 1/2 lime

2 tbsp chopped fresh cilantro

salt and black pepper

1 Make the tomato sauce. Heat the oil in a pan, add the onion, chili, and garlic, and fry over a high heat for a few minutes. Add the tomatoes and simmer without a lid over a low heat, stirring from time to time, for about 10 minutes until the mixture is fairly thick (the consistency of chutney). If it is still a little runny, reduce it by boiling over a high heat, stirring continuously. Add the lime zest and cilantro, and season with salt and pepper.

2 Take one tortilla and spread half of the tomato sauce over it to within 1 in (2.5 cm) of the edge. Top with half of the red kidney beans, and sprinkle half of both the cheeses over. Put another tortilla on top and press down a little with your hand so the 2 tortillas are sandwiched together. Make a separate tortilla sandwich (enchilada) with the remaining ingredients.

3 Heat the oil in a skillet with a wide bottom, so the tortillas fit in flat. Fry each enchilada for 3-4 minutes on each side or until the tortillas are golden brown and crisp, the filling is hot, and the cheese melted. Slice each enchilada into 6 wedges to serve.

MEXICAN BEAN SALAD

SERVES 6

2 cups (350 g) mixed beans, such as red kidney, navy, black eye, and aduki, soaked in cold water overnight, or 28 oz (800 g) canned beans

3 celery stalks, finely chopped

1 red onion, finely chopped

2 garlic cloves, crushed

DRESSING

4 tbsp olive oil

2 tbsp lime juice

2 tbsp chopped fresh cilantro

1 tsp Dijon mustard

1 tsp honey

salt and black pepper

1 Drain the soaked dried beans into a colander and rinse well under cold running water. Tip them into a large saucepan, cover with cold water, and bring to a boil. Half cover the pan and simmer for 1 hour or until all the beans are tender.

2 Drain the beans, rinse under hot water, and tip into a large bowl. If using canned beans, drain and rinse them before putting them in the bowl.

3 Whisk together all the dressing ingredients with plenty of salt and pepper, pour over the beans, and add the celery, red onion, and garlic. Toss well, cover the bowl, and leave to marinate until cold, or overnight.

REFRIED BEANS

Heat 1–2 tbsp sunflower oil in a skillet. Add 1/2 finely chopped onion, and cook for 8 minutes, until lightly browned. Add 1 crushed garlic clove, and cook for 2 minutes. Drain and rinse 14 oz (400 g) canned red kidney beans, and add to the pan. Cook over a gentle heat until warmed through, mashing the beans with a potato masher or fork and adding 1–2 tbsp water if necessary, to prevent sticking.

CLOCKWISE FROM TOP RIGHT: Vegetarian Enchiladas with guacamole, Refried Beans, Chargrilled Steaks with Red Vegetables, Mexican Bean Salad.

TERIYAKI BEEF

SERVES 4

1 lb (500 g) boneless sirloin steak, trimmed and cut into thin strips

2 tbsp sunflower oil

1 large onion, thinly sliced

1 red bell pepper, cored, seeded, and cut into strips

2 green onions, sliced, to garnish

MARINADE

½ cup (125 ml) dark soy sauce

6 tbls (90 ml) Japanese rice wine or dry sherry

2 tbsp sugar

1 Make the marinade: in a bowl, combine the soy sauce, rice wine, and sugar. Toss the steak strips in the marinade, cover, and leave in the refrigerator overnight.

2 Remove the steak strips from the marinade, reserving the marinade. Heat 1 tbsp of the oil in a wok, add the onion and red pepper, and stir-fry for about 2 minutes. Remove from the wok with a slotted spoon and set aside. Heat the remaining oil, and stir-fry the steak strips for 5 minutes or until just cooked through.

3 Return the onion and red pepper to the wok with the marinade and cook for 2 minutes or until heated through. Garnish with the green onions before serving.

FAJITAS

This Mexican speciality features slices of steak marinated in spices and fruit juice. Serve with tortillas, avocado, sour cream, and pico de gallo relish.

SERVES 4

500 g (1 lb) boneless sirloin steak

8 soft flour tortillas

chopped cilantro to garnish

1 avocado, pitted, peeled (page 370), and diced

sour cream

MARINADE

juice of 1 orange and 1 lime

3 garlic cloves, crushed

2 tbsp chopped fresh cilantro

a few drops of hot pepper sauce

salt and black pepper

PICO DE GALLO RELISH

6 tomatoes, diced

10 radishes, coarsely chopped

5 green onions, thinly sliced

1–2 green chilies, cored, seeded, and chopped

4 tbsp chopped fresh cilantro

juice of ½ lime

1 Make the marinade: in a large nonmetallic bowl, combine the orange and lime juice, garlic, cilantro, and hot pepper sauce, and season with salt and pepper. Turn the steak in the marinade, cover, and leave to marinate in the refrigerator overnight.

2 Make the pico de gallo relish: in a bowl, combine the tomatoes, radishes, green onions, chilies, cilantro, lime juice, and salt to taste. Cover and chill until ready to serve.

3 Remove the steak from the marinade and pat dry. Put the steak under a hot broiler, 3–4 in (7–10 cm) from the heat, and broil for 3 minutes on each side for rare steak, 4 minutes for medium steak, or 5–6 minutes for well-done steak. Cover with foil and leave to stand for 5 minutes.

4 Meanwhile, warm the tortillas (see box, right).

5 Slice the steak, arrange on serving plates, and sprinkle with cilantro. Serve with the tortillas, pico de gallo relish, diced avocado, and sour cream.

Warming tortillas

Sprinkle each soft flour tortilla with a little water, and stack the tortillas in a pile.

Wrap the tortillas in foil and warm in a preheated oven at 275°F (140°C) for 10 minutes.

WINTER BEEF CASSEROLE

SERVES 4–6

2 tbsp sunflower oil

2 lb (1 kg) boneless beef chuck, trimmed and cut into 1 in (2.5 cm) cubes

3 bacon slices, cut into strips

1 large onion, chopped

1/3 cup (45 g) all-purpose flour

2 cups (500 ml) tomato puree (sieved tomatoes)

2 cups (500 ml) beef stock

2/3 cup (150 ml) red wine

6 celery stalks, sliced

8 oz (250 g) carrots, cut into thin strips

1 garlic clove, crushed

1 tsp chopped fresh marjoram or 1/2 tsp dried marjoram or oregano

salt and black pepper

chopped parsley to garnish

1 Heat the oil in a large flameproof casserole, add the beef and bacon, and cook over a medium high heat for 2–3 minutes until browned all over. Remove with a slotted spoon, and drain on paper towels.

2 Add the onion and cook, stirring occasionally, for a few minutes until soft but not colored.

3 Add the flour and cook, stirring, for 1 minute. Add the tomato puree, stock, and wine and bring to a boil, stirring until smooth and thickened. Return the meat to the pan, add the celery, carrots, garlic, and marjoram, and season with salt and pepper.

4 Bring to a boil, cover and cook in a preheated oven at 325°F (160°C) for 2 hours or until the beef is tender. Taste for seasoning and garnish with chopped parsley before serving.

BOEUF BOURGUIGNON

SERVES 6

2 tbsp sunflower oil

2 lb (1 kg) boneless beef chuck, trimmed and cut into 2 in (5 cm) cubes

8 oz (250 g) thickly sliced smoked bacon, cut into strips

12 shallots

1/4 cup (30 g) all-purpose flour

1 1/4 cup (300 g) red Burgundy

2/3 cup (150 ml) beef stock

1 bouquet garni

1 garlic clove, crushed

salt and black pepper

8 oz (250 g) button mushrooms

1 Heat the oil in a large flameproof casserole or Dutch oven. Add the beef in batches, and cook over a high heat, turning occasionally, until browned on all sides. Remove with a slotted spoon and set aside to drain on paper towels.

2 Add the bacon and shallots and cook gently, stirring occasionally, for 3 minutes or until the bacon is crisp and the shallots are softened. Lift out and drain on paper towels.

3 Add the flour and cook, stirring, for 1 minute. Gradually blend in the wine and stock and bring to a boil, stirring until thickened.

4 Return the beef and bacon to the casserole, add the bouquet garni and garlic, and season with salt and pepper. Cover and cook in a preheated oven at 325°F (160°C) for 1 1/2 hours.

5 Return the shallots to the casserole, add the whole button mushrooms, and cook for 1 hour or until the beef is very tender.

6 Remove the bouquet garni and discard. Taste the sauce for seasoning before serving.

CARBONNADE OF BEEF

SERVES 6

2 tbsp sunflower oil

2 lb (1 kg) boneless beef chuck, trimmed and cut into 2 in (5 cm) cubes

2 large onions, sliced

1 garlic clove, crushed

2 tsp brown sugar

1 tbsp all-purpose flour

2 cups (500 ml) beer

2/3 cup (150 ml) beef stock

1 tbsp red wine vinegar

1 bouquet garni

salt and black pepper

thyme sprigs to garnish

1/2 baguette, cut into 1/2 in (1.25 cm) slices

Dijon mustard for spreading

1 Heat the oil in a large flameproof casserole or Dutch oven, add the beef in batches, and cook over a high heat for a few minutes until browned. Lift out with a slotted spoon.

2 Lower the heat and add the onions, garlic, and sugar. Cook, stirring, for 4 minutes or until browned. Add the flour and cook, stirring, for 1 minute. Add the beer and stock, and bring to a boil, stirring until thickened.

3 Return the meat to the casserole, add the vinegar and bouquet garni, and season with salt and pepper. Bring back to a boil, cover, and cook in a preheated oven at 300°F (150°C) for 2 1/2 hours or until the meat is really tender. Remove from the oven, lift out the bouquet garni, and discard. Taste for seasoning.

4 Increase the oven temperature to 375°F (190°C). Toast the baguette slices, and spread with mustard on one side. Put them, mustard-side up, in the casserole, and baste with sauce.

5 Return the casserole to the oven, uncovered, for 10 minutes or until the croutes are just crisp. Garnish with thyme sprigs before serving.

HUNGARIAN GOULASH

SERVES 6

2 tbsp sunflower oil

1 kg (2 lb) boneless beef chuck, trimmed and cut into 2 in (5 cm) cubes

2 large onions, sliced

1 garlic clove, crushed

1 tbsp plain flour

1 tbsp paprika

2 1/2 cups (600 ml) beef stock

14 oz (400 g) canned tomatoes

2 tbsp tomato paste

salt and black pepper

2 large red bell peppers, cored, seeded, and cut into 1 in (2.5 cm) pieces

4 potatoes, peeled and quartered

2/3 cup (150 ml) sour cream

paprika to garnish

1 Heat the oil in a large flameproof casserole, add the beef in batches, and cook over a high heat until browned.

2 Remove the beef with a slotted spoon. Lower the heat, and add the onions and garlic. Stirring occasionally, cook for a few minutes until soft but not colored.

3 Add the flour and paprika and cook, stirring, for 1 minute. Pour in the stock and bring to a boil, stirring.

4 Return the meat to the casserole, add the tomatoes and tomato paste, and season with salt and pepper. Bring back to a boil, cover, and cook in a preheated oven at 325°F (160°C) for 1 hour.

5 Add the red peppers and potatoes and continue cooking for 1 hour or until the potatoes and meat are tender.

6 Taste for seasoning, and stir in the sour cream. Sprinkle with a little paprika before serving.

Healthy option

Sour cream is the classic finish for goulash, but to reduce the fat content of this dish you can omit it. To compensate for its richness, add 8 oz (250 g) crimini mushrooms, sliced, in step 5, and stir in a good handful of chopped flat-leaf parsley with the sour cream in step 6.

CHIANTI BEEF CASSEROLE

SERVES 4–6

2 lb (1 kg) boneless beef chuck, trimmed and cut into 2 in (5 cm) cubes

2 large onions, roughly chopped

2 large garlic cloves, crushed

1/4 cup (45 g) all-purpose flour

2/3 cup (150 ml) Chianti

1 1/4 cup (300 ml) beef stock

2 oz (60 g) sun-dried tomatoes in oil, roughly chopped, with oil reserved

a few fresh thyme sprigs

salt and black pepper

14 oz (400 g) canned artichoke hearts, drained and halved

12 pitted black olives

1 heaped tbsp mango chutney

1 Heat 2 tbsp of the reserved oil from the sun-dried tomatoes in a large skillet, and brown the beef on all sides (you may need to do this in batches). Remove with a slotted spoon and keep warm.

2 Heat another 2 tbsp sun-dried tomato oil in a large flameproof casserole or Dutch oven, add the onions and garlic, and cook for 2–3 minutes.

3 Add the flour and cook, stirring, for 1 minute. Blend in the wine and stock, bring to a boil, and add the tomatoes and thyme (reserving a sprig for garnish). Season with salt and pepper.

4 Return the beef to the casserole, cover, and reduce the heat. Simmer for 1 1/2–2 hours or until the meat is tender.

5 Add the artichokes, olives, and mango chutney, and simmer for 10 minutes. Taste for seasoning and garnish with thyme before serving.

BEEF WITH HORSERADISH

SERVES 6

2 tbsp sunflower oil

2 lb (1 kg) boneless beef chuck, trimmed and cut into strips

12 shallots or button onions

1/4 cup (30 g) all-purpose flour

2 tsp mild curry powder

2 tsp light brown sugar

1 tsp ground ginger

2 1/2 cups (600 ml) beef stock

2 tbsp Worcestershire sauce

salt and black pepper

3 tbsp chopped parsley

2 tbsp horseradish cream

extra chopped parsley to garnish

1 Heat the sunflower oil in a large flameproof casserole, and cook the beef strips over a high heat until browned all over. Lift out with a slotted spoon and drain on paper towels.

2 Lower the heat, add the shallots, and cook gently, stirring occasionally, for a few minutes until softened. Lift out with a slotted spoon and drain on paper towels.

3 Add the flour, curry powder, sugar, and ginger to the casserole and cook, stirring, for 1 minute. Pour in the stock and bring to a boil, stirring until smooth and thickened. Add the Worcestershire sauce, season with salt and pepper, and return to a boil.

4 Return the beef and shallots to the casserole and stir in the parsley. Bring back to a boil, cover, and cook in a preheated oven at 325°F (160°C) for 2–2 1/2 hours until the meat is tender.

5 Stir in the horseradish cream, taste for seasoning, and garnish with parsley.

Healthy option

Horseradish cream is a mixture of grated horseradish with vinegar, seasonings, and cream. For a less rich finish, use just 1 tbsp bottled grated horseradish.

THAI RED BEEF CURRY

SERVES 6

3 tbsp sunflower oil

8 cardamom pods, split

1 in (2.5 cm) piece of cinnamon stick

6 cloves

8 black peppercorns

2 lb (1 kg) boneless beef chuck, trimmed and cut into 1 in (2.5 cm) cubes

1 large onion, chopped

2 in (5 cm) piece of fresh gingerroot, peeled and grated

4 garlic cloves, crushed

4 tsp paprika

2 tsp ground cumin

1 tsp ground cilantro

1 tsp salt

1/4 tsp cayenne pepper or 1/2 tsp chili powder

1 pint (600 ml) water

6 tbls (90 g) plain yogurt

14 oz (400 g) canned chopped tomatoes

1 large red bell pepper, cored, seeded, and cut into chunks

1 Heat the oil in a flameproof casserole, adding the cardamom, cinnamon, cloves, and peppercorns. Cook over a medium heat, stirring, for 1 minute. Remove with a slotted spoon and set aside on a plate.

2 Add the beef in batches, and cook over a high heat until browned all over. Lift out the beef with a slotted spoon and drain on paper towels.

3 Add the onion to the pan and cook over a high heat, stirring, for about 3 minutes until beginning to brown. Add the ginger, garlic, paprika, cumin, cilantro, salt, cayenne or chili, and 4 tbsp of the measured water. Cook, stirring, for about 1 minute.

4 Return the beef and spices to the casserole, then gradually add the yogurt, stirring. Stir in the remaining water. Add the tomatoes and red pepper, and bring to a boil. Cover and cook in a preheated oven at 325°F (160°C) for 2 hours or until the beef is tender. Taste for seasoning before serving.

Cook's know-how

If you are short of time, use 3–4 tbsp bottled Thai red curry paste instead of the whole and ground spices in this recipe. If you prefer, you can use coconut milk instead of the yogurt.

COUNTRY BEEF CASSEROLE

SERVES 8

3 tbsp sunflower oil

2 lb (1 kg) braising steak, trimmed and cut into 2 in (5 cm) cubes

1 lb (500 g) carrots, thickly sliced

8 oz (250 g) turnips, cut into large chunks

8 oz (250 g) parsnips, thickly sliced

2 onions, sliced

1 large leek, sliced

1 tbsp all-purpose flour

1 pint (600 ml) beef stock

14 oz (400 g) canned crushed tomatoes

2 tbsp chopped fresh herbs, such as parsley and thyme

1 large bay leaf

salt and black pepper

herb dumplings (see box, right)

1 Heat the oil in a large flameproof casserole, add the beef in batches, and cook over a high heat until browned. Lift out the beef with a slotted spoon.

2 Add the carrots, turnips, parsnips, onions, and leek, and cook over a high heat, stirring occasionally, for 5 minutes or until the vegetables are softened.

3 Add the flour and cook, stirring, for 1 minute. Add the stock and tomatoes, and 1 tbsp of the herbs, and season with salt and pepper. Bring to a boil, then return the meat to the casserole. Cover and cook in a preheated oven at 325°F (160°C) for 2 hours.

4 Place the dumplings on top of the meat. Increase the oven temperature to 375°F (190°C) and cook for 20–25 minutes until the dumplings are firm. Serve hot, sprinkled with the remaining chopped herbs.

Herb dumplings

Sift 1 cup (125 g) self-rising flour into a bowl, and add 4 tbls (60 g) shredded vegetable shortening, 1 tbsp chopped fresh thyme or parsley, and salt and pepper. Add 4–5 tbsp water to make a soft dough. Shape into 12–16 balls.

CHILI CON CARNE

SERVES 6

1 1/4 cups (250 g) dried red
  kidney beans

2 tbsp sunflower oil

1 1/2 lb (750 g) boneless beef chuck,
  trimmed and cut into large cubes

2 onions, chopped

2 fresh red chilies, cored, seeded,
  and finely chopped

1 garlic clove, crushed

1 tbsp all-purpose flour

3 3/4 cups (900 ml) beef stock

2 tbsp tomato paste

1 square of semisweet chocolate,
  grated

salt and black pepper

1 large red bell pepper, cored,
  seeded, and cut into chunks

chopped cilantro to garnish

1 Put the red kidney beans
into a large bowl, cover
generously with cold water, and
leave to soak overnight.

2 Drain the beans, rinse
under cold running water,
and drain again. Put the beans
into a large saucepan. Cover
with cold water and boil
rapidly for 10 minutes. Lower
the heat and simmer, partially
covered, for 50 minutes or until
the beans are tender. Drain.

3 Heat the oil in a large
flameproof casserole. Add
the beef and cook in batches
over a high heat for 5–7
minutes until browned. Lift out
with a slotted spoon.

4 Lower the heat, add the
onions, chilies, and garlic,
and cook, stirring occasionally,
for a few minutes until
softened.

5 Add the flour and cook,
stirring, for 1 minute. Add
the stock, tomato paste, and
chocolate, and season with salt
and pepper. Return the beef to
the casserole, add the beans,
and bring to a boil. Cover and
cook in a preheated oven at
300°F (150°C) for 1 1/2 hours.

6 Add the red pepper and
cook for 30 minutes. Taste
for seasoning, and garnish with
cilantro.

QUICK CHILI CON CARNE

Substitute 14 oz (400 g) canned
red kidney beans for the dried
beans, and ground beef for the
chuck steak. Simmer gently on the
stovetop for 45 minutes.

BEEF ROLLS WITH VEGETABLE JULIENNE

SERVES 6

8 thin slices of beef round, total
  weight about 1 1/2 lb (750 g)

2 tbsp sunflower oil

1/2 4-in (10 cm) piece of celery
  root, peeled and cut into
  matchstick-thin strips

8 oz (250 g) carrots, cut into
  matchstick-thin strips

2 small leeks, cut into matchstick-
  thin strips

salt and black pepper

1/4 cup (30 g) all-purpose flour

1 onion, sliced

1 garlic clove, sliced

2 cups (500 ml) beef stock

1 Pound each slice of beef
between 2 sheets of plastic
wrap with a rolling pin until
1/8 in (3 mm) thick

2 Heat 1 tbsp of the oil in a
large skillet, add the celery
root, carrots, and leeks, and
stir-fry over a high heat for 1
minute. Season with salt and
pepper, then lift out and drain.
Leave to cool.

3 Divide the vegetables
among the beef slices. Roll
up and secure with wooden
toothpicks.

4 Lightly coat the beef rolls in
half of the flour, shaking off
any excess. Heat the remaining
oil in a flameproof casserole,
add the beef rolls, and cook
over a high heat for 5–7
minutes until browned. Lift out
with a slotted spoon.

5 Add the onion and garlic
and cook gently until
softened. Add the remaining
flour and cook, stirring, for 1
minute. Gradually blend in the
stock, season with salt and
pepper, and bring to a boil,
stirring until thick.

6 Return the beef rolls to the
casserole, bring to a boil,
cover, and cook in a preheated
oven at 350°F (180°C) for 1 1/2
hours. Lift out the beef and set
aside. Strain the sauce, then
reheat. Thinly slice the beef,
removing the toothpicks. Serve
hot, with the sauce.

CORNED BEEF HASH

SERVES 4

4 tbls (60 g) butter

1 large onion, chopped

3 large potatoes, cut into small chunks

1¼ cups (300 ml) beef stock

salt and black pepper

12 oz (350 g) canned corned beef, cut into chunks

chopped parsley to garnish

1 Melt the butter in a large skillet, add the onion, and cook gently, stirring occasionally, for a few minutes until softened.

2 Add the potatoes and stir to coat in the butter. Pour in the stock, and season with salt and pepper. Simmer for 10–15 minutes until the potatoes are tender and the stock absorbed.

3 Stir in the meat and heat to warm through. Put the pan under a hot broiler, 3 in (7 cm) from the heat, to brown the top. Garnish with parsley

Cook's know-how

Corned beef hash can be made up to the broiling stage several hours ahead and then broiled until hot all the way through just before serving. You can add other vegetables, or a splash of Worcestershire or hot pepper sauce, and top each portion with a poached or fried egg.

TRADITIONAL STEAK & KIDNEY PIE

This pie is a classic, but for those who do not like kidneys you can omit them and use double the amount of mushrooms. For convenience, the meat can be cooked a day in advance, then all you have to do on the day of serving is make the pastry dough and bake the pie in the oven.

SERVES 6

2 tbsp sunflower oil

1 large onion, chopped

1½ lb (750 g) skirt steak, cut into 1 in (2.5 cm) cubes

8 oz (250 g) beef or lamb kidney, trimmed (page 240), and cut into 1 in (2.5 cm) cubes

¼ cup (30 g) all-purpose flour

1¼ cups (300 ml) beef stock

2 tbsp Worcestershire sauce

salt and black pepper

8 oz (250 g) button mushrooms

beaten egg for glazing

SHORTCRUST PASTRY

2 cups (250 g) all-purpose flour

½ cup (125 g) butter

about 3 tbsp cold water

1 Heat the oil in a large saucepan, add the onion, and cook, stirring from time to time, for a few minutes until soft but not colored.

2 Add the beef and kidney and cook until browned. Add the flour and cook, stirring, for 1 minute. Add the stock and Worcestershire sauce, season with salt and pepper, and bring to a boil, stirring. Partially cover, and simmer gently for 2 hours.

3 Add the mushrooms and cook for 30 minutes or until the meat is tender. Taste for seasoning, then leave to cool completely.

4 Make the pastry: sift the flour into a bowl. Add the butter and rub in lightly with your fingertips until the mixture looks like fine bread crumbs. Add the water and mix with a flat-bladed knife until the dough comes together to form a ball.

5 Roll out the pastry on a floured work surface until 2.5 cm (1 in) larger than the pie dish. Invert the dish over the dough and cut around the dish. Brush the rim of the dish with water and press on a strip of dough cut from the trimmings.

6 Put a pie funnel into the middle of the dish, then spoon in the meat mixture.

7 Lightly brush the dough strip with water and top with the dough lid, making a hole in the middle so the steam can escape through the pie funnel. Seal the dough edges and crimp with a fork, then decorate the top of the pie with dough trimmings, attaching them with beaten egg.

8 Brush the dough all over with beaten egg, and bake in a preheated oven at 400°F (200°C) for 25–30 minutes until the pastry is crisp and golden. Serve hot.

STEAK & KIDNEY PUDDING

Mix 2½ cups (300 g) self-rising flour, 1 cup (150 g) shredded suet, salt and pepper, and 1 scant cup (200 ml) water. Use ¾ of the dough to line a 1½ quart (1.7 liter) bowl. Add the uncooked filling, top with dough, and steam for 5 hours.

BRAISED MEATBALLS

SERVES 4

8 oz (250 g) ground beef

4 oz (125 g) ground pork

salt and black pepper

all-purpose flour for dusting

2 tbsp sunflower oil

2 large onions, sliced

1 garlic clove, crushed

1 1/4 cups (300 ml) hard cider

3 tbsp tomato paste

4 celery stalks, thickly sliced

1 large red bell pepper, cored, seeded, and cut into strips

4 oz (125 g) sliced mushrooms

2 tsp sugar

1 Mix together the beef and pork, and season with salt and pepper. On a floured work surface, shape the mixture into 16 even-sized balls.

2 Heat the oil in a flameproof casserole, add the meatballs, and cook over a high heat until browned. Remove and drain on paper towels. Lower the heat, add the onions and garlic, and cook, stirring occasionally, for a few minutes until softened.

3 Return the meatballs to the casserole and add the cider, tomato paste, celery, red bell pepper, mushrooms, and sugar. Season with salt and pepper, and bring to a boil. Cover and simmer for 20 minutes or until the meatballs are cooked through. Serve hot.

BEEF FLORENTINE

Bought phyllo pastry dough provides a quick and easy way to cover a pie, and it gives a crisp topping. If you prefer not to use butter, use olive oil instead and, to make a lighter dish, you can use lowfat Cheddar cheese and lowfat cream cheese, and omit the Gruyère or Swiss.

SERVES 8

11 sheets of phyllo pastry dough

4 tbls (60 g) butter, melted

BEEF LAYER

2 tbls (30 g) butter

2 lb (1 kg) lean ground beef

1 tbsp all-purpose flour

14 oz (400 g) canned chopped tomatoes

2 tbsp tomato paste

2 garlic cloves, crushed

1 tsp sugar

salt and black pepper

SPINACH & CHEESE LAYER

1 1/4 lb (625 g) spinach, tough stems removed, roughly chopped

3/4 cup (90 g) grated sharp Cheddar cheese

3/4 cup (90 g) grated Gruyère or Swiss cheese

1/2 cup (125 g) cream cheese

2 eggs, lightly beaten

1 Prepare the beef layer: melt the butter in a large saucepan, add the ground beef, and cook, stirring, for 10–15 minutes or until the meat is browned all over.

2 Add the flour and cook, stirring, for 1 minute. Add the tomatoes, tomato paste, garlic, and sugar, season with salt and pepper, and bring to a boil. Cover and simmer, stirring occasionally, for 35 minutes. Taste for seasoning.

3 Meanwhile, prepare the spinach and cheese layer: wash the spinach and put it into a large saucepan. Cook over a low heat until the spinach wilts. Drain thoroughly, squeezing to remove excess water. Mix the spinach with the Cheddar, Gruyère, cream cheese, and eggs, and season with salt and pepper.

4 Spoon the beef mixture into a shallow baking dish, then spoon the spinach mixture over the top.

5 Prepare the phyllo topping (see box, right).

6 Bake in a preheated oven at 400°F (200°C) for 20–25 minutes until the phyllo pastry is crisp and golden. Serve hot.

Preparing the phyllo topping

Brush 3 of the phyllo pastry sheets with a little of the melted butter and layer them on top of the spinach mixture, trimming to fit the dish if necessary.

Arrange the remaining 8 phyllo pastry sheets over the dish, lightly brushing with a little butter and scrunching each one up, in order to completely cover the lower layer of phyllo pastry.

THE BEST BURGERS

Burgers don't have to be made with plain ground beef, as these three recipes illustrate. They are very quick and easy to make, and will keep in the freezer for up to 3 months. If you want to be sure the burgers are seasoned enough, take a teaspoonful of the raw mixture and flatten it into a mini burger shape. Fry it for a minute, turning once, then taste it to see if it needs more seasoning or flavorings. If it does, add more to the raw mixture.

THAI BURGERS

SERVES 6

1 lb (500 g) best-quality ground beef

1 tbsp red Thai curry paste

2 tbsp chopped fresh cilantro

1 in (2.5 cm) piece of fresh gingerroot, peeled and finely grated

salt and black pepper

1 tbsp olive oil

1 Put the beef in a bowl with the curry paste, fresh cilantro, grated ginger and salt and pepper. Mix together thoroughly.

2 Shape the mixture into 6 even-sized burgers. Put on a large plate, cover and refrigerate for about 30 minutes (they will keep for up to 24 hours).

3 Heat the oil in a large, nonstick skillet or lightly coat a preheated ridged griddle pan with a little oil. Cook the burgers over a medium heat for 3–4 minutes on each side until they are brown. They are best served just pink in the middle, but they can be cooked another 1–2 minutes on each side if you prefer them more done than this.

LAMB BURGERS

SERVES 4-8

1–2 tbsp olive oil

1 small onion, finely chopped

1 garlic clove, crushed

500 g (1 lb) best-quality ground lamb

1 tsp ground cumin

2 tbsp chopped fresh mint

salt and black pepper

TO SERVE

4 warm pita breads, halved

about 8 tbsp tzatziki (ready made or see page 271)

1 Heat 1 tbsp oil in a skillet and cook the onion and garlic until completely softened – this can take up to 10 minutes. Allow to cool completely.

2 Mix the cooled onion and garlic with the remaining ingredients, then shape into 8 small burgers. Put on a large plate, cover and refrigerate for about 30 minutes (they will keep for up to 24 hours).

3 Heat a large, nonstick skillet or lightly coat a preheated ridged griddle pan with a little oil. Cook the burgers over a medium heat until browned and cooked through, 3–4 minutes on each side. Serve in warm pita pockets, with tzatziki.

VEGGIE BURGERS

SERVES 6

1 small red onion, finely chopped

3 tbsp chopped parsley

14 oz (400 g) canned cannellini beans, drained

10 oz (300 g) canned red kidney beans, drained

⅓ cup (60 g) no-need-to-soak dried apricots snipped into pieces

6 oz (175 g) grated carrots

½ cup (2 oz) grated Cheddar cheese

salt and black pepper

2 tbls (30 g) pine nuts, toasted

about 2–3 tbsp olive oil

1 Puree the onion and parsley in a food processor until fairly smooth. Add the remaining ingredients, except the pine nuts and oil, and blitz until smooth. (If you haven't got a processor, mash the beans and mix with the other ingredients except the pine nuts and oil.) Season really well.

2 Add the toasted pine nuts and pulse the machine to mix them in. Shape the mixture into 12 small burgers. Put on a large plate, cover, and refrigerate for about 1 hour (they will keep for up to 24 hours).

3 Place the burgers on a broiler pan lined with foil, under a hot broiler 3 in (7 cm) from the heat. Brush the burgers frequently with oil, for 4 minutes each side until until they are hot right through.

TOPPINGS FOR BURGERS

CHILI AIOLI

In a small bowl, combine 2 egg yolks, 1 tbsp lemon juice, 1 tsp Dijon mustard, and salt and pepper to taste, and whisk until thick. Gradually add 1 cup (250 ml) olive oil, whisking constantly until the mixture is thick. Stir in 1 crushed garlic clove, ½ tsp cayenne pepper, and ¼ tsp ground cumin. Taste for seasoning. Cover and refrigerate until ready to serve. Use on the day of making.

BARBECUE SAUCE

Heat 1 tbsp sunflower oil in a saucepan and cook 1 finely chopped onion and 1 crushed garlic clove until soft but not colored. Add 14 oz (400 g) canned chopped tomatoes, 2 tbsp water, 2 tbsp lemon juice, 1 tbsp brown sugar, 1 tbsp Worcestershire sauce, 2 tsp Dijon mustard, ½ tsp each paprika and chili powder, and salt and pepper. Bring to a boil, and simmer for 20 minutes. Serve warm or cold.

CLOCKWISE FROM TOP: Lamb Burgers in pita pockets with tzatziki, Veggie Burgers with a fresh tomato salsa, Thai Burgers with cucumber and carrot sticks, and a coconut milk, cilantro, and chili dip.

MEAT LOAF

SERVES 6

1 1/2 lb (750 g) ground beef

14 oz (400 g) canned chopped tomatoes

1 1/4 cup (90 g) herby stuffing mix

1 onion, chopped

1 carrot, coarsely shredded

3 garlic cloves, crushed

2 tbsp chopped parsley

1 egg, beaten

1 tbsp Worcestershire sauce

salt and black pepper

4–5 bacon slices

2 LB (1 KG) LOAF PAN

1 Combine the ground beef, tomatoes, stuffing mix, onion, carrot, garlic, parsley, beaten egg, and Worcestershire sauce, and season with salt and pepper.

2 Arrange bacon slices crosswise in the loaf pan, letting them hang over the sides. Put the beef mixture into the pan and fold over the bacon. Turn the loaf out into a roasting pan and bake in a preheated oven at 375°F (190°C), basting once or twice, for 1 hour.

3 Increase the heat to 450°F (230°C) and bake for 15 minutes or until the meat loaf is firm. Spoon off any fat, slice the loaf, and serve hot (or leave whole and serve cold).

MEAT PIES WITH CHEESY POTATO TOPPING

The ground beef mixture can be made a day ahead of serving, and kept in the refrigerator overnight. If you prefer you can omit the cheese in the potato topping, and use olive oil instead of butter.

SERVES 6

2 tbsp sunflower oil

1 large onion, finely chopped

1 celery stalk, finely chopped

1 large carrot, finely chopped

1 1/2 lb (750 g) ground beef

2 tsp all-purpose flour

1 1/4 cup (300 ml) beef stock

1 tbsp tomato paste

2 tbsp Worcestershire sauce

salt and black pepper

TOPPING

1 1/2 lb (750 g) potatoes, cut into chunks

2 tbls (30 g) butter

2–3 tbsp hot milk

1 cup (125 g) grated sharp Cheddar cheese

1 Heat the oil in a large saucepan, add the onion, celery, and carrot, and cook for 3 minutes. Add the ground beef, and cook for 5 minutes or until browned.

2 Add the flour and cook, stirring, for 1 minute. Add the stock, tomato paste, and Worcestershire sauce, season with salt and pepper, and bring to a boil. Cover and simmer, stirring occasionally, for 45 minutes. Remove from the heat and spoon into 6 individual baking dishes, or 1 large dish. Leave to cool.

3 Prepare the potato topping: cook the potatoes in boiling salted water for 20 minutes or until tender. Drain. Add the butter and hot milk to the potatoes and mash until soft, then stir in the cheese and season with salt and pepper.

4 Cover the ground beef mixture with the mashed potatoes (see box, right). Cook in a preheated oven at 400°F (200°C), allowing 20–25 minutes for small pies, 35–40 minutes for a large one, until the potato topping is golden brown and the meat mixture is bubbling. Serve hot.

Covering the pies

Spoon the mashed potatoes onto the beef mixture, and spread over the top to cover completely.

Score the surface of the mashed potatoes, using a fork, to make a decorative topping.

EXOTIC BEEF

SERVES 6–8

1 slice of white bread, crusts removed

1¼ cups (300 ml) milk

2 tbls (30 g) butter

1 large onion, chopped

2 garlic cloves, crushed

2 lb (1 kg) ground beef

1 tbsp medium-hot curry powder

½ cup (90 g) coarsely chopped ready-to-eat dried apricots

¾ cup (90 g) coarsely chopped blanched almonds

2 tbsp fruit chutney

1 tbsp lemon juice

salt and black pepper

2 eggs

¼ cup (30 g) slivered almonds

1 Put the bread into a shallow dish. Sprinkle 2 tbsp of the milk over and leave to soak for 5 minutes.

2 Meanwhile, melt the butter in a large skillet, add the onion and garlic, and cook gently, stirring occasionally, for a few minutes until soft.

3 Increase the heat, add the beef, and cook, stirring, for 5 minutes or until browned. Spoon off any excess fat.

4 Add the curry powder and cook, stirring, for 2 minutes. Add the chopped apricots and almonds, the chutney, lemon juice, and salt and pepper to taste.

5 Mash the bread and milk in the dish, then stir into the ground beef. Turn into a baking dish and bake in a preheated oven at 350°F (180°C) for 35 minutes.

6 Break the eggs into a bowl, and whisk in the remaining milk, and salt and pepper to taste. Pour over the ground beef mixture, sprinkle with the almonds, and bake for 25–30 minutes until the topping is set.

Healthy option

Almonds are the traditional topping for this South African recipe, but they can be omitted if you want to reduce the fat content of the dish.

BEEF TACOS

SERVES 4

1 tbsp sunflower oil

12 oz (375 g) ground beef

1 onion, chopped

3 garlic cloves, crushed

½ tsp chili powder

1 tsp paprika

½ tsp ground cumin (optional)

8 oz (225 g) canned crushed tomatoes

salt and black pepper

1 fresh green chili, cored, seeded, and thinly sliced

2 tbsp chopped fresh cilantro

8 taco shells

8 lettuce leaves, finely shredded

4 tbsp sour cream

chopped cilantro to garnish

1 Heat the oil in a large skillet, add the ground beef, onion, and garlic, and cook, stirring, for 5 minutes or until the beef is browned and the onion and garlic are softened.

2 Add the chili powder, paprika, and cumin (if using), and cook, stirring, for 2 minutes.

3 Stir in the tomatoes, cover, and cook over a medium heat for 5 minutes. Add salt and pepper to taste, remove from the heat, and stir in the chili and cilantro.

4 Warm the taco shells in a preheated oven at 350°F (180°C) for 2–3 minutes, or according to package instructions. Fill the taco shells (see box, below), and serve hot.

Filling taco shells

Holding each shell in one hand, put a layer of shredded lettuce into the bottom. Add a generous spoonful of the meat mixture and top with sour cream and a sprinkling of chopped cilantro.

PRESSED TONGUE

SERVES 10

4–5 lb (2–2.5 kg) salted ox tongue, trimmed

1 onion, quartered

1 bay leaf

1 tbsp unflavored gelatin

3 tbsp cold water

6 IN (15 CM) DEEP ROUND CAKE PAN OR STAINLESS STEEL SAUCEPAN

1 Put the ox tongue, onion, and bay leaf into a large saucepan, cover with cold water, and bring to a boil. Simmer very gently for 3–4 hours until tender. Test the water after 2 hours; if it is very salty, replace it with fresh water.

2 Lift the tongue out of the saucepan, reserving the cooking liquid, and leave to cool slightly. Remove and discard the skin, then cut the tongue in half lengthwise.

3 Sprinkle the gelatin over the measured water in a small bowl. Leave to stand for 3 minutes or until the gelatin is spongy. Put the bowl into a saucepan of gently simmering water and leave for 3 minutes or until the gelatin has dissolved.

4 Add 2/3 cup (150 ml) of the cooking liquid to the gelatin and mix well.

5 Squash one half of the tongue, cut-side down, into the cake pan or saucepan, and put in the other half, cut-side up. Pour in the gelatin mixture, cover with a small plate, and weigh down with weights or heavy cans. Chill in the refrigerator overnight.

6 Dip the base of the pan or saucepan into a bowl of hot water, just long enough to melt the gelatin slightly so it comes away from the bottom. Serve the tongue chilled, and very thinly sliced.

OXTAIL STEW

SERVES 6

1 tbsp sunflower oil

2 1/2 lb (1.25 kg) oxtail, cut into 2 in (5 cm) slices and trimmed

1/4 cup (30 g) all-purpose flour

1 1/2 pints (900 ml) beef stock

2 large onions, sliced

1 tbsp tomato paste

1 tbsp chopped parsley

1 tbsp chopped fresh thyme

1 bay leaf

salt and black pepper

8 celery stalks, thickly sliced

chopped parsley to garnish

1 Heat the oil in a large flameproof casserole, add the oxtail, and cook over a high heat for 10 minutes or until browned all over. Remove the oxtail and drain on paper towels.

2 Add the flour and cook, stirring occasionally, for about 1 minute. Blend in the beef stock and bring to a boil, stirring until the sauce has thickened.

3 Return the oxtail to the casserole, and add the onions, tomato paste, parsley, thyme, and bay leaf. Season with salt and pepper, and bring to a boil. Cover and simmer gently for 2 hours.

4 Add the celery and cook for 1 1/2–2 hours longer or until the meat can be removed from the bones easily. Skim off any fat, then taste the sauce for seasoning. Sprinkle with parsley before serving.

Cook's know-how

Oxtail stew needs long, slow cooking to develop its rich brown gravy and to make the meat so soft that it falls off the bone. If possible, make the stew the day before serving; the excess fat can then be easily lifted from the surface of the cooled stew before reheating. If you have any leftover stew, thin it down with stock or water to make a tasty and nutritious soup.

LEMON ROAST VEAL WITH SPINACH STUFFING

Loin of veal is a lean cut, so it has a tendency to be dry. Marinating for 2 days before roasting makes it more succulent. Loin of pork can be marinated and cooked in the same way.

SERVES 6–8

2 1/2 lb (1.25 kg) boneless veal roast, such as loin

2/3 cup (150 ml) dry white wine

2/3 cup (150 ml) chicken stock

MARINADE

3 tbsp olive oil

grated zest and juice of 1 lemon

4 thyme sprigs

black pepper

STUFFING

2 tbls (30 g) butter

1 shallot, finely chopped

2 bacon slices, finely chopped

6 cups (175 g) coarsely shredded spinach leaves

grated zest of 1 lemon

1 cup (60 g) fresh brown whole wheat bread crumbs

salt and black pepper

1 egg, lightly beaten

1 Combine the marinade ingredients. Turn the veal in the marinade, cover, and leave to marinate in the refrigerator for 2 days.

2 Make the stuffing: melt the butter, add the shallot and bacon, and cook for 5 minutes or until the shallot is softened. Stir in the spinach and cook for 1 minute. Remove from the heat, add the lemon zest and bread crumbs, and season with salt and pepper. Mix well, then bind with the egg. Leave to cool completely.

3 Remove the veal from the marinade, reserving the marinade. Spread the stuffing over the veal and roll up (see box, right).

4 Weigh the veal, insert a meat thermometer, if using, into the middle of the meat, and place in a roasting pan. Pour the marinade around the meat. Roast in a preheated oven at 350°F (180°C) for 25 minutes per pound (500 g), until the juices run clear or until the thermometer registers 175°F (80°C). Transfer to a platter, cover loosely with foil, and leave to stand in a warm place for 10 minutes.

5 Meanwhile, spoon the fat from the pan, and remove the thyme sprigs. Put the pan on the stovetop, add the wine and stock, and bring to a boil, stirring to dissolve the sediment from the bottom of the pan. Boil for 5 minutes or until thickened and reduced by about half.

6 Taste the gravy for seasoning, and pour into a warmed gravy boat. Carve the veal, and serve hot.

Rolling up the veal

Bring the 2 sides of the veal together, enclosing the stuffing. Tie fine string around the veal at regular intervals.

GRAVIES FOR MEAT

MUSHROOM GRAVY

Melt 2 tbls (30 g) butter in a saucepan. Add 1 finely chopped shallot and cook for 2 minutes until softened. Add 8 oz (250 g) sliced mushrooms and cook gently for 5 minutes. Pour in 1 1/4 cup (300 ml) beef stock, and simmer for about 5 minutes. Add 1 tbsp chopped parsley, 1 tsp chopped fresh thyme, and salt and black pepper to taste.

ONION GRAVY

Heat 1 tbsp sunflower oil and 2 tbls (30 g) butter in a saucepan. Add 1 sliced onion and cook for 5–7 minutes until golden. Add 1 tbsp all-purpose flour and cook, stirring, for 1 minute. Add 1 1/4 cup (300 ml) chicken stock. Simmer for about 5 minutes. Add salt and pepper to taste.

RED WINE GRAVY

Melt 2 tbls (30 g) butter in a saucepan. Add 1 sliced small onion and cook for 5 minutes or until beginning to brown. Add 1 tbsp all-purpose flour and cook, stirring, for 1 minute. Add 7 tbls (100 ml) red wine and 1 1/4 cup (300 ml) beef stock. Simmer for 5 minutes. Pour in any juices from the meat, and add salt and pepper to taste.

VEAL WITH TUNA MAYONNAISE

SERVES 8

3 lb (1.5 kg) boned rolled veal roast, such as loin

2 large rosemary sprigs

2 garlic cloves, cut into slivers

salt and black pepper

1 cup (250 ml) dry white wine

TUNA MAYONNAISE

7 oz (200 g) canned tuna in oil, drained

2 tbsp lemon juice

1 garlic clove, crushed

2 tbsp capers

1 tsp chopped fresh thyme

dash of hot pepper sauce

½ cup (125 ml) olive oil

1 cup (250 ml) mayonnaise

TO GARNISH

black olives

1 red bell pepper, cored, seeded, and cut into strips

fresh basil

1 Make incisions in the veal and push 1 or 2 rosemary leaves and a sliver of garlic into each incision. Season, and rub with any remaining rosemary and garlic.

2 Place the veal in a large roasting pan and pour the wine around it. Cover with foil and roast in a preheated oven at 325°F (160°C) for 2–2½ hours or until tender.

3 Remove the veal from the oven, and leave to cool completely in the cooking liquid. Remove any fat that solidifies on the surface. Slice the veal thinly and arrange the slices on a serving platter.

4 Make the tuna mayonnaise: puree the tuna, reserving a little for the garnish, with the lemon juice, garlic, capers, thyme, and hot pepper sauce in a food processor until smooth. Gradually blend in the oil, then add the mayonnaise, and season with salt and pepper. Pour over the veal. At this stage you can garnish and serve, or cover and refrigerate overnight to serve the next day.

5 To serve, garnish with the reserved tuna, the black olives, red bell pepper, and basil. Serve at room temperature (if refrigerated overnight, take it out for about 1 hour before serving).

VEAL CHOPS WITH MUSHROOMS & CREAM

SERVES 4

¼ cup (15 g) dried porcini mushrooms

1 cup (250 ml) warm water

2 tbsp all-purpose flour

salt and black pepper

4 veal loin chops, 8 oz (250 g) each

3 tbls (45 g) butter

8 shallots, chopped

3 garlic cloves, crushed

8 oz (250 g) thinly sliced button mushrooms (about 4 cups)

1 cup (250 ml) dry white wine

1¼ cup (300 ml) light cream

1 tbsp chopped fresh tarragon, plus extra to garnish

1 Put the dried mushrooms into a bowl, pour the warm water over, and leave to soak for 30 minutes or until soft.

2 Sprinkle the flour onto a plate, and season with salt and pepper. Lightly coat the chops with the flour.

3 Melt half of the butter in a skillet, add the veal chops, and cook for about 4 minutes on each side.

4 Remove the chops and keep warm. Melt the remaining butter in the pan, add the shallots and garlic, and cook gently, stirring occasionally, for a few minutes until softened.

5 Drain the dried mushrooms, reserving the soaking liquid. Add the dried and button mushrooms to the pan and cook for 3 minutes or until tender. Remove the shallots and mushrooms from the pan and keep warm.

6 Pour in the wine and boil until reduced to about 3 tbsp. Add the mushroom liquid and boil until reduced to about 125 ml (4 fl oz).

7 Stir in the cream and heat gently. Add the tarragon, and season with salt and pepper. Return the chops, shallots, and mushrooms to the pan and heat through gently. Transfer to serving plates, sprinkle with the extra chopped tarragon, and serve hot.

SALTIMBOCCA

SERVES 4

4 veal scallops, 2–3 oz (60–90 g) each

8–12 fresh sage leaves

4 thin slices of prosciutto

2 tbsp all-purpose flour

salt and black pepper

2 tbls (30 g) butter

1 garlic clove, crushed

1/2 cup (125 ml) dry white wine

4 tbsp heavy cream

1 Put each veal scallop between 2 sheets of waxed paper and pound until 1/8 in (3 mm) thick with a rolling pin.

2 Lay 2 or 3 sage leaves on each scallop, and press a slice of prosciutto firmly on top. Sprinkle the flour onto a plate and season with salt and pepper. Lightly coat both sides of the scallops with the flour, shaking off any excess.

3 Melt half of the butter in a large skillet until foaming. Add half of the scallops and cook for 2 minutes on each side, sprinkling them with half of the garlic as they cook. Lift out and keep warm while you cook the remaining scallops in the same way, with the remaining butter and garlic.

4 Pour the white wine into the empty pan and boil for a few minutes until it is reduced to about 2 tbsp.

5 Stir in the cream and heat gently, then taste for seasoning. Pour the sauce over the scallops on warmed plates, and serve at once.

Healthy option

Omit the ham, wine, and cream. Before serving, squeeze the juice of 1 lemon over the veal, and sprinkle with 2 tbsp shredded fresh basil and salt and pepper to taste.

WIENER SCHNITZEL

SERVES 4

4 veal scallops, 2–3 oz (60–90 g) each

salt and black pepper

1 egg, beaten

2 cups (125 g) fresh white bread crumbs

60 g (2 oz) butter

1 tbsp sunflower oil

TO SERVE

8 canned anchovy fillets, drained and halved lengthwise

2 tbsp coarsely chopped capers

lemon wedges

parsley

1 Put each veal scallop between 2 sheets of waxed paper and pound to a 1/8 in (3 mm) thickness with a rolling pin. Season with salt and pepper.

2 Spread the beaten egg over a plate, and sprinkle the bread crumbs over another plate. Dip each scallop into the beaten egg, then into the bread crumbs, to coat evenly. Chill in the refrigerator for about 30 minutes.

3 Melt the butter with the oil in a large skillet until foaming, add 2 of the scallops, and cook for 2 minutes on each side until golden. Drain on paper towels and keep warm while cooking the remaining scallops. Serve the veal scallops hot, with anchovy fillets, capers, lemon wedges, and parsley.

Healthy option

Traditonal Austrian Wiener Schnitzel is cooked in butter to give it a really good golden color, but if you use a nonstick skillet you can omit the butter and use 2 tbsp sunflower oil.

CALF'S LIVER WITH SAGE

SERVES 4

2 tbsp all-purpose flour

salt and black pepper

1 lb (500 g) calf's liver, sliced

4 tbls (60 g) butter

1 tbsp sunflower oil

juice of 1 lemon

3 tbsp roughly chopped fresh sage

sage leaves and lemon slices to garnish

1 Sprinkle the flour onto a plate and season with salt and pepper. Coat the liver slices in the seasoned flour, shaking off any excess.

2 Melt half of the butter with the oil in a large skillet. When the butter is foaming, add half of the liver slices and cook over a high heat for about 1 minute on each side until browned all over. Lift out with a slotted spoon and keep warm. Repeat with the remaining liver slices.

3 Melt the remaining butter in the pan, and add the lemon juice and sage, stirring to dissolve any sediment from the bottom of the pan. Pour the pan juices over the liver, garnish with sage leaves and lemon slices, and serve at once.

Cook's know-how

Overcooking liver will toughen it, so make sure the butter and oil are really hot, then the liver will cook quickly.

CALF'S LIVER WITH APPLE

Halve and slice 1 eating apple and add to the pan with the lemon juice and sage. Cook, stirring, for 3 minutes, and serve with the liver.

CREAMED SWEETBREADS

SERVES 6

1 lb (500 g) veal sweetbreads

2 tbsp lemon juice

1 small onion, chopped

a few parsley sprigs

1 bay leaf

salt and black pepper

3 tbls (45 g) butter

1/3 cup (45 g) all-purpose flour

1 1/4 cups (300 ml) milk

chopped parsley to garnish

1 Put the sweetbreads into a bowl, cover with cold water, add 1 tbsp of the lemon juice. Leave to soak for 2–3 hours.

2 Drain, rinse, and trim the sweetbreads (page 240).

3 Put the sweetbreads into a large saucepan with the onion, parsley, bay leaf, and a sprinkling of salt and pepper. Cover with cold water and bring slowly to a boil. Simmer gently for 5 minutes or until just tender, skimming off any scum as it rises to the surface.

4 Drain the sweetbreads, and reserve 1 1/4 cups (300 ml) of the cooking liquid. Cut the sweetbreads into bite-sized pieces.

5 Melt the butter in a saucepan, add the flour, and cook, stirring, for 1 minute. Remove the pan from the heat, and gradually blend in the milk and reserved cooking liquid. Bring to a boil, stirring constantly, and boil for 2–3 minutes until the mixture thickens. Add the remaining lemon juice and season with salt and pepper.

6 Add the sweetbreads to the sauce and simmer gently for about 5 minutes to warm through. Transfer to warmed plates and garnish with chopped parsley before serving.

ROAST LEG OF LAMB WITH RED WINE GRAVY

A rich gravy that incorporates all the flavorsome juices from the meat is traditonal with roast lamb. Red wine boosts the gravy's flavor, and you can add a spoonful of red-currant jelly too, plus a squeeze of lemon juice and a dash of Worcestershire sauce if you like.

SERVES 4–6

4 lb (2 kg) leg of lamb

salt and black pepper

2 tbsp chopped fresh rosemary

1 tbsp all-purpose flour

1¼ cups (300 ml) lamb or chicken stock

6 tbls (90 ml) red wine

mint sauce (see recipe, far right) to serve

rosemary and thyme to garnish

1 Trim the skin and excess fat from the lamb. Score the fat (see box, right).

2 Insert a meat thermometer, if using, into the middle of the meat. Put the lamb, fat-side up, on a rack in a roasting pan, and rub with salt and pepper and the rosemary.

3 Roast the lamb in a preheated oven at 400°F (200°C) for 20 minutes. Lower the oven temperature to 350°F (180°C) and roast for 20 minutes per pound (500 g) for medium-done meat, 25 minutes per pound (500 g) for well-done meat, until the meat thermometer registers 170–175°F (75–80°C), and the fat is crisp and golden.

4 Remove the lamb, cover with foil, and leave to stand for 10 minutes.

5 Meanwhile, make the gravy: spoon all but 1 tbsp fat from the pan. Put the pan on the stovetop, add the flour, and cook, stirring, for 1 minute. Pour in the stock and wine, and bring to a boil, stirring to dissolve any sediment.

6 Simmer the gravy for about 3 minutes, season with salt and pepper, then strain if you like. Serve the gravy and mint sauce with the lamb, garnished with rosemary and thyme.

Scoring the fat

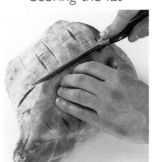

Score the fat in a criss-cross pattern using a small, sharp knife, making sure that only the fat is cut, and that the meat underneath remains completely untouched.

SAUCES FOR LAMB

MINT SAUCE

In a small bowl, combine 3 tbsp finely chopped fresh mint with 1–2 tbsp sugar, to taste. Add 3 tbsp white wine or apple cider and stir well to mix.

CUMBERLAND SAUCE

Put 4 tbsp red-currant jelly into a small saucepan and heat gently until melted. Add ½ cup (125 ml) red wine and the grated zest of 1 orange. Bring to simmering point, and simmer, whisking constantly, for 5 minutes. Add the juices of 1 orange and ½ lemon and simmer for 5 minutes longer. Strain, then add salt and pepper. Serve hot.

TZATZIKI SAUCE

Put ⅔ cup (150 g) plain yogurt, the grated zest and juice of 1 lemon, 1 crushed garlic clove, 1 tbsp chopped fresh mint, and salt and pepper into a small bowl. Mix well to combine, then taste for seasoning. Cover and chill until required.

GREEK ROAST LAMB

SERVES 6

4 lb (2 kg) leg of lamb

4 garlic cloves, cut into slivers

2 large rosemary sprigs, chopped

1 tbsp olive oil

salt and black pepper

chopped fresh rosemary to garnish

1 With a sharp knife, make small incisions in the lamb and insert a sliver of garlic into each incision.

2 Rub the lamb with the rosemary, olive oil, and salt and pepper, then put it in a roasting pan.

3 Roast in a preheated oven at 425°F (220°C) for 30 minutes or until the lamb is browned. Lower the oven temperature to 275°F (140°C), cover, and cook for 3¹/2 hours longer or until the lamb is very tender.

4 Cover the lamb with foil and leave to rest in a warm place for 10 minutes. Carve the lamb and serve hot, garnished with rosemary. Any cooking juices can be served with the meat, if you like.

SPINACH-STUFFED LAMB

The lamb in this recipe is distinctively flavored with spinach, wine, and anchovies. Stuffed mushrooms are a perfect accompaniment.

SERVES 6–8

4 lb (2 kg) leg of lamb, boned but left whole (page 237)

²/3 cup (150 ml) dry white wine

4 canned anchovy fillets, chopped

²/3 cup (150 ml) lamb or chicken stock

salt and black pepper

stuffed mushrooms (page 383)

SPINACH STUFFING

2 tbls (30 g) butter

3–4 garlic cloves, crushed

8 oz (250 g) coarsely shredded spinach leaves

1 cup (60 g) fresh whole wheat bread crumbs

1 egg, beaten

1 Make the stuffing: melt the butter in a pan. Add the garlic and cook, stirring, for 2–3 minutes until soft. Stir in the spinach, season with salt and pepper, and cook for 1 minute. Add the bread crumbs, cool, then mix in the egg.

2 Stuff the lamb (see box, right). Secure with fine skewers or kitchen string.

3 Put the lamb on a rack in a roasting pan and roast in a preheated oven at 400°F (200°C) for 15 minutes. Turn, insert a meat thermometer, if using, and cook for 15 minutes.

4 Drain the fat from the pan, then add the wine and anchovies. Cover the lamb loosely with foil, lower the oven temperature to 350°F (180°C), and cook for 1¹/2 hours or until the juices run slightly pink. The thermometer should register 170–175°F (75–80°C).

5 Remove the lamb from the pan. Leave to stand, covered with the foil, in a warm place for about 10 minutes.

6 Pour the cooking liquid into a measuring jug and make up to 1¹/4 cups (300 ml) with stock.

7 Return the cooking liquid to the pan. Bring to a boil, stirring to dissolve the sediment. Season, and strain into a warmed gravy boat. Serve the lamb with the stuffed mushrooms, and hand the gravy separately.

Stuffing the lamb

Season the cavity of the lamb with salt and pepper, then spoon in the cold spinach stuffing, packing it in tightly.

SHOULDER OF LAMB
WITH LEMON & OLIVES

SERVES 6–8

4 lb (2 kg) shoulder of lamb, boned
2 garlic cloves, cut into slivers
2/3 cup (150 ml) dry white wine
2/3 cup (150 ml) lamb or chicken stock

LEMON & OLIVE STUFFING

1 tbsp olive oil
1 shallot, finely chopped
2 cups (125 g) fresh bread crumbs
1/4 cup (30 g) pitted black olives, roughly chopped
finely grated zest of 1 lemon
1 tbsp chopped fresh thyme
1 tbsp chopped fresh rosemary
1 small egg, beaten
salt and black pepper

1 Make the stuffing: heat the olive oil in a small pan, add the shallot, and cook for about 5 minutes. Remove from the heat and add the bread crumbs, olives, lemon zest, herbs, and egg. Season with salt and pepper, stir, and leave to cool.

2 Make incisions in the meat side of the lamb, insert the garlic slivers into them, then sprinkle with salt and pepper and spread with the stuffing. Roll up and secure with skewers, then weigh the lamb.

3 Put the lamb into a roasting pan and insert a meat thermometer, if using, into the middle of the meat. Pour over the wine and stock and cook in a preheated oven at 400°F (200°C) for 20–25 minutes. Lower the temperature to 350°F (180°C) and cook for 20 minutes per pound (500 g) or until the juices run clear. The meat thermometer should register 170–175°F (75–80°C).

4 Remove the lamb, cover loosely with foil, and leave to stand for 10 minutes. Put the pan on the stovetop and spoon off any fat. Bring to a boil, and boil for 5 minutes, stirring to dissolve any sediment from the pan. Season, strain, and serve.

LEMON-BROILED LAMB

SERVES 6–8

4–5 lb (2 –2.5 kg) leg of lamb, butterflied (page 237)

MARINADE

juice of 3 lemons
4 tbsp honey
3 large garlic cloves, quartered
2 tbsp coarse-grain mustard

1 Make the marinade: in a nonmetallic dish, mix together the lemon juice, honey, garlic, and mustard. Turn the lamb in the marinade, cover, and leave to marinate in the refrigerator, turning the lamb occasionally, for 1–2 days.

2 Remove the lamb from the marinade. Strain and reserve the marinade. Cook the lamb under a hot broiler, 6 in (15 cm) from the heat, basting from time to time with the marinade, for 20–25 minutes on each side.

3 Test the lamb: insert a skewer into the thickest part – the juices will run clear when it is cooked.

4 Leave the lamb to stand, covered with foil, in a warm place for 5–10 minutes. Spoon the fat from the broiler pan, strain the juices into a gravy boat, and serve with the lamb.

Cook's know-how

Butterflied leg of lamb is a good cut for cooking on the barbecue, as well as under the broiler, because the meat is thin enough to cook quickly without becoming too charred on the outside. The marinade in this recipe works equally well for lamb chops, which can also be broiled or barbecued.

KEBABS ON THE BARBECUE

If you are having a barbecue party, threading the meat on skewers makes cooking, serving,
and eating really easy, so it is well worth the little extra time it takes to get them assembled.
You can choose from metal or bamboo skewers (see box below), as both are suitable for barbecuing.

BEEF & RED ONION

SERVES 4

1 lb (500 g) boneless sirloin, cut into chunks

2 red onions, cut into wedges

salt and black pepper

olive oil for brushing

MARINADE

4 tbls olive oil

4 tbls port wine, sherry, or Marsala

2 tbsp Dijon mustard

1 Combine the marinade ingredients, add the beef, and stir well. Cover and leave to marinate in the refrigerator for at least 2 hours, turning the meat occasionally.

2 Thread the beef and onions onto skewers, season, and brush with olive oil. Barbecue for 2–3 minutes on each side for rare beef, 3–4 minutes for medium, and 4–5 minutes for well-done.

CURRIED LAMB

SERVES 4

1 lb (500 g) boneless leg of lamb, trimmed and cut into chunks

lime wedges to serve

MARINADE

3 tbsp plain yogurt

juice of 1/2 lime

4 garlic cloves, crushed

3 tbsp chopped fresh cilantro

1 tbsp chopped fresh mint

2 tsp curry powder

1 Combine the marinade ingredients in a large bowl. Stir in the lamb, cover, and marinate in the refrigerator for at least 2 hours, turning the meat occasionally.

2 Thread the lamb onto skewers. Barbecue for 4 minutes on each side for medium lamb, or 5 minutes for well-done, basting with the marinade a few times. Serve with lime wedges.

ORIENTAL PORK

SERVES 4

1 lb (500 g) pork tenderloin, cut into chunks

1 red bell pepper, cored, seeded, and cut into chunks

1 green bell pepper, cored, and cut into chunks

1 onion, cut into chunks

1/4 fresh pineapple, peeled and cut into chunks

MARINADE

6 tbls (90 ml) sunflower oil

6 tbls (90 ml) soy sauce

juice of 1 lime

3 garlic cloves, crushed

3 tbsp sugar

1/4 tsp ground ginger

1 Combine the marinade ingredients in a bowl. Add the pork, peppers, onion, and pineapple, and stir well. Cover and chill for at least 2 hours.

2 Thread the meat onto skewers, alternating with peppers, onions, and pineapple. Baste with any remaining marinade. Barbecue for 4–5 minutes on each side, basting, until the pork is cooked.

SAUSAGE & SESAME

SERVES 4

16 link cocktail sausages, about 1½ in (4 cm) long

8 button mushrooms

8 cherry tomatoes

2 zucchini, each cut into 4 thick slices on the diagonal

salt and black pepper

olive oil, for brushing

about 2 tbsp mango chutney

about 2 tbsp toasted sesame seeds

1 Thread the sausages lengthwise onto skewers, putting 4 sausages on each skewer, then thread the vegetables onto 4 skewers, alternating the mushrooms, tomatoes, and zucchini. Season and brush with olive oil.

2 Barbecue for 4–5 minutes on each side, until cooked through. While the sausages are still hot, brush them with mango chutney and sprinkle with toasted sesame seeds.

SUCCESSFUL BARBECUES

Cooking over charcoal requires no special skills, but it helps to know a few simple rules before you start.

Meat is best if it is marinated before being cooked over a barbecue. The basis of a marinade should be an oil to keep the food moist, an acid such as lemon or lime juice to help tenderize the meat, and herbs, spices, or other seasonings to add flavor.

Basting or brushing with the marinade while the meat is cooking will help keep it moist.

Light the barbecue well before you want to start cooking – the coals should have stopped glowing and be covered in gray ash or the food may singe and burn on the outside before it is cooked inside. It takes about 30 minutes to get to this stage.

If you are using bamboo skewers for kebabs, soak them in warm water for 30 minutes before use so they don't burn.

TOP PLATTER: Beef & Red Onion (left) with Oriental Pork. BOTTOM PLATTER: Sausage & Sesame (top and middle); Curried Lamb.

SHOULDER OF LAMB WITH GARLIC & HERBS

SERVES 6

4 lb (2 kg) shoulder of lamb, trimmed of excess fat

creamed great northern beans (page 381) to serve

HERB BUTTER

6 tbls (90 g) butter, softened

2 garlic cloves, crushed

1 tbsp chopped fresh thyme

1 tbsp chopped fresh rosemary

1 tbsp chopped fresh mint

2 tbsp chopped parsley

salt and black pepper

GRAVY

1 tbsp all-purpose flour

2/3 cup (150 ml) red wine

2/3 cup (150 ml) lamb or chicken stock

1 Make the herb butter: mix the butter, garlic, thyme, rosemary, mint, and parsley, and season with salt and pepper.

2 Slash the lamb at regular intervals with a sharp knife, then push the herb butter into the cuts. Rub any remaining butter over the lamb. Weigh the lamb.

3 Put the lamb on a rack in a roasting pan and insert a meat thermometer, if using, into the middle of the meat. Cook in a preheated oven at 400°F (200°C) for 30 minutes.

4 Lower the temperature to 350°F (180°C) and cook for 20 minutes per pound (500 g). The thermometer should register 170–175°F (75–80°C).

5 Remove the lamb. Cover loosely with foil and leave to stand in a warm place for about 10 minutes.

6 Make the gravy: drain all but 1 tbsp of the fat from the tin. Set the pan on the stovetop, add the flour, and cook, stirring, for 1 minute. Pour in the wine and stock, bring to a boil, and simmer for 2–3 minutes. Taste for seasoning, and strain into a warmed gravy boat. Serve with the lamb and creamed great northern beans

INDIAN SPICED LAMB

SERVES 6

3 lb (1.5 kg) shoulder or leg of lamb

1 tsp lemon juice

salt and black pepper

cashew nuts and chopped cilantro to garnish

SPICED YOGURT MARINADE

4 garlic cloves, coarsely chopped

3 in (7 cm) piece of fresh gingerroot, peeled and grated

2 tbsp honey

1 tbsp lemon juice

seeds of 5 cardamom pods

1 tsp ground cumin

1 tsp turmeric

1/4 tsp cayenne pepper

1 tsp salt

1/2 tsp ground cinnamon

1/4 tsp ground cloves (optional)

2/3 cup (150 g) plain yogurt

1 Make the spiced yogurt marinade: purée the garlic, ginger, honey, lemon juice, cardamom, cumin, turmeric, cayenne, salt, cinnamon, cloves (if using), and yogurt in a blender or food processor.

2 Spread the mixture over the lamb (see box, right). Cover and leave to marinate in the refrigerator for at least 2 hours, or overnight.

3 Put the lamb on a rack in a roasting pan and cook in a preheated oven at 325°F (160°C) for 3 1/2 hours or until the meat is tender.

4 Remove the lamb and keep hot. Spoon the fat from the pan. Set the pan on the stovetop and stir in the lemon juice and enough water to make a sauce. Bring to a boil, stirring, and season with salt and pepper.

5 Cut the lamb from the bone, then cut the meat into chunks and mix with the sauce on the hob. Serve hot, garnished with cashew nuts and chopped cilantro.

Coating the lamb

Make incisions in the lamb, then spread the marinade over the whole joint, making sure it goes into the incisions.

RACK OF LAMB WITH A WALNUT & HERB CRUST

A favorite for dinner parties, a rack of lamb 8 bones, or chops. The bones should be scraped clean of all fat – this is called "French trimmed" by some butchers.

SERVES 4–6

2 prepared racks of lamb (page 238)

1 egg, beaten

WALNUT & HERB CRUST

1/2 cup (30 g) fresh whole wheat bread crumbs

1/2 cup (30 g) parsley, chopped

2 tbsp coarsely chopped walnut pieces

2 large garlic cloves, crushed

finely grated zest of 1 lemon

1 tbsp walnut oil

salt and black pepper

WINE & GRAPE SAUCE

2/3 cup (150 ml) dry white wine

2/3 cup (150 ml) lamb or chicken stock

4 oz (125 g) seedless green grapes, halved

1 Brush the outsides of the racks of lamb with some of the beaten egg.

2 Prepare the walnut and herb crust: combine the bread crumbs, parsley, walnuts, garlic, lemon zest, and oil, season with salt and pepper, and bind with the remaining egg. Chill for 30 minutes.

3 Coat the racks with the walnut and herb crust (see box, right), and put them crust-side up into a roasting pan. Cook in a preheated oven at 400°F (200°C) for 30 minutes.

4 Remove the lamb, cover with foil, and leave to stand in a warm place for 10 minutes. Meanwhile, make the sauce: spoon all but 1 tbsp of the fat from the roasting pan.

5 Set the pan on the stovetop, pour in the wine, and bring to a boil, stirring to dissolve any sediment from the bottom of the pan.

6 Add the stock and boil, stirring occasionally, for 2–3 minutes. Taste the sauce for seasoning, strain into a warmed sauce boat, and stir in the grapes. Serve with the lamb.

Coating the lamb

Press half of the walnut and herb crust mixture onto the meaty side of each rack of lamb, using a metal spatula.

LAMB WITH MINT GLAZE

SERVES 4

8 best end lamb chops, well trimmed

MINT GLAZE

3 tbsp dry white wine

1 tbsp white wine vinegar

4 mint sprigs, leaves stripped and chopped

1 tbsp honey

1 tsp Dijon mustard

salt and black pepper

1 Make the mint glaze: combine the wine, vinegar, mint, honey, and mustard, and season with salt and pepper. Brush the glaze over the chops, and leave to marinate for about 30 minutes.

2 Place the chops over a barbecue or under a hot broiler, 3 in (7 cm) from the heat, and cook, brushing often with the glaze, for 4–6 minutes on each side, until done to your liking.

LAMB WITH ORANGE GLAZE

Instead of the mint glaze, combine 3 tbsp orange juice with 1 tbsp each white wine vinegar, orange marmalade, and chopped fresh thyme, and 1 tsp Dijon mustard. Season with salt and pepper.

HERBED CHOPS

SERVES 4

4 sirloin lamb chops
1 tbsp olive oil
black pepper
4 rosemary sprigs
4 mint sprigs
4 thyme sprigs

1 Place the lamb chops on a broiler pan and brush each one with half of the oil. Sprinkle with black pepper and scatter with the herb sprigs.

2 Place the chops under a hot broiler, 4 in (10 cm) from the heat, and cook for 4–6 minutes. Remove from the heat, lift off the herbs, and turn the chops over.

3 Brush the chops with the remaining oil, replace the herbs, and broil for 4–6 minutes until done to your liking. Serve hot.

Cook's know-how

Sirloin chops are tender, meaty chops cut from the leg. Other suitable chops include those from the loin and ribs.

LAMB CHOPS WITH MINTED HOLLANDAISE SAUCE

Instead of the traditional mint sauce, lamb chops are served here with a creamy hollandaise sauce flavored with fresh mint. The sauce is easy to make, as long as you take care not to get the melted butter too hot.

SERVES 4

4 lamb chops
a little olive oil
salt and black pepper
minted hollandaise sauce to serve (see box, below)

1 Brush the chops on both sides with a little oil, and season with salt and pepper.

2 Put the chops under a hot broiler, 4 in (10 cm) from the heat, and cook for 3–4 minutes on each side for medium-rare chops, slightly longer for well-done.

3 Arrange the lamb chops on warmed serving plates and serve at once with the warm minted hollandaise sauce.

LEMON & THYME HOLLANDAISE

Substitute 1 tsp finely grated lemon zest and 1 tbsp chopped fresh thyme leaves for the chopped mint.

Minted hollandaise sauce

Whisk together 2 tsp lemon juice, 2 tsp white wine vinegar, and 3 egg yolks at room temperature. Put over a pan of simmering water and whisk until thick. In another pan, gently melt ½ cup (125 g) unsalted butter (do not let it get too hot). Pour into a jug.

Pour the melted butter, a little at a time, into the egg-yolk mixture, whisking constantly until the sauce thickens. Remove from the heat, stir in 2 tbsp chopped fresh mint, and season with salt and pepper. Pour into a sauce boat and serve at once.

MEAT HOT POT

SERVES 4

2 tbsp sunflower oil

2 lb (1 kg) shoulder lamb chops, trimmed

3 lamb's kidneys, trimmed (page 240) and halved

4 large potatoes, cut into 1/4 in (5 mm) slices

3 1/2 cups (500 g) sliced carrots

2 large onions, chopped

1 tsp sugar

salt and black pepper

1 bay leaf

1 rosemary sprig

a few parsley sprigs

2 1/3–3 cups (600–750 ml) lamb or chicken stock, or water

chopped parsley to garnish

1 Heat the oil in a flameproof casserole, add the lamb in batches, and brown over a medium heat for 5 minutes. Remove and set aside. Add the kidneys and cook for 3–5 minutes. Remove and set aside.

2 Add the potatoes, carrots, and onions, and cook for 5 minutes. Remove from the casserole.

3 Make layers of lamb chops, kidneys, and vegetables in the casserole, sprinkling with the sugar and a little salt and pepper, and putting the herbs in the middle.

4 Top with a neat layer of potatoes. Pour in enough stock or water to come up to the potato layer. Cover tightly and cook in a preheated oven at 325°F (160°C) for 2 hours or until the meat and vegetables are tender.

5 Remove the casserole lid, increase the oven temperature to 425°F (220°C), and cook for 20–30 minutes to brown the potato topping. Sprinkle with parsley before serving.

COUNTRY HOT POT

Omit the kidneys, and substitute 1/2 a peeled rutabaga for half of the carrots. Layer the meat and vegetables with 1/3 cup (60 g) pearl barley.

LAMB NOISETTES WITH ORANGE & HONEY

SERVES 4

8 lamb noisettes

2 lamb kidneys, trimmed (page 240) and quartered (optional)

chopped fresh thyme and rosemary to garnish

MARINADE

grated zest and juice of 1 orange

4 tbsp honey

3 tbsp olive oil

2 garlic cloves, crushed

1 tbsp chopped fresh thyme

1 tbsp chopped fresh rosemary

salt and black pepper

1 Make the marinade: in a shallow, non-metallic dish, combine the orange zest and juice, honey, oil, garlic, thyme, and rosemary, and season with salt and pepper. Add the lamb noisettes to the marinade, turn them, then cover, and leave to marinate in the refrigerator overnight.

2 Lift the lamb noisettes out of the marinade, reserving the marinade. Place a piece of kidney, if using, in the middle of each lamb noisette.

3 Put under a hot broiler, 4 in (10 cm) from the heat, and cook for 7 minutes on each side until the lamb is tender.

4 Meanwhile, strain the marinade into a small saucepan, bring to a boil, and simmer for a few minutes until it reaches a syrupy consistency. Taste for seasoning, spoon over the lamb noisettes, and garnish with thyme and rosemary.

Cook's know-how

Noisettes are taken from the loin of the lamb. The eye of meat is cut away, then rolled, tied, and cut into thick slices. It is an expensive cut but gives neat portions of tender, lean meat, with no waste.

IRISH STEW

SERVES 4

4 large baking potatoes, cut into 1/4 in (5 mm) slices

2 large onions, sliced

2 lb (1 kg) shoulder lamb chops, trimmed

a few parsley stalks

1 thyme sprig

1 bay leaf

salt and black pepper

1 1/4–2 cups (300–500 ml) water

chopped parsley to garnish

1 Put half of the potatoes into a flameproof casserole, cover with half of the onions, then add the chops, parsley, thyme, and bay leaf, and season with salt and pepper. Add the remaining onions, then the remaining potatoes, seasoning each layer with salt and pepper.

2 Pour in enough water to half-fill the casserole, and then bring to a boil. Cover tightly and cook in a preheated oven at 325°F (160°C) for 2–2 1/2 hours until the lamb and potatoes are just tender.

3 Remove the lid, increase the oven temperature to 425°F (220°C), and cook for 20–30 minutes to brown the topping. Sprinkle with parsley before serving.

CURRIED LAMB WITH ALMONDS

This aromatic lamb dish is enriched with yogurt instead of cream, which is traditionally used. The fresh mint and paprika garnish adds to both flavor and presentation. For an authentic accompaniment, serve with spiced red lentils.

SERVES 6

2 in (5 cm) piece of fresh gingerroot, peeled and grated

3 large garlic cloves, peeled

2 large green chilies, cored and seeded

1/2 cup (60 g) salted cashew nuts (optional)

2 tsp ground cumin

2 tsp ground cardamom

2 tsp turmeric

6 tbsp water

3 tbsp sunflower oil

2 lb (1 kg) lamb stew meat, trimmed and cut into 1 1/2 in (4 cm) cubes

2 large onions, roughly chopped

1 1/4 cups (300 ml) thick, plain yogurt

salt and black pepper

about 1 tbsp lemon juice

fresh mint and paprika to garnish

1 Place the ginger, garlic, chilies, cashew nuts (if using), cumin, cardamom, turmeric, and measured water in a food processor or blender, and puree until smooth.

Cook's know-how

To make this recipe even more special, experiment with other spices. The traditional garam masala powder is usually sold already mixed, and can include ground cilantro, cinnamon, cloves, mace, bay leaves, and pepper, as well as the three spices used in the recipe here. For a subtly different flavor, try adding 1 tsp ground cinnamon next time you make this recipe, or any of the other garam masala spices mentioned above.

2 Heat 2 tbsp of the oil in a large flameproof casserole, and brown the lamb on all sides (you might need to do this in batches). Remove with a slotted spoon and set aside to drain on paper towels.

3 Heat the remaining oil in the same pan, and fry the onions over a high heat for 2–3 minutes. Return the lamb to the pan, add the pureed spice blend, and stir in the yogurt. Season with salt and pepper, cover, and simmer gently for about 1 1/2–2 hours until the lamb is tender.

4 Just before serving, add the lemon juice, and check the seasoning. Garnish with a sprinkling of mint and paprika, and serve hot.

BLANQUETTE OF LAMB

SERVES 6

2 lb (1 kg) boneless shoulder of lamb, trimmed and cut into chunks

5 cups (1.25 liters) water

8 pearl onions

2 large carrots, thickly sliced

2 bay leaves

juice of 1/2 lemon

salt and black pepper

8 oz (250 g) button mushrooms

3 tbls (45 g) butter

1/3 cup (45 g) all-purpose flour

2/3 cup (150 ml) light cream

1 egg yolk

chopped parsley to garnish

1 Put the chunks of lamb into a large saucepan, cover with cold water, and bring to a boil. Drain, then rinse the meat thoroughly to remove the foam.

2 Return the meat to the saucepan and pour in the measured water. Add the pearl onions, carrots, bay leaves, and lemon juice, and season with salt and pepper. Bring to a boil, cover, and simmer gently for 1 hour.

3 Add the mushrooms and simmer for 30 minutes. Lift out the lamb and vegetables, reserving the liquid, and keep hot.

4 Melt the butter in a small pan. Add the flour and cook, stirring occasionally, for 1 minute. Gradually blend in the reserved cooking liquid, stirring constantly. Bring to a boil, stirring, then simmer until the sauce thickens.

5 In a bowl, whisk together the cream and egg yolk. Blend in 2 tbsp of the hot sauce. Take the saucepan off the heat, stir the cream mixture into the sauce, then reheat very gently. Taste for seasoning. Pour the sauce over the lamb and garnish with parsley before serving.

Healthy option

Substitute 14 oz (400 g) canned crushed tomatoes and 1 1/4 cups (300 ml) dry white wine for the water. Cook the lamb as in the recipe here, but do not make the white sauce. This will not be a classic blanquette, but it will cut down on the fat content.

AROMATIC LAMB WITH LENTILS

SERVES 8

3 lb (1.5 kg) boneless shoulder of lamb, trimmed and cut into chunks

2 tbsp olive oil

2 onions, chopped

2/3 cup (125 g) brown or green Puy lentils, rinsed

1 cup (175 g) dried apricots

salt and black pepper

2 1/2 cups (600 ml) lamb or chicken stock

MARINADE

3/4 cup (175 ml) orange juice

2 tbsp olive oil

3 garlic cloves, crushed

1 tsp ground ginger

1 tsp ground cilantro

1/2 tsp ground cinnamon

1 Make the marinade: in a large bowl, combine the orange juice, oil, garlic, ginger, cilantro, and cinnamon.

2 Turn the lamb in the marinade, cover loosely, and then marinate in the refrigerator overnight.

3 Remove the lamb from the marinade, reserving the marinade. Heat the olive oil in a large flameproof casserole, add the lamb in batches, and cook over a high heat for 5 minutes or until browned all over. Lift out the lamb chunks with a slotted spoon.

4 Lower the heat slightly, add the onions, and cook gently, stirring occasionally, for a few minutes until just soft but not colored. Lift out of the casserole.

5 Make layers of lamb, onions, lentils, and apricots in the casserole, sprinkling each layer with salt and pepper. Pour in the stock and the reserved marinade and bring to a boil. Cover and cook in a preheated oven at 325°F (160°C) for 2 hours or until the meat is tender. Taste for seasoning before serving.

LAMB TAGINE

SERVES 8

1/4 tsp saffron threads

2/3 cup (150 ml) hot water

3 tbsp olive oil

3 lb (1.5 kg) boneless shoulder of lamb, well trimmed and cut into 1-in (2.5-cm) cubes

1 fennel bulb or 4 celery stalks, trimmed and sliced crosswise

2 green bell peppers, cored, seeded, and cut into strips

1 large onion, sliced

1/4 cup (30 g) all-purpose flour

1/2 tsp ground ginger

2 cups (500 ml) lamb or chicken stock

grated zest and juice of 1 orange

2/3 cup (125 g) dried apricots

salt and black pepper

mint sprigs to garnish

1 Prepare the saffron (see box, right). Heat the oil in a flameproof casserole, add the lamb in batches, and cook over a high heat for 5 minutes or until browned. Lift out and drain on paper towels.

2 Lower the heat, add the fennel or celery, peppers, and onion, and cook gently, stirring, for 5 minutes.

3 Sprinkle the flour and ginger into the vegetables and cook, stirring occasionally, for 1 minute. Add the saffron liquid to the casserole, return the cubes of lamb, then add the stock and orange zest, and season with salt and pepper. Bring to a boil, cover, and cook in a preheated oven at 325°F (160°C) for 1 hour.

4 Add the orange juice and apricots and cook for about 30 minutes until the lamb is very tender. Taste for seasoning and garnish with mint sprigs before serving.

Preparing saffron

Put the saffron threads into a small bowl, add the measured hot water, and leave to soak for 10 minutes.

SPICED LAMB WITH COCONUT

SERVES 6

2 lb (1 kg) boneless shoulder of lamb, trimmed and cut into 1-in (2.5-cm) cubes

2 tbls (30 g) butter

1 tbsp sunflower oil

1 large Spanish onion, sliced

2 large garlic cloves, crushed

1 tbsp all-purpose flour

14 oz (400 g) canned crushed tomatoes

2/3 cup (150 ml) lamb or chicken stock

grated zest and juice of 1 lime

2 tbsp mango chutney

2 oz (60 g) creamed coconut, chopped

1 cup (250 g) thick, plain yogurt

cilantro sprigs to garnish

SPICE MIX

1-in (2.5-cm) piece of fresh gingerroot, peeled and grated

1 tbsp ground cumin

1 tbsp ground cilantro

1 tbsp mild curry powder

salt and black pepper

1 Toss the meat in the ginger, cumin, coriander, and curry powder, and season with salt and pepper.

2 Melt the butter with the oil in a large flameproof casserole. When the butter is foaming, add the lamb in batches, and cook over a high heat for about 5 minutes until browned all over.

3 Lift out with a slotted spoon and set aside. Lower the heat, add the onion and garlic, and cook gently, stirring occasionally, for a few minutes until soft but not colored.

4 Sprinkle in the flour and cook, stirring, for 1 minute. Add the tomatoes, stock, lime zest and juice, and chutney, and season with salt and pepper. Bring to a boil, stirring.

5 Return the lamb to the casserole, add the coconut, and bring back to a boil. Cover and cook in a preheated oven at 325°F (160°C) for 2 hours or until the lamb is tender.

6 Stir in the yogurt and taste for seasoning. Garnish with cilantro sprigs before serving.

SHEPHERD'S PIE

SERVES 6

1 1/2 lb (750 g) ground lamb	
1 1/2 cups (125 g) sliced mushrooms	
2 carrots, diced	
1 large onion, chopped	
1 garlic clove, crushed	
1/4 cup (30 g) all-purpose flour	
2/3 pint (150 ml) beef stock	
2 tbsp Worcestershire sauce	
salt and black pepper	
3 large potatoes	
about 4 tbsp hot milk	
2 tbls (30 g) butter	

1 Put the ground lamb into a large frying pan and heat gently until the fat runs. Increase the heat and cook, turning and mashing the meat, until it browns. Using a slotted spoon, lift the lamb out of the pan and spoon off the excess fat.

2 Add the mushrooms, carrots, onion, and garlic to the pan, and cook gently, stirring occasionally, for a few minutes until just beginning to soften.

3 Return the lamb to the skillet. Sprinkle in the flour and cook, stirring, for about 1 minute.

4 Add the stock and the Worcestershire sauce, and season with salt and pepper. Bring to a boil, cover, and simmer gently for 30 minutes.

5 Meanwhile, cook the potatoes in boiling salted water for 15–20 minutes until tender. Drain. Add the milk and butter to the potatoes and mash until soft, then season with salt and pepper.

6 Taste the lamb mixture for seasoning. Turn into a baking dish, then spread the potato on top. With a fork, score the potato in a decorative pattern. Cook in a preheated oven at 400°F (200°C) for about 20 minutes until the potato topping is golden and the meat mixture bubbling.

Cook's know-how

To make the pie more special, use half red wine and half beef stock.

LIGHT MOUSSAKA WITH FRESH MINT

SERVES 8

1 1/2 lb (750 g) lean minced lamb	
2 large onions, roughly chopped	
2 garlic cloves, crushed	
2 tsp ground cilantro	
1/4 cup (130 g) all-purpose flour	
2/3 cup (150 ml) red wine	
2 cups (500 ml) tomato puree	
2 tbsp tomato paste	
salt and black pepper	
2 tbsp chopped fresh mint	
2 large eggplants, thinly sliced	
olive oil, for brushing	
1 egg	
1 scant cup (200 g) plain yogurt	
1/2 cup (60 g) grated Parmesan cheese	

12 x 10 x 2 1/2 IN (30 x 25 x 6 CM) BAKING DISH

1 Put the lamb into a large skillet and heat gently until the fat runs. Increase the heat and cook, stirring, until browned. Spoon off excess fat.

2 Add the onions and garlic and cook for 2–3 minutes until softened. Add the ground cilantro and the flour and cook, stirring, for 1 minute.

3 Gradually blend in the wine, tomato puree, and tomato paste, and season with salt and pepper. Bring to a boil, stirring, until thickened. Cover and simmer for 20–30 minutes, then add the fresh mint.

4 Line the rack of a broiler pan with foil and place in the pan. Brush the eggplant slices with olive oil on both sides, and season with salt and pepper. Place the slices on the foil and cook under a hot broiler, 4 in (10 cm) from the heat, for 5–6 minutes until golden brown on both sides.

5 Lightly beat the egg with the yogurt, and season with salt and pepper. Spoon the meat mixture into the greased baking dish and level the top. Arrange the eggplant slices in an overlapping pattern over the meat. Pour the yogurt mixture over and spread to the edges so the eggplant is covered. Sprinkle with the cheese.

6 Bake in a preheated oven at 350°F (180°C) for about 45 minutes or until piping hot and golden.

KIDNEYS TURBIGO

SERVES 4

6 lamb kidneys

4 tbls (60 g) butter

8 oz (250 g) thin chipolata sausages

8 oz (250 g) button mushrooms

12 pearl onions, peeled, with roots left intact

1 tbsp all-purpose flour

1 1/4 cups (300 ml) lamb or chicken stock

3 tbsp medium sherry

2 tsp tomato paste

1 bay leaf

salt and black pepper

2 tbsp chopped parsley to garnish

croutes (page 49) to serve (optional)

1 Prepare the kidneys (page 214). Melt the butter in a large skillet, add the kidneys, and cook, stirring, over a high heat for about 3 minutes until browned.

2 Lift the kidneys out and drain on paper towels. Add the sausages and cook for 3 minutes or until browned. Lift out and drain on paper towels.

3 Add the mushrooms and onions to the pan and cook for 3–5 minutes until browned.

4 Sprinkle in the flour and cook, stirring, for 1 minute. Add the stock, sherry, and tomato paste, and bring to a boil, stirring constantly. Add the bay leaf, and season with salt and pepper.

5 Slice the sausages thickly. Return to the pan with the kidneys, cover and simmer for 20–25 minutes until tender.

6 Spoon the kidney mixture on to a warmed platter, garnish with parsley, and serve with croutes if you like.

SAUSAGES WITH POTATOES & PEPPERS

SERVES 4

3 large potatoes, unpeeled

salt and black pepper

1 red pepper

1 green bell pepper

8 oz (250 g) merguez (spicy sausages), cut into bite-sized pieces, or other sausages

3 garlic cloves, crushed

1/2 tsp ground cumin

1–2 tbsp olive oil, more if needed

chopped fresh cilantro to garnish

1 Put the potatoes into a large saucepan of boiling salted water and cook for 10 minutes. Drain and leave to cool.

2 Put the peppers under a hot broiler, 4 in (10 cm) from the heat, and broil, turning as needed, for 10–12 minutes until charred and blistered. Put the peppers into a plastic bag, seal, and leave to cool.

3 Cut the peppers lengthwise into strips, removing and discarding the skins, cores, and seeds. Pat the peppers dry.

4 Cut the potatoes into wedges and put into a casserole with the peppers and sausages. Stir in the garlic, cumin, and 1 tbsp oil, and season with salt and pepper. Cook in a preheated oven at 375°F (190°C), turning occasionally, for 45 minutes or until the potatoes are tender and the sausages cooked through, adding a little more oil if the potatoes look dry.

5 Remove the casserole from the oven, and spoon off any excess fat. Garnish with cilantro before serving.

BONED LOIN OF PORK WITH APRICOT STUFFING

Succulent boned loin of pork, with an apricot stuffing flavored with lemon juice and lemon thyme, is served here with a white wine gravy. The crackling is cooked separately, in the top half of the oven, to ensure that it is deliciously crisp.

SERVES 8

3 lb (1.5 kg) boned loin of pork, skin removed and scored at ¹/₂-in (1-cm) intervals

sunflower oil for brushing

APRICOT STUFFING

2 tbls (30 g) butter

1 small onion, finely chopped

¹/₂ cup (90 g) fresh whole wheat bread crumbs

¹/₂ cup (90 g) coarsely chopped dried apricots

1 tbsp chopped parsley

1 tbsp lemon juice

2 tsp chopped fresh lemon thyme

1 egg, beaten

salt and black pepper

GRAVY

1 tbsp all-purpose flour

²/₃ cup (150 ml) chicken stock

²/₃ cup (150 ml) dry white wine

1 Make the stuffing: melt the butter in a saucepan and cook the onion gently until soft.

2 Remove from the heat and add the bread crumbs, apricots, parsley, lemon juice, lemon thyme, and egg. Season with salt and pepper, mix well, and leave until cold.

3 Brush the scored side of the pork skin with a little oil, and sprinkle generously with salt and pepper. Place the skin on a rack in a roasting pan.

4 Remove as much fat as possible from the pork, expecially on the top where the skin has been removed. Season the meat well, then stuff and roll (see box, below right).

5 Place the pork skin in the top of a preheated oven at 350°F (180°C). Put the pork into another roasting pan, brush with oil, and season generously. Insert a meat thermometer, if using, into the middle of the loin, and cook the pork in the oven for 2 hours or until the thermometer registers 175°F (80°C).

6 Transfer the pork to a carving board, cover with foil, and leave to stand for 10 minutes. If the crackling is not really crisp, increase the oven temperature to 400°F (200°C) and let it continue to cook while making the gravy.

7 Put the roasting pan on the stovetop and spoon off all but 1 tbsp of the fat. Sprinkle in the flour, and cook, stirring to dissolve any sediment from the bottom of the pan, for 1 minute. Pour in the stock and wine, and bring to a boil, stirring constantly. Simmer for 3 minutes. Season to taste and strain into a gravy boat. Serve with the pork.

Stuffing and rolling a loin of pork

Open out the loin of pork and spread the stuffing over the meat.

Roll the pork around the stuffing and tie at intervals with kitchen string, or use skewers.

SAUCES FOR PORK

APRICOT SAUCE

Melt 2 tbls (30 g) butter, and cook 1 thinly sliced small onion until soft. Add ²/₃ cup (125 g) chopped dried apricots, ²/₃ cup (125 g) each chicken stock and dry white wine, and ¹/₄ tsp ground cinnamon. Season with salt and pepper, and simmer for about 20 minutes until pulpy.

APPLESAUCE

Peel, core, and slice 2 large cooking apples and put into a saucepan with the finely grated zest of 1 lemon and 2–3 tbsp water. Cover tightly and cook gently for about 10 minutes until soft. Stir in 2 tbls (30 g) sugar. Beat the sauce until smooth, then stir in 1 tbls (15 g) butter if you like.

SWEET & SOUR SAUCE

Finely slice 1 onion, 1 leek, and 2 celery stalks. Cut 2 carrots into matchstick-thin strips. Heat 2 tbsp sunflower oil in a pan and cook the vegetables for 3 minutes or until softened. Blend 2 tbsp ketchup, 1 tbsp soy sauce, 1 tbsp white wine vinegar, 4 tsp cornstarch, and 2 tsp sugar, then blend in 1 ¹/₄ cups (300 ml) water. Add to the pan and bring to a boil, stirring until thickened.

MARINATED LOIN OF PORK WITH PINEAPPLE

SERVES 8

3 lb (1.5 kg) boneless loin of pork, skin removed

broiled pineapple rings and parsley sprigs to serve

MARINADE

1 cup (250 ml) pineapple juice

2 tbsp maple syrup

2 tbsp soy sauce

2 garlic cloves, crushed

2 tbsp chopped fresh thyme

1 tsp ground cilantro

1 Make the marinade: in a large nonmetallic bowl, combine the pineapple juice, maple syrup, soy sauce, garlic, thyme, and cilantro. Add the pork, cover, and marinate in the refrigerator, turning occasionally, for 8 hours.

2 Remove the pork from the marinade, reserving the marinade. Put the pork flat, fat-side up, in a small roasting pan. Insert a meat thermometer, if using, into the middle of the pork. Cover loosely with foil and cook in a preheated oven at 425°F (220°C) for 1 hour.

3 Remove the foil and pour the marinade over the pork. Return to the oven and cook for 20–30 minutes or until the marinade has darkened and the juices run clear when the meat is pierced with a fine skewer. The meat thermometer should register 175°F (80°C).

4 Transfer the pork to a carving board, cover with foil, and leave to stand for 10 minutes. Strain the cooking juices and remove the fat (see box, below), then reheat. Serve the pork sliced, with the juices poured over, garnished with pineapple and parsley.

Removing the fat

Skim the layer of fat from the surface of the juices, using a skimmer or spoon.

ROAST FRESH HAM

SERVES 6–8

4 lb (2 kg) leg of pork, skin removed and scored at 1/2-in (1-cm) intervals

sunflower oil for brushing

salt and black pepper

1 carrot, thickly sliced

1 onion, thickly sliced

1 tbsp all-purpose flour

1 1/4 cups (300 ml) chicken stock

applesauce to serve (page 285)

1 Brush the scored side of the pork skin with a little oil, and sprinkle generously with salt and black pepper. Place on a rack in a small roasting pan.

2 Remove as much fat as possible from the pork, especially on top where the skin has been removed. Put the pork into another roasting pan, and arrange the carrot and onion around it. Brush the meat with a little oil, season well, and insert a meat thermometer, if using, into the middle of the pork.

3 Put both roasting pans in a preheated oven at 350°F (180°C), with the pork skin at the top.

4 Roast for 2 1/2 hours or until the thermometer registers 175°F (80°C). Transfer the pork to a carving board, cover with foil, and leave to stand for 10 minutes. If the crackling is not really crisp, increase the oven temperature to 400°F (200°C) and let it continue to cook while making the gravy.

5 Put the roasting pan on the stovetop. Remove the carrot and onion and spoon off all but 1 tbsp of the fat from the pan.

6 Add the flour and cook, stirring to dissolve any sediment from the bottom of the tin, for 1 minute. Pour in the stock and bring to a boil. Simmer for 3 minutes, then season, and strain into a gravy boat. Serve the pork with the gravy and applesauce.

Cook's know-how

The high oven temperature needed for crisp crackling can make meat tough and dry. Removing the skin and cooking it separately, above the pork, avoids this problem.

MADEIRA PORK WITH PAPRIKA

SERVES 4

2 tbls (30 g) butter

2 tbsp sunflower oil

1½ lb (750 g) pork, trimmed and cut diagonally into ½-in (1-cm) slices

1 onion, chopped

1 large red bell pepper, cored, seeded, and cut into strips

1 tbsp paprika

1 tbsp all-purpose flour

1¼ cups (300 ml) chicken stock

5 tbls (75 ml) Madeira

6 oz (175 g) button mushrooms

1 tsp tomato paste

⅔ cup (150 ml) light cream

salt and black pepper

1 Melt the butter with the oil in a large skillet. When the butter is foaming, add the pork slices, in batches if necessary, and cook over a high heat for about 3 minutes until just beginning to brown. Lift out with a slotted spoon and drain on paper towels.

2 Add the onion and red pepper and cook, stirring, for 2 minutes. Add the paprika and flour, and cook, stirring, for 1 minute. Remove the pan from the heat and blend in the stock. Return to the heat and add the Madeira, mushrooms, and tomato paste. Simmer for 2–3 minutes.

3 Return the pork to the pan and season with salt and pepper. Cover and simmer very gently for 20 minutes or until the pork is tender. Stir in the cream, taste for seasoning, and heat through gently. Serve hot.

Healthy option

The cream makes the sauce both look and taste rich, but it can be omitted and the sauce will still be good. Pork tenderloin is an excellent cut of meat to use if you are trying to cut down on fat because it is very lean and yet tender and succulent.

BACON-WRAPPED PORK IN VERMOUTH SAUCE

SERVES 6

2 pork tenderloins, about 12 oz (375 g) each, trimmed

2 tbsp Dijon mustard

salt and black pepper

12 oz (12 oz) bacon slices

VERMOUTH SAUCE

2 tbls (30 g) butter

1 tbsp olive oil

1 shallot, finely chopped

1 tbsp all-purpose flour

1 scant cup (200 ml) chicken stock

6 tbls (90 ml) dry vermouth

1½ cup (125 g) sliced crimini mushrooms

1 Spread the pork tenderloins with the mustard and season with salt and pepper. Stretch the bacon rashers with the back of a knife and wrap around the fillets (see box, right).

2 Place the tenderloins in a roasting pan and cook in a preheated oven at 425°F (220°C), turning them halfway through cooking, for 30–35 minutes until the juices from the pork run clear and the bacon is crisp and golden.

3 Meanwhile, make the sauce: melt the butter with the oil in a small pan. When the butter is foaming, add the shallot, and cook gently until softened.

4 Add the flour and cook, stirring, for 1 minute. Gradually blend in the stock and vermouth. Bring to a boil, add the mushrooms, and simmer for 15 minutes.

5 Transfer the pork to a warmed plate. Spoon off the fat from the roasting pan and strain the juices into the sauce. Heat through and taste for seasoning. Serve with the pork.

Wrapping tenderloins

Overlap half of the bacon slices on a work surface. Lay 1 tenderloin across the bacon and braid the bacon around the meat. Secure with a fine skewer. Repeat with the second tenderloin.

BROILED PORK CHOPS WITH MANGO SAUCE

SERVES 4

4 pork loin chops, on the bone

sunflower oil for brushing

salt and black pepper

1 ripe mango

flat-leaf parsley to garnish

MANGO SAUCE

1 ripe mango

2/3 cup (150 ml) chicken stock

1 tbsp mango chutney

1 Cut through the fat at regular intervals on the edge of each pork chop (this will help prevent the chops from curling up during cooking).

2 Brush the chops on each side with oil and sprinkle with black pepper. Put under a hot broiler, 4 in (10 cm) from the heat, and broil for 6 minutes on each side or until cooked through (timing depends on size of chops).

3 Meanwhile, make the mango sauce: peel, seed, and cube the mango (page 466), then puree in a food processor until smooth.

4 Put into a small saucepan with the stock, mango chutney, and salt and pepper. Bring to a boil and simmer for about 3 minutes until heated through. Taste for seasoning.

5 Peel the remaining mango and cut it into 2 pieces lengthwise, slightly off-center to miss the seed. Cut the flesh from around the seed. Slice the flesh into thin strips

6 Arrange the mango strips on the chops, garnish with flat-leaf parsley, and serve with the mango sauce.

PORK WITH CHILI & COCONUT

SERVES 6

1 1/2 lb (750 g) pork tenderloin, trimmed and cut into 1/4 in (5 mm) strips

2 tbsp sunflower oil

8 green onions, cut into 1 in (2.5 cm) pieces

1 large red bell pepper, halved, seeded, and cut into thin strips

14 oz (400 g) canned crushed tomatoes

2 oz (60 g) creamed coconut, coarsely chopped

4 tbsp water

2 tbsp chopped fresh cilantro

1 tbsp lemon juice

salt and black pepper

cilantro sprigs to garnish

SPICE MIX

1-in (2.5-cm) piece of fresh root ginger, peeled and grated

2 fresh red chilies, halved, seeded, and finely chopped

1 garlic clove, crushed

1 tbsp mild curry powder

1 Make the spice mix: in a bowl, combine the ginger, chilies, garlic, and curry powder, and season with salt and pepper. Turn the pork in the mix, cover, and leave to marinate in the refrigerator for 2 hours.

2 Heat a wok or large skillet, add the oil, and heat until hot. Add the strips of pork in batches, and stir-fry over a high heat for 5 minutes or until browned all over.

3 Add the green onions and stir-fry for 1 minute. Add the red pepper and stir-fry for 1 minute, then add the tomatoes, coconut, and measured water. Bring to a boil, cover, and simmer very gently for 15 minutes or until the pork is tender.

4 Add the chopped cilantro, lemon juice, and salt and pepper to taste. Garnish with cilantro sprigs before serving.

PORK CHOPS WITH SPINACH & MUSHROOM STUFFING

Tender pork loin chops are topped with a spinach and crimini mushroom stuffing mixture, and finished off under the broiler with Gruyère cheese. A wedge of the stuffing accompanies each chop as a delicious extra.

SERVES 6

6 lean pork loin chops, on the bone

olive oil for brushing

SPINACH AND MUSHROOM STUFFING

1 tbsp olive oil

1 large onion, chopped

1½ cups (150 g) roughly chopped crimini mushrooms

8 oz (250 g) shredded baby spinach leaves

2 cups (90 g) fresh bread crumbs

salt and black pepper

about 3 oz (90 g) Gruyère cheese, cut into 6 thin slices

1 Make the stuffing: heat the oil in a large skillet, add the onion, cover, and cook gently for about 15 minutes or until soft.

2 Uncover the pan, increase the heat, and add the mushrooms. Stir-fry for 2–3 minutes, then add the spinach and stir-fry until it has just wilted. Add the bread crumbs, season with salt and pepper, and stir well. Leave to cool.

3 Brush the chops on each side with oil, and season well. Put under a hot broiler, 4 in (10 cm) from the heat, and broil for 7–8 minutes each side or until cooked through and golden brown.

4 Spoon 1 tablespoon of the stuffing mixture on top of each chop, and top with a slice of cheese. Broil for 3–4 minutes until the cheese has melted.

5 Meanwhile, heat a little oil in a small nonstick skillet. Put the remaining stuffing into the pan, then press down and level with a wooden spoon so the stuffing forms a thick pancake.

6 Fry the stuffing for about 5 minutes until the underside is brown and crisp. Transfer the pan to the broil for 2–3 minutes to brown the top. Turn upside down onto a plate, and slice into 6 wedges. Serve a wedge of stuffing with each chop.

PORK CHOPS WITH ORANGES

SERVES 6

6 boneless pork loin chops

3 tbsp coarse mustard

2/3 cup (125 g) light brown sugar

3 small oranges

6 tbls (90 ml) orange juice

salt and black pepper

1 Spread both sides of each pork chop with the mustard, and sprinkle one side with half of the brown sugar. Arrange the chops, sugared-side down, in a single layer in a shallow baking dish.

2 With a sharp knife, carefully peel the oranges, removing all the pith. Cut the oranges into thin slices.

3 Cover the chops with the orange slices. Pour the orange juice over the top, season with salt and pepper, and sprinkle with the remaining sugar.

4 Cook, uncovered, in a preheated oven at 400°F (200°C) for about 35 minutes, basting the chops occasionally, until cooked through. Serve hot.

PORK CHOPS WITH MIXED PEPPERCORNS

SERVES 4

4 lean toploin chops

salt

3–4 tbsp mixed or black peppercorns

2 tbls (30 g) butter

1 1/2 cups (350 ml) dry white wine

1 1/2 cups (350 ml) chicken stock

3/4 cup (175 ml) heavy cream

1 Season the chops on each side with salt. Coarsely crush the peppercorns, spread them on a plate, and press the steaks into them to encrust the surface of the meat. Turn the steaks over and repeat on the other side. Cover and set aside for about 30 minutes, if you have the time.

2 Melt the butter in a large skillet, add the chops, and cook over a medium heat for 5 minutes on each side or until the meat is just cooked through but still juicy. Lift the steaks out, and keep hot.

3 Pour the wine into the pan and boil until it has reduced by half, stirring to mix in the peppercorns and the sediment from the bottom of the pan.

4 Pour in the stock and cook for 5 minutes. Strain the sauce to remove the peppercorns, then return to the pan and boil for 3 minutes or until the sauce is reduced but not too thick.

5 Add the cream and cook, stirring, over a high heat until the sauce is reduced and thickened. Return the pork chops to the pan, heat through, and serve at once.

SWEET & SOUR CHINESE SPARERIBS

SERVES 4

2 1/2 lb (1.25 kg) pork spareribs

salt and black pepper

green onions to garnish (optional)

SWEET & SOUR SAUCE

1-in (2.5-cm) piece of fresh gingerroot, peeled and grated

2 garlic cloves, crushed

2 tbsp soy sauce

2 tbsp rice wine or dry sherry

2 tbsp hoisin sauce

2 tbsp tomato paste

1 tbsp sesame oil (optional)

1 tbsp sugar

1 Lay the ribs in 1 layer in a roasting tin, season with salt and pepper, and cook in a preheated oven at 275°F (140°C) for 1 1/2 hours.

2 Make the sauce: combine all the ingredients in a small pan and heat gently.

3 Spoon the sauce over the ribs, turning them to coat. Increase the oven temperature to 350°F (180°C), and cook for 25–30 minutes. Serve hot, garnished with green onions if you like.

SPICY SPARERIBS

Add 1 tbsp brown sugar, 1/2 tsp grated nutmeg, and 1/4 tsp each ground cloves and ground cinnamon to the sauce.

Cook's know-how

Spareribs are excellent for a barbecue, but they are best partially cooked first or they will burn on the outside before the meat is properly cooked inside. Cook them in the oven as in step 1 and coat with the sweet and sour sauce, then cook over hot charcoal for 15 minutes on each side.

PORK IN RED WINE

SERVES 4

1 1/2 lb (750 g) boneless pork blade, cut into 1 1/2-in (3.5-cm) cubes

6 tbls (90 ml) olive oil

1 large onion, chopped

3 garlic cloves, crushed

1 cup (250 ml) beef or chicken stock

1 cup (250 ml) dry red wine

1/2 tsp cumin seeds

MARINADE

1 cup (250 ml) red wine

2 tbsp crushed cilantro seeds

1/2 tsp ground cinnamon

salt and black pepper

1 Make the marinade: in a large bowl, combine the red wine, coriander seeds, and cinnamon, and season with salt and pepper. Toss the pork in the marinade, cover, and leave to marinate in the refrigerator overnight.

2 Remove the pork from the marinade, reserving the marinade. Pat the pork dry with paper towels.

3 Heat the oil in a skillet, add the onion and garlic, and cook gently, stirring occasionally, for a few minutes until soft but not colored.

4 Add the pork and cook over a medium to high heat for 5 minutes or until golden brown all over. Discard any excess fat. Pour in the reserved marinade, the stock, and wine, and bring to a boil. Simmer for 1 hour or until the meat is tender.

5 Remove the meat with a slotted spoon and transfer to a shallow baking dish into which it just fits in 1 layer. Skim any fat from the sauce, then strain to remove the coriander seeds. Pour the sauce over the meat, sprinkle with cumin seeds and salt, and cook in a preheated oven at 400°F (200°C) for 40 minutes or until crisp and browned.

Healthy option

If you cook the pork in a nonstick skillet, you can reduce the amount of oil to 1–2 tbsp.

HEARTY PORK CASSEROLE

SERVES 8

2 tbsp sunflower oil

3 lb (1.5 kg) shoulder of pork, trimmed and cut into 1 1/2-in (3.5-cm) cubes

1/3 cup (40 g) all-purpose flour

2 cups (450 ml) chicken stock

4 tbsp white wine vinegar

3 tbsp honey

2 tbsp soy sauce

8 oz (250 g) large mushrooms, quartered

250 g (8 oz) pitted prunes

salt and black pepper

chopped parsley to garnish

1 Heat the oil in a large flameproof casserole. Add the pork in batches and cook over a medium to high heat for 5 minutes or until golden brown all over.

2 Return all of the meat to the casserole, sprinkle in the flour, and cook, stirring, for 1 minute.

3 Stir in the chicken stock, white wine vinegar, honey, and soy sauce, season with of salt and pepper, and bring to a boil. Cover and cook in a preheated oven at 325°F (160°C) for 2 hours.

4 Stir the mushrooms and prunes into the casserole and cook for 1 hour or until the pork is tender. Taste for seasoning and garnish with parsley before serving.

BOSTON PORK & BEAN CASSEROLE

Add 2 tbsp tomato paste with the stock and substitute 14 oz (400 g) canned great northern beans for the mushrooms and prunes.

Healthy option

Use lean pork fillet (tenderloin) instead of shoulder, which can be fatty, and reduce the cooking time to 50–60 minutes in the oven in step 3.

DANISH MEATBALLS

SERVES 4–6

I lb (500 g) ground pork
I small onion, very finely chopped
1/4 cup (30 g) all-purpose flour, plus extra for coating
I tsp chopped fresh thyme
1/4 tsp paprika
I egg, beaten
salt and black pepper
a little milk
2 tbls (30 g) butter
I tbsp sunflower oil
Plain yogurt or sour cream to serve
chopped fresh thyme to garnish

TOMATO SAUCE

2 tbls (30 g) butter
1/4 cup (30 g) all-purpose flour
2 cups (500 ml) chicken stock
14 oz (400 g) canned crushed tomatoes
I tbsp tomato paste
I garlic clove, crushed
I bay leaf

1 Mix the pork, onion, flour, thyme, paprika, and egg. Season, and add enough milk to give a soft, not sticky, texture.

2 Shape the mixture into 20 ovals, using 2 tablespoons or your hands. Roll lightly in flour, then chill in the refrigerator.

3 Make the tomato sauce: melt the butter in a pan, sprinkle in the flour, and cook, stirring, for 1 minute.

4 Blend in the stock, then add the tomatoes, tomato paste, garlic, and bay leaf, and season with salt and pepper. Bring to a boil, stirring until thickened. Cover and simmer for 20–25 minutes.

5 Meanwhile, melt the butter with the oil in a flameproof casserole. Cook the meatballs in batches, for 5 minutes or until browned all over. Lift out and drain on paper towels.

6 Pour the fat out of the casserole. Return the meatballs, add the sauce, and bring to a boil. Cover and cook in a preheated oven at 350°F (180°C) for 30 minutes. Spoon over a little yogurt or sour cream and garnish with thyme. Serve hot.

PASTICCIO

SERVES 6

I tbsp sunflower oil
I lb (500 g) ground pork or beef
2 onions, chopped
3 garlic cloves, crushed
14 oz (400 g) canned crushed tomatoes
6 tbls (90 g) tomato paste
6 tbls (90 ml) red wine
2 bay leaves
I tsp sugar
I tsp dried oregano
1/2 tsp ground cinnamon (optional)
2 cups (250 g) elbow macaroni
salt and black pepper

CHEESE SAUCE

2 tbls (30 g) butter
1/4 cup (30 g) all-purpose flour
1 1/4 cups (300 ml) milk
1 1/2 cups(175 g) grated sharp Cheddar cheese
I egg yolk
I tsp Dijon mustard

1 Heat the sunflower oil in a large skillet, add the meat, onions, and garlic, and cook over a medium heat for 5 minutes or until lightly browned.

2 Add the tomatoes, tomato paste, and wine. Bring to a boil and simmer for 15 minutes.

3 Add the bay leaves, sugar, oregano, and cinnamon (if using), and season with salt and pepper. Simmer gently for about 10 minutes or until the sauce is thickened.

4 Meanwhile, cook the macaroni in boiling salted water for 8–10 minutes until just tender. Drain and set aside.

5 Make the cheese sauce: melt the butter in a saucepan, sprinkle in the flour, and cook, stirring, for 1 minute. Remove from the heat and gradually blend in the milk. Bring to a boil, stirring constantly, until the mixture thickens. Simmer for 2–3 minutes. Remove from the heat and stir in the cheese, egg yolk, and mustard, and season with salt and pepper.

6 Spoon half of the meat mixture into an baking dish and add half of the macaroni. Cover with the remaining meat mixture, then top with the remaining macaroni and the cheese sauce.

7 Bake the pasticcio in a preheated oven at 350°F (180°C) for 40 minutes or until the topping is golden.

MUSTARD-GLAZED HAM

Ham tastes best when it is cooked on the bone, especially if it is home-baked. Here, ham slowly steam-roasts in its own juices, spiked with hard cider, and it is coated with a tangy glaze. Watercress and orange slices are the perfect finishing touch.

SERVES 16–20

8–10 lb (4–5 kg) smoked ham

1 1/3 cup (400 ml) hard cider or apple juice

3 tbsp English mustard

1/2 cup (90 g) light brown sugar

LEMON MUSTARD SAUCE

4 tbsp olive oil

juice of 1 lemon

1 tbsp sugar

2 tsp coarse mustard

salt and black pepper

2/3 cup (150 ml) sour cream

1 Put the ham into a large container, cover with cold water, and leave to soak for at least 12 hours.

2 Drain and rinse the ham. Arrange 2 pieces of foil, long enough to cover the ham, across a large roasting pan.

3 Pour the cider into the foil. Stand a wire rack on the foil and stand the ham on the rack. Insert a meat thermometer, if using, into the thickest part of the meat.

4 Wrap the foil loosely over the ham, leaving plenty of space for air to circulate. Place the ham just below the middle of a preheated oven and cook at 325°F (160°C) for 20 minutes per pound (500 g). The meat thermometer should register 170°F (75°C). Remove the ham from the oven and leave to cool for a few minutes.

5 Increase the oven temperature to 450°F (230°C). Transfer the ham to a carving board, drain the cooking juices from the foil, and discard. Glaze the ham with the mustard and sugar (see box, right).

6 Return the ham to the rack in the roasting pan. Cover any lean parts with foil, return to the oven, and cook, turning the roasting pan if necessary, for 15–20 minutes until the glaze is golden brown all over.

7 Meanwhile, make the lemon mustard sauce: put the olive oil, lemon juice, sugar, and mustard into a screw-top jar, season with salt and pepper, and shake vigorously to mix the ingredients together.

8 Put the sour cream into a bowl and stir in the lemon and mustard mixture. Taste for seasoning and leave to chill in the refrigerator until needed.

9 Carve the ham into slices and serve either warm or cold, with the lemon mustard sauce.

Glazing ham

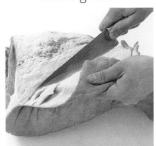

Cut away the skin with a sharp knife, leaving behind a thin layer of fat. Discard the skin.

Score the fat all over in a diamond pattern, so the glaze penetrates the fat.

Spread a generous layer of mustard over the fat, using a metal spatula or your hands.

Press the brown sugar onto the layer of mustard, making sure it is evenly coated all over.

BOSTON BAKED BEANS

SERVES 6–8

2 cups (375 g) dried great northern beans

¼ cup (60 g) dark brown sugar

2 tbsp tomato paste

2 tsp molasses

2 tsp maple syrup

2 tsp dry mustard

2 tsp salt

black pepper

8 oz (250 g) slab of bacon, cut into 1-in (2.5-cm) cubes

3 onions, quartered

2½ cups (600 ml) water

1 Put the beans into a large bowl, cover with plenty of cold water, and leave to soak overnight.

2 Drain the beans, and rinse under cold running water. Put them in a saucepan, cover with cold water, and bring to a boil. Boil rapidly for 10 minutes, then simmer for 30 minutes. Drain and set aside.

3 Put the sugar, tomato paste, molasses, maple syrup, and mustard into a large baking dish. Season with salt and pepper and heat gently, stirring constantly.

4 Add the bacon and onions to the casserole with the drained beans and measured water. Bring to a boil, cover tightly, and cook in a preheated oven at 275°F (140°C), stirring occasionally, for 4½–5 hours. Taste for seasoning before serving.

Healthy option

Boston baked beans traditionally contain pork side or bacon, which makes the dish quite high in fat. Without the pork or bacon, the beans make a tasty vegetarian main course that is much lower in fat, and if you serve it with crusty bread and a leafy green salad it makes a well-balanced, nutritious meal.

FARMER'S BACON BAKE

SERVES 6–8

1½ lb (750 g) slab of lean bacon

a few parsley stalks

6 black peppercorns

1 bay leaf

4 potatoes, cut into large chunks

4 carrots, thickly sliced

4 celery stalks, thickly sliced

chopped parsley to garnish

CHEESE SAUCE

3 tbls (45 g) butter

⅓ cup (45 g) all-pupose flour

1 scant cup (200 ml) milk

¾ cup (90 g) grated sharp Cheddar cheese

salt and black pepper

1 Put the bacon into a large pan, cover with cold water, and bring to a boil. Drain, rinse, and cover with fresh cold water. Add the parsley stalks, peppercorns, and bay leaf, and bring to a boil. Cover and simmer very gently for 45 minutes.

2 Add the potatoes, carrots, and celery and bring back to a boil. Cover and simmer very gently for 20 minutes or until the meat and vegetables are tender. Drain, reserving the cooking liquid, and allow the bacon to cool slightly.

3 Remove the rind and fat from the bacon, cut the meat into bite-sized pieces, and place in a shallow baking dish with the vegetables. Keep hot.

4 Make the cheese sauce: melt the butter in a saucepan, sprinkle in the flour, and cook, stirring, for 1 minute. Remove from the heat and gradually blend in the milk and 1 cup (250 ml) of the reserved cooking liquid. Bring to a boil, stirring constantly until the mixture thickens. Simmer for 2–3 minutes. Add three-quarters of the cheese, and season with salt and pepper.

5 Pour the sauce over the meat and vegetables and sprinkle with the remaining cheese. Bake in a preheated oven at 350°F (180°C) for 30 minutes or until the cheese topping is bubbling. Garnish with chopped parsley before serving.

SAUSAGE CASSOULET

Cassoulet is a hearty dish from Languedoc in the southwest of France.
This is a simple and satisfying version. The types of meat used in more traditional recipes
may include duck, goose, or lamb.

SERVES 8

2 cups (375 g) dried great northern beans

2 tbsp olive oil

1 lb (500 g) coarse pork sausages, such as Toulouse

8 oz (250 g) piece of smoked slab bacon, cut into strips

2 large onions, sliced

8 oz (250 g) piece of garlic sausage, cut into 1-in (2.5-cm) chunks

28 oz (800 g) canned crushed tomatoes

1¼ cup (300 ml) chicken stock

⅔ cup (150 ml) dry white wine

2 tbsp tomato paste

2 garlic cloves, crushed

1 bouquet garni

salt and black pepper

2–3 cups (125–175 g) fresh white bread crumbs

chopped parsley to garnish

1 Put the great northern beans into a large bowl, cover with plenty of cold water, and leave to soak overnight.

2 Drain the beans, and rinse under cold running water. Put the beans into a saucepan, cover with fresh cold water, and bring to a boil. Boil rapidly for 10 minutes, then simmer for 30 minutes or until just tender. Drain.

3 Heat the olive oil in a large flameproof casserole, add the sausages and bacon, and cook for 5 minutes or until browned all over. Lift out and drain on paper towels. Thickly slice the sausages.

4 Pour off all but 1 tbsp of the fat from the casserole. Add the onions and cook gently, stirring occasionally, for a few minutes until soft but not colored.

5 Return the bacon and sausages to the casserole, add the beans, the garlic sausage, tomatoes, stock, wine, tomato paste, garlic, and bouquet garni. Season with salt and pepper and bring to a boil.

6 Cover and cook in a preheated oven at 325°F (160°C) for 1 hour, then sprinkle the bread crumbs over the top and continue cooking, uncovered, for 30 minutes or until the topping is golden brown. Garnish with chopped parsley before serving.

SAUSAGE BAKE

SERVES 6

1 tbsp sunflower oil

2 lb (1 kg) coarse-cut pork sausages

4 trimmed leeks, thickly sliced

3 large potatoes, cut into ¼-in (5-mm) slices

½ cup (90 g) red lentils

salt and black pepper

2 bay leaves

2 cloves

1 garlic clove, crushed

3¾ cups (900 ml) chicken stock

chopped parsley to garnish

1 Heat the oil in a large flameproof casserole and brown the sausages. Lift out, then cut into thick slices.

2 Layer the leeks, potatoes, sausages, and lentils in the casserole, adding seasoning and placing the bay leaves, cloves, and garlic among the layers. Top with a layer of potatoes.

3 Pour in the stock and bring to a boil. Cover tightly and cook in a preheated oven at 325°F (160°C) for 2½ hours, checking the liquid level occasionally.

4 Remove the lid, increase the oven temperature to 400°F (200°C), and cook for 20–25 minutes until the potato is browned. Garnish with parsley and serve hot.

TOAD-IN-THE-HOLE WITH ONION SAUCE

SERVES 4

14 oz (400 g) bulk pork sausage

1 leek, finely chopped

2 tbsp chopped fresh sage or 1 tbsp dried sage

1 tbsp chopped parsley

3 tbsp sunflower oil

3 onions, chopped

2 tbsp all-purpose flour

1 1/4 cups (300 ml) milk

1 cup (250 ml) chicken stock

chopped parsley to garnish

BATTER

1 cup (125 g) self-rising flour

3 eggs, beaten

1 1/4 cups (300 ml) milk

1 tbsp chopped parsley

salt and black pepper

1 Make the batter: sift the flour into a bowl. Make a well in the middle and add the eggs and a little milk. Blend to a smooth paste, then gradually whisk in the remaining milk until the batter has the pouring consistency of heavy cream.

2 Add the chopped parsley, season with salt and pepper, and whisk again.

3 In another bowl, combine the sausage, leek, sage, and parsley, and season with salt and pepper. Shape into 12 balls and set aside.

4 Heat the oil in a saucepan, add the onions, and cook for a few minutes until soft but not colored. Transfer one-third of the onions to 4 small individual baking dishes or 1 large dish. Set aside the remainder.

5 Add the sausage balls to the dishes and bake in a preheated oven at 425°F (220°C) for about 10 minutes until brown.

6 Add the batter mixture, and return at once to the oven. Bake for 20–25 minutes until the batter is risen and golden.

7 Meanwhile, add the all-purpose flour to the onions in the pan and cook, stirring, for 1 minute. Remove from the heat and gradually blend in the milk and stock. Bring to a boil, stirring constantly, and simmer for 2–3 minutes until the mixture thickens. Serve the toad-in-the-hole hot, sprinkled with parsley, with the sauce handed separately.

SAUSAGE & LENTIL CASSEROLE

SERVES 6

1 1/2 cups (300 g) brown or green Puy lentils

2 bay leaves

2 tbsp sunflower oil

2 large onions, chopped

1 large potato, chopped

1 celery stalk, diced

1 carrot, diced

2 ripe tomatoes, diced

2 tbsp all-purpose flour

1 cup (250 ml) chicken or vegetable stock

2–3 tbsp chopped parsley

1 tbsp chopped fresh sage or 1 1/2 tsp dried sage

salt and black pepper

1 lb (500 g) herbed pork sausages

chopped parsley to garnish

1 Put the lentils and bay leaves into a saucepan, cover with water, and bring to a boil. Cover, simmer for 30 minutes or until the lentils are just tender, then drain.

2 Heat the oil in a large saucepan, add the onions, and cook gently, stirring occasionally, until softened.

3 Add the potato, celery, carrot, and tomatoes, and cook for 10 minutes or until the onions are browned and the other vegetables are softened. Using a slotted spoon, lift out the vegetables and set aside.

4 Sprinkle the flour into the pan and cook, stirring, for 1 minute. Remove the pan from the heat and gradually blend in the stock. Bring to a boil, stirring constantly, and simmer for 2–3 minutes until the sauce thickens.

5 Add the lentils to the sauce with the vegetables, parsley, and sage. Season with salt and pepper, mix well, and turn into a large ovenproof casserole.

6 Arrange the sausages on top and cook in a preheated oven at 375°F (190°C) for about 30 minutes until the sausages are browned all over and cooked through. Garnish with chopped parsley before serving.

7
VEGETARIAN
DISHES

UNDER 30 MINUTES

BARBECUE

HALLOUMI & VEGETABLE KEBABS

Cubes of halloumi cheese, cherry tomatoes, baguette slices, and red bell pepper threaded onto skewers, then broiled with a lemon-flavored baste.

SERVES 4 722 calories per serving

Takes 25 minutes · Page 321

RED BEAN & TOMATO CURRY

Rich and spicy: red kidney beans cooked with onion, garlic, chili, ginger, and curry powder, with a dash of cilantro to garnish.

SERVES 4 218 calories per serving

Takes 20 minutes · Page 320

VEGETABLE STIR-FRY WITH TOFU

Tofu is marinated in soy sauce and sherry, then stir-fried with carrots, ginger, mushrooms, bean sprouts, endove, and green onions.

SERVES 4 335 calories per serving

Takes 15 minutes, plus marinating · Page 322

30–60 MINUTES

COUSCOUS WITH ROASTED PEPPERS

Tasty and simple to make: couscous with chick peas, zucchini, carrots, and spices. Topped with peppers and almonds.

SERVES 4–6 418–279 calories per serving

Takes 45 minutes · Page 315

HIGH FIBER

FELAFEL WITH SESAME YOGURT SAUCE

Chick pea, green onion, herb, and spice patties, cooked until golden. Served with a creamy sauce.

SERVES 6 326 calories per serving

Takes 20 minutes, plus standing · Page 321

SPINACH & RICOTTA TRIANGLES

Light and crispy: spinach combined with ricotta cheese, onion, and nutmeg, and wrapped in strips of phyllo pastry until golden.

MAKES 4 307 calories per serving

Takes 40 minutes · Page 317

LOW FAT

MEXICAN CHILI WITH TOFU

Bite-sized pieces of tofu cooked with red kidney beans and tomato sauce, seasoned with garlic, chili, paprika, cumin, and oregano.

SERVES 6 257 calories per serving

Takes 35 minutes · Page 322

CARROT ROULADE

Fresh and creamy: carrot mixed with garlic, red bell pepper, tomatoes, and eggs, then baked and rolled around a cheese and cucumber filling.

SERVES 6–8 483–363 calories per serving

Takes 30 minutes, plus chilling · Page 327

FAMILY CHOICE

VEGETARIAN BURGERS

Lima beans with mushrooms, leeks, garlic, and chopped fresh chili. Shaped into burgers and pan-fried. Served with crunchy dressed lettuce.

SERVES 6 134 calories per serving

Takes 30 minutes, plus chilling · Page 323

30–60 MINUTES

HIGH FIBER

MIXED BEAN BAKE
Aduki and lima beans simmered with mushrooms, tomatoes, and parsley. Topped with leeks and a cheese sauce and baked until golden.

SERVES 6 376 calories per serving
Takes 60 minutes   Page 305

SPINACH ROULADE
Spinach, butter, and eggs, are combined and baked, then sprinkled with Parmesan and rolled with a sour cream and mushroom filling.

SERVES 6–8 250–187 calories per serving
Takes 30 minutes, plus chilling   Page 327

OVER 60 MINUTES

ITALIAN CLASSIC

EGGPLANT PARMIGIANA
Rich and tangy: eggplant slices layered with garlic- and basil-flavored tomato sauce, and topped with mozzarella and Parmesan cheeses.

SERVES 6 516 calories per serving
Takes 1¼ hours, plus standing   Page 308

ITALIAN STUFFED ZUCCHINI
Baked zucchini with a delicious tomato and basil stuffing and topped with capers and Fontina cheese.

SERVES 4 437 calories per serving
Takes 50 minutes   Page 310

RED LENTIL & COCONUT CURRY
Lentils cooked with coconut and seasoned with ginger, chili, garlic, and turmeric. Topped with mustard seeds.

SERVES 6 481 calories per serving
Takes 40 minutes   Page 320

BARBECUE

POLENTA WITH GRILLED VEGETABLES
Barbecued strips of Italian polenta served with marinated and barbecued zucchini, fennel, tomatoes, and red onion.

SERVES 6 319 calories per serving
Takes 45 minutes, plus marinating   Page 314

ROAST VEGETABLE NIÇOISE
Rich and aromatic: black olives, zucchini, tomatoes, red onion, and garlic, sprinkled with capers, herbes de Provence, and baked.

SERVES 4 237 calories per serving
Takes 60 minute   Page 304

Garnished with shredded fresh basil. It is delicious served hot or cold with croûtons or toasted baguette.

GLAMORGAN "SAUSAGES"
Cheddar and goat cheeses combined with fresh bread crumbs, leek, walnuts, sage, lemon zest, mustard, and eggs, and fried until golden.

SERVES 4 526 calories per serving
Takes 35 minutes, plus chilling   Page 323

OVER 60 MINUTES

MUSHROOM GOUGERE

Savory choux pastry with a filling of mixed mushrooms, flavored with tarragon, and baked until golden brown.

SERVES 4 558 calories per serving

Takes 1 1/2 hours, plus chilling   Page 316

SPINACH GNOCCHI WITH TOMATO SAUCE

Dumplings of spinach, ricotta and Parmesan cheeses, served with a smooth tomato sauce.

SERVES 4 738 calories per serving

Takes 1 1/4 hours, plus chilling   Page 314

ECONOMICAL

COUNTRY VEGETABLE PIES

Carrots and parsnips baked with onion, garlic, and parsley sauce. Topped with mashed potato to make a nourishing meal.

SERVES 6 428 calories per serving

Takes 1 1/4 hours   Page 305

HIGH FIBER

VEGETABLE & BARLEY CASSEROLE

Pearl barley, shallots, carrots, parsnips, zucchini, snow peas, and cauliflower are cooked with flavorsome stock, and then topped with dumplings.

SERVES 6 339 calories per serving

Takes 1 1/4 hours   Page 315

POTATO, CELERY ROOT, & PARMESAN GRATIN

Potatoes and celery root baked with a cream, ricotta cheese, bread crumbs, and Parmesan topping.

SERVES 6 451 calories per serving

Takes 1 3/4 hours   Page 308

CHESTNUT LOAF

Chestnuts baked with potatoes and celery, flavored with garlic, parsley, soy sauce, and tomato paste. Served with spicy tomato salsa.

SERVES 6 226 calories per serving

Takes 1 1/4 hours   Page 326

PICNIC FARE

TOMATO & OLIVE TART

Poppyseed pastry crust baked with a topping of onions, tomatoes, tomato paste, basil, garlic, mozarella cheese, and black olives.

SERVES 8 377 calories per serving

Takes 60 minutes, plus chilling   Page 316

STUFFED RED PEPPERS

Baked bell peppers with a nourishing stuffing of button mushrooms, onion, rice, red lentils, stock, pine nuts, and parsley.

SERVES 4 622 calories per serving

Takes 1 1/2 hours   Page 309

CHEESE-TOPPED BAKED EGGPLANT

Eggplant spiked with garlic slivers dipped in herbs and olive oil. Topped with blue and Cheddar cheeses.

SERVES 4 447 calories per serving

Takes 1 1/4 hours   Page 309

OVER 60 MINUTES

MUSHROOM LASAGNE
Lasagne layered with mushroom and tomato sauce, spinach, a creamy white sauce, and grated Cheddar cheese, then baked for a filling meal.

SERVES 6 684 calories per serving
Takes 1¼ hours Page 311

DAIRY-FREE LASAGNE
Tomato sauce layered with lasagne, lightly browned eggplant slices, and spinach, topped with zucchini, and baked until golden.

SERVES 4–6 364–243 calories per serving
Takes 60 minutes, plus standing Page 311

DINNER PARTY

SPICED EGGPLANT WITH PHYLLO CRUST
Diced eggplant, onions, feta cheese, lentils, red bell peppers, spices, and oregano, in phyllo pastry.

SERVES 6 569 calories per serving
Takes 1¼ hours, plus standing Page 317

HIGH PROTEIN

FESTIVE NUT LOAF
Brown rice blended with mushrooms, carrots, parsley, and rosemary, and baked in a loaf pan with walnuts, Brazil nuts, pine nuts, and Cheddar cheese.

SERVES 6–8 600–450 calories per serving
Takes 2½ hours, plus soaking Page 326

Garnished with rosemary sprigs, served in slices, and accompanied by cranberry sauce.

FAMILY CHOICE

CHEESE & VEGETABLE PIE
A variety of vegetables mixed with parsley and marjoram, in a Cheddar cheese and mustard sauce. Topped with cheese pastry.

SERVES 6 406 calories per serving
Takes 1½ hours, plus chilling Page 304

WINTER VEGETABLE TERRINE
Three colorful layers of baked pureed carrot, celery root, and broccoli, served in slices.

SERVES 4–6 142–95 calories per serving
Takes 1¾ hours, plus chilling Page 328

DINNER PARTY

MIDDLE EASTERN STUFFED SQUASH
Summer squash slices baked with a mixture of steamed couscous, mushrooms, lemon, green onions, yogurt, mint, and olives.

SERVES 4 247 calories per serving
Takes 1¼ hours Page 310

SUMMER VEGETABLE TERRINE
Eggplant and red and yellow bell peppers layered with a soft cheese mixture, wrapped in spinach leaves, and baked.

SERVES 8 194 calories per serving
Takes 2¼ hours, plus chilling Page 328

VEGETARIAN KNOW-HOW

THERE ARE TWO BASIC types of vegetarian diet. A vegan diet is the strictest – vegans do not eat any meat, poultry, fish, eggs, or dairy products – while a vegetarian diet excludes meat, poultry, and fish, but might include eggs and dairy products. In addition, there is the "semivegetarian" diet, which can include fish and even poultry. With such a great variety of foods from which to choose, vegetarian diets, based largely on complex carbohydrates, legumes, vegetables, fruits, nuts, and seeds, can be imaginative and nutritious.

MAINTAINING A BALANCED DIET

Fish, meat, poultry, dairy products, and eggs are high-quality protein foods – they contain all the essential dietary amino acids (the building blocks of protein) that the body needs. Many vegetarians replace fish, meat, and poultry with eggs, cheese, and other dairy products, but this is not the ideal solution as many dairy foods are high in saturated fats and calories.

A healthy alternative in a vegetarian diet is to focus on protein-rich legumes, nuts, and seeds. The protein these foods offer does not contain all 8 of the essential amino acids (with the exception of that from soy beans, which is "complete"), but it is easy to enhance their nutritional value – simply eat them with bread, pasta, and rice or other grains. Examples of vegetarian protein combinations drawn from cuisines around the world are beans or dhal (lentils) and rice, hummus and pita bread, or a mixed nut, lentil, and vegetable salad.

Another dietary interaction that vegetarians should be aware of is that between iron and vitamin C. The form of iron found in meat is easily absorbed by the body, whereas the iron in vegetables, nuts, grains, legumes, and eggs needs a helping hand. This is provided by vitamin C, which enhances iron uptake. So when planning meals, include vitamin C-rich foods such as fresh fruit (in particular citrus, berries, and kiwi fruit) and vegetables (bell peppers, tomatoes, broccoli, snow peas, and cabbages are good sources).

TOFU

Tofu is a high-protein food manufactured from soy beans. It is low in fat and calories, so can make a healthy basis for many vegetarian dishes. It is very bland (unless it is smoked), but easily absorbs flavors from marinades and sauces. Silken tofu has a soft, creamy texture: use it in sauces, dips, and puddings. Firm tofu, which has a texture similar to feta cheese, can be stir-fried, grilled, or casseroled. Other vegetarian meat substitutes include TVP (textured vegetable protein), which is also made from soy beans.

A gelatin substitute

Gelatin is a natural protein found in the bones, skin, and connective tissues of animals. Commercial unflavored gelatin is derived from pig skin, and is thus unacceptable in a vegetarian diet. The most common substitutes are agar-agar (or kanten) and carrageen (or Irish moss), both of which are derived from seaweeds. They have stronger setting properties than gelatin, so less is needed. Follow the package instructions for amounts to use.

VEGETABLE STOCK

Add any vegetable trimmings you have (celery tops or tomato skins, for example), or vary the ingredients to emphasize the flavor of the dish in which you plan to use the stock.

1 Coarsely chop 2 onions, 1 leek, 3 celery stalks, and 2–3 carrots. Put into a large saucepan or stockpot and add 1 large bouquet garni, plus 1 crushed garlic clove, if wished.

2 Add 5 cups (1.25 liters) water and bring to a boil. Skim any scum that rises to the surface, then lower the heat and simmer for 30 minutes.

3 Strain the stock through a strainer. If not using immediately, leave to cool, then cover and store in the refrigerator for up to 5 days or in the freezer for up to 1 month.

COOKING LEGUMES

Legumes are dried beans, peas, and lentils. Stored in a cool, dark place, they will keep for up to 6 months, but the older they are, the longer they take to become tender. They're easy to prepare, but if you want to save time you can use canned legumes, which are already cooked.

1 Put the legumes into a large bowl and cover with plenty of cold water. Leave to soak for the recommended time (see below). Drain and rinse in cold water.

2 Put into a saucepan and add cold water – about twice their volume. Bring to a boil and fast boil for 10–15 minutes. Cover and simmer until tender (see below).

WARNING

Most legumes contain toxins that we cannot digest, and these can cause symptoms of severe food poisoning. To destroy the toxins, boil the legumes rapidly for 10–15 minutes at the start of cooking, then reduce the heat to carry on cooking at a simmer. Chick peas, lentils, and split peas do not need this fast boil.

Legume know-how

Legumes are usually soaked for at least 8 hours, but you can speed up the process: boil for 3 minutes, then cover and soak for 1–2 hours.

Add salt toward the end of cooking: if it is added at the beginning, it can toughen the skins of the legume.

Legumes double in size and weight when cooked, so if a recipe calls for 8 oz (250 g) cooked legumes, you will need 4 oz (125 g) before cooking.

Adding baking soda before cooking to the cooking water can adversely affect the nutritional value of legumes.

SOAKING & COOKING TIMES OF LEGUMES

Cooking times depend on the variety of legume and whether it is recently dried or has been stored a long time and thus is very dry. The cooking times given below are therefore only a guide.

Legume	Soaking	Cooking
Adzuki beans	8–12 hours	45 minutes
Black-eyed peas	8–12 hours	1 hour
Chick peas	8–12 hours	2 hours
Flageolet beans	8–12 hours	1–1½ hours
Great northern beans	8–12 hours	1–1½ hours
Lentils, red	not required	20–30 minutes
Lentils, green	not required	30–45 minutes
Lima beans	8–12 hours	1–1½ hours
Mung beans (whole)	8–12 hours	45 minutes
Red kidney beans	8–12 hours	1¾ hours
Soy beans	10–12 hours	2½–4 hours
Split peas	not required	2 hours

GRAINS

Whole grains are first-class sources of carbohydrate, fiber, vitamins, and minerals.

Bulgur wheat
Also known as burghul wheat, this is made from steamed, dried, and crushed wheat kernels. It cooks very quickly, or can just be soaked and used in salads. Cracked wheat is similar, but is not precooked, so it takes longer to cook than bulgur wheat.

Couscous
Made from semolina, the wheat flour also used for pasta, couscous only needs to be soaked to allow the grains to swell and soften. For extra flavor, steam the couscous over a vegetable stew in a colander set over a large pot.

Pearl barley
The nutty flavor and chewy texture of this grain is delicious in vegetable soups and stews. The starch in the grain acts as a thickener too.

Polenta
Made from ground corn, polenta is added to simmering water and stirred constantly until it is very thick. Instant polenta takes only about 8 minutes to cook. Serve warm, or leave to cool and set, then slice and broil.

Millet
Available as flakes or whole grains, millet has a delicate, slightly nutty flavor. Add a small handful to soups to thicken them.

Oats
Oatflakes, also called rolled oats, are the basis of porridge and muesli. Fine steel-cut oats can be used to make cookies, bread, and oatcakes – and to thicken soups; coarser varieties can be cooked into oatmeal.

Quinoa
A tiny grain from South America with a slightly sweet taste, quinoa can be used like brown rice and other whole grains. Rinse it well before cooking.

ROAST VEGETABLE NIÇOISE

SERVES 4

1 1/2 lb (750 g) zucchini, sliced

1 large red onion, thinly sliced

3 garlic cloves, crushed

4 tbsp olive oil, more if needed

1 cup (125 g) black olives, pitted

2 tsp herbes de Provence

1 tbsp capers

black pepper

8 oz (250 g) cherry tomatoes, halved

1 tbsp shredded fresh basil

1 Put the zucchini, red onion, and garlic in a baking dish, drizzle with 4 tbsp oil, and toss to mix.

2 Arrange the black olives on top of the vegetables, then sprinkle with the herbs and capers, and plenty of pepper.

3 Roast in a preheated oven at 375°F (190°C) for 25 minutes, then add the tomatoes and roast for 20 minutes longer, checking occasionally to see if the surface is getting too dry. If it is, drizzle a little more olive oil over the vegetables.

4 Sprinkle the dish with the shredded fresh basil. Serve hot or cold.

CHEESE & VEGETABLE PIE

SERVES 6

2 tbls (30 g) butter

1 onion, chopped

2 carrots, sliced

1 lb (500 g) zucchini, sliced

2 large tomatoes, chopped

1/2 cup (125 g) sliced mushrooms

2 tbsp chopped parsley

1/2 tsp dried marjoram or oregano

salt and black pepper

CHEESE SAUCE

2 tbls (30 g) butter

1/4 cup (30 g) all-purpose flour

1 1/4 cup (300 ml) milk

1/2 cup (60 g) grated sharp Cheddar cheese

1 tsp English mustard

pinch of cayenne pepper

CHEESE PASTRY

1 cup (125 g) all-purpose flour

4 tbls (60 g) butter

1/2 cup (60 g) grated sharp Cheddar cheese

1 small egg, beaten

1 Make the cheese pastry: sift the flour into a bowl. Add the butter and rub in lightly until the mixture resembles fine bread crumbs. Stir in the cheese, then bind to a soft but not sticky dough with 1 tbsp of the beaten egg and 1 tbsp cold water. Chill for 30 minutes.

2 Melt the butter in a large pan, add the onion, and cook gently for 3–5 minutes until softened. Add the carrots and cook for about 5 minutes.

3 Add the zucchini, tomatoes, mushrooms, and herbs, and season with salt and pepper. Cook over a low heat, stirring occasionally, for 10–15 minutes until softened. Remove from the heat.

4 Make the cheese sauce: melt the butter in a saucepan, add the flour, and cook, stirring, for 1 minute. Remove from the heat and gradually blend in the milk.

5 Bring to a boil, stirring until the mixture thickens. Simmer for 2–3 minutes, then stir in the cheese, mustard, and cayenne, and season with salt and pepper. Stir the vegetables into the sauce, remove from the heat, and leave to cool.

6 Roll out the dough on a floured work surface. Invert a deep pie dish onto the dough and cut around the edge. Reserve the trimmings.

7 Transfer the vegetable and sauce mixture to the pie dish and top with the dough. Crimp the edges with a fork and make a hole in the top of the dough to allow steam to escape.

8 Decorate the pie with the dough trimmings, attaching them with beaten egg. Brush the dough all over with the remaining beaten egg. Bake in a preheated oven at 400°F (200°C) for 30 minutes or until the pastry is crisp and golden all over.

COUNTRY VEGETABLE PIES

SERVES 6

8 carrots, diced

8 parsnips, diced

1 1/4 cups (300 ml) vegetable stock

2 tbsp olive oil

1 onion, chopped

1 head of garlic, separated into cloves and peeled

3 large potatoes, diced

salt and black pepper

4 tbsp hot milk

3 tbls (45 g) butter

paprika to garnish

PARSLEY SAUCE

3 tbls (45 g) butter

1/3 cup (45 g) all-purpose flour

2/3 cup (150 ml) milk

4 tbsp chopped parsley

1 Blanch the carrots and parsnips in the stock for 1 minute. Drain, reserving the stock. Put the oil into a baking dish, add the vegetables and half of the garlic, and stir well. Roast in a preheated oven at 400°F (200°C) for 30 minutes.

2 Meanwhile, cook the potatoes and the remaining garlic in boiling salted water for 15–20 minutes until tender. Drain, return to the pan, and add the hot milk and 2 tbls (30 g) of the butter. Mash, and season with salt and pepper.

3 Remove the roasted vegetables with a slotted spoon, divide between 6 individual baking dishes, and season well.

4 Make the parsley sauce: melt the butter in a small pan, add the flour, and cook, stirring, for 1 minute. Remove from the heat and blend in the milk and reserved stock. Bring to a boil, stirring, until thick. Simmer for 2–3 minutes, then stir in the parsley and season with salt and pepper.

5 Pour the sauce over the vegetables, top with the potato, and dot with the remaining butter. Bake for 20 minutes. Serve hot, with paprika sprinkled on top.

MIXED BEAN BAKE

SERVES 6

2 tbsp olive oil

3 large leeks, trimmed and sliced

1 garlic clove, crushed

4 cups (250 g) sliced mushrooms

14 oz (400 g) canned adzuki or red kidney beans, drained and rinsed

14 oz (400 g) canned lima beans, drained and rinsed

14 oz (400 g) canned crushed tomatoes

3 tbsp tomato paste

4 tbsp chopped parsley

salt and black pepper

CHEESE SAUCE

2 tbls (30 g) butter

1/4 cup (30 g) all-purpose flour

1 1/4 cup (300 ml) milk

1 egg, beaten

1 cup (125 g) grated sharp Cheddar cheese

1 Heat the olive oil in a large saucepan. Add the leeks and cook gently, stirring, for a few minutes until softened but not coloured. Lift out with a slotted spoon and set aside.

2 Add the garlic and mushrooms and cook, stirring occasionally, for about 5 minutes. Add the canned beans, tomatoes, tomato paste, and 3 tbsp of the parsley. Season with salt and pepper. Bring to a boil, cover, and simmer very gently for about 20 minutes.

3 Meanwhile, make the cheese sauce: melt the butter in a small saucepan, add the flour, and cook, stirring, for 1 minute. Remove the pan from the heat and gradually blend in the milk. Bring to a boil, stirring constantly until the mixture thickens. Simmer for 2–3 minutes, then leave to cool slightly. Stir in the egg and cheese, and season with salt and black pepper.

4 Transfer the bean mixture to a baking dish and arrange the leeks on top. Pour the cheese sauce over the leeks, and bake in a preheated oven at 375°F (190°C) for 30 minutes or until the top is golden. Serve hot, sprinkled with the remaining parsley.

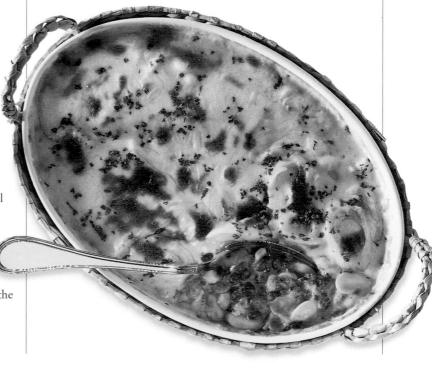

VEGETABLE CASSEROLES

Delicious, satisfying casseroles can be made from fresh vegetables whatever the season, particularly when herbs, spices, and flavorings are carefully chosen to complement their flavors. These recipes make hearty main courses, served with either hot crusty bread or boiled or steamed rice.

ROASTED VEGETABLE MEDLEY

SERVES 4

6 oz (175 g) small new potatoes, scrubbed and halved

8 baby carrots, scrubbed and trimmed

2 red onions, cut into wedges

2 garlic cloves, sliced

salt and black pepper

about 2 tbsp olive oil

a few rosemary sprigs

8 oz (250 g) cherry tomatoes

4 oz (125 g) thin green beans

1 small cauliflower, broken into florets

14 oz (400 g) canned lima beans, drained

2 tbsp balsamic vinegar

2 tbsp coarse mustard

a handful of chopped fresh herbs (such as parsley, chives, basil, and chervil)

1 Put the potatoes, carrots, onions and garlic in a roasting pan. Season and add the olive oil, then turn to coat. Tuck in the rosemary sprigs, and roast in a preheated oven at 375°F (190°C) for 40–45 minutes or until the vegetables are tender, stirring in the tomatoes about 15–20 minutes before the end.

2 Meanwhile, cook the green beans and cauliflower in boiling salted water for 4 minutes. Drain and set aside.

3 Mix the roasted vegetables with the green beans, cauliflower, and butter beans, then gently mix in the balsamic vinegar, mustard, and herbs. Serve hot.

ROASTED VEGETABLE GRATIN

Transfer the vegetables to a baking dish. Sprinkle with 3/4 cup (90 g) grated Cheddar cheese mixed with 1 cup (60 g) fresh bread crumbs. Return to the oven for about 10–15 minutes until golden.

MUSHROOM STROGANOFF

SERVES 4

3/4 oz (20 g) dried mushrooms (porcini)

2 tbsp olive oil

1 onion, chopped

1 garlic clove, crushed

1 lb (500 g) crimini mushrooms

2 red bell peppers, cored, seeded, and sliced

2 tsp paprika

salt and black pepper

2 tbls (30 g) cornstarch

1 1/4 cups (300 ml) cold vegetable stock

14 oz (400 g) canned artichoke hearts, drained

2 tbsp dry white or red wine

1 tbsp tomato paste

lowfat sour cream or plain yogurt to serve

1 Soak the dried mushrooms in 2/3 cup (150 ml) warm water for 20 minutes, then drain and reserve the soaking water.

2 Heat the oil in a flameproof casserole or Dutch oven, add the onion and garlic, and cook for 3–5 minutes until softened.

3 Add the mushrooms, peppers, and paprika, and season with salt and pepper. Cook, stirring, for 5 minutes. Mix the cornstarch and stock, add to the pan with the artichokes, wine, mushroom water, and tomato paste and bring to a boil. Simmer gently for 10–15 minutes. Taste for seasoning. Serve hot, with sour cream or yogurt.

MUSHROOM VOL-AU-VENT

When cooking the mushrooms, increase the heat to reduce and thicken the sauce. Warm through a store-bought puff pastry shell, and fill with the hot Mushroom Stroganoff.

SPICY PUMPKIN CASSEROLE

SERVES 4

2 tbsp olive oil

2 onions, cut into wedges

2 potatoes, cut into 1-in (2.5-cm) cubes

2 parsnips, cut into 1-in (2.5-cm) cubes

1 lb (500 g) pumpkin, peeled and cut into 1-in (2.5-cm) cubes

1–2 tbsp curry paste

1 3/4 cups (375 ml) vegetable stock

salt and black pepper

chopped fresh cilantro to garnish

1 Heat the olive oil in a flameproof casserole. Add the onions and cook gently for 3–5 minutes or until softened.

2 Add the vegetable cubes, curry paste, and stock. Season and bring to a boil. Cover and simmer, stirring, for 20 minutes.

3 Remove the vegetables with a slotted spoon and transfer to a warmed serving dish. Bring the sauce to a boil and boil until reduced and thickened. Spoon the sauce over the vegetables, garnish with cilantro, and serve hot.

CLOCKWISE FROM TOP: Spicy Pumpkin Casserole, Mushroom Stroganoff, Roasted Vegetable Medley.

SPICY PUMPKIN IN A PIE

Cool the vegetables and sauce, transfer to a pie plate, and top with store-bought pastry. Bake at 375°F (190°C) for 15 minutes or until the pastry is cooked and the filling is hot.

POTATO, CELERY ROOT, & PARMESAN GRATIN

SERVES 6

2 tbls (60 g) butter, plus extra for greasing

1 onion, sliced

2 garlic cloves, crushed

4 large potatoes, thinly sliced

12 oz (375 g) celery root, peeled and thinly sliced

1 1/4 cups (300 ml) light cream

2/3 cup (150 ml) milk

1 cup (250 g) ricotta cheese

3 tbsp snipped fresh chives

salt and black pepper

2 tbsp fresh bread crumbs

3 tbsp grated Parmesan cheese, plus extra for serving

1 Melt the butter in a skillet, add the sliced onion and crushed garlic, and cook gently, stirring occasionally, for 3–5 minutes until softened but not colored. Lightly butter a large gratin dish.

2 Arrange the potatoes, celery root, and the onion mixture in layers in the prepared gratin dish, finishing with a neat layer of potatoes.

3 In a large bowl, combine the cream, milk, ricotta cheese, and chives, and season with salt and pepper. Beat well together, then pour over the vegetables.

4 In a small bowl, combine the bread crumbs and 3 tbsp grated Parmesan cheese, and then sprinkle evenly over the potatoes.

5 Bake in a preheated oven at 350°F (180°C) for about 1 hour or until the potatoes and celery root are tender and the top is golden brown.

6 Serve the gratin hot, sprinkled with extra grated Parmesan cheese.

EGGPLANT PARMIGIANA

SERVES 6

3 lb (1.5 kg) eggplants

2 eggs, lightly beaten

1/2 cup (60 g) all-purpose flour

3 tbsp olive oil, more if needed

2 onions, chopped

2 lbs 7 oz (1.2 kg) canned crushed tomatoes, drained

2/3 cup (150 g) tomato paste

2 garlic cloves, crushed

2 tbsp chopped fresh basil

1/4 tsp sugar

salt and black pepper

10–12 oz (300–375 g) mozzarella cheese, sliced

1 cup (125 g) grated Parmesan cheese,

1 Cut the eggplants into 1/2 in (1 cm) slices. Dip into the beaten eggs, then into the flour, shaking off any excess.

2 Heat 1 tbsp olive oil in a large skillet, add the eggplant slices in batches, and cook for 3–4 minutes on each side until golden, adding more oil between batches if necessary. Lift out with a slotted spoon and drain on paper towels.

3 Heat another tablespoon of olive oil in a saucepan, add the onions, and cook gently until soft. Stir in the tomatoes, tomato paste, garlic, and basil. Bring to a boil, then simmer for 10–15 minutes until thickened. Add the sugar and season with salt and pepper.

4 Spoon some of the tomato mixture into a shallow baking dish and cover with a layer of eggplant slices, then with a layer each of mozzarella and Parmesan. Continue layering, finishing with tomato mixture, mozzarella, and Parmesan.

5 Bake in a preheated oven at 375°F (190°C) for 15–20 minutes until the cheese is lightly browned.

Healthy option

For a lighter version of this dish, omit the egg and flour coating for the eggplant in step 1. In step 2, lightly brush the slices with olive oil, and broil or chargrill them until golden brown on each side.

STUFFED RED PEPPERS

SERVES 4

8 small red bell peppers

4 tbsp water

STUFFING

4 tbsp olive oil

I large onion, finely chopped

I garlic clove, crushed

6 oz (175 g) button mushrooms, chopped

1¼ cups (250 g) long grain rice

½ cup (90 g) red lentils

2 cups (500 ml) vegetable stock

salt and black pepper

½ cup (60 g) pine nuts, toasted

4 tbsp chopped parsley

fresh cilantro to garnish

1 Slice the tops off the red peppers and reserve. Cut out and discard the cores, seeds, and white ribs, and set the peppers aside.

2 Make the stuffing: heat the oil in a pan. Add the onion and garlic and cook gently, stirring occasionally, for 3–5 minutes until soft but not colored. Add the mushrooms and cook for 10 minutes.

3 Add the rice and lentils and stir to coat in the oil. Pour in the stock, season with salt and pepper, and bring to a boil. Cover and simmer very gently for 15–20 minutes until the rice is tender and the liquid has been absorbed. Stir in the pine nuts and parsley, then taste for seasoning.

4 Divide the stuffing among the peppers, stand them upright in a baking casserole dish that just holds them upright, and replace the tops.

5 Pour the measured water into the bottom of the casserole, cover, and bake in a preheated oven at 350°F (180°C) for about 40 minutes until the peppers are tender. Serve at once, garnished with cilantro.

Healthy note

Using a nonstick pan in step 2 will enable you to halve the amount of oil to I or 2 tbsp, and cutting out the pine nuts will reduce the fat content even further.

CHEESE-TOPPED BAKED EGGPLANT

SERVES 4

3 tbsp chopped parsley

2 tbsp chopped fresh basil

2 tbsp olive oil

I tsp salt

4 medium eggplants

6 garlic cloves, cut into thin slivers

½ cup (175 g) crumbled Gorgonzola or Danish blue cheese

½ cup (175 g) grated Cheddar or mozzarella cheese

1 In a small bowl, combine the parsley, half of the basil, the olive oil, and salt.

2 Prepare the eggplants (see box, right). Put the eggplants into a baking dish and bake in a preheated oven at 350°F (180°C) for 40–50 minutes until they are very tender and soft to the touch.

3 Remove the eggplants from the oven, sprinkle with the Gorgonzola and Cheddar cheeses, and bake for 5 minutes or until the cheeses are melted. Serve at once, sprinkled with the remaining basil.

Preparing the aubergines

Cut diagonal slits one-third of the way into each eggplant. Stuff the garlic slivers and then the chopped herb mixture into each slit.

Healthy note

To reduce the fat content of these stuffed eggplants, use half the amount of Gorgonzola or Danish blue cheese and half the amount of Cheddar or mozzarella. You could even use reduced-fat or lowfat Cheddar or mozzarella to lower the fat content more – the strong flavors of the garlic and herbs will compensate for the lack of fat.

ITALIAN STUFFED ZUCCHINI

SERVES 4

4 large zucchini

2 tbls (30 g) butter

2 tbsp olive oil, plus extra for greasing

1 small onion, finely chopped

4 ripe tomatoes, finely chopped

4 tbsp chopped fresh basil

salt and black pepper

2 tbsp capers, drained and coarsely chopped

2 cups (250 g) grated Fontina cheese

1 Cut the zucchini in half lengthwise. Scoop out the flesh and chop finely.

2 Melt the butter with 1 tbsp of the olive oil in a saucepan.

3 When the butter is foaming, add the onion and cook gently, stirring occasionally, for 3–5 minutes until softened but not colored.

4 Add the zucchini flesh, tomatoes, and basil, and season with salt and pepper. Cook, stirring, for 5 minutes.

5 Brush the insides of the zucchini shells with the remaining oil and arrange in a lightly oiled shallow baking dish. Bake the shells in a preheated oven at 350°F (180°C) for 5–10 minutes.

6 Divide half of the tomato mixture among the zucchini shells. Cover with the chopped capers and a thin layer of cheese. Spoon the remaining tomato mixture over and top with the remaining cheese. Return to the oven and bake for 10–15 minutes until the cheese topping is bubbling.

MIDDLE EASTERN STUFFED SQUASH

SERVES 4

1 ⅓ cups (250 g) couscous

⅔ cup (150 ml) hot vegetable stock

2 lb (1 kg) summer squash

salt and black pepper

butter for greasing

1 tbsp olive oil

1 shallot, finely chopped

2 cups (125 g) sliced button mushrooms

grated zest and juice of ½ lemon

2 green onions, finely chopped

4 tbsp plain yogurt

1 tbsp chopped fresh mint

12 pitted green olives, chopped

chopped parsley to garnish

tomato sauce (page 314) to serve

1 Put the couscous into a bowl and pour in the hot stock. Stir well, and leave to stand for about 10 minutes.

2 Peel the squash, cut it crosswise into 2 in (5 cm)) slices, and scoop out and discard the seeds from each slice. Blanch the slices in boiling salted water for 2 minutes, then drain and arrange in a single layer in a lightly buttered ovenproof dish.

3 Heat the oil in a saucepan and cook the shallot gently for 2–3 minutes until softened. Add the mushrooms, lemon zest and juice, season with salt and pepper, and cook for about 8 minutes or until tender.

4 Drain the mushroom mixture and stir into the couscous. Add the green onions, yogurt, mint, olives, and salt and pepper to taste.

5 Spoon the mixture into the squash slices. Cover with foil and bake in a preheated oven at 375°F (190°C) for 20–25 minutes. Garnish with parsley and serve hot, with the tomato sauce.

MUSHROOM LASAGNE

SERVES 6

2 tbsp olive oil

I large onion, finely chopped

I lb (500 g) mushrooms, sliced

2 large garlic cloves, crushed

¼ cup (30 g) all-purpose flour

28 oz (800 g) canned crushed tomatoes

I tbsp chopped fresh basil

I tsp sugar

salt and black pepper

I lb (500 g) frozen leaf spinach, thawed and drained

White sauce (page 385), made with 6 tbls (90 g) butter, all-purpose flour, 3¾ cups (900 ml) milk, and I tsp Dijon mustard

3¾ cups (300 g) grated sharp Cheddar cheese

5 oz (150 g) lasagne noodles

1 Heat the oil in a saucepan, add the onion, mushrooms and garlic and cook for 10 minutes or until soft. Sprinkle in the flour and cook, stirring, for 1 minute.

2 Add the tomatoes, basil, and sugar, and season with salt and pepper. Cover and simmer for 20 minutes.

3 Season the spinach with salt and pepper. Taking 1 teaspoonful at a time, shape it loosely into 24 balls.

4 Spoon one-third of the mushroom mixture into a large baking dish, and place 8 of the spinach balls on top. Cover with one-third of the white sauce and one-third of the cheese. Arrange half of the lasagne on top. Repeat the layers, finishing with cheese.

5 Bake in a preheated oven at 375°F (190°C) for 35 minutes or until the pasta is tender. Serve hot.

Healthy option

This is a luxury lasagne for a special occasion. For everyday, halve the amount of white sauce and cheese.

DAIRY-FREE LASAGNE

SERVES 4–6

2–3 tbsp olive oil, more if needed

2 zucchini, sliced

salt and black pepper

I eggplant, cut into ¼ in (5 mm) slices

2 onions, chopped

I red bell pepper, cored, seeded, and diced

2 garlic cloves, crushed

28 oz (800 g) canned crushed tomatoes

⅔ cup (150 g) tomato paste

¼ tsp sugar

3 tbsp chopped fresh basil

5 oz (150 g) oven ready lasagne sheets

8 oz (250 g) frozen chopped spinach, thawed, drained, and seasoned well

1 Heat 1 tbsp olive oil in a large nonstick skillet, add the zucchini, and cook for 3 minutes. Turn into a bowl, and sprinkle with salt.

2 Heat another tablespoon of oil in the pan, and cook the eggplant slices for about 3–5 minutes on each side until golden. Remove and set aside.

3 Add the onions, red pepper, and garlic to the pan, with more oil if needed, and soften gently for 3–5 minutes. Add the tomatoes, tomato paste, and sugar and bring to a boil. Simmer for 10 minutes until thickened, stir in the basil, and season with salt and pepper.

4 Spoon one-third of the tomato sauce into a large ovenproof dish and cover with one-third of the lasagne. Add the eggplant, then half of the remaining tomato sauce. Add half of the remaining lasagne, then the spinach. Add the remaining lasagne and tomato sauce, and finish with an overlapping layer of zucchini.

5 Bake in a preheated oven at 375°F (190°C) for 35 minutes or until the pasta is tender and the top is golden.

VEGETARIAN BAKES

It is often difficult to find inspiration for vegetarian main meals, especially when you are entertaining meat eaters at the same time. These special "two-in-one" recipes are the perfect answer – the vegetarians in your party will love have something cooked especially for them, while the meat eaters will enjoy a spoonful or two alongside their own main course.

MAJORCAN TUMBET CASSEROLE

SERVES 6

1¼ lb (625 g) baby new potatoes

3 zucchini, thickly sliced

2 large Spanish onions, thickly sliced

3 large tomatoes, halved

3 fat garlic cloves, peeled and left whole

olive oil

salt and black pepper

3 tsp chopped fresh rosemary

1¾ cups (400 ml) tomato puree

hot pepper sauce sauce

3 fresh thyme sprigs, plus extra to garnish

3 PINT (1.8 LITER) BAKING DISH, ABOUT 8 × 11 × 2 IN (20 × 28 × 5 CM)

1 Boil the potatoes in salted water for about 15–20 minutes until not quite done. Drain and leave until cool enough to handle, then peel and cut in half.

2 Toss the zucchini, onions, tomatoes, and garlic cloves in a couple of tablespoons of olive oil and season well. Arrange cut-side down on a large baking sheet or in a shallow roasting pan. Roast in a preheated oven at 425°F (220°C) for about 30–40 minutes, turning once, until the vegetables are charred and soft.

3 Pick out the garlic, squash it with the back of a knife, and return it to the other vegetables. Layer the vegetables in a baking dish – first the potatoes with some seasoning and rosemary, about 6 tbsp passata, and a good dash of hot pepper sauce, then the onions, tomatoes, and zucchini with seasoning, rosemary, tomato puree, and hot pepper sauce as before. Push 3 sprigs of thyme in near the top.

4 Bake in a preheated oven at 400°F (200°C) for about 15–20 minutes, or at 325°F (170°C) for 30–40 minutes, until hot and bubbling. Before serving, replace the cooked thyme with fresh thyme. Good served with Vegetarian Burgers (see page 323).

KILKERRY PIE

SERVES 6

6 tbls (90 g) butter

1 lb (500 g) leeks, trimmed and thickly sliced

½ cup (60 g) all-purpose flour

1¼ cups (300 ml) apple juice

1¼ cups (300 ml) milk

1 tsp coarse mustard

salt and black pepper

4 hard-boiled eggs, roughly chopped

1¼ cups (150 g) grated sharp Cheddar cheese

3 large potatoes, cut into ¼ in (5 mm) slices (not peeled)

5 sheets of phyllo pastry dough, each about 10 × 15 in (25 × 38 cm)

SHALLOW BAKING DISH, ABOUT 10 IN (25 CM) SQUARE

1 Melt 4 tbls (60 g) of the butter in a large skillet, and cook the leeks for about 8–10 minutes until softened. Stir in the flour and cook for 1 minute, then gradually add the apple juice and milk, stirring constantly until boiling. It may look slightly curdled at this stage, but don't worry, it will come together. Reduce the heat, and simmer gently for 2–3 minutes. Add the mustard and season well.

2 Remove the sauce from the heat and stir in the roughly chopped eggs and the cheese. Now cook the potatoes in boiling salted water for 4–5 minutes until just tender. Drain, and mix into the sauce, then season, and pour into the dish.

3 Melt the remaining butter. Brush one of the phyllo sheets with butter and put it over the mixture in the dish, scrunching up the edges to fit. Repeat with the remaining phyllo sheets, scrunching up the last sheet before putting it on top of the pie. You can leave the pie for up to 6 hours at this stage, then bake it when you need it.

4 Bake in a preheated oven at 400°F (200°C) for 30–40 minutes until the phyllo is crisp and golden and the pie is hot right through.

TUSCAN CANNELLONI

SERVES 4

8 sheets of fresh lasagne, or dried lasagne cooked according to package directions

2 cups (500 g) tomato puree or store-bought fresh tomato and basil pasta sauce

2–3 tbsp grated fresh Parmesan cheese

a small handful of chopped fresh basil

FILLING

a little olive oil

2 shallots, finely chopped

1 garlic clove, crushed

20 oz (600 g) canned cannellini beans, drained

2 oz (60 g) sun-blushed or sun-dried tomatoes, snipped into pieces

5 oz (150 g) Dolcelatte cheese, roughly chopped

2 heaped tbsp chopped fresh basil

salt and black pepper

SHALLOW BAKING DISH, ABOUT 11 × 8 IN (28 × 20 CM)

1 Make the filling: heat the oil in a small pan, and cook the shallots and garlic until soft. Allow to cool. Crush the beans with a fork so that most are mashed but a few still retain some shape, then mix them with the shallots and garlic, tomatoes, Dolcelatte, and basil. Season well, taste, and add more seasoning if necessary.

2 Lay the lasagne sheets flat, divide the filling between them, and roll up from the short ends to enclose the filling. Put the cannelloni seam-side down into a greased or buttered baking dish – they should fit snugly. Season, then pour over the tomato puree or pasta sauce.

3 Cover and cook at 375°F (190°C) for 45–50 minutes until the pasta is cooked and the filling piping hot. (If pre-cooked pasta was used, bake for 25–30 minutes.) Scatter the Parmesan and basil over the top before serving.

CLOCKWISE FROM TOP RIGHT: Tuscan Cannelloni, Kilkerry Pie, Majorcan Tumbet Casserole.

SPINACH GNOCCHI WITH TOMATO SAUCE

SERVES 4

2 lb (1 kg) spinach

1 1/2 cups (375 g) ricotta cheese

3 eggs

4 tbsp grated Parmesan cheese

pinch of grated nutmeg

salt and black pepper

8–9 tbls (60–75 g) all-purpose flour

TOMATO SAUCE

2 tbl (30 g) butter

1 small onion, chopped

1 small carrot, chopped

1/4 cup (30 g) all-purpose flour

14 oz (400 g) canned crushed tomatoes

1 1/4 cups (300 ml) vegetable stock

1 bay leaf

1 tsp sugar

TO SERVE

1/2 cup (125 g) butter

grated Parmesan cheese and Parmesan shavings

1 Wash the spinach and put into a saucepan with only the water remaining on the leaves. Cook over a gentle heat until just wilted. Drain the spinach throughly, squeezing to remove any excess water.

2 Put the spinach, ricotta, eggs, Parmesan, and nutmeg into a food processor, season with salt and pepper and puree until smooth. Turn into a bowl and gradually add flour until the mixture just holds its shape.

3 Using 2 soup spoons, form the mixture into 20 oval shapes. Cover and chill in the refrigerator for 1 hour.

4 Make the tomato sauce: melt the butter in a pan, add the onion and carrot, and cook for 10 minutes or until softened. Sprinkle in the flour and cook, stirring, for 1 minute. Add the tomatoes, stock, bay leaf, and sugar, season with salt and pepper, and bring to a boil. Cover and simmer for 30 minutes. Puree in a food processor until smooth. Keep hot.

5 Cook the gnocchi in batches in boiling salted water for about 5 minutes or until they float to the surface. Lift out and keep hot. Melt the butter and pour over the gnocchi. Serve the gnocchi hot, with the tomato sauce, grated Parmesan, and Parmesan shavings.

POLENTA WITH GRILLED VEGETABLES

SERVES 6

1 cup (175 g) polenta

2/3 cup (150 ml) cold water

2 1/2 cups (600 ml) boiling salted water

2 tbls (30 g) butter

2 zucchini, halved and thickly sliced lengthwise

2 tomatoes, cored and sliced

1 fennel bulb, trimmed and quartered lengthwise

1 red onion, thickly sliced

melted butter for brushing

MARINADE

4 tbsp olive oil

2 tbsp red wine vinegar

3 garlic cloves, chopped

2–3 tbsp chopped parsley

salt and black pepper

1 Put the polenta into a saucepan, cover with the measured cold water, and leave to stand for 5 minutes.

2 Add the boiling salted water to the pan, return to a boil, and stir for 10–15 minutes, until smooth and thickened.

3 Sprinkle a baking tray with water. Stir the butter into the polenta, then spread the mixture over the tray in a 1/2 in (1 cm) layer. Leave to cool.

4 Combine the marinade ingredients in a bowl. Add the zucchini, tomatoes, fennel, and onion. Cover and marinate in the refrigerator for 30 minutes.

5 Lift the vegetables out of the marinade and cook over a hot barbecue for 2–3 minutes on each side. Cut the polenta into strips and cook over a hot barbecue, brushing with melted butter, for 1–2 minutes on each side until golden. Serve hot.

Cook's know-how

Instead of barbecuing the polenta and vegetables, you can cook them on a ridged cast-iron chargrill pan, or under a preheated broiler, for the same length of time.

COUSCOUS WITH ROASTED PEPPERS

SERVES 4–6

I large red bell pepper
I large yellow bell pepper
I cup (175 g) couscous
2½ cups (600 ml) hot vegetable stock
2 tbsp olive oil
½ cup (60 g) blanched almonds
2 zucchini, sliced
I large red onion, chopped
I large carrot, thinly sliced
1–2 garlic cloves, crushed
14 oz (400 g) canned chick peas, drained and rinsed
I tsp ground cumin
½ tsp curry powder
¼–½ tsp crushed dried red chilies
salt and black pepper
chopped cilantro to garnish

1 Cook the peppers under a hot broiler, 4 in (10 cm) from the heat, for 10 minutes or until charred. Seal in a plastic bag and leave to cool.

2 Put the couscous into a bowl and stir in the hot stock. Cover and leave to stand for 10 minutes.

3 Meanwhile, heat the oil in a large skillet, add the almonds, and cook gently, stirring, for 3 minutes or until lightly browned. Lift out with a slotted spoon and drain on paper towels.

4 Add the zucchini, onion, carrot, and garlic to the pan, and cook, stirring, for about 5 minutes.

5 Stir in the chick peas, cumin, curry powder, and crushed chilies, and cook, stirring occasionally, for a further 5 minutes. Stir in the couscous, and cook for 3–4 minutes until heated through. Season to taste.

6 Remove the skins, cores, and seeds from the broiled peppers, and cut the flesh into thin strips.

7 Divide the couscous among warmed serving plates and arrange the pepper strips on top. Serve at once, sprinkled with the almonds and chopped coriander.

VEGETABLE & BARLEY CASSEROLE

SERVES 6

4 tbls (60 g) butter
8 large shallots or small onions, halved
5 cups (1.25 liters) vegetable stock
8 oz (250 g) baby carrots
8 oz (250 g) baby parsnips
⅓ cup (60 g) pearl barley
I bay leaf
2 zucchini, sliced
I small cauliflower, separated into florets
4 oz (125 g) snow peas
I tbsp chopped fresh mixed herbs

DUMPLINGS

I cup (125 g) self-rising flour
¼ cup (60 g) shredded vegetable shortening
I tbsp chopped fresh mixed herbs
salt and black pepper

1 Make the dumplings: sift the flour into a bowl, add the shortening and herbs, and season with salt and pepper. Add enough water to make a soft, not sticky, dough. Shape into 16–18 balls. Cover and set aside.

2 Melt the butter in a large flameproof casserole or Dutch oven. When the butter is foaming, add the shallots and cook gently, stirring occasionally, for 3–5 minutes until soft but not colored.

3 Add the stock, carrots, parsnips, pearl barley, and bay leaf, and bring to a boil. Cover and bake in a preheated oven at 375°F (190°C) for about 30 minutes.

4 Remove the casserole from the oven, and stir in the zucchini, cauliflower, snow peas, and herbs. Season with salt and pepper.

5 Arrange the dumplings on top of the casserole, cover, and return to the oven for 20 minutes or until the dumplings are cooked. Discard the bay leaf before serving.

TOMATO & OLIVE TART

SERVES 8

3 tbsp olive oil

2 large onions, coarsely chopped

3 garlic cloves, crushed

14 oz (400 g) canned crushed tomatoes

2/3 cup (140 g) tomato paste

2 tsp chopped fresh basil

1 tsp sugar

1 cup (125 g) grated mozzarella cheese

3/4 cup (90 g) pitted black olives

shredded fresh basil to garnish

POPPY SEED CRUST

2 cup (250 g) all-purpose flour

1/2 cup (125 g) butter

6 tbls (90 g) poppy seeds

1 tbsp light brown sugar

salt and black pepper

about 4 tbsp cold water

1 Make the crust: put the flour, butter, poppy seeds, and sugar in a food processor, season with salt and pepper, and pulse until the mixture resembles fine bread crumbs.

2 Add the water and process until the mixture forms a ball. Turn out and knead lightly, then roll out to a 12 in (30 cm) circle on a baking sheet and pinch the edge to form a rim. Prick all over with a fork and chill for 30 minutes.

3 Heat the oil in a pan, add the onions and garlic, and cook gently for 3–5 minutes until soft. Add the tomatoes, tomato paste, basil, and sugar. Season and bring to a boil. Boil for 5–7 minutes until thick. Leave to cool slightly.

4 Bake the poppy seed crust in a preheated oven at 425°F (220°C) for 15 minutes. Spread the tomato mixture over the crust, sprinkle with the cheese and olives, and bake for 15–20 minutes. Serve hot or cold, sprinkled with basil.

Cook's know-how

If you are short of time, use store-bought piecrust dough instead of the poppy seed base. You will need 1 lb (500 g).

MUSHROOM GOUGERE

SERVES 4

4 tbls (60 g) butter

5 1/3 cups (375 g) sliced mixed mushrooms, such as oyster, shiitake, and button

1/2 cup (60 g) all-purpose flour

1 3/4 cups (450 ml) milk

1 tsp chopped fresh tarragon

tarragon leaves to garnish

CHOUX PASTRY

1 cup (125 g) all-purpose flour

salt and black pepper

1 1/4 cups (300 ml) water

4 tbls (60 g) butter, plus extra for greasing

4 eggs, beaten

1 Make the choux pastry dough: sift the flour with a pinch of salt. Put the measured water and butter into a saucepan and bring to a boil.

2 Remove the pan from the heat and add the flour. Beat well until the mixture is smooth and glossy and leaves the side of the pan clean. Leave to cool slightly.

3 Beat the eggs into the flour mixture until smooth and glossy. Make the gougère (see box, right). Cover and chill while preparing the filling.

4 Melt the butter in a large saucepan, add the mushrooms, and cook gently for 3–4 minutes. Lift out with a slotted spoon and set aside. Sprinkle in the flour and cook, stirring, for 1 minute. Remove from the heat and gradually blend in the milk. Bring to a boil, stirring until thickened. Simmer for 2–3 minutes.

5 Return the mushrooms to the pan, add the tarragon, and season with salt and pepper. Pour into the middle of the choux ring and bake in a preheated oven at 425°F (220°C) for 35–40 minutes until well risen and golden. Garnish with tarragon, and serve hot.

Making the gougère

Butter a large shallow baking dish, and lightly press the choux pastry dough around the edge with a spatula.

SPINACH & RICOTTA TRIANGLES

SERVES 4

4 sheets of phyllo pastry dough

4 tbls (60 g) melted butter, plus extra for greasing

FILLING

2 tbls (30 g) butter

1 small onion, finely chopped

10 oz (300 g) spinach, shredded

1/2 cup (125 g) ricotta cheese

pinch of grated nutmeg

salt and black pepper

tomato sauce (page 314) to serve

1 Make the filling: melt the butter in a saucepan, add the onion, and cook gently for 3–5 minutes until softened.

2 Add the spinach to the onion and cook for 1–2 minutes. Leave to cool. Add the ricotta and nutmeg, season with salt and pepper, and mix well. Divide into 8 portions.

3 Lightly butter a baking sheet. Cut each sheet of phyllo pastry dough lengthwise into 2 long strips. Brush 1 strip with melted butter, covering the remaining strips with a damp dish towel. Fill and fold the triangles (see box, right).

4 Bake in a preheated oven at 400°F (200°C) for 20 minutes or until the pastry is crisp and golden. Serve with the tomato sauce.

Filling and folding the triangles

Spoon 1 portion of filling onto a corner of the phyllo strip. Fold over opposite corner to form a triangle.

Fold the filled triangle until you reach the end of the strip. Brush with melted butter and put on to the baking sheet. Repeat with remaining phyllo strips.

SPICED EGGPLANT WITH PHYLLO CRUST

SERVES 6

2 tbsp olive oil

2 large onions, chopped

2 tbsp mild curry paste

2 eggplants, cut into 1/2 in (1 cm)

2 red bell peppers, cored, seeded, and diced

salt and black pepper

1 cup (175 g) red lentils

8 oz (250 g) feta cheese, diced

10 oz (300 g) phyllo pastry dough

4 tbls (60 g) melted butter

10 1/2 in (26 cm) SPRINGFORM CAKE PAN

1 Heat the oil in a large saucepan or deep skillet. Cook the onions over a low heat, stirring occasionally, for 3–5 minutes until softened. Stir in the curry paste, and cook for 2 minutes.

2 Add the eggplants and the red peppers and cook for 10–15 minutes until soft. Season with salt and pepper and leave to cool.

3 Meanwhile, put the lentils into a pan, cover with water, and bring to a boil. Simmer for 15 minutes or until just soft. Drain and cool.

4 Stir the lentils and diced cheese into the eggplant mixture. Taste for seasoning.

5 Using two-thirds of the dough, line the bottom and side of the cake pan, brushing each sheet with melted butter, and letting them overhang the rim of the pan. Spoon in the eggplant mixture and fold the phyllo over the top. Brush the remaining phyllo with butter, crumple, and arrange on top.

6 Bake in a preheated oven at 375°F (190°C) for 40 minutes or until the pastry is golden. Serve hot.

Cook's know-how

If you are short of time, omit the phyllo. Spread the eggplant, pepper, and lentil mixture in a baking dish and grate the cheese over the top.

VEGETARIAN CURRIES

The cuisine of India, with its use of aromatic spices to enhance the flavor of vegetables
and legumes, is one in which vegetarians can find a wide range of dishes to enjoy.
The tradition of eating a selection of small dishes, accompanied by rice and breads,
makes for well-balanced, nutritious meals.

NIRAMISH

SERVES 6

2 tbsp sunflower oil

3 tbsp curry paste

1/2 tsp cayenne pepper

1 in (2.5 cm) piece of fresh gingerroot, peeled and grated

1 large onion, chopped

2 garlic cloves, crushed

3 tbsp mango chutney

1 small cauliflower, cut into florets

2 potatoes, cut into chunks

2 large carrots, sliced

2 red bell peppers, cored, seeded, and cut into chunks

14 oz (400 g) canned crushed tomatoes

1 3/4 cups (400 g) canned coconut milk

1 1/2 cups (250 g) chopped green beans

salt and black pepper

juice of 1 lime

fresh cilantro leaves to garnish

1 Heat the oil in a large saucepan, add the curry paste and cayenne pepper, and cook, stirring constantly, for 1 minute. Add the ginger, onion, garlic, and mango chutney, and cook, stirring, for 3–5 minutes until the onion is softened but not colored.

2 Add the cauliflower, potatoes, and carrots to the pan, and stir well to coat in the spices. Cook, stirring occasionally, for 5 minutes.

3 Add the red peppers, tomatoes, and coconut milk to the pan and bring to a boil, then add the beans and season with salt and pepper. Stir well.

4 Cover and simmer gently for 25–30 minutes or until all the vegetables are tender. Stir in the lime juice and taste for seasoning. Serve hot, garnished with cilantro leaves.

SAG ALOO

SERVES 6

1 lb (500 g) new potatoes

salt

2 tbsp sunflower oil

1 tsp mustard seeds

1 tsp cumin seeds

2 onions, sliced

3 garlic cloves, chopped

1 in (2.5 cm) piece of fresh gingerroot, peeled and grated

1 small fresh green chili, halved, seeded, and finely chopped

2 tsp ground coriander

1/2 tsp turmeric

1 cup (250 ml) water

1 lb (500 g) fresh baby leaf spinach

2 tbsp lime or lemon juice

plain yogurt to serve

1 Cook the potatoes in a saucepan of boiling salted water for 10 minutes. Drain and leave to cool. Cut into bite-sized pieces and set aside.

2 Heat the oil in a large, heavy skillet. Add the mustard and cumin seeds and cook, stirring, for a few seconds until they pop. Add the onions, garlic, ginger, and chili and cook for about 5 minutes until soft.

3 Add 1 tsp salt, the ground coriander, and the turmeric Cook, stirring, for 1 minute. Add the potatoes and turn to coat in the spices, then pour in the water and bring to a boil. Cover and cook over a gentle heat for 15 minutes or until the potatoes are tender.

4 Remove the lid and stir in the spinach. Increase the heat and cook, stirring occasionally, for about 10 minutes or until the spinach wilts right down into the sauce. Stir in the lime or lemon juice and taste for seasoning. Serve hot, with yogurt.

DHAL

SERVES 4–6

1 1/4 cup (225 g) green lentils

1 bay leaf

2 tbsp vegetable oil

1 large carrot, chopped

1 large green bell pepper, cored, seeded, and chopped

1 large onion, chopped

1 garlic clove, crushed

1/2 in (1 cm) piece of fresh gingerroot, peeled and finely grated

1/2 tsp each ground cinnamon, cumin, and coriander

14 oz (400 g) canned crushed tomatoes

salt and black pepper

1 Rinse and drain the lentils, put them into a large saucepan, and cover with cold water. Bring to a boil and add the bay leaf. Cover and simmer for 30 minutes or until the lentils are tender. Drain and remove the bay leaf.

2 Heat the oil in the saucepan, add the vegetables, garlic, and ginger, and fry for 10 minutes, stirring occasionally. Add the lentils, ground spices, and tomatoes and cook gently for 10 minutes or until the carrot is soft.

3 Puree the mixture in 3 batches in a blender. Do not puree for longer than about 30 seconds for each batch because it should retain some of the texture of the lentils. Reheat in the rinsed-out pan, and add salt and pepper to taste.

ACCOMPANIMENTS

- tomato and cilantro relish
- yogurt and cucumber raita
- grated carrot salad
- mango chutney
- poppadoms
- basmati rice
- naan bread

CLOCKWISE FROM TOP RIGHT: Yogurt and cucumber raita, Niramish, Sag Aloo, Dhal.

RED LENTIL & COCONUT CURRY

SERVES 6

1²/₃ cup (300 g) red lentils

3³/₄ cup (900 ml) water

1 in (2.5 cm) piece of fresh gingerroot, peeled and grated

1¹/₂ fresh green chilies, cored, seeded, and finely chopped

4 garlic cloves

3 oz (90 g) creamed coconut, grated

¹/₂ tsp turmeric

1 tbsp lemon juice

salt

2 tbls (30 g) butter

4 tsp black mustard seeds

1 Put the lentils into a pan and add the water. Bring to a boil and simmer for about 20 minutes or until tender.

2 Using a pestle and mortar, crush the fresh gingerroot, two-thirds of the chilies, and 2 of the garlic cloves until smooth. Add to the lentils.

3 Add the creamed coconut, turmeric, lemon juice, and a pinch of salt. Cook gently, stirring, until the coconut dissolves, then increase the heat and cook for 5 minutes or until any excess liquid has evaporated. Taste for seasoning.

4 Crush the remaining garlic and set aside. Melt the butter in a skillet and add the mustard seeds. As soon as they begin to pop, remove the skillet from the heat and stir in the crushed garlic and the remaining chopped chili.

5 Transfer the lentil mixture to a warmed serving dish, top with the garlic, chili, and mustard seeds. Serve hot.

Cook's know-how

To save time grating a block of creamed coconut, use a carton of coconut milk. This can be poured straight into the lentils in step 3.

RED BEAN & TOMATO CURRY

SERVES 4

2 tbsp sunflower oil

1 large onion, sliced

3 garlic cloves, crushed

1–2 fresh green chilies, cored, seeded, and sliced

1 in (2.5 cm) piece of fresh gingeroot, peeled and grated

1 tbsp Madras or other hot curry powder

salt

14 oz (400 g) canned crushed tomatoes

28 oz (800 g) canned red kidney beans, drained and rinsed

1 tbsp lemon juice

fresh coriander leaves to garnish

1 Heat the oil in a large skillet, add the onion, garlic, chilies, and ginger, and cook, stirring occasionally, for a few minutes until all the aromas are released, and the onion is softened but not colored.

2 Add the curry powder and season with salt, then cook, stirring, for 2 minutes.

3 Add the tomatoes with most of their juice and cook for about 3 minutes. Add the beans and cook for a further 5 minutes or until the beans are warmed through and the sauce is thickened. Add the lemon juice and serve hot, garnished with cilantro.

FELAFEL WITH SESAME YOGURT SAUCE

SERVES 6

14 oz (400 g) canned chick peas, drained and rinsed

6 green onions, chopped

1 slice fresh white bread

1 egg

grated zest and juice of 1/2 lemon

1 garlic clove, roughly chopped

2 tbsp roughly chopped fresh cilantro

2 tbsp roughly chopped parsley

1 tbsp tahini paste

1 tsp ground coriander

1 tsp ground cumin

1/2 tsp ground cinnamon

pinch of cayenne pepper

salt and black pepper

sunflower oil for shallow-frying

chopped fresh cilantro to garnish

warmed mini pita breads to serve

SESAME YOGURT SAUCE

4 tbsp plain yogurt

2 tbsp olive oil

1 tbsp lemon juice

1 tbsp tahini paste

1 Put the chick peas into a food processor, add the onions, bread, egg, lemon zest and juice, garlic, cilantro, parsley, tahini, ground coriander, cumin, cinnamon, and cayenne pepper, and season with salt and pepper. Puree until smooth.

2 Turn into a bowl, cover, and leave to stand for at least 30 minutes.

3 Meanwhile, make the sesame yogurt sauce: in a bowl, combine the yogurt, oil, lemon juice, tahini, and salt and pepper to taste.

4 With dampened hands, shape the felafel mixture into balls about the size of a walnut, then flatten them into patties.

5 Pour enough oil into a nonstick skillet to just cover the base, and heat until hot. Shallow-fry the felafel in batches for 2–3 minutes on each side until golden. Lift out and drain on paper towels. Garnish with cilantro and serve warm, with mini pita breads and sesame yogurt sauce.

HALLOUMI & VEGETABLE KEBABS

SERVES 4

1 small baguette

8 oz (250 g) halloumi cheese

1 large red bell pepper, cored and seeded

2/3 cup (150 ml) olive oil, plus extra for greasing

16 large cherry tomatoes

grated zest and juice of 1 lemon

1 garlic clove, crushed

2 tbsp chopped fresh basil

1 tbsp snipped fresh chives

salt and black pepper

8 METAL SKEWERS

1 Cut the bread into 8 thick slices and cut each slice in half. Cut the halloumi into 16 cubes and cut the red pepper into 8 pieces.

2 Oil the skewers and thread alternately with the tomatoes, bread, cheese, and red pepper. Place in a shallow gratin dish.

3 Mix the oil, lemon zest and juice, garlic, and herbs, and season with salt and pepper. Drizzle over the kebabs.

4 Cook the kebabs under a hot grill, 4 in (10 cm) from the heat, turning once and basting with the marinade, for 3–4 minutes until the cheese is lightly browned.

Cook's know-how

Halloumi is a semi-firm Greek cheese which is usually made from ewe milk. It is best eaten hot, straight from the broiler, because it becomes rubbery when it cools down.

TOFU & VEGETABLE KEBABS

Substitute smoked tofu for the halloumi cheese, and 8 button mushrooms for the red pepper.

VEGETABLE STIR-FRY WITH TOFU

SERVES 4

8 oz (250 g) firm tofu, cut into bite-sized pieces

2 tbsp sesame oil

1 tbsp sunflower oil

1 head of endive, halved lengthwise

4 carrots, thinly sliced diagonally

2 in (5 cm) piece of fresh gingerroot, peeled and grated

3 1/2 cups (250 g) sliced shiitake mushrooms

8 green onions, sliced into 1 in (2.5 cm) pieces

8 oz (250 g) bean sprouts

3 tbsp toasted sesame seeds

MARINADE

3 tbsp soy sauce

3 tbsp dry sherry

1 garlic clove, crushed

salt and black pepper

1 Make the marinade: in a bowl, combine the soy sauce, sherry, and garlic, and season with salt and pepper. Turn the tofu in the marinade, cover, and leave to marinate at room temperature for at least 15 minutes.

2 Drain the tofu, reserving the marinade. Heat the sesame and sunflower oils in a wok or large skillet, add the tofu, and carefully stir-fry over a high heat for 2–3 minutes, being careful not to break up the tofu. Remove from the wok with a slotted spoon and drain on paper towels.

3 Separate the endive halves into leaves. Add the carrots and ginger to the wok and stir-fry for about 2 minutes. Add the mushrooms and green onions and stir-fry for a further 2 minutes, then add the bean sprouts and endive leaves and stir-fry for 1 minute.

4 Return the tofu to the wok, pour the reserved marinade over the top, and boil quickly until almost all of the marinade has evaporated and the tofu has warmed through. Generously sprinkle with the toasted sesame seeds, taste for seasoning, and serve at once.

MEXICAN CHILI WITH TOFU

SERVES 6

3 onions, chopped

3 garlic cloves, roughly chopped

1 fresh green chilli, halved, seeded, and roughly chopped

2 tsp paprika

1 tbsp chili powder

4 tbsp sunflower oil

14 oz (400 g) canned crushed tomatoes, drained and juice reserved

2 cups (500 ml) hot vegetable stock

1 1/4 lb (625 g) firm tofu, cut into bite-sized pieces

14 oz (400 g) canned red kidney beans, drained

salt and black pepper

chopped fresh cilantro to garnish

1 Put the onions, garlic, green chili, and spices into a food processor and process until fairly chunky.

2 Heat the oil in a skillet. Add the onion mixture and cook for a few minutes, stirring occasionally, until softened and fragrant.

3 Add the tomatoes to the pan and cook, stirring occasionally, until reduced and thickened. Pour in the stock and cook for 5–10 minutes more until thickened again.

4 Add the tofu, kidney beans, and the reserved tomato juice, and cook, spooning the sauce over the tofu pieces, for 5–8 minutes until heated through. Do not stir the tofu as it may break up. Season, and serve hot, sprinkled with cilantro.

Cook's know-how

Reducing a sauce involves cooking it over a high heat to let the moisture evaporate and the flavors to become concentrated.

VEGETARIAN BURGERS

SERVES 6

1 tbls (15 g) butter

1 3/4 cups (125 g) finely chopped crimini mushrooms

1 small leek, finely chopped

1 small green chili, cored, seeded, and finely chopped

1 tsp sugar

1 garlic clove, crushed

28 oz (800 g) canned lima beans or cannellini beans (or use one half of each), drained and rinsed

salt and black pepper

all-purpose flour for coating

4 tbsp olive or sunflower oil

DRESSED LETTUCE

4 tbsp reduced-calorie mayonnaise

2 tbsp Dijon mustard

dash of lemon juice

1/2 small iceberg lettuce, finely shredded

1 small onion, thinly sliced

1 Melt the butter in a skillet, add the mushrooms and leek, and cook over a high heat for 2–3 minutes until fairly soft. Add the chili, sugar, and garlic, and stir fry for 2–3 minutes. Add the beans and cook, stirring, for 1 minute.

2 Remove from the heat, season well, and mash with a potato masher until the beans are broken into a rough mixture with no large lumps. Shape into 6 burgers.

3 Spinkle some flour onto a plate and season with salt and pepper. Coat both sides of each burger in flour.

4 Heat the oil in a skillet, add the burgers, and cook for about 3–4 minutes on each side until golden brown and heated right through.

5 Make the dressed lettuce: combine the mayonnaise, mustard, and lemon juice. Stir in the lettuce and onion. Serve with the burgers.

GLAMORGAN "SAUSAGES"

SERVES 4

2 1/2 cups (150 g) fresh white bread crumbs

1 cup (125 g) grated Cheddar cheese

1 small leek, finely chopped

1/4 cup (30 g) walnuts, finely chopped

2 tbsp chopped fresh sage or parsley

1 tsp grated lemon zest

1 tsp dry mustard

1/2 cup (60 g) coarsely chopped goat cheese

2 eggs

1 tbsp milk

salt and black pepper

all-purpose flour for coating

2 tbsp sunflower oil

fresh sage or parsley to garnish

1 In a bowl, combine the bread crumbs, cheese, leek, walnuts, sage or parsley, lemon zest, and mustard. Blend the goat cheese into the mixture.

2 Separate 1 egg, reserving the white and adding the yolk to the remaining egg. Beat the egg and yolk into the cheese mixture with the milk, and season with salt and pepper.

3 Divide the mixture into 8 pieces and roll into sausages about 3 in (7 cm) long. Cover and chill for about 1 hour to allow the flavors to develop.

4 Sprinkle some flour onto a plate and season with salt and pepper. Brush the sausages with the reserved egg white, then dip into the seasoned flour until lightly coated all over. Shake off any excess flour.

5 Heat the oil in a skillet, add the sausages, and cook over a medium heat, turning occasionally, for 8–10 minutes until golden. Drain on paper towels, and serve hot, garnished with sage or parsley.

GOAT CHEESE NUGGETS

Cut the goat cheese into 16 cubes. Combine the bread crumbs with the other ingredients as above. Mold the mixture around the goat cheese cubes, forming small balls. Chill, then coat and cook as in steps 4 and 5.

ORIENTAL VEGETARIAN DISHES

Vegetarians fare better in the East than they do in the West because vegetarianism has been popular there for so much longer than in the West, and there are so many more dishes to choose from. These recipes from Thailand, Japan, and China are just a small sample to inspire you.

THAI CURRY

SERVES 4

I tbsp sunflower or sesame oil
I fresh green chili, cored, seeded, and finely chopped
I in (2.5 cm) piece of fresh gingerroot, peeled and grated
I tbsp Thai green curry paste
I large cauliflower, cut into bite-sized florets
12 oz (375 g) thin green beans, halved
1¾ cups (400 g) canned coconut milk
¼ pint (150 ml) vegetable stock
I fresh lemongrass stalk, bruised by bashing with a rolling pin
salt and black pepper
7 oz (200 g) canned water chestnuts
3 tbsp chopped fresh cilantro, to garnish
boiled or steamed Thai jasmine rice, to serve

1 Heat the oil in a wok or large nonstick skillet and stir-fry the chili and ginger for 2 minutes. Add the curry paste and stir-fry for a further minute.

2 Add the cauliflower and beans and stir to evenly coat the vegetables in the spices. Pour in the coconut milk and stock, then add the lemongrass and seasoning. Bring to a boil and simmer gently for about 20–30 minutes until the beans and cauliflower are just cooked (take care not to overcook them). Add the water chestnuts for the last 5 minutes. Remove and discard the lemongrass, scatter over the coriander and serve with rice.

JAPANESE NOODLE SOUP

SERVES 6

6 cups (1.5 liters) miso soup (3 sachets)
I tsp five-spice paste or I tsp five-spice powder mixed to a paste with a little water
10 oz(300 g) udon noodles (made from wheat flour)
8 oz (250 g) tofu, cut into ½ in (I cm) cubes
3 green onions, trimmed and shredded

1 Make up the miso soup, bring to a boil and add the five-spice paste. Simmer for 5 minutes, then add the noodles and simmer for 2 minutes, gently separating them with chopsticks or a fork.

2 Add the tofu and heat through for 1 minute. Ladle into soup dishes and scatter over the shredded spring onions before serving.

FIRECRACKER STIR-FRY

SERVES 4

250 g (8 oz) bok choy
2–3 tbsp sunflower or sesame oil
8 oz (250 g) sugarsnap peas, trimmed
I red bell pepper, cored, seeded, and cut into strips
I yellow bell pepper, cored, seeded, and cut into strips
2–3 hot fresh red chilies, cored, seeded, and sliced
4¼ cups (300 g) sliced shiitake mushrooms
2–3 tbsp soy sauce
salt and black pepper
boiled or steamed long grain rice, to serve

1 Cut the leafy tops off the bok choy, shred the leaves coarsely, and reserve. Slice the stems in half, or into quarters if they are large.

2 Heat the oil in a wok or large skillet. Add the peas, peppers and chili and stir-fry over a high heat for about 3–4 minutes. Add the mushrooms and bok choy stems and continue to stir-fry for another 2–3 minutes.

3 When the vegetables are just about tender, add the shredded bok choy leaves with a dash of soy sauce. Taste and add salt and pepper if needed, plus more soy sauce if you like. Serve immediately, with rice.

PEKING TOFU
WITH PLUM SAUCE

SERVES 6

sunflower oil, for frying
250 g (8 oz) tofu, cut into just over ½ in (1.5 cm) cubes
18 Chinese pancakes (store-bought or see page 212)
6 green onions, trimmed and cut into matchsticks
¼ cucumber, peeled, seeded, and cut into matchsticks

PLUM SAUCE

8 oz (250 g) dark red plums, halved and pitted
I small cooking apple, peeled, cored, and sliced
I fresh red chili, cored, seeded, and finely chopped
6 tbls (90 g) sugar
¼ cup (50 ml) white wine vinegar

1 Make the plum sauce. Put the plums, apple, chili, sugar, vinegar, and 2 tbls (25 ml) water into a pan. Heat gently to dissolve the sugar, then bring to a boil. Partially cover and simmer gently for 30–40 minutes until the fruits have cooked down and only a little liquid remains. Remove from the heat and allow to cool.

2 Pour enough oil into a nonstick skillet to cover the base. Heat until hot, then fry the tofu for 3–4 minutes until golden brown all over, turning carefully. Remove and drain on paper towels.

3 To serve, spread a pancake with a little plum sauce, top with a little crispy fried tofu, green onions, and cucumber and roll up to eat.

CLOCKWISE FROM TOP: Thai Curry with jasmine rice, Firecracker Stir-fry with long-grain rice, Japanese Noodle Soup, Peking Tofu with Plum Sauce.

CHESTNUT LOAF

SERVES 6

8 oz (250 g) frozen chestnuts, thawed

1 tbsp olive oil, plus extra for greasing

1 onion, coarsely chopped

2 celery stalks, chopped

2 garlic cloves, crushed

1 large potato, boiled and mashed

2 cups (125 g) fresh whole wheat bread crumbs

1 egg, beaten

2 tbsp chopped parsley

1 tbsp soy sauce

1 tbsp tomato paste

salt and black pepper

red bell pepper strips and watercress sprigs to garnish

spicy tomato salsa (see box, right) to serve

9 × 5 × 3 IN (23 × 12.5 × 7 CM) LOAF PAN

1 Coarsely chop half of the chestnuts, and finely chop the remainder.

2 Heat the oil in a pan, add the onion, celery, and garlic, and cook, stirring, for 3–5 minutes until soft. Remove from the heat.

3 Stir in the chestnuts, potatoes, bread crumbs, egg, parsley, soy sauce, and tomato paste, and season with salt and pepper.

4 Spoon the mixture into the greased loaf tin, and level the top. Cover with foil and cook in a preheated oven at 350°F (180°C) for 1 hour or until firm. Turn out, cut into slices, and garnish. Serve hot or cold, with the spicy tomato salsa.

Spicy tomato salsa

Dice 8 large tomatoes, and put into a bowl. Stir in 2 chopped green onions, 1 seeded and finely chopped fresh green chili, the zest and juice of 2 limes, 3 tbsp chopped fresh cilantro, and 1 tsp sugar. Season with salt and pepper, and chill.

FESTIVE NUT LOAF

SERVES 6–8

1/3 cup (75 g) brown rice

salt and black pepper

1/2 oz (15 g) dried ceps

2 tbls (30 g) butter

2 carrots, grated

1 small onion, finely chopped

1 garlic clove, crushed

3 1/2 cups (250 g) chopped button mushrooms

2 tbsp chopped parsley

1 tbsp chopped fresh rosemary

1 cup (125 g) walnuts, toasted and chopped

1 cup (125 g) Brazil nuts, toasted and chopped

1/2 cup (60 g) pine nuts, toasted

6 oz (175 g) grated Cheddar cheese

1 egg, beaten

sunflower oil for greasing

rosemary sprigs to garnish

cranberry sauce (page 202) to serve

9 × 5 × 3 IN (23 × 12.5 × 7 CM) LOAF PAN

1 Cook the rice in boiling salted water for 30–35 minutes until tender.

2 Meanwhile, soak the ceps in a bowl of warm water for about 20–30 minutes.

3 Drain the rice when it is ready. Drain the ceps, pat dry, and chop finely.

4 Melt the butter in a skillet, add the carrots, onion, and garlic, and cook gently, stirring occasionally, for 5 minutes. Stir in the chopped mushrooms, rice, ceps, parsley, and rosemary, and cook until softened.

5 Puree the mixture in a food processor. Stir in the walnuts, Brazil nuts, pine nuts, cheese, and egg. Season with salt and pepper.

6 Lightly grease the loaf pan, spoon in the mixture, and level the top. Cover with foil and bake in a preheated oven at 375°F (190°C) for 1 1/2 hours or until firm. Turn out, cut into slices, and garnish. Serve hot, with cranberry sauce.

SPINACH ROULADE

SERVES 6-8

1 lb 2 oz (560 g) fresh spinach

2 tbls (30 g) butter, plus extra for greasing

4 eggs, separated

¼ tsp grated nutmeg

1 tbsp finely grated Parmesan cheese

FILLING

1 tbls (15 g) butter

3½ cups (250 g) sliced button mushrooms

juice of ½ lemon

salt and black pepper

1 scant cup (200 ml) sour cream

2 tbsp chopped parsley

13 x 9 IN (33 x 23 CM) JELLY ROLL PAN

1 Make the filling: melt the butter in a pan, add the mushrooms and lemon juice, and season with salt and pepper. Cook for 3 minutes until just softened, then leave to cool.

2 Wash the spinach and put into a pan with only the water remaining on the leaves. Cook over a gentle heat for 1–2 minutes until the spinach has just wilted. Drain well, and squeeze out the excess water.

3 Butter the pan and line with parchment paper. Butter the parchment.

4 Coarsely chop the spinach, turn into a large bowl, and beat in the butter, egg yolks, and nutmeg. Season with salt and pepper. In another bowl, whisk the egg whites until firm but not dry, then fold gently into the spinach mixture.

5 Pour the spinach mixture into the jelly roll pan and bake in a preheated oven at 425°F (220°C) for 10–12 minutes until firm.

6 Sprinkle the Parmesan cheese onto a sheet of parchment paper. Turn the roulade out onto the cheese, leave to cool for 5–10 minutes, then peel off the lining paper. Trim the edges of the roulade.

7 Drain the mushrooms, reserving some of the cooking liquid. Put them into a bowl, add the sour cream, parsley, and season to taste. Add a little of the reserved liquid if too thick. Spread the filling over the roulade, leaving a 1 in (2.5 cm) border. Roll up from one long side. Cover and chill for 30 minutes. Cut into slices to serve.

CARROT ROULADE

SERVES 6-8

½ cup (125 g) butter, plus extra for greasing

1 large garlic clove, crushed

½ red bell pepper, cored, seeded, and finely chopped

7 oz (200 g) canned tomatoes

1½ lb (750 g) carrots, grated

6 eggs, separated

FILLING

1 cucumber, seeded and diced

salt and black pepper

4 oz (125 g) goat cheese

4 oz (125 g) cream cheese

3 green onions, thinly sliced

1 large garlic clove, crushed

2–3 tbsp finely chopped parsley

milk if needed

13 x 9 IN (33 x 23 CM) JELLY ROLL PAN

1 Put the diced cucumber into a colander, sprinkle with salt, and leave to stand for 20 minutes.

2 Butter the pan and line with parchment paper. Butter the parchment.

3 Melt the butter, add half of the garlic, the red pepper, and tomatoes, and cook gently for 5 minutes.

4 Add the carrots and cook gently for 2 minutes or until soft. Turn the carrot mixture into a large bowl and beat in the egg yolks. Season with salt and pepper. In another bowl, whisk the egg whites until firm but not dry, then fold into the carrot mixture.

5 Pour the carrot mixture into the jelly roll pan and bake in a preheated oven at 400°F (200°C) for 10 minutes or until golden. Cover and leave to cool.

6 Make the filling: rinse the cucumber and pat dry with paper towels. Turn into a bowl and combine with the goat cheese, cream cheese, green onions, garlic, parsley, and black pepper to taste. If the mixture is very thick, stir in 1–2 tbsp milk.

7 Turn the roulade out on to a sheet of baking parchment and peel off the lining paper. Trim the edges. Spread the filling over the roulade, leaving a 2.5 cm (1 in) border on each side. Roll up the roulade from one long side, using the parchment paper for support. Cover and chill for 30 minutes. Cut into slices to serve.

SUMMER VEGETABLE TERRINE

SERVES 8

12–16 large spinach leaves

salt and black pepper

1 eggplant, sliced lengthwise

1 tbsp olive oil, plus extra for greasing

2 large red bell peppers, cored, seeded, and halved

1 large yellow bell pepper, halved, seeded, and halved

2 cups (500 g) lowfat cream cheese

2 eggs, lightly beaten

4 tbsp light cream

1/4 cup (30 g) Parmesan cheese, grated

2 tbsp store-bought pesto

2 LB (1 KG) LOAF PAN OR TERRINE

1 Blanch the spinach in boiling salted water for 30 seconds. Drain, rinse in cold water, and pat dry. Line the loaf pan (see box, right).

2 Brush the eggplant with the oil, and cook under a hot broiler for 6–8 minutes on each side. Roast and peel the peppers (page 388). Cut the pepper halves into strips.

3 Combine the cream cheese, eggs, cream, grated Parmesan, and pesto. Season with salt and pepper.

Lining the loaf pan

Oil the loaf pan and line with the spinach leaves, letting 2 in (5 cm) overhang the sides.

4 Cover the base of the pan with some of the cheese. Layer in half of the red peppers and half of the eggplant slices, spreading cheese between each layer, then layer in the yellow pepper and repeat the layers of eggplant and red pepper, spreading the cheese between them as before. Finish with the remaining cheese. Fold over the spinach leaves.

5 Tightly cover the pan with oiled foil. Put the pan into a roasting pan and pour in boiling water to come halfway up the sides. Cook in a preheated oven at 350°F(180°C) for 1 1/2 hours or until firm. Remove from the water, cool, then chill thoroughly. Slice and serve.

WINTER VEGETABLE TERRINE

SERVES 4–6

12 oz (375 g) chopped carrots

1 in (2.5 cm) piece of fresh gingerroot, peeled and grated

salt and black pepper

12 oz (375 g) celery root, peeled and coarsely chopped

12 oz (375 g) broccoli

sunflower oil for greasing

3 eggs

2 LB (1 KG) LOAF PAN OR TERRINE

1 Cook the carrots with the ginger in boiling salted water for 10–15 minutes until the carrots are just tender. Cook the celery root in boiling salted water for 8–10 minutes until tender.

2 Cut the stems off the broccoli and cook them in boiling salted water for 8–10 minutes until almost tender, then add the broccoli florets and cook for 1 minute longer.

3 Drain all the the vegetables separately and rinse in cold water. Line the base of the greased loaf pan with parchment paper.

4 Put the broccoli in a food processor, add 1 egg, and season with salt and pepper. Puree until smooth, then turn the mixture into the loaf pan and level the surface.

5 Put the celery root in the food processor, add another egg, and season with salt and pepper, then puree until smooth. Spread over the broccoli mixture and level the surface.

6 Puree the carrots and ginger with the remaining egg and salt and pepper in the food processor until smooth. Spread over the celery root and level the surface.

7 Tightly cover the pan with greased foil. Put the pan into a roasting pan and pour in boiling water to come halfway up the sides. Cook in a preheated oven at 350°F (180°C) for 1 hour or until firm.

8 Remove from the water, and leave to cool in the loaf tin. Chill thoroughly in the refrigerator. Turn out the terrine, and cut into slices to serve.

8

PASTA & RICE

UNDER 30 MINUTES

PENNE WITH SPINACH & BLUE CHEESE

Pasta quills with mushrooms, cream, and garlic, mixed with spinach, and blue cheese.

SERVES 4 976 calories per serving

Takes 15 minutes Page 339

PASTA ALLA MARINARA

Pasta bows combined with squid, scallops, shrimp, button mushrooms, white wine, onion, and parsley. Enriched with cream.

SERVES 6 531 calories per serving

Takes 15 minutes Page 337

SPAGHETTI CARBONARA

Italian classic: crisp-cooked strips of bacon mixed with garlic, eggs, and Parmesan cheese, then tossed with spaghetti and light cream.

SERVES 4 906 calories per serving

Takes 20 minutes Page 344

DINNER PARTY

PASTA SHELLS WITH SCALLOPS

Scallops simmered with lemon juice, onion, peppercorns, and bay leaf. Served with a creamy mushroom sauce and pasta shells.

SERVES 4 753 calories per serving

Takes 25 minutes Page 338

TAGLIATELLE WITH VEGETABLE RIBBONS

Fine ribbons of zucchini and carrot cooked with tagliatelle. Mixed with pesto sauce.

SERVES 6 294 calories per serving

Takes 25 minutes Page 339

CHINESE CLASSIC

EGG-FRIED RICE

Delicious and simple: long-grain rice boiled and then stir-fried with bacon, peas, eggs, and bean sprouts. Sprinkled with green onions.

SERVES 4 441 calories per serving

Takes 25 minutes Page 360

PENNE WITH ASPARAGUS

Bite-sized pieces of asparagus and pasta quills in a light, aromatic mixture of olive oil, garlic, basil, and goat cheese.

SERVES 6 462 calories per serving

Takes 20 minutes Page 342

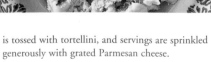

TORTELLINI WITH PEAS & BACON

Rich and creamy: peas and diced bacon combined with heavy cream, salt, black pepper, and a pinch of grated nutmeg. This delicious sauce is tossed with tortellini, and servings are sprinkled generously with grated Parmesan cheese.

SERVES 6 643 calories per serving

Takes 25 minutes Page 343

30–60 MINUTES

LOW FAT

STIR-FRIED CHINESE NOODLES

Egg noodles stir-fried with snow peas, bean sprouts, shiitake mushrooms, garlic, and ginger, served sprinkled with green onions.

SERVES 4 476 calories per serving

Takes 20 minutes, plus soaking   Page 343

CARIBBEAN RICE & PEAS

Traditional West Indian dish: rice cooked with kidney beans, stock, green onions, bacon, garlic, tomatoes, herbs, and spices.

SERVES 4–6 435–290 calories per serving

Takes 35 minutes   Page 351

RISI E BISI

Risotto rice cooked with peas, stock, and prosciutto. Flavored with garlic, onion, Parmesan cheese, and parsley.

SERVES 6 390 calories per serving

Takes 40 minutes   Page 354

SUMMER RISOTTO AL VERDE

Short-grain risotto rice cooked with stock and garlic, then mixed with cream, blue cheese, pesto, and pine nuts. Served sprinkled with basil.

SERVES 4 734 calories per serving

Takes 35 minutes   Page 357

TRADITIONAL

KEDGEREE

Anglo-Indian breakfast dish: long-grain rice baked with smoked haddock, hard-boiled eggs, cream, and lemon juice. Mixed with parsley.

SERVES 4 470 calories per scrving

Takes 45 minutes   Page 357

TAGLIATELLE WITH SHRIMP

Ribbon pasta served with a sauce of button mushrooms, tomatoes, prawns, and sour cream, garnished with parsley.

SERVES 4 734 calories per serving

Takes 35 minutes   Page 338

FAMILY CHOICE

CONFETTI RICE

Long-grain rice simmered with tomatoes, stock, corn, onion, carrot, and peas, and flavored with garlic.

SERVES 4 356 calories per serving

Takes 30 minutes   Page 351

PASTA SPIRALS WITH GROUND MEATBALLS

Ground turkey or chicken, bread crumbs, Parmesan cheese, parsley, and thyme in a tomato basil sauce.

SERVES 8 384 calories per serving

Takes 35 minutes   Page 345

PERSIAN PILAF

Rice cooked with cumin and cardamom seeds, cinnamon, cloves, and bay leaves. Combined with pistachio nuts and raisins.

SERVES 4 426 calories per serving

Takes 40 minutes   Page 355

30–60 MINUTES

SPAGHETTI ALLE VONGOLE

Fresh clams cooked in tomatoes and wine, and seasoned with onion, garlic, cayenne pepper, and parsley. Served with spaghetti.

SERVES 4 626 calories per serving
Takes 40 minutes   Page 337

VEGETARIAN

BAKED WILD RICE

Basmati and wild rice baked with broccoli, garlic, onions, sour cream, mozzarella and Parmesan cheeses, and rosemary.

SERVES 6 446 calories per serving
Takes 60 minutes   Page 354

FETTUCCINE PRIMAVERA

Asparagus, broccoli, zucchini, red and yellow peppers, garlic, tomatoes, peas, and cream mixed with fettuccine. Served with basil and Parmesan.

SERVES 4 831 calories per serving
Takes 35 minutes   Page 344

ITALIAN CLASSIC

RISOTTO MILANESE

Short-grain risotto cooked with stock and onion, flavored with saffron, and mixed with Parmesan cheese. Served with Parmesan shavings.

SERVES 6 403 calories per serving
Takes 45 minutes   Page 356

PORTUGUESE RICE WITH TUNA

Nourishing meal: brown rice simmered with stock, bacon, and onion. Combined with fresh tuna, pepper strips, and olives.

SERVES 4 603 calories per serving
Takes 45 minutes   Page 355

HIGH PROTEIN

CASSEROLE WITH FENNEL

A family favorite: fennel and onion baked with white sauce, pasta shells, tuna, eggs, and Cheddar cheese.

SERVES 6 512 calories per serving
Takes 45 minutes   Page 348

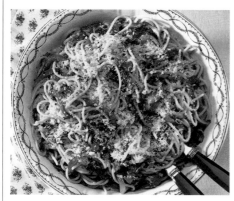

SPAGHETTI ALL' AMATRICIANA

Diced bacon cooked with tomatoes, garlic, red and green bell peppers, fresh chili, and herbs, then tossed with spaghetti.

SERVES 6 431 calories per serving
Takes 40 minutes   Page 342

CHICKEN LIVER RISOTTO

Wild and risotto rice cooked with stock and bacon. Combined with chicken livers, mushrooms, and sun-dried tomatoes.

SERVES 4–6 619–413 calories per serving
Takes 40 minutes   Page 356

VEGETARIAN

VEGETABLES NAPOLETANA

Broccoli, shiitake mushrooms, red bell pepper, zucchini, and mustard-flavored white sauce baked with pasta twists.

SERVES 4 713 calories per serving
Takes 55 minutes   Page 348

OVER 60 MINUTES

THREE-CHEESE MACARONI

Macaroni baked with a sauce flavored with smoked and sharp Cheddar and mozzarella cheeses, topped with bread crumbs.

SERVES 6–8 581–436 calories per serving

Takes 1 hour 5 minutes   Page 349

LASAGNE

Pasta layered with ground beef, simmered with stock, tomatoes, celery, white sauce, and Cheddar and Parmesan cheeses.

SERVES 8 641 calories per serving

Takes 1 1/2 hours, plus simmering   Page 350

CANNELLONI WITH RICOTTA & SPINACH

Cannelloni tubes filled with spinach and ricotta cheese, and topped with tomato sauce.

SERVES 6 462 calories per serving

Takes 40 minutes, plus simmering   Page 350

FISHERMAN'S LASAGNE

Pasta layered with haddock, shrimp, zucchini, and parsley sauce. Sprinkled with Cheddar and Parmesan cheeses.

SERVES 8 477 calories per serving

Takes 1 1/4 hours   Page 349

SPANISH CLASSIC

SPAGHETTI BOLOGNESE

Traditional Italian dish: spaghetti served with a sauce of ground beef simmered with celery, garlic, tomato, and red-currant jelly.

SERVES 4 904 calories per serving

Takes 15 minutes, plus simmering   Page 345

PAELLA

Chicken and rice are cooked in the oven with bacon, stock, tomatoes, onion, bell peppers, peas, and saffron. Mussels and shrimp are stirred in and cooked gently on top of the stove, then the dish is served garnished with jumbo shrimp, lemon wedges, olives, and parsley.

SERVES 6 718 calories per serving

Takes 1 1/4 hours   Page 360

PASTA & RICE KNOW-HOW

BOTH PASTA AND RICE are natural convenience foods: they are so quick to cook and they do not need any elaborate preparation. They are also endlessly versatile, working well with almost every ingredient imaginable to make appetizers, soups, main dishes, side dishes, salads, snacks, and even a few desserts.

Pasta and rice are very nutritious, being high in starchy carbohydrates, and in their wholegrain forms also offering vitamins, minerals, and fiber. As long as rich ingredients, such as butter, cream, and cheese, are kept to a minimum, pasta and rice dishes can be very low in fat and calories.

BUYING & STORING

Pasta is available both fresh and dried as well as vacuum-packed, in a huge variety of shapes, both plain and stuffed. The best commercial dried pasta is made from durum wheat. Egg is sometimes added to dried pasta, while the fresh pasta sold in packets in supermarkets is almost always enriched with eggs. Pasta is also colored and flavored – with spinach or tomato, for example. Fresh pasta is convenient because it cooks quickly, but its texture is not necessarily as good as some dried pasta. A good Italian brand of dried pasta, made from 100% durum wheat (*semola di grano duro*), is often of superior quality.

Dried pasta, in a tightly closed package, will keep almost indefinitely in the cupboard (up to 2 years); fresh pasta must be refrigerated and can only be kept for 2–3 days (check the use-by date). For longer storage, freeze it (see below).

Rice is another good cupboard stand-by. As long as it is stored in an airtight container in a cool, dry, dark place, it will keep for up to a year. But make sure that the container is tightly closed to prevent moisture or insects from getting in.

Store any leftover cooked pasta or rice in a tightly closed container in the refrigerator. Use pasta within 2 days. Rice should be eaten on the day it is cooked because it is susceptible to toxins and bacteria that cause food poisoning.

MICROWAVING

There is no advantage to cooking pasta in a microwave because it takes just as long as conventional cooking. However, many pasta sauces can be microwaved quickly and successfully, dishes containing layered or filled pasta cook really well in the microwave, and it is also an excellent way to reheat cooked pasta (be careful not to overcook it). The microwave is excellent for cooking rice, plain or turned into a pilaf or risotto, and the liquid does not have to be brought to a boil before the rice is added. Risotto turns out as tender and creamy as one made by the classic method that involves constant stirring, and yet it can be left totally unattended in the microwave.

FREEZING

Fresh uncooked pasta can be frozen for up to 3 months and then cooked from frozen. Layered or filled pasta dishes such as cannelloni, lasagne, and macaroni and cheese freeze very well and can also be stored for up to 3 months. Put them in foil or other freezerproof containers that can go straight from the freezer into the oven.

There is no advantage to freezing cooked rice as it takes a long time to thaw – longer than it would take to cook a fresh batch.

It is not advisable to freeze pasta and rice in soups and other dishes that contain a lot of liquid because the pasta and rice become mushy when thawed. Instead, add when reheating the soup or casserole.

ORIENTAL NOODLES

Oriental noodles are made from a variety of flours. The most popular types are available in supermarkets and delicatessens; others can be found in Chinese or Japanese food stores.

Wheat noodles
The most common of Oriental noodles, these are made from wheat flour usually enriched with egg. They are available both flat and round and in a variety of widths.

Cellophane noodles
Sometimes referred to as transparent noodles or bean thread noodles, these are very fine and white. They are made from ground mung beans.

Rice noodles
Rice vermicelli are long, thin, white strands made from rice flour. Sold dried or fresh in bundles, they are used in soups and can be deep-fried.

Rice sticks
Made from the same dough as rice noodles, rice sticks are broad ribbons. They are usually served in a broth or sauce.

Soba
These thin, brown Japanese noodles are made from buckwheat flour. They are often served with a dipping sauce.

Udon
Made from white wheat flour, these are also from Japan.

Noodles know-how
Store Oriental noodles in the same way as pasta.

•

Most Oriental noodles need only be soaked or briefly cooked in boiling water before being added to soups and broths, vegetable dishes and stir-fries.

PASTA SHAPES

Of the many pasta shapes available there are some that are traditionally served with certain sauces – spaghetti with bolognese sauce, for example. But you can mix and match as you wish.

Long, thin varieties
Capelli d'angelo or angel hair, vermicelli, spaghettini, spaghetti, and bucatini are best served with a thin oily sauce that clings without making the strands stick together.

Long flat ribbons
Pasta such as linguine, fettuccine, and tagliatelle is usually served with a creamy sauce, such as *alfredo*.

Tubular pasta
Macaroni, penne (quills), and rigatoni are best with rich sauces that will run inside their tubes.

Interesting shapes
There is a vast range of small pasta shapes, and more are being created every day. The most common include ditali (thimbles), fusilli (spirals), conchiglie (shells),

farfalle (bows), gnocchi (fluted shells), lumache (snails), orecchiette (ears), and radiatori (grills). Sauce them like tubular pasta.

Soup pasta
Very small pasta shapes, such as conchigliette, ditalini, farfallette and orzo, are used in soup.

Filled pastas
Agnolotti, capelletti, ravioli, and tortellini are some of the shapes stuffed with ground meats or mixtures such as spinach and ricotta, and served with a simple sauce.

Sheet pasta
Flat sheets of lasagne are layered with sauce and baked. Fresh lasagne, and cooked dried lasagne, can be rolled around a filling to make cannelloni.

COOKING PASTA

There is one golden rule when cooking pasta: use plenty of water and salt – at least 2 quarts (2 liters) water and 2 tsp salt for every 8 oz (250 g) of pasta.

1 Bring the salted water to a boil. Add the pasta and stir to separate. If cooking spaghetti, let the ends soften before stirring. Return the water to a boil as quickly as possible. Reduce the heat so the water is bubbling briskly and cook, uncovered.

2 When the pasta is al dente (see box, below), immediately tip it into a large colander, and shake to drain the pasta thoroughly.

3 Return the pasta to the pan or transfer to a warmed bowl. Toss with olive oil or butter, add plenty of ground black pepper and chopped fresh herbs, if liked, and serve immediately.

Pasta know-how

To test pasta, lift out a piece and bite it – it should be tender but still a little firm. The Italians call this al dente, literally "to the tooth."

If you are going to use cooked pasta in a baked dish, undercook it slightly before mixing it with sauce. This will help prevent it from being overcooked when it comes out of the oven.

OVEN-READY LASAGNE

The sheets of dried lasagne that are labeled "no pre-cooking required" or "oven-ready" are a great boon to the busy, time-stretched cook because they can be taken straight from the package and layered with the other ingredients. However, this lasagne needs to absorb liquid during cooking, so if you are using it in a recipe that calls for fresh pasta or for ordinary dried lasagne, increase the quantity of sauce and make it thinner and runnier. Or briefly soak the sheets in a dish of hot water for about 5 minutes to moisten and soften them before layering in the baking dish.

Colored & flavored pasta

Not only does pasta come in a vast range of shapes, you can also choose from a variety of colours and flavours. Green is the most common color, and is derived from spinach. Other colors include red, from tomato puree, pink, colored with beets, yellow, from saffron, and even black pasta, colored with squid ink. These colorings affect the taste very little. Flavored pasta usually has ingredients such as herbs, garlic, or black pepper added to the dough. Serve with a complementary sauce.

COOKING TIMES & QUANTITIES

These times can only be a guide because they depend on the freshness of fresh pasta and the age of dried pasta, as well as shape and thickness. Start timing as soon as the water returns to a boil, and for fresh pasta, start testing three-quarters of the way through the suggested cooking time. If using dried pasta, start testing as soon as the minimum time given on the package is reached. Fresh, store-bought pasta takes 2–4 minutes, 7–10 minutes if filled. Most dried pastas cook in 8–12 minutes (less for fine pasta such as capelli d'angelo and vermicelli).

In Italy, pasta is usually eaten as a first course. Use a pound (500 g) fresh or dried pasta (uncooked weight) to serve 6 people as a first course and 4 people as a main dish. If the dish has a rich sauce or filling it will stretch even further. As an accompaniment to another dish, this amount would serve 6–8 people.

COOKING WITH RICE

The length of the rice grain determines how it should be cooked and used. Short grain rice is almost round in shape and very starchy. It is best cooked by absorption, so it remains moist and sticky, and used for puddings, risottos, paella, stir-fried rice, and croquettes. The grains of long grain rice are separate, dry, and fluffy after cooking so it can be boiled and then used in pilafs, salads, and other savory dishes.

White rice has been milled to remove the husk, bran, and germ, whereas for brown rice only the tough outer husk has been removed, leaving the nutritious bran layer. This gives it its distinctive color and nutty flavor.

COOKING RICE BY ABSORPTION

Cook the rice very gently in simmering salted water. Use 2 parts water to 1 part rice.

1 Bring the salted water to a boil and add the rice. Return to a boil and stir once. Cover, reduce the heat, and cook gently until the water is absorbed.

2 Remove the pan from the heat and leave to stand, covered, for at least 5 minutes. Fluff up the rice with chopsticks or a fork just before serving.

BOILING RICE

Long grain rice should be rinsed well before and after boiling, to remove starch that would cause stickiness.

1 Put the rice into a large bowl of cold water. Swirl it around with your fingertips until the water becomes milky. Drain and repeat until the water stays clear. Drain again. Bring a large pan of salted water to a boil and add the rice.

2 Bring the water back to a boil. Reduce the heat so the water is simmering vigorously. Cook until the rice is just tender. Drain well and rinse with boiling water to remove any excess starch.

COOKING RISOTTO RICE

An authentic risotto requires constant attention as the hot liquid (usually stock) must be stirred into the rice very gradually. This basic technique can be varied in many ways by adding shellfish, mushrooms, herbs, ham, and so on.

1 Heat butter or oil in a large saucepan and soften the onion, garlic, or other flavorings as specified in the recipe.

2 Add the rice and stir to coat the grains with the fat (this will keep them separate during cooking). Cook, stirring, for 1–2 minutes or until the rice grains look translucent.

3 Add a ladleful, about 2/3 cup (150 ml), of the hot stock. Cook until absorbed. Add another ladleful and cook until absorbed.

4 Continue adding stock, stirring, for 25–30 minutes. When the rice is tender but still firm to the bite, you have added enough stock.

RICE VARIETIES

There are many varieties of rice, each with a distinct flavour and aroma. Here are the most common.

Camargue red
Similar to brown rice in texture, flavor, and cooking time.

Basmati
Available in brown or white varieties. Used mainly in Indian dishes. Cook for 10–15 minutes.

Brown
Has a slightly chewy texture with a mild nutty flavor. Cook for 30–35 minutes.

Easy-cook
Part-cooked so the grains stay separate. Cook for 10–12 minutes.

Long-grain
Mild in flavor. The most widely used type of white rice. Cook for 12–15 minutes.

Short-grain
Italian short-grain (such as arborio or carnaroli) is used for risotto; Spanish paella rice is similar but less creamy (the best is said to come from Valencia). Short-grain rice is also used for rice puddings. Cook for 20–25 minutes.

Wild
Not a true rice, but an aquatic grass. Cook for 35–40 minutes.

PASTA ALLA MARINARA

SERVES 6

1 lb (500 g) pasta bows

salt and black pepper

2 tbsp olive oil

1 large onion, finely chopped

1 large garlic clove, crushed

½ cup (125 ml) dry white wine

4 oz (125 g) squid, cut into strips or rings

1 scant cup (60 g) sliced button mushrooms

4 oz (125 g) scallops, halved

4 oz (125 g) cooked peeled prawns

⅔ cup (150 ml) heavy cream

4 tbsp chopped parsley

1 Cook the pasta bows in a large saucepan of boiling salted water for 8–10 minutes until just tender.

2 Meanwhile, heat the oil in a large pan, add the onion and garlic, and cook gently, stirring occasionally, for 3–5 minutes until softened but not colored.

3 Pour in the white wine and boil to reduce the liquid in the saucepan to about 2 tbsp, stirring constantly. Add the squid and cook for 1 minute, then add the mushrooms and scallops, and cook, stirring, for a further 2 minutes. Add the shrimp, cream, and half of the parsley, and heat through.

4 Drain the pasta bows thoroughly, and add to the seafood mixture, stirring well to combine. Season with salt and black pepper, and serve at once, garnished with the remaining chopped parsley.

Healthy option

Seafood and cream are a classic combination for a pasta sauce, but you may prefer a slightly less rich alternative. In fact, you can omit the cream altogether and use a few tablespoons of the pasta cooking water instead. Italian cooks often use this technique.

SPAGHETTI ALLE VONGOLE

SERVES 4

about 3 dozen fresh clams in their shells, cleaned (page 124)

2 tbsp olive oil, plus extra for tossing

1 onion, chopped

1 garlic clove, crushed

¼ tsp cayenne pepper

14 oz (400 g) canned crushed tomatoes

4 tbsp dry white wine

salt and black pepper

1 lb (500 g) spaghetti

2 tbsp chopped parsley

1 Holding each clam in a dish towel, insert a thin knife blade between the shells and twist the knife to open the shells. Reserve 4 clams for garnish. Remove the remaining clams from their shells, cut them into bite-sized pieces, and set aside with any juices.

2 Heat the olive oil in a large pan, add the onion and garlic, and cook gently, stirring occasionally, for 3–5 minutes until softened but not colored. Add the cayenne and cook gently, stirring, for 1 minute.

3 Add the tomatoes and wine, season with salt and pepper, and bring to a boil. Simmer, uncovered, for about 15 minutes or until the mixture has thickened.

4 Meanwhile, cook the spaghetti in a large saucepan of boiling salted water for 8–10 minutes until just tender. Drain, then toss the spaghetti in a little olive oil to prevent sticking. Transfer to warmed serving bowls.

5 Add the parsley, and the clams and their juices to the tomato mixture, and cook for 2 minutes. Do not cook longer or the clams will toughen.

6 Taste for seasoning, then spoon the sauce over the spaghetti. Serve at once, garnished with the reserved clams in their shells.

Cook's know-how

Live clams should be tightly closed in their shells. If any are open, give them a sharp tap on the work surface, then discard any that do not close.

TAGLIATELLE WITH SHRIMP

SERVES 4

2 tbsp olive oil

1 large onion, chopped

1 garlic clove, crushed

12 oz (375 g) button mushrooms, halved

1 lb (500 g) tomatoes, chopped into small pieces, cores removed

salt and black pepper

1 lb (500 g) tagliatelle

12 oz (375 g) cooked peeled shrimp

1/2 cup (125 ml) sour cream

4 tbsp chopped parsley to garnish

1 Heat the oil in a large pan, add the onion and garlic, and cook gently, stirring, for 3–5 minutes until softened but not colored. Add the mushrooms and cook over a high heat, stirring, for about 5 minutes.

2 Add the tomatoes, season with salt and pepper, and simmer gently, uncovered, for about 20 minutes or until the mixture has thickened.

3 Meanwhile, cook the tagliatelle in a large saucepan of boiling salted water for 8–10 minutes until just tender.

4 Add the shrimp and sour cream to the tomato mixture and cook gently for about 2 minutes until the prawns are heated through. Taste for seasoning.

5 Drain the tagliatelle thoroughly and pile onto warmed serving plates. Spoon the shrimp mixture on top, sprinkle with parsley, and serve at once.

PASTA WITH SMOKED SALMON & SHRIMP

Substitute 4 oz (125 g) smoked salmon, cut into bite-sized pieces, for 4 oz (125 g) of the shrimp. Add the smoked salmon after the shrimp have been heated through in step 4.

PASTA SHELLS WITH SCALLOPS

SERVES 4

8 large scallops, each cut into 3 slices

5 tbls (75 ml) water

juice of 1 lemon

1 slice of onion

6 black peppercorns

1 small bay leaf

1 lb (500 g) pasta shells

1 tbls (15 g) butter

chopped parsley and lemon slices to garnish

SAUCE

3 tbls (45 g) butter

1 1/2 cups (125 g) sliced button mushrooms

1/4 cup (30 g) all-purpose flour

2/3 cup (150 ml) heavy cream or sour cream

1 tbsp tomato paste

salt and black pepper

1 Put the scallops into a pan with the measured water, half the lemon juice, the onion, peppercorns, and bay leaf.

2 Bring to a gentle simmer, cover, and poach very gently for 2–3 minutes or until the scallops are opaque.

3 Remove the scallops with a slotted spoon, strain the liquid, and reserve.

4 Make the sauce: melt the butter in a saucepan, add the mushrooms, and cook gently, stirring occasionally, for 2 minutes. Sprinkle in the flour and cook, stirring, for 1 minute. Remove from the heat and blend in the strained poaching liquid. Cook, stirring, for 1 minute until thickened.

5 Add the cream and tomato paste and bring to a boil, stirring constantly until the mixture thickens. Simmer for 2 minutes, then add salt and pepper to taste.

6 Cook the pasta shells in a large saucepan of boiling salted water for 8–10 minutes or until tender. Drain, then toss with the butter and the remaining lemon juice. Add the scallops to the sauce, and heat through very gently.

7 Pile the pasta on warmed serving plates, and spoon the sauce on top. Serve at once, garnished with the parsley and lemon slices.

TAGLIATELLE WITH VEGETABLE RIBBONS

SERVES 4

2 medium zucchini

4 carrots, peeled

salt

12 oz (375 g) fresh tagliatelle

scant 1 tbsp olive oil

1 garlic clove, crushed

1 scant cup (200 ml) lowfat sour cream

2 tbsp pesto (page 388) or use ready made

1/2 cup (60 g) blue cheese

chopped parsley to garnish

1 Thinly slice the zucchini and carrots into wide, thin ribbons (page 369).

2 Bring a large pan of salted water to a boil, add the tagliatelle, zucchini, and carrots, and cook for 3 minutes. Drain and refresh under cold running water.

3 Heat the oil in a large skillet, add the garlic, and stir-fry for about 1 minute.

4 Add the sour cream and pesto, then crumble in the cheese. Simmer and stir the sauce for 2–3 minutes, then add the tagliatelle and vegetables. Mix gently, turn into a warmed serving dish, and sprinkle with chopped parsley. Serve immediately

Cook's know-how

Dolcelatte is a mild and creamy blue cheese from Italy. For a change, you could use gorgonzola, another Italian blue cheese, which has a stronger, saltier flavor. The French Roquefort could also be used.

PENNE WITH SPINACH & BLUE CHEESE

SERVES 4

1 lb (500 g) penne

salt and black pepper

3 tbls (45 g) butter

2 large garlic cloves, crushed

3 1/2 cups (250 g) sliced crimini mushrooms

1 1/4 cups (300 ml) heavy cream

1 egg, lightly beaten (optional)

1 3/4 cups (90 g) shredded fresh spinach leaves

3 oz (90 g) blue cheese, crumbled

juice of 1/2 lemon

pinch of grated nutmeg

1 Cook the penne in boiling salted water for 8–10 minutes until just tender.

2 Meanwhile, melt the butter in a large pan, add the garlic, and cook, stirring, for 1 minute. Add the mushrooms and cook, stirring occasionally, for 2 minutes. Stir in the cream and boil for 2–3 minutes until the mixture reaches a coating consistency.

3 Drain the pasta, add to the mushroom and cream mixture with the egg (if using), stir well, and heat through. Add the spinach, blue cheese, lemon juice, nutmeg, and pepper to taste, and stir well to coat the pasta. Serve at once.

Cook's know-how

Adding an egg to the sauce makes it richer and creamier, but you can omit it if you prefer a lighter consistency.

PENNE WITH BROCCOLI & STILTON

Substitute 1½ cups (125 g) small broccoli florets for the spinach. Cook in boiling salted water for 3–4 minutes or until just tender. Add to the pasta with the cheese, lemon juice, nutmeg, and pepper, omitting the egg. Stir well, and serve at once.

EASY PASTA SUPPER DISHES

Pasta is so popular with most people that you can never have enough recipes for tasty dishes to make with it. These three make delicious everyday meals, and are equally good for informal entertaining. All you need to accompany them is a tossed green salad and some good bread.

FUSILLI WITH DOUBLE TOMATOES

SERVES 4

12 oz (375 g) multicolored fusilli

8 oz (250 g) asparagus tips, cut into 2 in (5 cm) lengths

3 tbsp olive oil

2 garlic cloves, crushed

1 3/4 cups (90 g) sliced crimini mushrooms

1 lb (500 g) ripe cherry tomatoes, halved

2 oz (60 g) sun-blushed or sun-dried tomatoes, each piece snipped into three

salt and black pepper

TO SERVE

2 tbls (30 g) pine nuts, toasted

a small handful of fresh basil leaves, shredded

1 Cook the pasta in boiling salted water according to the package directions until just tender, adding the asparagus 2 minutes before the end of cooking. Drain the pasta and asparagus together and refresh under cold running water. Drain well.

2 Heat the oil in a large skillet, add the garlic and mushrooms, and fry over a high heat for a couple of minutes. Add both kinds of tomatoes and continue to stir-fry over a high heat until they are just heated through. Season well.

3 Quickly toss the pasta and asparagus through the tomato mixture in the pan until everything is hot, then scatter over the pine nuts and basil. Serve at once.

Healthy note

Tomatoes contain beneficial amounts of vitamins C and E. More importantly, they are a rich source of lycopene, a powerful antioxidant that can help to protect the body from harmful free-radical damage. Lycopene is most easily absorbed from tomatoes that have been heat processed in some way; a little oil helps absorption, too. Cherry tomatoes are also especially rich in antioxidants. All these ingredients make this recipe a perfect addition to a healthy diet.

RED HOT RAGU

SERVES 6

12 oz (375 g) rigatoni or other tubular pasta

1/2 cup (60 g) coarsely grated Parmesan cheese

3 tbsp chopped parsley, or 6 oz (175 g) young spinach leaves, shredded

SAUCE

1 lb (500 g) good-quality pork link sausages with herbs

a little olive oil

3 garlic cloves, crushed

2 small red chilies, cored, seeded and finely chopped

28 oz (800 g) canned crushed tomatoes

1 large onion, finely chopped

1 good tbsp sun-dried tomato paste

1 tbsp chopped fresh basil

1/2–1 tsp sugar, to taste

salt and black pepper

1 Make the sauce: cut long slits in each sausage and remove the casings. Heat a little oil in a nonstick skillet and add the garlic and sausage meat. Fry over a medium heat for 4–5 minutes, breaking the meat up with a wooden spatula until it is brown, with a minced pork consistency. Stir in the remaining sauce ingredients. Bring to a boil, cover, and simmer gently for 40–50 minutes or until the sausagemeat is cooked. Check the seasoning.

2 Meanwhile, cook the pasta in boiling salted water according to the package directions until just tender.

3 Drain the pasta and mix it into the sauce in the pan with half the Parmesan, then check the seasoning again. Scatter the parsley and remaining Parmesan over individual servings.

NOTE: If using spinach, stir it into the bubbling sauce and cook for a couple of minutes until it wilts before adding the pasta and half the Parmesan.

RIGATONI WITH MUSHROOMS AND ARUGULA

SERVES 6

12 oz (375 g) rigatoni or other tubular pasta

2/3 cup (150 ml) dry white wine

1 small onion, finely chopped

1 lb (500 g) mixed wild or cultivated mushrooms, such as shiitake, oyster, and ceps, coarsely sliced

salt and black pepper

6 tbsp whipping cream

4 tbsp good-quality pesto (bottled or see page 388)

2 oz (60 g) arugula leaves

coarsely grated Parmesan cheese, to serve

1 Cook the pasta in boiling salted water according to the package directions until just tender.

2 Meanwhile, pour the wine into a large skillet, add the onion and cook over a low heat until the onion has softened, 10–15 minutes. Add the mushrooms and stir over a high heat for a few minutes until the mushrooms are cooked and the liquid has reduced (there should be about 2 tablespoons left). Season with salt and pepper, add the cream and pesto, and stir to mix.

3 Drain the pasta and add to the mushroom mixture in the pan. Check the seasoning. At the last moment, stir in the arugula leaves and allow to wilt for about 2 minutes. Serve immediately, scattered with Parmesan.

NOTE: The warm, peppery, pungent taste of arugula is one people love or hate. If you love it and you're making your own pesto for this dish, try substituting arugula for basil in the pesto recipe on page 388.

CLOCKWISE FROM TOP: Red Hot Ragù, Rigatoni with Mushrooms & Arugula, Fusilli with Double Tomatoes.

PENNE WITH ASPARAGUS

SERVES 6

4 oz (125 g) goat cheese, cut into small pieces
3 tbsp olive oil
3 garlic cloves, crushed
3 tbsp shredded fresh basil
1 lb (500 g) penne or spaghetti
salt and black pepper
1 lb (500 g) asparagus

1 In a small bowl, combine the goat cheese, olive oil, garlic, and shredded fresh basil.

2 Cook the pasta in a large saucepan of boiling salted water for 8–10 minutes until just tender.

3 Meanwhile, trim any woody ends from the asparagus and peel the spears if they are not young. Cut the asparagus into bite-sized pieces and cook in boiling salted water for about 3 minutes until just tender.

4 Drain the pasta thoroughly, add the goat cheese mixture, and toss together. Drain the asparagus and add to the pasta mixture. Toss lightly together, season with salt and black pepper, and serve at once.

SPAGHETTI ALL' AMATRICIANA

A specialty of Amatrice, near Rome, this tomato-based sauce is spiked with chili and garlic, and richly flavored with diced bacon and roast peppers.

SERVES 6

1 red bell pepper
1 green bell pepper
4 tbsp olive oil
5 unsmoked thick bacon or pancetta slices, diced
1/2–1 fresh green chili, cored, seeded, and thinly sliced
3 garlic cloves, crushed
2 ripe tomatoes, finely chopped
2 tbsp chopped flat-leaf parsley
salt and black pepper
1 lb (500 g) spaghetti
shavings of Parmesan cheese to serve

1 Halve the red and green peppers, and remove the cores and seeds. Roast and peel the peppers (page 388). Cut the flesh into thin strips.

2 Heat the oil in a skillet, add the bacon, and cook over a high heat for 5 minutes or until crisp. Add the roasted pepper strips and the chili, and cook for 2 minutes. Stir in the garlic and cook for about 1 minute.

3 Add the tomatoes and parsley and cook for 3 minutes or until thickened. Remove from the heat and season with salt and pepper.

4 Cook the spaghetti in a large saucepan of boiling salted water for 8–10 minutes until just tender.

5 Drain the spaghetti thoroughly. Add the sauce and toss with the spaghetti. Serve at once, topped with Parmesan cheese shavings.

SPAGHETTI ALL' ARRABBIATA

Melt 2 tbls (30 g) butter with 2 tbsp olive oil in a skillet, add 3 crushed garlic cloves and 1/2–1 tsp crushed dried red chilies (chili flakes), and cook gently. Drain 14 oz (400 g) canned crushed tomatoes, stir the tomatoes into the pan, and bring slowly to a boil. Simmer until reduced and thickened, add 1/4 tsp dried oregano, and season with salt and black pepper. Toss with the spaghetti, and serve at once.

STIR-FRIED CHINESE NOODLES

SERVES 4

5 dried shiitake mushrooms

8 fl oz (250 ml) hot vegetable stock

12 oz (375 g) Chinese egg noodles

salt

about 2 tsp soy sauce

1 tbsp sunflower oil

8 oz (250 g) snow peas

3 garlic cloves, crushed

1/4 in (5 mm) piece of fresh
   gingerroot, peeled and grated

1/4 tsp sugar (optional)

4 oz (125 g) bean sprouts

about 1/2 tsp crushed dried red
   chilies (chili flakes)

TO SERVE

3 green onions, sliced

2 tsp sesame oil

1 tbsp chopped fresh cilantro

1 Put the mushrooms into a bowl, pour over the hot vegetable stock, and leave to soak for about 30 minutes.

2 Drain the mushrooms, reserving the liquid. Squeeze the mushrooms dry, then cut into thin strips.

3 Cook the noodles in a large saucepan of boiling salted water for 3 minutes or according to package directions. Drain the noodles, toss with soy sauce to taste, and set aside.

4 Heat the sunflower oil in a wok or large skillet, add the mushrooms, snow peas, garlic, and ginger, and stir-fry for 2 minutes. Add the sugar, if using, bean sprouts, crushed chilies to taste, and 3 tbsp of the reserved mushroom soaking liquid. Stir-fry for 2 minutes.

5 Add the egg noodles and stir-fry for 2 minutes or until heated through. Serve at once, sprinkled with the green onions, sesame oil, and cilantro.

TORTELLINI WITH PEAS & BACON

SERVES 6

1 lb (500 g) tortellini

salt and black pepper

1 tbsp sunflower oil

8 oz (250 g) thick bacon or
   pancetta slices, diced

175 g (6 oz) frozen peas

1 1/4 cup (300 ml) heavy cream

grated Parmesan cheese to serve

1 Cook the tortellini in boiling salted water for about 10–12 minutes, or according to package directions, until tender.

2 Meanwhile, heat the oil in a skillet, add the bacon, and cook over a high heat, stirring, for 3 minutes or until crisp.

3 Cook the peas in boiling salted water for about 2 minutes until just tender. Drain.

4 Drain the tortellini thoroughly and return to the saucepan. Add the bacon, peas, cream, and nutmeg, and season with salt and pepper. Heat gently for 1–2 minutes to warm through. Serve at once, sprinkled with grated Parmesan cheese.

Healthy option

Use just 2/3 cup (150 ml) lowfat sour cream instead of the heavy cream. Then do what the Italians do — splash a few ladlefuls of the pasta water into the sauce and stir vigorously to make enough sauce to coat the pasta.

FETTUCCINE PRIMAVERA

SERVES 4

4 oz (125 g) asparagus, trimmed and cut into bite-sized pieces

4 oz (125 g) broccoli florets

1 zucchini, sliced

salt and black pepper

3 tbsp olive oil

1/2 red and 1/2 yellow bell pepper, cored, seeded, and diced

3 garlic cloves, crushed

7 oz (200 g) canned crushed tomatoes

1/2 cup (90 g) frozen peas

1/2 cup (125 ml) heavy cream

1 lb (500 g) fettuccine

4 tbsp shredded fresh basil

90 g (3 oz) Parmesan cheese, grated, to serve

1 Cook the asparagus, broccoli, and zucchini in boiling salted water for 3 minutes or until just tender. Drain, rinse under cold running water, and set aside.

2 Heat the oil in a large, deep skillet, add the peppers and garlic, and cook, stirring, for 4 minutes or until the peppers are softened.

3 Add the tomatoes and the peas, and cook for 5 minutes or until the liquid in the pan is reduced by half.

4 Add the asparagus, broccoli, and zucchini, stir in the cream, and boil for 1–2 minutes to reduce the liquid and concentrate the flavor. Add salt and pepper to taste, and remove from the heat.

5 Cook the fettuccine in a large saucepan of boiling salted water for 8–10 minutes until just tender.

6 Drain the fettuccine thoroughly, add to the sauce, and toss over a high heat. Stir in the shredded basil and serve at once, sprinkled with Parmesan cheese.

Healthy option

For a lighter, less creamy, version of this classic dish, use 14 oz (400 g) canned crushed tomatoes and omit the cream. Instead of sprinkling with Parmesan to serve, sprinkle with more shredded fresh basil.

SPAGHETTI CARBONARA

SERVES 4

1 lb (500 g) spaghetti

salt and black pepper

6 thick slices of bacon, cut into strips

1 garlic clove, crushed

4 eggs

1 cup (125 g) grated Parmesan cheese

2/3 cup (150 ml) light cream

chopped parsley to garnish

1 Cook the spaghetti in a large saucepan of boiling salted water for 8–10 minutes until just tender.

2 Meanwhile, put the bacon into a skillet and heat gently for 7 minutes until the fat runs. Increase the heat and add the garlic. Cook for 2–3 minutes or until the bacon is crisp.

3 Break the eggs into a bowl. Add the bacon and garlic mixture, using a slotted spoon. Add the Parmesan cheese, season generously with salt and pepper, and whisk until well blended.

4 Drain the spaghetti and return to the hot pan. Stir in the bacon and egg mixture and toss quickly until the egg just begins to set. Stir in the cream and heat gently. Serve at once, sprinkled with parsley.

Cook's know-how

It is best to buy a whole piece of Parmesan cheese and grate the quantity you need for a given dish. Grated Parmesan in packages is less economical and lacks the flavor of freshly grated Parmesan.

SPAGHETTI ALFREDO

Heat 2/3 cup (150 ml) heavy cream with 2 tbls (30 g) butter until the mixture has thickened. Set aside. Cook the pasta, drain, then add to the cream mixture. Add 6 tbls (90 ml) more cream, 3/4 cup (90 g) Parmesan cheese, a pinch of grated nutmeg, and season with salt and pepper. Heat gently until thickened, and serve.

SPAGHETTI BOLOGNESE

SERVES 4

3 tbsp olive oil

1 lb (500 g) ground beef

1 large onion, finely chopped

2 celery stalks, sliced

1 tbsp all-purpose flour

2 garlic cloves, crushed

5 tbls (90 g) tomato paste

2/3 cup (150 ml) beef stock

2/3 cup (150 ml) red wine

14 oz (400 g) canned crushed tomatoes

1 tbsp red-currant jelly

salt and black pepper

1 lb (500 g) spaghetti

grated Parmesan cheese to serve

1 Heat 2 tbsp of the oil in a saucepan. Add the ground beef, onion, and celery, and cook, stirring, for 5 minutes or until the beef is browned. Add the flour, garlic, and tomato paste, and cook, stirring, for about 1 minute.

2 Pour in the stock and wine. Add the tomatoes and red-currant jelly, season with salt and pepper, and bring to a boil. Cook, stirring, until the mixture has thickened.

3 Lower the heat, partially cover the pan, and simmer very gently, stirring occasionally, for about 1 hour.

4 Meanwhile, cook the spaghetti in boiling salted water for 8–10 minutes until just tender. Drain thoroughly.

5 Return the spaghetti to the saucepan, add the remaining oil, and toss gently to coat.

6 Divide the spaghetti among warmed serving plates and ladle some of the sauce on top of each serving. Sprinkle with a little Parmesan cheese and hand the remainder separately.

PASTA SPIRALS WITH MEATBALLS

SERVES 8

1 lb (500 g) pasta spirals (fusilli)

shredded fresh basil to garnish

TOMATO BASIL SAUCE

1 tbsp olive oil

1 onion, coarsely chopped

2 garlic cloves, crushed

28 oz (800 g) canned crushed tomatoes

1 tsp sugar

salt and black pepper

MEATBALLS

1 lb (500 g) ground turkey or chicken

2 tbsp chopped parsley

1 tsp chopped fresh thyme

1/2 cup (60 g) grated Parmesan cheese

1 cup (60 g) fresh bread crumbs

1 egg, beaten

a little olive oil, for frying

1 Make the tomato basil sauce: heat the oil in a deep skillet, add the onion and garlic, and cook gently, stirring occasionally, for 3–4 minutes.

2 Add the tomatoes and sugar, season with salt and pepper, and stir well. Simmer, uncovered, for about 20 minutes, stirring occasionally, until the onion is soft and the sauce reduced.

3 Make the meatballs: in a large bowl, combine the ground turkey or chicken, parsley, thyme, Parmesan cheese, bread crumbs, and egg, then season with salt and pepper. With dampened hands, shape the mixture into balls about the size of large walnuts.

4 Heat a little oil in a large skillet, add the meatballs, and cook for about 8 minutes until browned and cooked through. Lift out with a slotted spoon and drain on paper towels. Add to the tomato sauce and heat gently for about 5 minutes.

5 Meanwhile, cook the pasta in a large pan of boiling salted water for 8–10 minutes until tender. Drain thoroughly, and top with the meatballs and sauce. Serve at once, garnished with shredded basil.

RAVIOLI

Ravioli is one of the easiest of homemade pastas to prepare because it does not need a pasta machine – simply roll out the dough by hand, then fill with a savory stuffing. Homemade ravioli is so delicious that it needs only a simple accompaniment of melted butter and freshly grated Parmesan.

BASIC PASTA DOUGH

SERVES 3

10 oz (300 g) Italian "00" flour or white bread flour
3 eggs
I tsp salt
I tbsp olive oil

1 Sift the flour into a mound on a work surface. Make a well in the middle of the flour and add the eggs, salt, and oil. Using your fingertips, gradually draw the flour into the egg mixture until a sticky ball of dough is formed.

2 Knead the dough on a floured work surface for 10 minutes or until the pasta dough is smooth and no longer sticks to the work surface.

3 Shape the dough into a ball, put into an oiled plastic bag, and leave to rest at room temperature for about 30 minutes.

4 Roll out the dough very thinly on a lightly floured work surface into a 15 in (37 cm) square. Leave the pasta uncovered for about 20 minutes to dry out slightly. Cut the pasta in half, fill, and cook the ravioli (see box, right).

CRAB & SHRIMP

3 oz (90 g) cooked white crabmeat, flaked
3 oz (90 g) cooked peeled shrimp, chopped
1/4 cups (60 g) cream cheese
I green onion, very finely chopped
salt and black pepper
cilantro sauce (page 339) to serve

1 Combine the crabmeat and shrimp with the cheese and green onion, and season with salt and pepper.

2 Fill and cook the ravioli (see box, right). Toss in cilantro sauce and serve at once.

CLOCKWISE FROM TOP: Chicken & Prosciutto with tomato basil sauce, Cheese & Spinach with grated Parmesan, Crab & Shrimp with cilantro sauce.

CHICKEN & PROSCIUTTO

I tbls (15 g) butter
1/2 cup (90 g) cooked ground chicken
2 1/2 oz (75 g) prosciutto, finely chopped
I tbsp fresh white bread crumbs
I tbsp chopped fresh flat-leaf parsley
2 tsp each water and tomato paste
salt and black pepper
I egg

TO SERVE

tomato basil sauce (page 345)
basil sprigs

1 Melt the butter in a saucepan. Add the chicken and fry for 5 minutes. Stir in the remaining ingredients.

2 Fill and cook the ravioli (see box, below). Toss in the tomato basil sauce, and serve at once, garnished with basil sprigs.

RICOTTA & SPINACH

1/2 cup (125 g) ricotta cheese
1/2 cup (60 g) grated Parmesan cheese
I egg, beaten
1/4 tsp grated nutmeg
8 oz (250 g) spinach leaves, cooked, squeezed dry, and chopped
salt and black pepper
2 tbls (30 g) butter to serve

1 Beat together the ricotta, half of the Parmesan, the egg, nutmeg, and spinach. Season with salt and pepper.

2 Fill and cook the ravioli (see box, below). Serve with butter, the remaining Parmesan, and black pepper.

Filling and cooking the ravioli

1 Place 18 spoonfuls of filling at regular intervals on to one half of the pasta. Lightly brush the pasta between the filling with water.

2 Roll the remaining pasta around a rolling pin and unroll over the filling. Press the pasta around the edges and the spoonfuls of filling.

3 With a knife, pastry wheel, or pastry cutter, cut into round or square ravioli. Leave for about 30 minutes, turning once, until dried out.

4 Add a little oil to a large saucepan of boiling salted water, add the ravioli, and cook for 4–5 minutes until just tender. Serve immediately.

TUNA CASSEROLE WITH FENNEL

SERVES 6

8 oz (250 g) pasta shells (conchiglie)

salt and black pepper

1 tbsp sunflower oil

1 fennel bulb, trimmed and finely sliced

1 onion, finely sliced

4 tbls (60 g) butter

1/2 cup (60 g) all-purpose flour

2 1/2 cups (600 ml) milk

7 oz (200 g) canned tuna in brine, drained and flaked

3 hard-boiled eggs, coarsely chopped

1 cup (125 g) grated sharp Cheddar cheese

2 tbsp chopped parsley to garnish

1 Cook the pasta shells in boiling salted water for 8–10 minutes until just tender. Drain thoroughly and set aside.

2 Heat the sunflower oil in a large skillet, add the fennel and onion, and cook for 3–5 minutes until softened but not colored. Set aside.

3 Melt the butter in a large saucepan, sprinkle in the flour, and cook, stirring, for 1 minute. Remove from the heat and gradually blend in the milk. Bring to a boil, stirring until the mixture thickens. Simmer for 2–3 minutes.

4 Stir in the pasta, the fennel and onion, tuna, eggs, and cheese. Season with salt and pepper, then turn the mixture into a shallow baking dish.

5 Bake in a preheated oven at 400°F (200°C) for about 30 minutes or until heated through and golden brown on top. Serve hot, sprinkled with chopped parsley.

Healthy option

To reduce fat, boil the fennel and onion with the pasta, make half the quantity of sauce in step 3, and make up the volume with pasta cooking water. You could also omit the eggs and halve the amount of cheese.

VEGETABLES NAPOLETANA

SERVES 4

8 oz (250 g) pasta spirals (fusilli)

salt and black pepper

8 oz (250 g) broccoli

1 tbls (15 g) butter

1 tbsp olive oil

1 large onion, chopped

2 large garlic cloves, crushed

5 oz (150 g) shiitake mushrooms, coarsely chopped

1 red bell pepper, cored, seeded, and sliced

2 zucchini, sliced

3/4 cup (75 g) grated Cheddar cheese

SAUCE

4 tbls (60 g) butter

1/2 cup (60 g) all-purpose flour

2 1/2 cups (600 ml) milk

1 tsp Dijon mustard

1 Cook the pasta in a large pan of boiling salted water for 8–10 minutes until just tender. Drain thoroughly.

2 Cook the broccoli stalks in boiling salted water for 3 minutes, then add the florets, and cook for 2 minutes longer. Drain and rinse in cold water.

3 Melt the butter with the oil in a large skillet. Add the onion and garlic and cook gently, stirring occasionally, for 3–5 minutes, until softened.

4 Add the mushrooms, red pepper, and zucchini slices, and cook, stirring occasionally, for 3 minutes. Remove from the heat and stir in the broccoli.

5 Make the sauce: melt the butter in a large saucepan, sprinkle in the flour and cook, stirring, for 1 minute. Remove from the heat and gradually blend in the milk. Bring to a boil, stirring constantly until thickened. Simmer for 2–3 minutes. Add the mustard, and season with salt and pepper.

6 Remove the sauce from the heat, add the vegetables and pasta, and stir well to coat.

7 Divide the mixture among 4 individual gratin dishes, sprinkle with the Cheddar cheese, and bake in a preheated oven at 400°F (200°C) for 20–25 minutes until golden. Serve hot.

Healthy option

For a lighter, and quicker, version of this baked pasta dish, make it without the sauce in step 5 and simply toss the hot vegetables with the freshly cooked pasta, moistening with a few spoonfuls of the pasta cooking water or 1–2 tbsp olive oil if you prefer. Serve at once.

FISHERMAN'S LASAGNE

SERVES 8

1 1/4 lb (625 g) haddock fillet

1 slice of onion

1 bay leaf

4 black peppercorns

1 1/4 cups (300 ml) dry white wine

8 oz (250 g) cooked peeled shrimp

2 tbls (30 g) butter

3 1/2 cups (500 g) zucchini, thickly sliced

1 garlic clove, crushed

6 oz (175 g) oven-ready lasagne noodles

1/2 cup (60 g) Cheddar cheese, grated

2 tbsp grated Parmesan cheese

SAUCE

6 tbls (90 g) butter

3/4 cup (90 g) all-purpose flour

1 1/4 cups (300 ml) light cream

3 tbsp chopped parsley

1 tbsp chopped fresh dill

salt and black pepper

1 Put the haddock into a large pan with the onion, bay leaf, peppercorns, and wine. Add enough water to cover, bring to a boil, and simmer for 5 minutes or until the fish is just cooked.

2 Lift out the fish, remove the skin and bones, and flake the flesh. Mix with the shrimp, strain the liquid, and make up to 3 3/4 cups (900 ml) with water. Set aside.

3 Melt the butter in a saucepan, add the zucchini and garlic, and cook for 3 minutes until beginning to soften.

4 Make the sauce: melt the butter in a saucepan, sprinkle in the flour, and cook, stirring, for 1 minute. Remove the pan from the heat, and gradually blend in the reserved cooking liquid. Bring to a boil, stirring until thickened. Simmer for 2–3 minutes. Stir in the cream, parsley, dill, and salt and pepper to taste.

5 Spoon one-third of the fish mixture into a shallow ovenproof dish, top with one-third of the zucchini, and pour over one-third of the sauce. Arrange half of the lasagne in a single layer. Repeat the layers, finishing with sauce.

6 Sprinkle with the cheeses and bake in a preheated oven at 400°F (200°C) for 40 minutes or until golden.

THREE-CHEESE MACARONI

SERVES 6–8

2 cups (375 g) short-cut macaroni

salt and black pepper

3 tbls (45 g) butter, plus extra for greasing

1/3 cup (45 g) all-purpose flour

3 3/4 cups (900 ml) milk

2 tsp Dijon mustard

1 1/2 cups (175 g) grated smoked Cheddar cheese

1/2 cup (60 g) chopped mozzarella cheese

3/4 cups (90 g) grated sharp Cheddar cheese

1 cup (60 g) fresh white bread crumbs

1 Cook the macaroni in boiling salted water for 8–10 minutes until just tender. Drain and set aside.

2 Melt the butter in a large saucepan. Add the flour and cook, stirring, for 1 minute. Remove the pan from the heat and gradually blend in the milk. Bring to a boil, stirring constantly until the mixture thickens. Simmer for about 5 minutes, stirring.

3 Stir in the mustard, smoked Cheddar and mozzarella cheeses, 1/2 cup (60 g) of the mature Cheddar cheese, and the cooked macaroni. Season with salt and pepper.

4 Lightly butter a large shallow baking dish and spoon in the macaroni mixture. Sprinkle with the bread crumbs and the remaining Cheddar cheese and bake in a preheated oven at 400°F (200°C) for about 15–20 minutes until golden and bubbling.

CHEESE & LEEK MACARONI

Omit the mozzarella cheese. Melt 2 tbls (30 g) butter in a saucepan, add 2–3 trimmed and finely sliced leeks, and cook gently for 3–5 minutes until softened. Add the leeks to the sauce with the two Cheddar cheeses and the cooked and drained macaroni.

CANNELLONI WITH RICOTTA & SPINACH

SERVES 6

butter for greasing

18 oven-ready cannelloni tubes

2 tbls (30 g) grated Parmesan cheese

TOMATO SAUCE

1 tbsp olive oil

2 celery stalks, chopped

1 small onion, chopped

1 carrot, chopped

1 garlic clove, crushed

1 1/4 cups (300 ml) chicken or vegetable stock

28 oz (800 g) canned crushed tomatoes

2 tbsp tomato paste

salt and black pepper

2 oz (60 g) sun-dried tomatoes in oil, drained and chopped

FILLING

2 tbsp olive oil

1 small onion, chopped

1 garlic clove, crushed

1 lb (500 g) spinach, chopped

2 cups (500 g) ricotta cheese

1/4 tsp grated nutmeg

1 Make the tomato sauce: heat the oil in a saucepan, add the celery, onion, carrot, and garlic, and cook gently for 3–5 minutes until softened. Stir in the stock, tomatoes, and tomato paste, season with salt and pepper, and bring to a boil. Cover and simmer, stirring occasionally, for 30 minutes.

2 Meanwhile, make the filling: heat the oil in a large pan, add the onion and garlic, and cook for 3–5 minutes until softened. Add the spinach and cook over a high heat for 1–2 minutes. Cool slightly, add the ricotta and nutmeg, and season with salt and pepper.

3 Puree the tomato sauce in a food processor, then stir in the sun-dried tomatoes.

4 Grease an baking dish. Spoon the spinach filling into the cannelloni. Arrange in the dish, cover with the sauce, and sprinkle with Parmesan. Bake in a preheated oven at 400°F (200°C) for 30 minutes. Serve hot.

LASAGNE

SERVES 8

1 cup (125 g) grated sharp Cheddar cheese

2 tbls (30 g) grated Parmesan cheese

6 oz (175 g) oven-ready lasagne noodles

chopped parsley to garnish

MEAT SAUCE

2 tbsp olive oil

2 lb (1 kg) ground beef

1/3 cup (45 g) all-purpose flour

1 1/4 cups (300 ml) beef stock

14 oz (400 g) canned crushed tomatoes

6 celery stalks, sliced

2 onions, chopped

2 large garlic cloves, crushed

4 tbsp tomato paste

1 tsp sugar

salt and black pepper

WHITE SAUCE

4 tbls (60 g) butter

1/3 cup (45 g) all-purpose flour

2 1/2 cups (600 ml) milk

1 tsp Dijon mustard

1/4 tsp grated nutmeg

1 Make the meat sauce: heat the oil in a saucepan, add the beef, and cook, stirring, until browned.

2 Sprinkle in the flour and stir for 1 minute, then add the stock, tomatoes, celery, onions, garlic, tomato paste, and sugar. Season with salt and pepper and bring to a boil. Cover and simmer for 1 hour.

3 Meanwhile, make the white sauce: melt the butter in a saucepan, sprinkle in the flour and cook, stirring, for 1 minute. Remove from the heat and gradually blend in the milk. Bring to a boil, stirring until the mixture thickens. Simmer for 2–3 minutes. Stir in the mustard and nutmeg, and season with salt and pepper.

4 Spoon one-third of the meat sauce into a large shallow baking dish, cover with one-third of the white sauce, and one-third of the Cheddar and Parmesan cheeses. Arrange half of the lasagne in a single layer. Repeat the layers, finishing with the Cheddar and Parmesan cheeses.

5 Bake in a preheated oven at 375°F (190°C) for 45–60 minutes until the pasta is tender and the topping is a golden brown color. Serve at once, sprinkled with parsley.

CARIBBEAN RICE & PEAS

SERVES 4–6

2 tbsp olive oil

8 green onions, sliced

3 smoked bacon slices, diced

2 garlic cloves, crushed

1 1/4 cups (250 g) long-grain rice

7 oz (200 g) canned tomatoes

3 tbsp chopped parsley

2 bay leaves

1 small green chili, cored, seeded, and thinly sliced

1/2 tsp turmeric

1/2 tsp cumin seeds

1/2 tsp dried thyme

14 oz (400 g) canned red kidney beans or black-eyed peas, drained and rinsed

1 1/2 cups (375 ml) chicken stock

1 lime, cut into wedges, to serve

1 Heat the oil in a pan, add the green onions and bacon, and cook for about 5 minutes or until the bacon is crisp. Add the garlic and cook for 2 minutes.

2 Add the rice and stir to coat the grains in the oil. Add the tomatoes with their juice, 2 tbsp of the parsley, the bay leaves, chili, turmeric, cumin, and thyme, and cook for 2 minutes.

3 Add the beans and stock and bring to a boil. Cover and cook over a low heat for 15 minutes until the rice is tender and the liquid has been absorbed.

4 Sprinkle with remaining parsley, and serve at once, with lime wedges.

Cook's know-how

Don't be misled by the name of this dish – there are no peas in it, but this is not a mistake. In the Caribbean the dish is traditionally made with small round beans, which are known as pigeon peas, hence the name of the dish. Red kidney beans make a good substitute when pigeon peas are not available.

CONFETTI RICE

SERVES 4

2 tbsp olive oil

1 onion, chopped

1 carrot, diced

1 cup (200 g) long-grain rice

1 large tomato, finely chopped

2 cups (500 ml) hot chicken or vegetable stock

1 cup (150 g) corn kernels

3/4 cup (90 g) frozen peas

2 tbsp tomato paste

salt and black pepper

1 garlic clove, crushed

chopped parsley to garnish

1 Heat the oil in a skillet, add the onion and carrot, and cook gently, stirring, for 3–5 minutes until the onion is softened but not colored.

2 Add the rice, and stir to coat the grains in the oil. Add the tomatoes and stock.

3 Add the corn, peas, and tomato paste, and bring to a boil. Simmer, stirring occasionally, for 12–15 minutes or until the rice is tender and the liquid has been absorbed.

4 Add salt and pepper to taste, and stir in the garlic. Serve at once, sprinkled with parsley.

Cook's know-how

Confetti rice is a delicious accompaniment to simple broiled or roasted foods, or it can make a tasty vegetarian meal on its own, to serve two people. For extra flavor just before serving, add a little chopped fresh cilantro, finely chopped green onions or raw red onion, or a sprinkling of crushed dried red chilies or hot pepper sauce. If you have any leftovers, spoon into hot chicken or vegetable soup to make them go farther.

ORIENTAL NOODLE DISHES

There is such a wide range of oriental noodles that it is often difficult to know which to choose and how to cook them. In fact, there is no mystery about them, and they are as quick and easy to deal with as Italian pasta. These three simple recipes will give you confidence to cook with them.

SINGAPORE NOODLES

SERVES 6

8 oz (250 g) rice noodles

2 tbsp sunflower oil

12 oz (375 g) pork tenderloin, cut into thin strips

1 tsp crushed dried red chilies (chili flakes)

1 1/4 cups (90 g) sliced shiitake mushrooms

7 oz (200 g) bok choy, coarsely chopped, keeping white and green parts separate

2 tbsp mild curry powder

2 tbsp soy sauce

2 tbsp oyster sauce

juice of 1/2 lime

4 tbsp coconut cream

chopped fresh cilantro to garnish

1 Cook the noodles according to package directions. Drain, refresh under cold running water, and set aside.

2 Heat 1 tbsp oil in a large wok or nonstick skillet and stir-fry the pork over a high heat for about 2 minutes until brown and cooked through. Remove from the pan with a slotted spoon and set aside.

3 Heat the remaining oil in the pan. Add the chilli flakes, mushrooms, and the white parts of the bok choy, and stir-fry for 1–2 minutes. Add the curry powder, soy, oyster sauce, lime juice, and coconut cream, and stir-fry for a few minutes longer.

4 Add the green parts of the bok choy, then return the pork and noodles to the pan. Stir-fry for a few minutes until piping hot, then scatter the cilantro over.

Cook's know-how

For a vegetarian version of Singapore Noodles, omit the pork and substitute the same weight of firm tofu, cut into strips. Add the tofu with the bok choy in step 3, omit the oyster sauce, and replace it with an extra tablespooon or two of soy sauce if you like.

SZECHUAN NOODLES WITH WATER CHESTNUTS

SERVES 6

12 oz (375 g) medium egg noodles

1 tbsp olive oil

250 g (8 oz) ground pork

1 in (2.5 cm) piece of fresh gingerroot, peeled and finely grated

2 garlic cloves, crushed

2 green onions, trimmed and sliced on the diagonal, keeping white and green parts separate

1 red bell pepper, cored, seeded, and finely sliced

3 tbsp soy sauce, or more to taste

3 tbsp black bean sauce

2 tsp sugar

3 oz (90 g) bean sprouts

7 1/2 oz (220 g) canned water chestnuts, drained and halved

salt and black pepper

1 Cook the noodles according to packet instructions. Drain, refresh under cold running water, and set aside.

2 Heat the oil in a wok or large nonstick skillet and stir-fry the pork for about 2 minutes until brown. Add the ginger, garlic, white parts of the green onions, and the red pepper, and stir-fry for a few minutes more.

3 Stir in the 3 tbsp soy sauce, the black bean sauce, sugar, and 5 tbsp water, and boil for few minutes. Add the bean sprouts and water chestnuts, and return the noodles to the pan, then toss over a high heat for about 2 minutes until everything is hot. Check the seasoning, and add more soy sauce if you like. Serve immediately, with the green parts of the green onions scattered on top.

PAD THAI WITH TIGER SHRIMP

SERVES 6

8 oz (250 g) thick rice noodles

2 tbsp olive oil

2 skinless, boneless chicken breast halves (about 4 oz/125 g each), cut into thin strips

1 small fresh red chilli, halved, seeded and finely chopped

1 in (2.5 cm) piece of fresh gingerroot, peeled and finely grated

1 in (2.5 cm) piece of fresh lemongrass from the lower part of the stalk, very finely chopped

125 g (4 oz) peeled raw tiger shrimp

1 1/4 cups (90 g) sliced oyster mushrooms

4 oz (125 g) sugarsnap peas, trimmed and sliced on the diagonal

3 tbsp soy sauce

2 tbsp lime juice

1 tbsp fish sauce

salt and black pepper

TO SERVE

2 tbls salted or unsalted peanuts, coarsely chopped

a handful of fresh cilantro, chopped

1 Cook the noodles according to the package directions. Drain, refresh under cold running water, and set aside.

2 Heat 1 tbsp of the oil in a wok or large nonstick skillet, and stir-fry the chicken over a high heat for 2 minutes or until golden brown and cooked through. Remove with a slotted spoon and set aside.

3 Heat the remaining oil in the pan, add the chili, ginger, lemongrass, shrimp, mushrooms, and peas and stir-fry for 1 minute. Add the soy, lime juice and fish sauce and season with salt and pepper. Return the noodles and chicken to the pan and stir-fry until the shrimp are pink and everything is piping hot, 2–3 minutes. Serve hot, scattered with peanuts and cilantro.

CLOCKWISE FROM TOP RIGHT: Singapore Noodles, Pad Thai with Tiger Shrimp, Szechuan Noodles with Water Chestnuts.

BAKED WILD RICE

SERVES 6

1³/4 cups (375 g) mixed basmati and wild rice
salt and black pepper
8–12 oz (250–375 g) broccoli
1 tbls (15 g) butter
2 onions, chopped
3 garlic cloves, crushed
¹/2 cup (125 ml) sour cream
1 cup (125 g) chopped mozzarella cheese
¹/2 cup (60 g) grated Parmesan cheese
1 tbsp chopped fresh rosemary

1 Cook the rice in boiling salted water for about 35 minutes, or according to the package directions. Drain thoroughly and rinse with cold water. Drain again.

2 Meanwhile, cut the stems off the broccoli and cook them in boiling salted water for 8–10 minutes until almost tender, then add the florets, and cook for 2 minutes longer. Drain and rinse in cold water. Drain again and set aside.

3 Melt the butter in a skillet, add the onions, and cook gently, stirring occasionally, for 3–5 minutes until softened. Add the garlic, and cook, stirring occasionally, for 3–5 minutes until the onions are lightly browned.

4 Coarsely chop the broccoli, then stir into the rice with the onion and garlic mixture, sour cream, three-quarters of the mozzarella and Parmesan cheeses, and the rosemary. Season with salt and pepper.

5 Turn the mixture into a baking dish and sprinkle with the remaining mozzarella and Parmesan cheeses. Bake in a preheated oven at 350°F (180°C) for about 20 minutes until the cheese has melted. Serve hot.

Healthy option

Reduce the fat content by using lowfat sour cream, reduced-fat mozzarella, and just 2 tbsp grated Parmesan.

RISI E BISI

SERVES 6

4 tbls (60 g) butter
1 onion, finely chopped
2 oz (60 g) prosciutto, diced, or 3 oz (90 g) unsmoked thick, lean bacon slices, diced
2 garlic cloves, crushed
1¹/2 cups (300 g) risotto rice
2 cups (300 g) frozen peas
salt and black pepper
1 quart (1 liter) hot chicken or vegetable stock
¹/2 cup (60 g) grated Parmesan cheese, and 2 tbsp chopped parsley to garnish

1 Melt the butter in a large pan. When it is foaming, add the onion, prosciutto, and garlic, and cook gently, stirring occasionally, for 3–5 minutes until the onion is soft but not colored.

2 Add the rice and stir to coat in the butter. Add the frozen peas and seasoning.

3 Pour in half of the stock and cook, stirring constantly, over a low heat until it is absorbed. Add a little more stock and cook, stirring, until it has been absorbed.

4 Continue adding the stock in this way until the rice is just tender and the mixture is thick and creamy. It should take about 25 minutes.

5 Serve hot, sprinkled with the grated Parmesan cheese and chopped parsley.

Healthy option

This is a classic Venetian rice dish, traditionally served with more liquid than a risotto. If you want to cut down on the fat content, use just 1 slice prosciutto, trimmed of all fat, and omit the Parmesan garnish. You can omit the ham altogether, but even a small amount will give the dish an authentic flavor.

PERSIAN PILAF

SERVES 4

1 small cinnamon stick

2 tsp cumin seeds

6 black peppercorns

seeds of 4 cardamom pods, crushed

3 cloves

2 tbsp sunflower oil

1 small onion, chopped

1 tsp turmeric

1 1/4 cups (250 g) long-grain rice

5 cups (1.25 liter) hot vegetable or chicken stock

2 bay leaves, torn into pieces

salt and black pepper

1/2 cup (60 g) shelled pistachio nuts, coarsely chopped

2 1/2 tbls (30 g) raisins

fresh cilantro to garnish

1 Heat a heavy pan and add the cinnamon stick, cumin seeds, peppercorns, cardamom seeds, and cloves.

2 Dry-fry the spices over a medium heat for 2–3 minutes until they begin to release their aromas.

3 Add the oil to the pan and, when it is hot, add the onion and turmeric. Cook gently, stirring occasionally, for about 10 minutes until the onion is softened.

4 Add the rice and stir to coat the grains in the oil. Slowly pour in the hot stock, add the bay leaves, season with salt and pepper, and bring to a boil. Lower the heat, cover, and cook very gently for about 10 minutes without lifting the lid.

5 Remove the saucepan from the heat and leave to stand, still covered, for about 5 minutes.

6 Add the pistachio nuts and raisins to the pilaf, and fork them in gently to fluff up the rice. Garnish with fresh cilantro, and serve at once.

PORTUGUESE RICE WITH TUNA

SERVES 4

3 bacon slices, cut into strips

3 tbsp olive oil

1 small onion, thinly sliced

1 1/4 cups (250 g) long-grain brown rice

2 1/2 cups (600 ml) hot chicken stock

salt and black pepper

12 oz (375 g) fresh tuna, cut into chunks

14 oz (400 g) canned pimientos, drained and cut into strips

16 black olives

dill sprigs and lemon slices to garnish

1 Heat the bacon into a large, heavy saucepan until it begins to sizzle. Add the olive oil and onion, and cook gently, stirring occasionally, for 3–5 minutes until soft but not colored. Add the rice and stir.

2 Pour the stock into the pan, season with salt and pepper, and bring to a boil. Cover and simmer for 25–30 minutes.

3 Add the tuna, pimientos, and olives, and cook for 5 minutes or until all the liquid has been absorbed and the rice and tuna are tender. Season, garnish with dill sprigs and lemon slices, and serve at once.

PORTUGUESE RICE WITH CANNED TUNA

Substitute 7 oz (200 g) canned tuna in brine for the fresh tuna. Drain the tuna well, and flake it roughly with a fork.

Cook's know-how

If you prefer, use a 10 oz (300 g) jar roasted peppers instead of the pimientos.

CHICKEN LIVER RISOTTO

SERVES 4–6

5 tbls (75 g) butter

I tbsp sunflower oil

4 oz (125 g) smoked bacon slices, diced

I onion, chopped

I garlic clove, crushed

I cup (175 g) risotto rice

¼ cup (60 g) wild rice

2½ cups (600 ml) hot chicken stock

8 oz (250 g) chicken livers, sliced

4 oz (125 g) wild mushrooms (see box, below right), sliced

2 oz (60 g) sun-dried tomatoes in oil, drained and chopped

salt and black pepper

2 tbls (30 g) Parmesan cheese, grated

I tbsp chopped fresh rosemary

1 Melt 4 tbls (60 g) of the butter with the oil in a large skillet. When the butter is foaming, add the bacon, onion, and garlic, and cook gently, stirring occasionally, for 3–5 minutes until the onion is soft but not colored.

2 Add the risotto rice and wild rice, stirring to coat the grains in the oil, then pour in the hot chicken stock. Cover and simmer for 25 minutes.

3 Meanwhile, melt the remaining butter in a saucepan. Add the chicken livers, and cook, stirring, for 2–3 minutes until a rich brown color. Add the mushrooms, and cook, stirring occasionally, for 5–7 minutes.

4 Stir the chicken livers into the rice. Add the sun-dried tomatoes, season with salt and pepper, and cook for 5 minutes or until all the liquid has been absorbed. Serve hot, garnished with Parmesan and rosemary.

Cook's know-how

Wild mushrooms add a special touch to this risotto. Chanterelles, ceps, and morels are all suitable, or you can use cultivated crimini mushrooms instead, if you prefer their flavor.

RISOTTO MILANESE

SERVES 6

6 tbls (90 g) butter

I onion, chopped

2 cups (375 g) risotto rice

5 cups (1.25 liters) hot vegetable or chicken stock

a few pinches of saffron strands

salt and black pepper

½ cup (60 g) grated Parmesan cheese

Parmesan shavings to serve

1 Melt 2 tbls (30 g) of the butter in a large saucepan, add the chopped onion, and cook gently, stirring occasionally, for 3–5 minutes until softened but not colored.

2 Add the rice, stirring to coat the grains in the butter, and cook for 1 minute. Add a ladleful of hot stock to the pan, and cook gently, stirring constantly, until all the stock has been absorbed.

3 Sprinkle in the saffron strands and season with salt and pepper. Continue to add the stock, a ladleful at a time, stirring constantly, until the risotto is thick and creamy and the rice tender. This will take 20–25 minutes.

4 Stir in the remaining butter and the Parmesan cheese, and season to taste with salt and pepper. Serve at once, topped with Parmesan shavings.

Cook's know-how

Risotto milanese is the traditional accompaniment to Osso buco (page 242), but you can serve it with any other dish of meat or poultry, or as a first course on its own. In the past, it was traditionally cooked with the marrow from the veal shanks used for the osso buco, but nowadays the finished risotto is sometimes topped with a few spoonfuls of the juices from a veal roast to give it a more traditional and authentic flavor. If you want to reduce the fat content in this recipe, omit the butter in step 4.

KEDGEREE

SERVES 4

1 cup (200 g) long-grain rice

1/4 tsp turmeric

12 oz (375 g) smoked haddock fillet

2 hard-boiled eggs

4 tbls (60 g) butter, plus extra for greasing

juice of 1/2 lemon

2/3 cup (150 ml) light cream

salt

cayenne pepper

2 tbsp finely chopped parsley

1 Simmer the rice and turmeric, covered, in boiling salted water for 12–15 minutes until tender. Rinse with boiling water, drain, and keep warm.

2 Meanwhile, put the haddock, skin-side down, in a skillet, cover with cold water, and poach for 8–10 minutes.

3 Cut 1 egg lengthwise into quarters and reserve for garnish. Coarsely chop the second egg.

4 Drain the haddock, remove the skin and bones, then flake the fish. Put the fish into a large bowl, add the rice, chopped egg, butter, lemon juice, and cream, and season with salt and cayenne pepper. Stir gently to mix.

5 Butter a baking dish, add the kedgeree, and bake in a preheated oven at 350°F (180°C), stirring occasionally, for 10–15 minutes.

6 To serve, stir in the parsley and garnish with the reserved egg quarters.

Cook's know-how

Some smoked haddock is dyed bright yellow, so look out for smoked haddock that is pale in color and labeled "undyed" if you want to avoid artificial colorings.

SUMMER RISOTTO AL VERDE

SERVES 4

1 tbls (15 g) butter

3 garlic cloves, crushed

1 1/5 cups (250 g) risotto rice

1 quart (1 liter) hot vegetable stock

3/4 cup (175 ml) single cream

3/4 cup (90 g) crumbled blue cheese

4 tbsp bottled pesto

3/4 cup (90 g) grated Parmesan cheese

4 tbsp pine nuts, lightly toasted

4 tbsp shredded fresh basil

1 Melt the butter in a large saucepan. When it is foaming, add the garlic and cook gently for 1 minute.

2 Add the risotto rice, stirring to coat the grains in the butter, and cook for 2 minutes. Add a ladleful of the hot vegetable stock, and cook gently, stirring constantly, until the stock has been absorbed. Continue to add the stock, a ladleful at a time, and cook for 20–25 minutes or until the rice is just tender.

3 Add the cream, and cook gently, stirring, until it has been absorbed. Stir in the blue cheese, then the pesto, Parmesan, and pine nuts. Garnish with shredded fresh basil, and serve.

CHICKEN & MUSHROOM RISOTTO

Add 1½ cups (125 g) sliced mushrooms to the saucepan with the garlic in step 1 and cook for 3–5 minutes until the mushrooms are soft. Substitute chicken stock for the vegetable stock, omit the blue cheese and pesto, then add 2 cups (250 g) cooked diced chicken with the cream in step 3.

ASPARAGUS RISOTTO

Add 1 finely chopped onion to the pan with the garlic in step 1, and cook for 3–5 minutes until soft. Omit the blue cheese and pesto, and add 12 oz (375 g) trimmed and chopped asparagus in step 2, about 5 minutes before the end of the cooking time.

NASI GORENG

The name of this Indonesian recipe simply means "fried rice." Prepared with a variety of ingredients, it is one of the best known Indonesian dishes, and one of the easiest to make. Traditional garnishes such as crushed peanuts, fried eggs, and omelet strips give contrasting flavors and textures to the dish.

CHICKEN NASI GORENG

SERVES 6

2 cups (400 g) long-grain rice

salt and black pepper

6 tbls (90 ml) olive oil

6 bacon slices, chopped

2 large onions, chopped

3 garlic cloves, crushed

1/4 tsp cayenne pepper

2 tsp mild curry powder

2 cooked chicken breast halves, skinned and cubed

6 tbls (90 ml) soy sauce

6 green onions, chopped

2 oz (60 g) cooked peeled shrimp

1/2 cup (60 g) almonds, halved, and toasted (page 186)

TO GARNISH

cilantro sprigs

6 fried eggs (optional)

shrimp crackers

1 Cook the rice in boiling salted water for 12–15 minutes until tender. Drain, rinse with boiling water, drain again, and set aside.

2 Heat 1 tbsp of the oil in a large skillet or wok, add the bacon, and cook for 3–5 minutes until browned. Add the remaining oil, the onions, and garlic, and cook over a gentle heat for 3–5 minutes until the onions are soft but not colored.

3 Add the cayenne and curry powders and cook, stirring, for 1 minute or until fragrant. Add the chicken and cook for 5–6 minutes until just beginning to brown.

4 Add the soy sauce and half of the rice and stir well. Add the remaining rice, and season with salt and pepper. Cook over a gentle heat, stirring, for 7–8 minutes until the rice is heated through. Stir in the green onions, shrimp, and almonds, and heat through.

5 Serve hot, garnished with cilantro sprigs, and fried eggs if you like. Serve prawn crackers in a separate bowl.

VEGETARIAN NASI GORENG

SERVES 6

2 cups (400 g) long-grain rice

salt

2 tbsp tamarind paste (optional)

2 tbsp vegetable oil

1 red bell pepper, cored, seeded, and thinly sliced

1 large onion, chopped

3 garlic cloves, crushed

1/2 in (1 cm) piece of fresh gingerroot, peeled and grated

2 tsp curry powder

1/4 tsp each crushed dried red chilies (chili flakes) and turmeric

1/2 small hard white cabbage, thinly sliced

7 oz (200 g) canned crushed tomatoes

3 tbsp soy sauce

TO GARNISH

3 tomatoes, cut into strips

1/2 cucumber, cut into strips

omelet strips (see right)

1 Cook the rice in boiling salted water for 12–15 minutes until tender. Drain, rinse with boiling water, and drain again. Stir in the tamarind paste (if using) and set aside.

2 Heat 1 tbsp of the oil in a large skillet or wok, add the red pepper and onion, and cook for 3–5 minutes until softened. Add the garlic, ginger, curry powder, crushed chilies, and turmeric, and cook gently, stirring, for 1 minute.

3 Add the cabbage and cook for 3–5 minutes. Add the tomatoes and cook for 2–3 minutes. Remove from the pan.

4 Heat the remaining oil in the pan, add the rice, and cook gently until lightly browned. Return the vegetables to the pan. Add the soy sauce and heat gently to warm through.

5 Serve hot, garnished with tomato, cucumber, and omelet strips.

QUICK NASI GORENG

SERVES 6

2 cups (400 g) long-grain rice

2 tbsp vegetable oil

1 onion, chopped

1/2 tsp paprika

1 tsp ground ginger

1 1/2 cups (125 g) sliced button mushrooms

2 oz (60 g) bean sprouts

1 tsp soy sauce

4 oz (125 g) cooked peeled shrimp

2 green onions, finely sliced

chopped cilantro to garnish

1 Cook the rice in boiling salted water, for 12–15 minutes until tender. Drain, rinse with boiling water, drain again, and set aside.

2 Heat 1 tbsp of the oil in a skillet or wok, add the onion, and cook for 3–5 minutes until soft. Add the paprika and ginger, and cook over a low heat for 1 minute. Add the mushrooms and bean sprouts and cook for 2–3 minutes until softened. Remove from the pan.

3 Heat the remaining oil in the pan, add the rice, and cook over a gentle heat, stirring, for 7–8 minutes to warm through. Stir in the soy sauce. Return the vegetables to the pan and add the shrimp and onions. Serve hot, garnished with coriander.

OMELET GARNISH

Whisk 2 eggs with plenty of salt and pepper. Melt 2 tbls (30 g) butter in an omelet pan or small skillet. Add the eggs to the pan and cook until set. Slide the omelet out of the pan and roll it up, then leave to cool before slicing across into fine strips.

CLOCKWISE FROM TOP: Chicken Nasi Goreng, Vegetarian Nasi Goreng, Quick Nasi Goreng.

EGG-FRIED RICE

SERVES 4

1¼ cups (250 g) long-grain rice

salt and black pepper

3 tbsp sunflower oil

2 oz (60 g) bacon slices, diced

1 cup (125 g) frozen peas

2 eggs, beaten

4 oz (125 g) bean sprouts

6 green onions, sliced

1 Cook the rice in boiling salted water for 12–15 minutes until tender. Drain.

2 Heat the oil in a wok or large skillet, add the bacon, and cook over a high heat, stirring, for 2 minutes. Add the rice and peas and cook, stirring, for 5 minutes.

3 Add the eggs and bean sprouts, and stir-fry for 2 minutes until the eggs have just set. Taste for seasoning, sprinkle with the sliced spring onions, and serve at once.

SPECIAL EGG-FRIED RICE

Add 4 oz (125 g) cooked peeled shrimp when you add the rice and peas in step 2, and sprinkle with ½ cup (60 g) toasted cashew nuts just before serving.

PAELLA

SERVES 6

3 tbsp olive oil

6 chicken thighs

8 oz (250 g) smoked slab bacon, cut into strips

1 large onion, chopped

1 quart (1 liter) chicken stock

1 large tomato, chopped

2 garlic cloves, crushed

a few pinches of saffron threads, soaked in a little hot water

3 cups (500 g) short-grain rice

1 red and 1 green bell pepper, cored, seeded, and sliced

1 cup (125 g) frozen peas

salt and black pepper

1 lb (500 g) mussels, cleaned (page 124)

4 oz (125 g) cooked peeled shrimp

TO FINISH

12 pitted black olives

6 large cooked shrimp, unpeeled

lemon wedges

2 tbsp chopped parsley

1 Heat the oil in a paella pan or a large, deep skillet or a Dutch oven. Add the chicken and cook over a medium heat for 10 minutes until browned all over. Add the bacon and onion and cook for 5 minutes.

2 Stir in the stock, tomato, garlic, and the saffron with its soaking liquid, and bring to a boil. Add the rice, red and green peppers, and peas, and season with salt and pepper. Cover and bake in a preheated oven at 350°F (180°C) for 35–40 minutes until the rice is nearly tender and the stock has been absorbed.

3 Meanwhile, put the mussels into a large pan with about ½ in (1 cm) water. Cover tightly, and cook, shaking the pan occasionally, for 5 minutes or until the shells open. Drain the mussels, and throw away any which have not opened: do not try to force them open.

4 Stir the peeled shrimp into the paella, cover, and cook gently on the stovetop for about 5 minutes. Taste for seasoning. Arrange the mussels around the pan, and the olives, large shrimp, and lemon wedges on top. Serve hot, sprinkled with parsley.

Healthy option

If you remove the skin from the chicken before cooking this will considerably reduce the fat content of the paella.

9

VEGETABLES & SALADS

UNDER 30 MINUTES

QUICK & EASY

CUCUMBER SALAD
Light and summery: thin cucumber slices in a vinaigrette dressing of white wine vinegar and sunflower oil, sprinkled with fresh dill.

SERVES 4–6 75–50 calories per serving
Takes 10 minutes   Page 393

CABBAGE WITH GARLIC
Light and nutritious: tender young cabbage cut into thin shreds, then blanched and stir-fried with olive oil and garlic.

SERVES 6 103 calories per serving
Takes 15 minutes   Page 379

AMERICAN CLASSIC

WALDORF SALAD
Fresh and fruity: celery and apple flavored with lemon and tossed with mayonnaise. Mixed with pieces of walnut.

SERVES 4 469 calories per serving
Takes 15 minutes, plus chilling   Page 390

GREEK SALAD
Tomato wedges with cucumber, green bell pepper, feta cheese, and olives. Flavored with olive oil, lemon, and oregano.

SERVES 4–6 503–335 calories per serving
Takes 10 minutes   Page 393

MIXED VEGETABLE STIR-FRY
Sliced zucchini stir-fried with yellow bell pepper and a variety of mushrooms. Flavored with lemon juice, and sprinkled with almonds.

SERVES 4 155 calories per serving
Takes 10 minutes   Page 384

CELERY ROOT SALAD
Matchstick-thin strips of celery root tossed with a yogurt and mayonnaise dressing flavored with capers and Dijon mustard.

SERVES 4–6 100–66 calories per serving
Takes 15 minutes   Page 391

MIXED GREEN SALAD
Crisp lettuce, mâche, watercress, and arugula leaves tossed with vinaigrette dressing, and sprinkled with herbs.

SERVES 4–6 117–70 calories per serving
Takes 10 minutes   Page 389

RED SALAD BOWL
Bite-sized pieces of radicchio and oak leaf and lollo rosso lettuces mixed with onion, grapes, and a balsamic vinegar dressing.

SERVES 4–6 387–258 calories per serving
Takes 15 minutes   Page 389

ECONOMICAL

CARROT JULIENNE SALAD
Matchstick-thin strips of carrot briefly cooked, then coated in a dressing of olive oil, white wine vinegar, garlic, and parsley.

SERVES 4–6 79–53 calories per serving
Takes 20 minutes   Page 391

UNDER 30 MINUTES

CABBAGE & MIXED PEPPER STIR-FRY
Crunchy and nourishing: shredded white cabbage stir-fried with onion, celery, red and yellow bell peppers, and mushrooms.

SERVES 6–8 128–96 calories per serving
Takes 15 minutes   Page 379

ITALIAN CLASSIC

THREE-COLOR SALAD
Thinly sliced beefsteak tomatoes arranged with slices of mozzarella cheese and avocado, then drizzled with olive oil.

SERVES 4 509 calories per serving
Takes 20 minutes   Page 392

OKRA WITH CHILI
Hot and spicy: okra, onion, garlic, and fresh red chili, stir-fried until just tender but still slightly crisp.

SERVES 4 152 calories per serving
Takes 15 minutes   Page 384

LOW CALORIE

SWEET & SOUR BEETS
Juicy and well-flavored: diced beets cooked with onions, garlic, lemon juice, and mint. Equally good served warm or cold.

SERVES 4 242 calories per serving
Takes 20 minutes   Page 378

FRENCH FRIES
Popular accompaniment or snack: potatoes, cut into sticks, deep fried until crispy and brown.

SERVES 6 281 calories per serving
Takes 20 minutes, plus soaking   Page 374

CRUNCHY ORIENTAL SALAD
Iceberg lettuce, bean sprouts, green onions, and green bell pepper tossed with ginger dressing and sprinkled with sesame seeds.

SERVES 6 141 calories per serving
Takes 10 minutes, plus soaking   Page 389

CREAMED SPINACH
Creamy and nutritious: lightly cooked spinach mixed with sour cream or crème fraîche, Parmesan cheese, chives, and nutmeg, then broiled.

SERVES 4 250 calories per serving
Takes 20 minutes   Page 378

AROMATIC BRUSSELS SPROUTS
Tender and tangy: Brussels sprouts simmered, then tossed with mustard-seed butter and flavored with lemon juice.

SERVES 6–8 125–94 calories per serving
Takes 15 minutes   Page 379

CAESAR SALAD
Pieces of romaine lettuce tossed with olive oil, lemon juice, and hard-boiled egg quarters. Mixed with croutons and Parmesan cheese.

SERVES 4 421 calories per serving
Takes 20 minutes   Page 390

30–60 MINUTES

SWEET & SOUR RED CABBAGE

Shredded red cabbage cooked with bacon, apple, sugar, red wine, vinegar, golden raisins, caraway seeds, cinnamon, and nutmeg.

SERVES 8 225 calories per serving
Takes 55 minutes
Page 380

FRENCH CLASSIC

POMMES ANNA

Thinly sliced potatoes, layered in a skillet, dotted with butter and seasoned with salt and pepper, then cooked until tender.

SERVES 6 205 calories per serving
Takes 55 minutes
Page 375

COUSCOUS SALAD

Couscous with golden raisins and ginger, flavored with chili oil, raspberry vinegar, tomatoes, onion, green onions, and mint.

SERVES 4–6 420–280 calories per serving
Takes 20 minutes, plus cooling
Page 397

GARLIC MASHED POTATOES

Hearty and satisfying: potatoes are boiled and then mashed with roasted garlic, warm milk, and butter. Sprinkled with chives.

SERVES 6 227 calories per serving
Takes 45 minutes
Page 375

CAULIFLOWER & BROCCOLI LAYERS

Florets of cauliflower and broccoli layered in rings, and molded in a bowl. Topped with almonds and bread crumbs.

SERVES 4–6 341–227 calories per serving
Takes 35 minutes
Page 380

FAMILY CHOICE

RICE SALAD

Long-grain rice in a dressing flavored with mustard and garlic. Mixed with peas, red bell pepper, corn, and chopped cilantro.

SERVES 4–6 517–345 calories per serving
Takes 25 minutes, plus cooling
Page 397

DINNER PARTY

ITALIAN FENNEL

Quartered fennel bulbs lightly cooked until tender, topped with mozzarella cheese and baked until golden.

SERVES 8 108 calories per serving
Takes 30 minutes
Page 383

GLAZED SHALLOTS

Whole shallots simmered in water, butter, sugar, and thyme until glazed and golden brown.

SERVES 6 150 calories per serving
Takes 30 minutes
Page 382

TABBOULEH

Fresh and herby: bulgur wheat mixed with vinaigrette dressing, lemon juice, tomatoes, green onions, parsley, and mint.

SERVES 4 276 calories per serving
Takes 10 minutes, plus standing
Page 397

OVER 60 MINUTES

TOMATO & BASIL SALAD
Assortment of tomatoes and chunks of yellow bell
pepper dressed in oil and balsamic vinegar, then
sprinkled with shredded basil.

SERVES 4–6 146–97 calories per serving
Takes 10 minutes, plus standing   Page 393

Page 393

TOMATO & ONION SALAD
Thinly sliced tomatoes and mild onion drizzled
with an olive oil and red wine vinegar dressing.
Sprinkled with snipped chives before serving.

SERVES 6 166 calories per serving
Takes 15 minutes, plus chilling   Page 393

EGGPLANT WITH FRESH PESTO
Mediterranean flavors: slices of eggplant broiled
until lightly browned, cooled, then spread with
pesto and sprinkled with basil.

SERVES 4 499 calories per serving
Takes 20 minutes, plus standing   Page 388

POTATO, APPLE, & CELERY SALAD
Hearty salad: pieces of boiled potato tossed with a
vinaigrette dressing, then mixed with apple, celery,
onion, and mayonnaise.

SERVES 6 332 calories per serving
Takes 30 minutes, plus chilling   Page 391

THREE-BEAN SALAD
Green beans, chick peas, and red kidney beans
combined with olives in a yogurt dressing, flavored
with vinegar and mustard.

SERVES 4 315 calories per serving
Takes 15 minutes, plus standing   Page 396

CRUNCHY COLESLAW
Shredded white cabbage tossed with onion, celery,
carrot, golden raisins, vinaigrette dressing, mustard,
and mayonnaise.

SERVES 8 245 calories per serving
Takes 15 minutes, plus chilling   Page 390

PASTA & MACKEREL SALAD
Pasta shells tossed with zucchini, thin green beans,
orange segments, mackerel, walnuts, and a dressing
of fragrant oils and orange juice.

SERVES 4–6 965–643 calories per serving
Takes 30 minutes, plus chilling   Page 398

POTATO SALAD
Tender boiled new potatoes and onion coated in an
oil-and-vinegar dressing, then mixed with chives
and mayonnaise.

SERVES 8 357 calories per serving
Takes 30 minutes, plus chilling   Page 392

MUSHROOM SALAD
Mushrooms cooked with ground coriander, then
dressed in yogurt flavored with mustard and garlic.
Chilled and mixed with thinly sliced celery.

SERVES 6 102 calories per serving
Takes 15 minutes, plus chilling   Page 392

OVER 60 MINUTES

SWISS ROSTI

Grated potatoes seasoned with pepper, and shaped into a cake. Lightly cooked in butter until golden.

SERVES 8 230 calories per serving

Takes 45 minutes, plus chilling   Page 373

POTATOES LYONNAISE

Mouthwateringly delicious: thickly sliced potatoes layered with onion. Baked until the potatoes are tender.

SERVES 6 246 calories per serving

Takes 1¾ hours   Page 374

LOW FAT

RATATOUILLE

Slices of eggplant, zucchini, and red bell pepper cooked with tomatoes. Flavored with onion, garlic, and basil.

SERVES 4–6 236–157 calories per serving

Takes 1½ hours, plus standing   Page 385

TRADITIONAL

ROAST POTATOES

Classic accompaniment to roast meat or poultry: briefly simmered pieces of potato roasted in a little fat until crisp and golden.

SERVES 6 192 calories per serving

Takes 1¼ hours   Page 374

SWEET POTATOES WITH GINGER BUTTER

Baked sweet potatoes, flavored with soy sauce, and served with melting ginger and garlic butter.

SERVES 4 381 calories per serving

Takes 1 hour 5 minutes   Page 377

SPINACH & CHEESE BAKED POTATOES

Hearty and healthy: baked potatoes scooped out and mixed with spinach, onion, and ricotta cheese.

SERVES 4–8 146–291 calories per serving

Takes 1¾ hours   Page 376

DINNER PARTY

HASSELBACK POTATOES

Simple to make: whole potatoes sliced almost through at intervals. Brushed with butter, sprinkled with Parmesan, and baked.

SERVES 8 183 calories per serving

Takes 1 hour 5 minutes   Page 376

CREAMED WHITE BEANS

Hearty dish: great northern beans simmered with carrot, onion, and herbs. Thickened with pureed beans and garnished with chopped parsley.

SERVES 6 167 calories per serving

Takes 1½ hours, plus soaking   Page 381

FRENCH CLASSIC

GRATIN DAUPHINOIS

Rich and creamy: thinly sliced potato layered with cream, garlic, and grated Gruyère cheese, then baked until golden.

SERVES 8 279 calories per serving

Takes 1¾ hours   Page 373

VEGETABLES & SALADS KNOW-HOW

ON EVERY SHOPPING TRIP there seem to be more new vegetables to try – strangely shaped squashes and roots like kohlrabi, tomatoes and bell peppers of all colors, exotic mushrooms, Chinese cabbages, and salad greens such as arugula, mizuna, and red chard – as well as different varieties of familiar vegetables like potatoes, each suitable for particular cooking methods. Imported produce adds to the bounty of our own seasonal vegetables. And for added convenience, chilled prepared vegetables and salads are widely available. This wonderful variety enables a cook to be innovative, creating nutritious, appetizing dishes with minimum effort.

BUYING AND STORING

When choosing vegetables and salad leaves, look for the freshest available. Their color should be bright and their texture firm and crisp. Any vegetables that are bruised or show distinct signs of age – those that are discolored, shriveled, or flabby – are past their best. In general, small, young vegetables are more tender than large, older ones, although very small baby vegetables can be tasteless.

Some vegetables, including onions, garlic, roots such as potatoes, parsnips, and rutabagas, and pumpkin, can be stored in a cool, dark, well-ventilated place. More perishable vegetables, such as peas, corn cobs, celery, salad leaves, spinach, and ripe tomatoes, should be chilled. Keep them in the special salad drawer in the refrigerator, unwrapping them or piercing their bags to prevent moisture buildup.

Many vegetables can be prepared ahead of time and kept in sealed plastic bags in the refrigerator. The exceptions to this are vegetables such as celery root and Jerusalem artichokes that discolor when cut and exposed to the air. Salad leaves can also be prepared in advance, but do not dress until ready to serve or they will wilt.

NUTRITION

A healthy, well-balanced diet should include plenty of vegetables, because they supply essential vitamins, minerals, fiber, and disease-fighting compounds. And vegetables are low in calories and fat. To get the maximum benefit from the vegetables you eat:
• choose the freshest produce
• keep in a cool, dark place, and do not store for too long (use within a few days of purchase)
• prepare as close to cooking or eating as possible
• leave on the peel or skin as it provides fiber, and nutrients are often concentrated just under the skin
• rinse thoroughly but don't soak before cooking, particularly if the vegetable is peeled or cut
• cut large pieces if boiling or steaming
• use the cooking liquid in a sauce or soup

CUTTING VEGETABLES

Keep vegetable pieces to a uniform size and shape so they cook evenly.

Julienne
Cut into 1/4 in (5 mm) slices. Stack the slices, then cut into sticks 1/4 in (5 mm) thick.

Dice
Cut into 1/2 in (1 cm) strips, then cut across the strips to form neat dice.

Ribbons
Using a vegetable peeler, carefully shave off thin, wide ribbons.

MICROWAVING

The microwave is ideal for cooking small quantities of vegetables: little water is used so they retain their nutrients as well as colors and flavors. Cut vegetables into uniform pieces, or pierce skins of those that are left whole. Arrange them so that the tender parts are in the middle of the dish, to prevent overcooking. Add salt when serving. Keep the dish tightly covered during cooking, and turn or stir once or twice if necessary.

FREEZING

Most vegetables freeze very well, whether plain, in a sauce, or in a prepared dish. The exceptions are potatoes and watery vegetables like cucumber and tomatoes. Vegetables that are to be frozen plain should be very fresh. Before freezing blanch them in boiling water, then cool quickly in iced water; this will set the fresh color. Vegetables can be kept in the freezer for 6–12 months, and can be cooked directly from frozen.

PREPARING VEGETABLES

Knowing the most efficient way to prepare vegetables will save you time and effort in the kitchen.
For most tasks, a cutting board and a sharp chef's knife, small knife, or vegetable peeler are all you'll need.
Here's how the professionals deal with more unusual vegetables.

Dicing fresh chilies

1 Cut the chili in half lengthwise. Remove the stem and core and scrape out the fleshy white ribs and seeds.

2 Set the chili cut-side up and cut into thin strips. Hold the strips together and cut across to make dice. (See know-how box below.)

Preparing bell peppers

1 Cut around the stem and the core. Twist and pull them out in one piece.

2 Cut the pepper in half. Scrape out the fleshy white ribs and the seeds.

Chopping fresh gingerroot

1 With a small knife, peel off the skin. Slice the ginger across the fibrous grain.

2 Set the flat of a knife on top of the slices and crush. Chop the crushed slices.

Preparing asparagus

Cut off any woody ends from the asparagus and make the spears uniform in length. You can peel them if you like: using a vegetable peeler, and working down from the tip toward the end of the spear, shave off the tough layer of skin from all sides.

Chopping garlic

1 Set the flat side of a knife on top of the clove and crush it lightly. Peel off the skin.

2 With a sharp chef's knife, chop the crushed garlic clove finely.

Preparing avocado

Cut the avocado in half lengthwise around the pit, twist the 2 halves to separate them, and ease out the pit. Or, if the avocado is to be mashed, the flesh can simply be scooped out of the skin with a teaspoon. To serve in slices, lightly score the skin into 2 or 3 strips, then peel off the strips of skin and slice the flesh.

Preparing vegetables know-how

The juices produced by fresh chilies can burn the skin, so it's best to wear rubber gloves when cutting them and to avoid touching your eyes or lips. If you do, rinse immediately with cold water.

•

The more finely you chop garlic, the stronger the flavor. Garlic crushed in a press will have the strongest flavor of all.

•

Avocados discolor quickly, so brush cut surfaces with lemon juice, and use as soon as possible after cutting. Other vegetables that discolor when cut and exposed to the air include globe artichokes, celery root, and Jerusalem artichokes.

COOKING VEGETABLES

Choose the right cooking method to bring out the best in vegetables and create exciting accompaniments or main dishes. If cooking a variety of vegetables at the same time, remember that some take longer to cook than others, so you might have to add them in stages.

Baking
Potatoes, sweet potatoes, eggplants, and pumpkin are all delicious baked. Prick the skins of whole vegetables or, if cut, moisten cut surfaces with oil or butter. Push a skewer through the centers of large vegetables to conduct heat and speed up cooking time.

Chargrilling
Many types of quick-cooking vegetables can be cooked on a chargrill, as well as under a broiler or on a barbecue. Halve the vegetables or cut into thick slices. Brush with oil and chargrill, turning at least once, until tender. For extra flavor, marinate vegetables first (page 386).

Braising
Carrots, celery, and other root vegetables are ideal for braising. Put the vegetables into a heavy pan or flameproof casserole, add a small amount of water or stock, and bring to the boil. Cover tightly and cook over a low heat until just tender. Boil to evaporate the liquid or drain.

Sautéing
Vegetables can be sautéed in oil or a mixture of oil and butter (butter alone burns if it becomes too hot). Cook the vegetables over a high heat, stirring and turning constantly, until they start to brown. Reduce the heat and continue cooking, stirring occasionally, until tender.

Roasting
Cut any root vegetables into large chunks and parboil them. Drain well. Put olive oil or duck fat into a roasting pan and heat in a preheated 350°F (180°C) oven. Add the vegetables to the pan and turn to coat with the fat. Roast, turning occasionally, until well browned.

Boiling
Drop vegetables (both greens and roots) into a large pan of boiling salted water and bring back to a boil as quickly as possible. Simmer until just tender, then drain. To stop longer cooking and set the color of green vegetables, rinse briefly under cold running water.

Deep-frying
Most vegetables (except roots like potatoes) need a protective coating such as batter before being deep-fried. Heat oil in a deep-fryer to the specified temperature. Add the vegetables in batches and fry until golden, bringing the oil back to the specified temperature between each batch. Drain on paper towels.

Stir-frying
Cut the vegetables into small, even-sized pieces. Heat a little oil in a wok. When it is hot, add the vegetables, starting with those that need the longest cooking time. Keep the heat high, and toss and stir the vegetables constantly. Cook for just a few minutes until the vegetables are tender but still crisp.

Steaming
This method is ideal for delicate vegetables such as cauliflower, broccoli, and asparagus. Bring water to the boil in a steamer base. Put the vegetables in a single layer on the rack, cover, and steam until just tender. If you don't have a steamer, use a large saucepan with a steamer basket, or a wok and a bamboo steamer.

MAYONNAISE

This always useful sauce is the base for many others – add crushed garlic and you have aioli – and for salad dressings. It can be made by hand, with a balloon whisk, or more quickly in a food processor or blender. For a lighter result use 1 whole egg rather than 2 egg yolks, and sunflower oil alone.

Traditional mayonnaise

1 Put a bowl on a dish towel to steady it. Add 2 egg yolks, 1 tsp Dijon mustard, and salt and pepper to taste, and beat together with a balloon whisk until the egg yolks have thickened slightly.

2 Whisk in 2/3 cup (150 ml) olive or sunflower oil, or a mixture of the two, just a drop at a time at first, whisking until the mixture is thick. Stir in 2 tsp white wine vinegar or lemon juice. Check the seasoning, adding sugar to taste if liked. Serve at once, or chill. This makes about 3/4 cup (175 ml).

Food processor mayonnaise

1 Put 2 whole eggs, 2 tsp Dijon mustard, and salt and pepper to taste in the bowl of a food processor or blender. Process briefly to combine.

2 With the blades turning, slowly add 1 1/4 cups (300 ml) olive or sunflower oil, or a mixture of the two. Finish as for traditional mayonnaise above.

SALAD DRESSINGS

Most salad dressings can be made in a matter of seconds – for vinaigrette the ingredients only need to be shaken together in a screw-topped jar, and the basic mixture can be endlessly varied. Other dressings are simply made by whisking flavourings into a creamy mixture based on mayonnaise.

Vinaigrette dressing

Put 6 tbsp olive oil, 2 tbsp white wine vinegar, 1 tbsp lemon juice, 1 tbsp Dijon mustard, 1/4 tsp sugar, and salt and pepper to taste into a screw-top jar. Shake until combined. This makes about 2/3 cup (150 ml).

Blue cheese dressing

Put 2/3 cup (150 ml) each of mayonnaise and sour cream into a bowl with 3 oz (90 g) mashed blue cheese, 1 tsp white wine vinegar, 1 crushed garlic clove, and black pepper to taste. Whisk until smooth.

Nutty vinaigrette

Use red wine vinegar instead of the white wine vinegar and lemon juice in the recipe above, and replace 2 tbsp of the olive oil with walnut or hazelnut oil.

Herb vinaigrette

Add 2 tbsp chopped fresh herbs, such as dill, tarragon, chervil, or flat-leaf parsley, to the vinaigrette just before serving.

Green mayonnaise dressing

Put 2 oz (60 g) each watercress

sprigs and flat-leaf parsley in a blender or food processor with 4 chopped green onions and 1 garlic clove. Process until the herbs are finely chopped. Whisk into a mixture of 2/3 cup (150 ml) each mayonnaise and sour cream or thick plain yogurt.

Easy coleslaw dressing

Whisk 5 tbsp apple cider vinegar and 1 tbsp sugar into 2/3 cup (150 ml) mayonnaise. Season with salt and pepper to taste. If liked stir in a pinch of caraway seeds.

Salad dressings know-how

If mayonnaise curdles, add 1 tbsp hot water and beat well, or start again with fresh egg yolks and oil and slowly add the curdled mixture once the eggs and oil thicken.

•

For best results have the eggs for mayonnaise at room temperature.

•

Keep homemade mayonnaise, tightly covered, in the refrigerator for no more than 1–2 days (remember that it contains raw eggs).

•

Vinaigrette dressing can be kept in its screw-top jar in the refrigerator for up to 1 week. Shake well before serving.

GRATIN DAUPHINOIS

SERVES 8

butter for greasing

⅔ cup (150 ml) light cream

⅔ cup (150 ml) heavy cream

1 large garlic clove, crushed

4 large baking potatoes

salt and black pepper

1 cup (125 g) grated Gruyère cheese

1 Lightly butter a shallow gratin dish. Put the light and heavy creams into a bowl, add the garlic, and stir to mix.

2 Thinly slice the potatoes, preferably with the slicing disk of a food processor.

3 Prepare the gratin dauphinois (see box, right).

4 Bake in a preheated oven at 325°F (160°C) for 1½ hours or until the potatoes are tender and the topping is golden brown. Serve at once.

Preparing the gratin dauphinois

Arrange a layer of potatoes, slightly overlapping, in the bottom of the gratin dish. Season with salt and pepper.

Pour a little of the cream mixture over the potatoes, then sprinkle with grated cheese. Continue layering the potatoes, cream, and cheese, and adding salt and pepper, then finish with a layer of cheese.

SWISS ROSTI

SERVES 8

6 large baking potatoes, very well scrubbed

black pepper

4 tbsp (60 g) butter

2 tbsp sunflower oil

fresh thyme to garnish

1 Cook the potatoes in boiling salted water for about 10 minutes until just tender. Drain the potatoes thoroughly, leave to cool, then peel. Cover and chill for about 4 hours.

2 Coarsely grate the potatoes into a large bowl, season with pepper, and stir carefully to mix.

3 Melt 2 tbsp (30 g) of the butter with 1 tbsp of the oil in a skillet, add the grated potato, and flatten into a cake with a spatula. Cook over a low heat for about 15 minutes until the base is crisp and golden brown. Turn out onto a large buttered plate.

4 Melt the remaining butter and oil in the skillet, slide in the potato cake, and cook for 5–10 minutes to brown the second side. Turn out onto a warmed platter, garnish, and serve cut into wedges.

CELERY ROOT ROSTI

Substitute 1½ lb (750 g) celery root for 3 of the potatoes. Before boiling in step 1, peel the celery root, and toss in lemon juice to prevent discoloration.

ONION ROSTI

Heat 1 tbsp sunflower oil in a skillet, add 1 large chopped onion, and cook for 3–5 minutes until softened but not colored. Fork the onion into the grated potato in step 2, season with pepper, and stir to mix.

POTATOES LYONNAISE

SERVES 6

6 tbsp (90 g) butter, plus extra for greasing

1 large onion, sliced

4 large baking potatoes, thickly sliced

salt and black pepper

chopped parsley to garnish

1 Lightly butter a gratin or other baking dish. Melt the butter in a skillet, add the onion, and cook gently, stirring occasionally, for 3–5 minutes until the onions are softened but not colored.

2 Layer the potatoes and onion in the gratin dish, seasoning each layer with salt and pepper, and finishing with a neat layer of potatoes.

3 Pour any butter left in the skillet over the potatoes. Bake in a preheated oven at 375°F (190°C) for 1–1½ hours until the potatoes are tender. Garnish with chopped parsley, and serve hot.

FRENCH FRIES

SERVES 6

3 large baking potatoes

sunflower oil for deep-frying

salt

DEEP-FRYER

1 Cut the potatoes into 2 x ½ in (5 x 1 cm) sticks, put into a bowl of cold water, and leave to soak for 5–10 minutes.

2 Heat the oil in a deep-fryer to 325°F (160°C). Dry the potato sticks thoroughly, then lower them into the deep-fryer, in batches if necessary, and deep-fry for 5–6 minutes until soft and very pale golden.

3 Lift the basket out of the fryer. Increase the temperature of the oil to 375°F (190°C). Carefully return the basket of fries to the fryer and deep-fry for 3–4 minutes until crisp and golden brown. Lift out the basket and drain the fries on paper towels. Sprinkle with salt, and serve hot.

POMMES FRITES

For these thin fries, cut the potatoes into 2 x ¼ in (5 cm x 5 mm) sticks and leave to soak as directed. Heat the oil as directed and deep-fry the sticks for 4–5 minutes. Lift out of the fryer, increase the heat as directed, return and deep-fry the sticks for 1–2 minutes. Serve at once.

Cook's know-how

Good French fries should be crisp and golden on the outside and soft and tender in the middle. The secret is to cook the potatoes first in medium-hot oil until tender, then lift them out, increase the temperature of the oil, and cook the chips quickly to brown and crisp the outsides. Drain well on paper towels before serving.

ROAST POTATOES

SERVES 6

4 large baking potatoes, cut into even-sized chunks

3 tbsp sunflower oil, or goose or duck fat

salt

1 Put the potatoes into a large saucepan, cover with cold water, and bring to a boil. Simmer for 1 minute, then drain thoroughly.

2 Return the potatoes to the saucepan and shake over a low heat to roughen the surfaces and dry the potatoes thoroughly.

3 Put the oil or fat into a roasting pan, heat until very hot, then add the potatoes, turning to coat them in the oil or fat. Roast the potatoes in a preheated oven at 425°F (220°C), turning and basting occasionally, for 45–60 minutes until tender, crisp, and golden. Sprinkle with salt, and serve at once.

Cook's know-how

Roughening the outside of blanched potatoes before roasting helps make them really crisp. If you like, you can also score them roughly with a fork.

POMMES ANNA

SERVES 6

3 large baking potatoes

6 tbsp (90 g) butter, plus extra for greasing

salt and black pepper

1 Slice the potatoes very thinly, preferably with the slicing disk of a food processor.

2 Butter the bottom and sides of an ovenproof skillet. Layer the potatoes in the skillet, seasoning each layer with salt and pepper, and dotting with the butter.

3 Cover the skillet tightly with buttered foil and the lid, and cook over a medium heat for about 15 minutes or until the base of the potato cake is light golden brown.

4 Transfer the skillet to a preheated oven and cook at 375°F (190°C) for 30 minutes or until the potato cake is tender.

5 Invert a warmed serving platter over the skillet, and turn out the potato cake so that the crisp layer is on the top. Serve at once, cut into wedges.

Cook's know-how

Arrange the potatoes in the skillet as soon as they have been sliced. Don't leave them to soak in water or the starch in them will leach out and they will not hold together properly to make the cake.

INDIVIDUAL POMMES ANNA

Layer the sliced potatoes in well-buttered individual ramekins, seasoning the layers and dotting with butter as in step 2. Omit the cooking on the stove-top in step 3, and bake, uncovered, in the top half of a preheated oven at 425°F (220°C) for 30–35 minutes or until the potatoes are tender and golden brown.

GARLIC MASHED POTATOES

SERVES 4

3 large baking potatoes, cut into large chunks

4 garlic cloves, unpeeled

salt and black pepper

about ⅔ cup (150 ml) milk

4 tbsp (60 g) butter

2 tbsp snipped fresh chives

1 Cook the potatoes and whole garlic cloves in boiling salted water for 20–30 minutes until tender. Drain thoroughly, and peel the skins off the garlic cloves.

2 Return the potatoes to the saucepan and toss over a low heat for a few seconds to dry thoroughly, shaking the saucepan so the potatoes do not burn. Add the garlic to the pan.

3 Mash the potatoes and garlic together, or work through a strainer for a finer puree, then push them to one side of the pan.

4 Pour the milk into the saucepan and heat until almost boiling. Beat the milk into the potatoes and garlic with the butter, and salt and pepper to taste. Sprinkle with chives, and serve hot.

HERB & CHEESE MASHED POTATOES

Omit the garlic, and add 2 tbsp chopped parsley and ½ cup (60 g) finely grated Cheddar cheese when you beat in the milk.

MASHED POTATOES WITH RUTABAGA

Omit the garlic and fresh chives. Substitute 8 oz (250 g) rutabaga, cut into small chunks, for 1 of the potatoes, and add a pinch of grated nutmeg just before serving.

HASSELBACK POTATOES

SERVES 8

8 large baking potatoes

4 tbsp (60 g) butter, melted, plus extra for greasing

salt and black pepper

4 tbsp grated Parmesan cheese

parsley to garnish

1 Peel the potatoes, then slice them (see box, right).

2 Put the potatoes into a buttered roasting pan and brush with the melted butter, separating the slices slightly so a little of the butter goes between them. Season with salt and pepper.

3 Bake in a preheated oven at 425°F (220°C) for 45 minutes, then sprinkle with the Parmesan cheese and return to the oven for 10–15 minutes or until the potatoes are tender.

4 Transfer to a warmed serving platter, garnish with parsley, and serve at once.

Slicing the potatoes

Cut a thin slice off one side of each potato, and place the potato cut-side down on a board. Make vertical cuts, three-quarters of the way through, at 1/4 in (5 mm) intervals.

Cook's know-how

To make it easier to slice the potatoes, push a skewer lengthwise through the lower part of each potato, and slice down almost as far as the skewer. Remove the skewer before cooking.

SPINACH & CHEESE BAKED POTATOES

SERVES 4–8

4 large baking potatoes, scrubbed

1 cup (250 g) fresh spinach

1 tbsp olive oil

1 small onion, finely chopped

1/2 cup (125 g) ricotta cheese

1/4 tsp grated nutmeg

salt and black pepper

1 Prick the potatoes all over with a fork. Bake in a preheated oven at 425°F (220°C) for 1–1 1/4 hours or until tender.

2 Meanwhile, wash the spinach and put it into a saucepan with only the water remaining on the leaves. Cook over a low heat for 1–2 minutes until the spinach has just wilted. Drain thoroughly, squeezing to remove excess water. Chop the spinach finely.

3 Heat the olive oil in a small saucepan, add the onion, and cook gently, stirring occasionally, for 3–5 minutes until softened but not colored.

4 Cut the potatoes in half lengthwise, scoop out the flesh and turn it into a bowl. Add the spinach, onion, any oil left in the pan, the ricotta cheese, and nutmeg. Season with salt and pepper, and mix thoroughly. Fill the potato skins with the mixture, return to the oven at the same temperature as before, and cook for 20 minutes or until piping hot. Serve hot.

GREEN ONION & HUMMUS BAKED POTATOES

Bake the potatoes, cut in half lengthwise, and scoop out the flesh. Mix with 4 finely chopped green onions, 2/3 cup (150 g) hummus, and season with salt and pepper. Fill the potato skins and bake as in step 4.

SWEET POTATOES WITH GINGER BUTTER

SERVES 4

4 sweet potatoes, scrubbed

4 tbsp (60 g) sesame seeds

soy sauce to taste

GINGER BUTTER

3 tbsp (45 g) butter, softened

1 garlic clove, crushed

1/2 in (1 cm) piece of fresh gingerroot, peeled and grated

1 Lightly prick the skins of the sweet potatoes with a fork. Bake in a preheated oven at 350°F (180°C) for 1 hour or until tender.

2 Meanwhile, make the ginger butter: put the butter into a small bowl and blend in the garlic and grated ginger.

3 Put the sesame seeds into a skillet and toss over a low heat for 2–3 minutes until golden brown. Remove from the skillet. Lightly crush about half of the sesame seeds to release more of their fragrance. Set aside.

4 Cut the sweet potatoes into wedges and arrange on a serving plate with the ginger butter. Sprinkle with soy sauce and sesame seeds, and serve at once.

Healthy note

Sesame seeds contain phytic acid, which may inhibit certain cancers, especially cancer of the colon. Dry-frying the seeds not only enhances their flavor but adds a sweet nuttiness to the dish.

SPICED YAMS

SERVES 4

3 tbsp (45 g) butter

2 garlic cloves, crushed

2 yams, total weight 2 lb (1 kg), trimmed but unpeeled, cubed

1 tsp mild chili powder

1/4 tsp paprika

1/4 tsp ground cinnamon

7 oz (200 g) canned crushed tomatoes

salt

plain yogurt and chopped parsley to serve

1 Melt the butter in a large pan. When it is foaming, add the garlic, and cook gently, stirring occasionally, for 1–2 minutes until soft but not colored.

2 Add the yams to the pan and toss over a medium to high heat for 1–2 minutes.

3 Stir in the chili powder, paprika, and cinnamon, then add the tomatoes, and cook the mixture over a medium heat for 1–2 minutes.

4 Season with salt, cover, and simmer for 15–20 minutes until the yams are tender. Turn the yams occasionally with a metal spatula, but do not stir or they will break up. Serve hot, topped with yogurt and parsley.

Cook's know-how

Yams and sweet potatoes are often confused, but they are not the same. Yams are a hard, starchy vegetable that comes in many different sizes, shapes, and colors, whereas sweet potatoes are softer and torpedo-shaped, with orange or yellow flesh. Sweet potatoes are rich in vitamins A and C (both antioxidants), whereas yams are not.

GINGER PARSNIPS

SERVES 8

2 lb (1 kg) parsnips, cut into matchstick-thin strips

salt and black pepper

4 tbsp (60 g) butter

1 in (2.5 cm) piece of fresh gingerroot, peeled and grated

1 1/4 cups (300 ml) sour cream or crème fraîche

1 Blanch the parsnips in a large saucepan of boiling salted water for 2 minutes. Drain the parsnips.

2 Melt the butter in the saucepan. Add the ginger and cook gently, stirring, for 2–3 minutes. Add the parsnips, tossing to coat in the butter. Season with salt and pepper, then turn the mixture into a large, shallow baking dish.

3 Pour the sour cream or crème fraîche over the parsnip mixture and bake in a preheated oven at 375°F (190°C) for 10–15 minutes until tender. Serve hot.

GLAZED CARROTS & TURNIPS

SERVES 4

4 carrots, cut into 2 in (5 cm) strips

12 oz (375 g) baby turnips

1 1/4 cups (300 ml) chicken stock

2 tbsp (30 g) butter

1 tsp sugar

salt and black pepper

1 tbsp mixed chopped fresh mint and parsley

1 Put the vegetables into a pan with the stock, butter, and sugar. Season with salt and pepper, and bring to a boil. Cover and cook for about 10 minutes until the vegetables are almost tender.

2 Remove the lid and boil rapidly until the liquid in the pan has evaporated and formed a glaze on the vegetables. Stir in the herbs, and serve hot.

CREAMED SPINACH

SERVES 4

1 1/2 lb (750 g) fresh spinach leaves

3 tbsp (45 g) butter

1/2 cup (125 ml) sour cream or crème fraîche

1/4 tsp grated nutmeg

salt and black pepper

1–2 tbsp grated Parmesan cheese

1 Cut any coarse stems off the spinach leaves and discard, then wash the leaves thoroughly in plenty of cold water.

2 Melt the butter in a saucepan, add the spinach, and stir until it has absorbed the butter.

3 Add half of the sour cream or crème fraîche, season with the nutmeg and salt and pepper, and heat through.

4 Transfer to a shallow gratin or other baking dish, pour the remaining sour cream or crème fraîche on top, and sprinkle with grated Parmesan. Put under a hot broiler for a few minutes until lightly browned. Serve hot.

SWEET & SOUR BEETS

SERVES 4

3 tbsp olive oil

2 onions, chopped

2 garlic cloves, crushed

2 tbsp sugar

4 cooked beets, diced

juice of 1 lemon

2 tsp chopped fresh mint

salt and black pepper

fresh mint to garnish

1 Heat the olive oil in a large saucepan, add the onions and garlic, and cook gently, stirring occasionally, for 3–5 minutes until the onions are softened but not colored.

2 Stir in the sugar, beets, half of the lemon juice, and the mint. Cook gently, stirring, for 10 minutes. Taste for seasoning, adding salt and pepper, and more lemon juice if needed.

3 Serve warm or cold, garnished with fresh mint.

CABBAGE & MIXED PEPPER STIR-FRY

SERVES 6–8

2–3 tbsp olive oil

1 large onion, finely sliced

6 celery stalks, sliced diagonally

2 red bell peppers, cored, seeded, and cut into thin strips

1 yellow bell pepper, cored, seeded, and cut into thin strips

6 oz (175 g) mushrooms, quartered

salt and black pepper

1 small white cabbage, finely shredded

1 Heat 1 tbsp olive oil in a wok or large skillet, add the sliced onion, and stir-fry over a high heat for about 2 minutes until beginning to brown.

2 Add the sliced celery and stir-fry for about 1 minute, then lower the heat and stir-fry for 2 minutes.

3 Add another tablespoon of olive oil to the pan. When it is hot, add the peppers and mushrooms, season with salt and pepper, and stir fry for 3 minutes.

4 Add the cabbage, with the remaining oil if needed, and stir-fry for 2 minutes or until tender-crisp. Taste for seasoning.

SAVOY CABBAGE STIR-FRY

Heat 1 tbsp sunflower oil in a wok and stir-fry 1 finely sliced large onion, and 2 crushed garlic cloves for a few minutes. Add another 1 tbsp sunflower oil, then 1 shredded small Savoy cabbage, and stir-fry for 2 minutes. Sprinkle with 2 tbsp soy sauce and 1 tsp sesame oil.

Cook's know-how

This is a good vegetable dish to serve when entertaining. Prepare and stir-fry the vegetables up to the end of step 3. The final cooking of the cabbage can be done just before serving.

CABBAGE WITH GARLIC

SERVES 6

2 lb (1 kg) cabbage leaves, tough stems removed

salt

2 tbsp olive oil

3 garlic cloves, coarsely chopped

1 Loosely roll up the cabbage leaves, a few at a time, and cut across into thin strips. Blanch in boiling salted water for 2 minutes.

2 Drain and rinse in ice water to cool. Drain thoroughly, gently squeezing to remove excess water.

3 Heat the olive oil in a large saucepan, add the garlic, and cook gently for 1 minute or until lightly browned. Add the cabbage, toss to coat thoroughly in the garlic and oil, and cook for 2–3 minutes until the cabbage is heated through.

4 Season with salt to taste. Serve hot or cold.

AROMATIC BRUSSEL SPROUTS

SERVES 6–8

2 lb (1 kg) Brussels sprouts

salt and black pepper

3 tbsp (45 g) butter

2 tsp mustard seeds

1 tbsp lemon juice

1 Cut a cross in the base of each sprout, and simmer the sprouts in boiling salted water for 5–10 minutes until just tender. Drain.

2 Melt the butter in a large saucepan, add the mustard seeds, cover, and cook over a low heat for 1–2 minutes until the mustard seeds have stopped popping and the butter is lightly browned. Do not let the butter burn.

3 Add the sprouts to the pan, tossing to heat them through and coat them in the mustard-seed butter. Add the lemon juice, season with salt and pepper, and serve at once.

CAULIFLOWER & BROCCOLI LAYERS

SERVES 6

1 lb (500 g) broccoli florets
1 lb (500 g) cauliflower florets
salt and black pepper
4 tbsp (60 g) butter, plus extra for greasing
1/2 cup (60 g) slivered almonds
4 tbsp fresh white bread crumbs
1 garlic clove, crushed
1 QUART (1 LITER) BOWL

1 Cook the broccoli and cauliflower in boiling salted water for 10 minutes or until just tender. Drain.

2 Butter the bowl and layer the cauliflower and broccoli (see box, right).

3 Cover the bowl with a small plate and press down lightly to mold the vegetables. Leave in a warm place for 5 minutes.

4 Melt the remaining butter in a skillet. Add the almonds, bread crumbs, and garlic, and cook, stirring, for 3–5 minutes until golden. Season with salt and pepper.

5 Invert the bowl onto a warmed platter. Serve with the almond mixture on top.

Layering the vegetables

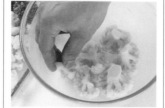

Arrange a layer of cauliflower florets, stem-sides up, in the bottom of the bowl.

Place a ring of outward-facing broccoli florets, then of cauliflower florets on top. Continue layering alternately. Tightly pack the middle of the bowl with the remaining florets.

SWEET & SOUR RED CABBAGE

SERVES 8

1 tbsp sunflower oil
4 bacon slices, diced
1/2 cup (125 g) packed soft brown sugar
2 onions, chopped
1 red cabbage, weighing about 2 lb (1 kg), shredded
1 tart apple, cored and diced
1 cup (250 ml) red wine
4 tbsp red wine vinegar
1/3 cup (60 g) golden raisins
2 tsp caraway seeds
1/4 tsp ground cinnamon
pinch of grated nutmeg (optional)
salt and black pepper

1 Heat the sunflower oil in a large saucepan, add the diced bacon, and cook for about 5 minutes until crisp and browned.

2 Stir in 6 tbsp (90 g) of the sugar and cook gently, stirring constantly, for 1–2 minutes, taking care that it does not burn.

3 Add the onions, cabbage, and apple, and cook, stirring occasionally, for about 5 minutes.

4 Pour in the wine and half of the wine vinegar, then add the golden raisins, caraway seeds, cinnamon, and nutmeg (if using). Season with salt and pepper. Cover and cook over a low heat for 30 minutes or until the cabbage is tender but still firm. If there is too much liquid, uncover, and boil rapidly until the liquid evaporates completely.

5 Stir in the remaining sugar and wine vinegar, heat through, and taste for seasoning. Serve hot.

VEGETARIAN RED CABBAGE WITH CHESTNUTS

Replace the bacon with 1 cup (125 g) coarsely chopped peeled chestnuts. Add to the pan in step 1, and cook for 3–4 minutes until golden. Continue as directed.

CREAMED WHITE BEANS

SERVES 6

1¼ cups (250 g) great northern beans

2 tbsp (30 g) butter

1 small carrot, finely chopped

1 small onion, finely chopped

1 bouquet garni or a bunch of fresh mixed herbs

salt and black pepper

2 tbsp chopped parsley

1 Put the beans into a large bowl, cover with cold water, then leave to soak for at least 8 hours.

2 Drain the beans. Rinse under cold water and drain again. Put the beans into a saucepan and cover with cold water. Bring to a boil and boil rapidly for 10 minutes. Drain.

3 Melt the butter in a heavy saucepan, add the carrot and onion, and cook, stirring, for 3–4 minutes until beginning to soften.

4 Add the beans and bouquet garni or fresh herbs, and pour in enough cold water to cover the beans generously. Bring to a boil, cover, and simmer gently for 1 hour or until the beans are soft but not breaking up.

5 Drain the bean mixture, reserving the cooking liquid. Discard the bouquet garni or herbs. Puree one-third of the bean mixture in a food processor.

6 Stir the puree back into the unpureed bean mixture in the pan, adding a little of the reserved cooking liquid to make a saucelike consistency. Season with salt and pepper. Reheat gently and serve hot, sprinkled with chopped parsley.

FRESH PEAS WITH LETTUCE

SERVES 4–6

1 small round lettuce, shredded

6 green onions, chopped

4 tbsp (60 g) butter

1 tbsp chopped parsley

1 tsp sugar

3 cups (500 g) shelled fresh peas (they must be young)

4 tbsp water

salt and black pepper

1 Line the bottom of a saucepan with the lettuce. Add the green onions, butter, parsley, and sugar, and top with the peas. Add the water, season with salt and pepper, and bring to a boil.

2 Simmer gently, uncovered, for 15–20 minutes until the liquid has evaporated and the peas are tender. Taste for seasoning and serve hot.

SUMMER PEAS & BEANS

SERVES 6–8

1½ cups (250 g) shelled fresh fava beans (they must be young)

salt and black pepper

1½ cups (250 g) shelled peas (they must be young)

1½ cups (250 g) thin green beans, halved

2 tbsp (30 g) butter

2 tbsp chopped fresh mint

fresh mint to garnish

1 Cook the fava beans in boiling salted water for a few minutes. Add the peas and green beans and cook for another 5–10 minutes or until tender (the timing depends on their freshness).

2 Drain all the vegetables, and return to the pan. Add the butter and mint and stir until the butter melts. Taste for seasoning, and serve hot, garnished with fresh mint.

GLAZED SHALLOTS

SERVES 6

1 1/2 lb (750 g) small shallots or pearl onions
6 tbsp (90 g) butter
1 tbsp sugar
1 tbsp chopped fresh thyme
salt and black pepper
chopped parsley to garnish

1 Place the shallots in a single layer in a large skillet and cover with cold water.

2 Add the butter, sugar, and thyme, and season with salt and pepper. Cover and bring to a boil. Uncover, and simmer gently for 10–15 minutes until the shallots are golden and the liquid almost evaporated. Shake the pan vigorously at intervals, to prevent the shallots sticking.

3 Garnish the shallots with parsley, and serve hot.

CELERY & LEEK STIR-FRY

SERVES 6

2 tbsp (30 g) butter
2 tbsp olive oil
4 young leeks, trimmed and thinly sliced
12 celery stalks, thinly sliced diagonally
salt and black pepper
2 tbsp snipped fresh chives
1 cup (125 g) salted cashew nuts to garnish

1 Melt the butter with the olive oil in a wok or large skillet.

2 When the butter is foaming, add the leeks, and cook over a high heat, stirring occasionally, for 5 minutes.

3 Add the celery, and cook for 3–5 minutes. Add salt and pepper, then stir in the snipped fresh chives. Garnish with the salted cashew nuts, and serve at once.

Healthy note

Celery is a good source of potassium, and is known to help prevent and reduce high blood pressure.

YANKEE SUCCOTASH

SERVES 6

2 tbsp sunflower oil
1 large onion, chopped
8 thick bacon slices, diced
3 cups (500 g) corn kernels
1 cup (250 ml) light cream
14 oz (400 g) canned beans, such as lima or fava, drained
salt
hot pepper sauce
3–4 tbsp snipped fresh chives
whole fresh chives to garnish

1 Heat the sunflower oil in a large skillet, add the onion and bacon, and cook gently, stirring occasionally, for 7 minutes or until lightly browned.

2 Stir in the corn and cream and simmer for 2 minutes. Puree 3–4 tbsp of the corn mixture in a food processor until just smooth (it should retain some bits), then stir back into the skillet.

3 Add the beans and return to a boil. Simmer, stirring occasionally, for 5–10 minutes until the mixture is thickened.

4 Add salt and hot pepper sauce to taste, and gently stir in the snipped chives. Serve at once, garnished with the whole chives.

Healthy option

Succotash is a native American dish. It is traditionally made rich with bacon and cream, but you can omit these two ingredients from this recipe and use low-sodium vegetable stock instead of the cream.

STUFFED MUSHROOMS

SERVES 6

8 oz (250 g) button mushrooms

4 tbsp (60 g) butter

I carrot, diced

I small zucchini, diced

I tbsp chopped parsley

salt and black pepper

1 Remove the stems from the mushrooms and chop the stems finely.

2 Melt the butter in a skillet. When it is foaming, add the mushroom stems, carrot, and zucchini, and cook, stirring, for 1 minute. Add the parsley and season with salt and pepper.

3 Put the mushroom cups in a single layer in a shallow baking dish. Fill with the vegetable mixture.

4 Cook in a preheated oven at 350°F (180°C) for 15 minutes. Serve hot.

GARLIC-STUFFED MUSHROOMS

Substitute I cup (60 g) fresh white bread crumbs and 4 crushed garlic cloves for the carrot and zucchini.

ITALIAN FENNEL

SERVES 8

4 fennel bulbs, trimmed and quartered lengthwise

salt and black pepper

butter for greasing

2 cups (250 g) grated mozzarella cheese

chopped parsley to garnish

1 Cook the fennel in boiling salted water for 3–5 minutes until just tender. Drain thoroughly.

2 Butter a shallow baking dish. Add the fennel and season with salt and pepper. Sprinkle the grated mozzarella cheese on top.

3 Bake in a preheated oven at 400°F (200°C) for 15–20 minutes until the cheese topping is golden and bubbling. Sprinkle with chopped parsley, and serve hot.

ASPARAGUS WITH PARMESAN

SERVES 4

1 1/4 lb (625 g) asparagus

3/4 cup (90 g) finely grated Parmesan cheese

lemon wedges and flat-leaf parsley sprigs to garnish

MARINADE

2 tbsp olive oil

2 tsp white wine vinegar

3 garlic cloves, crushed

salt and black pepper

1 Trim the woody ends from the asparagus.

2 Make the marinade: in a shallow dish, combine the oil, vinegar, garlic, a pinch of salt, and plenty of pepper.

3 Roll the asparagus in the marinade, cover, and leave to marinate for 15 minutes.

4 Sprinkle the Parmesan on a plate. Roll the asparagus in the Parmesan to cover all sides, then arrange in a single layer in a large baking dish.

5 Pour any remaining marinade over the asparagus, and roast in a preheated oven at 400°F (200°C) for 10–15 minutes until lightly browned and sizzling hot. Garnish with the lemon wedges and parsley sprigs, and serve hot.

Cook's know-how

As an alternative, you can omit the marinating and cook the Parmesan-rolled asparagus on a ridged cast-iron chargrill pan. The chargrilling will enhance the flavor of the asparagus, but take care that the cheese does not burn.

HERBED ROASTED TOMATOES

SERVES 4

1 lb (500 g) cherry tomatoes

fresh herb sprig to garnish

HERB BUTTER

3 tbsp (45 g) butter, softened

2 tbsp chopped fresh herbs, such as cilantro, basil, or flat-leaf parsley

1 garlic clove, crushed

1/2 tsp lemon juice

salt and black pepper

1 Arrange the tomatoes in a single layer in aa baking dish. Roast in a preheated oven at 450°F (230°C) for 15–20 minutes until the tomatoes are tender but still retain their shape.

2 Meanwhile, make the herb butter: put the butter into a small bowl and beat in the herb of your choice, garlic, and lemon juice. Season with salt and pepper, and mix well to blend. Dot the herb butter over the tomatoes, and serve hot.

GOLDEN ROASTED PUMPKIN

SERVES 6–8

2 lb (1 kg) piece of pumpkin, peeled, seeded, and cut into large chunks

2–3 tbsp olive oil

1 tsp balsamic or red wine vinegar

3 garlic cloves, crushed

1 tsp chopped fresh thyme

1 tsp paprika

salt and black pepper

fresh thyme to garnish

1 Put the pumpkin chunks on a baking sheet. Mix the oil, vinegar, garlic, thyme, and paprika, season with salt and pepper, and pour over the pumpkin.

2 Roast in a preheated oven at 375°F (190°C) for 15–20 minutes until the pumpkin is tender and lightly browned on top. Garnish with thyme, and serve at once. If preferred, leave to cool slightly and serve with a vinaigrette dressing (page 372).

OKRA WITH CHILI

SERVES 4–6

3 tbsp sunflower oil

1 small onion, sliced

1 garlic clove, crushed

1 lb (500 g) okra, trimmed

1 large fresh red chili, cored, seeded, and diced

salt and black pepper

1 Heat the oil in a wok or large skillet, add the onion, and stir-fry over a high heat for 3 minutes or until golden. Add the garlic and stir-fry for 1 minute.

2 Add the okra and chili and stir-fry over a high heat for 5–10 minutes until the okra is tender, but still retains some crispness. Add salt and pepper to taste. Serve hot.

Cook's know-how

Because of its shape, okra is also known as ladies' fingers. Trim the ends carefully so the juices and seeds are not exposed and released (they would make the dish sticky).

MIXED VEGETABLE STIR-FRY

SERVES 4

1 tbsp olive oil

1 large zucchini, sliced thinly on the diagonal

1 yellow bell pepper, cored, seeded, and thinly sliced

3 1/2 cups (250 g) sliced button or other small mushrooms

salt and black pepper

1 tbsp lemon juice

1/2 cup (60 g) slivered almonds, toasted

1 Heat the olive oil in a wok or large skillet, add the zucchini, and stir-fry for 3–4 minutes until the zucchini is just beginning to color.

2 Add the yellow pepper and mushrooms and stir-fry for 2 minutes. Add salt and pepper, stir in the lemon juice, and leave the mixture to bubble for about 1 minute. Sprinkle with the toasted slivered almonds, and serve hot.

TOMATO & ZUCCHINI BAKE

SERVES 4–6

2 zucchini, sliced

salt and black pepper

3 large juicy ripe tomatoes, sliced

snipped fresh chives to garnish

WHITE SAUCE

2 tbsp (30 g) butter

1/4 cup (30 g) all-purpose flour

1 1/4 cups (300 ml) milk

1/4 tsp grated nutmeg

1 Arrange half of the zucchini slices in the bottom of a shallow baking dish. Season with a little salt and pepper.

2 Arrange half of the tomato slices in a layer on top of the zucchini. Season again.

3 Layer the remaining zucchini and tomato slices in the dish, sprinkling them with salt and pepper.

4 Make the white sauce: melt the butter in a small saucepan. Sprinkle in the flour, and cook, stirring, for 1 minute. Remove from the heat and gradually blend in the milk. Bring to a boil, stirring, until the mixture thickens. Simmer for 2–3 minutes. Add the nutmeg, and season with salt and pepper.

5 Pour the white sauce over the vegetables. Cook in a preheated oven at 375°F (190°C) for 15–20 minutes until the vegetables are just cooked. Sprinkle with snipped chives, and serve hot.

Healthy option

Instead of the white sauce, layer the tomatoes and zucchini with ⅔ cup (150 g) grated reduced-fat mozzarella cheese and chopped fresh oregano, basil, or parsley (omit the chive garnish).

RATATOUILLE

SERVES 4–6

4 tbsp olive oil

1 large onion, sliced

1 large garlic clove, crushed

1 large eggplant, cut into 1/2 in (1 cm) slices

4 czucchini, sliced

6 juicy ripe tomatoes, sliced

1 large red bell pepper, cored, seeded, and sliced

1 tsp sugar

salt and black pepper

1 tbsp chopped fresh basil to garnish

1 Heat the olive oil in a large skillet, add the onion and garlic, and cook gently, stirring occasionally, for 3–5 minutes until softened.

2 Add the eggplant slices, cover, and simmer gently for 20 minutes.

3 Add the zucchini, tomatoes, red pepper, and sugar. Season with salt and pepper. Cover and cook gently, stirring occasionally, for 30 minutes or until the vegetables are soft.

4 Taste for seasoning and serve hot, warm, or cold, sprinkled with the chopped fresh basil.

Cook's know-how

Ratatouille is a summer dish from Provence in the south of France. You can make it at other times of the year, but if you cannot find good ripe, juicy tomatoes you will get a better flavor if you use 14 oz (400 g) canned crushed tomatoes instead of fresh ones. Some recipes for ratatouille include coriander seed. If you like its orangey flavour, add 1/4 tsp crushed seed in step 1 when softening the onion and garlic, and sprinkle some chopped fresh thyme over at the end, instead of the basil.

CHARGRILLED VEGETABLE PLATTER

Vegetables are delicious chargrilled – their flesh is tender and smoky in flavor. Serve them hot as a side dish with roast meat, poultry, or broiled fish, or cold as an unusual salad with picnics and barbecues. Experiment with different vegetables, oils, and marinades to suit your taste.

SERVES 4

4 small eggplants

salt and black pepper

4 small zucchini

1 red bell pepper

1 yellow bell pepper

1 large red or sweet onion

1 lb (500 g) asparagus

4 large mushrooms

6 oz (175 g) pattypan squash

olive oil for brushing

8–10 WOODEN TOOTHPICKS

1 Prepare the vegetables. Trim the eggplants, cut in half lengthwise, and score a crisscross pattern on the cut surfaces.

2 Cut the zucchini in half lengthwise. Cut the red peppers in half lengthwise and cut out the fleshy ribs and seeds. Peel the red or sweet onion and cut lengthwise into 4-6 wedges. Trim the woody ends from the asparagus and cut the spears to an even length.

3 Gently wipe the mushrooms with damp paper towels and remove the stems. Trim the squash if necessary.

4 Place the asparagus spears side by side in groups of 3 or 4 (depending on thickness). Gently push a toothpick through the asparagus, about 1/2 in (1 cm) from the tips, until they are all skewered. Insert a second toothpick at the bases of the spears. Repeat for the remaining groups of asparagus spears.

5 Brush all of the vegetables generously with olive oil and season with salt and pepper to taste.

6 Place a batch at a time over a hot barbecue or on a preheated ridged chargrill pan, and cook for 10–15 minutes, turning occasionally, until the vegetables are lightly charred. Keep each batch warm while you cook the remaining vegetables.

Cook's know-how

If you are using a ridged chargrill pan, either nonstick or cast iron, it is important to preheat it empty first, before laying the food on the ridges. Never oil the pan before preheating, as this will cause it to smoke. The secret is to oil the food, not the pan, and put the food in only when the pan is very hot. Press down hard on the food to help mark the ridges, and avoid moving the food in the pan as this will prevent the ridges from charring.

ADDING EXTRA FLAVOR

If you are cooking the vegetables over a barbecue, lay some woody herbs such as thyme or rosemary over the rack before you put the vegetables on. Another way of introducing flavor into the vegetables is to soak them in a robust marinade for about an hour before cooking – you can leave them overnight if this suits you better.

HERB & GARLIC MARINADE

Put 1 cup (250 ml) olive oil, 2 finely chopped garlic cloves, 1 tbsp chopped fresh rosemary, oregano, or thyme, and salt and pepper to taste into a bowl and whisk to mix thoroughly.

HONEY & MUSTARD MARINADE

Put 1 cup (250 ml) sunflower oil, 2 tbsp soy sauce, 1 tbsp honey, 2 tsp Dijon mustard, and salt and pepper to taste into a small bowl and whisk to mix.

THREE FLAVORED OILS

Flavored oils are easy to make and add an individual touch. Try using one of these flavored oils to baste the vegetables during chargrilling instead of the olive oil in the recipe above.

Thai perfumed oil
Lightly bruise 2–3 stems cilantro and 3 × 2 in (5 cm) pieces fresh lemongrass. Put the cilantro, lemongrass, and 2 dried chilies into a sterilized jar or bottle. Pour in 2 cups (500 ml) peanut oil or sunflower oil and seal the jar or bottle. Leave in a cool, dark place for 2 weeks, remove the cilantro and lemongrass, and use to baste as directed.

Paprika oil
Spoon 2 tbsp paprika into a sterilized jar or bottle. Pour in 2 cups (500 ml) extra-virgin olive oil and seal the jar or bottle. Leave in a cool, dark place, shaking the container from time to time, for 1 week. Line a funnel with a double layer of cheesecloth and then strain the oil into a clean bottle. Use the oil to baste as directed.

Mixed herb oil
Lightly bruise 1 rosemary sprig and 1 thyme sprig. Put the herbs, 1 bay leaf, and 6 black peppercorns into a sterilized jar or bottle. Pour in 2 cups (500 ml) extra-virgin olive oil and seal the jar or bottle. Leave in a cool, dark place for about 2 weeks, remove the herbs, and use to baste as directed.

FRESH & LIGHT SALADS

Some of the most interesting salads are made from vegetables, legumes, and grains rather than leaves.
They often have more flavor and texture, and they can be served as a meal in their own right.
These four recipes are light, healthy, and low in fat but still delicious.

PUY LENTIL SALAD

SERVES 6

1 1/2 cups (250 g) Puy lentils, rinsed

3 tbsp olive oil

2 tbsp balsamic vinegar

salt and black pepper

1 bunch of green onions, trimmed and finely sliced

3 tbsp chopped fresh flat-leaf parsley

1 Pour the lentils into a medium saucepan, cover with plenty of cold water, and bring to a boil. Reduce the heat, cover, and simmer for 15 minutes or until the lentils are tender.

2 Drain the lentils well, tip into a serving bowl, and add the olive oil and vinegar, and plenty of seasoning (warm lentils absorb the flavors of dressing better than cold lentils). Leave to cool, then mix in the green onions and chopped parsley just before serving.

TABBOULEH

SERVES 4

2/3 cup (125 g) bulgur wheat

3 tbsp extra virgin olive oil

juice of 2 lemons

salt and black pepper

1/4 bunch green onions, finely sliced

1/2 cucumber, peeled, seeded, and finely diced

6 tbsp chopped fresh mint

6 tbsp chopped fresh flat-leaf parsley

1 Soak the bulgur wheat in boiling water for 30 minutes. Drain well, tip into a serving bowl, and add the olive oil, lemon juice, and plenty of seasoning. Do this immediately while the wheat is still warm so it absorbs the maximum flavors.

2 Add the green onions, cucumber, and freshly chopped herbs to the bowl. Stir well and check the seasoning. Chill before serving so the flavors mingle.

ITALIAN PESTO SALAD

SERVES 4-6

2 heaping cups (375 g) broccoli, cut into bite-sized florets

2 heaping cups (375 g) cauliflower, cut into bite-sized florets

about 12 black olives, pitted

PESTO

1 cup (30 g) fresh basil

1 garlic clove

1 tbsp pine nuts

1/4 cup (30 g) grated Parmesan cheese

salt and black pepper

5 tbsp olive oil

1 Make the pesto: put the basil, garlic, pine nuts, Parmesan and seasoning into a small food processor and process until the basil is finely chopped. With the machine running, add the oil in a fine stream until the paste is creamy. Check the seasoning.

2 Blanch the broccoli and cauliflower florets in boiling salted water for about 2 minutes (they should retain plenty of bite, so take care not to overcook them). Drain and refresh under cold running water. Drain again, then toss with the pesto. Scatter with the olives and chill before serving.

Healthy note

Broccoli and cauliflower are both cruciferous vegetables (the name, crucifer, comes from the cross shape of their 4-petaled flowers), known to be excellent nutrition boosters. They are rich in the antioxidants vitamin C, vitamin E, and carotenes, which can help guard against heart disease and strokes, and they have a strong link to a lower risk of cancer. Cruciferous vegetables are also rich in folate and iron, minerals that help prevent and correct anemia, and in potassium, a mineral that helps avoid and regulate high blood pressure.

HERB SALAD WITH ORANGE & MUSTARD DRESSING

SERVES 4-6

4 oz (125 g) thin asparagus

salt and black pepper

1/2 romaine lettuce

2 oz (60 g) mâche

2 oz (60 g) arugula

1 small bunch of flat-leaf parsley, stems removed

1/2 cup (60 g) pine nuts, toasted

2 oz (60 g) sun-blushed or sun-dried tomatoes, snipped into small pieces

DRESSING

1 orange

2 tbsp olive oil

1 tsp pure maple syrup

1 tsp coarse mustard

1 Trim the asparagus and cut into 1 in (2.5 cm) pieces. Cook in boiling salted water for about 3 minutes until just tender. Drain and refresh under cold running water.

2 Break the romaine lettuce into bite-sized pieces and mix with the mâche, arugula, and parsley leaves in a salad bowl. Add the asparagus, pine nuts, and tomatoes, and toss gently.

3 Remove the zest of the orange with a zester and add the strips to the salad. Squeeze the juice from half of the orange to give about 3 tbsp, then mix with the remaining dressing ingredients and seasoning to taste. Toss the salad with the dressing just before serving.

CLOCKWISE FROM TOP: Herb Salad with Orange & Mustard Dressing, Puy Lentil Salad, Tabbouleh, Italian Pesto Salad.

PASTA & MACKEREL SALAD

SERVES 4–6

1 lb (500 g) pasta shells

salt and black pepper

2 zucchini, sliced

4 oz (125 g) thin green beans, cut in half crosswise

2 oranges

12 oz (375 g) smoked mackerel fillets, or other smoked fish

¼ cup (30 g) walnut pieces

DRESSING

juice of 1 orange

2 tbsp sunflower oil

1 tbsp walnut oil

2 tbsp chopped parsley

1 Cook the pasta shells in a large saucepan of boiling salted water for 8–10 minutes until just tender. Drain, rinse under cold running water, and drain again.

2 Cook the zucchini and green beans in another pan of boiling salted water for 4–5 minutes until tender. Drain, rinse, and drain again.

3 Peel and segment the oranges (page 466) and set aside. Remove the skin and any bones from the smoked fish, then flake the flesh into large pieces.

4 Make the dressing: combine the orange juice, sunflower and walnut oils, and parsley, and season with salt and pepper.

5 Put the pasta, zucchini, green beans, orange segments, flaked fish, and walnut pieces into a large salad bowl. Add the dressing and toss gently so the fish does not break up. Leave to chill in the refrigerator for at least 30 minutes before serving.

Cook's know-how

Smoked trout can be used instead of mackerel – it is less rich, and milder in flavor. Smoked eel (available from specialist fish markets) would also be a good choice. Ask to taste a bit before buying.

PASTA SALAD WITH PEPPERS

SERVES 4–6

1 lb (500 g) pasta bows

salt and black pepper

1 red bell pepper, cored, seeded, and diced

1 green bell pepper, cored, seeded, and diced

3 green onions, sliced diagonally

4 tbsp mayonnaise (page 372)

green onion tops, sliced, to garnish

1 Cook the pasta bows in a large saucepan of boiling salted water for 8–10 minutes until just tender.

2 Drain, rinse under cold running water, and drain again. Leave to cool.

3 Put the pasta, peppers, and green onions into a salad bowl, and season with salt and pepper. Add the mayonnaise, stir to coat all the ingredients evenly, then chill for 30 minutes. Garnish with green onion tops before serving.

PASTA SALAD WITH SNOW PEAS & SESAME SEEDS

Substitute 4 oz (125 g) blanched snow peas for the red and green peppers. Omit the mayonnaise. Mix together 2 tbsp white wine vinegar, 1 tbsp sunflower oil, and 1 tsp sesame oil, and pour over the salad. Taste for seasoning. Substitute 2 tbsp toasted sesame seeds for the green onion garnish, and serve at once.

Healthy option

If you prefer not to use mayonnaise for the dressing, use 2 tbsp olive oil whisked with the juice of 1 lemon, 1 tsp Dijon mustard, and a large handful of roughly chopped herbs. Fresh basil, dill, parsley, chervil, and chives can all be used, on their own or mixed together.

10

YEAST BAKING

OVER 60 MINUTES

FOCACCIA
Italian classic: flat pizzalike bread flavored with olive oil and fresh rosemary. Sprinkled with coarse sea salt just before baking.

MAKES 1 LARGE LOAF 2989 calories per loaf
Takes 35 minutes, plus rising   Page 411

TRADITIONAL

HOT CROSS BUNS
Slightly sweet spiced buns studded with dried currants and mixed peel, decorated with traditional pastry crosses, and baked until golden.

MAKES 12 279 calories each
Takes 35 minutes, plus rising   Page 422

DINNER ROLLS
White-flour dough shaped into rolls and baked until golden. Served warm or cool and spread with butter, if liked. An easy way to impress your guests.

MAKES 18 95 calories each
Takes 40 minutes, plus rising   Page 407

BRIOCHES
Classic and rich: an egg- and butter-enriched dough baked until dark golden brown in fluted molds to give the characteristic attractive shape.

MAKES 12 149 calories each
Takes 35 minutes, plus rising   Page 416

WHOLE-WHEAT COUNTRY LOAF
Hearty and flavorful: a close-textured loaf made from whole-wheat flour, shaped into a crown, and baked until golden. Great for toast and sandwiches.

MAKES 1 LARGE LOAF 2975 calories per loaf
Takes 50 minutes, plus rising   Page 408

CINNAMON ROLLS
Breakfast treat: a sweetened dough enriched with egg, kneaded with cinnamon and raisins, rolled into spirals, and baked then glazed.

MAKES 16 450 calories each
Takes 60 minutes, plus rising   Page 422

FAMILY CHOICE

SWEET BUNS
Rich dough sweetened with golden raisins and mixed peel. Shaped into buns, topped with crushed sugar, and baked until golden.

MAKES 18 196 calories each
Takes 40 minutes, plus rising   Page 421

DINNER PARTY

MILK ROLLS
Attractive rolls in a variety of shapes: knots, twists, and rosettes. Decorated with poppy seeds and sesame seeds, and baked until golden.

MAKES 18 188 calories each
Takes 50 minutes, plus rising   Page 407

CROISSANTS
Classic French breakfast roll: made rich and flaky with butter. Shaped into crescents, glazed, and baked until golden.

MAKES 12 352 calories each
Takes 55 minutes, plus chilling   Page 415

OVER 60 MINUTES

ENGLISH MUFFINS

Golden and fresh from the griddle: a simple batter cooked until light and tender. Served warm spread with butter.

MAKES 20 73 calories each

Takes 50 minutes, plus rising   Page 420

SANDWICH ROLLS

Soft-crusted rolls slightly sweetened with a little honey. Dusted with flour and baked until golden.

MAKES 16 135 calories each

Takes 45 minutes, plus rising   Page 406

CHEESE & HERB BREAD

Hearty and flavorful: Cheddar and Parmesan cheeses, chopped parsley, and mustard enhance this crisp-crusted bread.

MAKES 1 MEDIUM LOAF 2707 calories per loaf

Takes 55 minutes, plus rising   Page 410

CALZONE

A delicious and aromatic mixture of Mediterranean ingredients wrapped in pizza dough and baked until golden.

MAKES 4 637 calories each

Takes 35 minutes, plus rising   Page 414

SPICY DEEP-PAN PIZZA

Thick, crisp-crusted pizza covered with tomatoes, pepperoni sausage, mozzarella, and Parmesan cheeses. Spiked with green chilies.

MAKES 1 LARGE PIZZA 3596 calories

Takes 35 minutes, plus rising   Page 414

JELLY DOUGHNUTS

Old-fashioned favorite: doughnuts filled with raspberry jelly, deep-fried, and sprinkled with cinnamon and sugar.

MAKES 16 269 calories each

Takes 40 minutes, plus rising   Page 417

WALNUT BREAD

Hearty and rustic: a coarse-textured loaf studded with chopped walnuts and parsley. Slashed in a crisscross pattern, dusted with flour, then baked

MAKES 2 SMALL LOAVES 1657 calories per loaf

Takes 55 minutes, plus rising   Page 409

until golden brown. The classic accompaniment to wedges of sharp cheese, pickles, or relish – perfect for lunch or a quick snack.

COUNTRY BREAD

Simple to make: a white flour loaf with a large and tender crumb. Ideal for toast spread with your favorite preserve.

MAKES 1 LARGE LOAF 2790 per loaf

Takes 50 minutes, plus rising   Page 406

OVER 60 MINUTES

STICKY BUNS

A rich dough rolled with a filling of golden raisins, dried currants, orange zest, and apple-pie spice. Glazed with honey after baking.

MAKES 12 298 calories each
Takes 60 minutes, plus rising   Page 421

CHALLAH

Tender and golden: an egg-enriched dough, shaped into a braid, and baked until golden. Excellent toasted or used to make French toast.

MAKES 2 SMALL LOAVES 1144 calories per loaf
Takes 60 minutes, plus rising   Page 416

OLIVE & SUN-DRIED TOMATO BREADS

The flavors of Provence: pungent olives and sun-dried tomatoes are kneaded into a dough darkened with buckwheat flour.

MAKES 2 SMALL LOAVES 1139 calories per loaf
Takes 60 minutes, plus rising   Page 410

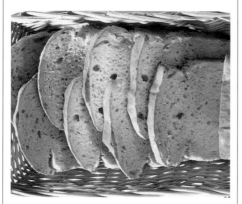

POTATO BREAD

Old-fashioned favorite: mashed potatoes and butter enrich this simple bread. Makes 2 hearty, coarse-textured loaves.

MAKES 2 SMALL LOAVES 1002 calories per loaf
Takes 60 minutes, plus rising   Page 409

SOURDOUGH RYE BREAD

A sourdough starter gives a slightly tangy edge to this robust loaf. Caraway seeds add extra flavor.

MAKES 2 LARGE LOAVES 3329 calories per loaf
Takes 1 hour 5 minutes, plus rising   Page 411

SHORTENING BREAD

Traditional English cake made tender and crisp with vegetable shortening and studded with mixed fruit. Baked until dark golden brown.

MAKES 1 LARGE LOAF 8186 calories per loaf
Takes 1 hour 5 minutes, plus rising   Page 417

TRADITIONAL

WHOLE-WHEAT ENGLISH MUFFINS

Savory quick bread cooked on a hot griddle. Served fresh from the oven spread with butter and jam.

MAKES ABOUT 12 158 calories each
Takes 60 minutes, plus rising   Page 420

HIGH FIBER

MULTIGRAIN LOAF

A nutritious, coarse-textured whole-wheat and white flour loaf studded with a combination of wheat flakes, linseed, and sunflower seeds. The loaves are lightly brushed with milk, generously sprinkled with wheat flakes, and baked until golden brown.

MAKES 2 SMALL LOAVES 1495 calories per loaf
Takes 60 minutes, plus rising   Page 408

YEAST BAKING KNOW-HOW

THE PLEASURE of baking bread is legendary. From making and kneading the dough to slicing a freshly baked loaf, the experience is a thoroughly satisfying one that cooks the world over have shared for centuries. Indeed, yeast baking is perhaps the most popular of all kitchen crafts.

From this rich history comes a wide variety of recipes, both sweet and savory, many of which are easily made; others are more time-consuming to prepare. Cinnamon rolls and sticky buns, Danish pastries and croissants, whole-wheat bread and crisp, thin-crusted pizzas are all equally delicious.

BREAD MACHINES

Although keen bakers maintain that bread made in a machine can never be as good to eat as a loaf made by hand, bread machines are increasingly popular, perhaps because they mean you can enjoy a freshly baked loaf at any time. Pop in the ingredients and the machine will mix, knead, raise, and bake for you. For perfect results, follow the manufacturer's recipes and directions.

FREEZING

It is a good idea to halve or quarter loaves before freezing so you can take out what you need. Pack in moisture-proof wrapping and seal well. Most loaves can be frozen for up to 4 months; if enriched with milk or fruit, storage time is 3 months. Thaw, still wrapped, at room temperature. Bread with a crust, such as baguette, does not freeze well because the crust lifts off.

Successful home baking

The quantity of liquid given in a recipe can only be a guide because the absorbency of flour can vary. The quantity of liquid that flour can absorb depends on several things: temperature and humidity; how much hard wheat the flour contains (proportions vary from one brand to another); and whether it is whole-wheat or white.

•

Dough can be kneaded in a food processor or an electric mixer fitted with a dough hook, as well as by hand.

•

Dough rises quickest in a warm environment. But a slow rise, such as in the refrigerator overnight, gives bread more flavor.

•

To test if dough has risen sufficiently, simply push in a clean finger; when withdrawn, an indentation should remain in the dough.

YEAST BAKING INGREDIENTS

There is a large range of flours to choose from, each with its own unique texture and flavor. The different types of yeast, on the other hand, vary simply in their method of preparation.

Flour

The best flours to use for yeast doughs are those labeled "bread flour". These are milled from hard wheat with a high gluten content and produce a good open-textured bread. Ordinary all-purpose flour, which contains a higher proportion of soft wheat, can be used for yeast doughs, but the result will be a more close-textured and crumbly loaf.

Even today, the flour most commonly used for bread-making is white flour. A lot of bread also is made from whole-wheat flour, which is milled from the entire wheat kernel, including the bran and germ, and so retains many of the vitamins and minerals lost in the process of producing white flour. Stone-ground flour is considered a nutritionally superior product because of the slow milling process. Look for it in natural food and specialty stores.

Other grains and cereals, such as barley, buckwheat, cornmeal, millet, oats, and rye, are milled into flour for bread-making. Soy beans are also ground into a flourlike powder. Most of these flours are low in gluten, or contain no gluten at all, so they are normally combined with wheat flour to prevent the bread from having too dense a texture.

Fresh yeast

This form of yeast, also know as compressed yeast or baker's yeast, looks like creamy-gray putty. It is perishable so requires refrigeration (keep it in an airtight container for up to 5 days). You will find it at a bakery where baking is done on the premises, or try a natural food store. Fresh yeast should be almost odorless, with only a slightly yeasty smell, and it should break apart cleanly. It needs to be blended

with warm liquid and "fed" with sugar, then left to become frothy before mixing with flour. Fresh yeast is sold in "cakes" of a standard weight. You can substitute one cake of fresh yeast for one envelope of dry yeast.

Dry yeast

Many home bakers prefer dry yeast, which is sold in sealed 1/4 oz (7 g) envelopes, for the convenience of buying and storing it. Dry yeast is available in two forms. Active dry yeast must be mixed with warm water before using (see below); quick-rising active dry yeast can be added directly to the other dry ingredients in the recipe. Dry yeast will keep for up to 6 months in a cool place.

To blend and dissolve both fresh and active dry yeast, always use water or other liquid that is lukewarm (105–110°F/40–43°C), not hot.

MAKING A YEAST DOUGH

Making bread is not difficult, nor does it take up a lot of time – the most lengthy parts of the procedure, the rising and baking, are done by the bread itself. Here are the basic techniques, using quick-rising active dry yeast.

1 Sift the flour into a large bowl, and then mix in the yeast and any other dry ingredients. Make a well in the middle and pour in almost all of the measured liquid (the precise amount is difficult to gauge).

2 Using your fingers, mix the liquid ingredients together, then gradually incorporate the flour. Mix thoroughly until a soft, quite sticky dough is formed, adding the remaining liquid if it is needed.

3 Turn the dough out onto a lightly floured work surface and knead: fold it over toward you, then push it down and away with the heel of your hand. Turn the dough, fold it, and push it away again. Continue kneading for 5–10 minutes until the dough is elastic and smooth. Bread flour doughs take longer to knead than those made with all-purpose flour.

4 Shape the dough into a ball. Put the dough into a lightly greased bowl and turn to coat it all over with oil. Cover with greased plastic wrap or a damp dish towel and leave to rise in a warm, draft-free place (or in a cool place for a longer time).

5 When the dough has doubled in size, turn it out onto a lightly floured work surface. Knock out the air by punching the dough gently, then knead the dough vigorously for 2–3 minutes until smooth and elastic.

6 Shape the dough as directed. Cover loosely with plastic wrap or a dry dish towel and leave in a warm, draft-free place to rise until doubled in size again. Bake according to the recipe.

BUTTER SHAPES

Impress your family and friends with butter that is shaped rather than just left in a stick. These shapes can be prepared in advance, frozen on a baking sheet, and packed in freezer bags, then thawed as needed. If you like, flavor the butter with herbs, mustard, or garlic to serve with savory breads, and spices, honey, or sugar for sweet breads.

Disks

Use butter at room temperature. Beat it with a wooden spoon until it is soft, then beat in any flavorings. Spoon onto a sheet of waxed paper and spread into a rough sausage, then roll in the paper until it forms a neat sausage shape. Wrap the butter tightly in the waxed paper and twist the ends to secure. Chill the butter in the refrigerator until firm. Unwrap and slice the butter across into thin disks. Use immediately or keep chilled; or freeze until required.

Curls

Use a well-chilled block of butter. Warm a butter curler in hot water, then dry it. Pull the curler lengthwise along the surface of the block, to shave off curls. Use the butter curls immediately, or keep them in ice water in the refrigerator until required.

GLAZES & TOPPINGS

Breads and rolls can be glazed before or after baking to add flavor and, depending on the glaze, to make the crust soft or shiny and crisp. Apply the glaze thinly, using a pastry brush. Here are a few suggestions for different glazes:
• water (before baking) for a crisp crust
• milk or cream (before baking) for a soft crust
• egg or egg yolk beaten with a pinch of salt (before baking) for a shiny, crisp crust
• butter (after baking) for a shiny crust
• sugar and water (after baking) for a shiny crust.

   Toppings such as wheat or barley flakes, woody herbs such as rosemary, sunflower or sesame seeds, poppyseeds, grated cheese, chopped nuts, and coarse sea salt can be sprinkled over glazed breads and rolls before baking. Sweetened breads are often sprinkled with sugar or a spice and sugar mixture after baking.

TESTING LOAVES

At the end of baking, bread should be well risen, firm, and golden brown. To test if it is thoroughly baked, tip it out of the pan or lift it off the baking sheet, and tap the bottom. The bread should have a hollow, drumlike sound. If it does not sound hollow, return it to the oven to bake for 5 minutes longer, then remove it and test again.

SHAPING LOAVES

Because of the elastic quality of dough, it can very easily be formed into a variety of different shapes. Here are some of the more traditional ones.

Cottage loaf

Cut off one-third of the dough. Roll each piece into a ball and put the small ball on top of the large ball. Push a forefinger through the middle all the way to the bottom.

Pan loaf

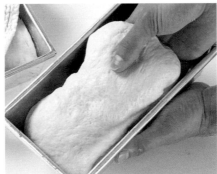

Shape the dough into a cylinder a little longer than the pan, then tuck the ends under so the shape just fits the pan. Place the dough in the pan, with the seams underneath.

Round loaf

Roll the dough into a ball, then pull up the sides of the ball to the middle, to make a tight, round ball. Turn the ball over and put onto a baking sheet, reshaping to form a neat ball if necessary.

Braided loaf

Divide and roll the dough into 3 strands. Place them side by side and pinch together at one end to join. Braid the strands, pinching them together at the other end to secure.

Crown loaf

Divide the dough into 9 even-sized pieces and shape each into a ball. Place 8 balls around the side of a deep cake pan, then place one ball in the middle to form a crown. The balls will rise to fill the pan.

COUNTRY BREAD

MAKES 1 LARGE LOAF

6 cups (750 g) white bread flour, plus extra for dusting

2 tbsp (30 g) butter or margarine

2 tsp salt

1/4 oz (7 g) envelope quick-rising active dry yeast

about 2 cups (500 ml) lukewarm water

sunflower oil for greasing

2 LB (1 KG) LOAF PAN

1 Put the flour into a bowl, rub in the butter with the fingertips until the mixture resembles bread crumbs, then stir in the salt and yeast, and make a well in the middle. Add enough water to mix to a soft, slightly sticky, dough.

2 Knead the dough on a lightly floured surface until smooth and elastic. Shape into a ball and place in a lightly greased large bowl.

3 Cover the bowl with greased plastic wrap and leave to rise in a warm place for 1–1 1/2 hours or until the dough has doubled in size.

4 Turn out the dough onto a lightly floured surface and punch down with your fists. Knead vigorously for 2–3 minutes until the dough is smooth and elastic.

5 Lightly grease the loaf pan. Shape the dough to fit the pan, tucking the ends under to give a smooth top, and place in the pan. Cover loosely with greased plastic wrap and leave to rise in a warm place for 30 minutes or until the dough reaches the top of the pan.

6 Lightly dust the top of the loaf with flour and bake in a preheated oven at 450°F (230°C) for 30–35 minutes until well risen and golden. Turn the loaf out and tap the bottom: it should sound hollow if it is baked. Leave the loaf to cool on a wire rack.

SANDWICH ROLLS

MAKES 16

4 cups (500 g) white bread flour, plus extra for dusting

3 tbsp (45 g) butter

1 tsp salt

1/4 oz (7 g) envelope quick-rising active dry yeast

about 2/3 cup (150 ml) very hot water

about 2/3 cup (150 ml) milk

1 tsp honey

sunflower oil for greasing

1 Put the flour into a large bowl. Add the butter and rub in with the fingertips until the mixture resembles fine bread crumbs. Stir in the salt and yeast, and make a well in the middle. Mix the water, milk, and honey together, and add to the flour until a soft dough is formed.

2 Knead the dough on a lightly floured surface until smooth and elastic. Shape into a ball and place in a lightly greased large bowl. Cover with greased plastic wrap and leave to rise in a warm place for 1–1 1/2 hours or until doubled in size.

3 Turn out the dough onto a lightly floured surface and punch down with your fists. Knead for 2–3 minutes until the dough is smooth and elastic.

4 Lightly grease 2 baking sheets. Divide the dough into 16 even-sized pieces. Knead and roll into balls and place well apart on the baking sheets. With the heel of your hand, flatten each ball so it measures 3 in (7 cm) across.

5 Cover loosely with greased plastic wrap and leave to rise in a warm place for about 30 minutes or until the dough has doubled in size.

6 Lightly flour the rolls and bake in a preheated oven at 400°F (200°C) for 15–20 minutes until golden. Leave to cool on a wire rack.

Cook's know-how

If you are short of time, just mix and shape these rolls, omitting the first rise in step 2 and giving them just one rise (step 5). The texture of the rolls will not be quite as light, but they will still be good.

MILK ROLLS

MAKES 18

6 cups (750 g) white bread flour, plus extra for dusting

4 tbsp (60 g) butter or solid vegetable shortening

2 tsp salt

1/4 oz (7 g) envelope quick-rising active dry yeast

about 1 3/4 cups (450 ml) lukewarm milk

sunflower oil for greasing

1 egg, beaten

poppy seeds and sesame seeds for sprinkling

1 Put the flour into a large bowl, rub in the butter, then stir in the salt and yeast. Make a well in the middle and add enough milk to mix to a soft dough.

2 Knead the dough on a lightly floured surface until smooth and elastic. Shape into a ball and place in a lightly greased large bowl. Cover with greased plastic wrap and leave to rise in a warm place for 1–1 1/2 hours or until doubled in size.

3 Turn out the dough onto a lightly floured surface and punch down with your fists. Knead for 2–3 minutes until smooth and elastic.

4 Divide the dough into 18 even-sized pieces and shape into balls, folding the sides to the middles to form tight, round balls, or shape as desired (see box, right).

5 Lightly grease 2 or 3 baking sheets. Arrange the rolls on the baking sheets, leaving enough room between them for the dough to expand, cover loosely with greased plastic wrap, and leave to rise in a warm place for 15–20 minutes or until doubled in size.

6 Brush the rolls with the beaten egg to glaze and sprinkle with poppy seeds and sesame seeds. Bake in a preheated oven at 450°F (230°C) for about 15 minutes until golden. Leave to cool on a wire rack.

Shaping milk rolls

Form each piece of dough into a long rope and tie into a single knot.

Roll each piece of dough into a thin strand. Fold in half and twist together, sealing the ends well to form a twist. Or, **shape** each piece of dough into a ball or an oval. Snip around the tops with scissors to form a pattern.

DINNER ROLLS

MAKES 18

4 cups (500 g) white bread flour

1 tsp salt

1/4 oz (7 g) envelope quick-rising active dry yeast

about 1 1/2 cups (350 ml) lukewarm water

sunflower oil for greasing

1 Put the flour into a large bowl, then stir in the salt and yeast. Make a well in the middle and pour in enough water to make a soft dough.

2 Knead the dough on a lightly floured surface until smooth and elastic. Shape into a ball and place in a lightly greased large bowl. Cover with greased plastic wrap and leave to rise in a warm place for 1–1 1/2 hours or until doubled in size.

3 Lightly grease 2 or 3 baking sheets. Divide the dough into 18 pieces. Shape into balls, folding the sides to the middles. Arrange on the baking sheets, leaving room for expansion. Cover loosely with greased plastic wrap and leave to rise in a warm place for 20 minutes or until doubled in size.

4 Bake in a preheated oven at 375°F (190°C) for 20 minutes or until golden. Leave to cool on a wire rack.

WHOLE-WHEAT COUNTRY LOAF

MAKES 1 LARGE LOAF

6 cups (750 g) whole-wheat flour, plus extra for dusting

2 tbsp (30 g) butter or margarine

1 tbsp sugar

2 tsp salt

1/4 oz (7 g) envelope quick-rising active dry yeast

about 1 3/4 cups (400 ml) lukewarm water

sunflower oil for greasing

milk for glazing

cracked wheat for sprinkling

8 IN (20 CM) DEEP ROUND CAKE PAN

1 Put the flour into a large bowl. Rub in the butter with the fingertips, then stir in the sugar, salt, and yeast. Make a well in the middle and add enough water to mix to a soft dough.

2 Knead the dough on a lightly floured surface until smooth and elastic, then shape into a ball.

3 Place the dough in a lightly greased large bowl, cover with greased plastic wrap, and leave to rise in a warm place for 1–1 1/2 hours or until the dough has doubled in size.

4 Turn out the dough onto a lightly floured surface and punch down with your fists. Knead for 2–3 minutes until smooth.

5 Shape the dough into a ball and put it into the lightly greased cake pan. Flatten with your hand, then mark into 8 wedges with a knife. Cover loosely with greased plastic wrap and leave to rise in a warm place for 1–1 1/2 hours or until doubled in size.

6 Brush the loaf with milk and sprinkle with cracked wheat. Bake in a preheated oven at 450°F (230°C) for 20–25 minutes. Tap the bottom to see if the loaf is baked: it should sound hollow. Leave to cool on a wire rack.

MULTI-GRAIN LOAF

MAKES 2 SMALL LOAVES

1/2 cups (150 g) wheat flakes

3 tbsp (45 g) linseed

1 1/4 cups (300 ml) boiling water

4 cups (500 g) white bread flour, plus extra for dusting

1 cup (125 g) whole-wheat flour

4 tbsp (60 g) sunflower seeds

2 tsp (15 g) salt

1/4 oz (7 g) envelope quick-rising active dry yeast

about 1 3/4 cups (350 ml) lukewarm water

sunflower oil for greasing

milk for glazing

wheat flakes to decorate

2 × 1 LB (500 G) LOAF PANS

1 Put the wheat flakes and linseed into a large bowl, pour the boiling water over, and stir. Cover and set aside for 30 minutes or until the water has been absorbed.

2 Stir the flours, sunflower seeds, salt, and yeast into the wheat-flake mixture. Make a well in the middle and add enough water to mix to a soft dough.

3 Knead the dough on a lightly floured surface until smooth and elastic. Shape into a ball and place in a lightly greased large bowl. Cover with greased plastic wrap and leave to rise in a warm place for 1–1 1/2 hours or until doubled in size.

4 Turn out the dough onto a floured surface and punch down with your fists. Knead for 2–3 minutes until smooth and elastic once again.

5 Grease the pans. Divide the dough in half, and shape into oblongs, tucking the ends under to give smooth tops. Place in the pans. Alternatively, shape into 2 balls and place on greased baking sheets. Cover loosely with greased plastic wrap and leave to rise in a warm place for 20–30 minutes.

6 Brush the loaves with milk to glaze and sprinkle with wheat flakes. Bake in a preheated oven at 450°F (230°C) for 10 minutes; reduce the oven temperature to 400°F (200°C), and bake for 20–25 minutes. Tap the bottoms to see if the loaves are baked: they should sound hollow. Leave to cool on a rack.

WALNUT BREAD

MAKES 2 SMALL LOAVES

5¼ cups (650 g) white bread flour, plus extra for dusting

2 tsp salt

2 tbsp (30 g) butter or margarine

1 cup (125 g) coarsely chopped walnut pieces

2 tbsp chopped parsley

¼ oz (7 g) envelope quick-rising active dry yeast

about 1¾ cups (400 ml) lukewarm water

sunflower oil for greasing

1 Put the flour and salt into a large bowl. Rub in the butter, then stir in the walnuts, parsley, and yeast. Make a well in the middle and add enough water to mix to a soft dough.

2 Knead the dough on a lightly floured surface until smooth and elastic. Shape into a ball and place in a lightly greased large bowl. Cover loosely with greased plastic wrap and leave in a warm place for 1–1½ hours or until doubled in size.

3 Lightly oil 2 baking sheets. Punch down the dough with your fists, then knead for 2–3 minutes until smooth and elastic.

4 Divide the dough in half, shape each half into a ball, and then place the 2 balls on a baking sheet.

5 Cover the balls loosely with greased plastic wrap, and leave to rise in a warm place for 20–30 minutes.

6 Dust each loaf with flour, slash the tops in a crisscross pattern, and bake in a preheated oven at 425°F (220°C) for about 10 minutes; reduce the oven temperature to 375°F (190°C), and bake for 20 minutes or until the bread is golden brown.

7 Tap the bottoms to see if the loaves are baked: they should sound hollow. Best eaten while still warm.

POTATO BREAD

MAKES 2 SMALL LOAVES

4 cups (500 g) white bread flour, plus extra for dusting

1 tsp salt

1 tbsp (15 g) butter

¼ oz (7 g) envelope quick-rising active dry yeast

1 large baking potato, cooked, peeled, mashed, and cooled

about 1 cup (250 ml) lukewarm water

sunflower oil for greasing

2 × 1 LB (500 G) LOAF PANS

1 Put the flour and salt into a large bowl, rub in the butter, then stir in the yeast. Add the potato, rubbing it loosely into the flour. Make a well in the middle of the ingredients and add enough water to mix to a soft dough.

2 Knead the dough on a floured surface until smooth and elastic, then shape into a ball. Place in a lightly greased large bowl, cover with greased plastic wrap, and leave to rise in a warm place for 1 hour or until doubled in size.

3 Turn out the dough onto a lightly floured surface and punch down with your fists. Knead until smooth and elastic.

4 Lightly oil the loaf pans. Divide the dough in half, and shape to fit the pans, tucking the ends underneath. Place in the pans. Cover loosely with greased plastic wrap and leave in a warm place to rise for 30 minutes or until the dough reaches the tops of the pans.

5 Bake in a preheated oven at 450°F (230°C) for 10 minutes; reduce the oven temperature to 400°F (200°C), and bake for 20–25 minutes until golden. Tap the bottoms of the loaves to see if they are baked: they should sound hollow. Serve warm or cold.

Cook's know-how

Always add the measured liquid gradually when making dough. Recipes cannot specify exact amounts because flours vary in how much liquid they will absorb.

CHEESE & HERB BREAD

MAKES 1 MEDIUM LOAF

4 cups (500 g) white bread flour, plus extra for dusting

3/4 cup (90 g) grated sharp Cheddar cheese

1/4 cup (30 g) grated Parmesan cheese

2 tsp dry mustard

2 tbsp chopped parsley

1 1/2 tsp salt

1/4 oz (7 g) envelope quick-rising active dry yeast

about 3/4 cup (350 ml) lukewarm milk

sunflower oil for greasing

beaten egg for glazing

2 tbsp grated sharp Cheddar cheese for sprinkling

1 Put the flour into a large bowl and stir in the cheeses, dry mustard, parsley, salt, and yeast, mixing thoroughly. Make a well in the middle and add enough milk to mix to a soft dough.

2 Knead the dough on a lightly floured surface until smooth and elastic.

3 Shape the dough into a ball and place in a lightly greased bowl. Cover with greased plastic wrap, and leave to rise in a warm place for 1–1 1/2 hours or until doubled in size.

4 Turn out the dough onto a floured surface and punch down. Knead for 2–3 minutes until smooth and elastic.

5 Lightly flour a baking sheet. Shape the dough into a 6 in (15 cm) ball and place on the baking sheet. Cover loosely with greased plastic wrap and leave to rise in a warm place for 20–30 minutes.

6 Brush with the egg to glaze, cut a shallow cross in the top, and sprinkle with the grated Cheddar cheese. Bake in a preheated oven at 450°F (230°C) for 10 minutes; reduce the oven temperature to 400°F (200°C), and bake for 20 minutes, covering the loaf loosely with foil halfway through baking if it is browning too much. Leave to cool on a wire rack.

OLIVE & SUN-DRIED TOMATO BREADS

MAKES 2 SMALL LOAVES

3 1/4 cups (400 g) white bread flour

1/2 cup (60 g) buckwheat flour

1 tsp salt

1/4 oz (7 g) envelope quick-rising active dry yeast

black pepper

about 1 1/4 cups (300 ml) lukewarm water

1 tbsp olive oil, plus extra for greasing

1 cup (125 g) coarsely chopped pitted black olives

4 oz (125 g) sun-dried tomatoes in oil, drained and chopped

1 tbsp chopped parsley

1 tbsp chopped fresh basil

1 tbsp coarse sea salt

1 Put the flours into a large bowl. Stir in the salt and yeast and season with black pepper. Make a well in the middle. Pour in the water and oil and mix to a soft dough.

2 Knead until smooth and elastic, shape into a ball, and place in a lightly greased large bowl. Cover with greased plastic wrap, and leave to rise in a warm place for 1–1 1/2 hours or until doubled in size.

3 Lightly oil a baking sheet. Punch down the dough, then knead for 2–3 minutes. Divide the dough into 2 pieces. Roll out each piece until about 9 x 10 in (23 x 25 cm). Spread one of the pieces with the olives and the other with the sun-dried tomatoes, parsley, and basil.

4 Roll up each piece of dough from one long end and place, seam-side down, on the sheet. Make 4 or 5 diagonal slashes on the top of each loaf, cover loosely with greased plastic wrap, and leave to rise in a warm place for 20–30 minutes.

5 Brush the top of each loaf with water and lightly sprinkle with sea salt. Bake in a preheated oven at 450°F (230°C) for 15 minutes; reduce the oven temperature to 375°F (190°C), and bake for 15 minutes longer or until golden.

6 Tap the bottoms to see if the loaves are baked: they should sound hollow. Leave to cool on a wire rack.

SOURDOUGH RYE BREAD

A satisfying and tasty country bread from Eastern Europe, especially good served with cheeses and pickles. It is not difficult to make but, because the starter has to be left to ferment for a few days, it does require a little forward planning.

MAKES 2 LARGE LOAVES

12 cups (1.5 kg) white bread, plus extra for sprinkling

1/4 oz (7 g) envelope quick-rising active dry yeast

1 cup (250 ml) lukewarm water

3 tbsp caraway seeds (optional)

1 tbsp salt

sunflower oil for greasing

fine cornmeal for sprinkling

SOURDOUGH STARTER

2 cups (250 g) white bread flour

1 tsp quick-rising active dry yeast

1 cup (250 ml) lukewarm water

SPONGE

1 3/4 cups (200 g) rye flour

1 cup (250 ml) lukewarm water

1 Make the sourdough starter: put the flour into a large bowl and stir in the yeast. Make a well in the middle, pour in the lukewarm water, and mix together.

2 Cover tightly and leave at room temperature for 2 days. Alternatively, leave the starter in the refrigerator for up to 1 week.

3 Make the sponge: put the rye flour into a large bowl, add the sourdough starter and the lukewarm water, and stir to mix. Cover tightly and leave at room temperature for 8 hours or chill in the refrigerator for up to 2 days.

4 Put the flour into a bowl, add the sponge mixture, yeast, lukewarm water, caraway seeds, if using, and salt, and mix to a soft but still slightly sticky dough.

5 Turn the dough into a large ungreased bowl, sprinkle the top with flour, cover loosely with greased plastic wrap, and leave to rise in a warm place for 2 hours or until doubled in size.

6 Lightly sprinkle 2 baking sheets with cornmeal. Turn out the dough onto a lightly floured surface and punch down with your fists. Knead for 3–4 minutes until smooth and elastic. Halve the dough and form into 2 balls. Score the tops with a sharp knife.

7 Place on the baking sheets, cover loosely with greased plastic wrap, and leave to rise in a warm place for 45 minutes or until doubled in size.

8 Place the loaves in a preheated oven at 425°F (220°C). Fill a roasting pan with boiling water and place at the bottom of the oven. Bake the loaves for about 35 minutes until they are lightly browned. Tap the bottoms to see if the loaves are baked: they should sound hollow. Leave to cool on wire racks.

FOCACCIA

MAKES I LARGE LOAF

6 cups (750 g) white bread flour, plus extra for dusting

1/4 oz (7 g) envelope quick-rising active dry yeast

3–4 tbsp chopped fresh rosemary

3 tbsp olive oil, plus extra for greasing

about 1 3/4 cups (450 ml) lukewarm water

2 tsp coarse sea salt

1 Put the flour into a bowl, and add the yeast and rosemary. Make a well in the middle, add the oil and enough water to make a soft but not sticky dough. Knead the dough until smooth and elastic, then shape into a ball.

2 Place the dough in a lightly greased large bowl, cover loosely with greased plastic wrap, and leave to rise in a warm place for about 1 hour or until the dough has doubled in size.

3 Turn out the dough onto a lightly floured surface and punch down. Knead for 2–3 minutes until smooth. Roll out the dough to a circle 2 in (5 cm) thick. Cover loosely with greased plastic wrap and leave in a warm place for 1 hour or until doubled in size.

4 Brush with olive oil and sprinkle with sea salt. Bake in a preheated oven at 375°F (190°C) for 20 minutes until golden. Best eaten warm.

THIN-CRUST PIZZAS

Tomatoes, cheese, herbs, and olive oil are just a few classic pizza toppings, but there are endless combinations. Pizza crusts can of course be bought already made, but if you follow the steps illustrated below you will have the satisfaction of making them at home.

NAPOLETANA

MAKES 1 LARGE PIZZA

14 oz (400 g) canned crushed tomatoes, drained

1 pizza crust (see box, below)

2 oz (60 g) canned anchovy fillets, drained

1 cup (125 g) shredded mozzarella cheese

2 tbsp olive oil

Spread the tomatoes over the pizza crust. Halve the anchovies and arrange on top with the remaining ingredients.

TUNA & CAPER

MAKES 1 LARGE PIZZA

14 oz (400 g) canned crushed tomatoes, drained

1 pizza crust (see box, below)

7 oz (200 g) canned tuna, drained

2 tbsp capers

1 cup (125 g) shredded mozzarella cheese

1 tsp dried oregano

2 tbsp olive oil

Spread the tomatoes over the pizza crust. Top with the remaining ingredients.

FOUR SEASONS

MAKES 1 LARGE PIZZA

14 oz (400 g) canned crushed tomatoes, drained

1 pizza crust (see box, below)

salt and black pepper

2 oz (60 g) thinly sliced salami

1/2 tsp dried oregano

1 cup (60 g) sliced small button mushrooms

1/4 cup (30 g) shredded mozzarella cheese

1 oz (30 g) canned anchovy fillets, drained

12 pitted black olives

2–3 pieces of bottled red peppers (in oil), thinly sliced

2 tbsp olive oil

grated Parmesan and fresh basil leaves to finish

1 Spread the tomatoes over the pizza crust and season to taste.

2 Put the salami and oregano on one quarter of the pizza, the mushrooms and mozzarella on a second quarter, the anchovies and olives on a third, the peppers on the fourth. Lightly sprinkle with olive oil. Sprinkle with Parmesan and basil, as desired, after baking.

MINI PIZZAS

MAKES 12

14 oz (400 g) canned crushed tomatoes, drained

1 quantity pizza dough (see box, below), shaped into 12 x 3 in (7 cm) circles

salt and black pepper

2 tbsp olive oil

GOAT CHEESE TOPPING

8 sun-dried tomatoes in oil, diced

6 pitted black olives, diced

2 garlic cloves, crushed

2 oz (60 g) goat cheese, diced

PROSCIUTTO TOPPING

2 slices of prosciutto, diced

6 artichoke hearts in oil, drained and sliced

Spread the tomatoes over the circles and season. Top 6 circles with the sun-dried tomatoes, olives, garlic, and goat cheese, and 6 with the prosciutto and artichokes. Sprinkle with the olive oil before baking.

CLOCKWISE FROM TOP: Mini Pizzas, Four Seasons, Tuna & Caper, Napoletana.

MAKING THE THIN PIZZA CRUST

1 Sift 2 cups (250 g) white bread flour onto a work surface and add a heaping 1/2 tsp quick-rising active dry yeast and 1/2 tsp salt. Make a well in the middle and add about 2/3 cup (150 ml) lukewarm water and 1 tbsp olive oil. Draw in the flour with your fingertips and work to make a smooth dough.

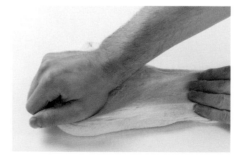

2 Lightly oil a large bowl. Knead the dough for 10 minutes until smooth. Shape into a ball and put in the bowl. Cover loosely with greased plastic wrap and leave in a warm place to rise for about 1 hour or until doubled in size. Turn out of the bowl and knead for 2–3 minutes on a lightly floured surface until smooth.

3 Roll and stretch the dough until it is about 14 in (35 cm) round and about 1/2 in (1 cm) thick. Make a rim around the edge. Put on a baking sheet, add the desired topping, and bake in a preheated oven at 425°F (220°C) for 20–30 minutes. Bake mini pizzas at 425°F (220°C) for only 12–15 minutes.

CHALLAH

MAKES 2 SMALL LOAVES

4 cups (500 g) white bread flour, plus extra for dusting

1 tbsp sugar

2 tsp salt

1/4 oz (7 g) envelope quick-rising active dry yeast

1 cup (250 ml) lukewarm water

2 eggs, beaten

2 tbsp sunflower oil, plus extra for greasing

beaten egg for glazing

poppy seeds for sprinkling

1 Put the flour, sugar, and salt into a bowl. Stir in the yeast. Make a well in the middle. Combine the water, eggs, and oil, and pour into the well. Mix to a soft dough.

2 Knead the dough on a lightly floured surface until firm and elastic. Shape into a ball and place in a greased bowl. Cover with greased plastic wrap and leave to rise in a warm place for 1–1 1/2 hours or until doubled in size.

3 Turn out the dough onto a lightly floured surface and punch down with your fists. Knead for 2–3 minutes until smooth and elastic. Divide the dough into 2 pieces.

4 Lightly oil a baking sheet. Divide each piece of dough into 3 even-sized strands, and shape into a braid (page 404). Place on the baking sheet, cover loosely with greased plastic wrap, and leave to rise in a warm place for 30 minutes or until doubled in size.

5 Brush the loaves with the beaten egg and sprinkle generously with poppy seeds. Bake in a preheated oven at 450°F (230°C) for 10 minutes; reduce the oven temperature to 400°F (200°C), and bake for 20 minutes, or until the loaves are a rich brown color. Tap the bottoms to see if the loaves are baked: they should sound hollow. Cool on a wire rack.

BRIOCHES

MAKES 12

2 1/2 cups (275 g) white bread flour, plus extra for dusting

2 tbsp sugar

4 tbsp (60 g) butter

1/4 oz (7 g) envelope quick-rising active dry yeast

2 eggs, beaten

about 3 tbsp lukewarm milk

sunflower oil for greasing

beaten egg for glazing

12 INDIVIDUAL BRIOCHE MOLDS

1 Sift the flour and sugar into a large bowl. Rub in the butter until the mixture resembles fine bread crumbs, then stir in the yeast. Make a well in the middle, then pour in the eggs and enough milk to mix to a soft dough.

2 Knead the dough on a lightly floured surface until smooth and elastic. Shape into a ball and place in a greased large bowl. Cover with greased plastic wrap and leave to rise in a warm place for 1–1 1/2 hours or until doubled in size.

3 Turn out the dough onto a lightly floured surface and punch down with your fists. Knead the dough for 2–3 minutes until smooth.

4 Lightly grease the brioche molds. Shape the brioches (see box, below).

5 Cover loosely with greased plastic wrap. Leave to rise in a warm place for 20 minutes or until doubled in size.

6 Brush the brioches with a little beaten egg and bake in a preheated oven at 400°F (200°C) for 10–12 minutes until golden brown. Tap the bottoms to see if the brioches are baked: they should sound hollow. Leave to cool on a wire rack. Best served warm.

Shaping brioches

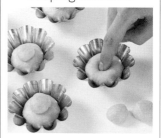

Divide the dough into 12 pieces, then cut one-quarter from each piece. Shape all the pieces into balls. Place the large balls in the molds, and indent the middle of each with your forefinger. Place the small balls on top and press down to seal.

JELLY DOUGHNUTS

MAKES 16

4 cups (500 g) white bread flour, plus extra for dusting

2 tbsp (30 g) butter or margarine

6 tbsp sugar

¼ oz (7 g) envelope quick-rising active dry yeast

about 6 tbsp (90 ml) milk

about 6 tbsp (90 ml) very hot water

2 eggs, beaten

sunflower oil for greasing and deep-frying

½ cup (150 g) raspberry jelly

½ cup (125 g) sugar

2 tsp ground cinnamon (optional)

1 Put the flour into a large bowl and rub in the butter with the fingertips until the mixture resembles fine bread crumbs. Stir in the sugar and yeast, and make a well in the middle. Mix the milk and hot water together. Pour the eggs into the well and mix with the flour, adding enough milk and water to make a smooth dough.

2 Knead the dough on a lightly floured surface until smooth and elastic. Shape into a ball and place in a lightly greased large bowl.

3 Cover with greased plastic wrap and leave in a warm place for 1–1½ hours until doubled in size. Turn out onto a lightly floured surface, and punch down with your fists. Knead for 2–3 minutes.

4 Divide the dough into 16 pieces. Shape each one into a ball, then flatten slightly. Fill the doughnuts (see box, below). Place on greased baking sheets, cover with greased plastic wrap, and leave to rise in a warm place for 30 minutes.

5 Heat the oil in a deep-fryer to 325°F (160°C), and cook the doughnuts in batches for 5 minutes until golden. Drain, toss in sugar and cinnamon, if using, and serve warm.

Filling the doughnuts

Place 1 tsp raspberry jelly in the middle of each flattened dough ball. Gather the edges over the jelly and pinch firmly to seal.

SHORTENING BREAD

MAKES 1 LARGE LOAF

4 cups (500 g) white bread flour, plus extra for dusting

1 tsp salt

¼ oz (7 g) envelope quick-rising active dry yeast

1 tbsp vegetable shortening

about 1¼ cups (300 ml) lukewarm water

sunflower oil for greasing

FILLING

6 tbsp (90 g) vegetable shortening

4 tbsp (60 g) butter, plus extra for greasing

½ cup (90 g) dried currants

½ cup (90 g) golden raisins

⅓ cup (60 g) chopped mixed candied peel

⅓ cup packed (60 g) dark brown sugar

GLAZE

1 tbsp sugar

1 tbsp boiling water

9 × 12 IN (23 × 30 CM) ROASTING PAN

1 Mix the flour, salt, and yeast in a bowl and rub in the shortening. Make a well in the middle and pour in enough water to mix to a soft dough.

2 Knead on a lightly floured surface until smooth and elastic, place in a greased large bowl, and cover with greased plastic wrap. Leave to rise in a warm place, 1–1½ hours.

3 Turn out the dough onto a lightly floured surface and roll out to a rectangle about ¼ in (5 mm) thick. Dot with one-third each of the vegetable shortening and butter. Sprinkle over one-third each of the dried fruit, mixed peel, and sugar.

4 Fold into three, folding the bottom third up and the top third down on top of it. Seal the edges to trap the air, then give the dough a quarter turn. Repeat the rolling and folding twice more, with the remaining shortening, fruit, peel, and sugar.

5 Lightly butter the roasting pan. Roll out the dough to fit the pan, and lift it carefully into the pan. Cover with greased plastic wrap and leave to rise in a warm place for about 30 minutes or until doubled in size.

6 Score the top of the dough in a crisscross pattern, and bake in a preheated oven at 400°F (200°C) for about 30 minutes or until golden brown. Leave to cool in the pan for about 10 minutes.

7 Meanwhile, make the glaze: dissolve the sugar in the measured water. Brush the glaze on top of the warm cake and leave to cool before serving.

DANISH PASTRIES

These melt-in-the-mouth, flaky pastries are surprisingly easy to make, and are a real treat for breakfast or any time of day. Vary the fillings, and bake them ahead, then freeze to save time. When you want to eat the pastries, warm them, loosely covered with foil, in a low oven.

MAKES 16

4 cups (500 g) white bread flour, plus extra for dusting

1/2 tsp salt

1 1/2 cups (375 g) butter, plus extra for greasing

1/4 oz (7 g) envelope quick-rising active dry yeast

4 tbsp sugar

2/3 cup (150 ml) lukewarm milk

2 eggs, beaten

beaten egg to glaze

FILLING & TOPPING

8 oz (250 g) white almond paste (marzipan)

4 apricot halves, canned or fresh

about 2 tsp water

1 cup (125 g) confectioners' sugar

1/2 cup (60 g) slivered almonds

1/3 cup (60 g) candied cherries

1 Put the flour and salt into a bowl and rub in 4 tbsp (60 g) of the butter. Stir in the yeast and sugar. Make a well in the middle, add the lukewarm milk and eggs, and mix to a soft dough.

2 Turn out the dough onto a floured surface and knead for 10 minutes or until smooth. Shape into a ball and place in a greased bowl. Cover with greased plastic wrap and leave in a warm place to rise for 1 hour or until doubled in size.

3 Turn out the dough onto a lightly floured work surface and knead for 2–3 minutes until smooth. Roll out into an 8 x 14 in (20 x 35 cm) rectangle. Dot the top two-thirds of the dough with half of the remaining butter. Fold the bottom third up and the top third down to form a package. Seal the edges, then give the dough a quarter turn so the folded side is to the left.

4 Roll out the dough into an 8 x 14 in (20 x 35 cm) rectangle as before. Dot with the remaining butter, fold, and chill for 15 minutes. Roll, fold, and chill twice more.

5 Divide the dough into 4 pieces. Shape and fill the pastries (see box, below). Arrange on buttered baking sheets and leave to rise in a warm place for 20 minutes. Brush with beaten egg and bake in a preheated oven at 425°F (220°C) for 15 minutes or until golden brown. Transfer to a wire rack.

6 Mix the water and confectioners' sugar and spoon a little over each pastry while still warm. Decorate kites with slivered almonds and pinwheels with candied cherries. Leave to cool.

CLOCKWISE FROM TOP: Pinwheels, Envelopes, Crescents, Kites.

SHAPING DANISH PASTRIES

Crescents

1 Roll out the dough into a 9 in (23 cm) circle. Cut into quarters. Place a small roll of almond paste at the wide end of each piece.

2 Starting from the wide end, roll up each dough quarter loosely around the almond paste, then curve the ends to form a crescent.

Kites

1 Roll out the dough into an 8 in (20 cm) square. Cut into 4 squares. Make cuts around 2 corners of each square, 1/2 in (1 cm) in from the edge.

2 Place a ball of almond paste in the middle of each square. Lift each cut corner and cross it over the almond paste to the opposite corner.

Pinwheels & Envelopes

For pinwheels: roll out dough and cut into 4 squares as for kites. Put almond paste in middle of each. Cut from the corners almost to the middle. Fold in alternate points.

For envelopes: roll out the dough, cut into 4, and fill as for pinwheels. Fold 2 opposite corners into the middle. Top with a half apricot, cut-side down.

WHOLE-WHEAT ENGLISH MUFFINS

MAKES ABOUT 12

4 cups (500 g) whole-wheat flour, plus extra for dusting

1 tsp salt

1/4 oz (7 g) envelope quick-rising active dry yeast

about 1 cup (250 ml) milk

about 1/2 cup (125 ml) very hot water

sunflower oil for greasing

3 IN (7 CM) PASTRY CUTTER

1 Put the flour into a large bowl, stir in the salt and yeast, and make a well in the middle. Mix the milk and water together, pour in all at once, and mix to a soft dough.

2 Knead on a lightly floured surface until smooth and elastic, then shape into a ball. Place the dough in a greased large bowl, cover with greased plastic wrap, and leave to rise in a warm place for 45–60 minutes until doubled in size.

3 Punch down the dough, then turn out onto a lightly floured surface and knead for 2–3 minutes until smooth and elastic.

4 Roll out the dough until 1/2 in (1 cm) thick. Using the cutter, cut into 12 circles, rerolling and kneading the dough as necessary.

5 Lightly dust 2 baking sheets with flour, arrange the circles on the sheets, and cover loosely with greased plastic wrap. Leave to rise in a warm place for about 30 minutes or until doubled in size.

6 Lightly oil a griddle or skillet, and cook the muffins over a medium heat, 3 or 4 at a time, for about 7 minutes on each side until golden and cooked through. Do not allow the griddle to get too hot or the outside of the muffins will burn before the inside is cooked.

ENGLISH MUFFINS

MAKES 20

3 cups (375 g) white bread flour

1/2 tsp salt

1/4 oz (7 g) envelope quick-rising active dry yeast

about 1 cup (250 ml) milk

about 1 1/4 cups (300 ml) very hot water

sunflower oil for greasing

4 × 3 IN (7 CM) BISCUIT CUTTERS

1 Put the flour into a large bowl, stir in the salt and yeast, and make a well in the middle. Mix the milk and water together, pour in, and beat to form a smooth, thick batter.

2 Cover and leave in a warm place to rise for 1 hour or until the surface is bubbling.

3 Beat the batter mixture for 2 minutes, then pour into a jug. Lightly grease the biscuit cutters and grease a griddle or skillet. Place the cutters on the griddle and then leave for 1–2 minutes to heat through.

4 Pour 3/4 in (2 cm) of batter into each cutter and cook for 5–7 minutes until the surface is dry and full of holes, and the muffins are shrinking away from the sides of the cutters.

5 Lift off the cutters, turn the muffins over, and cook for 1 minute until pale golden. Transfer the muffins to a wire rack and leave to cool.

6 Repeat with the remaining batter, lightly greasing the griddle and cutters between each batch. Best served warm.

STICKY BUNS

MAKES 12

4 cups (500 g) white bread flour

1 tsp salt

4 tbsp (60 g) butter

1/4 oz (7 g) envelope quick-rising active dry yeast

2 tbsp sugar

scant 1 cup (200 ml) lukewarm milk

1 large egg, beaten

sunflower oil for greasing

4 tbsp honey

FILLING

4 tbsp (60 g) butter

2 tbsp packed light brown sugar

1/3 cup (60 g) golden raisins

1/4 cup (60 g) dried currants

grated zest of 1 orange

1 tsp apple-pie spice

1 Put the flour into a large bowl and stir in the salt. Rub in the butter and yeast. Stir in the sugar. Make a well in the middle, pour in the milk and egg, and mix to a soft dough.

2 Knead the dough on a lightly floured surface until smooth and elastic, then shape into a ball and place in a lightly greased large bowl. Cover with greased plastic wrap and leave in a warm place for 1–1 1/2 hours or until doubled in size.

3 Make the filling: cream the butter with the brown sugar. In another bowl, combine the golden raisins, currants, orange zest, and spice.

4 Lightly grease a 7 x 11 in (18 x 28 cm) roasting pan. Turn out the dough onto a lightly floured surface, and punch down with your fists. Knead for 2–3 minutes until smooth.

5 Roll out into a 12 in (30 cm) square and dot with the butter mixture. Fold in half and roll out into a 12 in (30 cm) square. Sprinkle with the fruit mixture, then roll up.

6 Cut the roll into 12 pieces and arrange cut-side up in the roasting pan. Cover with greased plastic wrap. Leave in a warm place to rise for about 30 minutes or until the pieces are touching.

7 Bake in a preheated oven at 425°F (220°C) for 20–25 minutes, covering the buns loosely with foil after about 15 minutes to prevent them from browning too much. Transfer to a wire rack.

8 Warm the honey in a small saucepan and brush over the buns to glaze. Pull the buns apart, and serve warm.

SWEET BUNS

MAKES 18

4 cups (500 g) white bread flour

4 tbsp sugar

1 tsp salt

1/4 oz (7 g) envelope quick-rising active dry yeast

about 2/3 cup (150 ml) lukewarm milk

4 tbsp (60 g) butter, melted and cooled slightly

1 egg and 2 egg yolks, beaten

1 cup (150 g) golden raisins

1/2 cup (90 g) chopped mixed peel

sunflower oil for greasing

TOPPING

1 egg, beaten

2 tbsp coarsely crushed sugar cubes

1 Put the flour and sugar into a large bowl and stir in the salt and yeast. Make a well in the middle and add the milk, butter, egg and egg yolks, golden raisins, and mixed peel. Mix to a soft dough.

2 Knead the dough on a lightly floured surface until smooth and elastic.

3 Shape the dough into a ball and place in a greased bowl. Cover with greased plastic wrap and leave to rise in a warm place for 1–1 1/2 hours or until the dough has doubled in size.

4 Turn out the dough onto a lightly floured surface and punch down. Knead the dough for 2–3 minutes until smooth and elastic.

5 Lightly grease 2 or 3 baking sheets. Divide the dough into 18 pieces, shape into rolls, and place on the baking sheets. Cover loosely with greased plastic wrap and leave to rise in a warm place for about 30 minutes or until doubled in size.

6 Brush the tops of the buns with the beaten egg and sprinkle with the sugar. Bake in a preheated oven at 375°F (190°C) for 15 minutes or until golden brown.

7 Tap the bottoms of the buns to see if they are baked through: they should sound hollow. Leave to cool on a wire rack.

CINNAMON ROLLS

MAKES 16

8 cups (1 kg) all-purpose flour

4 tbsp sugar

1/4 oz (7 g) envelope quick-rising active dry yeast

1 tsp salt

about 3/4 cup (350 ml) lukewarm milk

2 eggs, lightly beaten

2 tbsp (30 g) butter, melted

1 1/3 cups (250 g) raisins

1 tbsp ground cinnamon

sunflower oil for greasing

milk for glazing

GLAZE

1 3/4 cups (200 g) confectioners' sugar

4 tbsp water

1 tsp vanilla extract

1 Sift the flour and 2 tbsp of the sugar into a bowl, then stir in the yeast and salt. Make a well in the middle, pour in the milk, eggs, and butter, and stir to make a sticky dough.

2 Knead the dough on a lightly floured surface until smooth and elastic.

3 Knead in the raisins and half of the cinnamon, then divide the dough into 16 even-sized pieces. Shape each piece into a 8–10 in (20–25 cm) strip, then flatten.

4 Combine the remaining sugar and cinnamon, sprinkle the mixture over the strips of dough, then roll up tightly into spirals.

5 Lightly grease 2 baking sheets. Arrange the rolls on the sheets, cover loosely with greased plastic wrap, and leave to rise in a warm place for about 1 hour or until doubled in size.

6 Brush the rolls with milk to glaze, then bake them in a preheated oven at 375°F (190°C) for 30–40 minutes until lightly browned. Transfer the rolls to a rack.

7 Meanwhile, make the glaze: in a small bowl, combine the confectioners' sugar, water, and vanilla extract. As soon as the cinnamon rolls come out of the oven, brush them with the glaze. Best served warm.

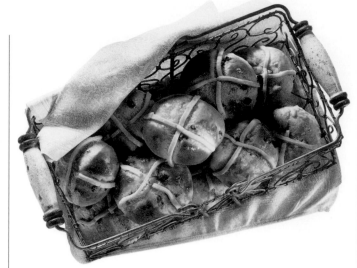

HOT CROSS BUNS

MAKES 12

4 cups (500 g) white bread flour

4 tbsp sugar

1/4 oz (7 g) envelope quick-rising active dry yeast

1 tsp salt

1 tsp apple-pie spice

1 tsp ground cinnamon

1/2 tsp grated nutmeg

about 2/3 cup (150 ml) milk

about 5 tbsp very hot water

4 tbsp (60 g) butter, melted and cooled slightly

1 egg, beaten

1/2 cup (90 g) dried currants

1/3 cup (60 g) chopped mixed peel

sunflower oil for greasing

2 oz (60 g) piecrust pastry dough, thawed if frozen

GLAZE

2 tbsp sugar

2 tbsp water

1 Sift the flour into a large bowl, stir in the sugar, yeast, salt, apple-pie spice, cinnamon, and nutmeg, and make a well in the middle. Mix the milk and water together and add to bowl with the butter, egg, currants, and mixed peel. Mix to make a soft dough.

2 Knead the dough on a lightly floured surface until smooth and elastic, then shape into a ball.

3 Put into a greased large bowl, cover with greased plastic wrap, and leave to rise in a warm place for 1–1 1/2 hours or until doubled in size.

4 Punch down the dough with your fists, then turn out onto a lightly floured surface and knead for 2–3 minutes until smooth and elastic. Divide the dough into 12 pieces and shape into rolls.

5 Roll out the pastry dough to 1/4 in (5 mm) thickness, cut it into 24 narrow strips, and press 2 strips crisscross on top of each bun, securing with a little water.

6 Lightly grease 2 baking sheets, arrange the buns on the sheets, and cover loosely with greased plastic wrap. Leave to rise in a warm place for 30 minutes or until doubled in size.

7 Bake the buns in a preheated oven at 425°F (220°C) for 15 minutes or until golden brown. Transfer the buns to a wire rack to cool. Serve warm or cold.

11

PIES, TARTS, &
HOT DESSERTS

UNDER 30 MINUTES

CHERRIES JUBILEE
Morello cherries simmered in sugar and flavored with almond extract and brandy. Served with vanilla ice cream.

SERVES 4 162 calories per serving
Takes 20 minutes   Page 435

JAMAICAN BANANAS
Banana halves coated in a rich caramel and cinnamon sauce, spiked with rum. Served warm with vanilla ice cream.

SERVES 4 269 calories per serving
Takes 15 minutes   Page 434

FRUIT FRITTERS
Bite-sized pieces of apple and banana coated in batter, and deep-fried until golden. Sprinkled with sugar and cinnamon.

SERVES 6 361 calories per serving
Takes 25 minutes   Page 435

30–60 MINUTES

FRENCH PANCAKES
Small golden pancakes, baked, then folded over a filling of apricot jam, and sprinkled with sugar.

SERVES 4 378 calories per serving
Takes 35 minutes   Page 436

TRADITIONAL

BAKED APPLES
Cooking apples filled with sugar and butter, then baked until soft and served hot with their juices spooned over.

SERVES 6 235 calories per serving
Takes 55 minutes   Page 433

FRENCH CLASSIC

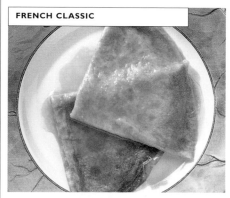

CREPES SUZETTE
Delicious crêpes coated with a sweet orange sauce including brandy or orange liqueur, folded in quarters, and served hot.

SERVES 4 604 calories per serving
Takes 55 minutes   Page 436

FAMILY CHOICE

SAUCY CHOCOLATE CAKE
Irresistible light chocolate cake flavored with cocoa and vanilla extract, and baked in a chocolate sauce.

SERVES 4 361 calories per serving
Takes 45 minutes   Page 440

APPLE BROWN BETTY
Layers of spiced apple slices and buttered bread crumbs sprinkled with sugar, then baked until golden brown.

SERVES 6 284 calories per serving
Takes 55 minutes   Page 433

PLUM CRUMBLE
Sweet and crunchy: juicy plums sprinkled with sugar and cinnamon, and baked beneath a golden brown topping.

SERVES 6 436 calories per serving
Takes 50 minutes   Page 434

OVER 60 MINUTES

MAGIC LEMON PUDDING

Fresh and tangy: a light lemony mixture separates
during cooking into a cake on top and a delicious
lemon sauce underneath.

SERVES 4 295 calories per serving
Takes 1 hour 5 minutes   Page 437

APPLE BREAD PUDDING

Slices of buttered bread covered with an apple and
apricot jam mixture, and topped with a layer of
bread triangles.

SERVES 6 428 calories per serving
Takes 1 hour 5 minutes   Page 432

DINNER PARTY

MILLE-FEUILLE

Melt-in-the-mouth puff pastry layered with
whipped cream, jam, and crème pâtissière, and
topped with glacé icing.

SERVES 6 486 calories per serving
Takes 45 minutes, plus chilling   Page 458

CLASSIC

KEY LIME PIE

Creamy, tangy lime-flavored filling is set in a baked
shell, then chilled and served decorated with lime
slices.

SERVES 8 489 calories per serving
Takes 60 minutes, plus chilling   Page 454

PINEAPPLE UPSIDE-DOWN CAKE

Pineapple rings and chopped apricots under a light
and springy sponge cake topping, turned out and
served "upside-down."

SERVES 8 375 calories per serving
Takes 1 hour 5 minutes   Page 437

SPECIAL SPONGE CAKE

Warming and filling: sweetened sliced cooking
apples, with lemon zest and juice, are topped with a
golden sponge cake.

SERVES 6 414 calories per serving
Takes 1 hour 5 minutes   Page 432

BANANA CREAM PIE

Rich and creamy: crushed crumb base with a
caramel filling, topped with banana slices, whipped
cream, and grated chocolate.

SERVES 6 653 calories per serving
Takes 20 minutes, plus chilling   Page 454

AUSTRIAN CLASSIC

APPLE STRUDEL

Sheets of phyllo pastry wrapped around apples,
lemon zest and juice, sugar, spices, and golden
raisins, and sprinkled with almonds.

SERVES 8 278 calories per serving
Takes 1¼ hours   Page 447

BANANA CUSTARD TART
WITH BERRIES

Pastry shell filled with layers of creamy custard and
fruit, and covered with whipped cream.

SERVES 6–8 787–590 calories per serving
Takes 60 minutes, plus chilling   Page 455

OVER 60 MINUTES

QUEEN OF PUDDINGS

Old-fashioned favorite: smooth, creamy custard is flavored with orange zest, spread with melted jam, and topped with meringue.

SERVES 6 386 calories per serving
Takes 60 minutes, plus standing   Page 441

SOUTHERN CLASSIC

MISSISSIPPI MUD PIE

Popular dessert: pastry shell with a sweetened chocolate and coffee filling, decorated with whipped cream. Served chilled.

SERVES 8–10 692–553 calories per serving
Takes 1¼ hours, plus chilling   Page 455

TREACLE TART

Rich and sweet: tart shell filled with dark corn syrup, bread crumbs, and lemon zest and juice. Served warm.

SERVES 8 386 calories per serving
Takes 60 minutes, plus chilling   Page 450

FAMILY CHOICE

DATE & WALNUT CAKE

Rich cake flavored with coffee extract, dates, and walnuts, and served with a deliciously sticky toffee sauce.

SERVES 8 690 calories per serving
Takes 1 hour 5 minutes   Page 440

HOT CHOCOLATE SOUFFLES

Light and airy: individual soufflés made from dark chocolate, baked until well risen and fluffy, then dusted with confectioners' sugar.

SERVES 4 494 calories per serving
Takes 1¼ hours   Page 441

GREEK CLASSIC

BAKLAVA

Traditional Greek pastry: baked layers of buttered phyllo pastry and walnuts soaked in honey and lemon juice, and cut into squares.

MAKES 20 SQUARES 249 calories per serving
Takes 60 minutes, plus cooling   Page 458

BAKED APPLE DUMPLINGS

Cooking apples filled with sugar and cinnamon, wrapped in decorative pastry case, and baked until golden.

SERVES 4 781 calories per serving
Takes 60 minutes, plus chilling   Page 445

TRADITIONAL

LEMON MERINGUE PIE

Deliciously sweet: golden brown pastry with tangy lemon filling, topped with light and fluffy meringue.

SERVES 8–10 537–430 calories per serving
Takes 1¼ hours, plus chilling   Page 453

APPLE PIE

Family favorite: light and golden puff pastry crusts above and below tender apple slices in this apple pie.

SERVES 6 432 calories per serving
Takes 60 minutes, plus cooling   Page 446

OVER 60 MINUTES

ALMOND TART

Traditional sweet dessert: pastry shell spread with jam, topped with an almond-flavored batter and dough lattice, and then baked.

SERVES 6 560 calories per serving

Takes 1 1/4 hours, plus chilling Page 451

TRADITIONAL

BREAD PUDDING

Slices of white bread thickly spread with butter, layered with dried fruit, lemon zest, and sugar, and baked in a custard.

SERVES 6 516 calories per serving

Takes 60 minutes, plus standing Page 442

STRAWBERRY & RHUBARB PIE

Sweet strawberries and rhubarb are lightly spiced, and baked in a pastry shell with a lattice topping.

SERVES 6–8 371–278 calories per serving

Takes 1 1/4 hours, plus chilling Page 445

DINNER PARTY

FRENCH APRICOT & ALMOND TART

French classic: poached apricot halves baked on a layer of pastry cream in a pastry shell. Glazed with brandy and slivered almonds.

SERVES 10 398 calories per serving

Takes 45 minutes, plus chilling Page 452

TARTE AU CITRON

Light and tangy: pastry shell with a cream and lemon filling, baked until set, and lightly dusted with confectioners' sugar.

SERVES 10–12 572–476 calories per serving

Takes 1 1/4 hours, plus chilling Page 453

FAMILY CHOICE

RICE PUDDING

Rich and creamy: short-grain rice, milk, sugar, and lemon zest mixed together, then sprinkled with freshly grated nutmeg and dotted with small pats of butter. Baked slowly in the oven until the top turns golden brown.

SERVES 4 210 calories per serving

Takes 2 3/4 hours, plus standing Page 442

OVER 60 MINUTES

PECAN PIE

Deliciously rich: pecan pie might come from the southern States of America, but it's a favorite all across the country. The buttery rich pecan nuts are toasted, then mixed with a lightly spiced syrup, and flavored with brandy and vanilla extract.

SERVES 6–8 611–458 calories per serving
Takes 1¼ hours, plus chilling   Page 451

FRENCH APPLE TART

Apple chunks, jam, sugar, and lemon zest, puréed, and spooned into a pastry shell, and topped with apple slices and jam glaze.

SERVES 8–10 593–474 calories per serving
Takes 2 hours, plus chilling   Page 450

STEAMED SYRUP PUDDING

Wonderfully sweet and sticky: a simple, traditional steamed pudding, deliciously sweetened with maple syrup.

SERVES 4–6 619–413 calories per serving
Takes 3¼ hours   Page 444

TARTE TATIN

Rich and fruity: crisp pastry baked over caramel and apple slices, then turned out with the glazed apples on top.

SERVES 6 511 calories per serving
Takes 60 minutes, plus chilling   Page 447

MINCEMEAT & ALMOND TART

A pastry shell filled with mincemeat and topped with a light, creamy almond mixture, then baked until golden.

SERVES 8–10 856–685 calories per serving
Takes 60 minutes, plus chilling   Page 444

STEAMED JAM PUDDING

Warm and filling: a temptingly light cake batter is steamed over jam. A firm family favorite.

SERVES 4–6 573–382 calories per serving
Takes 1¾ hours   Page 443

PLUM PUDDING

Rich, dark and fruity traditional British Christmas pudding: dried fruits are combined with nuts, and lemon zest and juice. Grated carrot makes sure the pudding stays deliciously moist. Once steamed, the pudding is liberally laced with rum.

SERVES 8–10 522–418 calories per serving
Takes 6¼ hours, plus storing   Page 443

PIES, TARTS, & HOT DESSERTS KNOW-HOW

DESSERTS MAY no longer be a feature of every family meal, but few people can say that they don't enjoy something sweet from time to time, especially to round off a special meal. Hot pastry desserts can take very little time to make these days as store-bought pastry dough, especially the already-rolled varieties, is so good. But if you have the time, and you enjoy it, then it's very satisfying to make your own, and you can try all the different types of pastry.

TYPES OF PASTRY

All pastries are based on a mixture of flour, fat, and a liquid to bind them. All-purpose flour is usually used, although whole wheat or a mixture of the two gives a "nuttier" pastry. The liquid used for binding may be water, milk, or egg; the fat may be butter, margarine, shortening, or a combination.

Piecrust pastry

A blend of 2 parts flour, 1 part fat, and usually water, piecrust pastry (page 430) is used for sweet and savory pies and tarts.

Pâte sucrée

Bound with egg yolks, pâte sucrée (page 430) is richer than piecrust pastry and is used for sweet tarts and tartlets. The classic method for mixing the dough is on a flat marble work surface.

Puff pastry

This light, flaky pastry is made by rolling and folding the dough many times to make paper-thin layers of dough and butter. Store-bought fresh or frozen dough is very convenient, but not all brands are made with butter. Puff pastry is often used as a top crust for sweet and savory pies, to wrap beef Wellington, and to make napoleons.

Flaky pastry

This is a shortcut version of puff pastry. The rolling and folding process is repeated only a few times. It is used for pies and tarts.

Quick puff pastry

Like puff and flaky pastry, this is rolled and folded, but the butter is added all at once, in large cubes. Quick puff pastry can be used in the same ways as flaky pastry and for dishes normally made with puff pastry.

Phyllo & strudel pastry

These are similar types of pastry made from a pliable dough that is stretched and rolled until extremely thin. It is then rolled around a filling or layered with melted butter. Phyllo and strudel pastries are difficult to make at home, but store-bought varieties are available fresh and frozen. Common uses include strudel and baklava.

MICROWAVING

The microwave can be a helpful tool when preparing pies, tarts, and hot desserts. For baking pastry-based pies and tarts, however, there really is no substitute for the conventional oven.

The microwave is perfect for cooking fruit fillings for pies and tarts. The fruit remains plump and colorful. It can also be used to melt or soften butter and to heat liquids in which fruit is left to soak. Under careful watch, the microwave can be used to melt chocolate and to make caramel.

FREEZING

Many desserts freeze well, particularly baked cakelike and steamed puddings (before or after cooking), bread pudding (before cooking), crumbles (before or after cooking), and crêpes. Custard-based and milk puddings are not as successful because they tend to separate.

Pastry dough is an excellent freezer standby; thaw before rolling out. Unbaked pastry shells are ideal for last-minute desserts as they can be baked from frozen. It's not a good idea to freeze baked pastries.

QUICK PUFF PASTRY

Ideal for both sweet and savory pies. These quantities make sufficient pastry for a 10 in (25 cm) double-crust pie.

1 Sift 2 cups (250 g) all-purpose flour into a bowl. Add 6 tbls (90 g) each of cubed butter and shortening, and stir to coat in flour. Add 2/3 cup (150 ml) cold water and, with a table knife, bind to a lumpy dough.

2 Roll out the dough into a rectangle 3 times as long as it is wide. Fold the bottom third up and the top third down. Press the edges with the side of your hand, to seal. Wrap and chill for 15 minutes, then place so the folded edges are to the sides.

3 Roll out the dough into a rectangle and fold as before. Turn the dough so the folded edges are to the sides again. Repeat the rolling, folding, and turning twice more. Wrap and chill for at least 30 minutes.

PIECRUST DOUGH

You can also make piecrust dough in a food processor: pulse the flour with the fat until like bread crumbs, then add the water and pulse again briefly (do this briefly or the pastry will be tough). Tip onto a floured surface and knead lightly to mix to a smooth dough. These quantities make sufficient pastry to line a 9–10 in (23–25 cm) quiche dish, tart pan, or pie plate.

1 Sift 1½ cups (175 g) all-purpose flour into a bowl. Cut 6 tbls (90 g) well-chilled butter, margarine, or shortening into small pieces and add to the bowl. Stir to coat the fat with flour.

2 Using your fingertips, quickly and lightly rub the fat into the flour, lifting the mixture to incorporate air, until it resembles fine bread crumbs. Sprinkle about 2 tbsp cold water over and stir gently with a table knife to mix. If the mixture seems too dry to bind together, add a little more water.

3 Gather the mixture together and knead very briefly until smooth (handle the dough as little as possible or the pastry will be tough. If the dough feels at all sticky, add a little more flour. Shape into a ball, wrap, and chill for at least 30 minutes.

PATE SUCREE

This French sweet pastry is traditionally made on a marble surface. These quantities make enough dough to line a 10 in (25 cm) quiche dish, tart pan, or pie plate.

1 Sift 1¾ cups (200 g) all-purpose flour on to a work surface. Make a well in the middle and add 6 tbls (90 g) softened butter, ¼ cup (60 g) sugar, and 3 egg yolks (for a less rich pastry, use just 1 egg yolk). With your fingertips blend together the butter, sugar, and egg yolks.

2 Using your fingertips, gradually work the sifted flour into the blended butter mixture until the mixture resembles coarse crumbs. If the mixture seems too sticky, work in a little more flour.

3 With your fingers or a pastry scraper, gather the dough into a ball, then knead briefly until it is smooth and pliable. Shape the dough into a ball again, wrap, and chill for at least 30 minutes or until it feels just firm.

MAKING A PASTRY SHELL

Careful handling of pastry dough should guarantee it does not shrink or distort when baking.

1 Put the pastry dough on a floured work surface and lightly flour the rolling pin. Roll out into a circle, starting in the middle each time and lifting and giving the dough circle a quarter turn after each roll.

2 If lining a pie plate, roll out the dough into a circle 2 in (5 cm) larger than the top of the pie plate; a pastry lid should also be 2 in (5 cm) larger. Roll the dough up loosely around the rolling pin, and unroll over the dish.

3 Gently ease the dough into the dish, pressing it firmly and neatly into the bottom edge. Be very careful not to stretch the dough. Carefully trim off the excess dough with a table knife. If there are any holes, patch them with bits of dough.

PREBAKING PASTRY

A pastry shell can be partly baked before adding a filling, to help it stay crisp, or it may be fully baked if the filling itself does not need to be cooked. The shell is filled with baking beans to weigh down the dough while it is in the oven.

1 Prick the pastry shell all over with a fork. Line with a piece of foil or waxed paper, letting it come high above the rim so it can be lifted out easily after baking.

2 Fill the shell with ceramic baking beans, dried legumes, or uncooked rice, and bake in a preheated oven at 375°F (190°C) for 10 minutes.

3 Remove the beans and foil. Return the shell to the oven and bake for 5 minutes (part baked) or 15 minutes (fully baked). If the pastry rises during baking, gently press it down with your hand.

STEAMED PUDDINGS

Light cakelike desserts and rich suet batters can both be gently cooked by steaming. Be sure to make the seal tight so moisture cannot get inside. It is important to keep the water in the saucepan topped up, so boil some water ready to add to the pan when needed.

1 Spoon the batter into a greased, heatproof bowl. Layer a piece of buttered waxed paper with a piece of foil and make a pleat across the middle, to allow for the pudding's expansion during cooking. Butter the paper.

2 Place the foil and paper, buttered-side down, over the top of the bowl. Secure by tying string tightly under the rim. Form a handle with another piece of string. Trim away excess paper and foil.

3 Put a trivet or upturned saucer or plate in the bottom of a saucepan and half fill with water. Bring to a simmer. Lower the bowl into the saucepan; add more boiling water to come halfway up the side of the bowl. Cover tightly and steam for the specified time. Make sure the water stays at simmering point and top up when necessary.

DECORATIVE EDGES

A simple way to give a decorative finish to a pie is to crimp the edge. Place the tips of your thumb and forefinger of one hand against the outside rim of the dish. With the forefinger of your other hand, gently push the dough edge outward between the thumb and finger, and pinch the pastry to make a rounded "V" shape. Repeat this action all around the top crust. Alternatively, push and pinch in the opposite direction, working from the outside of the edge inward.

Decorating pies & tarts

Keep dough trimmings to make small decorative shapes. Cut them freehand or use cutters. They can be fixed to the edge of a pastry shell or arranged on the top crust. If the dough has a glaze, attach the shapes with water, then apply the glaze all over the pie, brushing it on gently so the shapes are not disturbed.

•

A dough crust can be brushed with a glaze before baking. A little milk or beaten egg will give a shiny finish, as will egg white alone – this is a good way to use up whites when the dough is made with egg yolks. Sprinkle the crust with sugar for a crisp, sweet glaze.

APPLE BREAD PUDDING

SERVES 6

2 lb (1 kg) cooking apples, quartered, cored, peeled, and sliced

1/2 cup (125 g) sugar

3 tbsp water

2 tbsp apricot jam

1/2 cup (125 g) butter, softened, plus extra for greasing

12 slices of bread, crusts removed

6 IN (15 CM) SQUARE CAKE PAN

1 Put the apples, sugar, and measured water in a saucepan and cook over a medium heat for 10–15 minutes until the apples are soft but still holding their shape. Stir in the apricot jam.

2 Spread the butter on one side of each slice of bread. Lightly butter the cake pan and assemble the pudding (see box, right).

3 Bake in a preheated oven at 400°F (200°C) for about 40 minutes until crisp and golden. Serve hot.

Assembling the bread pudding

Use 8 of the bread slices to line the pan, cutting them into strips or squares as necessary, and placing them buttered-side down. Spoon in the apple mixture. Cut the remaining slices of bread into quarters diagonally. Arrange the quarters, buttered-side up, on top of the apple mixture.

SPECIAL SPONGE CAKE

SERVES 6

butter for greasing

1 lb (500 g) cooking apples, quartered, cored, peeled, and sliced

1/2 cup (90 g) packed brown sugar

grated zest and juice of 1 lemon

CAKE TOPPING

1/2 cup (125 g) baking margarine, straight from the refrigerator

1/2 cup (125 g) sugar

2 eggs, beaten

1 cup (125 g) self-rising flour

1 tsp baking powder

5 CUP (1.25 LITER) BAKING DISH

1 Lightly butter the baking dish and arrange the apples in the bottom. Sprinkle the brown sugar and the lemon zest and juice over.

2 Make the cake topping: put the margarine, sugar, eggs, flour, and baking powder in a large bowl, and beat until smooth and well blended. Spoon on top of the apple slices, and level the surface.

3 Bake in a preheated oven at 350°F (180°C) for about 45 minutes until the cake topping is well risen, golden, and springy to the touch. Serve hot.

SPICED SPONGE CAKE

Add 1 tsp ground cinnamon to the sponge topping, and 1/3 cup (60 g) raisins, 1 tsp ground cinnamon, and 1 tsp ground mixed spice to the apple mixture.

Cook's know-how

Instead of the brown sugar on top of the apples, you can use apricot jam, with the grated zest and juice of an orange rather than the lemon. To make a Christmas Sponge Cake, use mincemeat instead of the sugar or jam, or a mixture of chopped dried cranberries and apricots with 2 tbls (30 g) brown sugar and a splash of brandy, rum, or sherry.

APPLE BROWN BETTY

Easy to prepare from ingredients often on hand, this pudding is real comfort food, and it can be made with fruits other than apples if you prefer. Serve it with vanilla ice cream or whipped cream.

SERVES 6

2–3 tbls (30–45 g) butter

3 cups (175 g) fresh bread crumbs

2 lb (1 kg) cooking apples, quartered, cored, peeled, and thinly sliced

1/2 cup (125 g) sugar, plus extra for sprinkling

1 tbsp lemon juice

1–2 tsp ground cinnamon

DEEP 1 1/2–2 1/2 QUART (1.5–2 LITER) BAKING DISH

1 Melt the butter in a skillet. Add the bread crumbs and stir over a medium heat for 5 minutes or until the crumbs are crisp and golden. Remove from the heat.

2 Toss the apples with the sugar, lemon juice, and ground cinnamon.

3 Press one-quarter of the crisp bread crumbs over the bottom of the dish. Cover with half of the apple mixture and sprinkle with an additional one-quarter of the bread crumbs.

4 Arrange the remaining apple mixture on top of the bread crumbs, spoon any juices over, and cover with the remaining bread crumbs. Sprinkle the top of the dessert lightly with sugar.

5 Cover the dish with foil. Bake in a preheated oven at 400°F (200°C) for about 20 minutes.

6 Remove the foil and continue baking for 20 minutes longer or until the apples are tender and the top is golden brown. Serve warm.

APPLE & CRANBERRY BROWN BETTY

Add 6 oz (175 g) fresh or thawed frozen cranberries to the apple mixture. Add a little more sugar if necessary.

PEACH MELBA BROWN BETTY

Substitute 3 peeled, pitted, and sliced peaches, and 1½ cups (250 g) raspberries for the apples. Omit the lemon juice and cinnamon.

Cook's know-how

White or brown bread can be used for the bread crumbs. Whole wheat gives a nutty flavor, and mixed grain gives an interesting texture. For best results, the bread should be about 2 days old.

BAKED APPLES

SERVES 6

6 cooking apples

1/2 cup (90 g) packed brown sugar

6 tbls (90 g) butter, diced

3 tbsp water

1 Wipe the apples, and remove the cores using an apple corer. Make a shallow cut through the skin around the middle of each apple.

2 Put the apples into a baking dish and fill their middles with the sugar and butter. Pour the water around the apples.

3 Bake in a preheated oven at 375°F (190°C) for 40–45 minutes until the apples are soft. Serve hot, spooning all the juices from the dish over the apples.

CITRUS BAKED APPLES

Add the finely grated zest of 1 orange or 1 lemon to the brown sugar.

BAKED APPLES WITH MINCEMEAT

Use 4 oz (125 g) mincemeat instead of the sugar and butter.

433

JAMAICAN BANANAS

SERVES 4

2–3 tbls (30–45 g) unsalted butter

2–3 tbsp dark brown sugar

1/2 tsp ground cinnamon

1/4 cup (60 ml) dark rum

4 firm but ripe bananas, cut in half lengthwise

vanilla ice cream to serve

1 Put the butter and sugar into a large, heavy skillet, and heat gently until the butter has melted and sugar dissolved. Stir to blend together, then cook gently, stirring, for about 5 minutes.

2 Stir the cinnamon and rum into the caramel mixture, then add the banana halves. Cook for 3 minutes on each side until warmed through.

3 Transfer the bananas and hot sauce to serving plates. Serve at once, with scoops of vanilla ice cream.

Cook's know-how

If you want to serve these bananas to children, use the freshly squeezed juice of an orange instead of the rum, plus the grated orange zest, if you think they will like it. In summer you can bake the bananas wrapped in foil on the barbecue and make the sauce separately.

PLUM CRUMBLE

SERVES 6

2 lb (1 kg) plums, halved and pitted

1/4 cup (60 g) brown sugar

1 tsp ground cinnamon

CRUMBLE TOPPING

2 cups (250 g) self-rising whole wheat flour

6 tbls (90 g) butter

2/3 cup (150 g) brown sugar

1 Put the plums into a shallow baking dish and sprinkle with the sugar and cinnamon.

2 Make the topping: put the flour into a bowl, and rub in the butter with the fingertips until the mixture resembles fine bread crumbs. Stir in the sugar.

3 Sprinkle the topping evenly over the plums, without pressing it down. Bake in a preheated oven at 350°F (180°C) for 30–40 minutes until golden. Serve the crumble hot.

CRUNCHY APRICOT CRUMBLE

Substitute fresh apricots for the plums, and omit the cinnamon. Substitute oatmeal or muesli for half of the flour in the crumble topping, or use up to 1 cup (125 g) chopped toasted hazelnuts. You can also use half all-purpose and half whole wheat flour.

RHUBARB & GINGER CRUMBLE

Substitute 2 lb (1 kg) rhubarb, cut into 1 in (2.5 cm) pieces, for the plums. Put into a saucepan with the sugar, 2 tbsp water, and 1 tsp ground ginger instead of the cinnamon, and cook gently until the rhubarb is soft.

CHERRIES JUBILEE

SERVES 4

14 oz (400 g) Morello cherries in syrup from a jar or a can
2–3 tbsp sugar
5 tbls (75 ml) brandy
a few drops of almond extract
vanilla ice cream to serve

FRESH CHERRIES JUBILEE

Replace the Morello cherries with 1 lb (500 g) fresh cherries. Pit the cherries and poach them in 1 cup (250 ml) red wine and ½ cup (100 g) sugar until tender. Substitute the poaching liquid for the syrup.

1 Drain the cherries, reserving ½ cup (125 ml) of the syrup. Put the cherries into a saucepan with the measured syrup and the sugar.

2 Heat gently, stirring, until the sugar has dissolved, then bring to a boil. Simmer for about 5 minutes until the liquid has thickened and reduced by about half.

3 Pour the brandy over the cherries, and add the almond extract. Boil to evaporate the alcohol, then spoon the hot cherries and syrup over scoops of vanilla ice cream, and serve at once.

Cook's know-how

Instead of boiling the syrup until it is reduced in step 2, stir in 1 tsp cornstarch mixed to a paste with a little cold water. Bring to a boil, stirring, until thickened.
The cherries and their sauce are very versatile – serve them with meringues and cream, or spooned over slices of meringue or chocolate roulade, or over scoops of vanilla or frozen yogurt ice cream.

FRUIT FRITTERS

SERVES 6

2 apples
3 bananas
juice of ½ lemon
sunflower oil for deep-frying
¼ cup (60 g) sugar
1 tsp ground cinnamon
BATTER
1 cup (125 g) all-purpose flour
1 tbsp confectioners' sugar
1 egg, separated
2/3 cup (150 ml) mixed milk and water

1 Quarter, core, and peel the apples. Cut the apples and bananas into bite-sized pieces. Toss the pieces in the lemon juice to prevent discoloration.

2 Make the batter: sift the flour and sugar into a bowl, and make a well. Add the egg yolk and a little of the milk mixture and beat together. Whisk in half of the remaining milk mixture, drawing in the flour to form a smooth batter. Add the remaining milk.

3 Beat the egg white in a separate clean bowl until stiff but not dry. Fold into the batter until evenly mixed.

4 Heat the oil in a deep-fat fryer to 375°F (190°C). Pat the fruit dry. Dip each piece of fruit into the batter, lower into the hot oil, and cook in batches for 3–4 minutes until golden and crisp. Drain on paper towels and keep warm while cooking the remainder.

5 Combine the sugar and cinnamon, sprinkle generously over the fritters, and serve at once.

Cook's know-how

For a light, crisp batter, the egg white should be beaten and folded in just before you are ready to cook the fritters – don't leave the batter to stand or it will lose its airy texture.

FRENCH PANCAKES

SERVES 4

4 tbls (60 g) butter, softened, plus extra for greasing

1/4 cup (60 g) sugar

2 eggs, beaten

1/2 cup (60 g) self-rising flour

1 1/4 cups (300 ml) milk

apricot jam and sugar to serve

8-HOLE MUFFIN PAN WITH 3 IN (7 CM) CUPS

1 Combine the butter and sugar in a bowl and cream together until soft. Beat in the eggs, a little at a time, then fold in the flour.

2 In a small saucepan, heat the milk to just below boiling point. Stir into the creamed mixture.

3 Lightly butter the muffin pan molds, and divide the batter equally among them. Bake in a preheated oven at 375°F (190°C) for about 20 minutes until the pancakes are well risen and golden brown.

4 Slide the pancakes out of the molds, and serve with apricot jam and sugar. To eat, place a little jam in the middle of each pancake, fold in half, and sprinkle with sugar.

CREPES SUZETTE

SERVES 4

juice of 2 oranges

1/2 cup (125 g) unsalted butter

1/4 cup (60 g) sugar

3–4 tbsp orange liqueur or brandy

CREPES

1 cup (125 g) all-purpose flour

1 egg

1 tbsp oil, plus extra for frying

1 1/4 cups (300 ml) milk

7–8 IN (18–20 CM) SKILLET

1 Make the crêpes: sift the flour into a bowl. Make a well in the middle. Mix together the egg, 1 tbsp oil, and the milk, and pour into well. Gradually beat in the flour, to make a fairly thin batter.

2 Heat a little oil in the skillet, then wipe away the excess oil. Add 2–3 tbsp batter to the pan, tilting it to coat the bottom evenly. Cook for 45–60 seconds, then turn over, and cook the other side for about 30 seconds. Slide the crêpe out onto a warmed plate.

3 Repeat to make 7 more crêpes. Stack the crêpes on top of each other as soon as they are cooked (they will not stick together).

4 Make the orange sauce and add and fold the crêpes (see box, right). Heat to warm through.

Cook's know-how

In traditional French restaurants the crêpes are usually flambéed with orange liqueur or brandy at the table. At home this is not so practical, which is why the alcohol is simply heated with the other sauce ingredients in this recipe.

Making the sauce for the crêpes

Put the orange juice, butter, sugar, and liqueur or brandy into a large skillet, and boil for 5 minutes until reduced.
Place 1 crêpe in the pan, coat with sauce, fold in half, then in half again. Move to one side of the pan. Add another crêpe. Coat with the sauce, and fold as before. Repeat with the remaining crêpes.

MAGIC LEMON PUDDING

SERVES 4

60 g (2 oz) butter, softened, plus extra for greasing

grated zest and juice of 1 large lemon

1/2 cup (90 g) sugar

2 eggs, separated

1/4 cup (30 g) all-purpose flour

3/4 cup (175 ml) milk

lemon or lime slices to decorate

SHALLOW 2 1/2 CUP (600 ML) BAKING DISH

1 Put the butter, lemon zest, and sugar into a bowl and beat together until pale and fluffy.

2 Add the egg yolks, flour, and lemon juice, and stir to combine. Gradually stir in the milk until evenly mixed.

3 Beat the egg whites until stiff but not dry. Gradually fold into the lemon mixture batter.

4 Lightly butter the baking dish. Pour the lemon batter into the dish, and put the dish into a roasting pan. Add enough hot water to the roasting pan to come almost to the rim of the dish. Bake in a preheated oven at 325°F (160°C) for 40 minutes or until the cake topping feels springy. Serve hot, decorated with lemon or lime slices.

Cook's know-how

This "magic" pudding separates during cooking to form a cake topping with a tangy lemon sauce beneath.

PINEAPPLE UPSIDE-DOWN CAKE

SERVES 8

4 tbls (60 g) butter, softened, plus extra for greasing

1/2 cup plus 2 tbls (60 g) brown sugar

7 oz (200 g) canned pineapple rings in natural juice, drained, and juice reserved

4 dried apricots, coarsely chopped

SPONGE

1/2 cup (125 g) butter, softened

1/2 cup (125 g) sugar

2 eggs, beaten

1 1/2 cups (175 g) self-rising flour

1 tsp baking powder

7 IN (18 CM) DEEP, ROUND CAKE PAN

1 Lightly butter the pan and line the bottom with parchment paper. Cream together the butter and sugar and spread evenly over the parchment paper.

2 Arrange the pineapple rings on top of the butter and sugar mixture, and sprinkle the chopped dried apricots between the pineapple rings.

3 Make the cake: put the butter, sugar, eggs, flour, and baking powder into a bowl with 2 tbsp of the reserved pineapple juice. Beat for 2 minutes or until smooth and well blended. Spoon the batter on top of the pineapple rings and level the surface.

4 Bake in a preheated oven at 350°F (180°C) for about 45 minutes until the cake is well risen and springy to the touch. Invert the cake onto a warmed serving plate, and serve at once.

APRICOT UPSIDE-DOWN PUDDING

Substitute 14 oz (400 g) canned apricot halves for the pineapple, and 2 tbsp chopped ginger for the dried apricots.

DESSERT FONDUES

We are all used to savory fondues made with cheese or meat, but dessert fondues are less well known. This is a pity, because they are quick and easy to prepare and great fun to share at the end of an informal meal. Offer a good selection of dippers for dunking and you can't go wrong.

DARK CHOCOLATE FONDUE

SERVES 6

7 oz (200 g) good-quality semisweet chocolate

2 tbls (30 g) sugar

1/2 cup (125 ml) water

finely grated zest of 2 oranges (optional)

dippers of your choice (see box, below)

1 Break the chocolate into small pieces and put them into a heatproof bowl. Sit the bowl on top of a small saucepan of gently simmering water, making sure the bottom of the bowl does not touch the water or the chocolate might get too hot and "seize" into a ball. Heat very gently, stirring only once or twice, until the chocolate has just melted, then remove the pan from the heat, keeping the bowl over the hot water.

2 Put the sugar into another saucepan, pour in the measured water, and bring to a boil. Simmer for 5 minutes, then slowly stir this sugar syrup into the melted chocolate and whisk until smooth. Stir in the orange zest, if using.

3 Pour the chocolate fondue into a fondue pot and place over a low flame to keep warm. Serve with dippers of your choice.

WHITE CHOCOLATE FONDUE

SERVES 6

6 oz (175 g) good-quality white chocolate

2/3 cup (150 ml) heavy cream

dippers of your choice (see box, below)

1 Roughly chop the chocolate and put the pieces into a heatproof bowl. Sit the bowl on top of a small saucepan of gently simmering water, making sure the bottom of the bowl does not touch the water or the chocolate might get too hot and "seize" into a ball. Heat very gently, stirring only once or twice, until the chocolate has just melted, then remove the bowl from the pan and set aside.

2 Pour the cream into a heavy-based saucepan and bring almost to boiling point (you should see bubbles beginning to break around the edge of the cream). Slowly pour the hot cream onto the melted chocolate, stirring gently.

3 Pour the chocolate fondue into a fondue pot and place over a low flame to keep warm. Serve with dippers of your choice.

CHOCOLATE FUDGE FONDUE

SERVES 6

4 oz (125 g) caramel and fudge chocolate bar

3 oz (90 g) good-quality semisweet chocolate

1/2 cup (125 g) butter

3 tbls (60 g) maple syrup

4 tbsp heavy cream

dippers of your choice (see box, below left)

1 Roughly chop the caramel and fudge bar and the semisweet chocolate, and put the pieces into a small saucepan. Cut the butter into small cubes and drop them into the pan, then pour in the maple syrup.

2 Cook the mixture over a very low heat, stirring only once or twice, for 10–12 minutes. Remove from the heat and beat together until smooth, then beat in the cream.

3 Pour the chocolate fondue into a fondue pot and place over a low flame to keep warm. Serve with dippers of your choice.

Cook's know-how

When a recipe calls for good-quality chocolate, this means a chocolate with a high cocoa solids content. This will be given on the label, so always check before you buy. A chocolate with more than 50% cocoa solids will be good, but for the very best quality, look for one with around 70% cocoa solids.

White chocolate is not a true chocolate, so it is important to check the label carefully – to have a good "chocolatey" flavor it must contain cocoa solids among its ingredients.

DIPPERS

Increase the fun of your fondue by offering as wide a choice as possible of ingredients for dipping and dunking. You can be as creative as you like, but bear in mind that the ingredients need to be speared on small forks so they should not be too hard or crisp. Conversely, if the texture of the dippers is too soft and crumbly, they will drop into the pot and spoil the fondue. Here is a selection of tried-and-tested dippers.

- Strawberries with hulls intact, either whole fruits or halved if large
- Cherries, still on their stems if possible
- Banana slices (slightly underripe)
- Fig wedges
- Apricots and peaches, pitted and cut into quarters
- Kiwi fruits, cut lengthwise into eighths
- Pears, cut into chunky wedges and tossed in lemon juice

- Grapes, the large seedless variety
- Dried fruits, such as apricots, peaches, or mango
- Panettone cake, cut into cubes
- Brioche, cut into squares
- Long cookies, such as Viennese fingers, langues de chats, or cigarettes russes

CLOCKWISE FROM TOP: Dippers, Dark Chocolate Fondue, White Chocolate Fondue, Chocolate Fudge Fondue.

BREAD PUDDING

SERVES 6

12 thin slices of white bread, crusts removed

about ½ cup (125 g) butter, softened, plus extra for greasing

1 cup (175 g) mixed dried fruit

grated zest of 2 lemons

½ cup (125 g) granulated brown sugar

2½ cups (600 ml) milk

2 eggs

8 CUP (1.7 LITER) BAKING DISH

1 Spread one side of each slice of bread with a thick layer of butter. Cut each slice of bread in half diagonally. Lightly butter the baking dish and arrange 12 of the triangles, buttered-side down, in the bottom of the dish.

2 Sprinkle half of the dried fruit, lemon zest, and sugar over. Top with the remaining bread, buttered-side up. Sprinkle the remaining fruit, lemon zest, and sugar over.

3 Beat together the milk and eggs, and strain over the bread. Leave for 1 hour so that the bread can absorb some of the liquid.

4 Bake in a preheated oven at 350°F (180°C) for about 40 minutes until the bread slices on the top of the pudding are a golden brown color and crisp, and the custard mixture has set completely. Serve at once.

BREAD PUDDING WITH MARMALADE

Spread 6 of the slices of bread with thick-cut marmalade after spreading all of them with the butter. Halve the slices, and arrange the buttered ones buttered-side down in the dish. Sprinkle with the dried fruit, lemon zest, and sugar, then arrange the remaining triangles, marmalade-side up, on top.

BREAD PUDDING WITH APRICOTS

Add ½ cup (60 g) roughly chopped dried apricots to the dried fruit.

RICE PUDDING

SERVES 4

1 tbls (15 g) butter, plus extra for buttering the dish

⅓ cup (60 g) short-grain rice

2½ cups (600 ml) milk

2 tbls (30 g) sugar

1 strip of lemon zest

¼ tsp grated nutmeg

4 CUP (900 ML) BAKING DISH

1 Lightly butter the baking dish. Rinse the rice under cold running water and drain well.

2 Put the rice into the dish and stir in the milk. Leave for about 30 minutes to allow the rice to soften.

3 Add the sugar and lemon zest to the rice mixture, and stir to mix. Sprinkle the surface of the milk with freshly grated nutmeg and dot with small pats of butter.

4 Bake in a preheated oven at 300°F (150°C) for 2–2½ hours until the skin of the pudding is brown. Serve at once.

Cook's know-how

Short-grain rice absorbs the milk to give a rich, creamy consistency. For the creamiest pudding, use whole milk.

CHILLED RICE WITH PEARS

Let the pudding cool, then lift off the skin. Chill the pudding and serve in glass dishes, topped with slices of poached fresh or canned pears, topped with melted strawberry jam.

PLUM PUDDING

This is a rich, dark pudding, laden with dried fruit, spices, and alcohol – the traditional way to finish a British Christmas meal. Serve this with the easy-to-make hard sauce (see below).

SERVES 8–10

²⁄₃ cup (90 g) self-rising flour

¹⁄₂ cup (125 g) shredded shortening or grated chilled butter

¹⁄₄ cup (30 g) blanched almonds, shredded

2 carrots, grated

1¹⁄₃ cups (250 g) raisins

²⁄₃ cup (125 g) dried currants

²⁄₃ cup (125 g) golden raisins

2 cups (125 g) fresh bread crumbs

¹⁄₄ tsp grated nutmeg

¹⁄₂ cup (60 g) mixed candied peel, chopped

¹⁄₂ cup (90 g) packed brown sugar

grated zest and juice of 1 lemon

2 eggs, beaten

butter for greasing

5 tbls (75 ml) dark rum or brandy

hard sauce to serve

5 CUPS (1.25 LITER) PUDDING MOLD

1 In a large bowl, combine the flour, shortening or butter, almonds, carrot, raisins, currants, golden raisins, bread crumbs, nutmeg, candied peel, sugar, and lemon zest. Add the lemon juice and eggs, and stir until well combined.

2 Lightly butter the pudding mold. Spoon in the pudding mixture and level the surface.

3 Cover with buttered waxed paper, then foil, both pleated in the middle. Secure the paper and foil in place by tying string under the rim of the bowl (page 431).

4 Put the bowl into a steamer or saucepan of simmering water, making sure the water comes halfway up the side of the bowl. Cover and steam, topping up with boiling water as needed, for about 6 hours.

5 Remove the bowl from the steamer or pan and leave to cool. Remove the paper and foil covering. Make a few holes in the pudding with a fine skewer, and pour in the rum or brandy.

6 Cover the pudding with fresh waxed paper and foil. Store in a cool place for up to 3 months.

7 To reheat for serving, steam the pudding for 2–3 hours. Serve at once, with brandy butter.

Hard Sauce

Make your own hard sauce by creaming together 1 cup (200 g) each of unsalted butter and sugar, and 6 tbls (90 ml) brandy. The hard sauce can be frozen for up to 3 months.

STEAMED JAM PUDDING

SERVES 4–6

¹⁄₂ cup (125 g) soft butter or margarine, plus extra for greasing

3 tbsp jam

¹⁄₂ cup (125 g) sugar

2 eggs, beaten

1¹⁄₂ cups (175 g) self-rising flour

1 tsp baking powder

about 1 tbsp milk

5 CUP (1.25 LITER) PUDDING MOLD

1 Lightly grease the pudding mold, and spoon the jam into the bottom.

2 Put the butter or margarine, sugar, eggs, flour, and baking powder into a large bowl, and beat until smooth and thoroughly blended. Add enough milk to give a dropping consistency.

3 Spoon the batter into the pudding mold, and smooth the surface. Cover with greased waxed paper and foil, both pleated in the middle. Secure with string (page 431).

4 Put the bowl into a steamer or saucepan of simmering water, making sure the water comes halfway up the side of the bowl. Cover and steam, topping up with boiling water as needed, for about 1¹⁄₂ hours. Turn the pudding out onto a warmed plate, and serve hot.

STEAMED PUDDING

SERVES 4–6

butter for greasing

4 1/2 tbls (90 ml) maple syrup

1 cup (125 g) self-rising flour

1/2 cup (125 g) vegetable shortening cut into cubes or grated butter

2 cups (125 g) fresh white bread crumbs

1/4 cup (60 g) sugar

1/2 cup (125 g) milk

4 CUP (900 ML) PUDDING MOLD

1 Lightly butter the mold and spoon the maple syrup into the bottom.

2 Put the flour, shortening or butter, bread crumbs, and sugar into a bowl and stir to combine. Stir in enough milk to give a dropping consistency. Spoon into the bowl on top of the syrup.

3 Cover the bowl with buttered parchment paper and foil, both pleated in the middle. Secure by tying string under the rim of the bowl (page 431).

4 Put the bowl into a steamer or saucepan of simmering water, making sure the water comes halfway up the side of the bowl if using a saucepan. Cover and steam, topping up with boiling water as needed, for about 3 hours. Turn out the pudding, and serve.

MINCEMEAT & ALMOND TART

This is a rich dessert, ideal for a Chistmas dinner party or lunch.
For an everyday dessert you can use a little less mincemeat and add some stewed apple,
which will give a lighter texture and flavor.

SERVES 8–10

3/4 cup (175 g) butter, softened

3/4 cup (175 g) sugar

4 eggs

1/2 cup (175 g) ground almonds

1 tsp almond extract

about 8 tbsp good-quality, store-bought mincemeat

TART CRUST

2 cups (250 g) all-purpose flour

1/2 cup (125 g) chilled butter, cut into cubes

1/4 cup (60 g) sugar

1 egg, beaten

TOPPING

1 1/2 cups (175 g) confectioners' sugar, sifted

juice of 1/2 lemon

1–2 tbsp water

1/2 cup (60 g) slivered almonds

DEEP 11 IN (28 CM) FLUTED TART PAN

1 Make the crust: put the flour into a large bowl. Add the butter and rub in with the fingertips until the mixture resembles fine bread crumbs. Stir in the sugar, then mix in the egg to bind to a soft, pliable dough. Wrap the dough in plastic wrap and chill for about 30 minutes.

2 Roll out the dough on a lightly floured surface and use to line the pan. Prick the bottom with a fork. Cover and chill while preparing the filling.

3 Put the butter and sugar into a large bowl and cream together until pale and fluffy. Add the eggs one at a time, beating well after each addition, then mix in the ground almonds and almond extract.

4 Spread the mincemeat evenly over the bottom of the pastry shell. Pour the almond mixture over the mincemeat.

5 Bake in a preheated oven at 375°F (190°C) for about 40 minutes until the filling is golden and firm to the touch. Cover loosely with foil if it is browning too much.

6 Meanwhile, make the topping: stir together the confectioners' sugar, lemon juice, and enough water to make a thin glaze. Spread evenly over the tart, then sprinkle with the almonds.

7 Return to the oven for 5 minutes or until the glaze is shiny and the almonds lightly colored. Serve warm or cold.

STRAWBERRY & RHUBARB PIE

SERVES 6–8

3/4 cup (150 g) sugar, plus extra for sprinkling

1/3 cup (45 g) cornstarch

1 1/2 lb (750 g) rhubarb, cut into 1/2 in (1 cm) slices

1 cinnamon stick, halved

12 oz (375 g) strawberries, hulled and halved

PIECRUST DOUGH

4 1/2 cups (175 g) all-purpose flour

6 tbls (90 g) chilled butter, cut into cubes

about 2 tbsp cold water

9 IN (23 CM) TART PAN

1 Make the dough: put the flour into a large bowl, add the butter, and rub in with the fingertips until the mixture resembles fine bread crumbs. Add enough water to bind to a soft, but not sticky dough. Wrap the dough in plastic wrap and leave to chill in the refrigerator for at least 30 minutes.

2 Meanwhile, combine the sugar with the cornstarch and toss with the rhubarb, cinnamon, and strawberries. Leave to soak for 15–20 minutes.

3 On a lightly floured surface, divide the dough in half and roll out one half into a thin circle to line the bottom and sides of the tart pan.

4 Put the soaked fruit into the pastry shell, removing the cinnamon.

5 Roll out the second half of dough to the same size as the first circle. Cut a 1/2 in (1 cm) strip from around the edge of the dough.

6 Cut the remaining pastry into 1/2 in (1 cm) strips and arrange in a lattice on top of the pie. Brush the ends with water and attach the long strip around the rim of the pie. Sprinkle with 1–2 tbsp sugar.

7 Bake in a preheated oven at 425°F (220°C) for 10 minutes; reduce the oven temperature to 350°F (180°C), and bake for a further 30–40 minutes until the fruit is just cooked, and the pastry golden. Serve warm or cold.

BAKED APPLE DUMPLINGS

SERVES 4

4 cooking apples, peeled and cored

1/4 cup (60 g) brown granulated sugar

1/2 tsp ground cinnamon

milk for glazing

PIECRUST PASTRY DOUGH

3 cups (375 g) all-purpose flour

6 tbls (90 g) chilled butter, cut into cubes, plus extra for greasing

6 tbls (90 g) vegetable shortening, cut into cubes

3–4 tbsp cold water

1 Make the dough: put the flour into a large bowl. Add the butter and shortening, and rub in with the fingertips until the mixture resembles fine bread crumbs. Mix in enough water to make a soft, pliable dough. Wrap the dough in plastic wrap and chill for about 30 minutes.

2 Divide the dough into 4 pieces. Roll out each piece on a lightly floured surface and cut into an 7 in (18 cm) circle. Reserve the trimmings. Put an apple in the middle of each circle and make 4 dumplings (see box, above right).

Making the apple dumplings

Fill the apples with the brown sugar and cinnamon. Draw up a dough circle to enclose each apple, sealing the seams with a little water. Place, with the seams underneath, on a baking sheet.

3 Cut leaf shapes from the dough trimmings, and use to decorate the tops of the dumplings, attaching them with a little water. Make a hole in the top of each dumpling, and lightly brush all over with milk.

4 Bake in a preheated oven at 400°F (200°C) for 35–40 minutes until the pastry is golden and the apples tender. Serve hot.

SAUCES FOR PUDDINGS

SWEET WHITE SAUCE

Blend 1 tbsp cornstarch with 1 tbsp sugar, and a little milk taken from 1 1/4 cups (300 ml). Bring the remaining milk to a boil and stir into the cornstarch mixture. Return to the saucepan and heat gently, stirring, until thickened. If preferred, add flavorings such as grated orange zest, brandy, rum, or vanilla extract to the sauce. Serve warm.

CUSTARD SAUCE

Blend together 3 eggs, 2 tbls sugar, and 1 tsp cornstarch. Heat 2 1/2 cups (600 ml) milk to just below boiling and stir into the egg mixture. Return to the pan and heat gently, stirring, until thickened. Strain into a cold bowl to prevent additional cooking, and serve warm or cold.

SABAYON SAUCE

Put 4 egg yolks, 1/4 cup (60 g) sugar, and 2/3 cup (150 ml) dry white wine into a bowl over a saucepan of gently simmering water. Beat for 5–8 minutes or until the mixture is frothy and thick. Remove from the heat and beat in the grated zest of 1 orange. Serve at once or, to serve cool, continue beating the mixture until cool.

APPLE PIE

For a successful double crust pie, the pastry underneath should be properly baked and not soggy. Putting the dish on a hot baking sheet at the start of baking is the key.

SERVES 6

1 1/2 lb (750 g) cooking apples, quartered, cored, peeled, and sliced

2 tbls (30 g) sugar, plus extra for sprinkling

2 tbsp water

rough puff pastry (page 430)

milk for glazing

9 1/2 IN (24 CM) PIE PLATE

1 Put the apples into a large pan and add the sugar and water. Cover and cook gently, stirring, for about 10 minutes until the apples are soft and fluffy. Taste for sweetness and add more sugar if necessary. Turn into a bowl and leave the apples to cool.

2 Divide the dough into 2 portions, 1 portion slightly larger than the other. Roll out the larger portion on a lightly floured surface and use to line the pie dish.

3 Spoon the apple filling onto the pastry shell, spreading it almost to the edge and then doming it in the middle.

4 Roll out the remaining dough. Brush the edge of the pastry shell with a little water, then lay the dough lid over the apple filling. Trim the edge, then crimp to seal. Make a small hole in the dough lid to allow the steam to escape.

5 Use the dough trimmings to make leaves to decorate the pie, attaching them with milk. Brush the lid with milk and sprinkle with sugar.

6 Put a baking sheet in the oven and preheat the oven to 425°F (220°C). Put the pie plate on the hot baking sheet (this helps ensure a crisp pastry bottom) and bake for 25–30 minutes until the pastry is golden.

DUTCH APPLE PIE

When cooking the apples, substitute soft light brown sugar for the sugar, and add 1/2 cup (90 g) raisins, 1/2 tsp ground cinnamon, and 1/2 tsp apple pie spice to the apple filling.

CITRUS APPLE PIE

When cooking the apples, add the grated zest and juice of 1 large lemon, and 3 tbsp fine-cut orange marmalade to the apples.

TARTE TATIN

SERVES 6

6 tbls (90 g) butter

1/2 cup (90 g) granulated brown sugar

5–6 firm, sweet apples

grated zest and juice of 1 lemon

TART CRUST

1 1/2 cups (175 g) all-purpose flour

1/2 cup (125 g) chilled butter, cut into cubes

1/4 cup (30 g) confectioners' sugar

1 egg yolk

about 1 tbsp cold water

SHALLOW 9 IN (23 CM) ROUND CAKE PAN

1 Make the dough: put the flour into a large bowl and add the butter. Rub in until the mixture resembles fine bread crumbs. Stir in the confectioners' sugar, then mix in the egg yolk and enough water to make a soft, but not sticky, dough. Wrap and chill for 30 minutes.

2 Put the butter and sugar into a pan and heat very gently until the sugar dissolves. Increase the heat and cook gently for 4–5 minutes until the mixture turns dark golden brown and is thick, but pourable. Pour evenly over the bottom of the pan.

3 Peel, core, and slice the apples. Toss them with the lemon zest and juice. Arrange in the cake pan (see box, below).

4 Roll out the dough on a lightly floured surface into a circle slightly larger than the pan. Lay the dough over the apples, tucking the excess down the side of the pan.

5 Bake in a preheated oven at 400°F (200°C) for 25–30 minutes until crisp and golden. Invert a serving plate on top of the pan, turn the pan and plate over, and lift the pan to reveal the caramelized apples. Serve warm or cold.

Arranging the apples in the cake pan

Arrange a single layer of the best apple slices in a circular pattern on top of the caramel mixture. Cover evenly with the remaining apple slices.

APPLE STRUDEL

SERVES 8

4 10 x 18 in (25 x 45 cm) sheets of phyllo dough pastry

4 tbls (60 g) butter, melted

1 cup (30 g) fresh white bread crumbs

2 tbls (15 g) slivered almonds

confectioners' sugar for dusting

FILLING

1 1/2 lb (750 g) cooking apples, quartered, cored, peeled, and sliced

grated zest and juice of 1 lemon

3 tbsp brown sugar

1/2 tsp apple pie spice

1/2 tsp ground cinnamon

2/3 cup (125 g) golden raisins

1/2 cup (60 g) blanched almonds, roughly chopped

1 Make the filling: mix together the apples, lemon, sugar, spice, cinnamon, raisins, and almonds.

2 Lightly brush 1 sheet of phyllo pastry dough with melted butter. Cover with the remaining sheets, brushing each with butter. Add the filling and finish the strudel (see box, right).

3 Brush the strudel with melted butter and sprinkle with the almonds. Bake in a preheated oven at 375°F (190°C) for 40–45 minutes until crisp and golden. Dust with confectioners' sugar. Serve warm or cold.

Finishing the strudel

Sprinkle the bread crumbs over the dough. Spoon the apple mixture along the middle of the dough.

Fold the dough to enclose the filling, turn over onto a baking sheet, and bend into a horseshoe shape.

THE APPLE COLLECTION

Apples have a natural affinity with pastry, and they are the best of fruits to cook with. In these three recipes, pastry is used in different ways to show the apples off to their best advantage – and to make the fruit go farther. When you are feeling indulgent, serve with vanilla ice cream or custard sauce.

APPLE TARTE AU CITRON

SERVES 10

4 eggs

1 1/4 cups (250 g) sugar

finely grated zest and juice of 2 lemons

1/2 cup (125 g) butter, melted

2 large cooking apples – about 12 oz (350 g) prepared weight

2 red eating apples, quartered, cored, and thinly sliced (leave the red skin on)

about 2 tbls brown sugar

TART CRUST

2 cups (250 g) all-purpose flour

1/4 cup (30 g) confectioners' sugar

1/2 cup (125 g) butter, cubed

1 egg, beaten

1 Make the dough: sift the flour and confectioners' sugar into a bowl and rub in the cubes of butter until the mixture resembles bread crumbs. Stir in the egg and bring together to form a dough. (If making the pastry in a food processor, process the flour, butter, and confectioners' sugar until like breadcrumbs, pour in the beaten egg, and pulse until the dough forms a ball.) Form the dough into a smooth ball, put inside a plastic bag, and chill in the refrigerator for at least 30 minutes.

2 Roll out the chilled dough on a lightly floured surface and use to line a deep 10 in (25 cm) loose-bottomed tart pan. Chill again for 30 minutes.

3 Prepare the filling: beat the eggs, caster sugar, and lemon zest and juice in a bowl. Stir in the warm melted butter, then coarsely grate the cooking apples directly into mixture and mix well.

4 Spread the runny lemon mixture in the chilled tart shell. Level the surface with the back of a spoon and arrange the red-skinned apples around the outside edge.

5 Bake on a hot baking sheet in a preheated oven at 400°F (200°C) for about 40–50 minutes or until the center feels firm to the touch and the apples are tinged brown.

CLASSIC APPLE CRUMBLE

SERVES 6

5 large cooking apples

3/4 cup plus 2 tbls (175 g) sugar

finely grated zest of 1 lemon

6 tbsp water

TOPPING

1 1/2 cups (175 g) all-purpose flour

6 tbls (90 g) butter

3 tbls (60 g) brown sugar

1 Quarter, peel, and core the apples, then slice them fairly thinly. Toss the slices in the sugar, lemon zest, and water. Put in a shallow 8 in (20 cm) baking dish.

2 Make the topping: put the flour in a bowl and rub in the butter until the mixture resembles fine bread crumbs, then stir in the sugar.

3 Sprinkle the topping evenly over the apple mixture in the dish and bake in a preheated oven at 350°F (180°C) for 40–45 minutes until golden brown and bubbling.

Cook's know-how

For a crunchier topping on the Classic Apple Crumble, use 4 oz (125 g) whole wheat flour and 2 oz (60 g) porridge oats or muesli instead of the all-purpose flour.

To sweeten cooking apples, especially windfall apples that are not at their best, use apricot jam instead of some – or all – of the sugar. Apricot jam gives a gentle sweetness, and it improves the texture of the apples, especially if you are using them for a puree or a pie.

BLACKBERRY & APPLE COBBLER

SERVES 4

2 large cooking apples

1 lb (500 g) blackberries

1/4 cup (60 g) sugar

finely grated zest and juice of 1 lemon

COBBLER TOPPING

2 cups (250 g) self-rising flour

4 tbls (60 g) butter, cubed

1/2 cup (90 g) sugar

6 tbls (90 ml) milk, plus extra for glazing

5 CM (2 IN) ROUND FLUTED COOKIE CUTTER

1 Quarter, peel, and core the apples, then cut into large slices, about 1/2 in (1 cm) thick.

2 Put the apples into a saucepan with the blackberries, sugar, and lemon zest and juice. Cover and simmer gently for 10–15 minutes until the apple pieces are tender but not broken up.

3 Meanwhile, make the cobbler topping: put the flour into a bowl, add the cubes of butter, and rub in with the fingertips until the mixture resembles fine bread crumbs. Stir in the sugar, add the milk, and mix to form a soft dough.

4 Roll out the dough on a lightly floured surface until 1/2 in (1 cm) thick. Cut out as many shapes as you can with the cookie cutter, then re-roll the trimmings and cut out more. If you do not have a cookie cutter, stamp out circles with the rim of a glass or coffeemug.

5 Transfer the fruit to a baking dish, arrange the pastry shapes on top and brush with milk to glaze.

6 Bake in a preheated oven at 425°F (220°C) for 15–20 minutes until the cobbler topping is golden.

CLOCKWISE FROM TOP RIGHT: Classic Apple Crumble, Apple Tarte au Citron, Blackberry & Apple Cobbler.

TREACLE TART

SERVES 8

1 cup (375 g) dark corn syrup

3 1/2 cups (200 g) fresh white or whole wheat bread crumbs

grated zest and juice of 1 large lemon

TART CRUST

1 1/2 cups (175 g) all-purpose flour

6 tbls (90 g) chilled butter, cut into cubes

about 2 tbsp cold water

10 IN (25 CM) LOOSE-BOTTOMED FLUTED TART PAN

1 Make the dough: put the flour into a large bowl, add the butter, and rub in with your fingertips until the mixture resembles fine bread crumbs. Mix in enough water to make a soft, pliable dough.

2 Wrap the dough in plastic wrap and leave to chill in the refrigerator for about 30 minutes.

3 Roll out the dough on a lightly floured surface and use to line the tart pan.

4 Gently heat the syrup in a saucepan until melted, and stir in the bread crumbs and lemon zest and juice. Pour into the tart shell.

5 Bake in a preheated oven at 400°F (200°C) for 10 minutes; reduce the oven temperature to 350°F (180°C), and bake for a further 30 minutes or until the pastry is golden and the filling firm.

6 Leave to cool in the pan for a few minutes. Serve warm, cut into slices.

Cook's know-how

To weigh the syrup, put the pan on the scales set to zero and pour in the syrup from the can.

FRENCH APPLE TART

SERVES 8–10

6 tbls (90 g) butter

3 lb (1.5 kg) cooking apples, quartered, cored, and cut into chunks

3 tbsp water

6 tbsp apricot jam

1/2 cup (125 g) sugar

grated zest of 1 large lemon

APPLE TOPPING & GLAZE

12 oz (375 g) sweet apples, quartered, cored, peeled, and sliced

juice of 1 lemon

1 tbsp sugar

6 tbsp apricot jam

TART CRUST

2 cups (250 g) all-purpose flour

1/2 cup (125 g) chilled butter, cubed

1/2 cup (125 g) sugar

4 egg yolks

11 IN (28 CM) LOOSE-BOTTOMED FLUTED TART PAN

BAKING BEANS

1 Make the dough: put the flour into a bowl and rub in the butter until the mixture resembles fine bread crumbs. Stir in the sugar, then the egg yolks and a little cold water, if needed, to make a soft dough. Wrap and chill for 30 minutes.

2 Melt the butter in a large saucepan, and add the cooking apples and water. Cover and cook very gently for 20–25 minutes until the apples are soft.

3 Rub the apples through a nylon strainer into a clean pan. Add the jam, sugar, and lemon zest. Cook over a high heat for 15–20 minutes, stirring constantly, until all the liquid has evaporated and the apple puree is thick. Leave to cool.

4 Roll out the dough on a lightly floured surface and use to line the tart pan. Prebake with the baking beans (page 431) in a preheated oven at 375°F (190°C) for 10–15 minutes. Remove the beans and foil and bake for another 5 minutes. Cool.

5 Spoon the apple puree into the crust. Arrange the apple slices on top, brush with lemon juice, and sprinkle with caster sugar. Return to the oven and bake for 30–35 minutes until the apples are tender and their edges lightly browned.

6 Heat the jam, work through a strainer, then brush over the apples. Serve warm or cold.

ALMOND TART

SERVES 6

1/2 cup (125 g) butter

1/2 cup (125 g) sugar

1 egg, lightly beaten

1 cup (125 g) ground rice or semolina

1/2 tsp almond extract

2 tbsp raspberry jam

confectioners' sugar for sprinkling

TART CRUST

1 1/2 cups (175 g) all-purpose flour

3 tbls (45 g) chilled butter, cut into cubes

3 tbls (45 g) chilled shortening, cut into cubes

about 2 tbsp cold water

milk for glazing

19 CM (7 1/2 IN) LOOSE-BOTTOMED FLUTED TART PAN

1 Make the dough: put the flour into a large bowl. Rub in the butter and shortening until the mixture resembles fine bread crumbs. Mix in enough water to make a soft, pliable dough. Wrap in plastic wrap and chill for 30 minutes.

2 Roll out the dough on a lightly floured work surface and use to line the tart pan. Reserve the trimmings.

3 Melt the butter in a saucepan, stir in the sugar, and cook for about 1 minute. Remove from the heat, leave to cool a little, then gradually stir in the egg, ground rice or semolina, and almond extract.

4 Spread the jam evenly over the bottom of the tart shell, and pour the almond filling on top.

5 Roll out the reserved dough trimmings, and cut into thin strips, long enough to fit across the tart. Arrange the strips on top of the almond filling to form a lattice, attaching them to the edge of the tart shell with a little milk.

6 Bake in a preheated oven at 400°F (200°C) for 45–50 minutes until the filling is well risen and golden and springs back when lightly pressed with a finger. If the pastry is browning too much, cover the tart loosely with foil.

7 Remove the tart from the oven. Sprinkle with confectioners' sugar and serve the tart warm or cold.

PECAN PIE

SERVES 6–8

1 1/4 cups (150 g) pecan halves

2 tbls (30 g) unsalted butter

1/4 cup (60 g) brown sugar

2 tbls (30 g) sugar

1/3 cup (125 ml) light corn syrup

3 tbsp brandy

1 tsp vanilla extract

2 tbsp light cream

1/4 tsp ground cinnamon

pinch of grated nutmeg

1 extra large egg, lightly beaten

2 egg yolks

TART CRUST

1 1/2 cups (175 g) all-purpose flour

6 tbls (90 g) chilled butter, cubed

about 2 tbsp cold water

1 egg white, lightly beaten

9 IN (23 CM) LOOSE-BOTTOMED FLUTED TART PAN

BAKING BEANS

1 Make the dough: put the flour into a bowl, add the butter, and rub in with your fingertips until the mixture resembles fine bread crumbs. Add enough water to make a soft dough. Leave to chill for about 30 minutes.

2 Roll out the dough on a lightly floured work surface and line the tart pan. Prebake with the beans (page 431) in a preheated oven at 350°F (180°C) for 10 minutes.

3 Remove the beans and foil, lightly brush the pie shell with egg white, and return to the oven for 1–2 minutes.

4 Meanwhile, toast the pecans in a preheated oven at 350°F (180°C), turning occasionally, for 10–15 minutes. Reserve a few pecan halves and coarsely chop the remainder.

5 Put the butter into a heavy saucepan and cook over a gentle heat until it turns golden brown. Add the sugars and corn syrup, and heat gently until the sugars dissolve. Add the brandy, bring to a boil, and cook for 5 minutes.

6 Remove from the heat and stir in the vanilla extract, cream, cinnamon, and nutmeg.

7 Beat together the egg and egg yolks. Beat a little hot syrup into the eggs. Add half of the syrup, little by little, then add the remainder. Leave to cool.

8 Arrange the chopped pecans and pecan halves in the pie shell. Pour the syrup and egg mixture over them. Bake in a preheated oven at 350°F (180°C) for about 40 minutes until golden brown and set. Leave to cool before serving.

FRENCH APRICOT & ALMOND TART

So often the star of the pastry counter, this golden fruit tart is easy enough to make at home. Fresh apricots really make it special, but if they are not available, canned apricots can be used instead.

SERVES 10

pastry cream (see box, right)

TOPPING

2 lb (1 kg) fresh apricots, halved and stoned

juice of 1 lemon

1/2 cup (125 ml) water

5 tbsp sugar

1 tsp arrowroot

1 tbsp brandy

2 tbsp toasted slivered almonds

TART CRUST

1 cup (250 g) all-purpose flour

1/2 cup (125 g) chilled butter, cubed

1/4 cup (60 g) sugar

1 egg, beaten

11 IN (28 CM) LOOSE-BOTTOMED FLUTED TART PAN

BAKING BEANS

1 Sift the flour into a large bowl. Add the butter and rub in until the mixture resembles fine bread crumbs.

2 Stir in the sugar, then mix in the egg to make a soft, pliable dough. Wrap in plastic wrap and chill for 30 minutes.

3 Roll out the dough on a lightly floured surface and use to line the tart pan. Prebake (page 431) in a preheated oven at 400°F (200°C) for 10 minutes until the tart shell is beginning to brown at the edge. Remove the beans and foil and bake for another 5–10 minutes. Leave to cool.

4 Put the apricots, cut-side down, in a shallow pan with the lemon juice, measured water, and sugar. Cover tightly and bring to a boil. Lower the heat and simmer gently for 3 minutes or until just soft.

5 Remove the apricots with a slotted spoon, reserving the juices. Drain on paper towels, and leave to cool.

6 Remove the tart shell from the pan and put on a serving plate. Spread the pastry cream over the pastry shell, and smooth the surface.

7 Arrange the apricots, cut-side down, on the pastry cream. Combine the arrowroot and brandy in a small bowl and stir in the reserved apricot juices.

8 Return the mixture to the pan and bring to a boil, stirring until thick. Add the toasted slivered almonds.

9 Spoon the glaze over the apricots, making sure they are evenly coated. (Add a little water to the glaze if it is too thick.) Leave to stand until the glaze has cooled and set. Serve the tart cold.

Pastry cream

Put 3 eggs, 1/2 cup (90 g) sugar, 1/2 cup (60 g) all-purpose flour, and 1 tsp vanilla extract into a bowl. Add 2 tbsp milk taken from 1 3/4 cups and mix until smooth. Pour the remaining milk into a heavy pan and bring almost to a boil. Pour onto the egg mixture, whisking well.

Rinse out the pan to remove any milk residue. Return the egg mixture to the pan, and cook over a gentle heat, stirring continuously, until thickened.

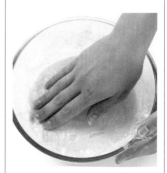

Pour into a bowl and cover with plastic wrap, gently pressing it over the surface of the cream to prevent a skin from forming. Leave to cool.

LEMON MERINGUE PIE

SERVES 8–10

grated zest and juice of 4 large lemons

generous ³/4 cup (90 g) cornstarch

2¹/2 cups (600 ml) water

4 egg yolks

1³/4 cups (175 g) sugar

MERINGUE

5 egg whites

1¹/4 cups (250 g) sugar

TART CRUST

2 cups (250 g) all-purpose flour

¹/4 cup (30 g) confectioners' sugar

¹/2 cup (125 g) chilled butter, cut into cubes

1 egg yolk

2 tbsp cold water

10 IN (25 CM) LOOSE-BOTTOMED FLUTED TART PAN

BAKING BEANS

1 Make the dough: sift the flour and confectioners' sugar into a large bowl. Add the butter and rub in with the fingertips until the mixture resembles fine bread crumbs.

2 Mix in the egg yolk and enough cold water to make a soft, pliable dough. Wrap the dough in plastic wrap and chill in the refrigerator for about 30 minutes.

3 Roll out the dough on a lightly floured surface and use to line the tart pan. Prebake (page 431) in a preheated oven at 400°F (200°C) for 10 minutes.

4 Remove the baking beans and foil and bake the tart shell for 5 minutes or until the bottom has dried out. Remove from the oven and reduce the temperature to 300°F (150°C).

5 Mix the lemon zest and juice with the cornstarch. Bring the water to a boil, then stir into the lemon mixture. Return to the pan and bring back to a boil, stirring, until the mixture thickens. Remove from heat.

6 Leave to cool slightly, then stir in the egg yolks and sugar. Return to a low heat and cook, stirring, until just simmering. Pour into the tart shell.

7 Make the meringue: beat the egg whites until stiff but not dry. Beat in the sugar 1 tsp at a time. Pile on top of the filling and spread over evenly. Bake for 45 minutes or until the meringue is crisp and brown. Serve the pie warm or cold.

TARTE AU CITRON

SERVES 10–12

9 eggs

1¹/4 cups (300 ml) heavy cream

grated zest and juice of 5 large lemons

1³/4 cups (375 g) sugar

confectioners' sugar for dusting

lemon twists to decorate

TART CRUST

2 cups (250 g) all-purpose flour

¹/2 cup (125 g) chilled butter, cut into cubes

¹/4 cup (60 g) sugar

1 egg

11 IN (28 CM) LOOSE-BOTTOMED FLUTED TART PAN

BAKING BEANS

1 Make the dough: put the flour into a large bowl. Add the butter and rub in with the fingertips until the mixture resembles fine bread crumbs.

2 Stir in the sugar, then bind together with the egg to make a soft, pliable dough. Wrap in plastic wrap and chill for at least 30 minutes.

3 Roll out the dough on a lightly floured surface and use to line the tart pan. Prebake (page 431) in a preheated oven at 400°F (200°C) for 10 minutes.

4 Remove the baking beans and foil and bake the tart shell for 5 minutes or until the bottom has dried out. Remove from the oven and reduce the oven temperature to 350°F (180°C).

5 Beat the eggs in a bowl and add the cream, lemon zest and juice, and sugar. Stir until smooth, and carefully pour into the tart shell.

6 Bake for 35–40 minutes until the lemon filling has set. Cover the tart loosely with foil if the dough begins to brown too much.

7 Leave the tart to cool for 20 minutes, then dust with confectioners' sugar. Decorate with lemon twists, and serve warm or at room temperature.

KEY LIME PIE

SERVES 8

1 1/4 cups (300 ml) heavy cream

1 3/4 cups (400 ml) sweetened condensed milk

grated zest and juice of 1 lime

lime slices to decorate

TART CRUST

1 1/2 cups (175 g) all-purpose flour

6 tbsp (90 g) chilled butter, cut into cubes

about 2 tbsp cold water

9 IN (23 CM) LOOSE-BOTTOMED FLUTED TART PAN

BAKING BEANS

1 Make the dough: put the flour into a large bowl, add the butter, and rub in until the mixture resembles fine bread crumbs. Add enough cold water to make a soft dough.

2 Wrap the dough in plastic wrap or foil and chill in the refrigerator for 30 minutes.

3 Roll out the dough on a lightly floured surface and use to line the tart pan.

4 Prebake the tart shell (page 431) in a preheated oven at 400°F (200°C) for about 10 minutes. Remove the baking beans and foil and return the shell to the oven for 5 minutes. Cool slightly.

5 Beat the cream to soft peaks in a large bowl and mix together with the condensed milk. Slowly stir in the lime zest and juice until the mixture thickens.

6 Pour the mixture into the tart shell and smooth the top, or create a pattern with a metal spatula. Chill in the refrigerator for at least 2 hours or until the filling is set firm.

7 Serve the pie chilled, decorated with lime slices.

BANANA CREAM PIE

SERVES 6

6 tbsp (90 g) butter

1 3/4 cups (400 ml) sweetened condensed milk

2 bananas, peeled and sliced

2/3 cup (150 ml) heavy cream, lightly whipped

1 oz (30 g) semisweet chocolate, grated, to decorate

CRUMB CRUST

4 tbsp (60 g) butter

5 oz (150 g) gingersnaps, crushed

7 IN (18 CM) LOOSE-BOTTOMED FLUTED TART PAN

1 Make the crumb crust (see box, right).

2 Melt the butter in a small saucepan over a low heat. Stir until the butter has melted.

3 Add the condensed milk to the pan, and heat gently, stirring constantly, until the mixture is a pale caramel color, about 10 minutes. Leave to cool slightly, and beat well to mix if the filling has separated.

4 Pour the warm caramel filling into the crumb crust and leave to cool. Chill until the filling is set.

5 Arrange the banana slices evenly over the caramel filling. Top with the whipped cream, and decorate with the grated chocolate. Serve chilled.

Making the crumb crust

Melt the butter in a saucepan, add the crushed gingersnaps, and stir well to combine. Press onto the bottom and side of the tart pan. Chill until set.

MISSISSIPPI MUD PIE

SERVES 8–10

7 oz (200 g) semisweet chocolate

1/2 cup (125 g) butter

1 tbsp coffee extract

3 eggs

2/3 cup (150 ml) light cream

3/4 cup packed (175 g) soft dark brown sugar

2/3 cup (150 ml) heavy cream to decorate (optional)

TART CRUST

2 cups (250 g) all-purpose flour

1/2 cup (125 g) chilled butter, cut into cubes

about 2–3 tbsp cold water

10 IN (25 CM) LOOSE-BOTTOMED FLUTED TART PAN

BAKING BEANS

1 Make the dough: put the flour into a large bowl. Add the butter and rub in until the mixture resembles fine bread crumbs. Add enough cold water to make a soft pliable dough.

2 Wrap the dough and chill for 30 minutes.

3 Roll out the dough on a lightly floured surface and use to line the tart pan.

4 Prebake the tart shell (page 431) in a preheated oven at 400°F (200°C) for about 10 minutes until the edge of the crust begins to brown.

5 Remove the baking beans and foil and bake for a further 5 minutes or until the bottom has dried out. Remove the shell from the oven, and reduce the oven temperature to 375°F (190°C).

6 Break the chocolate into pieces, and place in a heavy pan with the butter and coffee extract. Heat gently, stirring occasionally, until the chocolate and butter have melted. Remove from the heat. Leave the mixture to cool slightly.

7 Beat the eggs, then add to the saucepan with the cream and sugar. Stir thoroughly to mix the ingredients together.

8 Pour the filling into the pastry shell. Bake for 30–35 minutes until the filling has set. Leave to cool.

9 If liked, pipe whipped cream around the edge of the pie before serving.

BANANA CUSTARD TART WITH BERRIES

SERVES 6–8

1 cup (200 g) sugar

3 tbsp cornstarch

1 tbsp all-purpose flour

pinch of salt

2 egg yolks, lightly beaten

3/4 cup (175 ml) milk

3/4 cup (175 ml) heavy cream

1 tsp vanilla extract

2 ripe bananas, peeled and sliced

4 oz (125 g) raspberries

1 cup (250 ml) heavy cream, chilled

2 tbsp sugar

TART CRUST

1 1/2 cups (175 g) all-purpose flour

6 tbsp (90 g) chilled butter, cubed

3 tbsp muesli

about 2–3 tbsp cold water

9 IN (23 CM) LOOSE-BOTTOMED FLUTED TART PAN

BAKING BEANS

1 Make the dough: put the flour into a bowl, add the butter, and rub in with the fingertips until it resembles fine bread crumbs. Mix in the muesli. Add enough cold water to make a soft pliable dough. Chill for at least 30 minutes.

2 Roll out the dough on a lightly floured work surface and use to line the tart pan (patch it with your fingers if the dough breaks).

3 Prebake the pastry shell (page 431) in a preheated oven at 400°F (200°C) for 10 minutes. Remove the beans and foil and bake for 10–15 minutes longer.

4 Combine the sugar, cornstarch, flour, and salt. Mix together the egg yolks, milk, and cream, and beat into the cornstarch mixture.

5 Cook over a medium heat, stirring constantly, until the mixture boils and thickens. If the egg begins to curdle or the mixture sticks, lower the heat. Remove from the heat and stir in the vanilla extract. Cool.

6 Spread half of the custard over the tart shell. Arrange the bananas and raspberries on top, reserving some berries for decoration. Spread with the remaining custard. Chill until serving time.

7 Before serving, beat the cream with the sugar until it forms stiff peaks. Spread over the pie, and decorate with the reserved berries.

FRUIT TARTLETS

A mouth-watering combination of crisp golden pastry, creamy filling, and refreshing fruits always makes a special treat, whether served for dessert or as part of an elegant afternoon tea. To save time and effort, use the same crust and filling, but vary the toppings for a colorful display.

RASPBERRY TARTLETS

MAKES 16

I cup (250 g) cream cheese
2 tbsp sugar
12 oz (350 g) raspberries
3 tbsp red-currant jelly
1–2 tsp lemon juice to taste

TART CRUST

2 cups (250 g) all-purpose flour
1/2 cup (125 g) chilled butter, cut into cubes
2 tbsp sugar
3–4 tbsp cold water
7 CM (3 IN) BISCUIT CUTTER
16 x 2 1/2 IN (6 CM) ROUND TARTLET PANS

1 Make the dough: put the flour into a bowl, add the butter, and rub in with the fingertips until the mixture resembles fine bread crumbs. Stir in the sugar, then add enough cold water to bind to a soft pliable dough. Wrap and chill for at least 30 minutes.

2 On a lightly floured surface, roll out the dough thinly. Using the biscuit cutter, cut out 16 circles.

3 Gently press the dough circles into the tartlet pans. Prick all over with a fork and bake in a preheated oven at 375°F (190°C) for 12–15 minutes until golden. Leave in the pans for 10 minutes, then remove and transfer to a wire rack. Leave to cool completely.

4 Beat together the cream cheese and sugar and spoon into the pastry shells. Top with the raspberries, pressing them gently into the filling.

5 Melt the red-currant jelly with lemon juice to taste in a small pan, then spoon over the raspberries. Leave to cool and set before serving.

BLUEBERRY PUFFS

MAKES 8

I lb (500 g) store-bought puff pastry dough, thawed if frozen
beaten egg
4 oz (100 g) blueberries
2/3 cup (150 ml) heavy cream
I tbsp sugar
I ripe nectarine or peach, pitted and sliced
confectioners' sugar for dusting (optional)

1 Roll out the dough until 1/4 in (5 mm) thick on a lightly floured surface. Cut into strips 3 in (7 cm) wide, then cut the strips diagonally into 8 diamond shapes.

2 Using a sharp knife, score each dough diamond 1/2 in (1 cm) from the edge, taking care not to cut all the way through. Sprinkle a baking sheet with water. Place the dough shapes on the sheet and glaze with beaten egg.

3 Bake in a preheated oven at 450°F (230°C) for 10–15 minutes until golden. Transfer to a wire rack. The pastry centers will have risen away from the shells. Remove the centers, reserving them for lids if desired. Leave to cool.

4 Divide half of the blueberries among the pastry shells. Beat the cream and sugar and divide among the shells. Top with nectarine or peach slices, and the remaining blueberries. If desired, dust the pastry lids with confectioners' sugar, and replace on top of the filling before serving.

TROPICAL TARTLETS

MAKES 10

about 2 1/2 cups (600 ml) store-bought thick vanilla custard sauce
7 oz (200 g) canned mandarin orange segments in natural juice, well drained
7 oz (200 g) canned apricot halves in natural juice, well drained and cut into pieces
about 3 tbsp apricot jam
about 1/2 cup (60 g) toasted slivered almonds

ALMOND TART CRUST

1/2 cup (60 g) ground blanched almonds
I cup (125 g) all-purpose flour
2 tbsp sugar
6 tbsp (90 g) chilled butter, cut into cubes
about 3 tbsp cold water
10 x 3 IN (7 CM) ROUND TARTLET PANS OR BOAT-SHAPED PANS

1 Make the dough: combine the almonds, flour, and sugar in a bowl. Add the butter and rub in with the fingertips until the mixture resembles fine bread crumbs. Add enough cold water to make a soft pliable dough. Wrap and chill for 1 hour.

2 Put the dough on a floured surface and flatten slightly. Place a large sheet of parchment paper on top and roll out the dough, under the parchment, until about 1/8 in (3 mm) thick. Line the tartlet pans with dough and chill for 2 hours.

3 Prick the dough all over and bake in a preheated oven at 375°F (190°C) for 10 minutes. Leave the shells to cool in the pans for 10 minutes. Remove and transfer to a wire rack. Leave to cool.

4 Spoon vanilla custard sauce into each shell, then top with the mandarin orange segments and apricot pieces. Melt the jam in a small pan, strain, and spoon over the fruit. Sprinkle with the almonds and leave to set before serving.

CLOCKWISE FROM TOP: Raspberry Tartlets, Blueberry Puffs, Tropical Tartlets.

NAPOLEON

SERVES 6

8 oz (250 g) puff pastry dough, thawed if frozen

3 tbsp raspberry jam

2/3 cup (150 ml) heavy cream, whipped

PASTRY CREAM

2 eggs, beaten

4 tbsp (60 g) vanilla-flavored sugar

1/4 cup (30 g) all-purpose flour

1 1/4 cups (300 ml) milk

ICING

1 cup (125 g) confectioners' sugar

about 1 tbsp water

1 Make the pastry cream (page 452), using the quantities listed above.

2 Roll out the dough on a floured surface to make a thin 11 x 13 in (28 x 33 cm) rectangle. Sprinkle a baking sheet with water. Place the dough rectangle on the sheet.

3 Prick the dough with a fork. Bake in a preheated oven at 425°F (220°C) for 10–15 minutes until the pastry is crisp and a deep brown color.

4 Remove from the oven and leave to cool. Reduce the oven temperature to 350°F (180°C).

5 Trim the pastry edges, then cut into 3 equal rectangles, 4 in (10 cm) wide. Crush the pastry trimmings to make fine crumbs and set aside.

6 Mix the confectioners' sugar and enough water to make a smooth glacé icing. Spread over 1 of the rectangles, and place on a baking sheet.

7 Bake for 2 minutes or until the icing has just set and has a slight sheen. Leave to cool.

8 Place a second pastry rectangle on a serving plate. Spread evenly with the jam and then the whipped cream. Set the third rectangle on top and cover with the pastry cream.

9 Top with the iced pastry rectangle. Decorate the long edges of the rectangle with thin rows of pastry crumbs.

10 Chill the napoleon in the refrigerator until ready to serve, cut into individual slices with a very sharp knife.

Cook's know-how

Always bake puff pastry dough on a dampened baking sheet. The steam will produce extra light, crisp pastry.

BAKLAVA

MAKES 20 SQUARES

2 cups (250 g) finely chopped walnut pieces

1/4 cup packed (60 g) light soft brown sugar

1 tsp ground cinnamon

3/4 cup (175 g) butter, melted, plus extra for greasing

24 sheets of phyllo pastry dough, weighing about 1 lb (500 g)

4 1/2 tbsp (90 ml) honey

2 tbsp lemon juice

SHALLOW 7 x 9 IN (18 x 23 CM) RECTANGULAR CAKE PAN

1 Mix together the walnuts, sugar, and cinnamon.

2 Lightly butter the cake pan and lay 1 sheet of phyllo pastry dough in the bottom of the pan, allowing it to come up the sides (if necessary, cut the sheets to fit the pan). Brush the dough with a little melted butter.

3 Repeat with 5 more phyllo dough sheets, layering and brushing each one with the butter. Sprinkle with one-third of the nut mixture.

4 Repeat this process twice, using 6 more sheets of phyllo dough each time, brushing each sheet with butter and sprinkling the nut mixture over each sixth sheet. Finish with 6 buttered sheets of phyllo dough. Lightly brush the top with melted butter.

5 Trim the edges of the phyllo dough, then, using a very sharp knife, cut about halfway through the dough layers to make 20 squares.

6 Bake in a preheated oven at 425°F (220°C) for 15 minutes, then reduce the oven temperature to 350°F (180°C) and bake for 10–15 minutes until the pastry is crisp and golden brown. Remove the baklava from the oven.

7 Heat the honey and lemon juice in a heavy saucepan until the honey has melted. Spoon over the hot baklava. Leave to cool in the pan for 1–2 hours. Cut into the marked squares, and serve the baklava at room temperature.

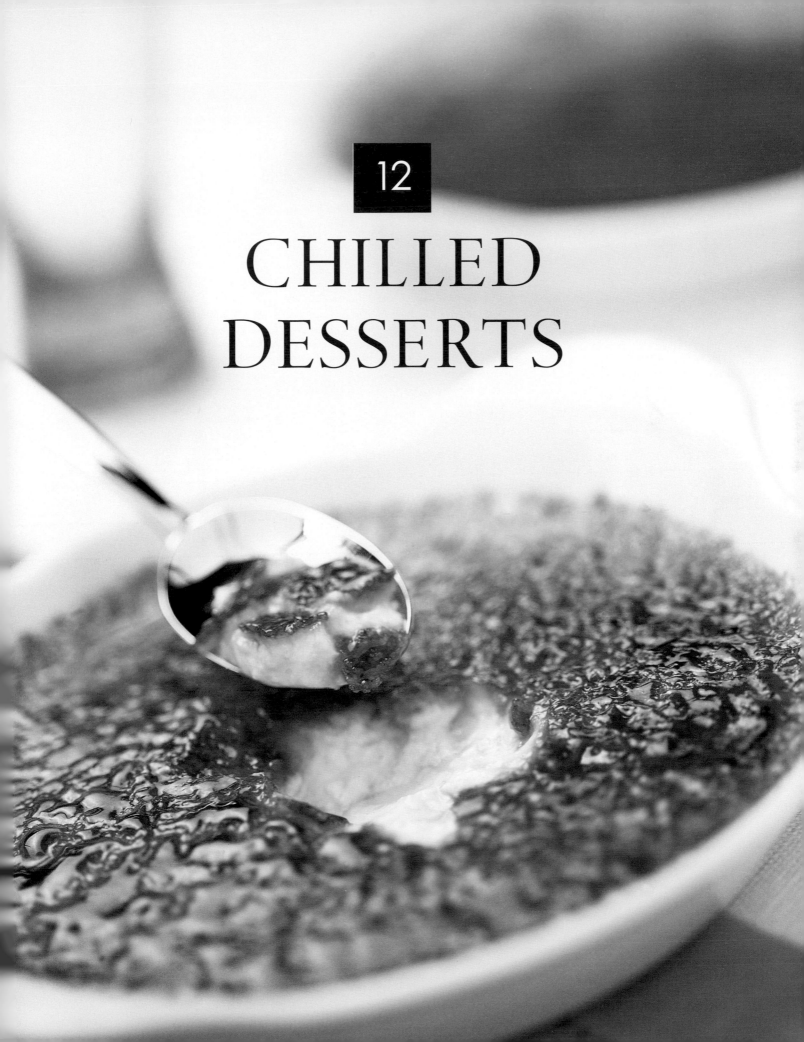

12
CHILLED
DESSERTS

UNDER 30 MINUTES

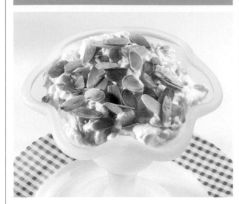

SCOTCH MIST
Rich heavy cream whipped with whiskey and crushed meringues, chilled, and sprinkled with toasted slivered almonds.

SERVES 6 446 calories per serving
Takes 10 minutes, plus chilling Page 474

ITALIAN CLASSIC

ZABAGLIONE
Light dessert: egg yolks, sugar, and Marsala beaten until creamy, and served with ladyfingers.

SERVES 6 114 calories per serving
Takes 20 minutes Page 485

PEACH MELBA
Deliciously ripe peaches and raspberries, topped with large scoops of vanilla ice cream and a sweetened raspberry sauce.

SERVES 4 273 calories per serving
Takes 15 minutes Page 492

30–60 MINUTES

DINNER PARTY

BAKED ALASKA
Impressive dessert: sponge cake filled with layers of raspberries, strawberries, or other summer fruits, topped with ice cream and meringue, and browned.

SERVES 8 256 calories per serving
Takes 30 minutes Page 493

BERRY FOOL
Fresh berries are lightly cooked with fragrant elderflowers until soft, mixed with whipped cream, and decorated with lime zest.

SERVES 6 396 calories per serving
Takes 30 minutes, plus chilling Page 469

TRADITIONAL

LEMON SYLLABUB
Lemon zest and juice, whipped heavy cream, sweet white wine, and beaten egg whites, are folded together, and topped with lemon zest.

SERVES 4 470 calories per serving
Takes 20 minutes, plus standing Page 473

OVER 60 MINUTES

MOCHA PUDDING
Easy and delicious: chocolate and coffee-flavored bread crumbs are layered with whipped cream, and sprinkled with chocolate.

SERVES 6 510 calories per serving
Takes 15 minutes, plus chilling Page 486

LOW CALORIE

FRESH FRUIT SALAD
Light and refreshing: a variety of fruit, including pink grapefruit, oranges, green grapes, pears, and bananas coated in syrup.

SERVES 6 173 calories per serving
Takes 25 minutes, plus chilling Page 468

POTS AU CHOCOLAT
Rich and smooth: chocolate, coffee, butter, egg yolks, and vanilla extract combined with egg whites and decorated with whipped cream.

SERVES 6 324 calories per serving
Takes 15 minutes, plus chilling Page 484

OVER 60 MINUTES

FROZEN LEMON SHERBERT

Whipped heavy cream, lemon zest and juice, sugar, and milk, frozen, and then decorated with strips of lemon zest.

SERVES 4 391 calories per serving

Takes 20 minutes, plus freezing   Page 494

CHOCOLATE & BRANDY MOUSSE

Smooth and delicious: an egg and whipped cream mousse flavored with chocolate and brandy. Topped with cream and chocolate.

SERVES 6 585 calories per serving

Takes 45 minutes, plus chilling   Page 487

RICH PEACHY TRIFLE

Family favorite: cake slices layered with peaches or pears, crisp cookies, custard, and whipped cream. Decorated with toasted almonds.

SERVES 8 401 calories per serving

Takes 35 minutes, plus chilling   Page 468

LOW FAT

SUMMER PUDDING

Ripe and juicy strawberries, blackberries, blueberries, cherries, and raspberries wrapped in juice-soaked bread.

SERVES 6 240 calories per serving

Takes 35 minutes, plus chilling   Page 469

FAMILY CHOICE

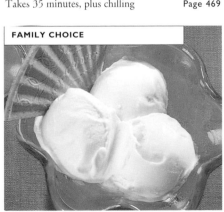

QUICK VANILLA ICE CREAM

Plain and simple: fresh eggs and heavy cream flavored with vanilla sugar, beaten until light and creamy, and frozen.

SERVES 4–6 799–533 calories per serving

Takes 20 minutes, plus freezing   Page 489

CHOCOLATE CHIP CHEESECAKE

Rich and delicious: a granola crust is topped with a creamy mixture enriched with both melted chocolate and chocolate chips. The cheesecake is decorated with piped rosettes of whipped cream and chocolate caraque for a luscious finish.

SERVES 8 628 calories per serving

Takes 50 minutes, plus chilling   Page 484

OVER 60 MINUTES

PAVLOVA WITH PINEAPPLE & GINGER

Crisp meringue case filled with whipped heavy cream and ginger, and topped with pineapple rings and strips of ginger.

SERVES 6–8 504–378 calories per serving
Takes 2½ hours, plus cooling   Page 474

TIRAMISU

Traditional Italian dessert: a spongecake base layered with creamy mascarpone cheese flavored with brandy, chocolate, and coffee.

SERVES 8 508 calories per serving
Takes 45 minutes, plus chilling   Page 487

FRENCH CLASSIC

CREME BRULEE

Simple and delicious: egg and cream custard baked until tender, finished with crisp, caramelized sugar on top.

SERVES 6 302 calories per serving
Takes 45 minutes, plus chilling   Page 488

MANGO & LIME MOUSSE

Light and refreshing: mangoes and tangy lime zest and juice mixed with whipped cream. Decorated with lime slices and cream.

SERVES 6 354 calories per serving
Takes 40 minutes, plus chilling   Page 472

CHOCOLATE ROULADE

Rich and creamy: a chocolate-flavored sponge with a deliciously rich cream and chocolate filling.

SERVES 6 677 calories per serving
Takes 60 minutes, plus cooling   Page 485

TUTTI-FRUTTI BOMBE

Easy and delicious: dried fruit, apricots, cherries, and brandy combined with custard and whipped cream, and then frozen.

SERVES 8 437 calories per serving
Takes 20 minutes, plus freezing   Page 493

LOW FAT

CARAMELIZED ORANGES

Quick and easy: oranges caramelized and served in their own juices, and decorated with strips of orange zest.

SERVES 4 388 calories per serving
Takes 30 minutes, plus chilling   Page 472

CHILLED LEMON SOUFFLE

Light and fluffy: refreshing, smooth dessert with a citrus tang, decorated with whipped cream and toasted almonds.

SERVES 4 883 calories per serving
Takes 40 minutes, plus chilling   Page 473

FLOATING ISLANDS

Fluffy oval-shaped meringues are served floating on a smooth and creamy vanilla-flavored custard. Decorated with almonds.

SERVES 4 412 calories per serving
Takes 40 minutes, plus cooling   Page 479

OVER 60 MINUTES

AUSTRIAN CHEESECAKE
Smooth and creamy: beaten cottage cheese, butter, egg, almonds, and semolina studded with golden raisins and lightened with egg whites.

SERVES 8 331 calories per serving
Takes 50 minutes, plus cooling   Page 481

DINNER PARTY

CHOCOLATE LAYERED TERRINE
Two chocolate and brandy mousselike layers sandwiched with white chocolate. Decorated with whipped cream and chocolate shavings.

SERVES 8–10 641–513 calories per serving
Takes 45 minutes, plus chilling   Page 486

TROPICAL FRUIT CHEESECAKE
Crunchy coconut cookie crust topped with a creamy mango mixture, and decorated with tropical fruits.

SERVES 10 396 calories per serving
Takes 1¼ hours   Page 481

FRENCH CLASSIC

CREME CARAMEL
Easy and delicious: velvety vanilla-flavoured custard coated with a tempting golden brown caramel sauce.

SERVES 6 255 calories per serving
Takes 60 minutes, plus chilling   Page 488

CHERRY CHEESECAKE
Black cherries flavored with kirsch top a slightly sweet and creamy cheese filling with a crisp crumb crust.

SERVES 8 530 calories per serving
Takes 60 minutes, plus chilling   Page 479

FAMILY CHOICE

RICH VANILLA ICE CREAM
Creamy and irresistible: rich egg custard mixed with heavy cream, flavored with vanilla extract, churned, and then frozen. A delicious and versatile recipe every cook should know. Colorful strawberry fans highlight each serving.

SERVES 4–6 577–385 calories per serving
Takes 30 minutes, plus freezing   Page 492

OVER 60 MINUTES

MANGO & PASSION FRUIT MERINGUE
Two light and crunchy meringue circles are sandwiched together with cream, mango slices, strawberries, and passion fruit.

SERVES 6 503 calories per serving
Takes 1½ hours, plus cooling   Page 475

ITALIAN CLASSIC

CASSATA
Layers of ice cream, rum-soaked fruit, and sorbet are frozen to make this traditional Italian dessert.

SERVES 8 364 calories per serving
Takes 30 minutes, plus freezing   Page 494

MARBLED RASPBERRY CHEESECAKE
Crunchy crust of walnuts and oatmeal cookies is topped with a creamy raspberry and cheese filling. Decorated with whipped cream.

SERVES 10 439 calories per serving
Takes 45 minutes, plus chilling   Page 480

PREPARE AHEAD

CHOCOLATE & MERINGUE BOMBE
Delicious layers of vanilla and chocolate ice cream with a surprise center of whipped cream and crushed meringue.

SERVES 8 413 calories per serving
Takes 45 minutes, plus freezing   Page 489

HAZELNUT MERINGUE GATEAU
Toasted hazelnuts add a rich flavor to meringue layers, which are sandwiched with cream and served with raspberry sauce.

SERVES 8 429 calories per serving
Takes 1¼ hours   Page 478

DINNER PARTY

STRAWBERRY MERINGUE ROULADE
A light meringue layer scattered with slivered almonds, spread with whipped heavy cream and strawberries, and rolled into a roulade. Chilled, then lightly dusted with confectioners' sugar just before serving. A perfect and attractive end to a special dinner.

SERVES 8 349 calories per serving
Takes 55 minutes, plus chilling   Page 475

CHILLED DESSERTS KNOW-HOW

CHILLED DESSERTS can be made well in advance so are great for dinner parties. Fruit salads and fools, trifles, creamy mousses and light chilled soufflés, meringue baskets, luxurious cheesecakes, layered terrines, ice creams, and sorbets – all can be kept in the refrigerator or freezer, to be served when you're ready.

BEATING EGG WHITES

A balloon whisk is the classic tool for beating egg whites, but an electric mixer saves time and effort. Ensure all your equipment is clean, dry, and grease-free, and that the egg whites are at room temperature.

Beat the whites as forcefully as possible (on maximum speed if using an electric mixer) right from the start. When they look like a cloud, add any sugar little by little. The mixture will get stiffer and stiffer as you add sugar and whisk.

FREEZING

Many completed desserts, as well as ingredients and accompaniments for desserts, can be stored in the freezer. Freeze chocolate, caramel, or fruit sauces; thaw at room temperature, or reheat from frozen if serving warm. Tray freeze piped rosettes of cream, then pack in a freezer bag; pack chocolate decorations in rigid containers. Both can be used frozen – they will thaw in minutes. Freeze citrus zest, and thaw, unwrapped, at room temperature. Tray freeze baked meringue shells, cake layers, and cheesecake; unwrap and thaw in the refrigerator. Crème caramel can be frozen uncooked in the mould and baked from frozen, allowing extra time.

Egg safety

Some of the chilled desserts in this book, such as mousses and soufflés, contain uncooked eggs. Because of the risk of salmonella poisoning, it is usually recommended that those in vulnerable groups should not eat raw or undercooked eggs (see also page 32).

DISSOLVING GELATIN

Gelatin is a flavorless setting agent used in chilled desserts, such as mousses. It is most commonly available as a powder, sold in envelopes. Leaf gelatin can also be used (4 sheets in place of 1 envelope): soften in cold water for 5 minutes, then drain and melt in the hot dessert mixture, whisking well.

1 Put the specified quantity of cold water or other liquid into a small heatproof bowl and sprinkle the specified quantity of gelatin over the surface. Leave to soak for about 10 minutes until the gelatin has absorbed the liquid and become "spongy."

2 Put the bowl of gelatin into a pan of hot water and heat until the gelatin has dissolved and is clear. Use a metal spoon to check that there are not any granules left. Use the gelatin at the same temperature as the mixture it is setting.

PREPARING A SOUFFLE DISH

To give a chilled soufflé the appearance of having risen above the rim of the dish, it is set with a raised collar.

Cut out a piece of foil or waxed paper 2 cm (5 cm) longer than the circumference of the dish and wide enough to stand 2 in (5 cm) above the rim when the paper is folded. Fold in half. Wrap around the dish and secure with tape or string. Remove before serving.

FOLDING EGG WHITES

To retain as much air as possible, egg whites should be folded gently and quickly into a mixture.

Mix a spoonful of the whites into the heavy mixture to lighten it. Using a rubber spatula or metal spoon, fold in the remaining whites using a "figure-eight" motion, cutting straight through the mixture, then turning it over until well blended.

PREPARING CITRUS FRUITS

When taking the zest from citrus fruits (even if they are unwaxed), first scrub the fruit with hot soapy water, rinse well, and dry.

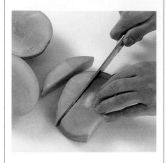

Grating

Hold the grater on a plate. Rub the fruit over the medium grid of the grater, removing just the zest and leaving behind the bitter white pith. Use a pastry brush to remove all the zest from the grater.

Paring

Use a vegetable peeler or small knife to pare off strips of zest, trying not to take any of the white pith with the zest. Cut the pieces of zest lengthwise into very fine strips or "julienne."

Zesting

For speedy removal of zest in tiny strips, use a citrus zester or a flat ultrasharp grater.

Peeling

Use a small sharp knife. Cut off a slice of peel across the top and the base, cutting through to the flesh. Set the fruit upright on a cutting board and cut away the peel from top to bottom, following the curve of the fruit and cutting away the white pith as well.

Segmenting

Hold the peeled fruit over a bowl to catch the juice. With a sharp knife, cut down one side of a segment, cutting it from the dividing membrane. Cut away from the membrane on the other side, and remove the segment. Continue all around the fruit.

Citrus tips

To get the maximum juice from citrus fruits, first roll the fruit gently on a work surface, pressing lightly. Or heat in the microwave, on HIGH (100% power) for 30 seconds, just until the fruit feels warm.

If a recipe includes citrus zest, add it immediately after grating or zesting, preferably to any sugar in the recipe. Then the zest won't discolor or dry out, and all the flavorsome oils from the zest will be absorbed by the sugar.

PREPARING MANGOES

Mangoes have a large, flat central seed and the flesh clings to it tightly. There are 2 methods of preparation, depending on how the flesh is to be used.

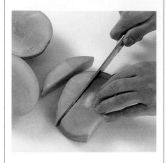

Slicing

For flesh to be used sliced or pureed, cut the flesh from each side of the seed with a sharp knife. Also cut the flesh from the edges of the seed. Then peel and slice or puree.

Dicing

1 Cut the unpeeled flesh away from each side of the seed. With a sharp knife, score the flesh in a crisscross pattern, cutting just to the skin but not through it.

2 Press in the middle of the skin to open out the cubes of flesh, then cut them away from the skin with a sharp knife.

PREPARING A PINEAPPLE

When peeling pineapple, cut away the skin in strips, taking out all the "eyes." If there are any left after peeling, cut them out with the tip of a knife.

Wedges or cubes

Rings

1 Cut off the green crown, then cut a slice from the bottom. Set the pineapple upright on a cutting board and cut away strips of skin, cutting from top to bottom.

2 To remove the core, cut the pineapple into quarters lengthwise. Cut the central core from each quarter. Cut the quarters into wedges or cubes as required.

Do not cut the pineapple lengthwise, but cut crosswise into 1/2 in (1 cm) slices. Stamp out the central core from each slice using a cookie or pastry cutter.

DECORATING WITH CHOCOLATE

Chocolate decorations can transform a dessert, and you don't have to reserve them for desserts made only
from chocolate – fruit fools and mousses can also benefit from a contrasting finishing touch.

Grating chocolate

Use chilled chocolate and hold it firmly in a piece of waxed paper. Hold the grater on a sheet of waxed paper and rub the chocolate over the large holes of the grater.

Chocolate curls

Have the chocolate at room temperature, and use a vegetable peeler to shave off long curls onto a sheet of waxed paper. Lift the paper to tip the curls onto the dessert.

Chocolate caraque

1 Spread a smooth, thin layer of melted chocolate, about 1/16 in (1.5 mm) thick, onto a cool work surface (preferably marble), and leave to cool until nearly set.

2 Using a long, sharp knife held at an angle, push across the chocolate with a slight sawing action, to shave it into "caraque" curls. Use a toothpick to pick up the caraque.

MELTING CHOCOLATE

Care is needed when melting chocolate, especially white chocolate. Don't allow it to overheat or come into contact with any steam because this could cause it to scorch or harden.

Chop the chocolate and put it into a heatproof bowl set over a pan of hot, not boiling, water. The base of the bowl should not be touching the water. Heat slowly, without stirring, until the chocolate becomes soft. Remove from the heat, but leave the bowl over the water. Stir until the chocolate is very smooth and creamy.

DECORATING WITH CREAM

Piped whipped cream adds a professional touch to desserts and cakes, and with a little practice
and some confidence this is not difficult to do. A star-shaped tip is the most useful.

1 Drop the tip into the piping bag, then tuck the lower half of the piping bag into the tip, to prevent the cream from leaking out when filling the bag.

2 Hold the bag in one hand, folding the top of the bag over your hand. Spoon in the whipped cream.

3 When the bag is full, twist the top until there is no air left. Pipe the cream as desired, gently squeezing the twisted end to force out the cream in a steady stream.

Rosette
Hold the bag upright, just above the surface of the cake. Squeeze gently, moving the bag in a small circle. Stop squeezing and lift the tip away.

Swirl
Hold the bag upright, just above the surface of the cake. Squeeze the bag and pipe the cream in a steady stream, guiding the tip in an "S" shape.

Rope
Hold the bag at a 45° angle. Pipe a short length of cream to 1 side. Pipe another length of cream to the opposite side, overlapping the first one.

RICH PEACHY TRIFLE

SERVES 8

14 oz (400 g) canned peach or pear halves

6 individual sponge cakes

4 tbsp red fruit jam

2 oz (60 g) amoretti cookies or macaroons

5 tbls (75 ml) sherry

3 egg yolks

2 tbls (30 g) sugar

1 tsp cornstarch

1 1/4 cups (300 ml) milk

1 1/4 cups (300 ml) heavy or whipping cream

1/4 cup (30 g) slivered almonds, toasted, to decorate

1 Drain and slice the fruit, reserving the juice.

2 Cut the sponge cakes in half horizontally and sandwich the halves together with the jam.

3 Line the bottom of a glass serving bowl with the cake slices, and arrange the fruit and biscuits on top. Drizzle the sherry and reserved fruit juice over, and leave to soak while you make the custard.

4 In a bowl, mix together the egg yolks, sugar, and cornstarch. Warm the milk in a heavy saucepan, then pour it into the egg yolk mixture, stirring constantly. Return the mixture to the pan and cook over a low heat, stirring constantly, until the custard thickens. Leave the custard to cool slightly.

5 Pour the custard over the cakes, fruit, and cookies in the glass bowl. Cover the surface of the custard with a sheet of plastic wrap, to prevent a skin from forming, and chill until set, preferably overnight (to let the flavors mingle).

6 Whip the cream until thick and spread over the custard. Scatter the almonds over the top to decorate. Serve chilled.

APRICOT & GINGER TRIFLE

Use 14 oz (400 g) canned apricot halves. Sandwich the cakes with apricot jam and sprinkle with 1 piece of ginger in syrup, chopped, instead of the almonds.

FRESH FRUIT SALAD

SERVES 6

1/4 cup (60 g) sugar

6 tbls (90 ml) water

pared zest of 1/2 lemon

2 pink grapefruit

2 oranges

8 oz (250 g) seedless green grapes, halved

2 ripe pears, peeled, cored, and sliced

2 bananas, sliced

1 Put the sugar and measured water into a saucepan and heat gently until the sugar has dissolved. Add the lemon zest and bring the syrup to a boil. Boil for 1 minute, then strain into a serving bowl. Leave to cool.

2 Using a sharp serrated knife, cut the peel and pith from each grapefruit and orange. Remove the segments by cutting between each membrane. Add the segments to the bowl.

3 Add the grapes, pears, and bananas to the serving bowl and gently mix to coat all of the fruit in the sugar syrup.

4 Cover and chill the fruit salad for up to 1 hour before serving.

SUMMER BERRY SALAD

Cut 1 1/2 lb (750 g) strawberries in half, then mix them with 8 oz (250 g) raspberries and 8 oz (250g) blueberries. Sift 3 tbsp confectioners' sugar over the fruit, and pour the juice of 2 oranges on top. Stir gently, cover, and chill for 1 hour.

Cook's know-how

If you are short of time you can just sprinkle the fruit with sugar to taste rather than making a sugar syrup. To prevent the pears and bananas from discoloring when sliced and exposed to the air, toss the pieces in lemon juice.

468

SUMMER PUDDING

This classic English summertime treat is very easy to make, and not at all high in calories. For a perfect, evenly colored result, reserve half of the cooking juices and pour them over any pale patches of bread after unmolding the dessert.

SERVES 6

8 slices of stale medium-sliced white bread, crusts removed

1³⁄₄ lb (875 g) mixed summer fruits such as strawberries, blueberries, blackberries, cherries, and raspberries

³⁄₄ cup (150 g) sugar

5 tbls (75 ml) water

2 tbsp framboise or crème de cassis liqueur

whipped cream, sour cream, or plain yogurt to serve

5 CUPS (1.25 LITER) BOWL

1 Set 2 slices of bread aside for the top of the dessert, then use the remaining slices to line the bowl (see box, right).

2 Hull and halve the strawberries if large, strip the currants from their stalks, and pit the cherries.

3 Place the blueberries, blackberries, and cherries in a saucepan with the sugar and measured water. Heat gently until the juices begin to run. Stir until the sugar has dissolved, and cook until all of the fruit is just tender.

4 Remove from the heat and add the strawberries, raspberries, and liqueur.

5 Spoon the fruit and half of the juice into the lined bowl, reserving the remaining juice. Cover the top of the fruit with the reserved bread slices.

6 Stand the bowl in a shallow dish to catch any juices that may overflow, then put a saucer on top of the bread lid. Place a kitchen weight (or a can of food) on top of the saucer. Leave to chill for 8 hours.

7 Remove the weight and saucer and invert the dessert onto a serving plate. Spoon the reserved juices over the top, paying particular attention to any pale areas, and serve with either whipped cream, sour cream, or yogurt.

Lining the bowl

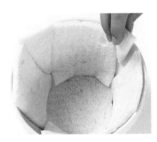

Put a slice of bread in the bottom of the bowl, cutting it to fit if necessary, then use the remainder to line the side. The slices should fit snugly together.

BERRY FOOL

SERVES 6

1 lb (500 g) strawberries, topped and tailed

1 tbsp water

4 tbls (60 g) butter

2 elderflower heads (optional)

sugar to taste

1¹⁄₄ cups (300 ml) heavy cream, whipped until thick

strips of blanched lime zest to decorate

1 Put the strawberries into a pan with the measured water, butter, and elderflowers, if using. Cover and cook gently for 5–10 minutes until the gooseberries are soft.

2 Beat with a wooden spoon until smooth, and add sugar to taste. Leave to cool.

3 Fold the mixture into the cream. Turn into serving glasses and chill for 30 minutes. Decorate with lime zest.

RHUBARB & ORANGE FOOL

Substitute 1 lb (500 g) chopped rhubarb for the strawberries and omit the elderflowers. Cook the rhubarb until soft with sugar to taste and the finely grated zest and juice of 1 large orange.

RED FRUIT DESSERTS

There is nothing more stunning than a dessert made with red fruits. The color speaks for itself, so there is very little you have to do – the less the better. There are endless variations if you use with different fruits as they come into season. There are no hard-and-fast rules.

PORT & WINE MOLD

SERVES 8

8 sheets of leaf gelatin (scant 1 oz/about 25 g)

1¼ cups (250 g) sugar

2 cups (500 ml) water

2 tbsp red-currant jelly

1 cinnamon stick

2 cups (500 ml) red wine from Bordeaux

300 ml (½ pint) ruby port

TO SERVE

small seasonal red fruits, such as raspberries, cherries, red-currants, wild strawberries

cream (optional)

6 CUP (1.5 LITER) JELLY MOLD OR 8 WINE GLASSES

1 Put the sheets of gelatin in a medium bowl and cover with cold water. Leave to soak for about 5 minutes until softened.

2 Meanwhile, put the sugar into a large saucepan, pour in the measured water, and add the red-currant jelly. Heat gently until the sugar and jelly have dissolved, then add the cinnamon stick, wine, and port. Bring to a boil, bubble for 1 minute, then remove the pan from the heat.

3 Pour the wine through a strainer lined with a double layer of cheesecloth into a bowl. Lift the gelatin out of the water, squeeze it, then add to the wine and stir until the gelatin has dissolved. Cool a little, pour into a mold or glasses, and leave until completely cold. Cover, and chill until set, at least 4 hours. Serve with seasonal fruits, and cream if you like.

Cook's know-how

If you want to use powdered gelatine instead of gelatin leaves, for the Port & Wine Mold you will need to sprinkle 2 tbsp gelatin powder over 6 tbsp cold water in a small bowl, and for the Cranberry & Vodka Sparkle you will need to sprinkle 1½ tsp gelatine powder 1½ tbsp cold water. Leave to sponge for 10 minutes before stirring into the hot liquid.

RASPBERRY PASSION

SERVES 6

3 ripe passion fruit

2 cups (500 g) plain yogurt

1 cup (250 g) reduced-fat sour cream

12 oz (375 g) raspberries

⅔ cup (90 g) light brown sugar

6 x 1¼ CUP (300 ML) STEMMED GLASSES

1 Using a teaspoon, scoop the seeds and flesh from the passion fruit into a bowl, and mix with the yogurt and sour cream.

2 Put an equal quantity of raspberries in each glass, then fill with the sour cream mixture. Cover and refrigerate for up to 8 hours.

3 An hour or so before serving, sprinkle with sugar and return to the refrigerator until ready to serve.

CRANBERRY & VODKA SPARKLE

SERVES 4

2 sheets of leaf gelatin

¾ cup (175 ml) cranberry juice

½ cup (125 ml) vodka

squeeze of lime juice

dainty red fruits (such as raspberries, cherries, red-currants, and wild strawberries) to serve

4 GLASSES

1 Put the sheets of gelatin into a medium bowl and cover with cold water. Leave to soak for about 5 minutes until softened.

2 Heat the cranberry juice in a pan. Lift the gelatine out of the water, squeeze it, then add to the cranberry juice and stir until the gelatin has dissolved. Cool slightly, then add the vodka and lime juice. Cool completely, then pour into glasses, cover and chill until set, about 6 hours. Serve topped with dainty red fruits.

JUBILEE TRIFLE

SERVES 6

8 individual sponge cakes

about 7 tbsp black cherry jam or jelly

14 oz (400 g) cannned pear quarters in natural juice, drained with the juice reserved

14 oz (400 g) canned red cherries, drained with the juice reserved

4 tbsp kirsch or other cherry liqueur

2 cups (500 ml) custard sauce (store-bought or see page 446 and use double the amount of cornstarch)

⅔ cup (150 ml) whipping cream

6 INDIVIDUAL GLASS DISHES, OR A 5 CUP (1.5 LITER) SHALLOW GLASS DISH, ABOUT 8 IN (20 CM) IN DIAMETER

1 Split the cake slices in half, spread generously with about 4 tbsp jam, and sandwich together again. Place 4 in the bottom of 6 individual glass dishes, cutting them to fit.

2 Chop each pear quarter into small pieces, and put some of the pieces around the edges of the dishes, and some in between the sponges. Dot with the cherries.

3 Mix the 5 tbsp of the pear juice with the kirsch, and pour half of it over the sponges. Arrange the last 4 sponges in the dishes, again cutting them to fit, then pour the remaining juice and kirsch over. Leave for a few minutes, then gently squash flat with the back of a spoon. Pour the custard over, level gently, and chill for 1 hour.

4 Lightly whip the cream – it should still be soft and floppy – and spread over the custard. Cover and chill for at least 4 hours (or up to 24 hours).

5 To serve, warm 3 tbsp cherry jam in a small pan with 2 tbsp of the reserved cherry juice until the jam has dissolved. Leave to cool, then strainer to remove any lumps, and drizzle over the trifles.

CLOCKWISE FROM TOP LEFT: **Port & Wine Mold**, **Raspberry Passion, Cranberry & Vodka Sparkle, Jubilee Trifle.**

CARAMELIZED ORANGES

SERVES 4

1 1/4 cups (250 g) sugar

2/3 cup (150 ml) cold water

2/3 cup (150 ml) lukewarm water

3 tbsp orange liqueur

8 thin-skinned oranges

1 Put the sugar and measured cold water into a heavy pan and heat gently until the sugar dissolves.

2 When all the sugar has dissolved, bring to a boil and boil steadily until a rich brown color. (If the caramel is too light in color it will be very sweet, but be careful not to let it burn.)

3 Protect your hand by covering it with a cloth, and remove the pan from the heat. Pour the measured lukewarm water into the caramel.

4 Return the pan to the heat and stir to melt the caramel. Pour the caramel into a heatproof serving dish. Leave to cool for 30 minutes. Stir in the orange liqueur.

5 Pare the zest from 1 of the oranges, using a vegetable peeler. Cut the zest into very thin strips (page 466). Cook for 1 minute in boiling water, drain, rinse thoroughly under cold running water, and set aside.

6 Using a sharp knife, remove the peel and pith from each orange, catching any juice to add to the caramel in the dish. Cut each orange into slices crosswise, then reassemble the oranges, holding the slices together with toothpicks.

7 Place the oranges in the dish of caramel and spoon the caramel over them. Scatter the strips of orange zest over the top. Chill for about 30 minutes. Remove the toothpicks before transferring the oranges to individual bowls to serve.

MANGO & LIME MOUSSE

SERVES 6

2 large ripe mangoes

grated zest and juice of 2 limes

2 x 1/4 oz (7 g) envelope unflavored powdered gelatin

3 eggs, plus 1 egg yolk

3 tbls (45 g) sugar

2/3 cup (150 ml) heavy or whipping cream, whipped until thick

DECORATION

2/3 cup (150 ml) heavy or whipping cream, whipped until thick

1 lime, thinly sliced

1 Slice the mango flesh away from the seeds (page 466). Peel the flesh, then puree in a blender or food processor. Add the lime zest to the puree.

2 Put the lime juice into a small bowl, sprinkle the gelatin over the top, and leave for 10 minutes until it becomes spongy.

3 Stand the bowl in a pan of hot water and heat until the gelatine has dissolved.

4 Combine the eggs, egg yolk, and sugar in a large bowl and beat vigorously for about 10 minutes until the mixture is pale and very thick. Gradually add the mango puree, whisking between each addition to keep the mixture thick.

5 Fold the whipped cream into the mango mixture. Add the dissolved gelatine in a steady stream, stirring gently to mix. Pour the mixture into a glass serving bowl and chill until set.

6 To decorate, pipe rosettes of whipped cream (page 467) on top of the mousse. Cut the lime slices in half, place 2 slices between each rosette of cream, and serve chilled.

LEMON SYLLABUB

SERVES 4

2/3 cup (150 ml) dessert wine or sweet white wine

2 large lemons

scant 1/2 cup (90 g) sugar

1 1/4 cups (300 ml) heavy cream

2 egg whites

1 Put the wine into a bowl with the grated zest and juice of 1 of the lemons, and the sugar. Stir to mix, then leave to stand for about 15 minutes, stirring occasionally, until the sugar has dissolved.

2 Meanwhile, remove the zest from the remaining lemon in long, very thin strips. Blanch the strips in a small saucepan of boiling water for 1 minute. Drain, rinse under cold running water, and pat dry.

3 In a medium bowl, whip the cream until it just holds its shape. Add the wine mixture very slowly, whisking well between each addition so the mixture remains thick.

4 In a separate bowl, beat the egg whites until stiff but not dry. Carefully fold into the cream and wine mixture. Spoon into 4 tall glasses. Decorate the top of each syllabub with a strip of lemon zest, and serve at once.

Cook's know-how

For a less rich syllabub, use half whipped heavy cream and half plain yogurt. Do not use whipping cream instead of heavy cream because it will not be heavy enough to hold the weight of the wine. Serve with shortbread cookies, if you like.

CHILLED LEMON SOUFFLE

SERVES 4

3 tbsp cold water

2 x 1/4 oz (7 g) envelope unflavored powdered gelatin

3 large eggs, separated

1 1/4 cups (250 g) sugar

grated zest and juice of 3 lemons

1 1/4 cups (300 ml) heavy or whipping cream, whipped until thick

DECORATION

1/4 cup (30 g) chopped almonds

2/3 cup (150 ml) heavy or whipping cream, whipped until stiff

1 QUART (1 LITER) SOUFFLÉ DISH

1 Prepare the soufflé dish: tie a band of double thickness waxed paper or foil around the outside so it stands about 2 in (5 cm) above the top of the dish (page 465).

2 Put the water into a small bowl and sprinkle the gelatin over the top. Leave for 10 minutes until it becomes spongy. Stand in a pan of hot water and heat until dissolved.

3 Put the egg yolks and sugar into a heatproof bowl and put over a pan of gently simmering water. Do not let the bottom of the bowl touch the water. Using an electric mixer, beat together. Add the lemon zest and juice and whisk at full speed until the mixture is pale and thick.

4 Fold the whipped cream into the lemon mixture, then fold in the dissolved gelatin.

5 In a separate large bowl, beat the egg whites until stiff but not dry. Fold into the lemon mixture, and carefully pour into the prepared soufflé dish. Level the surface, then chill for about 4 hours until set.

6 Carefully remove the paper collar. Decorate the outside edge of the soufflé with the lightly toasted almonds and sprinkle some in the middle. Pipe the cream (page 467) around the edge of the soufflé, and serve chilled.

SCOTCH MIST

SERVES 6

2 cups (500 ml) heavy or whipping cream

4 tbsp whiskey

3 oz (90 g) meringues, coarsely crushed

1/4 cup (30 g) slivered almonds, toasted

1 Whip the cream with the whiskey until it just holds its shape. Fold in the crushed meringues.

2 Spoon the mixture into 6 glass serving bowls, cover, and chill for about 20 minutes or until firm.

3 Scatter the toasted slivered almonds over the desserts just before serving.

ETON MESS

Substitute 4 tbsp brandy for the whiskey, and add 1 lb (500 g) chopped strawberries to the cream mixture. Decorate with strawberry halves and mint leaves instead of the almonds.

PAVLOVA WITH PINEAPPLE & GINGER

Pavlova meringue is crisp on the outside, soft and slightly chewy like marshmallows inside. This pineapple and ginger topping is good in winter, but if you want to make a summer pavlova, use sweetened fresh red berries instead – and omit the ginger.

SERVES 6–8

4 egg whites

1 1/4 cups (250 g) sugar

1 1/2 tsp cornstarch

1 1/2 tsp white wine vinegar

TOPPING

1 3/4 cups (375 ml) heavy or whipping cream

4 tbls (60 g) ginger in syrup, cut into matchstick-thin strips

14 oz (400 g) canned pineapple rings, drained

1 Preheat the oven to 325°F (160°C). Mark a 9 in (23 cm) circle on a sheet of non-stick parchment paper, turn the paper over, and line a baking tray.

2 Beat the egg whites until stiff, then add the sugar, 1 tsp at a time, beating the mixture constantly.

3 Blend the cornstarch and vinegar and beat into the egg white mixture.

4 Spread the mixture inside the circle on the parchment paper, building the sides up so they are higher than the middle. Place in the oven, then immediately reduce the temperature to 300°F (150°C).

5 Bake the meringue for 1 hour or until firm to the touch. Turn off the oven and leave the meringue inside for another hour.

6 Peel the lining paper from the meringue, and transfer the meringue to a serving plate. Leave to cool.

7 Before serving, whip the cream until stiff, and stir in half of the ginger strips. Spoon the whipped cream into the middle of the meringue. Top with the pineapple rings and the remaining ginger strips.

Cook's know-how

Keep the oven door closed when you leave the meringue to dry out, but if you have a convection oven, you should leave the door slightly open. The meringue base can be made a day in advance and kept in an airtight container in a cool place until needed. Add the cream and fruit topping just before serving.

MANGO & PASSION FRUIT MERINGUE

SERVES 6

4 egg whites

1 1/4 cups (250 g) sugar

FILLING

1 ripe mango

1 passion fruit

1 1/4 cups (300 ml) whipping cream, whipped until thick

1 cup (125 g) strawberries, sliced

DECORATION

2/3 cup (150 ml) heavy or whipping cream, whipped until stiff

a few strawberries

1 Mark 8 in (2 x 20 cm) circles on 2 sheets of nonstick parchment paper, turn the paper over, and use to line 2 baking sheets.

2 Beat the egg whites until stiff but not dry. Add the sugar, 1 tsp at a time, and continue to beat until all the sugar has been incorporated and the mixture is stiff and glossy.

3 Pipe the meringue, in concentric circles, inside the marked circles on the paper-lined baking sheets.

4 Bake the meringue circles in a preheated oven at 275°F (140°C) for 1–1 1/4 hours until crisp and dry. Leave to cool, then carefully peel off the paper.

5 Dice the mango very fine (page 466). Halve the passion fruit and scoop out the pulp.

6 Spread the whipped cream over 1 of the meringue circles. Arrange the mango, passion fruit pulp, and strawberries on top, and top with the remaining meringue circle.

7 Decorate with piped rosettes of whipped cream (page 467), strawberry slices, and a whole strawberry.

PEACH MERINGUE

Substitute 2 peeled and sliced peaches for the mango, and 4 oz (125 g) raspberries for the strawberries. Decorate the top of the peach meringue with a few whole raspberries.

STRAWBERRY MERINGUE ROULADE

SERVES 8

sunflower oil for greasing

4 egg whites

1 1/4 cups (250 g) sugar

1/3 cup (45 g) slivered almonds

confectioners' sugar for dusting

FILLING

2/3 cup (300 ml) heavy or whipping cream, whipped until thick

8 oz (250 g) strawberries, quartered

9 x 13 IN (23 x 33 CM) JELLY ROLL PAN

1 Lightly grease the jelly roll pan and line with a sheet of baking parchment.

2 Beat the egg whites until stiff but not dry. Add the sugar, 1 tsp at a time, and continue to beat, until all the sugar has been incorporated and the mixture is stiff and glossy.

3 Spoon the meringue into the lined pan and tilt to level the surface. Sprinkle over the flaked almonds.

4 Bake near the top of a preheated oven at 400°F (200°C) for about 8 minutes until the top is golden brown.

5 Reduce the oven temperature to 325°F (160°C), and continue baking for 10 minutes or until the meringue is firm to the touch.

6 Remove the meringue from the oven and turn out onto a sheet of parchment paper. Peel the lining paper from the base and leave the meringue to cool for 10 minutes.

7 Spread the whipped cream evenly over the meringue, and scatter the strawberries over the cream.

8 Roll up the meringue from a long side, using the parchment paper to help lift it. Wrap the roulade in the parchment and leave to chill in the refrigerator for about 30 minutes. Lightly dust with sifted confectioners' sugar before serving.

MERINGUES

Meringues are very quick and easy to prepare, and they can be made weeks in advance and kept in the freezer, so they are ideal for impromptu entertaining and special occasions of all kinds. The picture shows Mocha Meringue Mille-Feuilles (top left), Chocolate Meringue Shells (top right), and Fresh Fruit Baskets (below).

FRESH FRUIT BASKETS

MAKES 8

I quantity basic meringue (see below right)
1/2 cup (250 ml) heavy cream
berries and mint sprigs (optional) to decorate

RASPBERRY SAUCE

8 oz (250 g) fresh or frozen raspberries
2 tbsp confectioners' sugar
a squeeze of lemon juice, to taste

1 Make the raspberry sauce: puree the raspberries in a blender or food processor, then push the puree through a strainer with a spoon into a bowl (discard the seeds in the strainer). Stir in the sugar and lemon juice to taste. Chill in the refrigerator until ready to use.

2 Pipe 8 meringue baskets (see box, below). Bake in a preheated oven at 250°F (120°C) for 1–1 1/2 hours until firm. Leave to cool.

3 Whip the cream until it forms stiff peaks. Fill the baskets with the cream, top with berries, and decorate with mint sprigs if you like. Serve with the chilled raspberry sauce.

MOCHA MERINGUE MILLE-FEUILLES

MAKES 6

I quantity basic meringue (below right)
I cup (125 g) slivered almonds
confectioners' sugar for dusting

COFFEE-FLAVORED CREAM

I cup (250 ml) heavy cream
I tsp instant coffee, dissolved in I tbsp water
2–3 tbsp sugar

1 Spoon 18 mounds of meringue onto nonstick parchment paper, then spread them flat with a spatula until they are very thin and about 3 in (7 cm) in diameter. Sprinkle over the almonds. Bake in a preheated oven at 250°F (120°C) for 1–1 1/2 hours until firm. Cool.

2 Make the coffee-flavored cream: whip the cream until it forms soft peaks. Add the coffee and sugar to the cream and whip until stiff peaks form.

3 Sandwich the meringue disks together in threes, with the coffee-flavored cream in between. Dust with a little confectioners' sugar before serving.

CHOCOLATE MERINGUE SHELLS

MAKES 12

I quantity basic meringue (below)
2 squares (60 g) semisweet chocolate, chopped

CHOCOLATE GANACHE

125 g (4 oz) plain chocolate, chopped
1/2 cup (125 ml) heavy cream

1 Pipe 24 shells (see box, below left). Bake in a preheated oven at 250°F (120°C) for 1–1 1/2 hours until firm. Leave to cool. Put the chocolate into a heatproof bowl over a pan of hot water and heat until melted. Drizzle over the meringues and leave to set.

2 Make the ganache: put the chopped chocolate and the cream into a heavy-bottomed saucepan and heat gently, stirring occasionally, until the chocolate has melted.

3 Remove the pan from the heat and beat the ganache for about 5 minutes until the mixture is fluffy and cooled. Sandwich the meringues together with the chocolate ganache.

BASIC MERINGUE

4 egg whites
1 1/4 cups (250 g) sugar

1 Beat the egg whites in a scrupulously clean large bowl, with an electric mixer on maximum speed, until the whites are stiff and look like clouds.

2 Keeping the mixer on maximum speed, add the sugar a teaspoon at a time and continue beating until the mixture is stiff and shiny.

3 Pipe, spoon, or spread the meringue as preferred and bake as in the recipes above. All ovens vary, so baking times cannot be exact. You will know the meringues are cooked when they can be lifted easily from the parchment paper.

PIPING MERINGUE SHAPES

Baskets

Mark 4 in (8 x 10 cm) circles on nonstick parchment paper; turn over. Spoon the meringue into a pastry bag fitted with a medium star tip, and pipe inside the circles, building up the sides to form baskets.

Shells

Spoon the meringue into a pastry bag fitted with a medium star tip. Pipe 24 even-sized shells, about 2 in (5 cm) in diameter at the base, onto nonstick parchment paper .

MARBLED RASPBERRY CHEESECAKE

The crunchy crust of this cheesecake, made with crushed oatmeal cookies and walnuts, provides a delicious contrast to the creamy filling, marbled with streaks of fresh raspberry puree. It is a delicate cheesecake, so for best results be sure to chill it well before slicing and serving.

SERVES 10

3 tbsp cold water

2 x 1/4 oz (7 g) envelope unflavored powdered gelatin

1 lb (500 g) raspberries

4 tbsp framboise (raspberry liqueur)

1 cup (250 g) cream cheese, at room temperature

2/3 cup (150 ml) sour cream

2 eggs, separated

1/2 cup (125 g) sugar

COOKIE CRUST

1 1/3 cups (125 g) coarsely crushed oatmeal cookies

4 tbls (60 g) butter, melted

2 tbls (30 g) light brown sugar

1/3 cup (45 g) walnuts, chopped

DECORATION

2/3 cup (150 ml) whipping cream, whipped until stiff

a few raspberries

mint sprigs

9 IN (23 CM) LOOSE-BOTTOMED OR SPRINGFORM CAKE PAN

1 Make the cookie crust: mix together the cookies, butter, brown sugar, and walnuts and press evenly over the bottom of the pan.

2 Put the measured water into a heatproof bowl, sprinkle the gelatin over the top, and leave for about 10 minutes until spongy.

3 Meanwhile, puree the raspberries in a food processor, then push them through a strainer to remove the seeds. Stir in the liqueur. Set aside.

4 Put the cream cheese into a large bowl, and beat until soft and smooth. Add the sour cream and egg yolks, and beat until well blended.

5 Stand the bowl of gelatin in a saucepan of hot water and heat gently until it dissolves. Stir into the cheese mixture.

6 Make the filling (see box, right).

7 Use a spatula to loosen the side of the cheesecake from the pan, then remove the cheesecake. Slide it onto a serving plate. Pipe whipped cream (page 467) around the edge and decorate with raspberries and mint sprigs.

Cook's know-how

To achieve an attractive marbled effect, fold in the raspberry puree lightly but thoroughly, so it forms thin streaks. If there are large areas of raspberry puree, they will not set with the rest of the mixture.

Making the filling

Beat the egg whites until stiff but not dry. Add the sugar, 1 tsp at a time, and keep beating until all the sugar is incorporated and the meringue mixture is stiff and glossy.

Turn the cheese mixture into the meringue and fold together, blending well. Leave the mixture to thicken slightly.

Fold in the raspberry puree, swirling it in just enough to give an attractive marbled effect.

Pour the mixture carefully onto the cookie crust and chill until set.

AUSTRIAN CHEESECAKE

SERVES 8

6 tbls (90 g) butter, at room temperature, plus extra for greasing

3/4 cup (150 g) sugar

1 1/4 cups (300 g) cottage cheese

2 eggs, separated

1/2 cup (60 g) ground almonds

2 tbsp semolina

grated zest and juice of 1 large lemon

1/3 cup (60 g) golden raisins

confectioners' sugar for dusting

8 IN (20 CM) LOOSE-BOTTOMED OR SPRINGFORM CAKE PAN

1 Lightly butter the pan and line the bottom with a circle of parchment paper.

2 Beat the butter with the sugar and cottage cheese until light and creamy. Beat in the egg yolks, then stir in the almonds, semolina, and lemon zest and juice. Leave to stand for 10 minutes, then fold in the golden raisins.

3 In a separate bowl, beat the egg whites until stiff but not dry. Carefully fold into the cheese mixture.

4 Turn into the prepared pan and level the surface. Bake in a preheated oven at 375°F (190°C) for 30–35 minutes until browned and firm to the touch. Turn off the oven and leave the cheesecake inside to cool for about 1 hour. Chill before serving.

5 Use a spatula to loosen the side of the cheesecake from the pan, then remove the cheesecake. Slide on to a plate, and dust with sifted confectioners' sugar (see below).

Cook's know-how

For a decorative pattern on top of the cheesecake, place a doily on top, dust with confectioners' sugar, then carefully lift off the doily.

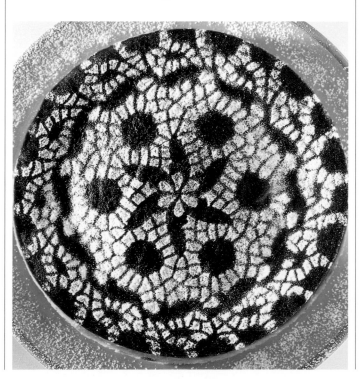

TROPICAL FRUIT CHEESECAKE

SERVES 10

2 ripe mangoes

2/3 cup (150 ml) mango and apple fruit juice combined

2 x 1/4 oz (7 g) envelope unflavored powdered gelatin

1 cup (250 g) cream cheese, at room temperature

generous 1 cup (125 g) sugar

2 eggs, separated

2/3 cup (150 ml) whipping cream, whipped until thick

COOKIE CRUST

2 cups (125 g) crushed coconut cookies

4 tbls (60 g) butter, melted

2 tbls (30 g) light brown sugar

DECORATION

2 kiwi fruit, peeled and sliced

8 oz (250 g) canned pineapple pieces in natural juice, drained

9 IN (23 CM) LOOSE-BOTTOMED OR SPRINGFORM CAKE PAN

1 Make the cookie crust: mix together the cookies, melted butter, and sugar, and press over the bottom of the pan.

2 Slice the mango flesh away from the seeds (page 466). Peel, then puree in a food processor.

3 Pour the fruit juice into a heatproof bowl, and sprinkle the gelatin over the top. Leave for about 10 minutes until it becomes spongy. Stand the bowl in a small pan of hot water, and heat gently until the gelatin has dissolved.

4 In a large bowl, beat the cream cheese until smooth and creamy. Beat in half of the sugar, the egg yolks, and the mango puree. Gradually beat in the gelatin mixture.

5 In a separate bowl, beat the egg whites until stiff but not dry. Beat in the remaining sugar, 1 tsp at a time, and continue to beat at high speed until the sugar is incorporated and the mixture is stiff and glossy.

6 Fold the whipped cream into the cheese and mango mixture, then fold in the egg whites. Pour onto the cookie crust and chill until set.

7 Use a spatula to loosen the side of the cheesecake, then remove from the pan. Slide onto a serving plate. Decorate the top with slices of kiwi fruit and pieces of pineapple before serving.

FRUIT SALADS

A fruit salad is welcome at the end of any meal any time of year, whether it is a simple family supper or a special occasion. All of these fruit salads can be made well in advance and served just as they are, or with cream or ice cream, sour cream, or yogurt.

TROPICAL ISLAND FRUIT SALAD

SERVES 6

1 small ripe pineapple

1 ripe cantaloupe melon

1 ripe mango

8 oz (250 g) seedless black grapes

⅔ cup (150 ml) pineapple and coconut juice or pineapple juice

4 oz (125 g) cape gooseberries

2 ripe guavas, preferably pink-fleshed

2 Asian pears

1 Cut the top and bottom off the pineapple. Remove the skin with a sharp knife, then cut out the brown eyes. Cut the pineapple lengthwise into 4 pieces and remove and discard the hard inner core. Cut the flesh into chunks and put into a large glass serving bowl.

2 Cut the melon into quarters, remove and discard the seeds with a spoon. Cut each melon quarter in half, remove the skin with a sharp knife, and cut the flesh into chunks. Add to the pineapple.

3 Peel the mango, cut either side of the large flat seed, and neatly cut the mango flesh into pieces. Add to the bowl with the grapes. Pour the fruit juice over, cover, and chill in the refrigerator for about 4 hours, or overnight.

4 Peel back the paper lanterns on the cape gooseberries. Remove the fruits from about half of the cape gooseberries, wipe gently with paper towels, and add to the bowl.

5 Peel the guavas, halve the fruits, and remove the seeds. Cut the flesh into neat pieces and add to the bowl. Peel and quarter the pears, remove the cores, and slice the flesh neatly into the bowl.

6 Stir the fruits gently together, making sure the pear is submerged in juice or it will discolor. Cover and chill in the refrigerator for about 1 hour. Serve chilled, decorated with the remaining cape gooseberries.

SPICED FRUIT SALAD

SERVES 4–6

1 lb (500 g) mixed ready-to-eat dried fruits, such as pears, peaches, mango, prunes, pineapple, figs, and apple

about 3¾ cups (900 ml) apple juice

2–3 star anise, to taste

1 vanilla bean

½ cup (75 g) dried cranberries

½ cup (75 g) dried cherries

1 Put the mixed fruits into a saucepan with 3¾ cups (900 ml) apple juice, the star anise, and vanilla bean. Bring to a boil and simmer gently for about 15 minutes.

2 Add the dried cranberries and cherries to the pan and continue cooking for about 15 minutes, adding more apple juice (or water) if necessary. Serve hot or cold.

ORANGE PASSION SALAD

SERVES 6

8 thin-skinned oranges

juice of 1 small lime

2 ripe papayas (pawpaws)

3 ripe passion fruit

1 Remove the thin orange skin from 2 of the oranges with a zester and set the strips of zest aside. Peel all the oranges and remove all the skin and pith. Slice into circles and remove any seeds.

2 Put the orange slices into a fairly shallow glass bowl with any juice from the oranges and the lime juice.

3 Halve the papayas lengthwise and scoop out the seeds. Peel the halves, cut crosswise into fairly thick slices, and add to the bowl. Cut the passion fruit in half crosswise and scoop the juice and seeds over the fruit in the bowl. Top the salad with the orange zest, cover, and chill in the refrigerator for at least 2 hours. Stir before serving – there is no need for sugar.

FRUITS-OF-THE-FOREST SALAD

SERVES 6–8

8 oz (250 g) fresh cranberries

¼ cup (60 g) sugar

8 oz (250 g) strawberries, hulled and halved if large

4 oz (125 g) blueberries

8 oz (250 g) raspberries

8 oz (250 g) blackberries

8 oz (250 g) loganberries, or increase the amount of the other berries if loganberries are unavailable

2–3 tbsp balsamic vinegar

1 tsp green peppercorns in brine or oil, rinsed and lightly crushed

1 Put the cranberries into a stainless-steel pan with 5 tbsp water. Cook gently for 5–10 minutes or until the cranberries pop and are just soft. Remove from the heat, stir in the sugar, and leave until the sugar has dissolved and the mixture has cooled slightly (do not add the sugar at the beginning or it will make the cranberry skins tough).

2 Put the remaining fruit into a serving bowl, add the cooled cranberries and juice, and mix gently together.

3 Add the balsamic vinegar and green peppercorns and mix gently. Cover and chill in the refrigerator for at least 4 hours (or overnight) to allow to juices to develop and the flavors to mellow.

CLOCKWISE FROM TOP RIGHT: Spiced Fruit Salad, Orange Passion Salad, Tropical Island Fruit Salad, Fruits-of-the-Forest Salad.

MOCHA PUDDING

SERVES 6

2 cups (125 g) fresh whole wheat crumbs

2/3 cup (90 g) light brown sugar

1/3 cup (75 g) sweetened cocoa powder

2 tbsp instant coffee

1 1/4 cups (300 ml) heavy cream

2/3 cup (150 ml) light cream

2 oz (60 g) semisweet chocolate, grated

1 In a bowl, mix together the bread crumbs, sugar, cocoa powder, and coffee granules. In another bowl, whip the creams together until they form soft peaks.

2 Spoon half of the cream into 6 glass serving dishes. Cover with the bread crumb mixture and then with the remaining cream. Chill for at least 6 hours, or overnight for best results.

3 Sprinkle generously with the grated chocolate just before serving.

Cook's know-how

To make grating chocolate easy, chill it well in the refrigerator before you grate it, and use the largest holes on the grater.

CHOCOLATE LAYERED TERRINE

This rich and creamy dessert is ideal for a dinner party or weekend treat. A layer of white chocolate and heavy cream is sandwiched between layers of semisweet chocolate and heavy cream made heady with brandy.

SERVES 8–10

DARK CHOCOLATE LAYERS

8 oz (250 g) semisweet chocolate

2 tbsp brandy

2 eggs

1 3/4 cups (375 ml) heavy cream

WHITE CHOCOLATE LAYER

3 oz (90 g) white chocolate

1 egg

2/3 cup (150 ml) heavy cream

DECORATION

2/3 cup (150 ml) heavy or whipping cream, whipped, grated chocolate, and mint sprigs to decorate

2 LB (1 KG) LOAF PAN

1 Make the dark chocolate layers: break the semisweet chocolate into pieces and place in a heatproof bowl with the brandy over a pan of hot water. Heat gently to melt, then leave to cool.

2 Line the loaf pan with plastic wrap. Set aside.

3 Put the eggs into a heatproof bowl over a pan of hot water. Beat until the eggs are thick and mousselike, and leave a trail when the whisk is lifted. Remove from the heat and beat until the bowl is completely cold.

4 Whip the cream until it just holds its shape. Fold the whisked eggs into the cooled chocolate mixture, then fold in the cream.

5 Pour half of the dark chocolate mixture into the prepared pan, then place in the freezer for about 15 minutes until firm. Reserve the remaining semisweet chocolate mixture.

6 Meanwhile, make the white chocolate mixture in the same way as the semisweet chocolate mixture.

7 Pour the white chocolate mixture on top of the firm layer in the pan, and freeze for 15 minutes.

8 Spoon the reserved semisweet chocolate mixture on top of the white chocolate layer and freeze for about 30 minutes until it is firm enough to slice.

9 Invert the pan onto a serving plate, and remove the plastic wrap. Decorate the terrine with piped rosettes of whipped cream (page 467), grated chocolate, and mint sprigs. Slice thinly to serve.

Healthy option

To make this chocolate terrine slightly less rich and calorific, use plain yogurt in place of one-third of the heavy cream. Omit the cream and chocolate decoration, and dust with unsweetened cocoa powder instead.

CHOCOLATE & BRANDY MOUSSE

SERVES 6

8 oz (250 g) semisweet chocolate, broken into pieces
3 tbsp brandy
3 tbsp cold water
2 x 1/4 oz (7 g) envelope unflavored powdered gelatin
4 eggs, plus 2 egg yolks
6 tbls (90 g) sugar
2/3 cup (150 ml) whipping cream, whipped until thick

DECORATION

2/3 cup (150 ml) heavy or whipping cream, whipped until stiff
chocolate curls or caraque (page 467) to decorate

1 Put the chocolate and brandy into a heatproof bowl over a pan of hot water. Heat until melted. Leave to cool.

2 Put the cold water into a heatproof bowl and sprinkle the gelatin over the top. Leave for 10 minutes until spongy. Put the bowl in a pan of hot water and heat gently until dissolved.

3 Combine the eggs, egg yolks, and sugar in a large heatproof bowl, and put over a saucepan of simmering water. Beat with an electric mixer until the egg mixture is very thick and mousselike. Beat in the dissolved gelatin.

4 Fold the whipped cream into the cooled chocolate, then fold into the egg mixture. Carefully pour into a glass serving bowl, cover, and leave in the refrigerator until set.

5 Decorate with piped rosettes of cream and chocolate curls or caraque (page 467). Serve the mousse chilled.

Cook's know-how

Buy a good-quality semisweet chocolate. For the best flavor, look for a brand with at least 70% cocoa solids.

TIRAMISU

SERVES 8

1 1/2 tsp instant coffee granules
1/2 cup (125 ml) boiling water
3 tbsp brandy
2 eggs
1/3 cup (65 g) sugar
1 cup (250 g) mascarpone cheese
1 1/4 cups (300 ml) heavy cream, whipped until thick
16 ladyfingers or plain cake slices
2 oz (60 g) semisweet chocolate, coarsely grated
1 oz (30 g) white chocolate, coarsely grated, to decorate

1 Dissolve the coffee in the measured boiling water and mix with the brandy.

2 Combine the eggs and sugar in a large bowl and beat together until thick and light, and the mixture leaves a trail on the surface.

3 Put the mascarpone into a bowl and stir in a little of the egg mixture. Fold in the rest, then fold in the cream.

4 Cut the ladyfingers horizontally in half. Layer the tiramisu (see box, below) with half the ladyfingers, half the coffee and brandy mixture, half the mascarpone mixture, and half the semisweet chocolate.

5 Repeat the layers with the remaining ingredients, decorating the top with the grated white chocolate and the remaining semisweet chocolate. Cover and chill for at least 4 hours before serving.

Layering the tiramisu

Line the bottom of a large glass serving bowl with half of the ladyfingers or cake slices. Drizzle half of the coffee and brandy mixture over them.

SORBETS

Light and refreshing, sorbets are the perfect ending to a rich meal. Flavored with fresh fruits and made from a basic mixture of sugar, water, and egg white, they're also low in fat. Decorate each sorbet with its key ingredient or with an ingredient complementary in flavor.

LIME

SERVES 6–8

| 1 1/4 cups (250 g) sugar |
| 2 1/2 cups (600 ml) water |
| finely grated zest and juice of 6 limes |
| 2 egg whites |
| strips of lime zest to decorate |

1 Put the sugar and measured water into a saucepan and heat gently until the sugar dissolves. Bring to a boil and boil for 2 minutes. Remove from the heat, add the lime zest, and leave to cool completely. Stir in the lime juice.

2 Strain the lime syrup into a shallow freezerproof container and freeze for about 2 hours until just mushy. Transfer the mixture into a bowl and beat gently to break down any large crystals.

3 Beat the egg whites until stiff but not dry, then fold into the lime mixture. Return to the freezer, and freeze until firm. Transfer the sorbet to the refrigerator to soften for about 30 minutes before serving, and top with strips of lime zest.

APRICOT

SERVES 6–8

| 6 tbls (90 g) sugar |
| 1 1/4 cups (300 ml) water |
| juice of 1 lemon |
| 1 1/2 lb (750 g) apricots, halved and pitted |
| 2 egg whites |

1 Put the sugar, measured water, and lemon juice into a saucepan and heat gently until the sugar has dissolved. Bring to a boil, add the apricots, and simmer for 15 minutes or until very tender. Cool.

2 Peel and slice a few apricots for decoration, and set aside. Press the remainder through a strainer. Mix with the syrup in a freezerproof container, then follow steps 2 and 3 of Lime Sorbet (above). Decorate with the sliced apricots before serving.

PEAR & GINGER

SERVES 6–8

| 6 tbls (90 g) sugar |
| 1 1/4 cups (300 ml) water |
| 1 tbsp lemon juice |
| 1 1/2 lb (750 g) pears, peeled and cored |
| 1 piece of ginger in syrup, finely chopped |
| 2 egg whites |
| strips of ginger in syrup to decorate |

1 Put the sugar, measured water, and lemon juice into a saucepan and heat gently until the sugar dissolves. Bring to a boil, add the pears, and poach gently, basting with the sugar syrup from time to time, for 20–25 minutes until the pears are tender. Cool, then puree in a food processor.

2 Add the chopped ginger to the pear puree. Pour the pear mixture into a freezerproof container, then follow steps 2 and 3 of Lime Sorbet (left). Decorate with stem ginger before serving.

RASPBERRY

SERVES 6–8

| 1 lb (500 g) raspberries |
| 1 scant cup (175 g) sugar |
| 2 1/2 cups (600 ml) water |
| juice of 1 orange |
| 3 egg whites |
| raspberries and mint sprigs to decorate |

1 Puree the raspberries in a food processor, then push through a strainer to remove the seeds. Put the sugar and measured water into a saucepan and heat gently until the sugar dissolves. Bring to a boil, then boil for 5 minutes. Pour into a bowl and cool.

2 Stir in raspberry puree and orange juice. Pour into a freezerproof container, then follow steps 2 and 3 of Lime Sorbet (left). Decorate with raspberries and mint sprigs before serving.

GRANITAS

Italian granitas are similar to sorbets but even easier to make: they are simply flavored ice crystals.

COFFEE

Put 4 tbls (60 g) sugar and 4 tbsp instant coffee granules into a pan with 3 cups (750 ml) water and bring to a boil. Simmer for about 5 minutes. Leave to cool, then pour into a freezerproof container. Freeze, stirring occasionally, for 5 hours.

LEMON

Put 1 cup (200 g) sugar into a saucepan, add 3 cups (500 ml) water, and bring to a boil. Simmer for 5 minutes. Leave to cool. Add 2 tsp finely grated lemon zest and the juice of 4 lemons to the sugar syrup. Pour into a freezerproof container and freeze, stirring occasionally, for 5 hours.

WATERMELON

Remove and discard the rind and seeds from 2 lb (1 kg) watermelon. Puree the flesh in a food processor. Pour into a freezerproof container and mix in 1/4 cup (30 g) confectioners' sugar and 1 1/2 tsp lemon juice. Freeze, stirring occasionally, for 5 hours.

CLOCKWISE FROM TOP RIGHT: Lime, Raspberry, Pear & Ginger, and Apricot Sorbets.

PEACH MELBA

SERVES 4

4 ripe peaches, peeled, pitted, and sliced

8 scoops of vanilla ice cream

mint sprigs to decorate

MELBA SAUCE

12 oz (375 g) raspberries

about 4 tbsp confectioners' sugar

1 Make the Melba sauce (see box, below).

2 Arrange the peach slices in 4 glass serving dishes. Top each with 2 scoops of ice cream and some sauce. Decorate with mint sprigs and the remaining raspberries.

Making Melba sauce

Puree 8 oz (250 g) of the raspberries. Push through a strainer to remove the seeds.

Sift the confectioners' sugar over the puree and stir in.

RICH VANILLA ICE CREAM

Homemade ice cream tastes better than commercially made ice cream, and it keeps for up to a month in the freezer. If you have an electric ice-cream maker, you will get a smoother result.

SERVES 4–6

4 egg yolks

generous ¹/₂ cup (125 g) sugar

1¹/₄ cups (300 ml) milk

1¹/₄ cups (300 ml) heavy cream

1¹/₂ tsp vanilla extract

strawberries to decorate

1 Put the egg yolks and sugar into a bowl and beat until light in color.

2 Heat the milk in a heavy pan to just below boiling point. Add a little of the hot milk to the egg-yolk mixture and stir to blend, then pour in the remaining milk.

3 Pour back into the pan and heat gently, stirring, until the froth disappears and the mixture coats the back of a spoon. Do not boil.

4 Leave the custard to cool, then stir in the cream and vanilla extract.

5 Pour into a container and freeze for 3 hours. Tip into a bowl and mash to break down the ice crystals. Return to container. Freeze for 2 hours. Mash and freeze for another 2 hours. Remove from the freezer 30 minutes before serving, and decorate.

CHOCOLATE ICE CREAM

In step 2, heat the milk with 4 oz (125 g) chopped semisweet chocolate. Let it melt before adding to the egg-yolk mixture.

CHOCOLATE CHIP ICE CREAM

In step 2, heat the milk with 4 oz (125 g) chopped white chocolate. Let it melt before adding to the egg-yolk mixture. Stir 2 oz (60 g) semisweet chocolate chips into the custard with the cream in step 4.

BANANA & HONEY ICE CREAM

Mash 1 lb (500 g) bananas with 3 tbsp lemon juice and 2 tbsp honey. Add to the custard with the cream in step 4.

BAKED ALASKA

SERVES 8

1 x 8 in (20 cm) sponge cake case

8 oz (250 g) raspberries, sliced strawberries, or other summer fruits

1 pint (500 ml) vanilla ice cream

2 egg whites

generous 1/2 cup (125 g) sugar

whole berries to decorate

1 Put the sponge cake case into a shallow ovenproof serving dish. Arrange the fruits in the case.

2 Put the ice cream on top of the fruits and put in the freezer to keep the ice cream frozen while making the meringue.

3 Beat the egg whites (an electric mixer can be used) until stiff but not dry.

4 Add the sugar, 1 tsp at a time, and continue to beat until the sugar has been incorporated and the meringue mixture is stiff and glossy.

5 Pipe or spoon the meringue over the ice cream, covering it completely.

6 Bake immediately in a preheated oven at 450°F (230°C) for 3–4 minutes until the meringue is tinged with brown. Serve at once, decorated with raspberries and strawberries.

Cook's know-how

A block of firm ice cream is needed for this recipe – do not use soft-scoop ice cream. Make sure the ice cream is completely covered by the egg white, which stops the ice cream from melting.

TUTTI-FRUTTI BOMBE

SERVES 8

1 cup (175 g) mixed dried fruit

1/3 cup (60 g) dried apricots, chopped

1/3 cup (60 g) candied cherries, halved

3 tbsp brandy

3 eggs

generous 1/2 cup (125 g) sugar

2 cups (500 ml) milk

1 3/4 cups (450 ml) heavy cream

2/3 cup (150 ml) light cream

7 1/2-CUP (1.75 LITER) BOMBE MOLD

1 Combine the dried fruit, apricots, cherries, and brandy. Cover and soak for 8 hours.

2 In a large bowl, beat together the eggs and sugar. Heat the milk in a heavy saucepan to just below boiling point. Pour into the egg mixture, stirring.

3 Pour back into the pan. Cook gently, stirring with a wooden spoon, until the froth disappears and the mixture thickens. Do not boil. Remove from the heat and leave to cool.

4 Whip 1 1/4 cups (300 ml) heavy cream and the light cream together until they are just beginning to hold their shape. Fold into the custard with the fruit and brandy mixture.

5 Turn into a shallow freezerproof container and freeze for 2 hours or until beginning to set but still slightly soft.

6 Remove the mixture from the freezer and mix well to distribute the fruit evenly. Spoon into the bombe mold, cover, and return to the freezer. Freeze for 3 hours or until firm.

7 Remove from the freezer about 20 minutes before serving to soften. Turn out onto a serving plate, and spoon the remaining cream, lightly whipped, on top. Slice and serve at once.

CASSATA

SERVES 8

1 oz (30 g) candied angelica, rinsed, dried, and chopped

2 tbls (30 g) candied cherries, rinsed, dried, and chopped

2 tbls (30 g) chopped mixed candied peel

2 tbsp dark rum

2¹/2 cups (600 ml) raspberry sorbet

²/3 cup (150 ml) heavy cream, whipped until thick

2¹/2 cups (600 ml) vanilla ice cream

3³/4 CUP (900 ML) TERRINE

1 Chill the terrine. Put the angelica, candied cherries, and candied peel in a bowl.

2 Add the rum and stir well, then leave to soak while preparing the ice-cream layers.

3 Allow the sorbet to soften, then spread it evenly over the bottom of the chilled terrine. Chill in the freezer until solid.

4 Fold the fruit and rum mixture into the whipped cream. Spoon into the terrine and level the surface. Return to the freezer until firm.

5 Allow the vanilla ice cream to soften, then spread it evenly over the fruit layer. Cover and freeze for 8 hours.

6 To turn out, dip the terrine into warm water and invert the cassata onto a large serving plate. Slice, and serve at once.

Cook's know-how

This is not a true cassata, but a layered ice-cream "sandwich" that has borrowed its name. A true Sicilian cassata is a bombe of liqueur-soaked sponge cake filled with ricotta cheese studded with candied fruits and grated chocolate. It is often served at wedding feasts and other celebrations.

FROZEN LEMON SHERBERT

SERVES 4

²/3 cup (150 ml) heavy cream

finely grated zest and juice of 1 large lemon

1 cup (175 g) sugar

1¹/4 cups (300 ml) milk

thinly pared zest of 1 lemon, cut into strips, to decorate

1 Whip the cream until it forms soft peaks. Add the lemon zest and juice, sugar, and milk, and mix until evenly blended.

2 Pour into a shallow freezerproof container, cover, and freeze for at least 6 hours or until firm.

3 Cut the mixture into chunks, then transfer to a food processor and blend until smooth and creamy. Pour into 4 individual freezerproof dishes and freeze for about 8 hours.

4 Blanch the strips of lemon zest in a pan of boiling water for 1 minute only. Drain, rinse, and pat dry.

5 Decorate the sherbert with the strips of lemon zest and serve.

FROZEN ORANGE SHERBERT

Substitute the finely grated zest and juice of 1 orange for the lemon, and reduce the sugar to 4 oz (125 g). Decorate with blanched strips of orange zest.

13

CAKES &
QUICK BREADS

30–60 MINUTES

OVER 60 MINUTES

ECONOMICAL

WHOLE-WHEAT PANCAKES

Family favorite: a simple batter made with whole-wheat flour, cooked in moments on a hot griddle or in a skillet. Delicious with maple syrup.

MAKES 20 55 calories each

Takes 30 minutes   Page 519

TRADITIONAL

VICTORIA LAYER CAKE

Two light and golden layers of sponge cake sandwiched with jam, and sprinkled generously with sugar.

CUTS INTO 8 SLICES 386 calories each

Takes 35 minutes, plus cooling   Page 510

FORK COOKIES

Plain and simple: a butter-enriched dough, imprinted with a fork pattern and baked until crisp and golden.

MAKES 32 104 calories each

Takes 30 minutes, plus cooling   Page 521

BRANDY SNAPS

A delicate batter with the zesty bite of ground ginger and lemon juice, baked until golden, then rolled and left to get crisp.

MAKES 15 107 calories each

Takes 40 minutes, plus cooling   Page 521

CORNBREAD

An old-fashioned favorite: a slightly sweet batter made from cornmeal. Baked until golden and served warm.

MAKES 9 SQUARES 230 calories each

Takes 40 minutes, plus cooling   Page 516

WALNUT COOKIES

Crisp and sweet: a walnut-studded dough, shaped into a roll, cut into thin slices, and baked until golden. Very easy to make.

MAKES 50 59 calories each

Takes 35 minutes, plus chilling   Page 524

FRENCH CLASSIC

ALMOND TUILES

Crisp and delicate: a sweet, almond-flavored batter baked until golden brown, then shaped into curves resembling old-fashioned roof tiles.

MAKES 30 45 calories each

Takes 30 minutes, plus cooling   Page 520

FAMILY CHOICE

BISCUITS

A treat at any time: featherweight biscuits baked from a dough made in moments. Perfect spread with butter and jam.

MAKES 12 133 calories each

Takes 30 minutes, plus cooling   Page 518

MINCEMEAT MUFFINS

Rich and fruity: a miniature and quick version of traditional British mince pies. Baked in individual cupcake cases.

MAKES 32 137 calories each

Takes 40 minutes, plus cooling   Page 512

OVER 60 MINUTES

JELLY ROLL

A time-honored favorite: a light golden cake spread generously with a layer of raspberry jam, rolled up, and decorated with confectioners' sugar.

CUTS INTO 8 SLICES 195 calories each

Takes 45 minutes, plus cooling   Page 507

VIENNESE FINGERS

Pretty and delicious: a rich butter dough piped into finger shapes, baked until golden brown, then each end dipped in melted chocolate.

MAKES 12 215 calories each

Takes 30 minutes, plus cooling   Page 520

PINWHEEL COOKIES

Attractive and easy: vanilla and coffee doughs rolled together, then cut into thin slices and baked.

MAKES 18 98 calories each

Takes 45 minutes, plus chilling   Page 524

COCONUT MACAROONS

Almonds as well as coconut flavor these cookies. Crisp and golden on the outside and deliciously tender on the inside.

MAKES 26 116 calories each

Takes 40 minutes, plus cooling   Page 520

POTATO ROLLS

An unusual treat: a dough made with mashed potatoes and baked until crisp. Simple and delicious.

MAKES 12 113 calories each

Takes 40 minutes, plus cooling   Page 519

FAMILY CHOICE

FLAPJACKS

Rich, chewy, and very easy to make: an oatmeal studded batter is spread into a roasting pan, baked, and cut into slices.

MAKES 24 102 calories each

Takes 45 minutes, plus cooling   Page 524

GINGERSNAPS

Crisp and rich: ginger and cinnamon spice up the buttery dough that is baked until dark golden brown.

MAKES 15 81 calories each

Takes 30 minutes, plus cooling   Page 521

FRUIT & CREAM CAKE

Two layers of golden sponge cake filled with freshly whipped cream, sweet, juicy strawberries, and tropical passion fruit.

CUTS INTO 8 SLICES 260 calories each

Takes 60 minutes, plus cooling   Page 507

ECONOMICAL

SWEET GRIDDLE CAKES

Old-fashioned griddle cakes studded with dried currants and flavored with apple-pie spice. Served hot from the pan or left to cool slightly.

MAKES 12 204 calories each

Takes 30 minutes, plus cooling   Page 518

OVER 60 MINUTES

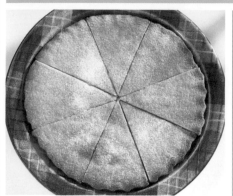

SHORTBREAD

A Scottish classic: a dough made rich with butter, baked until golden, and sprinkled with sugar.

MAKES 8 WEDGES 233 calories each

Takes 55 minutes, plus cooling   Page 516

DEVIL'S FOOD CAKE

Layers of moist, rich chocolate cake spread with a sweet, fluffy white frosting. Perfect for large family gatherings.

CUTS INTO 12 SLICES 513 calories each

Takes 60 minutes, plus cooling   Page 504

CARROT CAKE

Moist cake made with mashed bananas and grated carrot; chopped walnuts add crunch. Cream cheese frosting is spread on top.

CUTS INTO 10 SQUARES 412 calories each

Takes 1 1/4 hours, plus cooling   Page 503

MARBLED COFFEE RING CAKE

Two batters, one coffee flavored and one plain, swirled together, baked, and topped with coffee frosting and melted white chocolate.

CUTS INTO 12 SLICES 471 calories each

Takes 1 1/4 hours   Page 505

IRISH SODA BREAD

A traditional quick bread enhanced with the tang of buttermilk. Scored and baked until golden brown.

CUTS INTO 8 WEDGES 227 calories each

Takes 45 minutes, plus cooling   Page 519

GINGERBREAD

A batter cake made moist, dark, and delicious with molasses and spices. Best baked ahead and stored in an airtight tin for a few days before eating.

MAKES 15 SQUARES 349 calories each

Takes 1 1/4 hours, plus cooling   Page 516

LIME SHEET CAKE

Light and delicious: a lime-flavored cake batter baked in a rectangular pan, topped with tangy lime frosting, and cut into squares.

MAKES 12 SQUARES 340 calories each

Takes 50 minutes, plus cooling   Page 510

CHOCOLATE & ORANGE MOUSSE CAKE

Two layers of delicate chocolate cake filled with chocolate- and orange-flavored mousse.

CUTS INTO 12 SLICES 417 calories each

Takes 1 1/4 hours, plus chilling   Page 506

CREAMY CHOCOLATE CAKE

Rich and attractive; delicious whipped cream hides a cocoa-flavored cake. Decorated with white chocolate curls if you like.

CUTS INTO 14 SLICES 391 calories each

Takes 1 1/4 hours, plus cooling   Page 505

OVER 60 MINUTES

FRUITED BANANA BREAD

Ripe bananas, spices, and succulent dried fruit give this hearty loaf special appeal. Serve sliced and spread with butter.

CUTS INTO 12 SLICES 334 calories each

Takes 1½ hours, plus cooling · Page 513

ZUCCHINI BREAD

An all-time summer favorite: zucchini baked until sweet and tender in a deliciously spiced and walnut-studded batter.

CUTS INTO 12 SLICES 331 calories each

Takes 1½ hours, plus cooling · Page 503

DATE & WALNUT LOAF

Sweet dates and crunchy walnuts are baked in a lightly sweetened batter. Delicious sliced and spread with butter.

CUTS INTO 12 SLICES 269 calories each

Takes 1¾ hours, plus cooling · Page 517

CHECKERBOARD CAKE

Classic cake made from chocolate- and vanilla-flavored batters wrapped with almond paste.

CUTS INTO 8 SLICES 425 calories each

Takes 60 minutes, plus cooling · Page 511

FRUIT LOAF

A deliciously tender loaf studded with tea-soaked dried fruit. Serve sliced and spread with butter.

CUTS INTO 12 SLICES 257 calories each

Takes 2 hours, plus soaking · Page 517

SIMNEL CAKE

Moist and tender fruitcake, brushed with apricot jam, topped with almond paste, and decorated with balls of almond paste.

CUTS INTO 12 SLICES 494 calories each

Takes 2¾ hours, plus cooling · Page 512

DUNDEE CAKE

Rich and fruity: golden raisins, dried currants, raisins, candied cherries, and lemon, baked in a batter until golden, and decorated with almonds.

CUTS INTO 12 SLICES 384 calories each

Takes 1¾ hours, plus cooling · Page 513

HEAVENLY CHOCOLATE CAKE

A rich chocolate and almond cake cut in half, filled and covered with fudge frosting, and decorated with white chocolate curls.

CUTS INTO 8 SLICES 615 calories each

Takes 1½ hours, plus cooling · Page 504

RICH FRUITCAKE

Classic and good: raisins, golden raisins, candied cherries, spices, and brandy flavor this moist cake. Best when baked ahead.

CUTS INTO 10 SLICES 570 calories each

Takes 2–2¼ hours, plus cooling · Page 511

CAKES & QUICK BREADS KNOW-HOW

CAKE MAKING is often seen as the test of a cook's skills, but there are lots of cakes and quick breads, as well as biscuits, cookies, and muffins that are very simple to make, and just as delicious as more elaborate creations. If you are a beginner, just remember to follow recipes carefully, and make sure you measure ingredients accurately. Use the correct equipment and pan, and take the time to prepare the batter or dough properly so you'll achieve perfect results every time. You'll find that once you've gained confidence, you'll be able to experiment with more challenging recipes.

STORING

Most cakes are best eaten freshly made, particularly sponge cakes made without fat, but if you do want to keep a cake, be sure to store it in an airtight container. Put the cake on the upturned lid of the cake tin, then put the tin over the top. This makes it easy to remove the cake from the tin. Fruitcakes and cakes made by the melting method, such as gingerbread, actually improve with keeping (store in an airtight tin). Wrap fruitcake in waxed paper and then overwrap in foil. Don't put foil directly in contact with a fruitcake because the acid in the fruit might react with the foil. Any cake that has a filling or frosting of whipped cream, buttercream, or cream cheese should be kept in the refrigerator. Biscuits, muffins, and most quick breads are best eaten the day you make them – just out of the oven, if you like.

Most cookies can be stored in an airtight tin for a few days; if they soften, crisp them up in a warm oven. Leave cakes and cookies to cool completely on a wire rack before putting them into a tin. Do not store cakes and cookies together because the moisture from the cake will soften the cookies.

MICROWAVING

Microwave-baked cakes and cookies can be disappointingly pale in color and gluey in texture. With baking, the microwave comes into its own when used as an accessory to the conventional oven. Here are good things to use it for:
• Melting chocolate: break chocolate into small pieces, put into a bowl, and cook on LOW for 3–5 minutes until melted and shiny; stir halfway.
• Melting crystallized honey or syrup: heat on HIGH for 1–2 minutes. If kept in the jar, take off the lid.
• Softening hardened sugar: cook on HIGH for 30–40 seconds.
• Skinning and toasting hazelnuts: place them on paper towels and cook on HIGH for 30 seconds, then remove skins. To toast, cook again until golden.

FREEZING

If baked goods are not eaten immediately, freezing is a good way to keep them fresh. Cakes, quick breads, cookies, muffins, and biscuits all freeze well.

Wrap plain cakes, fruitcakes and quick breads in foil or freezer paper. If a cake has been frosted or decorated, open freeze it, then place in a rigid container or freezer bag. Fruitcakes can be stored for up to 12 months; unfrosted cakes for 4–6 months; frosted cakes for 2–3 months. Unwrap decorated cakes before thawing, but leave other cakes in their wrapping.

Cookies, muffins, and biscuits can be stored for 6 months. Interleave cookies with foil or freezer paper to keep them separate. Thaw cookies and muffins at room temperature. Biscuits can be successfully reheated or toasted from frozen.

BAKING INGREDIENTS

In baking it is important to use the ingredients specified in a recipe. Choose the best quality available.

Butter and other fats
In simple cakes, cookies, and quick breads, where flavor is important, always use butter. In other cakes, margarine is acceptable. For one-bowl batters, soft margarine is best since it is made up of 80% fat and blends easily. Diet spreads are not suitable for baking because of their high water content, so check before you buy. If a recipe requires oil, use a mild, light oil such as sunflower oil or sweeter corn oil.

Flour
Both all-purpose and self-rising flours are used in baking, either white or whole-wheat. Self-rising flour includes a leavener (usually a mixture of baking soda and cream of tartar). If you want to substitute all-purpose flour for self-rising flour, add 2 tsp baking powder to each 2 cups (250 g) flour.

Leaveners
Baking powder and baking soda are used to raise cakes, quick breads, cookies, biscuits, and muffins. When a recipe calls for baking powder or self-rising flour, be sure to bake without delay, while the chemicals are still active.

Sugar and other sweeteners
For most mixtures, it is essential to use a sugar that dissolves easily, such as granulated sugar or soft, light brown sugar. Superfine sugar is useful when making meringues. Coarse sugar or sugar crystals are fine for melted mixtures and ideal for sprinkling on the top of cakes, as is confectioners' sugar. Other sweeteners used in baking include maple syrup, honey, molasses, and malt extract, and concentrated fruit puree or juice.

Eggs
Eggs at room temperature are more easily aerated than cold eggs taken straight from the refrigerator. Cold eggs can also cause some cake batters to curdle.

BAKING COOKIES

When arranging cookies on prepared baking sheets, leave enough space between them to allow for spreading, if necessary. As cookies bake quickly, they can easily be made in batches if you don't have enough baking sheets.

At the end of the baking time, many cookies will still feel a little soft in the middle: they will continue to bake on the hot sheet after being removed from the oven. If the recipe directs, leave them to firm up for 1–2 minutes before transferring to a wire rack. Avoid letting cookies cool completely on the sheet or they might stick.

ONE-BOWL CAKES

Be sure to use a soft margarine for this quick, simple technique.

Put all the ingredients into a large bowl and beat together with an electric mixer until combined. You can also do this in a food processor or by hand.

BEATEN CAKES

These light, fatless sponge cakes are raised by air whisked into the eggs. Use a hand-held or stand electric mixer. If using a hand-held mixer, set it at high speed.

1 Whisk the eggs, or egg yolks, with the sugar until the mixture is light, pale, and thick enough to leave a trail on the surface. This can take up to 5 minutes.

2 Gently fold in the flour and any other ingredients. If the eggs have been separated, the whisked egg whites should be folded into the mixture last of all.

CREAMED CAKES

The creaming method is used for both cakes and cookies. A wooden spoon, rubber spatula, or electric mixer are all suitable. Be sure to soften the butter or margarine first.

1 Cream the fat and sugar together until the mixture is pale in color and fluffy in texture. Keep scraping the side of the bowl with a spoon or spatula to incorporate all of the mixture.

2 Lightly beat the eggs. Gradually add the eggs to the creamed mixture, beating well between each addition. If the mixture curdles, which will result in a dense-textured cake, beat in a spoonful of the flour.

3 Sift over the flour and any other dry ingredients. Using a wooden spoon, gently fold in the flour until it is well combined with the creamed mixture. Any liquid ingredients should also be added at this stage.

PREPARING CAKE PANS

Lightly greasing the pan makes turning out the baked cake easier. Some recipes also call for the pan to be floured or lined with waxed paper or parchment paper.

Greasing and flouring

Use melted or softened butter or margarine, or oil, according to the recipe. Brush over the bottom and side of the pan using a pastry brush or paper towels. If flouring, add a spoonful of flour and tilt the pan to coat it with a thin layer. Tip out any excess flour.

Lining

1 Set the cake pan on a sheet of waxed paper or parchment paper and mark around the base with a pencil or the tip of a knife.

2 Cut out the shape, cutting just inside the line, then press smoothly over the bottom of the pan. Lightly grease if directed in the recipe.

BAKING, TESTING, & COOLING CAKES

Before baking cakes, quick breads, and cookies, be sure to preheat the oven to the specified temperature. If you need to, adjust the position of the shelves before you turn on the oven.

1 As soon as the batter is ready, turn it into the pan and level the surface. Tap the pan on the work surface to break any large air bubbles. Transfer immediately to the oven.

2 When done, a cake will shrink slightly from the side of the pan. To test, lightly press the middle with a fingertip; the cake should spring back. Rich cakes should feel firm to the touch.

3 Set the cake pan on a wire rack and leave to cool for about 10 minutes. Run a knife around the side of the cake to free it from the pan.

4 Hold a wire rack over the top of the pan, then invert the rack and pan so the cake falls onto the rack. Carefully lift the pan away from the cake.

5 Peel off the lining paper. With a light-textured cake, turn it over again so the bottom is on the rack; this will prevent the rack marking the top.

6 To cut the cake into two or more layers, steady it by setting one hand gently on top. Cut the cake horizontally, using a gentle sawing action.

Baking know-how

Be sure to use the correct size pan, as specified in the recipe. To check the dimensions of a cake pan, measure inside the top rim. To work out the depth, measure from the bottom to the top rim on the inside of the pan. To check the capacity of a pan, measure how much water is needed to fill it to the brim.

•

Bake for the minimum time specified in the recipe before opening the oven door. If the door is opened too soon it can cause some cakes to deflate.

•

If a cake looks as though it is browning too quickly, cover the top loosely with foil.

•

If baking several cake layers, stagger them on the oven shelves so one pan is not directly under another.

•

When measuring ingredients with a spoon, don't hold the spoon directly over the bowl or you may accidentally add too much.

TESTING FRUITCAKES

For fruitcakes and fruited quick breads, insert a metal skewer or long wooden toothpick into the middle: the skewer or toothpick should come out clean, without any moist crumbs sticking to it.

FILLING & FROSTING CAKES

Whipped cream, fresh or canned fruit, jam, or chocolate frosting make quick and easy fillings for a sponge cake. Buttercream can be made in a variety of flavors, to complement the flavor of the cake.

Chocolate buttercream
In a bowl, soften ⅔ cup (150 g) butter. Add ¼ cup (30 g) unsweetened cocoa powder and 2 cups (250 g) sifted confectioners' sugar. Beat together to make a smooth, spreading consistency. For a citrus buttercream, omit the cocoa powder and add finely grated orange or lemon zest.

Spreading frosting
Frost a cake only when it has cooled completely. Use a large metal spatula and spread the frosting with long, smooth strokes over the top and side of the cake, or as specified in the recipe. Dip the spatula in warm water if the frosting sticks to it.

ZUCCHINI BREAD

CUTS INTO 12 SLICES

1 large zucchini
2 eggs
1/2 cup (125 ml) sunflower oil, plus extra for greasing
1 1/4 cup (250 g) sugar
1/4 tsp vanilla extract (optional)
3 cups (375 g) self-rising flour
1 tsp ground cinnamon
1/2 tsp salt
1/2 cup (60 g) walnut pieces, coarsely chopped
2 LB (1 KG) LOAF PAN

1 Coarsely grate the zucchini, put it into a strainer set over a plate, and leave for about 30 minutes to drain.

2 Beat the eggs until light and foamy. Add the sunflower oil, sugar, vanilla extract (if using), and zucchini and mix lightly until combined.

3 Sift the flour, cinnamon, and salt into a large bowl. Make a well in the middle, pour in the zucchini mixture, and stir to mix thoroughly. Add the chopped walnuts and stir again to combine.

4 Pour the batter into the greased loaf pan and bake in a preheated oven at 350°F (180°C) for about 50 minutes until firm. Turn out and cool.

Cook's know-how

For best results, the grated zucchini should be thoroughly drained. Press it into the strainer with your hand or the back of a spoon to extract as much juice as possible.

CARROT CAKE

CUTS INTO 10 SQUARES

2/3 cup (150 ml) sunflower oil, plus extra for greasing
2 cups (250 g) whole-wheat self-rising flour
2 tsp baking powder
2/3 cup packed (150 g) soft light brown sugar
1/2 cup (60 g) walnuts, coarsely chopped
2 carrots, grated
2 ripe bananas, mashed
2 eggs
1 tbsp milk

TOPPING

1 cup (250 g) low-fat cream cheese, at room temperature
2 tsp honey
1 tsp lemon juice
chopped walnuts to decorate
8 IN (20 CM) SQUARE CAKE PAN

1 Lightly grease the cake pan and line the bottom with parchment paper.

2 Combine all the cake ingredients in a large bowl. Mix until thoroughly blended. Turn into the prepared cake pan and level the surface.

3 Bake in a preheated oven at 350°F (180°C) for about 50 minutes until the cake is well risen, firm to the touch, and beginning to shrink away from the sides of the pan.

4 Leave the cake to cool in the pan for a few minutes. Turn out on to a wire rack, peel off the lining paper, and leave to cool completely.

5 Make the topping: mix together the cheese, honey, and lemon juice. Spread on top of the cake and sprinkle the walnuts over the top. Store the cake in the refrigerator until ready to serve.

Healthy option

A cream cheese frosting is the traditional topping for carrot cake, but the lower-fat version suggested in this recipe tastes equally good. If you prefer a cake without frosting, spread melted honey on top of the cake while it is hot from the oven, and sprinkle with chopped walnuts. Or leave the cake plain. It will be moist and delicious just as it is.

HEAVENLY CHOCOLATE CAKE

CUTS INTO 8 SLICES

1/2 cup (125 g) butter, plus extra for greasing

7 oz (200 g) semisweet chocolate, broken into pieces

2 tbsp water

3 eggs, separated

1/2 cup (125 g) sugar

3/4 cup (90 g) self-rising flour

1/2 cup (60 g) ground blanched almonds

FUDGE FROSTING

4 tbsp (60 g) butter

1/3 cup (30 g) cocoa powder

2 cups (250 g) confectioners' sugar, sifted

3 tbsp milk

white chocolate curls (page 467) to decorate

DEEP 8 IN (20 CM) CAKE PAN

1 Lightly butter the pan and line the bottom with parchment paper.

2 Put the butter, chocolate, and water into a bowl. Put the bowl over a pan of hot water and heat gently, stirring, until melted. Cool.

3 Combine the egg yolks and sugar in a large bowl and beat together with an electric mixer until fluffy and very light in color. Stir in the cooled chocolate mixture. Carefully fold in the flour and ground almonds.

4 In a separate bowl, beat the egg whites until stiff but not dry. Fold into the cake batter, gently but thoroughly. Pour the batter into the prepared pan. Bake in a preheated oven at 350°F (180°C) for 50 minutes or until well risen and firm to the touch.

5 Leave the cake to cool in the pan for a few minutes, turn out onto a wire rack, and peel off the lining paper. Cool completely. Make the fudge frosting: melt the butter in a pan, add the cocoa powder, and cook, stirring, for 1 minute. Stir in the confectioners' sugar and milk. Beat until smooth. Leave to cool until thickened.

6 Split the cake in half horizontally and sandwich the layers together with half of the fudge frosting. With a spatula, spread the remaining frosting over the top and side of the cake. Decorate with white chocolate curls.

DEVIL'S FOOD CAKE

CUTS INTO 12 SLICES

3/4 cup (175 g) soft butter or margarine, plus extra for greasing

3 oz (90 g) semisweet chocolate, broken into pieces

3/4 cup (175 ml) hot water

2 cups unpacked (300 g) soft light brown sugar

3 eggs, beaten

2 1/2 cups (300 g) all-purpose flour

1 1/2 tsp baking soda

1 1/2 tsp baking powder

1 tsp vanilla extract

2/3 cup (150 ml) sour cream

FROSTING

2 cups (400 g) sugar

2 egg whites

4 tbsp hot water

pinch of cream of tartar

3 x 8 IN (20 CM) ROUND CAKE PANS

1 Grease the pans with butter and line the bottoms with parchment paper.

2 Put the chocolate into a pan with the water. Heat gently, stirring, until the chocolate melts. Cool.

3 Combine the butter and sugar in a bowl and beat until light and fluffy. Gradually add the eggs, beating well.

4 Stir in the cooled melted chocolate. Sift together the flour, baking soda, and baking powder. Fold into the chocolate mixture until evenly blended, then fold in the vanilla extract and sour cream.

5 Divide the batter evenly among the prepared pans. Bake in a preheated oven at 375°F (190°C) for about 25 minutes until well risen, springy to the touch, and just shrinking away from the sides of the pans.

6 Turn out the cakes onto wire racks, peel off the lining papers, and leave to cool.

7 Make the frosting: put all the ingredients into a large heatproof bowl. Set the bowl over a pan of hot water and beat with an electric mixer for 12 minutes or until the frosting is white, thick, and stands in soft peaks.

8 Use half of the frosting to sandwich the three cake layers together, then spread the remainder over the top and side of the cake, pulling the frosting into decorative peaks with the flat of a small metal spatula.

MARBLED COFFEE RING CAKE

CUTS INTO 12 SLICES

1 cup (250 g) soft butter, plus extra for greasing

1 1/4 cups (250 g) sugar

4 eggs

2 cups (250 g) self-rising flour

2 tsp baking powder

2 tsp instant coffee powder

1 tbsp hot water

1 oz (30 g) white chocolate

FROSTING

4 tbsp (60 g) butter, softened

3 tbsp milk

2 tbsp instant coffee powders

2 cups (250 g) confectioners' sugar, sifted

7-CUP (1.75 LITER) RING MOLD

1 Lightly grease the ring mold with butter.

2 Combine the butter, sugar, eggs, flour, and baking powder in a large bowl. Beat until smooth.

3 Put half of the batter into another bowl. Dissolve the instant coffee in the measured hot water and stir into one half of the cake batter.

4 Drop tablespoonfuls of the plain batter into the ring mold, then tablespoonfuls of the coffee batter on top of the plain batter. Make the marble effect by swirling the two together with a skewer.

5 Bake in a preheated oven at 350°F (180°C) for 40 minutes or until well risen and firm to the touch. Leave to cool for a few minutes, then turn out onto a wire rack set over a baking sheet, and leave to cool completely.

6 Make the frosting: combine the butter, milk, and coffee in a pan and heat, stirring, until smooth. Remove from the heat and beat in the confectioners' sugar until smooth and glossy.

7 Leave to cool, then pour over the cake, spreading it over the side with a spatula to cover completely. Leave to set.

8 Melt the white chocolate in a heatproof bowl over a pan of hot water. Cool slightly, then spoon into a plastic bag. Snip off a corner of the bag and drizzle the chocolate over the cake. Leave to set.

CREAMY CHOCOLATE CAKE

CUTS INTO 14 SLICES

6 tbsp (90 g) butter, melted and cooled slightly, plus extra for greasing

6 large eggs

3/4 cup plus 2 tbsp (175 g) sugar

1 cup (125 g) self-rising flour

1/4 cup (30 g) cocoa powder

2 tbsp cornstarch

FILLING AND TOPPING

1 1/4 cups (300 ml) heavy cream, whipped until thick

white chocolate curls (optional – page 467)

DEEP 9 IN (23 CM) ROUND CAKE PAN

1 Lightly butter the cake pan and line the bottom of the pan with parchment paper.

2 Put the eggs and sugar into a large bowl and beat together with an electric mixer on high speed until the mixture is pale and thick enough to leave a trail on itself when the beaters are lifted out.

3 Sift together the flour, cocoa powder, and cornstarch, and fold half into the egg mixture. Pour half of the cooled butter around the edge; fold in gently.

4 Repeat with the remaining flour mixture and butter, folding gently.

5 Turn the batter into the prepared cake pan and tilt the pan to level the surface. Bake in a preheated oven at 350°F (180°C) for 35–40 minutes until the cake is well risen and firm to the touch. Turn out onto a wire rack, peel off the lining paper, and cool.

6 Cut the cake in half horizontally and sandwich the layers together with half of the whipped cream. Cover the cake with a thin layer of cream, then pipe the remainder around the top and bottom edges.

7 Press the white chocolate curls, if using, over the top and side of the cake.

CHOCOLATE & ORANGE MOUSSE CAKE

This delectable creation is made of chocolate sponge cake layers sandwiched together with a fluffy chocolate and orange mousse. When making the mousse, do not overbeat the egg whites; when they just flop over at the tip they are ready to fold into the chocolate mixture.

CUTS INTO 12 SLICES

butter for greasing

4 eggs

1/2 cup plus 2 tbsp (125 g) sugar

3/4 cup (90 g) self-rising flour

1/3 cup (30 g) cocoa powder

MOUSSE

6 oz (175 g) semisweet chocolate, broken into pieces

grated zest and juice of 1 orange

1 tsp unflavored powdered gelatin

2 eggs, separated

1 1/4 cups (300 ml) heavy cream, whipped until thick

DECORATION

1 1/4 cups (300 ml) heavy cream, whipped until thick

strips of orange zest, blanched

DEEP 9 IN (23 CM) SPRINGFORM CAKE PAN

1 Lightly butter the pan and line the bottom with parchment paper. Make the batter (see box, right).

2 Bake in a preheated oven at 350°F (180°C) for 40–45 minutes until the cake is well risen and beginning to shrink away from the sides of the pan. Turn out onto a wire rack, peel off the lining paper, and leave to cool.

3 Cut the cake in half horizontally. Put one half back into the clean pan (with the cut side up).

4 Make the mousse: put the chocolate into a heatproof bowl set over a pan of hot water. Heat gently, stirring occasionally, until the chocolate has melted. Leave to cool slightly.

5 Strain the orange juice into a small heatproof bowl and sprinkle the gelatin over. Leave for 3 minutes or until spongy, then stand the bowl in a saucepan of gently simmering water for 3 minutes or until the gelatin has dissolved.

6 Stir the egg yolks and orange zest into the cooled melted chocolate. Slowly stir in the dissolved gelatin, then fold in the whipped cream. In a separate bowl, beat the egg whites until stiff but not dry, then gently fold into the chocolate mixture until well blended.

7 Pour the mousse on top of the cake layer in the pan. Put the remaining cake layer on top, cut side down. Cover and chill in the refrigerator until the mousse filling is set.

8 Remove the side of the pan and slide the cake onto a serving plate. Decorate with whipped cream and orange zest.

Making the batter

Put the eggs and sugar in a large bowl and beat with an electric mixer at high speed until the mixture is pale and thick enough to leave a trail on the surface when the beaters are lifted out.

Sift the flour and cocoa powder over the surface.

Fold in the flour and cocoa to lightly blend the ingredients.

Turn the batter into the prepared pan and tilt to level the surface.

FRUIT & CREAM CAKE

CUTS INTO 8 SLICES

butter for greasing

3 eggs

1 scant cup (90 g) sugar

3/4 cup (90 g) self-rising flour

FILLING AND TOPPING

1 1/4 cups (300 ml) heavy cream, whipped until thick

4 oz (125 g) strawberries, sliced

1 passion fruit, halved and pulped

strawberries, halved, to decorate

2 x 7 IN (18 CM) ROUND CAKE PANS

1 Lightly butter the cake pans, line the bottoms with parchment paper, then lightly butter the paper.

2 Put the eggs and sugar into a large bowl. Beat with an electric mixer at high speed until the mixture is pale and thick enough to leave a trail when the beaters are lifted out.

3 Sift half of the flour over the surface and fold in gently. Repeat with the remaining flour.

4 Divide the batter between the pans. Tilt to spread the mixture evenly.

5 Bake in a preheated oven at 375°F (190°C) for 20–25 minutes until the cake is well risen, golden, and beginning to shrink away from the sides of the pans. Turn out onto a wire rack, peel off the lining papers, and leave to cool.

6 Spread half of the whipped cream over 1 of the cakes. Top with the sliced strawberries and passion fruit pulp. Put the other cake on top and press down gently.

7 Spread the remaining cream thinly on top of the cake, smoothing it neatly with a metal spatula. Decorate with strawberry halves.

JELLY ROLL

CUTS INTO 8 SLICES

butter for greasing

4 large eggs

1/2 cup plus 2 tbsp (125 g) sugar, plus extra for sprinkling

1 cup (125 g) self-rising flour

confectioners' sugar for sprinkling

FILLING

about 4 tbsp raspberry jam, slightly warmed to soften

9 x 13 IN (23 x 33 CM) JELLY ROLL PAN

1 Lightly butter the pan, line with parchment paper, then lightly butter the paper.

2 Put the eggs and sugar into a large bowl. Beat together with an electric mixer at high speed until the mixture is pale and thick enough to leave a trail on the surface when the beaters are lifted out.

3 Sift the flour into the egg mixture and fold in gently but thoroughly.

4 Turn the batter into the prepared pan and tilt to spread the batter evenly, particularly into the corners.

5 Bake in a preheated oven at 425°F (220°C) for 10 minutes or until the cake is golden and starting to shrink away from the side of the pan.

6 Invert the cake onto a large piece of parchment paper that has been liberally sprinkled with sugar. Peel off the lining paper and trim the edges of the cake with a sharp knife.

7 Roll up the cake and the parchment paper together, from one of the short ends. Leave to rest for 2–3 minutes.

8 Carefully unroll the cake, and remove the parchment paper. Spread the unsugared surface of the cake with warmed jam and roll up again. Wrap in parchment paper and leave to cool. Unwrap the cake, dust with confectioners' sugar, and serve cut in slices.

SMALL CHOCOLATE CAKES

All chocolate cakes are irresistible, but these chocolate brownies, cupcakes, and muffins look twice as tempting as a large cake, and they're quicker and easier to make, too. The muffins are at their very best eaten warm, and the cupcakes will keep fresh for a day or two. Brownies will last longer, and will even improve if you keep them several days, stored in an airtight container.

BEST-EVER BROWNIES

MAKES 24

12 oz (375 g) semisweet chocolate, broken into pieces

1 cup (250 g) margarine

2 tsp instant coffee powder

2 tbsp hot water

2 eggs

1¼ cups (250 g) sugar

1 tsp vanilla extract

¾ cup (90 g) self-rising flour

1½ cups (175 g) walnut pieces

8 oz (250 g) semisweet chocolate chips

1 Grease a 12 x 9 in (30 x 23 cm) roasting pan, line the base with parchment paper, and grease the paper.

2 Put the chocolate and margarine in a heatproof bowl set over a pan of gently simmering water. Melt the chocolate, then remove the bowl from the pan and leave the chocolate to cool.

3 Put the coffee in another bowl, pour in the hot water, and stir to dissolve. Add the eggs, sugar, and vanilla extract. Slowly beat in the chocolate mixture. Fold in the flour and walnuts, then the chocolate chips.

4 Pour the batter into the prepared pan and bake in a preheated oven at 375°F (190°C) for about 40–45 minutes or until firm to the touch. Don't overbake: the crust should be dull and crisp, but the middle may seem still underdone. Leave to cool in the pan, then cut into 24 pieces.

Cook's know-how

The secret of really good brownies is to not overbake them. Take them out of the oven just before you think they are done. The middle should be soft and squidgy, not baked firm. Do not worry if there is a dip in the middle and the top is cracked because this is how it should be. You will find the brownies firm up while cooling.

CHOCOLATE CUPCAKES

MAKES 24

⅓ cup (40 g) cocoa powder

about 4 tbsp boiling water

3 eggs

¾ cup (175 g) margarine

¾ cup plus 2 tbsp (175 g) sugar

1 scant cup (115 g) self-rising flour

1 heaping tsp baking powder

FROSTING

4 tbsp (60 g) butter

2 tbsp cocoa powder

about 3 tbsp milk

2 cups (250 g) confectioners' sugar

2 x 12-HOLE MUFFIN PANS AND 24 CUPCAKE CASES

1 Line the 2 muffin pans with cupcake cases. Sift the cocoa powder into a large bowl, pour in the boiling water, and mix into a thick paste. Add the remaining cake ingredients and beat with an electric mixer (or use a wooden spoon).

2 Divide the batter equally among the 24 cupcake cases. Bake in a preheated oven at 400°F (200°C) for about 10 minutes until the cupcakes are well risen and springy to the touch. Leave in the cases to cool on wire racks.

3 Make the frosting: melt the butter, and pour it into a bowl. Sift in the cocoa powder and stir to mix well. Stir in the milk and then sift in the confectioners' sugar a little at a time to make a glossy, spreadable frosting. Spread the frosting on top of the cupcakes, smoothing it with a metal spatula. Leave to set before serving.

DOUBLE-CHOCOLATE MUFFINS

MAKES 12

melted butter for greasing

2 eggs, lightly beaten

½ cup (125 g) plain yogurt

½ cup (125 ml) strong brewed coffee

½ cup (125 ml) milk

2 cups (250 g) self-rising flour

1¼ cups (250 g) sugar

¾ cup (75 g) cocoa powder

pinch of salt

3½ oz (100 g) semisweet chocolate chips

12-HOLE MUFFIN PAN

1 Generously butter each cup of the muffin pan.

2 Combine the eggs, yogurt, coffee, and milk in a large bowl.

3 Sift the flour, sugar, cocoa powder, and salt over the the milk mixture. Mix well to combine the ingredients. Stir in the chocolate chips.

4 Spoon the batter into the muffin cups, filling them almost to the tops.

5 Bake the muffins in a preheated oven at 400°F (200°C) for about 10 minutes, then reduce the oven temperature to 350°F (180°C), and continue to bake for about 15 minutes until the muffins are risen and firm. Serve warm.

CLOCKWISE FROM TOP LEFT: Double-chocolate Muffins, Best-ever Brownies, Chocolate Cupcakes.

VICTORIA LAYER CAKE

CUTS INTO 8 SLICES

3/4 cup (175 g) soft butter or margarine, plus extra for greasing

3/4 cup plus 2 tbsp (175 g) sugar

3 eggs

1 1/2 cups (175 g) self-rising flour

1 1/2 tsp baking powder

FILLING

4 tbsp raspberry or strawberry jam

caster sugar for sprinkling

2 x 7 IN (18 CM) ROUND CAKE PANS

1 Lightly grease the pans and line the bottoms with parchment paper.

2 Combine all the cake ingredients in a large bowl. Beat well for about 2 minutes until smooth.

3 Divide the batter between the prepared pans and tilt to spread evenly. Bake in a preheated oven at 350°F (180°C) for about 25 minutes or until the cake layers are well risen, golden, and springy to the touch.

4 Turn out onto a wire rack, peel off the lining paperss, and leave to cool.

5 Sandwich the 2 cakes together with jam and sprinkle the top of the cake with sugar before serving.

LEMON LAYER CAKE

Add the finely grated zest of 1 lemon to the cake ingredients before beating. Sandwich the cakes together with lemon curd and 2/3 cup (150 ml) heavy cream, whipped until thick. Dust with sifted confectioners' sugar.

Cook's know-how

For a special occasion, sandwich the cake layers together with cream cheese or mascarpone (a rich Italian cheese), sweetened with sugar to taste and beaten until light and fluffy with the pulp of 2 passionfruit. Dust the top of the cake with sifted confectioners' sugar to finish.

LIME SHEET CAKE

MAKES 12 SQUARES

3/4 cup (175 g) soft butter or margarine, plus extra for greasing

3/4 cup plus 2 tbsp (175 g) sugar

2 cups (250 g) self-rising flour

1 1/2 tsp baking powder

3 eggs

3 tbsp milk

finely grated zest of 2 limes

FROSTING

2 cups (250 g) confectioners' sugar

juice of 2 limes

9 x 12 IN (23 x 30 CM) CAKE PAN

1 Lightly grease the pan and line the bottom with parchment paper.

2 Combine all the cake ingredients in a large bowl and beat well for about 2 minutes or until smooth and thoroughly blended.

3 Turn into the prepared pan and level the surface. Bake in a preheated oven at 350°F (180°C) for 35–40 minutes until the cake is well risen, springy to the touch, and beginning to shrink away from the sides of the pan.

4 Leave to cool slightly in the pan, then turn out onto a wire rack, peel off the lining paper, and leave to cool.

5 Make the frosting: sift the confectioners' sugar into a bowl. Mix in the lime juice little by little to give a runny consistency (you may not need it all). Pour over the cooled cake, spreading carefully with a spatula, and leave to set. Cut into squares to serve.

CHOCOLATE & MINT SHEET CAKE

Mix 4 tbsp cocoa powder with 4 tbsp hot water and leave to cool. Add to the cake batter ingredients with 4 tbsp chopped fresh mint, and mix well. Bake as directed. For the frosting, break 8 oz (250 g) semisweet chocolate into pieces and combine with 6 tbsp (90 g) butter and 4 tbsp hot water in a heatproof bowl. Put the bowl over a pan of hot water and heat gently until the chocolate and butter have melted. Beat together until smooth and shiny, then spread over the top of the cooled cake. Leave to set before serving.

CHECKERBOARD CAKE

CUTS INTO 8 SLICES

1/2 cup (125 g) soft butter or margarine, plus extra for greasing

1/2 cup plus 2 tbsp (125 g) sugar

2 large eggs

1/2 cup (60 g) ground rice

1 cup (125 g) self-rising flour

1/2 tsp baking powder

a few drops of vanilla extract

1 1/2 tsp cocoa powder

3 tbsp apricot jam

8 oz (250 g) almond paste

SHALLOW 7 IN (18 CM) SQUARE CAKE PAN

1 Lightly grease the cake pan with butter. Line the bottom of the tin with parchment paper.

2 Beat the butter, sugar, eggs, ground rice, flour, baking powder, and vanilla extract in a large bowl for 2 minutes or until the batter is smooth and evenly combined.

3 Spoon half of the mixture into another bowl. Dissolve the cocoa in a little hot water to make a thick paste and add to one half of the batter. Mix well. Spoon the plain batter into one half of the prepared pan, and the chocolate batter into the other half of the pan.

4 Bake the batter in a preheated oven at 325°F (160°C) for 35 minutes or until the cake is risen and springy to the touch. Turn out onto a wire rack, peel off the lining paper, and cool.

5 Trim the edges of the cake. Cut between the plain and chocolate cakes, then cut both of the cakes lengthwise into 2 equal strips.

6 Warm the apricot jam in a small saucepan. Stack the cake strips, alternating the colors to give a checkerboard effect, and sticking their sides together with apricot jam.

7 Roll out the almond paste into an oblong that is the same length as the cake and wide enough to wrap around it. Brush with jam, then put the cake on top. Wrap the paste around the cake (see box, below).

8 Score a crisscross pattern in the almond paste on the top of the cake to make a decorative finish.

Wrapping the cake

Press the almond paste gently around the cake, making the seam in one corner. Turn the cake over to hide the seam.

RICH FRUITCAKE

CUTS INTO 10 SLICES

1 cup (250 g) soft butter or margarine, plus extra for greasing

1 3/4 cup unpacked (250 g) soft light brown sugar

4 eggs

2 cups (250 g) self-rising flour

1 1/2 cups (250 g) raisins

1 1/2 cups (250 g) golden raisins

3/4 cup (125 g) candied cherries, halved and rinsed

1/2 tsp ground apple-pie spice

1 tbsp brandy or water

DEEP 8 IN (20 CM) ROUND CAKE PAN

1 Lightly grease the pan and line the bottom and side with waxed paper.

2 Combine the ingredients in a large bowl and mix well. Turn the batter into the pan and level the surface.

3 Bake in a preheated oven at 275°F (140°C) for 2–2 1/4 hours. Cover the top of the cake loosely with foil after about 1 hour to prevent the top becoming too brown.

4 To test for doneness, insert a fine skewer into the middle of the cake: it should come out clean. Leave the cake to cool in the pan before turning it out onto a wire rack. Store in an airtight container.

MINCEMEAT MUFFINS

MAKES 32

1 cup (375 g) bottled mincemeat

1 1/2 cups (250 g) dried currants

2 eggs

3/4 cup (150 g) sugar

2/3 cup (150 g) soft butter or margarine

2 cups (250 g) self-rising flour

32 PAPER CUPCAKE CASES

1 Combine all the ingredients in a large bowl and beat well for about 2 minutes.

2 Divide the batter evenly among the paper cupcake cases, putting them into muffin pans if preferred.

3 Bake in a preheated oven at 325°F (160°C) for 25–30 minutes until golden and springy to the touch. Transfer the muffins in their cases to wire racks and leave to cool.

Cook's know-how

Mincemeat (which now doesn't actually contain meat) is traditionally made with beef suet but a vegetarian version, made with vegetable fat, is available (read the label). You can improve on store-bought mincemeat by adding finely chopped nuts and dried fruit such as apricots or peaches.

SIMNEL CAKE

Originally this cake was given by girls to their mothers on Mother's Day but it has now become a celebratory cake for Eastertide, closely aligned to the Christian tradition. The almond paste balls represent the 11 disciples of Christ (the disgraced Judas Iscariot is excluded).

CUTS INTO 12 SLICES

3/4 cup (175 g) soft butter or margarine, plus extra for greasing

3/4 cup packed (150 g) soft light brown sugar

3 eggs

1 1/2 cups (175 g) self-rising flour

1 cup (175 g) golden raisins

1/2 cup (90 g) dried currants

1/2 cup (90 g) candied cherries, quartered, rinsed, and dried

1/4 cup (30 g) candied peel, roughly chopped

grated zest of 1 large lemon

1 tsp apple-pie spice

FILLING AND DECORATION

1 lb (500 g) almond paste

2 tbsp apricot jam

1 egg white, lightly beaten

DEEP 7 IN (18 CM) ROUND LOOSE-BOTTOMED CAKE PAN

1 Roll out one-third of the almond paste. Using the bottom of the cake pan as a guide, cut out a 7 in (18 cm) circle, and set aside.

2 Grease the cake pan and line the bottom and side with waxed paper.

3 Combine all the cake ingredients in a bowl. Beat well until thoroughly blended. Spoon half of the cake batter into the prepared pan and smooth the surface. Top with the circle of almond paste.

4 Spoon the remaining cake batter on top and level the surface.

5 Bake in a preheated oven at 300°F (150°C) for 2 1/4 hours or until golden brown and firm to the touch.

6 Cover the top of the cake with waxed paper if it is browning too quickly. Leave to cool for 10 minutes, then remove from the pan, and leave to cool completely.

7 Warm the jam and brush it over the top of the cake.

8 Decorate the cake: roll out half of the remaining paste, and use the cake pan as a guide to cut out a 7 in (18 cm) circle. Press on top of the cake and crimp the edges (page 431). Roll the remaining almond paste into 11 small balls. Place around the edge of the cake, attaching them with egg white.

9 Brush the tops of the balls and the almond paste with egg white. Place under a hot broiler for 1–2 minutes, until the balls are golden.

FRUITED BANANA BREAD

CUTS INTO 12 SLICES

1/2 cup (125 g) butter or margarine, plus extra for greasing
2 cups (250 g) self-rising flour
3/4 cup plus 2 tbsp (175 g) sugar
2/3 cup (125 g) golden raisins
1/2 cup (60 g) walnuts, roughly chopped
2/3 cup (125 g) candied cherries, quartered, rinsed, and dried
2 large eggs, beaten
1 lb (500 g) bananas (weight with peel), peeled and mashed
2 LB (1 KG) LOAF PAN

1 Lightly grease the loaf pan and line the bottom with waxed paper.

2 Put the flour into a bowl, add the butter, and rub in with the fingertips until the mixture resembles fine bread crumbs. Mix in the sugar, golden raisins, chopped walnuts, and candied cherries.

3 Add the eggs and mashed bananas and beat the mixture until well blended. Spoon into the prepared pan.

4 Bake in a preheated oven at 325°F (160°C) for about 1 1/4 hours until well risen and firm to the touch. To test for doneness, insert a fine skewer into the middle of the loaf. It should come out clean.

5 Leave the loaf to cool slightly in the pan, then turn out onto a wire rack, and peel off the lining paper. Leave the loaf to cool completely before slicing and serving.

Cook's know-how

If you like, you can add some grated orange or lemon zest or 1 tsp apple-pie spice to the batter, for extra flavoring.

DUNDEE CAKE

CUTS INTO 12 SLICES

2/3 cup (150 g) butter, at room temperature, plus extra for greasing
2/3 cup packed (150 g) soft light brown sugar
3 eggs
2 cups (250 g) all-purpose flour
1 tsp baking powder
1 cup (175 g) golden raisins
1/2 cup (90 g) dried currants
1/2 cup (90 g) raisins
1/3 cup (60 g) candied cherries, quartered, rinsed, and dried
1/3 cup (60 g) chopped candied peel
2 tbsp ground blanched almonds
grated zest of 1 large lemon
1/2 cup (60 g) whole almonds, blanched and halved, to decorate
DEEP 8 IN (20 CM) ROUND LOOSE-BOTTOMED CAKE PAN

1 Lightly butter the cake pan and line the bottom with waxed paper.

2 Put the butter, sugar, eggs, flour, and baking powder in a bowl and beat for 2 minutes or until well blended. Stir in the fruit, candied peel, ground almonds, and lemon zest.

3 Spoon the batter into the prepared pan. Level the surface and arrange the halved almonds in a decorative pattern on top.

4 Bake in a preheated oven at 325°F (160°C) for 1 1/2 hours or until well risen, golden, and firm to the touch. A fine skewer inserted into the middle of the cake should come out clean. Cover the cake with foil halfway through baking if it is browning too quickly.

5 Leave the cake to cool in the pan for a few minutes, then turn out onto a wire rack and leave to cool completely. Store in an airtight container for about 1 week before eating.

FESTIVE FRUITCAKES

Celebrate the holidays with one of these festive cakes. Rich fruitcakes are perfect for serving over a period of days, so the decorations also need to store well without refrigeration. The picture shows two different presentation ideas – Candied Fruitcake (above) and Snow White Cake (below). Both are easy to adapt according to the ingredients available and your personal taste.

RICH FRUITCAKE

CUTS INTO ABOUT 30 SLICES

2 1/2 cups (425 g) dried currants

1 1/3 cups (250 g) golden raisins

1 1/3 cups (250 g) raisins

1 3/4 cups (300 g) candied cherries, quartered, rinsed, and dried

1 cup (150 g) soft dried apricots, snipped into small pieces

1/2 cup (75 g) mixed candied peel, roughly chopped

4 tbsp brandy or orange juice, plus extra brandy for soaking cake (step 5, optional)

2 1/2 cups (300 g) all-purpose flour

1 tsp apple-pie spice

1/2 tsp grated nutmeg

1 1/4 cups (300 g) soft butter, plus extra for greasing

1 1/3 cups packed (300 g) soft dark brown sugar

5 eggs

1/2 cup (60 g) whole unblanched almonds, roughly chopped

1 tbsp molasses

finely grated zest of 1 large lemon

finely grated zest of 1 large orange

DEEP 9 IN (23 CM) ROUND OR 8 IN (20 CM) SQUARE CAKE PAN

1 Put the fruit and candied peel in a large bowl. Add the brandy or orange juice, and stir to mix. Cover and leave overnight.

2 Put the remaining ingredients into a large bowl and beat well with an electric mixer until thoroughly blended. Stir in the soaked fruits and any liquid.

3 Grease the cake pan with margarine, line the bottom and side with a double layer of parchment paper, and grease the paper. Spoon the batter into the prepared pan. Level the surface and cover the top of the cake with parchment paper.

4 Bake in a preheated oven at 275°F (140°C) for 4 3/4–5 hours until firm to the touch and a skewer inserted into the middle of the cake comes out clean. Leave the cake to cool in the pan.

5 When the cake has cooled, pierce the top in several places with a fine skewer and pour a little brandy over. Remove the cake from the pan, but leave the lining papers on. Wrap the cake in waxed paper, then overwrap with foil. Store the cake in a cool place for up to 3 months, to mature, unwrapping and spooning more brandy (1–2 tbsp) over occasionally.

6 Decorate the cake with candied fruit (see below) or almond paste and royal icing (see below and recipes, right).

CAKE DECORATIONS

Whichever cake you choose, you need to warm and strain about 1/2 cup (90 g) apricot jam before you apply the candied fruit or almond paste. The jam prevents the cake from drying out and keeps crumbs out of the decoration.

CANDIED FRUITCAKE

This looks most dramatic if it is made in a square cake pan. Brush the strained jam over the top of the cake and then arrange nuts and whole or sliced candied fruits and peel in a decorative pattern while the jam is still warm and sticky. Glaze with more jam and leave until set firmly before tying a ribbon around the side of the cake.

SNOW WHITE CAKE

Brush the strained jam over the top and side of the cake. Roll out the almond paste into a circle that is big enough to cover the top and side of the cake. Smooth it in place with your hands and trim off any excess. Let the almond paste dry out for a few days before covering with royal icing. Use a metal spatula to spread the icing over the top and around the side of the cake, then swirl it into soft peaks with the spatula. If using store-bought decorations for the top (here, silver dragees and fresh cranberries), gently press them onto the icing before it sets.

ALMOND PASTE

MAKES ENOUGH FOR A 9 IN (23 CM) ROUND OR 8 IN (20 CM) SQUARE CAKE

2 cups (250 g) ground blanched almonds

1 1/4 cups (250 g) sugar

2 cups (250 g) confectioners' sugar, sifted

6 drops of almond extract

about 4 egg yolks, or about 2 whole eggs

1 Mix the ground almonds in a bowl with the sugar and confectioners' sugar until evenly combined. Lightly beat together the almond extract and egg yolks or whole eggs. Add almost all of the egg mixture to the dry ingredients and mix together until a stiff paste forms (add the remaining egg mixure if needed).

2 Dust a work surface lightly with sifted confectioners' sugar, turn out the almond paste onto it, and knead with your hands just long enough to make a smooth ball (take care not to overknead or the paste will be oily). Wrap in plastic wrap and store in the refrigerator until required.

ROYAL ICING

MAKES ENOUGH FOR A 9 IN (23 CM) ROUND OR 8 IN (20 CM) SQUARE CAKE

2 egg whites

4 cups (500 g) confectioners' sugar, sifted

4 tsp lemon juice

1 Lightly whisk the egg whites in a large bowl with a fork until bubbles begin to form on the surface. Add about half the confectioners' sugar and all of the lemon juice and beat well with a wooden spoon for about 10 minutes until brilliant white.

2 Stir in the remaining confectioners' sugar a s at a time until the icing is very thick but still spreadable (you may not need all of the sugar). If not using at once, keep the bowl covered with a damp cloth to prevent the icing drying out.

CORN-BREAD

MAKES 9 SQUARES

sunflower oil for greasing

1 1/2 cups (175 g) fine yellow cornmeal

1 cup (125 g) all-purpose flour

2–3 tbsp brown sugar

2 tsp baking powder

1 tsp salt

1 1/4 cups (300 ml) lukewarm milk

2 eggs, lightly beaten

4 tbsp (60 g) butter, melted and cooled slightly

7 IN (18 CM) SQUARE CAKE PAN

1 Lightly oil the cake pan. Put the cornmeal, flour, sugar, baking powder, and salt into a large bowl. Pour in the milk, eggs, and butter, and beat the ingredients to form a batter.

2 Pour the batter into the cake pan and bake in a preheated oven at 400°F (200°C) for 25–30 minutes until golden. Leave to cool in the pan, then cut into squares.

SHORT-BREAD

MAKES 8 WEDGES

1 cup (125 g) all-purpose flour

1/2 cup (60 g) ground rice

1/2 cup (125 g) butter, plus extra for greasing

5 tbsp (60 g) sugar, plus extra for sprinkling

1 Mix the flour and ground rice in a bowl. Add the butter and rub in with the fingertips. Stir in the sugar. Knead to a smooth dough.

2 Lightly butter a baking sheet. Roll out the dough on a lightly floured work surface into a 7 in (18 cm) circle. Lift onto the baking sheet. Crimp the edges (page 431), prick all over with a fork, and mark into 8 wedges with a sharp knife. Chill until firm.

3 Bake in a preheated oven at 325°F (160°C) for 35 minutes or until pale golden brown. Mark the wedges again, and sprinkle with sugar.

4 Allow the shortbread to cool on the baking sheet for about 5 minutes, then lift off carefully with a metal spatula and transfer to a wire rack to cool completely. Cut into wedges to serve.

GINGERBREAD

MAKES 15 SQUARES

1 cup (250 g) butter or margarine, plus extra for greasing

1 cup plus 2 tbsp packed (250 g) soft dark brown sugar

2/3 cup (250 g) molasses

3 cups (375 g) all-purpose flour

5 tsp ground ginger

2 tsp ground cinnamon

1/2 tsp ground allspice

2 eggs, beaten

1 1/2 cups (300 ml) milk

2 tsp baking soda

9 x 12 IN (23 x 30 CM) CAKE PAN

1 Lightly grease the pan and line the bottom with waxed paper.

2 Heat the butter, sugar, and molasses in a pan, stirring, until smooth. Cool slightly.

3 Sift in the flour and ground spices. Stir well, then beat in the beaten eggs.

4 Warm the milk in a small heavy saucepan, and add the baking soda. Pour into the gingerbread mixture and stir gently until thoroughly blended.

5 Pour the batter into the prepared pan. Bake in a preheated oven at 325°F (160°C) for about 1 hour until well risen and springy to the touch.

6 Leave to cool in the pan for a few minutes, then turn out onto a wire rack, and peel off the lining paper. Leave until cold, then store in an airtight container for 2–3 days (the cake improves with keeping). Cut into squares to serve.

FRUIT LOAF

CUTS INTO 12 SLICES

| 2 cups (375 g) mixed dried fruit |
| I cup plus 2 tbsp packed (250 g) soft light brown sugar |
| I 1/4 cups (300 ml) strong hot tea, strained |
| butter for greasing |
| 2 1/2 cups (300 g) self-rising flour |
| I egg, beaten |
| 2 LB (I KG) LOAF PAN |

1 Combine the dried fruit, sugar, and hot tea in a large bowl. Stir well, then cover and set aside for at least 8 hours.

2 Lightly butter the loaf pan and line the bottom with waxed paper. Stir the flour and egg into the dried fruit and tea mixture, mixing thoroughly. Turn the batter into the loaf pan and level the surface.

3 Bake in a preheated oven at 300°F (150°C) for 1 1/2–1 3/4 hours until well risen and firm to the touch. A fine skewer inserted into the middle should come out clean.

4 Leave to cool in the pan for about 10 minutes, then turn out onto a wire rack, and peel off the lining paper. Leave to cool completely. Serve sliced, with or without butter.

Cook's know-how

The mixed dried fruit is steeped in tea so it is moist and well plumped up by the time the batter is mixed.

DATE & WALNUT LOAF

CUTS INTO 12 SLICES

| 6 tbsp (90 g) soft butter or margarine, plus extra for greasing |
| 8 oz (250 g) dates, pitted and roughly chopped |
| 2/3 cup (150 ml) boiling water |
| 1/2 cup (90 g) sugar |
| I egg |
| 2 cups (250 g) self-rising flour |
| I tsp baking powder |
| 3/4 cup (90 g) walnuts, roughly chopped |
| 2 LB (I KG) LOAF PAN |

1 Lightly grease the loaf pan with butter and line with waxed paper.

2 Put the dates into a bowl, pour over the measured boiling water, and leave for about 15 minutes.

3 Combine the butter, sugar, egg, flour, and baking powder in a large bowl and beat until well blended. Add the date mixture and walnuts, and stir to mix thoroughly.

4 Spoon into the prepared loaf pan and bake in a preheated oven at 350°F (180°C) for 1 1/4–1 1/2 hours until well risen and firm to the touch. A fine skewer inserted into the middle of the loaf should come out clean.

5 Leave to cool in the loaf pan for a few minutes, then turn out onto a wire rack, and peel off the lining paper. Leave to cool completely. Serve sliced, with or without butter.

CHERRY & BANANA LOAF

Omit the dates (and boiling water) and walnuts, and add 2/3 cup (125 g) quartered candied cherries and 2 mashed large ripe bananas in step 3.

BISCUITS

MAKES 12

4 tbsp (60 g) butter, plus extra for greasing
2 cups (250 g) self-rising flour
2 tsp baking powder
2 tbsp (30 g) sugar
1 egg
about ²/3 cup (150 ml) milk, plus extra for glazing
butter and jam to serve
2 IN (5 CM) COOKIE CUTTER

1 Lightly butter a large baking sheet.

2 Sift the flour and baking powder into a bowl. Rub in the butter with the fingertips until the mixture resembles fine bread crumbs. Stir in the sugar.

3 Break the egg into a measuring jug and make up to ²/3 cup (150 ml) with milk. Beat lightly to mix. Add to the bowl and mix to a soft dough.

4 Lightly knead the dough until smooth. Roll out to ¹/2 in (1 cm) thick, cut into circles with the cookie cutter, and put on the baking sheet. Brush with milk.

5 Bake in a preheated oven at 425°F (220°C) for about 10 minutes until risen and golden. Cool on a wire rack. Serve on the day of making, if possible, with butter and jam.

CHEESE BISCUITS

Omit the sugar, and add 1 cup (125 g) grated sharp Cheddar cheese and ¹/2 tsp dry mustard to the dry ingredients before mixing in the egg and milk. Roll out the dough into a 6 in (15 cm) circle and cut it into wedges. Brush with milk and sprinkle with finely grated cheese. Bake as directed.

SWEET GRIDDLE CAKES

MAKES 12

2 cups (250 g) self-rising flour
1 tsp baking powder
¹/2 cup (125 g) butter
¹/2 cup (90 g) sugar
¹/2 cup (90 g) dried currants
¹/2 tsp apple-pie spice
1 egg, beaten
about 2 tbsp milk
sunflower oil for greasing
3 IN (7 CM) COOKIE CUTTER

1 Sift the flour and baking powder into a large bowl. Add the butter and rub in with the fingertips until the mixture resembles fine bread crumbs.

2 Add the sugar, currants, and spice, and stir to mix. Add the egg and enough milk to form a soft, but not sticky, dough.

Cook's know-how

If preferred, serve the griddle cakes hot, lightly sprinkled with sugar, straight from the griddle or skillet.

3 On a lightly floured work surface, roll out the dough to ¹/4 in (5 mm) thick. Cut into circles with the cookie cutter.

4 Heat a flat griddle or heavy skillet and grease with a little oil. Cook the griddle cakes on the hot griddle or in the skillet over a low heat for about 3 minutes on each side until cooked through and golden brown.

5 Leave to cool on a wire rack. Best served on the day of making, if possible.

WHOLE-WHEAT PANCAKES

MAKES 20

1 1/2 cups (175 g) whole-wheat self-rising flour

2 tsp baking powder

3 tbsp (45 g) sugar

1 large egg

1 scant cup (200 ml) milk

sunflower oil for greasing

butter and maple syrup or jam to serve

1 Combine the flour, baking powder, and sugar in a bowl, and stir to mix. Make a well in the middle of the dry ingredients and add the egg and half of the milk. Beat well to make a smooth, thick batter.

2 Add enough milk to give the batter the consistency of thick cream.

3 Heat a flat griddle or heavy skillet and grease with oil. Drop spoonfuls of batter onto the hot griddle or skillet, spacing them apart. When bubbles rise to the surface, turn the pancakes over and cook until golden.

4 As each batch is cooked, wrap the pancakes in a clean dish towel to keep them soft. Serve warm, with butter and maple syrup or jam.

PLAIN PANCAKES

Substitute white self-rising flour, and use only 1 tsp baking powder and a little less milk.

Cook's know-how

These pancakes freeze well if you have any leftovers, or you could make a batch to freeze and use as required. Interleave with freezer wrap or waxed paper and freeze for up to 6 months. Warm the pancakes on a griddle or in a skillet or toaster oven before serving.

IRISH SODA BREAD

CUTS INTO 8 WEDGES

4 cups (500 g) all-purpose flour, plus extra for dusting

1 tsp baking soda

1 tsp salt

1 1/4 cups (300 ml) buttermilk, or half milk and half plain yogurt

6 tbsp (90 ml) lukewarm water

sunflower oil for greasing

1 Sift the flour, baking soda, and salt into a large bowl. Pour in the buttermilk, or milk and yogurt, and the measured water. Mix with a metal spatula or wooden spoon to form a very soft dough.

2 Lightly grease a baking sheet. Turn out the dough onto a lightly floured work surface and shape into a circle 7 in (18 cm) in diameter.

3 Place the dough on the prepared baking sheet and cut a deep cross in the top.

4 Bake in a preheated oven at 400°F (200°C) for 30 minutes. Turn the bread over and bake for 10 minutes longer or until it sounds hollow when tapped on the bottom. Cool on a wire rack. Serve on the day of making (best used for toast on following days).

POTATO ROLLS

MAKES 12

1 1/2 cups (175 g) all-purpose flour

1 tbsp baking powder

4 tbsp (60 g) butter, plus extra for greasing

3 tbsp (45 g) sugar

1 1/3 cups (125 g) freshly made mashed potatoes

about 3 tbsp milk

1 Sift the flour and baking powder into a bowl. Rub in the butter until the mixture resembles fine bread crumbs. Stir in the sugar and mashed potatoes. Add enough milk to form a soft dough.

2 Turn out the dough onto a floured surface and knead lightly until blended. Roll out until 1/2 in (1 cm) thick and cut into rectangles or triangles.

3 Place the rolls on a greased baking sheet and bake in a preheated oven at 425°F (220°C) for 12–15 minutes until risen and golden. Leave to cool on a wire rack. Serve on the day of making.

ALMOND TUILES

MAKES 30

| 2 egg whites |
| 1/2 cup (125 g) sugar |
| 1/2 cup (60 g) all-purpose flour |
| 1/2 tsp vanilla extract |
| 4 tbsp (60 g) butter, melted and cooled |
| 1/4 cup (30 g) slivered almonds |

1 Line a baking sheet with parchment paper. Put the egg whites into a bowl and beat in the sugar until frothy. Stir in the flour and vanilla extract, then add the melted butter.

2 Put 6 single teaspoonfuls of the batter onto the baking sheet, spacing them well apart to allow for spreading. Flatten each with a fork.

3 Sprinkle with the almonds. Bake in a preheated oven at 350°F (180°C) for about 6 minutes until golden brown around the edges but still pale in the middle.

4 Allow the cookies to cool on the baking sheet for a few seconds, then lift off with a spatula and gently lay them over a greased rolling pin to give the curved shape.

5 Allow the cookies to set, then carefully lift off them off the rolling pin onto a wire rack. Leave to cool.

6 Bake and shape the remaining batter in batches, baking one batch while another is setting on the rolling pin.

Cook's know-how

These dainty cookies take their name from the French word "tuile," meaning roof tile (curved roof tiles are common in rural parts of France). If you prefer, omit the shaping in step 4 and leave the cookies to cool flat on a wire rack. They will be just as delicious.

VIENNESE FINGERS

MAKES 12

| 3/4 cup (175 g) butter, plus extra for greasing |
| 1/4 cup (60 g) sugar |
| 1 1/2 cups (175 g) self-rising flour |
| 3 oz (90 g) semisweet chocolate, broken into pieces |

1 Lightly butter 2 baking sheets. Combine the butter and sugar in a bowl and cream together until pale and fluffy. Stir in the flour and beat until well combined.

2 Spoon the mixture into a pastry bag with a medium star tip. Pipe into 3 in (7 cm) lengths on the baking sheets. Bake in a preheated oven at 325°F (160°C) for about 20 minutes until golden. Cool on a wire rack.

3 Put the chocolate into a heatproof bowl. Set the bowl over a pan of hot water and heat gently until the chocolate has melted. Dip both ends of each cookie into the chocolate. Leave to set on a wire rack.

COCONUT MACAROONS

MAKES 26

| 3 egg whites |
| 1 1/2 cups (175 g) confectioners' sugar |
| 1 1/2 cups (175 g) ground blanched almonds |
| a few drops of almond extract |
| 1 1/3 cups packed (175 g) shredded coconut |
| 13 blanched almonds, halved |

1 Line 2 baking sheets with parchment paper.

2 Whisk the egg whites until stiff but not dry. Sift in the confectioners' sugar and fold it in gently. Fold in the ground almonds, almond extract, and shredded coconut.

3 Put teaspoonfuls of the coconut batter onto the baking sheets. Top each with an almond half.

4 Bake in a preheated oven at 300°F (150°C) for about 25 minutes until golden brown and crisp on the outside but still soft in the middle.

5 Leave the cookies to cool on a wire rack. Best served on the day of making.

BRANDY SNAPS

MAKES 15

6 tbsp (90 g) butter

3/4 cup unpacked (90 g) soft light brown sugar

1/4 cup (90 g) light corn syrup

2/3 cup (90 g) all-purpose flour

3/4 tsp ground ginger

3/4 tsp lemon juice

1 Line a baking sheet with parchment paper.

2 Combine the butter, sugar, and corn syrup in a small saucepan and heat gently until the ingredients have melted and dissolved. Cool slightly, then sift in the flour and ginger. Add the lemon juice and stir well.

3 Place 3 or 4 teaspoonfuls of the batter on the baking sheet, leaving plenty of room for the cookies to spread out.

4 Bake in a preheated oven at 325°F (160°C) for about 8 minutes until the batter spreads out to form large, thin, dark golden circles. While the cookies are baking, grease the handles of 3 or 4 wooden spoons.

5 Remove the cookies from the oven and leave for 1–2 minutes to firm slightly.

6 Lift a cookie from the paper using a metal spatula, and wrap it around one of the spoon handles. Repeat with the remaining cookies. Transfer to a wire rack and cool until firm, then slip the cookies from the spoon handles.

7 Continue baking, shaping, and cooling the remaining batter in batches.

GINGER-SNAPS

MAKES 15

4 tbsp (60 g) butter, plus extra for greasing

1/4 cup (90 g) light corn syrup

1 cup (125 g) self-rising flour

2 tsp ground ginger

1 tsp ground cinnamon

1/2 tsp baking soda

1 tbsp sugar

1 Lightly grease 2 baking sheets with butter.

2 Combine the butter and corn syrup in a small saucepan and heat gently until melted. Leave the mixture to cool slightly.

3 Sift the flour, spices, and baking soda into a bowl, and stir in the sugar. Add the cooled butter and corn syrup mixture, and stir to mix to a soft but not sticky dough.

4 Roll the dough into balls about the size of walnuts and place well apart on the baking sheets. Flatten the dough balls slightly with the palm of your hand.

5 Bake in a preheated oven at 375°F (190°C) for about 15 minutes. Leave the cookies to cool on the baking sheets for a few minutes, then transfer them to a wire rack and leave to cool completely.

FORK COOKIES

MAKES 32

1 cup (250 g) butter, at room temperature, plus extra for greasing

1/2 cup (125 g) sugar

2 1/2 cups (300 g) self-rising flour

1 Lightly grease 2 baking sheets with butter.

2 Put the butter into a large bowl and beat with a wooden spoon to soften it. Gradually beat in the sugar, then stir in the flour. Use your hands or a metal spatula to gather the mixture together into a soft dough.

3 Roll the dough into balls about the size of walnuts and place well apart on the baking sheets. Dip a fork into cold water and press on top of each ball to flatten it and imprint a pattern.

4 Bake in a preheated oven at 350°F (180°C) for 15–20 minutes until the cookies are a very pale golden color. Transfer the cookies from the baking sheets to a wire rack and leave to cool completely.

CHOUX PASTRIES

Unlike any other pastry, choux pastry (also called pâte à choux and cream-puff pastry) is a thick paste that can be piped into any shape you like. When baked, the pastry puffs up into a light-as-air creation that literally melts in the mouth. The three classic recipes here are all-time favorites.

COFFEE ECLAIRS

MAKES 10–12

butter for greasing

1 quantity choux pastry (see box, below)

1 egg, beaten

1 1/4 cups (300 ml) heavy cream, whipped

COFFEE FROSTING

1 tsp instant coffee powder

1 tbsp (15 g) butter

2 tbsp water

3/4 cup (90 g) confectioners' sugar

1 Butter a baking sheet and sprinkle with water. Spoon the pastry into a pastry bag fitted with a 1/2 in (1 cm) plain tip, pipe into 3 in (7 cm) lengths and brush with beaten egg. Bake in a preheated oven at 425°F (220°C) for 10 minutes, then reduce the temperature to 375°F (190°C) and bake for 20 minutes longer. Split the éclairs in half and cool on a rack.

2 Spoon the whipped cream into the bottom halves of the éclairs. Make the frosting: put the coffee, butter, and water in a bowl over a pan of water. Heat gently until the butter melts. Remove from the heat and beat in the confectioners' sugar. Dip the top half of each éclair in the frosting, then place on top of the cream. Leave the frosting to cool before serving.

CHOCOLATE CREAM PUFFS

MAKES 12

butter for greasing

1 quantity choux pastry (see box, below)

1 egg, beaten

1 1/4 cups (300 ml) heavy cream, whipped

CHOCOLATE FROSTING

5 oz (150 g) semisweet chocolate, chopped

2/3 cup (150 ml) heavy cream

1 Butter a baking sheet and sprinkle with water. Put 12 tablespoonfuls of pastry on the sheet and brush with beaten egg. Bake in a preheated oven at 425°F (220°C) for 10 minutes, then reduce the temperature to 375°F (190°C) and bake for 20 minutes longer. Split each cream puff in half and cool on a rack.

2 Make the chocolate frosting: gently melt the chocolate with the heavy cream in a bowl over a pan of simmering water, stirring until smooth and shiny (take care not to let the mixture get too hot). Leave to cool slightly.

3 Fill the cream puffs with whipped cream, sandwiching the two halves of each puff together. To serve, place the cream puffs on individual plates, and drizzle with the warm chocolate frosting.

TOP-HAT CREAM PUFFS

MAKES 10

butter for greasing

1 quantity choux pastry (see box, below)

1 egg, beaten

1 1/4 cups (300 ml) heavy cream, whipped

1 quantity warm Chocolate Frosting (left)

1 Butter a baking sheet and sprinkle with water. Spoon the pastry into a pastry bag fitted with a 1/2 in (1 cm) plain tip, pipe 10 large and 10 slightly smaller balls, and brush with beaten egg. Bake in a preheated oven at 425°F (220°C) for 10 minutes, then reduce the temperature to 375°F (190°C) and bake for 20 minutes longer. Split one side of each ball and cool on a rack.

2 Reserve about 3 tbsp of the whipped cream. Fill the balls with the remaining whipped cream, spooning it in the sides.

3 Dip the tops of a large and small ball in frosting. Fit a pastry bag with a 1/2 in (1 cm) star tip and pipe the reserved cream on top of a large ball. Gently press a small ball on top of the cream, with the frosting facing up. Repeat with the other balls.

CLOCKWISE FROM TOP LEFT: Coffee Eclairs, Top-Hat Cream Puffs, Chocolate Cream Puffs.

BASIC CHOUX PASTRY

1 Put 4 tbsp (60 g) butter, cut into cubes, into a saucepan with 2/3 cup (150 ml) water and heat until the butter melts. Bring to a boil.

2 Remove from the heat and add 9 tbsp (75 g) sifted all-purpose flour and a pinch of salt. Stir vigorously until the mixture forms a soft ball.

3 Leave to cool slightly, then gradually add 2 lightly beaten eggs, beating well between each addition, to form a smooth, shiny paste.

FLAPJACKS

MAKES 24

1/2 cup (125 g) butter, plus extra for greasing

1/4 cup (90 g) light corn syrup

scant 3/4 cup packed (90 g) soft light brown sugar

3 cups (250 g) rolled oats

SHALLOW SHEET CAKE PAN, ABOUT 8 x 12 IN (20 x 30 CM)

1 Lightly grease the sheet cake pan with butter.

2 Combine the butter, corn syrup, and sugar in a pan and heat gently until all of the ingredients have melted and dissolved. Stir in the rolled oats and mix well.

3 Spoon into the prepared pan and smooth the surface with a metal spatula. Bake in a preheated oven at 350°F (180°C) for about 30 minutes.

4 Leave to cool in the pan for about 5 minutes, then mark into 24 bars. Leave in the pan to cool completely, then cut and remove from the pan.

WALNUT COOKIES

MAKES 50

2 cups (250 g) all-purpose flour

1 tsp baking powder

1/2 cup (125 g) butter, plus extra for greasing

3/4 cup plus 2 tbsp (175 g) sugar

1/2 cup (60 g) walnuts, finely chopped

1 egg, beaten

1 tsp vanilla extract

1 Sift the flour and baking powder into a bowl. Rub in the butter with the fingertips until the mixture resembles bread crumbs. Mix in the sugar and walnuts. Add the beaten egg and vanilla extract, and stir to form a smooth dough.

2 Shape the dough into a roll about 2 in (5 cm) in diameter. Wrap in foil and refrigerate for about 8 hours.

3 Lightly butter several baking sheets. Cut the dough roll into thin slices and place the cookies on the baking sheets. Bake in a preheated oven at 375°F (190°C) for 10–12 minutes until golden.

PINWHEEL COOKIES

MAKES 18

VANILLA DOUGH

4 tbsp (60 g) butter, at room temperature

2 tbsp (30 g) sugar

3/4 cup (90 g) all-purpose flour

a few drops of vanilla extract

about 1 tbsp water

COFFEE DOUGH

4 tbsp (60 g) butter, at room temperature

2 tbsp (30 g) sugar

3/4 cup (90 g) all-purpose flour

1 tbsp coffee extract

milk for brushing

1 Combine the ingredients for the vanilla dough in a bowl and mix well, adding just enough water to bind. Knead lightly, then wrap and chill for at least 2 hours until very firm.

2 Mix the ingredients for the coffee dough, using the coffee extract to bind. Wrap and chill for at least 2 hours until very firm.

3 On a lightly floured work surface, roll out each dough to a rectangle about 7 x 10 in (18 x 25 cm).

4 Brush the coffee dough with a little milk, then place the vanilla dough on top. Roll up together like a jelly roll, starting at a narrow end.

5 Wrap the roll tightly in foil and leave to chill in the refrigerator for about 30 minutes or until firm.

6 Lightly grease 1 or 2 baking sheets. Cut the dough roll into about 18 thin slices and place them well apart on the baking sheets.

7 Bake in a preheated oven at 350°F (180°C) for about 20 minutes until the vanilla dough is a very pale golden color.

8 Leave the cookies to cool on the baking sheets for a few minutes, then lift off onto a wire rack and leave to cool completely.

Cook's know-how

If you don't have time to chill the doughs (steps 1 and 2), roll out each piece between sheets of waxed paper so it won't stick to the rolling pin.

COOK'S NOTES

All the recipes in this book have been carefully tested so they produce successful results. When selecting a dish, shopping for ingredients, and making a recipe at home, take note of the following essential points.

- Use only one set of measurements. Cup measures and metric measurements are not exact equivalents, so never combine the two.
- Tablespoons are 15 ml, and teaspoons are 5 ml. Spoon measurements are always level unless otherwise stated.
- Eggs are large unless otherwise stated.
- All flours are measured unsifted and spooned into the cup measure. Use a knife to level the surface.
- Always preheat the oven before the food goes in for successful results. Recipes in this book have been tested (where appropriate) in a preheated oven.

- No two ovens are alike, so temperatures and cooking times may need to be adjusted to suit your oven. For convection ovens, lower the temperature according to the manufacturer's instructions.
- When a dish is cooked in the oven, always use the middle shelf unless otherwise stated.
- Calorie counts are approximate and given for guidance only.
- Serving suggestions and accompaniments given with the recipes are optional, for guidance only, and are not included in the calorie counts.

CONVERSION TABLES

MEASUREMENTS

STANDARD	METRIC
¼ in	5 mm
½ in	1 cm
1 in	2.5 cm
2 in	5 cm
3 in	7 cm
4 in	10 cm
5 in	12 cm
6 in	15 cm
7 in	18 cm
8 in	20 cm
9 in	23 cm
10 in	25 cm
11 in	28 cm
12 in	30 cm

LIQUID MEASURES

STANDARD	METRIC
½ cup	125 ml
⅔ cup	150 ml
¾ cup	175 ml
1 cup	250 ml
1¼ cup	300 ml
1½ cup	350 ml
1¾ cup	400 ml
15 oz	450 ml
2 cups	500 ml
2¼ cups	550 ml
2½ cups	600 ml
3 cups	750 ml
3¾ cups	900 ml
1 quart	1 liter

WEIGHT

STANDARD	METRIC
½ oz	15 g
1 oz	30 g
2 oz	60 g
3 oz	90 g
4 oz	125 g
6 oz	175 g
8 oz	250 g
10 oz	300 g
12 oz	375 g
13 oz	400 g
14 oz	425 g
1 lb	500 g
1½ lb	750 g
2 lb	1 kg

OVEN TEMPERATURES

FAHRENHEIT	CELSIUS	DESCRIPTION
225°	110°	Cool
250°	120°	Cool
275°	140°	Very slow
300°	150°	Very slow
325°	160°	Slow
350°	180°	Moderate
375°	190°	Moderate
400°	200°	Moderately hot
425°	220°	Hot
450°	230°	Hot
475°	240°	Very hot

INDEX

RECIPE NOTES

PAGE NO	RECIPE NAME	COMMENTS

PAGE NO	RECIPE NAME	COMMENTS

ACKNOWLEDGMENTS

AUTHOR'S ACKNOWLEDGMENTS
For the first edition, I would like to thank Fiona Oyston for her expertise in writing and testing recipes, and for all her hard work helping me produce the book. I would also like to thank managing editor Gillian Roberts for help in preparing the second edition.

PUBLISHER'S ACKNOWLEDGMENTS
The first (1995) edition of this book was created by Carroll & Brown Limited for Dorling Kindersley.
Thanks to the following people for their help:
Editorial consultant Jeni Wright
Project editor Vicky Hanson
Editors Jo-Anne Cox, Stella Vayne, Anne Crane, Sophie Lankenau, Trish Shine
Cookery consultants Valerie Cipollone & Anne Hildyard
Art editors Louise Cameron & Gary Edgar-Hyde
Designers Alan Watt, Karen Sawyer, Lucy De Rosa
Photography David Murray & Jules Selmes
Assisted by Nick Allen & Sid Sideris
Production Wendy Rogers & Amanda Mackie
Food preparation Eric Treuille, Annie Nichols, Cara Hobday, Sandra Baddeley, Elaine Ngan
Assisted by Maddalena Bastianelli Sarah Lowman
Additional recipes/Contributors Marlena Spieler, Sue Ashworth, Louise Pickford, Cara Hobday, Norma MacMillan, Anne Gains
Nutritional consultant Anne Sheasby

The second (2003) edition of this book was created by Dorling Kindersley. Thanks to the following people for their help:
Editorial contributor Norma MacMillan
Editorial assistance Hugh Thompson
DK Picture Library Claire Bowers & Charlotte Oster
DK India Dipali Singh (project editor), Kajori Aikat (editor), Romi Chakraborty (project designer), Rashmi Battoo (designer), Narender Kumar, Rajesh Chibber, Nain Singh Rawat (all DTP), Ira Pande (managing editor), Aparna Sharma (managing art editor)
Nutritional consultant Wendy Doyle
Index Helen Smith
Loan of props Villeroy & Boch (+44 (0) 20 8871 0011), Thomas Goode & Co. (+44 (0) 20 7499 2823), Chomett (+44 (0) 20 8877 7000)

All images © Dorling Kindersley
Discover more at www.dkimages.com
DK Images is part of the Pearson Asset Library